WAR OF A THOUSAND DESERTS

RECENT TITLES

The Comanche Empire, by Pekka Hämäläinen
Frontiers: A Short History of the American West, by Robert V. Hine and
    John Mack Faragher
Bordertown: The Odyssey of an American Place, by Benjamin Heber Johnson and
    Jeffrey Gusky
Emerald City: An Environmental History of Seattle, by Matthew Klingle
Making Indian Law: The Hualapai Land Case and the Birth of Ethnohistory,
    by Christian W. McMillen
The American Far West in the Twentieth Century, by Earl Pomeroy
Fugitive Landscapes: The Forgotten History of the U.S.–Mexico Borderlands,
    by Samuel Truett
Bárbaros: Spaniards and Their Savages in the Age of Enlightenment, by David J. Weber

FORTHCOMING TITLES

The Bourgeois Frontier, by Jay Gitlin
Defying the Odds: One California Tribe's Struggle for Sovereignty in Three Centuries,
    by Carole Goldberg and Gelya Frank
Under the Tonto Rim: Honor, Conscience, and Culture in the West, 1880-1930, by
    Daniel Herman
William Clark's World: Describing America in an Age of Unknowns, by Peter Kastor
César Chávez, by Stephen J. Pitti
Geronimo, by Robert Utley
The Spanish Frontier in North America, Brief Edition, by David J. Weber

WAR OF
A THOUSAND DESERTS

Indian Raids and the U.S.—Mexican War

Brian DeLay

Published in Association with
The William P. Clements Center for Southwest Studies,
Southern Methodist University

Yale University Press
New Haven & London

Published with assistance from the foundation established in memory of
Philip Hamilton McMillan of the Class of 1894, Yale College.

Set in Electra type by Tseng Information Systems, Inc.

Printed in the United States of America.

Library of Congress Cataloging-in-Publication Data
DeLay, Brian, 1971–
War of a thousand deserts : Indian raids and the U.S.–Mexican War / Brian DeLay.
p. cm. — (The Lamar series in western history)
Includes bibliographical references and index.
ISBN-13: 978-0-300-11932-9 (alk. paper)
ISBN-10: 0-300-11932-1 (alk. paper)
1. Mexican-American Border Region—History, Military—19th century.
2. Mexico, North—History, Military—19th century. 3. Mexican War,
1846–1848—Indians. 4. Mexican War, 1846–1848—Mexican-American Border
Region. 5. Mexican War, 1846–1848—Mexico, North. 6. Indians of North
America—Wars—Mexican-American Border Region. 7. Indians of North
America—Wars—Mexico, North. 8. Mexican-American Border Region—
Ethnic relations—History—19th century. 9. Mexico, North—Ethnic
relations—History—19th century. I. Title.
F800.D45 2008
972′.100497—dc22
2008011982

A catalogue record for this book is available from the British Library.

This paper meets the requirements of ANSI/NISO Z39.48-1992 (Permanence of Paper).
It contains 30 percent postconsumer waste (PCW) and is certified by the Forest
Stewardship Council (FSC).
10 9 8 7 6 5 4 3 2 1

To
Dilianche, Noah, and Alethea
For my Life

Such is the peace of the barbarians in an old one's expression: When they have reduced the settlements to the silence of the deserts, this they call peace.

—"Aster Phylos," *El Ancla: Seminario de Matamoros*, March 1, 1841

CONTENTS

Part Three. Convergence

A Note on Names

Like everyone else, the people who populate this book had multifaceted identities. Depending on context, they might have identified themselves in reference to their immediate family, gender, occupation, linguistic or ethnic group, age, social circle, religion, or nation. Sometimes a whole framework of identities could shift radically, as when a person was taken captive by enemies. It is impossible to talk about other people, especially those outside of one's culture, without doing damage to the subtleties of their lives. In this book I discuss many groups of people and often have to refer to them in broad terms.

Sometimes I discuss views that one group held about another. When, for example, I examine Mexicans referring to native peoples as "savages" or Americans referring to Mexicans as "mongrels," I follow the lead of the people doing the talking. Insults like these reveal little about the people they refer to but can speak volumes about those who invoke them.

I usually refer to the citizens of the United States as Americans. Latin Americans rightly object that the Yankees unilaterally monopolized this term that the rest of the hemisphere had long laid claim to, but, alas, there is no elegant alternative. I use the more precise term *Anglo-American* when referring to the actions of or the racial arguments made by Americans of English descent, and *norteamericano* when discussing Mexican concerns about or perceptions of U.S. citizens. *Tejanos* here refers to residents of Texas whose main language is Spanish, and *Texans* refers to the colonial newcomers, most from the United States, who began arriving in 1821 and won political control of Texas in 1836. Northern Mexico's sedentary population consisted of Indians from different backgrounds (most Hispanicized in important regards by the 1830s), Spanish-Americans, some Africans, and especially people of mixed Indian, African, and

European heritage. Occasionally I refer to a particular subset of this population by an ethnic affiliation. Usually, though, I refer to those who recognized the pre-eminence of Mexican secular and religious authorities as Mexicans, northern Mexicans, or northerners or as residents of particular states.

Most difficult have been terms of reference for indigenous communities. Many of the native peoples discussed in this book are commonly known by names given to them by other peoples, often enemies. Apaches, Navajos, and Comanches are examples. Moreover, in the early nineteenth century, the people now referred to as Comanches were far more likely to identify with smaller so-cial units, for example, a band or a division (tribe), than with their larger linguis-tic community. I use the more specific terms when possible. Most often I refer to the division we know the most about for this period: the Hois, later known as Penatekas. For Comanche names, I follow Thomas W. Kavanagh's *Comanche Political History* (1996).

While I endeavor to be as precise as possible when identifying Indian peoples, much of this story concerns Indian raids upon Mexican settlements. The Mexi-can sources that describe these activities almost never identify raiders with pre-cision. Attackers are described as "Comanches," "Navajos," "Apaches" or with even vaguer terms like "Indian," "enemy," "savage," or "barbarian." In most cases, therefore, it has been impossible to refer to the groups of men who carried out raiding activities in terms that they themselves would have found most meaning-ful. I console myself with the conviction that, for all these actors, actions reveal more about identity than names.

INTRODUCTION: A LITTLE DOOR

The U.S.–Mexican War ended with a handshake on May 30, 1848, when representatives of the two republics exchanged ratifications of the Treaty of Guadalupe Hidalgo. The treaty spelled out terms for the withdrawal of the U.S. Army, the new boundary, the money Mexico would receive for surrendering territory, and the promised rights of Mexicans living above the new border. The first time I read the treaty it all seemed straightforward, until I got to article 11. Article 11 explained that since lands transferred to the United States through the treaty were occupied by "savage tribes" whose "incursions within the territory of Mexico would be prejudicial in the extreme[,] it is solemnly agreed that all such incursions shall be forcibly restrained by the Government of the United States." Moreover the treaty's authors bound the U.S. government to rescue any Mexicans held captive by these tribes, and, most surprising, felt compelled to make it illegal for inhabitants of the United States "to purchase or acquire any Mexican . . . who may have been captured by Indians inhabiting the territory of either of the two Republics." I later learned that Mexico's minister to the United States worked tirelessly to see article 11 fulfilled, calling it "the only advantage" in the treaty that could compensate Mexico for its vast losses in the war.[1]

This all struck me as curious and fascinating. As someone interested in both nation-states and native peoples, I immediately wanted to learn more about the international alarms over Indians. Yet making sense of article 11 turned out to be harder than I expected. Over the past generation historians have done a great deal of work recovering the roles native peoples played in interimperial conflicts in eastern North America. Sometimes native peoples influenced these conflicts directly, by lending military support to particular European powers. But one of the chief virtues of the groundbreaking recent work on this subject has been an insistence that Indian polities could just as often influence imperial designs and colonial realities indirectly, by pursuing independently their own complicated and shifting agendas. Over the course of the eighteenth century, however, the geopolitical significance of North America's autonomous Indians supposedly wore away, peaking with the Seven Years' War, declining with the American Revolution, and all but disappearing after the War of 1812.[2] Thus historians in the United States who have written about westward expansion, Manifest Destiny, and the U.S.–Mexican War have ignored Indian raids in northern Mexico and say almost nothing about the native peoples that so preoccupied the architects of article 11.[3] Indians are more visible in Mexican than in U.S. history, by a matter of demographic necessity. Indigenous peasants are increasingly prominent, for example, in the literature on early nineteenth-century Mexico. But the tens of thousands of independent Indians who controlled the vast northern borderland region rarely make it into books about Mexico's early national period or into Mexican scholarship on the War with the United States.[4]

Of course scholars who specialize in this region have had much to say about independent Indians and their conflicts with northern Mexicans. Violence between native peoples and colonizers has long been a major theme of the literature on Spanish borderlands. But three gaps in this work, having to do with place, period, and connections, left me still puzzled that relations between native peoples and northern Mexicans would have been of such concern in Mexico City and Washington. First, borderlands historians tend to read the modern border backward into history. Though this is now changing, scholars of the borderlands in the United States have generally focused on the present-day Southwest while those in Mexico concentrate on states south of the Rio Grande, despite the fact that the border did not exist before 1848. This approach has hidden from view important historical problems, including those that concerned the architects of article 11. Second, though a generation has passed since David Weber's pathbreaking book *The Mexican Frontier* invited more scholarly attention to the era of Mexican rule in what would become the American Southwest (1821–46), relatively few writers since have concentrated on the period except as part of much longer chronological studies. Finally, while regional specialists have been sensitive to the ways in which outside forces shaped the lives of the region's communities, they have been less inclined to ask whether the influence ever went the other way around. The state is conspicuously absent from much of the recent work on borderlands and native peoples, and, despite calls from prominent scholars of American foreign relations to take Indians and borderlands more seriously, few specialists in international history do so. Consequently, except for the Texas rebellion, events in northern Mexico prior to 1846 are rarely analyzed in terms of their national, let alone international, significance.[5]

But, as the authors of the Treaty of Guadalupe Hidalgo well knew, many things happened in the Mexican north during these years that had national and international ramifications. As I made my way through sources from the states of Tamaulipas, Coahuila, Nuevo León, Durango, Texas, and New Mexico and from Mexico City and Washington, I came to realize that article 11 was a little door into a big story, one told only in pieces by borderlands anthropologists and historians and forgotten altogether by the broader national and international histories of the era.

In miniature, the story goes like this. In the early 1830s, for a variety of reasons, Comanches, Kiowas, Apaches, Navajos, and others abandoned imperfect but workable peace agreements they had maintained with northern Mexicans since the late eighteenth century. Men from these Indian communities began attacking Mexican ranches and towns, killing and capturing the people they found there and stealing or destroying the Mexicans' animals and property. When able, Mexicans responded by doing the same to their indigenous enemies. The conflicts intensified through the 1830s and 1840s, until much of the northern third of Mexico had been transformed into a vast theater of hatred, terror, and staggering loss for independent Indians and Mexicans alike. By the eve of the U.S. invasion these varied conflicts spanned all or parts of ten states. They had claimed thousands of Mexican and Indian lives, made tens of thousands more painful and often wretched, ruined northern Mexico's economy, stalled its demographic growth, and depopulated much of its countryside. The consequences were far-reaching. I argue that the bloody interethnic violence that preceded and continued throughout the U.S.–Mexican War influenced the course and outcome of that war and, by extension, helped precipitate its manifold long-term consequences for all the continent's peoples.[6]

Thoughtful northern Mexicans living through the insecurity of the 1830s and 1840s recognized a unity in their many struggles with groups of independent Indians, despite the fact that the struggles unfolded in a thousand encounters throughout the north. I follow the lead of those observers who referred to their conflicts collectively as a war. They had different names for it: the Indian war, the war of the savages, the barbarian war. I call it the War of a Thousand Deserts. The name comes from something Mexicans recognized as an alarming but inevitable consequence of ongoing Indian raids: the creation of man-made deserts where once there had been thriving Mexican settlements. In this context the term referred not to aridity, but to emptiness, silence, fruitlessness, desolation, to the absence of industry and improvement and of human mastery over nature. A prominent author from Chihuahua, for example, said that raiders had "destroyed the haciendas, the temples, the cities, all the work and glory of many generations, in order to recreate the desert which the Apache eye delights in." Likewise Mexico's minister of war, who referred to once-rich properties depopulated and destroyed by Mescalero Apache and Comanche raids as "immense deserts."[7]

Northern Mexicans rarely described these deserts in writing, perhaps because, to their sorrow, they came to see them as drearily familiar. But occasionally foreigners passed by abandoned places and, being struck, wrote about them in stark detail. In the autumn of 1846, with the U.S.–Mexican War raging elsewhere in the north, a young British traveler in Durango named George Ruxton set out to visit "a tract of country laid waste by the Comanches, and but little known, and which is designated, par excellence, *'los desiertos de la frontera.'*" Ruxton and his companion rode thirty-six miles from the town of Mapimí to the small, silent settlements of Jaral Grande and Jaral Chiquito. Entering Jaral Grande, they wandered through a "perfect forest of crosses, many of them thrown down or mutilated by the Indians." They found flowers still growing in the gardens, struggling skyward from a carpet of weeds and melon vines. Most of the town's small houses had fallen into ruin, though a few remained intact. In front of one house they frightened off a rabbit from a doorstep and saw several more scampering across the earthen floor inside. The walls of the "ruined houses were covered with creepers, which hung from the broken roofs and about the floors."[8]

Passing through another derelict home, Ruxton found something that gave him pause: a warm fire-pit, some arrows and drinking gourds, and a discarded human scalp—evidence that raiders had revisited the place only a short while before. One can imagine that Ruxton's paid companion began regretting the trip at this point, no matter the coins in his pocket, and that even the superhumanly confident young Englishman might have heard his heart beating in his ears. Still, the nervous pair continued on to Jaral Chiquito and found the humble settlement "entirely burned by the Indians, with the exception of one house which was still standing, the roof of which they had torn off, and from the upper walls had shot down with arrows all the inmates." Inside, Ruxton saw the skeleton of a dog and a confusion of human bones. "A dreary stillness reigned over the whole place, unbroken by any sound, save the croaking of a bullfrog in the spring, round which we encamped for a few hours."[9]

The houses of Jaral Grande and Jaral Chiquito were not the only homes in northern Mexico to lose their voices, to have "a dreary stillness" replace the sounds of roosters, mules, and barking dogs and of women and men at work, the chatter of children, the hushed conversations of parents before bed. As the War of a Thousand Deserts progressed, Mexicans across the north, from Tamaulipas in the east to Sonora in the west, and from New Mexico in the north to San Luis Potosí in the south, fled their farms, ranches, haciendas, and small towns for the relative safety of larger cities and settlements to the south. These refugees left deserts behind them. For Ruxton, a man happily risking his life for thrills and for glimpses of someone else's misery, these deserts were curiosities, fodder for his memoirs and his expansive ego. But northern Mexico's ruined communities had more complicated and more consequential meanings for the Mexicans, Americans, and independent native peoples in this book.

Collectively, those meanings form a story that is, at its heart, political. For Mexicans, the War of a Thousand Deserts was both a life-and-death struggle against Indian enemies and a political struggle between Mexicans over how best to confront *los indios bárbaros*. As deserts multiplied throughout the north, the region's beleaguered residents began asking a number of basic questions: Who was a Mexican? what did Mexicans owe local, state, and national governments, and what did these governments owe them? what did Mexicans owe each other? These remained open questions throughout the 1830s and 1840s, and fierce disagreements, even armed rebellions, failed to settle them. The violence ate away at fragile connections that bound Mexicans to one another at local, state, regional, and national levels, and, by 1846, northerners found themselves divided, exhausted, and embittered in the face of another, very different kind of invasion.

Politicians in the United States took a keen interest in Mexico's troubles with independent Indians and, like their Mexican counterparts, used the term *desert* to describe much of northern Mexico. But in American mouths the term became an indictment rather than a lament. When they looked at places like Jaral Grande and Jaral Chiquito Americans saw perversion and opportunity: perversion because Mexican settlers seemed to be reversing the arc of history by falling back before Indians, and opportunity because, characteristically, Americans thought they could do better. Throughout the late 1830s and early 1840s, editors, diplomats, congressmen, and administration officials invoked Mexicans' manifest inability to control Indians in order to denigrate Mexico's claims to its northern territories, first in Texas and, later, across the whole of the Mexican north. These fateful attitudes reached their logical conclusion in 1846 and 1847, when the United States invaded Mexico and exploited the tensions and tragedies of the ongoing war with Comanches, Kiowas, Apaches, and Navajos to conquer the north and to frame the dismemberment of Mexico as an act of salvation. Americans had come to conquer not Mexico, but a desert—to defeat the savage Indians and redeem the Mexican north from what they saw as the Mexicans' neglect.

So Mexicans and Americans had much in common. They both sought information about the crisis in northern Mexico, they both engaged in public dialogues about its significance, and they both argued about what their respective national communities ought to do in response. These political processes unfolded through various means and to very different ends in the two republics, but each began in response to the actions of independent Indians. In this regard both republics seemed to be reversing the arc of history. Thanks to a generation of careful scholarship, we now know much about the complicated struggles of native peoples to resist, cope with, and even profit from the activities of Europeans and their descendents. This book reverses that now-familiar pattern, exploring the efforts of Mexicans and Americans to resist, cope with, and sometimes profit from the activities of Indians.[10]

Thus the starting place for making sense of article 11 is to ask why and how northern Mexico's independent Indians did what they did. The answers to these questions are also part of a political story, though Mexicans and Americans from the period almost never thought of Indians as political beings. Mexicans variously conceived of *los salvajes* as disorganized, psychotic animals with "no more policy than robbery and assassination" or as disorganized, wayward children in need of paternalistic instruction. Americans, too, held disparaging views of Indians generally, but, in comparison to the "civilized" Indians they were just then forcibly removing from eastern North America, U.S. observers held Comanches, Apaches, and others across Mexico's far north in special contempt. It is true that at the time most of North America's indigenous communities lacked the formal, overtly coercive political structures that characterized European-style politics. But that means only that Indians and Europeans had diverse political traditions, not that politics was any less important to Native American than to European life. Modern writers are far more likely to stress the cultural and, especially, economic context of native activities than the political mechanisms that helped bring them about. And yet if one defines politics broadly, not as a matrix of particular institutions, positions, or mechanisms, but rather as a process, one of establishing and pursuing public goals, then it is clear that, despite their differences, the Americans, Mexicans, and independent Indians in this story were all engaged in political endeavors.[11]

Understanding the interplay of those endeavors is a central goal of this book. My aim is not to argue for the incidental significance of Indian activities to Mexico and the United States, but to demonstrate that Mexican, American, and indigenous politics came together in a forgotten nexus that reshaped North

American boundaries for all of its peoples. The trouble is that historians know much less about the workings of native politics in the 1830s and 1840s than they do about political maneuvers in Mexico and the United States, where editors, diplomats, representatives, and administration officials wrote about the nature and significance of northern Mexico's security crisis. The vast majority of sources from the period were written by Mexicans, Texans, and Americans who had little insight into the dynamics of native political cultures. But, when used carefully, the written evidence can reveal a great deal about what native peoples did. Once enough evidence has been gathered about actions, it is then possible to turn to other, more intimate sources to try to explain them.

This method of getting at politics through actions requires too narrow a lens to allow an investigation of all of northern Mexico's many indigenous protagonists. For that reason, I have narrowed my analysis of native politics to a loose coalition of peoples on the plains: Kiowas, Kiowa Apaches, and, especially, Comanches. Men from these societies raided across all or part of eight Mexican states, becoming by the 1840s the archetypal *bárbaros* in the minds of Mexican and American observers alike.[12] More important, from the historian's perspective, Plains Indians generated an enormous amount of anxiety and hence an enormous amount of documentation throughout the Mexican north. Long ignored, the Mexican source material on raids by Comanches and their allies has recently drawn the attention of careful scholars, most from Mexico, who have begun tracing out local and regional consequences of raiding in close detail.[13]

I have integrated and extended this innovative work in an attempt to reconstruct the broader history of what southern plains Indians did in northern Mexico during the 1830s and 1840s. Sometimes Comanches and their allies engaged Mexicans in huge, pitched battles. But often encounters were small and quick. Collectively, these interactions generated thousands of documents, mostly correspondence between local and state officials describing in spare language sightings of or hostilities with raiders. I have extracted data from northern Mexican newspapers and archival materials as well as from the scholarship of Mexican and American researchers to assemble a quantitative picture of the larger war.

While the Mexican materials indicate what happened, they say little about why or how Comanches and Kiowas did the things they did. I address the dual questions of motivations and politics by combining the quantitative data from northern Mexico with other, more qualitative sources produced north of the Rio Grande. Mexican officials during these years usually wrote about southern plains Indians at war, but the traders, agents, army officers, Texan officials, diplomats, and travelers who met with them in peace tended to offer more revealing insights into the workings of their communities. I have also relied upon captivity narratives, several remarkable descriptions of Comanches written during the late 1820s, a few invaluable native sources, and important ethnographic material gathered among Comanches and Kiowas in later years. These materials have helped me make sense of the striking patterns visible in the Mexican data and to reconstruct a far richer picture than either type of source could reveal on its own.

The result of the larger exercise, of following a single drama across geopolitical boundaries and across the intellectual boundaries separating American, Mexican, and Indian histories, implicates all three peoples in the midcentury transformation of the continent. Including Texas, the United States wrested away more than one-half of Mexico's territory in the 1840s. The war with Mexico helped make the United States a world power, made possible the eventual American dominance of the Pacific basin, and, through the immense and varied resources of the conquered territory, would contribute in perpetuity to the prosperity and might of the United States. Critics from the period would have added that the war poisoned the nation's republican soul and fixed it on a path of insatiable economic imperialism. "Contemplating this future," one contemporary critic of Manifest Destiny predicted, "we behold all seas covered by our fleets; our garrisons hold the most important stations of commerce; an immense standing army maintains our possessions; our traders have become the richest, our demagogues the most powerful, and our people the most corrupt and flexible in the world." Now as then such judgments depend on one's politics, but it is objectively the case that America's feast upon Mexican land in 1848 helped bring about the redemptive cataclysm of the Civil War thirteen years later.[14]

The consequences for Mexico were equally momentous, though more difficult to talk about. The war produced an immediate and lasting psychological shock, as every new map testified to a great failure of the Mexican national project. Eventually the trauma of the war would help forge a newly coherent nationalism in Mexico, an energized sense of collective purpose. But in the short and medium term the conflict only contributed to troubles that fed decades more instability and serial crisis. And whatever the odd blessings of loss for Mexico's national identity, they are poor consolation for the incalculable advantages that its citizens could eventually have wrung from their far north had it not become the American southwest. It is in fact nearly impossible to speculate about what Mexico would be like had it not lost half its territory because the exercise quickly produces too many what ifs to sort through. However dense the tangle of historical possibilities, the indisputable fact that Mexico would have been quite different is annually attested to by the great numbers of Mexicans who are literally dying to get to this place that was once their patrimony.

The native peoples who lived in the territories that the United States and Mexico warred over eventually had their own lives transformed by the outcome of that war. Comanches, Navajos, Apaches, and others who enjoyed dominion over millions of acres of land before the American invasion would, within a few decades of the Treaty of Guadalupe Hidalgo, be living impoverished, bounded lives on policed reservations. In their raids of the 1830s and 1840s, Indians helped conjure up this transformation. By shattering northern Mexico's economy, depopulating its countryside, and opening up great wounds in Mexico's body politic, by giving Americans more reasons to despise Mexicans and be contemptuous of their claim to North America, by indirectly facilitating the conquest and occupation of the Mexican north in 1846 and 1847, and by creating for the invaders a noble cause in which to dress their territorial ambition, indigenous peoples were indispensable in the reshaping of the continent.

This is a shared story. This is American history, Mexican history, and Indian history. To stress that point and to set the stage for the unfamiliar, I begin on the outside looking in—with the ambitions and anxieties of empires and nation-states, with a hopeful meeting, and with a proposition.

Prologue

EASY STORIES

Aaron Burr helped kindle Andrew Jackson's enduring interests in wine and Texas. In 1805, a year after killing Alexander Hamilton in their infamous duel and just months after ending his term as Thomas Jefferson's vice president, Burr traveled to Nashville, Tennessee, seeking support for a conspiracy to wrest Florida and Texas from Spain. Westerners liked Burr. He had championed Tennessee's statehood, and, insofar as Hamilton had supposedly promoted eastern aristocrats over western farmers, the blood on Burr's hands only greased his entry into Nashville society. He lodged with Jackson and his beloved wife, Rachael, and extended sly feelers in search of men, material, and money for his grand but shifting plans against the Spanish. Andrew Jackson knew Burr from Washington and had been introduced to the civilizing charms of fine wine at one of Burr's parties. He reveled in having such an esteemed and cultivated guest and became accomplice to Burr's scheme, identifying recruits and securing supplies. But he distanced himself from the conspiracy shortly before it collapsed, aborted by rumors that the former vice president had treasonously planned to seize New Orleans as well as Spanish territories. Still, Jackson never lost his taste for good wine. In later years his Tennessee mansion, the Hermitage, became known as "the wine center of the west," and, after his presidential election in 1828, Jackson built a wine cellar underneath the state dining room in the White House.[1]

Jackson never lost his interest in Texas either, and one wonders whether he had wine on hand on August 13, 1829, when he summoned Secretary of State Martin Van Buren and Anthony Butler to his office to help him buy Texas from Mexico. Years before in Tennessee, Jackson had become guardian to Butler and his siblings after their father's death. Now grown, the ward shared with his old patron a passion about western land and a settled contempt for the "Spaniards"

1

who for so long had stopped American citizens from getting at it. At a time when few in Washington knew anything about Texas, Butler represented expert opinion at the meeting. The trio set to work talking about what they wanted from Mexico, why they wanted it, and how they were going to get it. Or, rather, get it back.[2]

MORE THAN TWENTY FLORIDAS: THE ALLURE OF TEXAS

Like many westerners, Jackson maintained that the United States had a long-standing claim on Texas. In 1685, the French explorer René-Robert Cavelier, Sieur de La Salle had shipwrecked on the Texas coast and thrown up a few ramshackle buildings before being murdered by his starving men. It was anxiety over La Salle's presence that had prompted Spain to establish missions and settlements in Texas in the late seventeenth and early eighteenth centuries, and by the time Jackson convened his meeting some of the missions and settlements were more than a century old. Still, like Jefferson before him, Jackson insisted that La Salle gave primacy to France's claim and that the United States had acquired that claim through the Louisiana Purchase. Spain thought this argument absurd, but the U.S. government clung to it until signing the Adams-Onís Treaty in 1819. John Quincy Adams had negotiated the agreement in his capacity as James Monroe's secretary of state and considered the treaty a triumph because it secured U.S. sovereignty over the Southeast, extinguished Spain's lingering claims to the Missouri country, and finally gave the United States unquestioned overland access to the Pacific.[3]

Andrew "Old Hickory" Jackson initially approved of the treaty, unsurprisingly, since he had done more than anyone else to pave its way. Even before the fiasco with Burr, Jackson had dreamed of obtaining for the United States all of Spanish Florida (divided into East and West Florida, roughly present-day Florida state and coastal Alabama, respectively) and driving the "dons" out of the Southeast forever. During the War of 1812 the United States obtained de facto control of West Florida, but Jackson was forbidden from pushing east. As more and more Seminoles, free blacks, and runaway slaves converged there after the war, Jackson insisted that these confederated threats could be vanquished only if the territory belonged to the United States. This argument gained traction with the inauguration of the first Seminole War in 1817, when American militia destroyed an Indian town north of the Florida border and Seminoles responded by killing a boatful of Americans on the Apalachicola River. Secretary of War John C. Calhoun put Jackson in command of U.S. forces, and Jackson entered the field determined to seize Florida. "The Spanish government is bound by treaty to keep her Indians at peace with us," he reasoned. "They have acknowledged their incompetency to do this, and are consequently bound, by the law of nations, to yield us all facilities to reduce them." Jackson's forces moved through Florida destroying Seminole towns, capturing and killing Hillis Hadjo and other prominent Creek leaders, and then evicting Spanish authorities from their fort at Pensacola. Spain was outraged, naturally, and critics in Washington denounced Jackson as a would-be despot. The hero defended himself by invoking butchered frontier women and babies whose "cradles [were] stained with the blood of innocence." Minus the hyperbole, Adams embraced Jackson's logic about rampaging Indians and the right of self-defense to persuade his counterpart Onís to sign the transcontinental treaty.[4]

So in securing Florida the Adams-Onís Treaty achieved one of Jackson's main goals. Before long, however, Old Hickory joined Thomas Hart Benton, Henry Clay, and others who denounced Adams for surrendering Texas. These critics bemoaned the loss of a region where a single league of land was supposedly "of more value to the U. States . . . than the whole territory west of the Rocky Mountains," an ideal region for producing export commodities such as sugar and coffee, a place "worth more than twenty Floridas." As the language suggests, American advocates of "regaining" Texas had optimistic and rather narrow ideas about what and where Texas was. Jackson's Texas was what today would be thought of as east Texas, part of the Mississippi drainage and an ecological extension of the American Southeast. The president therefore wanted to "regain the Territory as far south and west as the great Desert." Butler concurred, observing that as it ran through a desert, the Nueces River would be the ideal southern U.S.–Mexico border.[5]

The Jackson administration's desire for east Texas was motivated by a set of interlocked concerns that all harmonized with a coherent national project. Most broadly, Jackson saw himself as champion of the common man. He believed that the federal government's first obligation was to expand opportunities for white Americans to improve their situation in life, most especially through owning and developing land. Acquiring Texas would obviously advance that aim. Second, Jackson wanted Texas for reasons of security. Like many public men, he continued to see Europe, especially England, as a threat to the United States and viewed Mexican Texas as a point of insecurity from which an enemy, perhaps allied with Indians, could menace the Mississippi Valley. Moreover, the absence of a natural boundary between Mexico and the United States, of the kind Butler recognized in the desert surrounding the Nueces, would sooner or later bring the two republics into disagreement. According to this logic, the United States needed Texas to ensure future harmony with Mexico.[6]

Jackson's third rationale for acquiring Texas had to do with his convictions about who did and did not belong in the republic. Most Indians did not belong, as far as Jackson was concerned, and the tens of thousands still residing east of the Mississippi would need somewhere to go. The president himself had inspired previous Indian exoduses when he and his men crushed the Red Stick Creeks at the Battle of Horseshoe Bend in 1814 and afterward forced Creeks to surrender half of their territory. Later campaigns against Seminoles and coercive treaties with native peoples throughout eastern North America convinced thousands to abandon their homes for good. By the 1820s, large numbers of Shawnees, Delawares, Kickapoos, Creeks, Cherokees, Choctaws, and Chickasaws had relocated west of the Mississippi. Some had even immigrated to Spanish and then Mexican Texas. In 1825, with "voluntary" removal proceeding apace, the federal government formally established Indian Territory where refugees from the East would supposedly enjoy permanent sanctuary from the insatiable American appetite for land.[7]

Several months into his first term as president, Jackson knew that removal had run into problems. Relocated families had become embroiled in conflicts with western Indians, with Osages and Pawnees from the prairies and, increasingly, with Wichitas from the southern plains. Jackson had reason to intervene because negative reports from Indian Territory would likely dissuade other Indians from moving west. Indeed, the bilingual newspaper the *Cherokee Phoenix*, whose editors opposed voluntary removal, ran excited reports of attacks by savage Plains Indians precisely to discourage more Cherokees from migrating. With comprehensive removal in the works (Jackson would set the Indian Removal Bill before Congress in December), the acquisition of Texas could help solve two problems. The purchase might include some marginal lands suitable for native emigrants. More important, if the United States possessed Texas it could more effectively manage conflicts between western and immigrating Indians.[8]

If Texas figured into Jackson's vision of how to keep the wrong people out of the republic, it also had something to do with keeping the right people in. In 1821, just months before losing their continental possessions to Latin American independence, Spanish officials had approved a request by Moses Austin of Missouri to relocate three hundred *norteamericano* families to Texas. Authorities in newly independent Mexico extended the offer to Austin's son Stephen following his father's death. Austin and many other early immigrants sought to maximize their advantages in Texas by nominally becoming Catholic, learning Spanish, and embracing Mexican citizenship. What began as a trickle had become a deluge by Jackson's presidency, and it is easy to see why. During the 1820s it could have been said that Mexican Texas was more Jacksonian in the opportunities it offered ambitious men than the United States. Above all, Mexican Texas offered cheap land. Coahuila y Texas's colonization law of 1825 (the two provinces were fused into one state in 1824) provided immigrant families with nearly 4,500 acres of grazing land and 177 acres of farmland, all for nominal fees and no payments for four years. Moreover, the financial panic of 1819 had ruined families throughout the western United States, and Texas offered a haven from steadily increasing taxes, rapacious bankers, and debtors' prisons.[9]

Jackson surely knew this. And yet soon after taking office (presumably before his meeting with Butler and Van Buren), the president scribbled a note in his personal memorandum book that "early attention" needed to be given to altering the unsatisfactory boundary line between the United States and Mexico, "as by it part of our citizens are thrown into the province of Texas." The language here is instructive. Even in a note to himself he insisted on the fiction that English speakers in Texas were loyal Americans overtaken by events rather than enthusiastic émigrés seeking a better life under a different flag. In fact, just months after Jackson's meeting, Austin expressed his view that annexation to the United States would be "the greatest misfortune that could befall Texas at this moment." Still, requited or no, Jackson wanted Austin and the other émigrés back.[10]

By regaining Texas, therefore, the president thought he could expand the area of opportunity for white men, inoculate the United States against the intrigues of the British and future conflicts with Mexico, advance his project of excluding Indians from the republic, and redeem good Americans languishing under alien government. The remaining question was how to convince Mexico to sell.

I SCARCELY EVER KNEW A SPANIARD: JACKSONIAN CONFIDENCE

Van Buren and Butler helped Jackson settle on a set of complementary strategies to play on Mexico's anxieties, exploit its problems, and bribe its leaders. In an unofficial, solicitous way, the American negotiator was to point out the inevitability of colonial insurrection in Texas. In fact, American colonists had already attempted rebellion in late 1826, when an ineffectual and disgruntled *empresario* (colonization agent) named Hayden Edwards reacted to the cancellation of his grant by rechristening most of Texas the independent Republic of Fredonia. Edwards enlisted a prominent mixed-blood Cherokee trader and promised that masses of discontented American and Cherokee immigrants would "make this government shake to its centre." Bold talk, but in truth neither man enjoyed their peoples' support. Austin denounced Edwards's scheme and his "unnatural and bloody alliance with Indians," and the movement collapsed in early 1827, as soon as Mexican forces arrived on the scene. Fredonia had been desperate, even comic, but, with the American colonial population surging, Jackson could argue that a more serious rebellion was only a matter of time. Prompt sale would rescue Mexico from this fate, along with the complications rebellion would naturally create for U.S.–Mexico relations.[11]

Moreover, Jackson and his collaborators knew that Mexico was at that moment under attack from a Spanish force intent on reconquering its former colony. Still refusing to recognize Mexican independence and possessed of the curious if not uncommon idea that they would be greeted as liberators, Spanish authorities had landed thirty-five hundred men near the port of Tampico at the end of July. At the time of Jackson's Texas meeting the outcome of their campaign was unknown. So, in a novel interpretation of his responsibilities under the Monroe Doctrine, Jackson reasoned that the threat ought to make Mexico welcome a quick infusion of dollars from the sale of Texas.[12]

Finally, if impending rebellion or national emergency would not motivate a sale, personal remuneration might. Jackson cast his thoughts back to his days dealing with the Spanish in Florida. "I scarcely ever knew a Spaniard who was not the slave of avarice," he later wrote Butler, "and it is not improbable that this weakness may be worth a good deal to us, in this case." Though the president and his supporters would later express shock at accusations of improper conduct, Butler sensibly took this note as instruction to bribe Mexican officials and, inspired, scrawled across the back of the letter, "Gen. Jackson—remarkable communication."[13]

After the session adjourned and Jackson had dismissed his two confidants, it fell to Secretary Van Buren to craft a letter of instruction to the U.S. minister in Mexico, Joel Poinsett. As he did so, he added an argument that seems to have received slight attention at the meeting: that if the United States possessed Texas, it could do Mexico the favor of subduing the Comanches. This was not a new strategy. Four years earlier, when President John Quincy Adams had attempted to buy Texas, his secretary of state, Henry Clay, hastily made the same argument. Van Buren's version had more color, thanks to a letter he had recently received from Poinsett. It included parts of a report that a prominent general had written for authorities in Mexico City concerning the dismal condition of Texas's defenses. Van Buren worked the general's anxieties into the instructions he sent Poinsett in late August. "The Comanche Indians," the secretary noted, "a numerous and daring tribe, have, for years, been a scourge to Texas. They have, more than once, swept every article of livestock from their owners, and killed the inhabitants of San Antonio, on the commons, in front of the public square." Such threats had forced Mexico to maintain an expensive but ultimately ineffective military presence in the region. "It is said that the soldiers are insulted by the savages at the muzzles of their guns; and that, when complaints are made, the officers frankly acknowledge their inability to give redress." The secretary asserted that Indians had long since stopped attacking the American newcomers in Texas because, unlike Mexicans, Americans invariably punished Indian raiders. Indeed, local Mexicans had grown jealous, imagining that the peace Americans enjoy, peace "attributable solely to that hardihood, courage, and enterprize which distinguish our border men, arises from a sinister understanding with the Indians." By relinquishing Texas, he concluded, Mexicans would not only be relieved of these misunderstandings and a costly, interminable military obligation, "but will secure protection to their own territory, by interposing the United States between the Indians and their eastern frontier."[14]

The secretary's confidence came easy. Born just months after his country achieved independence from Great Britain, Van Buren came of age watching (from afar) as the United States vanquished and displaced native peoples across half a continent. This outcome may have seemed steady and inevitable looking backward from 1829, with America's greatest Indian fighter in the White House crafting a comprehensive removal plan. Success is easily read into the past. In fact, as a child, Van Buren would have heard of great calamities in his country's Indian wars. When he was seven, Miamis and Shawnees forced Brigadier General Josiah Harmar into a humiliating retreat from the Forks of the Maumee in Northwest Territory. A year later the brilliant Miami leader Little Turtle killed at least six hundred American soldiers under Major General Arthur St. Clair, losing only twenty-one of his own men. In 1794 American forces finally gained a narrow victory over the region's Indians at the Battle of Fallen Timbers (in present-day Ohio) and in so doing appropriated much of the Northwest for American settlement.[15]

But at the same time Americans in Tennessee and Kentucky, embroiled in bloody feuds with southeastern Indians, denounced the federal government for its inability or unwillingness to save them from savages. Indeed, Washington's failure to protect southerners as they encroached on Indian lands encouraged many southern men to talk incautiously about leaving the Union and courting Spain or England instead. "This Country is Declining [fast]," went a typical complaint in 1794, "and unless Congress lends us more am[ple] protection this Country will have at length [to break] or seek a protection from some other Source than the present." This from an ambitious and impatient young lawyer named Andrew Jackson.[16]

Even in the War of 1812, the conflict that turned Jackson from a courtly frontier tough with uncertain loyalties into the towering patriot of his age and that supposedly placed the seal on American triumph and native defeat—even here contingencies and narrow victories betrayed the fragility of American dominion over native peoples. Early in the war, militia leaders from Tennessee, Alabama, and Mississippi waged successful campaigns against the towns of the Red Stick Creeks but by the end of 1813 began to be abandoned by their men. Hungry, weary, concerned about their families and interests, and convinced they had fulfilled their duty, southern militiamen deserted in droves. By early January, an apoplectic Jackson sat in Fort Strother with fewer than 150 men to complain to. Had the Red Sticks seized the moment, Andrew Jackson would have been little more than a footnote in Tennessee's history. More broadly, had events in Europe not dissuaded Spain and England from doing more to support their native allies in the South and the North, Hillis Hadjo, Tecumseh, and Tenskwatawa might have sustained their movements and defended their rights to land and autonomy. Such a victory, even a temporary one, could have fractured the Union and revived European power in the continent by convincing frontier Americans, especially in the South, that the hapless U.S. government could not defend their interests and that they did indeed need to seek protection "from some other Source than the present."[17]

In other words, had Van Buren reflected on his own country's fragile, lurching struggle against Indians in the first decades after independence, he might have managed some sympathy for Mexico and its troubles with Comanches. After all, Mexico had been independent for all of eight years when the secretary sat down to write his letter. Eight years after America won independence Little Turtle was slaughtering U.S. soldiers in heaps and turning Washington's cheeks red with rage. But as he bent to his task Van Buren had less use for the road his republic had traveled than for the destination it had reached. What mattered was that Jackson did get his reinforcements in 1814 and that he took them to Horseshoe Bend, where he famously "glutted" his vengeance by killing perhaps 850 Indians. His soldiers helped keep count by slicing off the noses of the dead. British forces failed their native allies on the battlefield in the North, and Kentucky militia shot Tecumseh and left his body to trophy seekers who tore strips from his "yellow hide" to use as souvenirs and razor strops.[18]

Whatever the war's ambiguous international consequences, Van Buren and other like-minded Americans could henceforth rest easy in the knowledge that prior frontier humiliations had been anomalies; that the native peoples of eastern North America were "their Indians" to do with as they would. In the years after the War of 1812, this meant negotiating more and more treaties for land and convincing more and more Indians to move west—activities in which Jackson and his allies assumed leading roles. "Once a formidable and terrible enemy," the famed explorer William Clark observed in 1825, Indians in the East had seen their power broken, "their warlike spirit subdued, and themselves sunk into objects of pity and commiseration." By the time Jackson occupied the White House, these outcomes seemed inevitable to many Americans. In his lifetime Van Buren had seen his countrymen defeat and dispossess the most powerful native peoples in eastern North America. Why should Comanches be any different?[19]

IMAGINARY DOMINIONS: THE LATE BOURBON INSIGHT

Van Buren knew little about Texas, less about Mexicans, and nothing about Comanches. He was groping. But when he linked his republic's territorial designs to northern Mexico's troubles with independent Indians, he hit a nerve. For more than two centuries, the administrators of New Spain had endured considerable distraction, cost, and embarrassment as they sought to protect scattered northern enclaves amid a host of unconquerable Indians. The predicament the secretary sought to exploit had been long in the making.

Throughout the Americas, European powers relied on the private ambitions of their subjects to extend empires. In this way Spanish power leapt north from the shattered capital of the Aztecs to dominate and often enslave Indians, open silver mines, and found cities farther and farther away. Silver translated into investment, ranches, slavers, armies, and a sustained will for war—things that, combined with unceasing epidemics, wrecked many native societies and forced others into a wary "colonial pact." Over the decades and centuries of colonial rule northern New Spain underwent a profound transformation as peoples indigenous to the area declined, fled, submitted, or assimilated, and newcomers moved in. Critically, the crown convinced thousands of Indians from central Mexico to move north to new mines, ranches, and towns. These Tlaxcalans, Tarascans, Otomis, and others were joined by growing populations of Spanish descent, enslaved and free Africans, and other migrants of mixed heritage. As a result, the provinces of Sonora, Nueva Vizcaya (including the present-day state of Durango, most of Chihuahua, and part of Coahuila), Nuevo León, and Nuevo Santander (present-day Tamaulipas) developed quickly. They also had remarkably diverse populations. Across most of this huge region peoples of mixed Indian/African and Indian/European descent predominated by the late colonial period, followed by Indians indigenous to the region, native peoples from elsewhere in Mexico, "full-blood" Spaniards, and relatively small numbers of Africans. The conquest of indigenous populations, the development of the mining and ranching economy, and the rise of such a mixed regional society all testified to Spain's capacity to transform the New World.[20]

When the crown pushed far north of the mining frontier, however, into what is today the American Southwest, it discovered places that broke European ambitions. To the northwest Spaniards found deserts and dry, difficult mountains, to the northeast an eternity of grass, and in both directions mobile indigenous peoples who used the arid land and eventually Spanish horses to extraordinary tactical advantage. Spain managed to colonize the sedentary Pueblo villages on the upper Rio Grande and to establish missions and even modest civilian settlements in Texas and, less so, in present-day Arizona. These remained islands of royal power, disconnected from each other and encompassed by dangers. Aggrieved by Spanish slave raids, alienated from their customary trade with the now-colonized and diminishing Pueblos, and empowered by Spanish horses and occasionally firearms, the mobile Athapaskans, whom Spaniards came to call Apaches and "Apaches del Navahu" (Navajos), became skilled raiders and helped to confine Spanish power. Lacking huge native populations to exploit and significant exportable resources to excite and sustain individual aspirations and investment, the vast majority of the territory Spain claimed in the far north would remain immune from European conquest.[21]

Spain's frustrations in the far north were not simply a matter of imperial exhaustion or preoccupation with other realms. Even in the inordinately confident atmosphere of 1820s United States, imaginations staggered and ambitions shrank before the arid west. Americans moving beyond the Appalachians had long used trees to gauge the agricultural possibilities inherent in any new landscape, so it is little wonder they responded to the Great Plains with such pessimistic awe. In 1810, the publication of Zebulon Montgomery Pike's report of his trek across northern New Spain advertised the region as rich in commercial possibilities but utterly unsuited to agriculture and hence unsuited to American life. This was supposed to be a good thing. For Pike, this dry, alien, nearly treeless expanse would ensure "a continuation of the Union" by preventing a fatal overextension of the United States. Stephen H. Long, who explored parts of the Trans-Mississippi West in 1818–19, thought much the same and dubbed the region "the Great American Desert." Authors high and low, including such luminaries as James Fenimore Cooper and Washington Irving, concurred. Jackson's desire for the relatively well-watered *east* Texas resonated with their views. Well into the nineteenth century, most Americans thought it probably impossible and certainly undesirable for their country to expand into the arid west.[22]

In this light, New Spain's limited accomplishments in its own arid north seem impressive, even audacious. But these accomplishments were fueled more by

anxiety than by ambition. The crown submitted to the expense and the indig-
nity of maintaining unprofitable settlements amid people it could not control
because it feared other states. Though specific anxieties changed over time, the
perennial worry was that another empire would align with independent Indians,
move through northern New Spain, and seize what mattered most in Mexico,
the silver mines in places like Zacatecas and Chihuahua. France was first to set
off alarms, as its agents made alliances with native peoples throughout much of
the Mississippi Valley in the late seventeenth and early eighteenth centuries.
Realists in the Spanish administration had wanted to abandon the useless and
troublesome colony of New Mexico for good after Pueblo Indians orchestrated
a devastating rebellion in 1680, killing hundreds of Spaniards and driving survivors out of the region. But news of French activities west of the Mississippi
worried enough Spaniards that their European enemies planned to "settle as far
as New Mexico and make themselves Lords of many Kingdoms and Provinces."
Preventing these imagined landgrabs justified a permanent royal commitment
in New Mexico, and La Salle's mishap activated the same thinking in regard to
Texas.[23]

Once Spaniards returned to the upper Rio Grande in the early 1690s, they soon
learned that their colonial endeavor was indirectly transforming native communities throughout western North America. In the summer of 1706, Pueblos and
Apaches complained to Spanish officials that their people had endured devastating attacks from new mounted warriors they called Comanches, a term probably
deriving from the Ute word *komántica* (meaning "enemy" or, literally, "anyone
who wants to fight me all the time"). They called themselves Nʉmʉnʉʉ, the
people. Originally Northern Shoshones living in small kin groups in the Great
Basin, the people embarked on an economic and cultural revolution once they
obtained horses. Emerging onto the plains, Comanches displaced horticultural
Apaches from the Arkansas Valley and soon began probing bison-rich grasslands
below that river. Comanches forged partnerships with allied tribes collectively
known as the Wichitas. Wichitas were farmer-hunters who occupied a strategic
position on the Red River between French traders in Louisiana and Indians on
the plains. Armed with French guns, Comanches and their Wichita allies spent
the next decades forcing most Apaches out of the hunting grounds on the plains
and onto the margins of the Rio Grande, where the refugees increasingly stole
Spanish animals to survive. Meanwhile, Spain's inconsistent policies, underfunded military, and, not least, the slaving, thefts, and aggression that its subjects directed against Indians led to mounting conflicts. By the 1760s Spanish
authorities found themselves submerged in ruinous wars with Comanches and
Apaches alike.[24]

All sides suffered. In just six years, between 1771 and 1776, Spanish authorities calculated that in the province of Nueva Vizcaya Apaches killed 1,674 people, took 154 captives, seized more than 66,000 head of cattle, and forced the abandonment of more than a hundred ranches and haciendas. Between 1767 and 1777, Pedro Fermín de Mendinueta, the governor of New Mexico, recorded 106 attacks by Comanches, 77 by Apaches, and 12 by Navajos. Together these raids resulted in the captivity of 94 Spaniards and Pueblo Indians and the deaths of 382 others. Raiders stole so many horses that too few remained to effect pursuit. Maps from the time show abandoned settlements throughout the upper Rio Grande. Casualties among independent Indians are harder to estimate, though Mendinueta claimed to have killed hundreds of Comanche men and to have sold into slavery over 100 Comanche women and children. Everyone in the region had cause to seek peace.[25]

Mounting losses contributed to shifts in Spanish policy. Spain's energetic King Carlos III (1759–88) took a keen interest in his American possessions, understood the connection between frontier security and interimperial rivalry, and, as early as the 1760s, had empowered several able subordinates to be creative in an attempt to end the Indian wars. One of these, the Marqués de Rubí, traveled overland seventy-five hundred miles visiting nearly the whole of New Spain's northern frontier. This tour convinced Rubí that the crown had wasted its finite resources trying to exert power over "imaginary" dominions in the north, those places claimed by Spain but controlled by Indians. The marqués suggested measures to better defend New Spain's real dominions, and officials experimented with and refined Rubí's suggestions over the next two decades. Critically, new regulations centralized military command and institutionalized coordination of resources and policies throughout northern New Spain. Just as important, this centralized command began adopting more flexible policies inspired by the French—policies stressing trade over war and deception over confrontation. At the close of the Seven Years' War, Spain took possession of Louisiana west of the Mississippi from France. It did so lest the English have it and because it wanted an unambiguous boundary—the Mississippi—to keep off Anglo-American encroachments and minimize the possibility of a future war with England. The transfer gave Spanish administrators an intimate look at how the French had been interacting with native peoples in North America and inspired a new generation of administrators to shift course.[26]

The French influence found its most important expression in 1786, with the publication of the *Instructions for Governing the Interior Provinces of New Spain*, by Viceroy Bernardo de Gálvez. A former governor of Louisiana and a man with experience fighting Apaches at the frontier, Gálvez ordered that Indians be courted through gifts, diplomacy, and trade: "It is my intention to establish with the Indians a commerce which will attract them to us, which will interest them, and which in time will put them under our dependency." On the other hand, the viceroy instructed frontier officials to continue waging war against those who refused entreaties and in doing so to side with certain native communities against others: "I am certain that the vanquishment of the heathen consists in obliging them to destroy one another." Once intransigents sought a respite from attacks, they were to be forgiven and made dependent through gifts, for example, low-quality firearms in hopes that skills with bow and arrow would diminish and that want of ammunition and repairs would keep Indians tractable.[27]

The viceroy's reforms were well timed because far to the north Comanches had been rethinking their positions as well. In 1779, Governor Mendinueta's able successor Juan Bautista de Anza led an attack that killed the feared Comanche leader Cuerno Verde, organizer of numerous deadly assaults on New Mexico. Cuerno Verde had championed continued war with the Spanish, and his death presented an opportunity for Comanches with different views. A year later smallpox killed one-fifth or even a quarter of New Mexico's population and took a grave toll on Comanches as well. Considering their losses from the epidemic and the war as well as the potential diplomatic and economic benefits of a Spanish alliance, proponents of peace began to push the case. They took the extraordinary step of calling a huge, multidivisional meeting and electing one of their leaders, Ecueracapa, to represent Comanches in peace talks with Governor Anza. The two signed a peace treaty in 1786. Comanches in the east signed a similar treaty in San Antonio, though the peace would never be as firm with Texas as with New Mexico. Spanish authorities tried to police trading to ensure that Comanche families were treated fairly and respectfully when they came into towns. Anza and his counterpart in Texas also honored Comanche leaders with gifts, including imported cloth, blankets, clothes, colored capes, medallions, hats, cigars, metal tools, pipes, candles, sugar, and gear for horses. Such presents were indispensable for forging and maintaining diplomatic and personal relationships between Indians and non-Indians. Just as important, regular gifts provided Comanche leaders with crucial resources that they in turn would redistribute to their kin and followers.[28]

For their part, Comanches agreed to help Spaniards destroy Apaches. This was hardly a concession, as it furthered the long-term project of driving Apaches from the plains and thereby monopolizing access to bison and to markets in New Mexico and Texas. Together the allies managed to coerce Navajos into joining their new coalition, and then all three groups launched unforgiving campaigns against Apaches. By the 1790s, desperate Apache families began seeking asylum at Spanish peace establishments, where military authorities promised to feed and protect them if they foreswore raiding. Many stayed away but remained relatively quiet and obtained rations indirectly from relatives. Raiding never ceased entirely anywhere in the north, but thefts became far rarer than they had been and kidnappings and killings rarer still. In the 1780s, then, New Mexico and Texas entered a new era of security, growth, and prosperity. The same was true for provinces further south by the 1790s. None of this would have happened without Comanche leaders such as Ecueracapa who saw more advantage in peace with New Spain than in war. Prominent Comanches expended considerable energy over the coming decades to police the relationship, restrain their young men, and smooth over the inevitable disagreements.[29]

But the enduring peace also represented a triumph for New Spain's administrators. By financing frontier defense and infrastructure, by thinking creatively and flexibly, by centralizing command, and by acting respectfully toward native allies and treating them as sovereign peoples, they left the frontier in remarkable shape on the eve of the nineteenth century. These administrative accomplishments all emerged from an insight that Carlos III realized more keenly than other Spanish monarchs. In a world of competitive states and shifting boundaries, New Spain's security depended upon the security of the thinly populated northern frontier; and the security of the frontier hinged on good relations with the real masters of that vast, difficult realm—Apaches, Navajos, Wichitas, and, especially, Comanches. In North America, interimperial rivalries were inextricably bound up in relations with independent Indians.[30]

Spain would be reminded of this logic as its fortunes changed in the early nineteenth century. When Carlos III died, his weak son Carlos IV took the throne and soon came under the spell of audacious but inept advisors. Spain started and quickly lost an ill-conceived war against Republican France and, in defeat, had to abandon an alliance with England. England's navy responded by cutting Spain off from its American markets. In 1800, with Spain's economy in shambles, Carlos IV bowed to pressure from Napoleon Bonaparte to return Louisiana to France—on the condition that Napoleon would never sell it to the Americans. Four years later, he did precisely that. Jefferson's administration immediately launched its belligerent campaign to see Texas included in the purchase, and U.S. and Spanish forces nearly came to blows on the Texas–Louisiana border.[31]

In 1805, in the midst of these tensions, General James Wilkinson warned the American secretary of war that the United States would have to consider Comanches in its calculations regarding Texas. Wilkinson was many things— the ranking general in the west, a double agent for the Spanish crown, partner to Aaron Burr, and the man who finally betrayed Burr to Jefferson—all of which meant he knew much that other Americans did not. He considered Comanches, with whom he had traded horses in Texas, "the most powerful nation of savages on this continent." The general insisted that it was "in their power to impede our march to New Mexico, should such movement ever become necessary." Wilkinson likened the current standoff with Spain over Texas to the standoff with England over the Ohio Valley, where mighty native peoples controlled strategic territory between the two powers. From his perch in Louisiana, he doubted that the United States could take Texas as it had the Ohio country: "The Theatre before us is much more extensive—we are here feeble and far removed from substantial succor—The Savages are as ten to one—They are known to the Spaniards and unknown to us—and their Habits of Life [their nomadism], put it out of our Power to destress or destroy them."[32]

This was sound counsel. Spaniards and Comanches had both suffered greatly during their intermittent conflicts, and in the years since had come to place considerable value on each other's friendship. Indeed, when news about Meriwether Lewis's and William Clark's expedition set off alarms in New Spain, a Comanche party traveled as far north as the Missouri River seeking news of "Captain Merry" for their anxious allies. And when they learned of New Spain's brewing border dispute with the United States in 1806, thirty-three Comanche headmen and more than two hundred warriors came to San Antonio and reaffirmed their support for the crown. The Comanche–Spanish alliance seemed sufficiently robust to withstand Jefferson's pressure.[33]

Once the king's subjects started killing each other, however, things got complicated. Quiet New Mexico remained virtually untouched by the War of Independence, but because men and materials could be obtained from neighboring Louisiana, royalists and insurgents fought fiercely over Texas. Some Comanches initially sided with royal officials and even campaigned against insurgents in Coahuila in 1811. But the logic of the old alliance quickly unraveled as experienced frontier soldiers deserted their posts to fight for or against the uprising, as military commanders and administrators switched sides depending on who seemed to be winning, and as funding for Indian diplomacy vanished. Groups of Comanches, Wichitas, and Lipán Apaches began raiding settlements in Texas and Coahuila, and campaigns were particularly intense in 1814 and 1815. The region became even more volatile after smallpox arrived in 1815 and 1816. One influential leader reportedly claimed he had lost four thousand of his people, though it is unclear whether he spoke only of his own division or of all Comanches. The epidemic of 1780–81 had surely contributed to the political consolidation and reorientation that resulted in the seminal peace with the Spanish in that decade. This time smallpox disrupted and fragmented Comanche politics instead of uniting it. The disease killed many of the men who had forged and regulated the Spanish peace, including four principal chiefs in Texas. For the moment, New Spain's civil war left other influential men with little reason to rebuild the alliance. The late colonial system had broken.[34]

TO ALL BE BROTHERS: MEXICAN INDEPENDENCE

After Mexico finally achieved independence in 1821, it fell to Anastacio Bustamante to rebuild the broken system. Like most prominent men of his time, Bustamante made a name for himself fighting for the crown during Mexico's War of Independence. When Father Miguel Hidalgo y Costilla issued his famous Grito de Dolores in 1810, Bustamante and most others of his class viewed the padre and his allies as criminal zealots turning indigenous peasants against their betters. A medical doctor by training, Bustamante became an officer in the royal army and, as the movement fractured into regional insurgencies following Hidalgo's capture and execution, spent the next decade killing insurgents. By 1821, however, continued instability in Spain seemed to threaten the very social privileges Bustamante and his contemporaries had been fighting to maintain. They turned on the king. General Agustín de Iturbide brokered a compromise with the rebels, helped defeat the remaining royal forces, and secured for Mexico an independence safely devoid of any sweeping social reforms. According to the compromise plan, Mexico was to be a constitutional monarchy. In early 1822 Iturbide and his followers convinced a sufficient number in Congress to make him the monarch, Emperor Agustín I.[35]

Bustamante had been an early supporter of Iturbide's plan and served as a key lieutenant in the final military campaigns. Soon after independence Iturbide rewarded him with the highest rank in the Mexican army and appointed him captain general of the eastern and western internal provinces, jurisdictions that embraced California, New Mexico, and Texas as well as the present-day northern tier of Mexican states. Before he even assumed this position Bustamante began making inquiries about the independent Indians of the frontier and taking steps to reopen lines of communication. In August of 1821 he sent circulars to frontier officials urging them to dispatch "envoys to the pueblos of the belligerent nations of the North, that they may be instructed, by way of captives or emigrants that exist among them, of our happy political regeneration." The time had arrived, Bustamante continued, "to all be brothers, to put away arms, return prisoners," and restore peace and harmony.[36]

Frontier officials had anticipated the order, and within a year Bustamante finally got to meet some of his proud "brothers" face to face. Lipán Apache representatives traveled from the lower Rio Grande to Mexico City for Iturbide's coronation in July 1822 and afterward sat down with Bustamante to sign a peace treaty. A few months later Comanche delegates arrived in the capital in the company of a remarkable tejano named José Francisco Ruiz. Educated in Spain, Ruiz had been a teacher in Texas around the turn of the century and in 1813 joined the insurgents against the crown. When royalists gained the upper hand and placed a five-hundred-peso bounty on his head, he fled to Louisiana. Thereafter, Ruiz made a living trading with Indians. By independence he probably knew more about the native peoples of the southeastern plains than any of his contemporaries and was the obvious choice for frontier officials seeking a cultural intermediary. Ruiz convinced southern Comanche leaders to send delegates to Mexico City and, once they arrived there he helped the lead Comanche representative, Guonique, conclude a treaty. Among other things, the agreement provided for peace, return of prisoners, trade, the education of select Comanche youth in Mexico City, and defense of Mexican territory against rival states.[37]

Guonique stayed in the capital for weeks. He impressed his hosts as "enterprising, truthful, observant, prudent, and resolute" and also proved to be a man with an eye for opportunity. Somehow he heard that a trio of prominent generals had initiated a rebellion against the emperor. The delegate slyly informed Iturbide that if need be, he and a Comanche counterpart named Paruakevitsi could put twenty-seven thousand armed men at the emperor's disposal. Communicating through Ruiz, Guonique insisted that the "Comanche nation of the East" and its subordinates and allies "know how to keep their word; they destroy the enemies of the Empire with the rifle, the lance, and the arrow, in the same way that they destroy the wild beasts." The capital press enjoyed the idea that the exalted hero of Mexican independence might need saving by savages. But Guonique's inflated claims about Comanche manpower (probably exaggerated by a factor of ten) were likely meant as a gentle threat to an ally who obviously knew too little about northern Indians. Only a few months earlier, Iturbide had hosted a man calling himself Botón de Fierro, or Iron Button, and claiming to be a Comanche chief who could broker a lasting peace. A few months after Iron Button earned the emperor's enthusiastic confidence it came to light that he was really José Rafael Guadalupe del Espíritu Santu Iglesias y Parra, a carpenter from Alta California with a very long name but no connection whatever to Comanches. Bustamante's energy and initiative notwithstanding, newly independent Mexico was a long way from recapturing Bourbon New Spain's informed and effective Indian policy.[38]

Still, while the new government might confuse carpenters for Comanches and be hoodwinked by imaginary Indian legions, at least it was taking independent native peoples into account. As influential Mexicans set about debating, imagining, and constructing a sovereign state in the early 1820s, part of the conversation proceeded from the old Bourbon insight linking security against rival states to frontier security and frontier security to Indian relations. At the same time, Mexicans saw colonization as the long-term solution. In 1822 a committee on foreign relations submitted a report suggesting that foreign colonization of the north could help with the pacification of the "barbarian nations." Such a solution was particularly urgent in Texas, the committee concluded, because Texas was the buffer between Mexico and the United States, and it was norteamericanos, not native peoples, who posed the greatest threat in the long run. In the early 1820s it was still an open question, though, just who those colonists should be. Some insisted on recruiting from elsewhere in Mexico or from Catholic Europe. Others thought these hopes unrealistic, arguing that most colonists must inevitably come from the United States with its booming nearby population of mobile, land-hungry farmers.[39]

As to whether norteamericano colonists could be trusted, several would-be empresarios traveled to Mexico City to convince the emperor and his people that they could. Stephen F. Austin, always the shrewdest of the lot, arrived in the spring of 1822 and immediately set about cultivating allies. Soon after unpacking his bags he wrote Bustamante a long letter seeking favor and offering opinions on Texas Indians. Austin dwelt on the American markets that encouraged Comanches to steal horses and mules and insisted that increased population would be necessary to interdict the trade. If the government approved his colonization plan, Austin concluded, "I will obligate myself as stated in my memorial to organize the settlers into Rifle Companies and arm them, and to hold them in readiness at all times to march against the Indians within said Province whenever called on." At the dawn of independence, then, Mexican policy makers and would-be empresarios alike understood Texas to be a point of special vulnerability for Mexico, and that they had to view Indian relations, colonization, and potential threats from foreign powers—especially the United States—as interlocked issues.[40]

Bustamante would go on to play an important role in this delicate intersection, but not in quite the way he or his would-be client expected. The brewing rebellion that Guonique found so interesting forced Iturbide from power in early 1823. In October of the following year congressional delegates approved the Constitution of 1824, making Mexico a federal republic. As one of the few high-ranking officials to stick with the emperor to the end, Bustamante felt compelled to relinquish his captain generalship following the abdication. After a time in state government the general became involved in a plot allegedly aimed at returning Iturbide to the throne, which led to his arrest, imprisonment, and finally release in early 1825 as part of a general amnesty for political criminals. Unsure what to do with this able but suspect man, the government of President Guadalupe Victoria got him out of the capital by appointing him commander general of the eastern internal provinces (comprised of Coahuila y Texas, Tamaulipas, and Nuevo León).[41]

When he arrived to take up his responsibilities Bustamante experienced firsthand the complexity of Indian affairs in postindependence Mexico. Initially the treaty Guonique had signed in Mexico City seemed to inaugurate a new era of peace, and for the next few years Comanche leaders were regaled by individual towns in Texas and along the lower Rio Grande. In 1825 the leader Hoyoso received a Mexican tricolor flag as a personal gift from President Victoria, and he and two others were made honorary officers in the Mexican militia. But during the same year and into the next other Comanches, Wichitas, and Kiowas stole and slaughtered animals and occasionally even killed Mexicans in Texas, Coahuila, Chihuahua, and New Mexico. Peoples on the southern plains evidently disagreed about how to treat Mexicans. The inconsistencies and contradictions confounded Mexican authorities, who expected clear distinctions between enemies and friends. By 1825 one exasperated official despaired of sorting it out and denounced all Comanches as "a class of people that know no . . . other occupation than to roam the deserts, robbing and killing." Solicitous Comanche leaders responded apologetically to the raids, returned livestock and captives, and blamed Kiowas or ungovernable youths. A large mixed party of hundreds of Comanche men, women, and children came into San Antonio in July 1825 seeking trade and a reaffirmation of the peace, and Comanches signed new treaties in Santa Fe and in Chihuahua City in late 1826. Meanwhile, hostilities continued in Texas, where Austin and others expressed alarm over rumors that Comanches and Wichitas were "going to make a grand effort" at a massive, coordinated assault.[42]

Then in late 1826 Bustamante seized an opportunity to confront the Indians from a position of strength. Though eventually a fiasco, Hayden Edwards's Fredonia Rebellion began in a manner serious enough to warrant the mobilization of military and civilian resources from across Texas and the lower Rio Grande. Once the rebellion collapsed, the commander general pivoted to challenge Comanches and Wichitas. Bustamante wrote Austin congratulating him for his loyalty during the rebellion and enlisting him in the next step. "What now remains[,] my friend," he wrote, "is to pacify the Comanches and other tribes that threaten our settlements." Bustamante had local officials organize defenses, sought to recruit Texas Cherokees in the effort, and declared the necessity of fighting Comanches "in their own villages with an energy equivalent to the per- fidy and cruelty of their outrages."[43]

A small victory in the field and the general threat of Mexicans, colonists, and possibly Texas Cherokees campaigning across *la comanchería* worked to the ad- vantage of Comanche leaders who had been trying to restore a broad consensus for peace. That summer Comanche representatives signed an armistice, and in the following year the peace was formalized in San Antonio by the prominent leader Paruakevitsi. He stated that he had spent the year "examining the inten- tions of the different tribes of his nation" and insisted that they all supported peace. The ceremony at San Antonio echoed the historic peace ceremonies of the 1780s. The assembled Comanche leaders came together in a circle, swearing "in the presence of the sun and the earth, that they would do no more harm to the inhabitants of Mexico." They dug a hole in the center of the circle, deposited broken arrows, daggers, gunpowder, and ammunition and covered the weapons with dirt "to signify that henceforth weapons would be buried forever between their people and the Mexican nation." While Paruakevitsi could not speak for all Comanches, he was undoubtedly one of the most influential men on the south- ern plains and he invested considerable energy in peace. He maintained contact with high-ranking Mexican officials and, accompanied by Ruiz, traveled to New Mexico and helped arrange conferences between other Comanche leaders and Mexican officials in an attempt to prevent raids into Chihuahua and along the lower Rio Grande. Comanches and Mexicans enjoyed a basically cooperative relationship for the rest of the decade and into the early 1830s, one fortified by trade, gift giving, and energetic diplomacy. In August 1830, the military com- mandant of Texas noted that Comanches had made no incursions for at least two years, nor behaved badly in any way. The only thing the commandant and his colleagues had to complain about was the mounting cost of regaling Coman- che visitors.[44]

The peace gave Mexican authorities an opportunity to assess the increasingly complicated situation in east Texas. Mexico's Congress appropriated funds for a *comisión de límites* to travel to Texas, determine its precise boundary with Louisi- ana (something left undone from the 1819 Adams-Onís agreement), investigate its natural resources, and gather information about its diverse peoples. Busta- mante welcomed the commission in early 1828, three hundred years after the first Spaniard set foot in Texas. Drawing on their observations, on conversations with Indians, Mexicans, and Texans, and on the deep knowledge of key figures such as Bustamante and, especially, Ruiz, the commission members eventually

1. Comanche Family. Watercolor by Lino Sánchez y Tapia after a sketch by José María Sánchez y Tapia. Courtesy of the Gilcrease Museum, Tulsa, Oklahoma.

produced a trove of information about Comanches and other native peoples. José María Sánchez, a military man and the draftsman for the commission, kept a detailed diary and produced sketches of Indians that, while now lost, guided another artist, José María Sánchez y Tapia, who painted an invaluable series of extant watercolors depicting all of the major native cultures of Texas in the late 1820s. A remarkable Frenchman named Jean Louis Berlandier accompanied the commission as a botanist and distinguished himself through his focused and learned curiosity about indigenous peoples. Berlandier gained tremendous insight from Ruiz and others, made a brief sojourn hunting with Comanches (an experience he wrote about for Mexican audiences), and collected examples of native material culture. He married a Mexican woman and spent his remaining years in Matamoros, refining a manuscript destined to be the greatest borderland ethnography of the first half of the nineteenth century.[45]

Finally, the leader of the expedition, General Manuel Mier y Terán, wrote a report and several influential letters about Texas that alarmed important people

2. Comanches in War Dress. Watercolor by Lino Sánchez y Tapia after a sketch by
Jean Louis Berlandier. Courtesy of the Gilcrease Museum, Tulsa, Oklahoma.

in Mexico City. Terán was an intense patriot worried about the future of his
nation. He had been a member of the congressional committee that submitted
plans for the colonization of Texas in 1822 and had long felt uneasy with the
virtually unregulated immigration of American citizens. His tour of Texas only
deepened these worries, hence the letters that interested so many in the capital, including Joel Poinsett. It was Terán's writing that Poinsett sent to Secretary
of State Van Buren in August 1829 and that Van Buren hastily drew upon to
argue that if Mexico sold Texas, the United States would control the Comanches. Having just helped coordinate a fragile but hopeful alliance with Comanches and other Indians in Texas, Bustamante might have taken exception to Van
Buren's portrait of the ravaged and helpless Mexican frontier. And as it turned

out, by the time Jackson's proposition received a hearing in Mexico City Bustamante would occupy his republic's highest office.[46]

THE POLITICAL EXISTENCE OF OUR COUNTRY:
MEXICAN POLITICS

The commander general was able if uninspired. Few begrudged Bustamante's
loyalty and integrity, and he was well liked in the north, where he served with
energy and determination. Northerners winked at rumors that he had several
mistresses on the frontier; long after he left the region, it was said, "there remained live examples of his cult of love." Fanny Calderón de la Barca, a diplo-
mat's wife living in Mexico City and an insightful observer of Mexico and its
people, found Bustamante decidedly less seductive: "simple in his manners, and
not at all like a hero." She thought his conversation tedious—he had too much to
say about medicine—but nonetheless found him "frank, open, and unreserved.
It is impossible to look in his face without believing him to be an honest and
well-intentioned man." Still, whatever his qualities, Bustamante could attribute
his five-year pilgrimage from prison to the presidency to nothing so much as the
quickening turmoil of Mexican politics. To make sense of Bustamante's ascen-
sion, his response to Jackson's offer, and, most broadly and importantly, the way
he and other Mexicans would react to Comanches, Kiowas, Apaches, Navajos,
and other northern Indians in the years to come, one must know something of
Mexico's early political history.[47]

In the broadest sense, most of Mexico's political elites subscribed to the same
goals. They wanted Mexicans to enjoy safety, stability, and prosperity. They
wanted the Mexican Republic to be a modern nation-state, one that could defend its borders, provide internal security to persons and property, enact and
enforce necessary laws, and command the loyalty and allegiance of its citizens.[48]
Manifold obstacles stood in the way of these goals. The country's population
consisted of diverse indigenous peoples (perhaps 40 to 60 percent of the country), *creoles* (American-born persons of European descent) and Spaniards (20
percent), mestizos or *castas* (persons of mixed ancestry, 20 to 40 percent), and
smaller populations of African descent concentrated on the coasts. Unlike the
United States, which excluded native peoples from the polity as a matter of
course and defined most African Americans as fractional persons lacking political rights, independent Mexico decoupled race from citizenship. In the eyes
of the government everyone born in Mexico was a Mexican citizen, whether
or not they knew or cared. José María Luis Mora, a prominent liberal thinker
of the period, insisted that from a legal standpoint "Indians no longer exist." In

practice, however, politicians were hardly blind to race. They variously saw the country's poor indigenous and mestizo majority as malleable constituents, as compatriots in waiting, lacking only education and institutional reforms, or as dangerous children to be isolated from the national political arena at all costs.[49]

Demography and racism were not the only barriers to the emergence of a strong, coherent, and stable Mexican nation-state. The independence struggle had left Mexico with hundreds of thousands dead, with mining and other critical sectors of the economy damaged and depressed, and with fiscal crises besetting the new government. While the U.S. economy surged in the first half of the nineteenth century thanks to immigration, improvements in industrial technology and transportation, and legal innovations protecting property and encouraging investment and commerce, Mexico fell behind in all these regards. Mexico lacked the navigable river systems so critical to the U.S. economy. Just as important, it also suffered from political instability, which retarded investment and the institutional reforms necessary for economic growth. For more than a decade after independence, Mexico's elites refused to contribute meaningfully to the government's tax base, and foreign trade proved woefully inadequate. A stagnant national economy made it all the more difficult for governments to achieve fiscal solvency; insolvency contributed to political instability; and unstable governments could do little to promote the investments needed to revive the stagnant economy. This ruinous cycle shaped much of Mexico's early history and would be of central importance in years to come when northern Mexicans became desperate for national assistance against mounting Indian raids. Indeed, fiscal and political crises became so entrenched that not until the last quarter of the nineteenth century did Mexicans have the same per capita income their grandparents had enjoyed in 1800.[50]

Thus politicians in postindependence Mexico City faced tremendous challenges, and, naturally, they disagreed about how to meet them. Most basically they disagreed about the geography of political power. Important figures in Mexico City argued that given the population's political immaturity and the danger of territorial dissolution, the country's political power should be concentrated in the capital. Other elites, especially those dominating the provinces, insisted on a federalist system that dispersed power among states. Centralists tended toward oligarchical politics while federalists did more to cultivate popular support. Centralists were often associated with conservative politics while federalism was more regularly associated with liberalism—though these labels can obscure more than they illuminate. Certainly, some politicians, newspapers, and thinkers identified so strongly with centralism or federalism as to become nearly synonymous with it. During the 1820s, for example, Lorenzo de Zavala was for many the champion of federalism and radical social reforms, while his contemporary Lucas Alamán worked consistently for centralized political authority and conservative social policy. But for most of Mexico's political class federalism and centralism were not fixed, irreconcilable ideological camps. For instance, the pragmatic Bustamante advocated federalism unless he or one of his close allies had power, in which case centralism seemed the prudent course. Participants in this decades-long controversy over governance often held complex and contradictory views about the organization of the nation-state, views that could shift with changing opportunities and political realities. Still, in the critical period following Iturbide's abdication, federalists had the upper hand. The constitution of 1824 established a republic composed of semiautonomous states and centrally administered territories, governed by a president (elected by the state legislatures) and a bicameral national congress.[51]

Political debates sharpened during Victoria's presidency in 1824–28. Shifting political coalitions emerged in response to controversies over the powers of the central government as well as over tax policy, tariffs, corporate privileges, military budgets, church property, and, most divisively during these years, the fate of the many European-born Spaniards remaining in Mexico. The rancor of the period—characterized by bitter feuds in the press, personal attacks, and the physical menacing of rival politicians—fueled the elite's anxieties and even provoked a failed coup.[52] The election of 1828 set the war hero General Vicente Guerrero against Manuel Gómez Pedraza. Seeking to blunt fears that Guerrero and his close advisor Zavala would pursue a radical agenda, the general's supporters sought to recruit a prominent vice presidential candidate: someone perceived to be a friend to the elite, someone safe, competent, and untouched by the acrimony of recent capital politics. They recruited Anastacio Bustamante.[53]

The choice cast light on how Mexicans and Americans viewed their respective Indian frontiers. While Guerrero's backers made their election-year calculations, Jackson was roaring toward his goal of defeating Adams and becoming president of the United States. Old Hickory had national appeal for a variety of reasons, including his populist economic and political platform. But Jackson the hero was at bottom an Indian fighter, the man who had broken the Creeks, seized Florida, "liberated" millions of acres of farmland, and, as president, would liberate millions of acres more. Jackson's handlers sought maximum advantage from his Indian-fighting past. So did his opponents, who styled him a butcher: a famous editorial cartoon from the era depicts Jackson's likeness made out of scores of naked Indian corpses, beneath which appears a quote from Shakespeare's *Richard III:* "Methought the souls of all that I had murder'd came to my tent." Many in Mexico City saw appeal in Bustamante's frontier experience, but,

crucially, that appeal had little if anything to do with his accomplishments fighting and negotiating with independent Indians. Bustamante's frontier sojourn
simply meant that he had been absent from the capital and hence unsullied by
the messy disputes of the mid-1820s. By the end of the decade almost no one in
Mexico City was talking about Comanches, Apaches, or Navajos. Thus while
Bustamante's record influenced the vote in the frontier states, his interactions
with native peoples had little or no political significance, either positive or negative, elsewhere in the country. Independent Indians on distant frontiers had little
hold on Mexico's national imagination.[54]

The addition of Bustamante left Guerrero's backers confident of victory. Then
Gómez Pedraza won the election. Guerrero refused to accept the outcome and
led a coup. Gómez Pedraza eventually concluded that he could not prevail, resigned as president-elect, and sailed into exile. In early January 1829, Congress
recognized Guerrero as president and Bustamante as vice president, legitimat-
ing the violent nullification of a fair election and setting a ruinous precedent.
Guerrero entered office about the same time that Jackson began his first term
and right away started aggravating existing enemies and creating new ones.
Zavala, now minister of finance, initiated a host of tax reforms that alienated the
Catholic Church, the wealthy, state and local governments, business owners,
foreign merchants, and powerful editorialists. In August 1829 the Spanish invasion that Jackson and Van Buren would seek to exploit materialized on the
Gulf coast. Mexican forces handily defeated the ill-conceived campaign, but, to
his chagrin, the embattled president enjoyed none of the credit. By November
army officers began plotting against the government and soon prevailed upon
Vice President Bustamante to lead the movement. Though supported by the
same faction in the election, Bustamante and Guerrero had no close personal or
political relationship, and the moderate vice president felt uneasy with Zavala
and the administration's supposed excesses. By Christmas Guerrero had abandoned the fight, and, on New Year's Day, 1830, Anastacio Bustamante became
chief of state.[55]

The upheavals of the past two years had left Mexicans with an understandable
craving for stability, and Bustamante's government proceeded to placate frightened elites and move strongly against crime and social unrest. The conservative
champion Alamán served as foreign secretary and became the most active and
important figure in Bustamante's administration. Long convinced that Mexico
was unsuited to U.S.-style federalism, Alamán began concentrating power in
the executive. Newspapers friendly to the administration expounded on the deficiencies of the federalist system, opposition deputies in Congress started receiving threats and consequently missing sessions, and Alamán worked to secure

compliant legislatures in the states. The administration rounded up petty criminals and made public executions commonplace. Bustamante's was to be a government in control of its country.[56]

And its borders. Bustamante brought to the presidency his familiarity with the rapidly changing northeastern frontier, and the findings of Terán's border commission deeply troubled Alamán and many others in the capital. Like Terán, Alamán had long opposed liberal immigration laws. Indeed, it had obviously been too easy to populate Texas with norteamericanos. By 1830 there were more than seven thousand colonists and enslaved Africans in Texas, compared to a tejano population of perhaps three thousand. Terán found many of the newcomers ignorant or contemptuous of Mexico's laws, and the commission's draftsman, Sánchez, thought the colonists "a lazy people of vicious character." Stopping at Austin's settlement, Terán and his men had made the acquaintance of a wealthy norteamericano named Gross, who had come to Texas fleeing creditors. Gross had brought with him "innumerable" hogs, many cattle and horses, and 116 (mostly stolen) slaves, whom he treated with "great cruelty." Gross and some companions introduced the Mexican commissioners to his three dogs, Ferdinand VII, Napoleon, and Bolivar. "The indignation at seeing the name of the Colombian Liberator thus debased," wrote Sánchez, provoked the team's mineralogist to "utter a violent oath, which the impudent fellows did not understand or did not wish to understand." While not all norteamericano dogs seemed so objectionable to the commissioners, most of their owners did. Ignoring the rules governing colonization, the newcomers had appropriated lands adjacent to the U.S. border and along the seacoast and, disdaining the company of Mexicans, had established themselves in enclaves apart from the older settlements of San Antonio and Goliad. Expedition members noted strong colonist discontent with the Mexican government, and many became distressed. Terán warned that the colonists would "be the cause for the Mexican federation to lose Tejas unless measures are taken soon." Sánchez agreed, predicting that "the spark that will start the conflagration that will deprive us of Texas, will start from [Austin's] colony. All because the government does not take vigorous measures to prevent it. Perhaps it does not realize the value of what it is about to lose."[57]

Warnings such as these informed the Bustamante administration's reaction to Jackson's offer. In August 1829 Secretary of State Van Buren had instructed Ambassador Poinsett to open negotiations on purchasing Texas for the United States, but the Spanish expedition, Guerrero's mounting crisis, and Poinsett's own troubles got in the way. Poinsett had long been perceived as a meddler in Mexico's politics, and Guerrero came under intense popular pressure to have him replaced. The despised ambassador stepped down in December just as

Guerrero was forced from office. It speaks to Jackson's single-mindedness that he appointed his crony Anthony Butler as a replacement. Butler arrived in Mexico in late 1829 determined to secure a deal for Texas. He aggressively courted Foreign Minister Alamán and wrote confidently to Van Buren that "we can gain as much from the present administration as from any subsequent one."[58]

This perception can be attributed to Alamán's dissembling and Butler's credulity. Bustamante and Alamán viewed Jackson's offer more as an insult to bear than a proposition to consider—yet another installment in a long sequence of threats, bombast, and disdainful ploys expressive of U.S. designs upon Mexican territory. As early as 1805, in the heat of his argument with Spain over Louisiana's boundary, Thomas Jefferson stood before Congress and denounced Spain's perfidious, unjust conduct toward the United States. "And if we have kept our hands off her till now," Jefferson had growled, "it has been partly out of respect for France, and from the value we set on the friendship of France. We ask but one month to be in possession of the city of Mexico." In 1819 the official newspaper in Mexico City published translations of editorials written by the prominent newspaperman and future Missouri senator Thomas Hart Benton proclaiming the justice and inevitability of an American Texas. In 1822 independent Mexico's new Committee on Colonization warned that Texas would meet "the same fate that the Floridas experienced, or, at least, it will be converted into a rendezvous for pirates," if U.S. designs remained unchecked. Two years later Mexico's first chargé d'affaires in Washington told his superiors that Jackson was ready to invade Texas as he had Florida, in order to force Mexico into a cession. And only two days after Poinsett had first presented himself in Mexico City in 1825, he approached one of President Victoria's confidants about U.S. "dissatisfaction" with the Adams-Onís line.[59]

Butler's mission, then, was an outrage but not a surprise. Newspapers and political figures in the capital expressed indignation at the suggestion that Mexicans would sell part of their own country. Terán, the commander general of the eastern internal provinces following Bustamante's elevation, captured the wounded cynicism with which many Mexicans had come to view the United States by the late 1820s. He explained how "the most avid nation in the world" had employed a variety of subtle means to "dispossess the powers of Europe of vast territories" in North America. Instead of force, "these men lay hands on means that, if considered one by one, would be rejected as slow, ineffective, and at times palpably absurd." First, they appeal to history to make spurious territorial claims, as they did with La Salle's "absurd fiasco" in Texas. Obscure writers recommend these claims to their countrymen, and the territory in question "begins to be visited by adventurers and empresarios." Before long these newcomers express dissatisfaction and begin complaining to the legitimate settlers, "discrediting the efficiency of the existing authority and administration." Then "diplomatic maneuvers begin." U.S. authorities incite uprisings and "manifest a deep concern for the rights of the inhabitants," all the while masking their aims with "equitable and moderate" communications to the other power. Then, "with the aid of other incidents, which are never lacking in the course of diplomatic relations, finally comes the desired conclusion of a transaction as onerous for one side as advantageous for the other."[60]

Terán observed that such tactics succeeded with European colonies, but "the question with respect to Mexico is quite different." How could a *republic* sell part of itself? How could Mexico "cut itself off from its own soil?" Terán saw Texas both as a strategic buffer and as a land with tremendous agricultural and commercial potential. By scheming to obtain Texas the United States was "attacking primary interests intimately tied up with the political existence of our country." Should Mexico "consent to this base act, it would degenerate from the most elevated class of American powers to that of a contemptible mediocrity, reduced to the necessity of buying a precarious existence at the cost of many humiliations." As to the republic's leaders, "he who consents to and does not oppose the loss of Texas is an execrable traitor who ought to be punished with every kind of death."[61]

Neither Bustamante nor his foreign secretary aspired to be execrable, traitorous, or dead. In early February 1830, Alamán had a bill introduced in Congress criminalizing further norteamericano immigration into Texas. In March he read a speech before Congress repeating many of Terán's formulations and adding some of his own to dissect the sly processes of U.S. expansion. "Sometimes more direct means are resorted to," the secretary explained, "and taking advantage of the enfeebled state, or domestic difficulties of the possessor of the soil, they proceed upon the most extraordinary pretext, to make themselves masters of the country, as was the case in the Floridas." On April 6, 1830, a version of Alamán's bill became law, encouraging Mexican and European immigration to the troubled region and criminalizing further American immigration into Texas. While Bustamante and Alamán took drastic measures, Butler pressed on, assuring his intense patron Jackson that he had nearly secured a sale.[62]

All four men indulged in easy stories. The story that Jackson and Butler told themselves was one in which corrupt Mexican dons could be bullied or bribed into selling Texas, thus facilitating the inexorable march to greatness by the United States. Bustamante and Alamán cherished a narrative in which wise, determined Mexican leaders would foil the disingenuous, sinister tactics through which norteamericanos proposed to expropriate their republic's northern lands. Neither story gave a meaningful role to the people who still controlled so much of North America, including most of the territory in question. For Jackson and his subordinates, Comanches and other native peoples in the Mexican northeast entered the story only as an afterthought—as bogeymen meant to frighten Mexico into a sale. Perhaps in part because independent Indians had proved so difficult to predict and understand, Mexico's leaders increasingly thought of them as regional actors: obviously important to the frontier but largely irrelevant to—or, more exactly, incomprehensible within—the logic of national and international politics. Hence while Terán had come to know and to write a good deal about native peoples in Texas, the thumbnail sketch of the continent's history he crafted for his superiors in Mexico City had everything to do with scheming norteamericanos and virtually nothing to do with Indians. Alamán and others promoted the same North American tale, even in regard to a place like Florida whose long, complex, and tortuous history had been forged precisely at the volatile intersection of imperial and native pasts. Mexicans often turned to Florida's history in this period for helpful parallels, and when they did they took away simple stories about norteamericano deceit and aggression.

There is irony in this. Jackson's offer signaled the imminent materialization of a threat that Spaniards and then Mexicans had anticipated for nearly 150 years. Northern New Spain's security and prosperity during this long watch depended in large part on the ability of its authorities to recognize the limits of their own power. This meant seeing Indians as more than wandering savages or pawns in interimperial struggles. Instead it meant taking them seriously as independent polities; complex and fractious to be sure, but polities nonetheless with geopolitical goals relevant to the geopolitics of European empires. That Rubí, Gálvez, Anza, and like-minded Bourbon-era officials embraced this outlook in hopes of better manipulating Indians is beside the point. To secure the frontier against all enemies and forward the slow project of extending real dominion, they had to entertain complicated stories about regional and continental power, stories in which native peoples could play decisive roles. Independent Mexico seemed initially to adopt the same viewpoint, seeking out native leaders, regaling them in the capital, and celebrating treaties that acknowledged Indian power and autonomy while gesturing hopefully at a broader Mexican unity.

And yet by 1830, with the hopes of the treaties frayed by bouts of raiding, the budget crisis deepening, domestic politics unraveling, and international relations growing more and more precarious, ambivalence had set in. Mexicans were increasingly unsure not only of how to treat independent Indians but even how to think about them. By the time Butler began his vain negotiations with

Alamán, most of Mexico's national leaders had quietly forgotten the late colonial insight that unconquerable indigenous peoples held the keys to their imperiled and still imaginary dominion in the North. Like their norteamericano rivals, the members of Mexico's political elite had come to explain their emerging predicament through a story about nation-states, one that effectively denied that stateless Indian peoples could be meaningful geopolitical actors.

While pushed to the imaginative margins by politicians in Washington and Mexico City, Comanches and other independent Indians in Mexico's north controlled strategic territory in what was becoming the epicenter of international tension in North America. They had seen their own histories shaped directly and indirectly by the interimperial contests of previous decades and centuries. Indeed, at the very moment that they were being written out of the story they found themselves more connected to continental events than ever before. By 1830 Comanches were grappling with new threats and new opportunities as population movements, market expansion, and state formation in the United States and Mexico all worked changes upon their world. How they responded to these changes would put the lie to easy stories and throw into stark relief the complications that still lashed together the histories of states and indigenous polities in nineteenth-century North America.

Part One

NEIGHBORS

Danger and Community

Early on October 18, 1831, Capitán Manuel Lafuente paced around San Antonio's plaza and reviewed his little army: two hundred men, give or take a few, milling about with guns and provisions, doing their best to calm several hundred snorting horses and mules. The assembly included professional soldiers, militiamen, and volunteers from ranches and towns across Texas. They came to kill Indians. In just three weeks they would get their chance and, in seizing it, make a colossal mistake. For the moment, though, all was optimism and celebration: drums and bugles, flags and handshakes, prayers, good-byes, and bravado. It was a morning of collective purpose. Tejanos thought this campaign long overdue, that the region's Indians had forgotten that Mexicans could be terrible in their wrath. Of that, God willing, Lafuente would remind them. Those with the courage, tools, and time volunteered. Lieutenant Francisco de Castañeda, imprisoned for fraud, successfully petitioned for temporary release. Others donated horses, money, guns, ammunition, and food. Everyone wanted a part.[1]

The camaraderie and confidence must have been good for the spirit because Lafuente and his men were living in a time of decline. The oldest tejanos watching the procession might have recalled an era of even greater violence and insecurity in the 1760s and 1770s, recalled how their fathers helped usher in a long period of peace by doing what Lafuente was about to do: riding out to kill Indians, showing them that tejanos should be feared. But their fathers had the crown behind them. Apache, Wichita, and Comanche attacks during the War of Independence had gone unanswered, and Comanche raids in the mid-1820s ended only when Bustamante's show of force empowered Paruakevitsi and other leaders to build consensus for yet another treaty. Even this agreement had not stopped Wichitas, especially Tawakonis and Wacos, from plundering tejano herds. The robberies had led to a punishing cycle of raids and counterraids by the late 1820s and early 1830s, and locals began clamoring for a decisive campaign.[2]

Mexican authorities had to revisit their delicate equations of force and friendship. They had authorized Lafuente's expedition, belatedly, but found themselves in a difficult position. The recent insults and raids had been trying, to be sure, and tragic for those directly affected. But this was not war—not yet. War was what had happened in the mid-eighteenth century, when large-scale Indian campaigns in New Mexico and Texas shattered regional economies, demolished flocks and herds that had taken generations to build, turned scores of settlements into ghostly deserts, and consigned hundreds of Spanish women and children to bondage in native camps. Mexican authorities had to be realistic about their diminished resources and use force carefully, lest they turn tension and scattered acts of violence into outright war.

So while they urged Lafuente to track Tawakoni raiders and leave them "so severely punished that they can never be hostile to us again," Comanches were off-limits. Certain frontier officials resented this, convinced that Comanches had been thieving along with their Wichita allies. Resentment and complacency made some Mexicans cavalier about maintaining diplomatic relationships even with Comanches. After spending 365 pesos entertaining Guonique and a small group of followers at Saltillo, for example, the tightfisted governor of Coahuila y Texas requested that Comanche leaders be prevented from traveling so far south. Even José Francisco Ruiz was losing patience. Two months before Lafuente embarked, news arrived that smallpox was raging in several Wichita villages. The renowned cultural intermediary declared, "May it be God's will that not a one of them will be left," adding, "I hope that the same thing is happening to the Comanches."[3]

Despite growing ill will, Paruakevitsi and other leaders continued visiting San Antonio to affirm peace and apologize for their young men. In March of 1830 he had arranged for a Mexican escort to take his brother Chuparú to visit Bustamante in Mexico City. Several months later he stopped a party of Wichitas on the road, relieved them of thirty horses they had stolen, and returned the animals to the authorities in San Antonio. So, for the time being, if Texan officials found Comanches raiding, they were to employ diplomacy first by lodging protests with Paruakevitsi, "the most celebrated and valiant captain among all the Comanches."[4]

Lafuente's eager men rode out from San Antonio and soon added eighteen Caddos, Kickapoos, and Ionis to their troop. The diverse group located the village of the Tawakoni raiders three weeks out. Spies reported that the Indians were absorbed in a dance. Lafuente ordered most of his men to withdraw quietly while others reconnoitered the village, locating the best avenues for attack. At 2:00 a.m., the spies returned to say that the Tawakonis had all fallen asleep. Lafuente ordered his men to load their weapons and advance. "As soon as we drew near," Lafuente later reported, "we opened fire with a dense volley, and we continued to pour bullets into them so fast that within a few minutes it was necessary to cease fire because the field had been completely abandoned by the savages, who only occupied themselves with putting themselves and their families in safety, without making any resistance."[5]

The tejanos had another reason to cease fire. As soon as the volley began, shocked voices cried out, "Comanches, amigos amigos Españoles!" Lafuente maintained in his report that he had not realized Comanches were present in the camp, but this is difficult to believe. The report noted distinctive Comanche tepees among those of the Tawakonis, and it is highly unlikely that Mexican and Indian spies would have missed this crucial detail while reconnoitering the village. After three weeks of searching, Lafuente likely decided he was not going to forgo his opportunity to kill Wichitas just because a few Comanches had got in the way. But the captain could not have known *which* Comanches had got in the way. Once the smoke cleared, Mexican soldiers made their way to where wailing women hovered over a pair of bodies. They looked down and, to their dismay, saw that they had killed the great man himself, Chief Paruakevitsi, along with one of his sons.[6]

One can imagine that Lafuente's mind began to race at this moment. That Paruakevitsi had likely been urging Tawakonis to adopt a conciliatory stance toward tejanos only underscored the magnitude of the error. The attack "left the entire tribe completely terrified, [and] plunged all of them, especially the families of the deceased, into inconsolable sorrow." The Mexicans' anxiety shone through in the impromptu conference they arranged, at which they nervously explained to Paruakevitsi's people that "we were not to blame for these deaths, and that they alone had caused them because they had united with the [Tawakonis], our enemies." Lame as it was, the Comanches seemed amenable to this explanation—given that the large Mexican force maintained its threatening position opposite the camp. Still worried, the Mexicans gave the dead chief's kin "a large part of the booty" taken from the Wichitas and then left them to grieve.[7]

Lafuente's men pursued the fleeing Tawakonis, killed nine, hung the corpses from two oak trees, and returned as conquerors to San Antonio. The citizen-soldiers who volunteered for the campaign came home with enhanced reputations and even with some plundered Indian ponies. But the little victory came at great cost. Bustamante congratulated Lafuente yet lamented the death of Parua-kevitsi, "the most beloved of all the Comanches, the one who obeyed better than anyone else." Mexican authorities could no longer rely on him to admonish ag-gressive young warriors or to make the case for peace among other native leaders. And, of course, tejanos now had reason to expect Comanche reprisals.[8]

None came. To the puzzled relief of authorities throughout northeastern Mexico, two months after the attack hundreds of Comanche men, women, and children came into San Antonio to trade "a large number of loads of furs, bear grease, meat and other things," reaffirming peace despite Paruakevitsi's killing. Prominent Comanches said the same, and, in case any doubt remained, one of the dead chief's sons even came into San Antonio to express his continued good-will. Comanches were doing everything they could to ease Mexican minds.[9]

The question is why. If, as most Mexicans seemed to think, Comanche policy toward Texas depended primarily on how Mexicans acted, then the careless kill-ing of one of the region's preeminent leaders would surely have had negative repercussions. At the very least Comanches might have demanded restitution, but they did not. In fact, peace had come to depend upon factors that Mexican authorities neither understood nor controlled. While neither side felt satisfied with the actions of their inconsistent allies, Comanches and Mexicans lived in a dynamic world of dangers that for the time being required both to maintain community with each other. Why their unsatisfactory peace continued to lurch along, and why it finally collapsed when it did, may be discerned in this shifting landscape of danger and community.

TO SPOIL THE SPOILER:
DANGERS ON THE SOUTHERN PLAINS

In the early 1830s, there were probably ten to twelve thousand Comanches living on the plains. Their population was far short of its peak in 1780, when the first in a series of major epidemics ravaged their camps. In rebuilding they had be-come increasingly diverse, assimilating indigenous and Mexican captives as well as Indians and non-Indians who chose to become Comanche. Moreover, in the early nineteenth century Comanches allowed their former enemies the Kiowas and Kiowa Apaches to dwell peacefully beside them on the southern plains. Lin-guistically, sociopolitically, and ceremonially distinct from each other and from Comanches, the fifteen hundred to two thousand people who comprised these tribes nonetheless integrated themselves with their hosts—occasionally through

1. Comanches and their neighbors, ca. 1830

marriage, often through camping and hunting together, and usually through cooperation against those their partners considered enemies.[10] By 1830 all three peoples spent most of the year south of the Arkansas River. The rough outlines of their territory stretched from the high Llano Estacado of eastern New Mexico and the Texan Panhandle, south along the Pecos River to the Rio Grande, east and north along the rim of the Balcones Escarpment, northwest to the edge of the Cross Timbers, and north again some distance above the Arkansas. Though the Numunuu homeland, like their population, had been much reduced from what it was a half century before, *la comanchería* remained vast, diverse, and bountiful.[11]

As did most plains peoples, Comanches and their resident allies depended upon bison hunting for their primary caloric needs and for most of their clothing and shelter. Their position on the southern plains gave them privileged access to immense herds of bison. But access to another animal is what made Comanches so wealthy in comparison to their Indian neighbors. By the eighteenth century and early nineteenth, horses had transformed native societies across the plains. To secure their territories, maintain their economies, and live comfortable, dignified lives within their own communities, plains peoples had to constantly acquire new horses. A few, Comanches included, increased their herds somewhat through controlled breeding. Another method was to capture and break wild mustangs, especially abundant on the southern plains. But by the early nineteenth century, the ranches and haciendas of northern Mexico remained the most important supplier of horses for plains societies. In the Mexican north, with its relatively mild winters and an economy driven by animal breeding, horses seemed nearly innumerable. Proximity gave Comanches and their allies a near-monopoly on this resource and more horses per capita than any other native people in North America. Berlandier wrote that even the poorest Comanche families had between six and ten of the animals. Wealthier Comanches supposedly had between thirty and forty, in addition to eight or ten mules. Some of the richest men on the southern plains owned hundreds of horses each.[12]

Through impressive community organization and military prowess Comanches had come to dominate this most strategically valuable territory on the Great Plains. They thus had access to critical hunting and trading resources and, most important, had become rich in animal wealth in comparison to their neighbors. Notwithstanding these accomplishments, great wealth had "aroused the envy of the other nations" and put the residents of la comanchería in considerable danger. Non-Indian observers had little information about war between native peoples, so documentary evidence for these conflicts is fragmentary. Still, combined with other sources, these fragments make it clear that by the 1820s and early 1830s several Indian peoples threatened the families and fortunes on the southern plains.[13]

Their most immediate threats from the north and northwest were relative new-comers to the region. The Cheyennes lived in present-day Minnesota during the seventeenth century, were pushed west by enemies during the eighteenth, and subsequently adopted the classic equestrian, bison-hunting culture of the plains while moving into the Black Hills of South Dakota. By the early nineteenth century they occupied a position of power on the high plains in southeastern Wyoming, and a portion of the Cheyenne began to expand their hunting and raiding activities to the area between the Platte and Arkansas rivers in present-day Colorado. By the late 1820s the Southern Cheyenne and their allies, princi-pally the Arapahos, had helped push the regular Comanche range south of the Arkansas.[14]

According to George Bent, son of the prominent Cheyenne Owl Woman and the Missouri trader Charles Bent, Cheyennes saw the southern plains herds as the natural place for a warrior to acquire horses, just as surely as Comanches and their allies saw Mexican herds in the same light. Bent recalled that the Coman-ches and Kiowas were "famous throughout the plains for the size and quality of their herds." As a boy he had been told that the southern tribes preferred horse meat to bison and used horse hides as others used buffalo hides. For wide-eyed Cheyenne boys who dreamt of owning a few horses of their own some day such tales must have evoked the same disbelieving wonder that urban urchins felt upon hearing about tycoons who lit cigars with twenty-dollar bills. Chey-enne elders recalled that Blackfeet often came through their camps in the early 1820s, boasting about the horses they had taken from Comanches and Kiowas. In 1826 the famous leader Yellow Wolf led one of the first Cheyenne raids into la comanchería. Soon other parties followed, until Comanches and their allies were, according to Bent, "constantly being plundered" by Cheyennes, Arapahos, Blackfeet, Gros Ventres, and others. These raids produced tales of bravery and daring told well into the reservation era.[15]

Farther east, Osages had been raiding la comanchería for much longer. David G. Burnet, future president of Texas and one of the first Americans to live among Comanches voluntarily, reported constant warfare between his hosts and Osages, who regularly ventured south to "spoil the spoiler of his prey." A traveler among the Osage heard one leader boast of having stolen five hundred Coman-che horses in a single night. Violence often attended these raids. In 1820 Lieu-tenant Stephen H. Long's exploratory troop encountered a Comanche party that had just been attacked by Osages. The raiders had killed three men and wounded six more. One of the Comanche men had "cut more than one hun-

3. Cheyenne Killing Two Kiowa Women. Cheyenne ledger art, unknown artist.
Courtesy of the Frontier Army Museum, Fort Leavenworth, Kansas.

dred parallel and transverse lines on his arms and thighs, of the length of from
three to four inches, deep enough to draw blood" in mourning for a slain brother.
Comanche leaders complained on multiple occasions to American traders that
the United States provided arms and ammunition to Osages, "but we can get
none, or very few of them. This is wrong . . . very wrong." American weapons
helped give Osages a deadly advantage. Berlandier reported that in 1828 Osages
executed thirty Comanche women and children they had captured in a previous
raid.[16]

A most extraordinary native source attests to this violence. From at least
1833 on, Kiowas recorded their history on calendars that memorialized two key
events each year, one in summer and one in winter. One of the earliest surviving
records is for summer 1833, the "summer that they cut off their heads." In early
spring, when most of the men were away on a journey, Kiowa families gathered
in a single camp. At some point news arrived that Osages were about. Terrified
and largely undefended, the families fled in four directions. At dawn the next
morning Osage warriors surprised one of these parties, taking a brother and sister
captive and killing five men and many more women and children. The raiders

set the camp on fire and then hacked off the heads of their victims and stuffed them into several brass buckets for horrified kin to discover on their return.[17]

Awful and threatening as they were, it seemed by 1830 that these foes would soon be eclipsed by native immigrants arriving daily from the East. Berlandier noted that "almost all of the peoples who came here originally from the United States of North America make war on the Comanches." An early Anglo-Texan newspaper reported in 1830 on the outbreak of "a kind of exterminating war" between Cherokees, Shawnees, Delawares, and others against Comanches and their allies. In the early 1830s, Mexican officials were paying very close attention to a particularly bloody feud between Comanches and Shawnees. Eastern Indians had more and better firearms than peoples on the southern plains, including guns and ammunition that came from U.S. government annuities given in return for ceded lands. This advantage enabled small parties of native immigrants to best much larger groups of Comanches. In 1832, for example, twenty-nine Koasatis (a division of the Upper Creeks) fought one hundred and fifty Comanches, apparently killing or wounding upward of one-half. A year later another Koasati party brought back seventy scalps from Comanche country. As grave as the situation seems in light of these scattered references, the full reality was undoubtedly worse.[18]

While the Comanches' herds lured enemies into their territory, the requirements of hunting and of caring for horses made it difficult for families on the southern plains to protect themselves and their property. Killing frosts came later to the southern than to the central and northern plains, and new, nutritious short grasses could appear weeks or even months earlier in the southern reaches of la comanchería than farther north. Despite these relative advantages, herds had basic requirements that shaped life and vulnerability on the plains. Each week a mustang needs a pound of salt. Each day the animals drink ten to twelve gallons of water, and they need enough grass to equal twenty-five pounds of good hay. One study has found that a camp with a thousand horses in western Kansas would have consumed seven acres of grass daily during periods of average rainfall. During drought, horses could consume six times that much. The threat of disease also resulted in the dispersion of animals. Parasites, lice, blood-sucking louse, and chewing louse all pestered plains horses, and the longer the animals stayed in one place, or the more quickly they returned to it, the greater the risk of the herd becoming infected. Beyond the requirements of sustenance and health, horses are simply very choosy eaters, often straying far from camp to find their favorite grasses.[19]

Though they were a populous people, Comanches thus out of necessity

4. Koasatis. Watercolor by Lino Sánchez y Tapia.
Courtesy of the Gilcrease Museum, Tulsa, Oklahoma.

spent most of the year separated from each other in mobile groups vulnerable to enemy raiders. That did not mean, however, that families on the southern plains were autonomous, isolated people at the mercy of adversaries. Community made them something much more dangerous than that.

COALESCE WITH THEIR KINDRED:
COMMUNITY ON THE SOUTHERN PLAINS

Comanches made meaningful decisions together at several organizational levels. Immediate, or nuclear, families occasionally sojourned on their own, but more commonly the most stable residence group was an extended family of ten to thirty people. Extended families generally camped with other extended families to form residence *rancherías*, or bands, that spent the greater part of the year together. Band members were connected by webs of kinship obligations and by an institutionalized form of friendship that not only produced a fictive kinship between two people, but obligated the families of those two people to honor the obligations of family relations as well. The size of the bands fluctuated, ranging from approximately two dozen to several hundred residents.[20]

Within families and bands, Comanches looked to particular senior men for direction on matters of community interest. Each family had a de facto leader, or *paraibo*, usually an older though not elderly man who had proven his honor to his family members. Men obtained honor through the possession of medicine power, or *puha*, through daring and success in war, through the generous redistribution of gifts and resources, and through wise, eloquent, and balanced counsel. A man who would obtain such political power strove to arrange good marriages for kin and otherwise increase his pool of dependents and followers. While each band recognized a senior paraibo, there were also younger men in every ranchería who had gained reputations and social influence for successfully leading war or raiding parties against the Comanches' many enemies.[21]

The most prominent leader of the central extended family in a residence band would be looked to as the head chief of that band. Before making decisions of consequence about moving camp, performing important ceremonies, hunting, or regulating trade, he would seek consensus informally and in council with the other men of the band. Though very rarely paraibos may have threatened or even used coercive force on other Comanches, their authority depended entirely upon the voluntary allegiance of family and supporters. Comanche families regularly moved between bands, so leaders' political power always fluctuated. Comanche politics at this level was therefore highly fluid and sensitive to the opinions and fortunes of individual families.

Throughout most of the year, the band remained the largest political unit of everyday relevance. During the summer months, however, Comanche bands assembled as tribes or divisions to renew social bonds, perform rituals of community integration, and engage in communal bison hunts.[22] Each division had a distinct name and a particular territory. By the second quarter of the nineteenth century there were four Comanche divisions: Kotsotekas (Buffalo Eaters), Yamparikas (Yampa-Root Eaters), Hois (Timber People), and Tenewas ([those who stay] Downstream).[23]

The annual period of divisional socialization and cooperation served to bind bands together. Men's and possibly women's societies of several kinds recruited members from within divisions and fostered social and material connections between bands. War leaders often recruited men from different bands to go on expeditions against enemies, and they formed temporary communities united in ambition, risk, and honor that laid the groundwork for future cooperation. Most fundamentally, Comanches tended to marry outside the band but inside the division. Brides would generally live with their husband's families, and children recognized the families of both their parents as relatives. Marriages created kinship obligations and political support networks that connected bands at a variety of levels. If they looked deep enough, nearly every Comanche could have recognized any other as some kind of relative.[24]

These mechanisms for integrating community fostered within Comanche divisions a framework for coordinated action in relations with outsiders. War and peace, trade relationships, territory and resource use—these issues affected all families within a division, and the shared interests of these families and their bands would be represented by their own leaders when they met in council during divisional gatherings. Such councils unfolded with much ceremony and served to promote unified policies vis-à-vis other peoples in a variety of ways. First, they provided an opportunity to share and evaluate intelligence about outsiders gathered by the several paraibos over the intervening months. Second, divisional councils served a kind of policing function, putting checks on the activities of individual leaders by calling them to account for their actions and periodically reevaluating their public honor in the context of the interconnected interests of the entire division. Finally, councils served as public forums where paraibos could articulate the concerns of their people and work to achieve consensus on important issues, particularly concerning policies relative to non-Comanches.[25]

The members of the divisions chose a principal chief from among their most prominent paraibos to facilitate this consensus and to serve as the highest representative of divisional policy to outsiders. Paruakevitsi may have occupied this position among the Tenewa. While the principal chief did have special influence in matters of external policy, the office itself implied no particular authority in internal Comanche affairs: political power in this sphere depended entirely upon the principal chiefs' positions as prominent band leaders in their own right. Like all political positions within Comanche society, the authority and influence of a leader derived from his personal reputation and honor and also from the contingencies of the times—not from the office itself.[26]

While the position of principal chief was the highest office Comanches recognized, the division was not the highest organizational unit within which they could coordinate policies and actions. Most broadly, all Comanches spoke the same language and shared material, political, and religious cultures. Though each division had a particular territory, the boundaries of these territories shifted with the seasons and over time and always remained porous to other Comanches. Interaction between Comanches on the overlapping fringes of divisional territories would have been common. Families moved freely between divisions temporarily or permanently and may have done so as a consequence of the perpetual competition between paraibos for new followers. Death, too, occasioned movement between bands and divisions. Families tended to separate themselves from their resident band and seek other, more distant associations while in mourning for immediate kin. Finally, Comanches would have been connected to other Comanches outside of their division through material relationships. Scholars have followed Euro-American observers in stressing the existence of trade ties between Comanches and outsiders, but the huge Comanche community was itself a still more regular arena for gift giving and exchange.[27] Most redistribution and trading would have taken place at the band and divisional levels, but because of their different territories, divisions often had access to diverse kinds and amounts of plant, animal, and manufactured goods. These variations encouraged the movement of people and products across the whole of la comanchería and strengthened far-flung networks of kinship, patronage, and obligation that constituted an established base for the coordination of policy.[28]

Such policy coordination was generally passive. Most visibly the several divisions nearly always respected the demands of each other's external relations. The norm seems to have been to consider serious enemies of one, enemies of all. An informed observer noted that if any Comanche division was attacked by a formidable enemy, it would "retire to, and coalesce with, their kindred, who would adopt the quarrel without an inquiry into its justice or expediency." Likewise, peoples who were important friends of one division became, if not friends of all, at least a group whom no Comanches should wage war upon. Scattered thefts and occasional acts of violence aside, one does not hear of Hois, for example, laying waste to New Mexican ranches where Kotsotekas had close ties, or of Yamparikas besieging San Antonio while Hois were at peace there, or even of Tenewas trading for horses that Osages had stolen from Kiowas. Young men may have driven off animals in inconvenient places from time to time, and divisional and interdivisional consensus might be altogether lacking in transitional periods. But Comanches nonetheless tended to coordinate broad external policy across divisions. Usually this coordination remained passive and negative, tacit agreement about what not to do. But given the right circumstances and leaders, this force became active, creative, and potent.

This potential for coordination extended to non-Comanches. Kiowas often cooperated with Comanches in matters of war, and they too had a segmentary social structure that could be mobilized when necessary. Like Comanches, Kiowas spent most of the year in residence bands, or *topotóga*, of perhaps 130 people, most of whom were members of an extended family. Individuals always married outside their extended family and often outside of bands, and Kiowas regularly moved between different residence groups for short periods. Most important, all Kiowas gathered nearly every summer for an elaborate ceremonial and social occasion known as the Sun Dance. The Sun Dance gave Kiowas an opportunity to renew tribal bonds, revitalize their sense of common identity, and maintain the relationships that bound people together across the different topo-tóga. Having a far smaller population than their allies, Kiowa Apaches generally resided near Kiowas and often participated with them in their Sun Dances.[29]

In addition to Kiowas and Kiowa Apaches, the Comanches' longtime horticultural allies the Wichitas had long been reliable trading partners and friends. Sometimes Wichitas, especially Tawakonis, accompanied Comanches on raids against Mexicans. Indeed, with their economy and population undermined in the early nineteenth century some Wichitas chose to become Comanches themselves. José María Sánchez remarked that Comanches seemed "very considerate of the small tribes with which they have friendly relations, protecting them, teaching them their habits and customs, and finally amalgamating them into their nation." Last, Shoshone families often sojourned with Comanches, their linguistic kin, and cooperated with them in matters of war and peace. Mexican observers such as Ruiz and Berlandier knew that "Sonsores" could be found in Comanche villages, but most non-Indians failed to notice any difference between these closely related peoples. For example, one of the most famous captivity narratives from the nineteenth century, Rachael Plummer's *Narrative of Twenty-One Months Servitude as a Prisoner among the Commanchee Indians*, is almost certainly an account of Shoshone, not Comanche, captivity.[30]

Families of Kotsotekas, Yamparikas, Hois, Tenewas, Kiowas, Kiowa Apaches, Tawakonis, Shoshones, and others on the southern plains thus cooperated and communicated through a variety of social mechanisms. Collectively, these connections created the potential for the coordination of formidable offensive power; and offense was the key to territorial security. Because southern plains peoples, like New Mexicans, Navajos, and nearly all pastoralists, found it difficult to mount effective and consistent defense against raiding parties, they had to take the fight to their enemies. They had to rely on offensive campaigns to demonstrate to their foes that attacks on any of their number could provoke the wrath of hundreds or even thousands. Large parties of Comanches and Kiowas were known to campaign in Cheyenne and Arapaho country, pursuing horse raiders even to the Platte. More regularly, southern plains Indians came together in the summer for what seems to have been a nearly annual campaign against their old enemies, the Osages. Ruiz was present for such an event in 1824. By his estimate there were twenty-five hundred warriors present: two thousand for the campaign and five hundred to guard an enormous, sprawling camp. Assuming one fighting man for every five Comanches, Kiowas, and Kiowa Apaches, this assembly must have represented nearly the whole of the fighting force on the southern plains.[31]

These massive campaigns advertised the power and coherence of the greater Comanche and Kiowa communities to their many enemies and may have dissuaded other groups from escalating their raiding into a territorial war for control of the southern plains. But these exercises tended to last only several days and rarely resulted in significant changes to the power dynamics of the region. It was not in the martial tradition of any of these peoples to engage in set battles between infantry or cavalry, and this made extended campaigns and numerous minor engagements prerequisite to any really effective offense against hostile enemies. Moreover, groups of thousands or even hundreds of men traveling together would have had difficulty feeding themselves on the plains during most of the year, especially if they were hunting enemies rather than game. Finally, the warriors' families and animals would be safe in a single camp with a five-hundred-man guard, but the demands of hunting and grazing meant that this kind of security could be only a very temporary luxury. If several hundred or a thousand men left for weeks or months at a time to fight any one of their many enemies, then their families and fortunes would be exposed to attacks by the others in their absence. For instance, the Kiowa men who returned to camp in the summer of 1833 and found the severed heads of loved-ones stuffed into brass buckets had been away campaigning against Utes.

In sum, Comanches and their allies had a serious problem by 1830. The same resource that had made them rich had also attracted powerful enemies from the north and east. Their impressive ability to coordinate offensively had been ideally suited to attacking Spanish ranches or the Apaches' fixed, horticultural settlements during the eighteenth century, but ecological and defensive constraints had frustrated an effective military response to their many new adversaries by 1830. This problem was fundamental to the peace that plains families maintained with their Mexican neighbors. La comanchería had become a dangerous place to live, and Comanches could not profitably fight their indigenous enemies and Mexico at the same time.

Having so many hostile peoples on their borders, Comanches and their allies relied on the markets they found in Mexican settlements to their west and south, where they could dispose of their dressed skins and furs and obtain foodstuffs and manufactured goods. The Republic of Mexico had been inconsistent in its respect for the alliance, but frontier settlements often depended upon Comanches for their trade and especially for their friendship because war would be ruinous. While national and state officials might be haughty, indifferent, or hostile, Mexicans who lived on the margins of la comanchería had reason to please.

AHI VIENE EL COMANCHE:
DANGERS IN NORTHERN MEXICO

If in 1830 a Comanche or Kiowa party used the peace as an opportunity to tour the Mexican towns and villages to the west and south of la comanchería, it would have found them growing and hopeful but nervous. Riding west, these plains ambassadors would first have visited the Indian pueblos and Mexican villages and towns on the upper Rio Grande. Most sat somewhere between the river and mountains: the Sangre de Cristos, Sandias, Manzanos, and San Juans. By 1830 Comanches and their allies seem to have had little interaction with settlements west of the river. Among the two dozen or so to the east, populations varied greatly. Santa Fe and Santa Cruz de la Cañada had the most inhabitants, over five thousand each. The settlements closest to la comanchería, San José del Vado, San Miguel del Vado, and Anton Chico, villages that had crept onto the plains along the Pecos Valley following the Comanche peace of 1786, probably had a combined population of nearly three thousand in 1830. Kiowas called New Mexicans K'o´pt'a'ka´i. The first element, k'o´p, means "mountain." The second, t'a'ka´i, is common to all the Kiowa terms for specific groups of Mexicans. Its literal meaning is obscure but might be rendered as "mule-people." By the late nineteenth century t'a'ka´i was more often translated as "whiteman," though the term identified cultural difference, not skin color (hence the term Ko´ñkyäo´ñt'a'ka´i, literally "black whitemen," to refer to Africans).[32]

South of Socorro and the emptiness of the Jornada del Muerto, El Paso and the declining presidios of San Elizario and El Norte were aging gateways to Chihuahua's haciendas and towns, peopled by the Toñhe´ñt'a'ka´i, or "Waterless whitemen," as Kiowas called them. El Paso probably had over five thousand residents in 1830. Beyond El Norte, following the course of the Rio Grande, riders found no significant Mexican populations for more than one hundred kilometers on either side of the hard, spectacular Big Bend country.[33]

In the next cluster of ranches and towns along the river lived the P'aedalt'a'ka´i, or "Rio Grande whitemen." The towns of Rio Grande, Nava, and Guerrero sat on the south bank of the great river. These were mirrored by other towns a few miles into the interior, toward the ranches and haciendas in the shadows of the Santa Rosa Mountains, the country of the Do´'ka´ñit'a'ka´i, or "Bark whitemen." Next on the river came Laredo, situated on the north bank. A still denser settlement area existed farther down river, including the towns of Revilla, Mier, Camargo, Reynosa, and, finally, the unhealthy but booming gulf city Matamoros. Kiowas called the inhabitants of the far lower Rio Grande Ä´t'a'ka´i, "Timber whitemen," a term that also applied more broadly to residents of Tamaulipas and Nuevo León. The principal towns from Rio Grande to Camargo had populations ranging from several hundred to over three thousand, while Matamoros and its ranching hinterlands were home to ten thousand. All told, twenty-five to thirty thousand Mexicans lived along the lower Rio Grande in 1830, in between the more populous Mexican cities, towns, villages, haciendas, and ranches in the interior of northeastern Mexico, and powerful native peoples to the north.[34]

The final area of Mexican settlement in the far north that Comanches and Kiowas could have visited was located more than one hundred miles north of the Rio Grande, between the Nueces and Colorado rivers in Texas. There were two principal towns, San Antonio de Béxar and Goliad. These towns and their associated ranches existed just on the eastern fringe of the prairies. Behind them, in the timbered country beyond the bison range, newly arrived Anglo-American colonists had their settlements, plantations, and farms. There were a few older Mexican settlements even farther east, though Plains Indians rarely visited these places. The Mexican population between the Nueces and the Colorado, with which they regularly interacted, amounted to between three and four thousand in 1830.[35]

Some of the Mexican settlements surrounding la comanchería accumulated their wealth through agriculture. While farming mattered across the north, however, in many areas it was not productive enough even for self-sufficiency. Many river towns had to import grains and vegetables. Some had access to other resources, such as rich salt deposits, that could be mined for trade. Most families supplemented their incomes through handicrafts, especially weaving, which women along the river were renowned for. Above all, these people worked as ranchers and herders. Northern Mexicans recognized cash money as the ultimate medium through which to reckon wealth, but the typical paucity of hard currency on the frontier meant that land and, especially, animals remained the de facto measure of wealth in the north. New Mexicans accumulated wealth in sheep, in particular. Below El Paso, the stock was more mixed. Mexicans there also kept some sheep and goats, but they had more cattle, horses, and mules than most New Mexicans. Residents of the lower Rio Grande used horses and mules in farming, commerce, travel, and defense and also to measure and distribute family wealth. They exchanged animals for all kinds of goods, for land, and for services. Moreover, they made dowry payments in horses and also in mules, which many valued at twice the price of mounts.[36]

Across the whole of arid northern Mexico, two dangers threatened the expansion of ranching and grazing economies: drought and war. Drought, the War of Independence, and Indian raids had together contributed to a significant contraction in animal populations along the lower Rio Grande in the early nineteenth century. Berlandier estimated that the whole of northern Mexico lost 1$\frac{1}{2}$ million animals in the independence era. Texas had been especially hard-hit. By 1830 the Mexican population of Texas had shrunk to perhaps one-third of what it had been at the end of the eighteenth century. Another commentator calculated that Texas had 40,000 to 50,000 tame horses and nearly 100,000 head of cattle in 1806. In 1828 San Antonio, the principal town in Mexican Texas, had only 150 horses and mares and 1,322 cattle.[37]

By the late 1820s, however, the prospects for the northeast and for northern Mexico more broadly seemed much improved. After several serious droughts in the first two decades of the century, most of northern Mexico enjoyed abundant rainfall from the late 1820s through 1846. Authorities in Coahuila, for example, did not record a single year of drought from 1829 to 1846. The tenuous Comanche peace held out the promise that northern Mexicans from Chihuahua to the gulf coast were poised to capitalize on the rain and the end of the War of Independence to exploit an economic and demographic expansion the likes of which had not been seen in generations.[38]

Mexican settlements spread out into new or abandoned areas in the 1820s, almost with a sense of relief. One report estimated that more than three million head of stock grazed the ranches of the lower Rio Grande by 1835. Settlers established new ranches between the river towns and in the sparse fields between the Rio Grande and the Nueces, where most of the new livestock grazed. Ranches were usually composed of a handful of families who built houses relatively near each other. There were a few large landholders, but the typical holding in Texas and the lower Rio Grande included two *sitios*, or 8,856 acres, of grazing land per family. That individual families would routinely receive such large grants is indication of the poor quality of soil and pasture in much of northern Mexico, even in wet years.[39]

While most of the grazing land along the lower Rio Grande and in Texas belonged to families of modest means, wealthy, politically connected families had by the 1830s gained control of the major rivers in Tamaulipas, Nuevo León, Coahuila, Chihuahua, and Durango. They consequently owned the great majority of land in these states, nearly all of it fit only for grazing. The largest of these estates—indeed, the largest such estate ever to exist in the Western Hemisphere—was in Coahuila. The Sánchez-Navarro family began buying water rights and land in the sixteenth century, and, by the most conservative estimate, their holdings encompassed 16.5 million acres, or 25,780 square miles by 1840. Connecticut, Massachusetts, New Jersey, Rhode Island, and Delaware possess less land combined than did the Sánchez-Navarros. By comparison, the largest ranch in U.S. history, the XIT ranch in Texas, was less than one-fifth the size of the Sánchez-Navarro property at its height. This enormous estate and others like it employed thousands of laborers, many bound to their employers by debts that could carry over from generation to generation. These people lived and worked near the estate houses and ranches at the hearts of the great haciendas. Some of these settlements were quite large, but as a rule ranches were smallish and scattered throughout the estate. Since the rural economy revolved around animals and animals had to be well spaced because of the relatively nutrient-poor grasses in the north, their caretakers also had to be scattered and well spaced.[40]

The nature of the ranching economy thus meant that families in northern Mexico and the wealth they possessed or protected were extraordinarily vulnerable to attacks by enemies. In this they had much in common with their Comanche neighbors. Herders and shepherds were the most exposed link in the ranching economy chain because their far-flung animal charges required them to work alone or in small parties. Small to medium-sized ranches rarely had advance warning of attacks and seldom repulsed raiders without loss of life or property. Outside of fortified estate complexes and the larger towns and cities, defense as such remained practically impossible.

Decisions the previous generation had made about Apaches aggravated this structural insecurity. While the Spanish had come to an understanding with several tribes of Apaches by the late eighteenth century and early nineteenth, Comanches had not. The intensity of Apache–Comanche feuds had cooled by the 1790s but still presented problems for Spanish and, later, Mexican authorities, who styled themselves benefactors to the first and allies to the second. The Jicarillas living in and around the Sangre de Cristos seem not to have endangered relations between Comanches and area Mexicans in the early nineteenth century, but Mescaleros on the northeastern border of Chihuahua did. The troubling Comanche raids in the north of the state during the mid-1820s seem to have started as attacks upon Mescaleros. Comanche leaders later explained that their young warriors simply could not resist the tempting Mexican herds once they were in the neighborhood.[41]

Lipán Apaches posed even keener problems. In return for promises of peace, Spanish authorities had grudgingly granted Lipanes protection and safe haven south of the lower Rio Grande in the years before Mexican independence. Of the two main Lipán communities, the first ranged north from Laredo to Mescalero territory near El Paso, and the second south from Laredo nearly to the coast. The two groups probably consisted of 750 to 1,000 people each. Relative to population size the southern Lipanes must surely have been the most dangerous people in all of northern Mexico. No other community knew so much about the terrain, resources, and weaknesses of both la comanchería and the Mexican northeast. After they had been driven from the plains, abandoned and preyed upon by the Spanish in the late eighteenth century, and impoverished and nearly annihilated by Comanches, the remaining Lipanes became consummate survivors. They stayed among Mexicans for a generation, wandering between towns and ranches and living off wild game, petty trade, handouts, and pilfered animals. They learned everything they could about the region and then made peace with Comanches, moving back onto the plains during the independence era. This was a nightmare for northeastern Mexicans, but a diplomatic triumph for Comanches. They had several of their men marry Lipán women and, unusually, go and live with the families of their new wives, perhaps to keep a closer watch on these dangerous new allies. Comanches seem to have sought this alliance so that they might exploit the Lipanes' key resource—intelligence. Lipán scouts introduced Comanche raiding parties to all the best watering holes, safest routes, and most exposed settlements below the river, to the very doorsteps where Lipán families spent a generation bartering and begging. Comanche raiding along the lower Rio Grande in the 1810s seems to have been facilitated by Lipán scouts. But it was the Lipanes themselves who raided northeastern Mexico most severely during these years, especially in 1817.[42]

With the advent of independence, when Ruiz was dispatched to invite Comanche leaders to parley in Mexico City, Comanches apparently expected the Lipanes to travel with them and negotiate jointly as one of the groups Guonique referred to as the Comanches' subordinates. But Cuelgas de Castro, leader of the Southern Lipanes, went ahead of his erstwhile allies. Castro was proficient in Spanish, like most of his people, and described by one Euro-American observer as a "sagacious, shrewd, and intelligent man." He met Anastacio Bustamante and negotiated separately for the southern Lipanes, receiving a commission into the Mexican army and promising to help fight Comanches if necessary. Soon after Castro's return from Mexico City, he slit the throats of all the Comanche men who had married into his community and hurried his people back south across the Rio Grande. Given the renewed commitment from Mexican authorities to protect and indulge the Southern Lipanes and to honor Castro personally, peace with Mexico seems to have offered more security and prosperity than peace with Comanches. There was doubtless more to the Comanche–Lipán breach than Mexicans understood, but, whatever the causes, the Lipanes had revised their own calculations of danger and community and become allies of Mexico once again.[43]

Northern Mexicans were perhaps more careful about how they spoke to and dealt with the Lipanes after these events, but they feared and hated them more than ever. One observer said that the *vecinos* (citizens or neighbors) despised

5. Lipanes. Watercolor by Lino Sánchez y Tapia after a sketch by José María
Sánchez y Tapia. Courtesy of the Gilcrease Museum, Tulsa, Oklahoma.

the Lipanes and wanted them exterminated "because they recognize them as
the authors of the desolation of the pueblos in the last war and of their present
misery." More to the point, the Lipanes' very existence threatened peace with
Comanches, and everything depended on peace with Comanches. Plains families grew nervous about visiting Mexican settlements with Lipanes about. In
1828 Berlandier and his companions saw a large Comanche party break camp
in San Antonio's central square and flee in a rush because of a rumor that Lipanes were nearby. Soon after when a band of Comanches allowed Berlandier to
accompany them on a bison hunt he noted that the party seemed perpetually
anxious about the possibility of a Lipán attack.[44]

Most ominously, Comanches occasionally sent war parties south of the Rio
Grande to attack and plunder their Apache enemies. Indeed, during the first
recorded Comanche raid below the river, in 1799, they killed eight Lipanes and
seven Spaniards. In 1824, Paruakevitsi led a campaign of at least six hundred warriors against Lipanes on the lower Rio Grande. Mindful of the peace, he visited
the military commander at Laredo to insist he had no quarrel with Mexicans.
Other war parties had less discipline, and by 1825 Comanches in Coahuila were
striking Mexicans as well as Lipanes. Mexican authorities acknowledged their
friendship with Comanches and Apaches alike but wanted to "remain neutral

in their debates." Lipanes boasted that they did not fear Comanches, but Lipán mothers could be heard to silence crying children by whispering "ahi viene el comanche" (here comes the Comanche). Whatever they thought, the Mexican families below the river knew Comanche raids on resident Apaches threatened the fragile peace that was prerequisite to their growth and prosperity.[45]

A BAZAAR GOING ON AMONG THEM:
COMMUNITY IN NORTHERN MEXICO

Like Comanches, then, northern Mexicans lived in considerable danger because of the character of their history, their economy, and their arid homeland. Like Comanches, they turned to several kinds of community for protection against threats. Ranches were the smallest and most common unit of settlement in northern Mexico, usually consisting of a few extended families living near each other and cooperating with labor and defense. Ranches forged and maintained social, economic, and familial connections to other ranches in the area through trade, strategic marriages, and a form of fictive kinship called *compadrazgo* (co-godparenthood). These same mechanisms created bonds of kinship and mutual obligation between towns or cities and the ranches in the hinterlands around them. Moreover, many of the wealthier town folk had farms and ranches in the countryside run by client families, and thus the wealth and interests of the towns and the ranches intertwined. Whether because of familial or economic ties or both, Northern Mexicans could call upon extensive support networks to help them through hard times and to send them men and aid in crises.

These networks had been built over generations from the bottom up and were in many ways similar to community bonds on the plains. The most important similarity might have been their mutual vulnerability to raiders and thieves, despite the manifold ways they cooperated and helped one another. But Spanish speakers in northern Mexico could call upon another, parallel system of community that was far larger, more formal, and imposed from the top down. Thanks to the federalist constitution of 1824, Tamaulipas, Nuevo León, Chihuahua, Durango, Occidente (later the states of Sonora and Sinaloa), and Coahuila y Texas all had governors and state legislatures. New Mexico had territorial status during these years, meaning that the national congress was finally responsible for its governance, but it nonetheless had high officials and an assembly. States and territories were further subdivided into departments, and departments into *partidos*. Governors appointed a prefect to administer each department, and the prefects assigned a subprefect to administer each partido. Thus every settlement in northern Mexico belonged to a state (or a territory), a department, and a partido, and residents of every settlement had some claim upon the attention of a governor, a prefect, and a subprefect, either directly or through intermediaries. Settlements located within this political geography also had their own representatives, who dealt with local matters and communicated with higher authorities. Cities and towns of sufficient size had *alcaldes* (mayors) and formal, elected councils called *ayuntamientos*. Smaller towns and ranches elected justices of the peace. At haciendas the owner, or *hacendado*, usually appointed subalterns to handle organization and representation at different levels.[46]

All of these units were fractions of the supercommunity called Mexico that, nominally, everyone born within the limits of the Mexican Republic belonged to. The potential cooperation among these units in the name of Mexican nationhood was a threat that Mexican officials regularly tried to impress upon independent Indians. For every Comanche living in 1830 there were nearly one thousand Mexicans in the republic. Mobilizing the entire republic would obviously be impossible, but Mexicans had the advantage Comanches lacked of being able to coordinate the resources of their population through taxation. Under ideal conditions they could concentrate and support professional soldiers, horses, weapons, and supplies for extended periods against their enemies, as they did with Bustamante's campaign in Texas in 1827. Every diplomatic visit Comanches made to Santa Fe or San Antonio in the late 1820s and early 1830s gave frontier officials another opportunity to argue for the reality and relevance of the Mexican nation-state; to insist that all Spanish speakers across the frontier were one people.[47]

In theory Spanish speakers in northern Mexico could therefore turn to many levels of community integration to help fend off surrounding dangers. And they depended on one final kind of community to keep them safe: the personal relationships many among them maintained with Comanches themselves. Plains families regularly came into settlements all along the northern frontier to trade and maintain social ties with individual Mexican communities. These were not Comanche–Mexican relationships per se, but local, place-specific connections between Comanche families and members of individual Mexican settlements, what one scholar calls "borderlands communities of interest." The settlers of San Miguel del Vado in eastern New Mexico, for example, had long-standing economic, social, and even kinship ties to Comanches. At least three Christian marriages took place between Comanche men and Vado women in the 1810s and 1820s. Other frontier towns, such as San Carlos in Chihuahua and Guerrero in Tamaulipas, were likewise places of special relationships between Comanches and Mexicans. The Kiowas had particular and regular enough connections with Mexicans at El Paso (Pä´suñt'a'ka´i, "Paseño whitemen") and Laredo

(Tso´ñt'a'ka´i, "Light-haired whitemen") to give them their own names. Often such towns had translators or soldiers who had spent time with Comanches either as captives or, like Ruiz, as guests and had gone on to become invaluable cultural intermediaries.[48]

Trade was the bedrock of these relationships. Hundreds of Comanche men, women, and children regularly made visits to the eastern New Mexican settlements, to towns on the lower Rio Grande, and to San Antonio bringing mules loaded with commodities for barter. Comanche families brought a variety of goods to exchange, most of them the products of women's work—especially dried meats and processed animal skins. Comanche women were renowned for the suppleness of their bison hides. Many women added artistry and value to their trade hides by painting them with elaborate designs. Skillful painting could triple the price hides fetched in certain markets. There was also a brisk trade in bear grease, especially in Texas. Berlandier estimated that tejanos killed around four hundred black bears annually, but that Comanches killed far more. A large bear could render up to one hundred pounds of grease, which Mexicans used as lard for cooking, for medicinal applications, and also as an exotic trade item to ship south. There were even ads for the grease in Mexico City's papers, one highlighting the "extraordinary effect that this bear oil possesses in beautifying the hair." Finally, Comanches occasionally brought Mexican and Anglo-American captives to trade at the frontier settlements, and relatives or middlemen often paid high prices for these lost kin.[49]

In return for such goods and captives, Mexicans offered a variety of things Comanches did not produce, including tobacco, corn, other vegetables and fruits, baked breads, and brown sugar in the form of little loaves called *piloncillo*. They traded metal objects, such as knives and sword blades to affix to lances, and barrel hoops that Indians made into arrowheads. Impoverished frontier soldiers even traded their guns, powder, and shot to Comanche visitors on occasion, and in periods of peace Comanches and their allies eagerly bartered for horses and mules. Finally, Comanches and their allies sought textiles made by Mexican women. This trade rarely drew the attention of Mexican or Anglo-American observers, but the surviving references indicate that textiles were one of the goods Comanches most desired. In September 1831, for example, a party of twenty Comanches and Kiowas came into Cuesta, New Mexico, and traded a number of horses for several woven blankets and some gunpowder. In times of war, Mexican officials often found Mexican clothes and blankets among the spoils taken from defeated Comanches. It is also likely that Navajo blankets were making their way to Comanches via New Mexican traders by the early nineteenth century.[50] Sometimes this trade happened in reverse, with Mexican *comancheros* from eastern New Mexico leading loaded mule trains onto the plains. The great trade fairs at Pecos and Taos during the eighteenth century had declined by the nineteenth, and most trade happened in la comanchería instead. New Mexican authorities occasionally tried to control this commerce, but it would continue until the late nineteenth century.[51]

Wherever the traffic commenced, trading visits presented opportunities to renew mundane but critical relationships between individuals and families that rarely made it into the documentary record. This diverse commerce created bonds of interethnic community relations across the frontier that surely did more to preserve peace between northern Mexicans and Plains Indians than Mexico's meager gift giving and inconstant diplomacy. By the early 1830s, for example, the main exports of San Antonio district were hides and pelts, perhaps ten thousand annually, the great majority obtained from native peoples. New Mexico had a longer history of dependence upon Plains Indian trade than Texas. Through the eighteenth century, New Mexico's export of furs and hides seems to have generated considerably more trading revenues for the province than even the sheep trade. One eighteenth-century official described New Mexico's textile and hide trade "the rich mines of the kingdom." While New Mexican commerce became much more dynamic in the nineteenth century, especially following the advent of trade between Santa Fe and Missouri along the famous Santa Fe Trail, New Mexico continued to profit from the hide and animal trade with the southern plains. In a treatise on his adopted homeland, a newcomer to New Mexico insisted with great enthusiasm that "vermilion, knives, biscuit, bread baked in ovens, gunpowder, awls, and other trifles purchase most valuable furs which may be sold at great profit." Trade with plains peoples presented New Mexicans with seemingly unlimited opportunities: "Even those remote places occupied by wild Indians offer us rich products with which we are as yet unfamiliar."[52]

Comanche families likewise depended upon the trade, so their leaders tried to restrain violent protests against the mounting inadequacy of official Mexican diplomacy. Since the 1780s, diplomatic gifts from Spanish and Mexican authorities provided Comanche leaders with prestige items and manufactured goods that they redistributed to their people. Redistribution of diplomatic gifts was an important tool in solidifying a popular following or political base. From the independence period onward, Mexican authorities in the north had trouble acquiring the quality, quantity, and variety of gifts that Comanche leaders had come to expect. This failure is often seen as a chief motivation for Comanche raiding during the Mexican period. But local markets with individual Mexicans and Mexican communities represented an even more important political resource for Comanche paraibos. Unlike the undependable dividends of state-

and national-level diplomacy, Mexicans on the frontier usually welcomed commerce with Plains Indians. Surrounded by enemies to the north and east, many Comanches still depended upon the Mexican trade in 1830. Every ambitious paraibo had to locate and maintain reliable markets for the goods his people, especially the women in his community, produced. Insofar as individual Comanche families relied on Mexicans this way, paraibos had to respect and cultivate the commerce if they wanted to retain or grow their followings. As much as they resented the inconstancy and parsimony of Mexican officials, then, Comanches kept coming in to trade. Observing one such visit to San Antonio, Berlandier remarked that "it is like a little fair to see a town square covered with the tents of a tribe, with all the hustle and bustle of a bazaar going on among them."[53]

In the early 1830s, then, Comanches and northern Mexicans had common problems and common interests. Their huge animal herds and the aridity of their homelands left them vulnerable to similar dangers, and their trading relationship made them mutually dependent. Individual northern Mexican towns and villages went to considerable trouble to receive Comanches with respect and hospitality, comancheros made regular visits to Comanche camps, and local leaders on both sides had compelling reasons to maintain and police a healthy relationship. But peace by the early 1830s had come to depend upon other factors that neither Comanches nor northern Mexicans could master. No matter the care, attention, and respect given to the relationship on the ground, it was still indirectly shaped by the actions of the Comanches' Indian enemies and by the financial and political crises that distracted Mexico City from its obligations in the north. In this sense the effort, goodwill, and energy that went into local relationships between Mexicans and Comanches were all tentative, marked by hope but also apprehension over what neither side could fully anticipate or control. Meanwhile, men in Washington and Arkansas were trying to decide what to do about the Indians of the southern plains.

BUFFALO-HIDE QUIVER

Imagine for a moment that every time Comanches and their allies stole a Mexican horse or mule, attacked a ranch, or wounded, captured, or killed a Mexican a light flashed in the darkness. If we could stare down at a nighttime map of Mexico and watch years unfold in minutes, most of 1830 would be black. Toward the end of the year, pinpricks of light coming from northeastern Chihuahua might catch our eyes. From 1831 to early 1834, the flashes become slightly more pronounced and predictable, though still dull and mostly contained in Chihuahua, until late in 1834 much of the state suddenly catches fire. Something changed. Another change takes place during 1836 and 1837, when the lights spill east out of Chihuahua and race like electric current down the lower Rio Grande to the gulf. Several years of protective shadows are cast back on either side of the river, illuminating the isolated ranches and towns from El Paso to Matamoros in a hard, white light. Then, just as suddenly, the map starts to dim. In 1838 we see occasional flashes all across the north of present-day Mexico, but by 1839 only a handful of isolated, if bright, bursts are visible in Nuevo León. Finally, in 1840 a third, momentous change takes place. As if someone threw a switch, Chihuahua, Durango, Coahuila, Nuevo León, Tamaulipas, and parts of Zacatecas and San Luis Potosí are suddenly ablaze.

The data from northern Mexico from the early 1830s through the early 1840s reveal three critical moments of transition moving the Comanche–Mexican relationship from imperfect peace to sustained war. The three dramatic expansions in Comanche raiding correspond to geopolitical events on or around the southern plains. These events helped convince most Comanches, Kiowas, and Kiowa Apaches to abandon their ongoing efforts at manipulating Mexico's government into acting differently. Over the course of the decade, proponents of

peace with Mexico lost all their best arguments, and Plains Indians stopped talking to Mexico and started taking from it.

OUT OF THEIR SPONTANEOUS WILL:
THE PRECARIOUS ALLIANCE

Comanches made a difficult decision in the late 1820s: they decided to ask
their imperfect Mexican allies for help against the raiders plundering their territory. Anastacio Bustamante's Texas campaign in 1827 had the desired result
of signaling a more vigorous Mexican military presence in the region, but it
also seems to have heightened Comanche expectations. At least twice, in 1828
and 1829, Comanches and their allies requested direct military assistance from
Mexican authorities. These requests would not have been made lightly. Southern plains Indians put themselves in a vulnerable position by advertising their
problems. By asking for help they offered Mexico a small but significant opportunity to be something of a benefactor. To fight side by side with Comanches
would have proved that Mexico took its northern frontier seriously and viewed
Plains Indians as critical allies in policing it against outsiders. Here was a chance
to forge a more meaningful relationship.

Mexican officials denied both requests. Some canny authorities seemed to
understand that the settlements were safer because of the Comanches' defensive crisis and thought it madness to intervene. That logic made perfect sense,
so long as the goal of a genuine and lasting alliance with Comanches had already been abandoned. Whether or not most felt this way, Mexican officials had
another, more basic reason to decline the invitations to help. The Comanches'
native enemies lived on the other side of the international border, and joint
operations against them could ultimately mean sending Mexican troops into
U.S. territory. International politics always trumped Indian relations in independent Mexico.[1]

An important opportunity had come and gone. If Comanches hoped that
the renewed alliance with Mexicans might lead to military cooperation like the
Spanish peace had fifty years before, now they knew better. The typically meager gifts Mexican frontier officials could afford did little to ease disappointment
that had been building for some time. Growing ambivalence in the early 1830s
fueled renewed raids on Mexican herds. Starting in late 1830 southern plains
raiders again began stealing animals in Texas, along the lower Rio Grande, and
especially in Chihuahua. Alarmed Mexican authorities from across the north
responded aggressively. Forces under Capitán José Ronquillo marched from
Chihuahua and killed five Comanches on the Rio Pecos, and other parties went

out from El Paso in early 1833 and 1834 to kill enemies and retake horses and mules.[2] President Bustamante gave provisional approval to the desire of Chihuahua's governor "to open up a general campaign in which a simultaneous attack can be made upon these tribes." An official in Tamaulipas even drew up an elaborate campaign plan, involving perhaps two thousand men surging into la comanchería from every state and territory bordering the plains. While nothing so ambitious ever materialized, forces from Texas and the lower Rio Grande did launch several modest but successful campaigns onto the southern plains in the early 1830s and killed dozens of Comanches in the process.[3]

Mexican officials also tried to leverage the trading relationships Comanches maintained with frontier settlements to check raiding. Starting in 1831 authorities in Coahuila stopped issuing licenses to Comanche families eager to trade below the Rio Grande and refused to resume licensing until all raiding ceased. New Mexico's governor likewise put an official ban on the comanchero trade with the plains. These sorts of official orders could and did cut down on the volume of commerce, but trading relations quietly endured in places across the frontier. Seasoned northern officials knew that this was a good thing. Ronquillo and others understood that insofar as commerce forged community between Comanches and Mexicans, it protected peace where peace endured and created opportunities to reestablish it where it did not. To discourage raiding, Mexico had to threaten Comanches on the plains and deny them certain trading opportunities, but lines of communication needed to be kept open so that paraibos who wanted venues for conversation had them.[4]

Resilient relationships between individual Comanches and Mexicans eventually led to a breakthrough. On July 23, 1834, two Comanche leaders (probably Kotsotekas or Yamparikas), one Kiowa "general," and a number of warriors came to El Paso to sign a treaty with Chihuahua. The Indian leaders said they were making peace "out of their own spontaneous will, and in thanks for the services that the inhabitants of El Paso had rendered in regaling them." They singled out a soldier named Guillermo Treviño, possibly a former captive, insisting that he had special influence among their peoples. The plains representatives offered "friendship, peace, and commerce" with Chihuahua and also promised to speak to the eastern divisions and try to bring them into the agreement. By 1834 the Apache peace had long since dissolved in Chihuahua, and Mexican officials urged the plains warriors to wage war upon Mescaleros and Chiricahuas. Mexican negotiators offered to affix special brands onto any horses taken from Apaches, even animals that once belonged to Mexican ranchers, so Comanches could lawfully trade the beasts in Mexican settlements. This significant concession promised a dramatic expansion in commerce. Given Chihuahua's dismal financial situation, the plains negotiators generously agreed to forgo the customary diplomatic presents that had been a traditional dividend of peace. They had more interest in unrestricted trade and unfettered access to their Apache enemies.[5]

As long as Mexicans could exert military power in the plains and offer Comanches and Kiowas things they needed in trade, peace would have advocates on both sides. Just as important, when trade was brisk, Comanches and Mexicans met and talked regularly, and it was from just such interactions that the treaty of 1834 had emerged. Still, these material bases for peace all depended on a commercial landscape where Mexicans remained key trading partners for the residents of la comanchería. Such was the case in the 1820s and early 1830s because Comanches were at war with the peoples to the north and east with whom they might otherwise have been doing business. The Comanches' defensive problems were therefore the Mexicans' defensive solutions, and this fact snapped into focus once southern plains Indians started finding solutions of their own.

THE BEADS SHOW THE ROAD IS CLEAN:
PEACE IN THE EAST

Since the early 1830s, it had been the desire of the U.S. government to arrive at a peace treaty with the Comanches and their allies. Raids and counterraids between Osages, Comanches, Wichitas, and Indians emigrating from eastern North America had forced an expensive buildup of army personnel and resources on the southwestern frontier. What is more, the violence stood in the way of the ostensible long-term goal of seeing removed Indians establish vigorous economies and stable governments and eventually a self-sufficient, peaceful Indian confederacy subordinate to the U.S. government. Finally, though Mexico had denied Comanche requests for military assistance against Indians residing in the United States, Mexican officials pressured their counterparts in Washington to stop "their" Indians from making raids upon the peoples of the southern plains.[6]

The U.S. effort got off to a curious start in early 1833, when Sam Houston traveled to San Antonio and met with several Comanches on behalf of President Andrew Jackson. As a young man Houston had fought under Jackson at Horseshoe Bend, where he suffered multiple wounds and nearly died on the field. He earned Jackson's trust and became a protégé, even leading the pallbearers at Rachael Jackson's funeral. With the help of his benefactor, Houston eventually won two terms in the House of Representatives and, in 1827, became governor of Tennessee. There was talk about bigger things, perhaps even the presidency. But then his marriage collapsed in 1829, and, distraught, Houston abandoned his governorship and moved out west to live with a Cherokee band that had adopted him in his youth. He dabbled in various schemes, took a native wife, drank scandalously, and started thinking big. Much to Jackson's embarrassment, word reached Washington that Houston was claiming he "would conquer Mexico or Texas, and be worth two millions in two years." Indeed, some believed Houston's failed marriage and retreat to the Cherokees had been an elaborate ruse, an early detail in a grand plan to conquer part of Mexico. Whatever his or his patron's larger goals, Houston arrived in San Antonio in January 1833 and somehow convinced Mexican authorities to facilitate and translate a meeting with "Kimanches." He reported that Comanches held Americans in high regard but viewed Mexicans with "the most supreme contempt." He presented the Indians with a Jackson peace medal, and they promised to return in three months with more senior paraibos to accompany him east for a formal conference. Optimistic, Houston worried only about his hosts. "If anything can defeat the present expectations, it will be the indirect influence of the Spaniards, who are jealous of everybody and everything." Indeed, tejano officials soon thought better of helping two potential adversaries make peace and informed the American that he had outstayed his welcome. Houston's conference never materialized. He left San Antonio and turned his attention to the simmering cauldron of Texas politics.[7]

Americans kept trying to impress southern plains Indians. One year later U.S. rangers marched onto the plains to force or intimidate Comanches into moving west, away from the borders of Indian Territory. The expedition failed spectacularly—Indians even captured and killed one of the rangers. At last in the summer of 1834 a huge dragoon expedition under Colonel Henry Dodge entered the southern plains to negotiate with Comanches and their allies. Eight Cherokees, seven Senecas, six Delawares, and eleven Osages accompanied Dodge as scouts and as their peoples' representatives to talk peace. The party also included Jefferson Davis, the future president of the confederacy (who ate so much bison on the trip that later in life the mere thought of it made him ill), the shrewd and well-connected trader Auguste Pierre Chouteau, and an artist who would become famous for his paintings of Indians, George Catlin. Finally, Dodge brought along two Wichita captives and a Kiowa girl named Gunpä´ñdamä who had been kidnapped by Osages the year before, during the "summer that they cut off their heads."[8]

The expedition crossed into Mexican Texas, made its way to a Wichita village, held talks with Comanche, Kiowa, and Wichita representatives, and handed out a great many presents. Perhaps most important, Dodge set the tone for the

6. Comanche Meeting the Dragoons, George Catlin, 1834–35. Courtesy of the
Smithsonian American Art Museum, Gift of Mrs. Joseph Harrison, Jr.

meetings by returning Gunpä´ñdamä and the Wichita children to their astonished and overjoyed kin. Catlin described the reaction of a taciturn Wichita
leader on seeing his lost relatives redeemed. "The heart of the venerable chief
was melted at this evidence of the white man's friendship, and he rose upon his
feet, and taking Colonel Dodge in his arms and, placing his left cheek against
the left cheek of the colonel, held him for some minutes without saying a word,
whilst tears were flowing from his eyes." Dodge had not been empowered to sign
treaties, so formal peace with the United States would have to wait for another
council at Camp Holmes the following year. In any case the peace between
southern plains Indians and the Osages and refugees from the East mattered
more, and, given the violence of past years, all parties had reason to welcome
it. Refugees from the East needed to be able to hunt the prairies without fear of
Comanche, Kiowa, or Wichita retaliation. To Comanches and their allies, the
U.S. government held out gifts and commercial incentives. Most important, the

7. Túnkahtóhye, Thunderer, a boy, and Wunpántomee, White Weasel, a Girl. George Catlin, 1834. Captured by Osages in 1833, this Kiowa girl (Gunpä´ñdamä) and her brother were purchased a year later by the U.S. Dragoons preparing to treat with southern plains Indians. A ram killed the boy the day after Catlin executed this painting, and just days before the expedition got under way. Courtesy of the Smithsonian American Art Museum, Gift of Mrs. Joseph Harrison, Jr.

prospect of turning bitter enemies into trading partners seemed the key benefit for all of the native peoples involved. Comanches and Kiowas had long been bound to dull Mexican markets, and peace with eastern Indians meant access to a wider variety and steadier supply of U.S. and European manufactures. In return, Comanches and their allies offered access to a seemingly inexhaustible supply of horses and mules, animals that newcomers from the East needed more than ever as they tried to rebuild their lives and fortunes in Indian Territory.[9]

The initial peace concluded with much ceremony. The eastern Indians gave Kiowas and Comanches white beads and tobacco. "The beads and tobacco, you must take home to your people . . . tell them, 'the beads show the road is clean,' and let them smoke the tobacco in remembrance of us who send it." Even the long-standing enmity between Osages and Comanches and Kiowas went to rest when, after much prodding, southern plains representatives embraced their old enemies in council. More formal negotiations would take place with Comanche representatives in 1835 and with Kiowas and Kiowa Apaches in 1837. And the peace had its strains. Disputes would arise over hunting rights and, rarely, over acts of violence. Nonetheless, a basically cooperative relationship existed between southern plains Indians and their eastern and northeastern neighbors from the summer of 1834 onward.[10]

This peace became the catalyst for the first major expansion of Comanche raiding into Mexico during the 1830s, for two reasons. The first has to do with trade. The peace transformed multiple, increasing, and terrible threats into cautious friendships and turned thieves into trading partners with high expectations. Comanches and their allies suddenly had viable, even preferable, alternatives to trading in the Mexican settlements. The second consequence was more basic but perhaps less obvious. Peace meant that the requirements on men's labor had become very different by mid-1834 than they had been only months earlier. Before the peace, southern plains men had obviously been responsible for the active pursuit of hunting, but also important was the passive duty of simply being present in camp to deter attacks on the community and its property. In other words, enemies had limited the movement of Comanche and Kiowa men. Some few young warriors might be able to leave without endangering their communities, but large numbers of Comanche and Kiowa men could not embark on prolonged ventures confident of their families' security. With the pressure off from the east and northeast, more and more men on the southern plains gained the freedom to leave camp on prolonged expeditions. As a second consequence the peace therefore set hundreds of Comanche and Kiowa warriors at liberty to attend raiding campaigns into Mexico.

Meanwhile, Mexican officials still felt optimistic that things were trending their way. But while certain Comanches and Kiowas signed papers at El Paso, others dealt with Dodge. By fall it became clear which agreement would most influence southern plains policy. In October, more than one hundred Comanche raiders stole horses from points in western and central Chihuahua. Another campaign, more wide-ranging than the first, got under way in the state two months later. Raids continued through the New Year, and southern plains men struck ranches and haciendas in Chihuahua every month from January through July of 1835.[11]

The most dramatic campaign took place in May, when eight hundred warriors invaded the state's eastern and southern districts. One episode from the campaign illustrates how quickly raids could poison relationships. On May 21, a portion of the eight-hundred-man force encountered a Mexican detachment of thirty-six soldiers near the Rancho de la Mula. The raiders raised a white flag and dispatched a captive to ask for peace, but the Mexican commander insisted on speaking to the Comanche leader first. When the captive returned to relay the message, additional Comanche warriors came into view. Spooked perhaps, or simply determined to seize their chance, the Mexicans fired a cannon loaded with ball and shrapnel. The astonished warriors, who had thought they enjoyed the protection of a formal parley, watched in horror as companions fell before the blast. The survivors rode off with their dead and wounded, slaughtering Mexican animals in their path.[12]

Thereafter the campaign took on a different quality. More than simply stealing animals and seizing captives, the raiders went out of their way to destroy what they did not want. They laid waste to the Hacienda de las Animas in early June, killing men, stealing horses and mules, sacking nine houses and burning others, and destroying all the storage bins of beans and corn they could find. When they finally withdrew, they took thirty-nine captive Mexicans with them. Most never saw their families again. Josiah Gregg, the great chronicler of the Santa Fe trade, was in Chihuahua when the attack took place and long remembered the shock and disbelief that washed over the state once the news broke. Five years after the event he found himself trading with a large Comanche band that was home to six of the Las Animas captives. He asked each if they wanted to be ransomed. One boy named Bernardino Saenz refused, insisting, "I've already become too brutish to live among Christians." In the end only one of the six, "a stupid boy . . . who had probably been roughly treated on account of his laziness," accepted Gregg's offer and returned with him to Chihuahua.[13]

It took Mexican authorities some time to connect their misfortune with

Dodge's diplomatic mission. Tejano officials were the first Mexicans to learn the foreboding news that Comanches had made peace with the Osages, Cherokees, Delawares, and others through the good offices of the U.S. Army and this helped explain why local trade was drying up. By mid-1835 Comanche families only came into Texan towns seeking sugar, apparently the one thing they had trouble getting from their new native and Anglo-American allies. But just as new dangers had been forged on the borders of Texas, so too might solutions be found there. As bad as the violence in Chihuahua had become, conflict in Texas remained relatively minor. Mexicans had launched several small but destructive campaigns into la comanchería from Texas and the lower Rio Grande in the early 1830s, and the threat of more campaigns apparently made distant Chihuahua a safer target for southern plains raiders. Authorities in Chihuahua and the rest of Mexico became increasingly hopeful that Mexican Texas might hold the key to reestablishing peace.[14]

In 1834, Colonel Juan Nepomuceno Almonte traveled from Mexico City to east Texas and met with the Cherokees, Shawnees, Kickapoos, Creeks, Delawares, and others who had established themselves there years before. They seem not to have taken part in the peace negotiations between their counterparts in Indian Territory and Comanches and Kiowas. For years, Cherokees and others in Texas had been negotiating with Mexican authorities to gain legal title to their lands. They promised to punish the Plains Indians if Mexico confirmed their titles. Officials in Texas urged their constituents to contribute funds to outfit the Cherokees and others in a campaign against Comanches.[15]

While authorities in Texas tried to threaten Indians out of raiding, tejano officials endeavored to please Hois who still came in to conduct trade—often in animals taken from Chihuahua. Authorities in Texas aimed to convince Hois leaders of the value of a general peace with Mexico, one based on expanded commerce and more diplomatic gifts. If the Hois could be won over, perhaps they would try to convince other divisions to stop raiding. Recognizing that Indian "quietude depends for a major part" on gifts, a prominent general in Coahuila ordered authorities in San Antonio to lavish presents upon Comanche leaders. Talks about a new treaty got under way, and by August three hundred Comanches had visited San Antonio with the intention of proceeding on to Matamoros to finalize a peace agreement. After the terrible summer of 1835, then, hope existed in Chihuahua and elsewhere in Mexico that Texas could be critical to a renewed Comanche peace, peace born of threatened war and the application of skilled diplomacy. But discontent within the Mexican Republic itself would dash those hopes for good.[16]

TO CONQUER THIS DESERT: THE TEXAS REBELLION

There was no such thing as an unpopular leader in la comanchería; leaders were either popular or they were no longer leaders. While prominent Comanche men injected politics into most of what they did, Comanches wasted little time and few resources struggling over the structure of their political system. They debated policy, of course, but had no divisive contests—let alone civil wars— over how politics ought to work. Most contemporary non-Indians would have explained this as part of the political vacuum that characterized all barbarian societies. But such inattention to the forms of governance was one dividend among many of a political tradition that freed up the energies and resources of its people for other activities, like attacking Mexicans.

Mexico had a very different political experience during the 1830s. Bustamante's government had proceeded vigorously with its program of enhancing domestic stability and frontier security from 1830 into early 1832. But Bustamante and his key minister Lucas Alamán alienated important constituencies by attacking the opposition press, behaving sympathetically toward Mexico's remaining Spaniards, courting the church, passing draconian anticrime laws, and meddling in state politics to augment Mexico City's power.[17]

Moreover, Bustamante alienated General Antonio López de Santa Anna, a constituency unto himself. Only fifteen when the War of Independence began, by the end of the war Santa Anna had distinguished himself through his bravery, his seemingly inexhaustible energy, and his remarkable talent for raising and organizing soldiers. After independence he rose to national prominence by initiating the movement that deposed the emperor Iturbide and led to the establishment of the federal republic in 1824. In 1829 he played a critical role in repulsing the Spanish invasion and became the most popular figure in Mexico. Bustamante began to worry. Santa Anna had mountainous personal ambition and a ruthless streak that contrasted sharply with Bustamante's amiable, some would say naïve, sincerity. "There cannot be a greater contrast," wrote Fanny Calderón de la Barca, "both in appearance and reality, than between him and Santa Anna. There is no lurking devil in [Bustamante's] eye." Convinced that Bustamante was undermining him in his home state of Veracruz and exquisitely alert to political opportunities, Santa Anna initiated a protest against the administration. The protest became a rebellion, and the rebellion a brief but destructive civil war. By December 1832 Bustamante had been forced from power, and in March of the following year Santa Anna was elected president. Never a man enamored of policy and keenly aware that a cultivated disdain for politics would put him heroically above the fray in the public's eyes, Santa Anna returned to his hacienda in Veracruz. He left the government in the hands of his vice president, the prominent federalist Valentín Gómez Farías.[18]

Gómez Farías proceeded with a reform program perceived by many elites to be radical and dangerous, one including the promotion of state autonomy and advocacy of state-controlled militias as an alternative to the bloated national army. Bustamante had left behind an empty treasury and a debt of more than eleven million pesos, and Gómez Farías tried to boost revenues by forcing the church to sell most of its properties and taxing the sale. Church leaders resisted and cast about for help in ridding themselves of this latest threat. There emerged a conservative coalition of men convinced that the instability of the past several years and the many crises that plagued that nation, including the brewing trouble in Texas, could be remedied only through the centralization of political power and decision making in Mexico City. They chose as their leader (or figurehead) none other than Antonio López de Santa Anna, who in the spring of 1834 forced his own vice president out of power, annulled most of the recent reforms, and reinvented himself as a staunch centralist. Santa Anna and his allies moved vigorously to stifle dissent and rein in the states, provoking several rebellions in the process. The most serious erupted in Zacatecas, where the powerful governor raised four thousand militiamen in defense of state autonomy. In April 1835 Santa Anna marched north, crushed the militia, and sacked the state capital.[19]

These events sent Coahuila y Texas into a panic. Coahuila had been an unrivaled bastion of federalism since independence. The constitution of 1824 left the state with remarkable latitude in distributing lands in Texas to would-be colonists and empresarios, and successful applicants invariably had respectable federalist credentials. The ideological affinity facilitated joint business ventures and helped create a web of relationships binding prominent norteamericano colonists to elites in Coahuila. The changes in national politics began tearing this web apart. Colonists had already begun to question their pact with Mexico as a result of Bustamante's and Alamán's Law of April 6, 1830, which criminalized American immigration into Texas. The law proved a farce (the norteamericano population of Texas doubled between 1830 and 1834 despite the ban), but it did have the effect of alienating moderate Texans from the government and empowering the arguments of a separatist minority that had long been preaching secession. Once Santa Anna came into power, federalists in Coahuila denounced his government. Santa Anna's allies established a rival government in Saltillo, and the federalists fled to the city of Monclova, where they frantically started selling off lands in Texas to pay for men and weapons, worrying little about prior claims or the interests of established empresarios. These land schemes poisoned relationships that bound colonists to Coahuila's federalist elite.[20]

Feeling betrayed, despairing of Mexico's political trajectory, and lacking viable allies to support in Coahuila's federalist/centralist contest, Anglo landholders in Texas began talking seriously about independence. Separatists seized a garrison near the Texan coast, and Mexican officials below the Rio Grande initiated plans to suppress the rebellion. Rumors spread that Santa Anna would free the slaves and that he would loot Texas just as he had Zacatecas. As late as 1830, Stephen F. Austin had been assuring Mexican authorities that "it has been my ambition to conquer this desert and add in this way to the prosperity, wealth, and physical and moral strength of this Republic that I have adopted as my country." But by late 1835 even this great empresario, heretofore the voice of restraint in Texas, advocated secession. Texan forces seized Goliad and San Antonio, and in March of 1836 they issued a declaration of independence. Several tejanos, including José Francisco Ruiz, signed the document. War was under way.[21]

Santa Anna marched six thousand weary soldiers into Texas and laid siege to the defenders of San Antonio, holed up in a dilapidated Franciscan mission known as the Alamo. Though they lost many of their own men, Mexicans killed as many as 200 defenders in taking the Alamo. The colorful backwoods congressman Davy Crockett survived, along with 6 other Texan men. All were summarily shot. Mexican forces also fought a Texan contingent near Goliad and quickly compelled it to surrender along with another battalion nearby. Ignoring a plea for clemency from a senior Mexican officer, Santa Anna had 342 Texan captives shot dead on Palm Sunday.[22]

The Mexican president now set out to crush the remainder of the Texan force, about 1,200 men under Sam Houston, the politician and Indian agent who had come to Texas three years earlier courting Comanches. Santa Anna brashly divided his forces and led a portion in pursuit of the enemy. On April 20, 1836, Houston's spies reported that Santa Anna's forces were resting unawares near the San Jacinto River. The Texans surprised the overconfident Mexicans and, enraged no doubt by Santa Anna's massacres, slaughtered more than 600 hapless Mexicans and captured more than 700 others. The Texans lost 8 men killed in the "Battle" of San Jacinto. Santa Anna tried to flee the scene dressed as an enlisted man but was soon recognized and apprehended. He formally surrendered to Houston, and in the Treaty of Velasco ordered the remainder of the Mexican forces south of the Rio Grande. Texans would later claim that this clause in the treaty amounted to Mexican recognition of the Rio Grande as the legitimate southern and western boundary of independent Texas. Mexico City refused to recognize the treaty at all, let alone the extraordinary claim about the river, and the two republics went on to harass each other along the border for another decade. But the Mexican government would never again control Indian policy, or anything else, in Texas.

The Texas revolt became the catalyst for the second major expansion in Comanche raiding into Mexico, and its significance can hardly be overstated. Since the eighteenth century, Spanish and Mexican diplomacy with Comanches had been supported by the twin pillars of Santa Fe and San Antonio. The rebellion threw that diplomacy into imbalance and confusion. Most immediately, the centerpiece of Mexico's strategy for ending the current Comanche hostilities had literally vanished from the national map. The project of enlisting Cherokees and other eastern Indians in Texas against plains peoples would now have to proceed quietly, in enemy territory, or not at all. And the peace negotiations that had been painstakingly nurtured with Comanches in San Antonio had become irrelevant.

As grave as these immediate complications were, in the loss of Texas the long-term consequences for Comanche diplomacy mattered more. Mexico could no longer deal with Plains Indians in the context of an implicit threat of military action from Texas or from the lower Rio Grande. Retaliatory raids from these places during the early 1830s had helped coax Comanche leaders back to negotiations in 1834 and 1835. With Texas lost, however, any military campaign into la comanchería would have to begin from the west, in isolated New Mexico or distant Chihuahua, or else march through the Republic of Texas first. Perhaps most disastrously, the intercultural resources Mexican Texas had possessed— resources of ritual place, personality, and history, of which only New Mexico had a greater share—were now beyond the reach of the Mexican state. Comanches had made several thousand peaceful visits to San Antonio since 1790, and these had been crucial in maintaining lines of communication. Go-betweens such as Ellis P. Bean, Juan N. Seguín, and especially Ruiz, the most prominent Comanche intermediary in all of Mexico, now worked for Mexico's newest enemy. Others, unnamed tejano traders, farmers, and ranchers who remained in Texas after the rebellion and who may have done even more at the local level to guard the lower Rio Grande and northeastern Mexico from Comanche hostility, simply found their world much contracted. Tejanos from San Antonio and elsewhere would continue trading and communicating with friends, business partners, and relatives below the river. They would even act as spies, informing Mexican authorities about the movements of hostile Comanches, and occasionally offer assistance against raiders attacking the lower Rio Grande. Yet whereas they once interacted with the peoples of the plains as Mexican nationals, henceforth they were an increasingly isolated minority living under alien government.[23]

With Mexican authority driven from Texas and the fighting force in northeastern Mexico in disarray, Comanche and Kiowa raiding parties shifted their focus from eastern Chihuahua, already stripped of much of its animal wealth, to the growing towns and ranches along the lower Rio Grande. While these campaigns in the northeast resulted in fewer Mexican casualties than had campaigns in Chihuahua, raiders devastated the region's animal herds. They took more than one thousand horses and mules from Laredo alone, totaling more than four-fifths of the horses possessed by the city and its surrounding ranches. The Indians burned huts and fields between the Nueces and the Rio Grande, compelling the ranching families lately established there to retreat south of the great river. Raiders slaughtered animals they had no interest in driving off. The number of sheep and goats owned by families in Laredo plummeted from nearly six thousand in late 1835 to a mere fifteen hundred by 1837. In just two years, raids stalled and in some cases reversed the economic and demographic growth the lower Rio Grande had enjoyed since the 1820s.[24]

As debilitating as the attacks had been along the river, officials in northeastern Mexico discerned an even more alarming trend by 1837. Comanches and their allies began extending their raids farther south, probing Tamaulipas, Nuevo León, and Coahuila to discover better herds in the interior. The Indians seemed poised for a major expansion in their raiding territory, and Nuevo León's governor warned the minister of war that each day brought the region "closer to its total destruction." But the anticipated escalation did not come. Raiding activity decreased dramatically from late summer 1837 through mid-1838, and in May 1838 five Comanche men even held peace talks with officials in northern Coahuila. They acknowledged that some of their people would inevitably continue raiding but nonetheless signed a treaty promising peace in return for trading privileges. And while Nuevo León suffered heavy casualties in a particularly violent campaign the following winter, southern plains Indians sent only two major expeditions below the river in 1839 and confined them to well-known territory in that one state. Something seemed to be holding the raiders back.[25]

SLAUGHTERING THE ENEMY IN THEIR BEDS: RENEWED CRISES

Northern Mexicans once again reaped benefits from warfare and misfortune in la comanchería. To the east, Tenewas and especially Hois plunged into nightmarish confrontations with the newly independent Republic of Texas. During the Texan rebellion, Comanches and their allies took the opportunity to avenge prior Anglo-Texan hostilities and disperse new settlements trespassing on their hunting grounds. The following few years were marked by occasional raids and counterraids, but also by cautious negotiation. Houston, now president of Texas, championed a policy of coexistence and diplomacy with Indians. Comanches held a number of talks with Houston's representatives and expressed anger over encroachment onto the eastern fringes of la comanchería, but the president had little desire or ability to arrest this movement. At the same time, Shawnee traders assured Comanches that the Texans intended to take their lands and even that Mexico had fought the Texan rebellion over the issue of native land rights. With suspicions and tensions mounting in 1838, an autumn attack upon a Comanche party by Texas Rangers led to a cycle of retaliatory raids. The violence helped discredit Houston's peace policies just in time for a new election. Constitutionally forbidden from holding the presidency in consecutive terms, Houston put his energy into electing a successor. But after an improbable series of misfortunes (Houston's first pick committed suicide, and then a hastily recruited replacement mysteriously drowned), the Indian hater Mirabeau B. Lamar ascended to the presidency. Lamar repudiated the agreements Houston had made with Cherokees and other immigrant Indians in east Texas and drove them from the republic. In the west, he employed plunder-hungry rangers in a program of active campaigning designed to terrorize Comanche families and drive them away from the rapidly expanding line of Texan settlement.[26]

Lamar depended on a shrewd new ally for many of his victories. Cuelgas de Castro and his Lipanes had undoubtedly suffered from increasing Comanche raiding like everyone else along the lower Rio Grande. In late 1837 they had moved farther south, seeking shelter with Mexican communities deep inside Nuevo León. Recalling perhaps that Lipanes had guided Comanche raiders in the 1820s, local Mexicans soon grew suspicious of their new guests and drove them north. Three months later, Castro signed a treaty of peace, commerce, and friendship with the Republic of Texas. By early 1839, Lipán scouts were back out on the plains hunting bison and spying on Comanche families. During the winter of 1838–39 Lipán spies discovered "the place where the women and children of the hostile Comanches are stationed." In January, the editors of the popular newspaper *Telegraph and Texas Register* informed readers that "the warriors are now absent on an excursion" and that a force of Texans, Lipanes, and Tonkawas were outfitting to take advantage of the opportunity. Two weeks later, this force attacked the Comanche camp without warning, "throwing open the doors of the wigwams or pulling them down and slaughtering the enemy in their beds."

The Texan and Indian force estimated that they killed or wounded eighty to one hundred Comanches but made little of the fact that most of the victims were women, children, and aged men.[27]

The Hois war leaders Potsanaquahip, Saviah, and Pia Kusa led minor retaliatory raids and patrolled the eastern section of la comanchería against hostile Texan parties, but it was obvious that Texans and Mexicans could not be fought at the same time, at least not profitably. In early 1840 Hois sent emissaries to San Antonio. Officials there told them to bring in every Texan captive they had and to send negotiators to conclude a definitive peace treaty. Once the emissaries left, Texan authorities agreed that when Comanche negotiators came in they should be detained until all Texan captives went free. Lamar's secretary of war further insisted that Comanches henceforth avoid the settlements, accept the permanent cessation of diplomatic gifts, and stay away from surveyors or settlers who ventured into Comanche territory (which, according to the secretary, did not exist).[28]

In March, the prominent paraibo Muguara led a large party of men, women, and children into San Antonio for negotiations. He brought with him a young woman named Matilda Lockhart, captured two years before, and Muguara insisted he had no other Texan captives. Decades later, Mary Maverick, a pioneer and diarist who had tended Lockhart in San Antonio, claimed the young woman had been beaten and disfigured by her captors: "Her head, arms, and face were full of bruises, and sores, and her nose was actually burnt off to the bone. The nostrils were wide open and denuded of flesh." It is a shocking image, one suspiciously absent from other firsthand accounts. Whether or not Lockhart really came in with so frightful a look, the Texans present did not need her as an excuse for what they were about to do. Already convinced that their guests held other Texans in bondage (a suspicion Lockhart confirmed), the commanding officer, Hugh McLeod, asked his tejano translator to inform the Comanches that they were now prisoners. The translator looked at McLeod, walked to the entrance, opened the door, and translated the message as he hurried outside. After a moment of stunned silence, a Comanche man tried to escape and a fight broke out. McLeod's men killed 35 Comanches, including Muguara, and imprisoned 27 others. Seven Texans were killed. The massacre drew condemnations in newspapers across the United States and an unmistakable reaction from Comanche warriors. A few months after the killings, 500 plainsmen attacked the town of Victoria and nearly destroyed the nearby settlement of Linnville. But Texan forces intercepted the triumphant Comanche party on its return north, killing at least a dozen warriors. In October 1840, Lipán scouts again led a large Texan force to yet another Comanche camp, where they took 35 Indians prisoner and massacred 140 more. When shocked survivors made for the Colorado River, many were shot or drowned while crossing to the other side. Texan attackers suffered 2 men wounded.[29]

To the north and west, Kiowas, Kiowa Apaches, Yamparikas, and Kotsotekas struggled with their own crises and tragedies in the late 1830s. The Southern Cheyennes and Arapahos, who had stolen so many horses from the southern plains during the early 1830s, seem to have relaxed their assaults by mid-decade, possibly thanks to the intervention of a third party. In the early 1830s both peoples had become intimately associated with the American trading enterprise of Bent, St. Vrain, and Company. The Bent brothers Charles and William grew up in Missouri and spent their youths in the western fur trade. Together with their fellow Missourian Ceran St. Vrain they opened stores in Santa Fe and Taos and constructed a formidable adobe fort in present-day Colorado, just north of what was then the international border, the Arkansas River. In 1830 William Bent helped two young men associated with the Cheyenne leader Yellow Wolf escape a party of Comanches who had come to punish them for stealing horses. Southern Cheyennes and their Arapaho allies became the Bents' main native clients, but the brothers also looked south. They knew that southern plains families produced an enormous number of processed hides and that they had access to far more horses and mules than anyone on the central plains. In the summer of 1835 William ventured south and traded with upward of two thousand Comanches on the Red River. He clearly had an interest in ending the conflict that Cheyennes and Arapahos had with Comanches and Kiowas, and though there is no direct evidence, he may have tried to initiate a truce as part of this trading endeavor in 1835. If so, that would help explain the large Comanche campaigns into Mexico during those years, campaigns which took so many men away from their families for weeks at a time.[30]

Whether or not there had been a temporary truce between peoples of the central and southern plains in the mid-1830s, by the summer of 1837 fighting escalated once again. The Kiowa calendar attests to the violence of these years and to the shift in focus on the southern plains. Whereas the key events from the previous few seasons had emerged from the Mexican campaigns, the memorialists devoted 1837–39 entirely to enemies from the north. They called summer 1837 the "summer that the Cheyenne were massacred" and winter 1837/1838 the "winter that they dragged the head." Summer 1838 was the "summer that the Cheyenne attacked the camp on Wolf River," an attack in which Lokota Sioux supposedly helped Cheyennes and Arapahos kill hundreds of Kiowa and Comanche men and women. The winter of 1838/1839 was memorialized by yet another storied battle with the Arapaho. While the defenders garnered significant victories in these years, the conflicts nonetheless kept southern plains families in a state of anxiety and alarm and made it exceedingly dangerous for men to leave on campaigns into Mexico.[31]

Two other factors likely contributed to the lull in raiding during the late 1830s. First, many of the men who had been eager raiders in the previous few years may have found that they had as many horses and mules as they could manage by late decade. A major trade outlet disappeared when Choteau's posts were closed following his death in 1838. Those families who failed to dispose of excess trade animals had to expend labor caring for them and make difficult choices about camping in large, relatively safe groups and moving constantly or abiding in smaller, more manageable rancherías and hoping for the best. This dilemma became keen in winter and could mean life or death so long as enemies harried the region. Second, the Kiowa calendar for winter 1839/1840 depicts a man covered from head to foot in spots; that is, a man suffering from smallpox. Brought to the southern plains by Osage traders, this was the same epidemic that virtually destroyed the Mandans. As is so often the case during the 1830s and early 1840s, surviving sources tell us little of this event's consequences in la comanchería, but it is fair to assume that the tragedy complicated short-term plans for campaigning.[32]

Families across the southern plains therefore experienced a defensive crisis by the late 1830s. Hois and Tenewas suffered major losses to Lipán and Texan raiders, Kiowas, Kiowa Apaches, Kotsotekas, and Yamparikas faced an increasingly aggressive threat from the central plains, and it is probable that smallpox visited all of these communities. Before war leaders could escalate their campaigning into Mexico, Comanches and their allies had to come to terms with their other, more threatening enemies. Moreover, war with Texans and with Cheyennes and Arapahos held out few benefits to Comanches and their allies. The Texans were too close, too many, and too dangerous to attack directly, as the aftermath of the Linnville and Victoria raids demonstrated. Moreover, Lipán scouts and warriors enabled Texans to track and attack Comanche families in their home ranges. Likewise, nearly all of the violence between peoples of the central and southern plains during the late 1830s seems to have taken place in la comanchería. Comanches and their allies might seek to plunder their northern enemies, but it simply was not worth the risk of sending raiding parties north when it was so much easier and more profitable to steal horses and mules from Mexico. By early 1840 southern plains Indians were looking to change the regional dynamic.

WE WILL GO AND BRING MORE HANDSOME LADS:
PEACE AND WAR IN 1840

The breakthrough came in 1840, when Comanches and Kiowas made peace with their formidable Cheyenne and Arapaho enemies. Oral traditions disagree about who initiated the peace, but southern plains peoples undoubtedly had the more compelling interest. The peace put a stop to years of violence, freed families on both sides of the Arkansas from much suffering and uncertainty, and inaugurated an intense commercial relationship. It is also likely that the epidemic facilitated peace. Insofar as plains families lost kin to the disease, they also found themselves more vulnerable to enemies. Just as the calamitous smallpox epidemic of 1780-81 seems to have empowered the proponents of an alliance with New Spain, disease in 1839 probably resulted in a reconsideration of policy and a greater willingness to come to terms with dangerous foes.

The former adversaries celebrated at a huge ceremony near the Arkansas River. Cheyennes and Arapahos gave their new allies blankets, guns, ammunition, beads, calico, and brass kettles. The Kiowas and Comanches gave—what else?—horses. Even "unimportant" Cheyenne and Arapaho men and women got four, five, six horses each. So many animals changed hands that recipients lacked ropes enough to lead them all home. Perhaps there had indeed been a glut of horses on the southern plains. After giving presents and seeing to the more formal aspects of the ceremony, the participants engaged in a great trading session that anticipated partnerships lasting into the reservation era.[33]

Cheyennes and Arapahos had lost many men on raids into la comanchería, and doubtless some among them wanted to stop the bloodletting. But their enthusiasm for peace probably had less to do with casualties than with an economic reorientation toward commercial bison hunting. The Bents provided Cheyennes and Arapahos with an almost inexhaustible market for hides and robes. Through the 1830s and 1840s both groups increasingly spent their time hunting and processing hides for sale. War with Comanches and Kiowas had made hunting in the region between the Platte and Arkansas rivers dangerous for several years, and consequently the region became a buffer zone where game flourished. Peace gave Cheyenne and Arapaho hunters safe access to this rich territory.[34] Given the paucity of source material for fleshing out the Great Peace of 1840 (historians do not even know in which month it took place), scholars have speculated that southern plains negotiators were motivated by strategic threats from Texans and immigrant tribes. The trouble with this interpretation is that the Kiowas, Kiowa Apaches, Kotsotekas, and Yamparikas in closest communication with Cheyennes and Arapahos had little to fear from these eastern

8. The Great Peace of 1840. Ledger art by Howling Wolf, Southern Cheyenne
(ca. 1878–1881). Late twentieth-century Cheyenne informants identified this image
as a representation of the second day of the ceremonies surrounding the peace of
1840, when Cheyennes received gifts of horses from Kiowas (see Moore,
Cheyenne Nation, 6–7). Image courtesy Joslyn Art Museum, 1991.19.

threats. Moreover, with one possible but unlikely exception, they seem not to
have turned their attentions eastward in the aftermath of the Great Peace.[35]

They did, however, look south. Soon after the ceremonies on the Arkansas,
southern plains warriors dramatically expanded their attacks below the Rio
Grande. The first campaign got under way in early September 1840, crossing
the river near the town of Guerrero in Tamaulipas, and, over the course of the
next two or three weeks, plundered ranches and haciendas across eastern Nuevo
León. Another crossed the river in the beginning of October, rode through northern Coahuila, swept down the eastern border of Nuevo León, and then drove
toward the center of the state, to the very outskirts of the capital, Monterrey,
before retreating. In December and January Comanches raided the length of
Coahuila into northern Zacatecas and San Luis Potosí, while another, separate
group struck targets throughout Nuevo León. Raiders returned to Nuevo León
in February, and that same month a reported eight hundred Comanches and

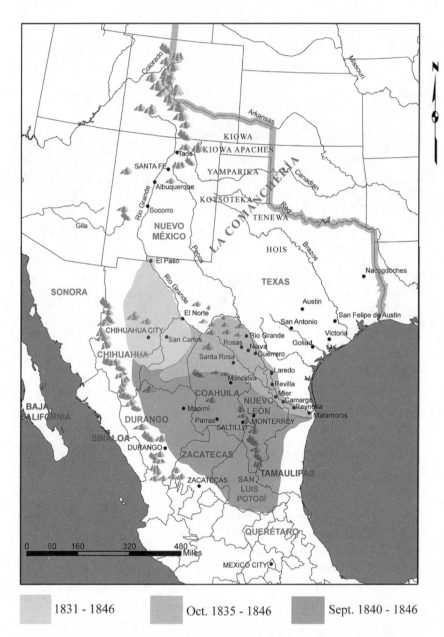

1831 - 1846	Oct. 1835 - 1846
	Sept. 1840 - 1846

2. Territorial expansion of Comanche and Kiowa raiding, 1831–46

Kiowas campaigned throughout Chihuahua and Durango. This dramatic expansion in raiding would have been impossible without improved security, and the Great Peace gave thousands of men on the southern plains both freedom to resume large-scale, long-distance raids, and a new and lucrative market for stolen horses and mules. In other words, strategic concerns did motivate Comanches and Kiowas to seek peace with their central plains adversaries, but these concerns had more to do with Mexico than with Texas or eastern Indians.[36]

It is unclear whether many Hois men participated in the campaigns of 1840 and 1841, given their ongoing collisions with Lamar's Texans. But for them, too, security would soon improve. In 1841 Sam Houston won a second term as president of Texas and put a stop to state-sanctioned raids by Lipanes and rangers. Hois leaders understandably harbored intense ill will against Texans and refused Houston's early requests for peace talks. Nonetheless, by late 1841 the threat from Texas had much diminished. More broadly, la comanchería as a whole was more secure than it had been in a generation. Men had unprecedented freedom to leave their families for prolonged raiding campaigns and embraced the opportunity to plunder new territories. As campaigns pushed into previously unknown areas Comanches and Kiowas became astonished at the animal wealth they discovered. Following a raid into Zacatecas in 1842, for example, an escaped Mexican captive reported that these Indians had never been this far south before and that one warrior had said, "We will go and bring more handsome lads and come back here, for there are many horses." This they certainly did. From 1840 through 1847, Comanches and Kiowas sent more than twice as many large campaigns below the river as they had in the previous eight years. All the while, Mexicans could do little to convince Comanches and Kiowas to change their policies and restore the peace.[37]

The Kiowa symbol for the winter of 1840/1841 is a quiver made of buffalo hide. Put into context, this simple drawing is an eloquent marker for the changing relationships between southern plains Indians and Mexicans from 1830 to 1840. By 1830 Mexico's frontier defenses had declined considerably, and the Mexican government had little to offer Comanches and their allies in diplomatic gifts or military support. The peace limped along nonetheless, with prominent Comanche leaders working to restrain young men and negotiate with Mexican authorities. But the peace had come to depend upon the extensive trade plains families conducted with Mexican citizens and, especially, upon the limits that conflicts with other Indians placed on the activities of Comanche and Kiowa men. The breakthrough with Osages and eastern Indians in 1834 secured alternative markets while at the same time freeing up hundreds of warriors to attend raids in

9. Winter 1840–41, Hide Quiver War Expedition Winter.
The black bar below the quiver indicates dead vegetation,
hence winter. From Mooney, *Calendar*, 276.

Mexico. Rebellion in 1836 destroyed any hope that Mexico would be able to use Texas as a diplomatic and military base from which to refashion the Comanche alliance. Finally, peace with Cheyennes and Arapahos and, more gradually and warily, with the Texans opened up new markets and brought unprecedented security to the southern plains, which meant that more men than ever were free to ride south into Mexico for prolonged campaigns.[38]

Of course, Comanches, Kiowas, and Kiowa Apaches had complicated and divergent motives for making peace with Indians and Texans in this period, these motives changed over the 1830s and 1840s, and not everyone in la comanchería supported the agreements in any case. The alliances may also be seen as part of a broader effort by native peoples across the Great Plains in this period to forge strong partnerships in the face of demographic, ecological, and economic change. Moreover, the negotiations that led to peace were themselves complex and contingent events, and it is easy enough to imagine different outcomes. Still, while the sources do not give us access to high-level deliberations about regional strategy, the convergence of events above and below the river makes it clear that Mexico played an increasingly important role in the geopolitical decisions of the period. Surely southern plains leaders anticipated the ways in which security and expanded markets would facilitate and reward raiding campaigns into Mexico. How else explain the speed with which so many of them capitalized on geopolitical change by leading their men below the Rio Grande? or the tremendous resources they devoted to this dangerous, complicated, and labor-intensive project year after year? By 1840 the war with Mexico had become a key fact of economic and political life on the southern plains.[39]

The consequences of these changes can be seen hiding behind the drawing of the buffalo-hide quiver. By the 1840s, young Kiowa warriors preferred quivers made of sleek Mexican leather or panther skin to those made of buffalo hide, which only old men used. The symbol for "Hide-quiver war expedition winter" memorializes a campaign comprised of older men who headed south into Mexico. Traditionally, older men were the minimum defense Kiowas and Comanches would leave behind to guard women, children, and herds. But the changes of the past six years had produced such freedom of movement and such enthusiasm for war that even aged warriors joined the campaigns, bearing their rough, outmoded quivers made of buffalo hide to the scattered ranches and haciendas south of the Rio Grande. They rode off to join their sons and nephews in a series of campaigns marking the definitive end of a transition begun in the early 1830s. In the intervening years, Comanches and their allies had finally abandoned an unprofitable peace with Mexico and adopted a policy of aggressive war. The war in turn would revitalize their economy and transform the southern plains into a busy plunderer's bazaar.

3

PLUNDER AND PARTNERS

On September 12, 1843, Juan Antonio de Olaciregui wrote to inform Juan
Meléndez that several Comanches had attacked the Rancho de Torreón in Durango. The Indians "gravely wounded a shepherd and took his woman captive,"
though the terrified woman soon escaped her captors and returned home, "very
broken down." Before the Comanches left the vicinity they robbed eight horses
from the nearby Estancia de Salgado. Olaciregui had no way of knowing what
became of these eight animals, and, since his letter is the only record of this incident, neither do we. This is a shame because their histories would offer a glimpse
into the complex and far-flung network of material interests that helped propel
Comanches into Mexico.[1]

If we could indeed follow the journeys of these eight horses, we might see
something like this:

The raiders were Yamparikas, including a man of Mexican descent who had
been captured as a boy and raised Yamparika, and were accompanied by one
free Mexican—a resident of San Carlos, Chihuahua. After attacking Torreón,
the party took the eight horses and headed north along the border between
Coahuila and Chihuahua. The first division of booty took place when the
Mexican from San Carlos departed and took one horse as a fee for having
guided the Comanche party to Torreón. San Carlos was notorious for its ties to
Indian raiders, so this man thought it safer to bring the horses to a discrete hacienda farther south where the operator bought animals without asking questions. Three years later Chiricahua Apaches attacked the hacienda and stole
the horse a second time. The animal spent the rest of its life with an Apache
family in what is now southern New Mexico.[2]

The Yamparika party, meanwhile, had driven their seven remaining animals along a familiar trail system to a crossing near the Big Bend in the Rio Grande. While camping in the rough country between the Pecos River and the Big Bend they were hailed by a handful of Hois who had returned along the same trail system from Coahuila. The Yamparikas agreed to exchange three of their seven remaining horses for two Mexican girls, sisters the Hois had captured near Patos. The Hois drove these three horses back to their ranchería on the upper Brazos River in Texas. Thereafter these three animals met very different fates. One, an old, weak beast, was given to an elderly woman who used it as a packhorse for three seasons before it died. A second joined the herd of one of the more senior raiders. He eventually gave the animal to a poor nephew, who used it as part of a bride price for a young Hois woman he wished to marry. The father of this girl kept the horse for one year and then traded it for a knife, some clothing, and a bolt of patterned cloth at a Texan trading post on the Brazos. From there the horse was purchased by a trader, who took the animal to the city of Austin and sold it to a newly arrived farmer from Alabama who wanted the horse to help him clear land on his new property and to transport crops to market. The horse stayed with the farmer until its death. The third animal was the strongest of the trio, and its owner sold it to a Delaware man for a quantity of gunpowder, several bars of lead, some tobacco, six yards of red ribbon, and a large brass kettle. The Delaware drove the horse east and sold it to another Delaware trader, who took it north and sold it to a Cherokee family in present-day Oklahoma. The family kept the horse until it died in a hard winter.

The original group of Yamparika raiders returned to their residence band in what is now northeastern New Mexico with four Mexican horses. One stayed in the band for life, becoming the favorite mount of one of the raiders' wives. Another remained in a local herd for two years until it was given to an ambitious young man who wished to participate in a raid but had no horses of his own. He rode off into Tamaulipas, where, following a successful attack on a ranch outside Matamoros, his party was surprised the next day at sunrise by Mexican militia. A middle-aged rancher shot and killed the young man, captured the dead youth's horse, and, effacing the old Durango brand by burning it with gunpowder, claimed it as his own. The rancher kept the horse for six months and then gave it to a neighbor to settle a long-standing debt. The animal stayed with this last owner for the rest of its life.[3]

The Yamparikas traded the two remaining Durango horses to a Cheyenne, who kept them both for one year. At the end of that year the Cheyenne met with a party of Oglala Sioux who gave him a British-made rifle and several knives for one of the two horses. The Oglala owner kept the horse for a few years and then sold it to a trader at Fort Laramie in early 1849. Soon after, the horse was purchased by a party of miners traveling on the Oregon Trail to the goldfields in California. The old horse broke a leg somewhere in present-day Idaho. The would-be miners shot the animal and, running low on rations, ate it on the trail.

The Cheyenne man who had one horse remaining from the two he obtained from the Yamparikas traded it to William Bent at Bent's Fort on the Arkansas River in the summer of 1845. Bent had the animal taken east to a business associate in St. Louis, Missouri, where it remained until it was purchased along with several hundred other horses (and far more mules) by the U.S. Army in June of 1846. A minor officer rode the horse to participate in the conquest of New Mexico and Chihuahua. Somewhere between Parras and Buena Vista the horse became ill, and the young officer left it with a local rancher who, remarkably, recognized the original brand from Durango and contemplated returning the horse to its rightful owner. In the end the rancher decided to keep the horse, and the animal stayed on his land for almost a year before Comanche raiders stole it again in the winter of 1848. Pursued by Mexican militia, the Comanches drove their herd of captured animals unrelentingly, and this most well traveled of horses died of thirst and exhaustion ten miles south of the Rio Grande.[4]

It may seem unlikely that the eight Mexican horses taken from la Estancia de Salgado could have gone on to lead such exciting lives, but this imaginary history suggests the very real complexities of the trading network that helped fuel Comanche raids into Mexico. The Durango horses in particular may not have traveled thousands of miles and changed hands so many times, but others did. The horses, mules, and captives that Comanches and their allies robbed from northern Mexico entered a vast network of markets. Once inside the network, these animals and people traveled throughout la comanchería, to the central and northern plains and even to Canada; throughout Anglo-Texas, Missouri, and the U.S. South; to New Mexico, to present-day Arizona west to the Colorado River drainage and even back into northern Mexico.

Animals and people underwent transformations on these journeys. From the perspective of their temporary owners, markets transformed horses into prestige and deference, or into cash or titles to land, or into clothes, blankets, brass buttons, and tobacco. Mules turned into gunpowder and lead, dried corn, jackets, mirrors, knives, and silver coins. Captives became bridles, bread, iron pots, and rifles or wives, daughters, sons, slaves, and warriors. The variety of these transformations testifies to the diversity of the network's participants. While dynamic, profitable, and far-reaching, this network was not a single market with a coherent set of values and meanings. It was rather a system of trails and human relation-

3. Trading partners in and around *la comanchería*

ships that bound together very different economic cultures and value systems without imposing any one set of meanings on the whole. Animals and captive Mexicans had different significance and utility and were assigned different material values among the Kiowas, Chihuahuans, Hois, Kiowa Apaches, Cheyennes, Oglalas, Texans, Yamparikas, Osages, Missourians, Tenewas, Creeks, Kotsotekas, Delawares, Arapahos, comancheros, and other peoples active in the trading network.

The several Comanches who attacked the Rancho de Torreón in September 1843 obviously had distinct ambitions of their own. And yet the attack must be understood as a manifestation of a far larger and more diverse collection of material interests implicating dozens of different peoples in the violence, losses, and sorrows afflicting northern Mexicans throughout the 1830s and 1840s. To understand the material dimension of the raiding campaigns that did so much damage to the Mexican north, it is necessary to look both at the economic context on the southern plains and the markets it intersected with—markets that could make raiders insatiable by turning captives, mules, and horses into almost anything they wanted.

CAUGHT HIM ON THE RIO GRANDE:
COMANCHES AND CAPTIVES

For Comanches themselves, the immediate material incentives that drove raids into northern Mexico can be divided into three categories, in increasing order of significance: miscellaneous plunder, captives, and animals. Miscellaneous plunder is often overlooked in discussions of raiding because it was so varied, seldom recorded in detail, and not immediately implicated in far-flung trade networks, as captives and, especially, animals were. Raiding provided southern plains Indians with many of the things they had once acquired peacefully at places like San Antonio. In 1836, for example, Comanches attacked a party of travelers heading north from a failed settlement near the Rio Grande, killing most of the party's men and taking several women and children captive. Sarah Ann Horn, one of the captives, later recalled that the raiders took all the dead men's clothes and even stripped the party's wagons, boxes, and trunks of every piece of metal that could be used, as barrel hoops from San Antonio had been used, for making arrow and lance heads. Dolly Webster, another redeemed captive, remembered that after Comanches overwhelmed her party they seized various items of interest, including mirrors: "Our looking-glasses were broken into small pieces and divided amongst them as the most valuable property we had."[5]

Indians sacking homes in towns and ranches probably sought food, among other things, including corn and other grains, and goods like sugar that remained difficult to acquire elsewhere. Raiders also collected weapons and ammunition whenever they could find them and sometimes took papers and books to stuff their shields. On more than one occasion they carried off a large quantity of silver coin. And just as textiles had been key items in the Comanche–Mexican trade, raiders hauled off clothes and cloth whenever they won access to Mexican homes. Horn's captors forced her to alter linens and dresses taken from a Mexican house. Webster remembered that raiders returning from Mexico brought silks, clothes, calicoes, and "a large quantity of jewelry." In one of the bold raids into Nuevo León during 1840 a Mexican woman witnessed Comanches leaving plundered houses with, among other things, pillows, silk tunics, sheets, dyed wool, shirts, printed calico tunics, and bedspreads.[6]

Comanches also acquired several hundred Mexican captives during the 1830s and 1840s, and many things could befall Mexicans once their captors brought them across the Rio Grande. Most simply, captives could become commodities. Sometimes Comanches brought captives into Mexican towns along the Rio Grande to fish for an appealing ransom. The Bent brothers often purchased Mexican captives from Comanches and Kiowas and had them manage animals, do maintenance work, and assist in commerce at the fort. Comancheros regularly attempted to acquire Mexicans from Plains Indians, and Americans and Mexicans resident in eastern New Mexico also sought to buy and "rescue" non-Indian captives. A Mexican man purchased Sarah Ann Horn near San Miguel del Vado for a horse, four fine bridles, two blankets, two looking glasses, two knives, some tobacco, and a quantity of powder and balls. Eastern markets were even more important in this trade. After Comanches and their allies destroyed Parker's fort in Texas and captured several women and children, James Parker spent years looking for his family. He covered hundreds of miles following rumors and newspaper reports of children who had been sold by Comanches to eastern Indian traders or to prairie Indians like the Osage and who were then bought by officials or private citizens in western frontier towns in the United States. Parker's wanderings encompassed only one section of la comanchería's perimeter, but they begin to suggest the scope of the trading networks implicated in Comanche raiding.[7]

Comanches and others found considerable profits in this trade. For example, Burnet bought four Mexican captives from Comanches at an average price of $200 in goods each. In 1842 General Zachary Taylor, at Fort Smith in Arkansas, issued a standing offer of $200 for any white children purchased from Comanches. In 1844 American residents of Jasper County, Missouri, paid native intermediaries $100 and a good horse for a Mexican girl, and in the following year a

Delaware paid a Comanche paraibo $300 for a Texan boy named Gillis Doyle. Anglo-Texan traders on the borders of la comanchería purchased Mexican captives who seemed useful or who managed to convince them that family members would reward their kindness. A Mexican boy from Presidio de Rio Grande escaped the Comanches this way. When his brothers learned he had been purchased they journeyed to Texas in order to "return" the $120 ransom that the "kind hearted" trader said he had paid, so that they could bring the boy back home. Pity no doubt motivated some such transactions. But whether through manipulation of the supposed value of goods paid to Indians or through outright lies, the rescue business could be profitable indeed.[8]

While Comanches sold many of their captives, it seems that the majority remained in la comanchería for life. The principal material dividends of captive taking came from the additional labor it brought to plains households, and gender structured this labor. Captors almost always required boys to tend horses and mules. Most boys from northern Mexico would have had prior experience working with animals, and even at a young age their skills could be especially valuable on the plains. Boys tried to keep the animals from wandering away, to see that they got sufficient pasture in the daytime, and to keep them safe from thieves. One observer estimated that each boy had responsibility for around 150 animals. This hard work became considerably harder in winter — Sarah Ann Horn's son froze to death watching over a Comanche herd. Young Mexican males also worked as trainers and breakers of horses and mules. Two Mexican youths that a Texan trader purchased from Comanches excelled everyone else in his outfit at breaking mules. Comanches usually killed the men they captured but occasionally took younger males old enough to have acquired other important skills, like making or mending saddles. Mexican boys who grew to manhood among Comanches were often sought after by prominent men to become husbands for low-status female kin. It was said that Mexicans made ideal husbands in such circumstances because they generally had little wealth or social standing of their own and could thus be depended upon to obey their fathers-in-law and help with their herds and their interests more broadly.[9]

Captured females performed very different tasks. They labored at a variety of daily chores, including gathering wood, fetching water, cooking, tending to children, repairing clothing, collecting wild foods and medicines, and disassembling, packing, moving, and reassembling camp. Their most significant economic contribution was in processing bison and other animals for meat and hides. New Mexicans, tejanos, and Mexicans along the lower Rio Grande had always bartered for Comanche skins. Even as these transactions became complicated by war, new partnerships to the east and north deepened connections between southern plains Indians and the ravenous international market for skins. While market demand for beaver declined in the early 1830s, demand and prices for bison robes and hides increased considerably, peaking for a time in the early 1840s. Bent's Fort became the epicenter of this trade for the southern and central plains, but comancheros, Texans, and eastern Indian traders also sought hides and robes.[10]

It took tremendous labor to produce such hides in quantity. Comanche and Kiowa women obviously had a great deal of work to do besides the processing of skins. Successful participants in the hide trade therefore had several female "dependents" that together could complete chores with dispatch and devote much or most of their time to hide production. Cooperation paid dividends. Among the Blackfeet, for example, it was said that eight wives working together could produce nearly double the number of hides produced by eight women working alone. Because of high mortality in wars and raiding, women outnumbered men in Comanche and Kiowa residence bands. Since raiders almost never brought Mexican men back to la comanchería, captive raiding probably contributed to this imbalance. Some prominent Comanche men had as many as ten wives, or even more. Captive Mexican females therefore provided critical labor at a moment when Comanches had more market outlets for women's work than ever before. There is also some evidence that Comanches had an unusually low birth rate per capita, for a variety of reasons, and Mexican wives who became mothers thus helped recreate population on the southern plains.[11]

These boys and girls and women labored long and hard for their captors, who under some circumstances held them as chattel slaves in the long term. It seems that older boys or adolescents who resisted assimilation were especially vulnerable to this social condition. A good number of male captives eventually escaped and resumed their lives in Mexican ranches, towns, and cities. But the risks were considerable. A Texan captive recalled that two twelve-year-old Mexican boys who ran away from their Comanche captors "were caught, brought back to camp, and hung until nearly dead." Given the danger of flight and the traumas captives endured, it is not surprising that nineteenth-century observers often found young captives to be resigned to and even happy with life as Comanches. As one put it, "Even the born frontiersman, taken prisoner and given a few years to live with the natives, no longer cares for civilization once he has had a taste of the desert life." Most captives eventually became family: low-status kin who shared the rights and responsibilities of membership in Comanche communities. Mexican women became wives; children became sons and daughters and brothers and sisters and eventually husbands and wives in their own right. In this way, captive taking strengthened not only the Comanche economy, but also the

10. Comanche Village, Women Dressing Robes and Drying Meat.
George Catlin, 1834–35. Courtesy of the Smithsonian American
Art Museum, Gift of Mrs. Joseph Harrison, Jr.

community itself. As family members rather than simple laborers, captives freely
made contributions of great importance in mediating between the plains and
the Anglo-American and Mexican worlds.[12]

They also made critical contributions to the war Comanches waged on
Mexico. Literate captives could translate intercepted documents and newspapers reporting engagements and troop movements. After some years, captive
males could themselves participate in raids in northern Mexico. For example,
Comanches captured Sabás Rodríguez on the lower Rio Grande in 1844, when
he was a teenager. The young man spent three years guarding horses and mules
before being allowed to accompany minor raids against Americans and other
Indians. After two years more he started raiding his former countrymen south
of the river. It became a truism among observers of the southern plains that
"Comanche" raiders like Rodríguez were far crueler toward other Mexicans
than their captors were. Josiah Gregg believed that captives became "the most
formidable savages. Combining the subtlety of the Mexican with the barbarity
of the Indian, they sometimes pilot into their native frontier and instigate horrid
outrages." The captive-turned-Comanche phenomenon produced some striking
scenes. While a captive among Comanches, Dolly Webster met a blue-eyed,

blond-haired boy named Lyons who had supposedly been seized on the Texas frontier some time before. In Webster's estimation Lyons had already become "almost a savage," and she noted acidly that he spied on other captives in camp for his captors. A German visitor to Texas met Lyons eight or nine years later, in 1847, in la comanchería. An eight-year-old Mexican boy rode behind Lyons on his horse, "half starved and shivering in the cold north wind, because of his scanty dress." The German inquired about the child, and the Comanche Lyons answered quietly, "'I caught him on the Rio Grande.' This was said in a tone of voice, as if he were speaking of some animal."[13]

THE PURPOSE OF GIVING IT TO OTHERS: WEALTH IN HORSES

Horses and mules made for less complicated spoils than captives, but these animals were the most important objects in the raiding economy. Between 1830 and 1846 Comanches and their allies robbed tens of thousands of horses and mules from northern Mexican ranches and haciendas, and the total number probably exceeded one hundred thousand during this period. Still, the number of horses and mules raiders drove off far exceeded the number they got back across the river. Comanches seem to have discriminated very little in the animals they stole. Young or old, weak or strong, each horse and mule that could be driven off was driven off. Weaker animals were sometimes eaten in camp. More important, as living plunder the creatures were mobile but fragile. Harried by Mexican pursuers, Comanches inevitably drove their hundreds or thousands of captured animals hard, often to death, as they raced around northern Mexico. Herds diminished through accidental drowning, heat stroke, thirst, and simple exhaustion. David G. Burnet estimated that only half of the animals plains raiders rounded up ever made it back to la comanchería alive.[14]

Those they did get home became the key commodities in the political economy of the southern plains. In order to appreciate what happened to stolen animals after they shook the water from their coats on the north bank of the Rio Grande, we first have to look more closely at this political economy and contrast it with the international market economy with which it intersected. Horses were prerequisite for the hunting and raiding that allowed men to feed families and accumulate wealth and honor of their own. Horses also became the standard payment family heads required when giving female dependents away in marriage. If they lacked horses, in other words, young men were shut out of the most fundamental aspects of social and economic life on the plains. These indispensable creatures were unequally distributed within Comanche and Kiowa society.

It has been suggested that peoples on the plains needed a minimum of six horses per capita to lead a fully nomadic, equestrian lifestyle, and they needed as many as twelve each for comfort and security. Most established Comanche and Kiowa families would have had such wealth, owning several horses and mules they used as pack animals, several more for riding transportation, and a select handful of strong horses reserved for hunting and raiding. Many young men and poor families, however, did not have sufficient animals to meet these various needs. Some owned none.[15]

Kiowas observed finer social distinctions than Comanches, and one's ability to ascend from lower to higher social ranks depended to a considerable extent on family wealth in animals. Men achieved membership in the most distinguished social category, *óngop*, by being independently wealthy, generous, handsome, dignified, and gracious. Above all, this preeminent rank demanded remarkable accomplishments in war: counting first coup against an enemy, for example, charging while others fled, recovering slain or wounded comrades before retreating, or rushing a party of adversaries alone. Young men whose fathers belonged to the óngop grade invariably had access to horses—prominent Kiowa families sometimes had several hundred horses in their herd, most unbroken and reserved for future use. Consequently, children of the elite had means to go on raids and, just as important, could concentrate on acquiring war honors rather than on stealing more animals. Ambitious men of lower ranks often had to borrow horses from wealthier relatives and, once in enemy territory, necessarily prioritized horses over war deeds. Moreover, they often had to split their spoils with their patrons once they returned to camp. Thus, while material wealth was only one facet of a complex system for evaluating social worth, horses empowered the relatively wealthy to achieve nonmaterial distinction.[16]

Given the necessity of horses for every Kiowa and Comanche family and for junior men in particular, established men used their large herds to get what they valued most: social prestige and political power. It was not, therefore, material accumulation, even accumulation of horses and mules, but rather the broad redistribution of animals and other goods as gifts that helped secure the social prestige and political following that every ambitious man on the southern plains strove for. Once accepted, such gifts generally required reciprocation, not through repayment in kind, but through perpetual deference, respect, occasional service, and political obedience. Gifts produced solidarity, and the giver had the power to dictate the ends to which solidarity would be turned.[17]

Generosity was therefore prerequisite for the acquisition of political power in la comanchería. Ambitious men needed to accumulate animals, but more than that they needed to accumulate followers, primarily through the obligations

conferred by gifts. As has been said of similar economic values in another context, "successful entrepreneurs in the end turned their 'profits' back into people:
dependent kin, clients, and slaves." One of the distinguishing characteristics between such "gift economies" as opposed to the market economy was thus that
the "rich" stayed rich by getting rid of their possessions. Non-Indians marveled
at these values. One sensitive observer of nineteenth-century Comanches remarked, in puzzled precision, "From the liberality with which they dispose of
their effects . . . it would induce the belief that they acquire property merely for
the purpose of giving it to others."[18]

Throughout the plains the perpetual contest over prestige and followers led to
acts of conspicuous generosity in a number of contexts. At its most nakedly political, animals could be given in the manner suggested above, to needy juniors
or indigent families, who then became clients to the giver. Most venues for gift
giving were subtler, mediated by cultural traditions. Once a warrior returned
from a successful raid, for example, young women often came to his tent, dancing and chanting his glories, appealing for a share of his spoils. Comanches considered these visits public honors, and proud warriors or their fathers would rise
to the occasion by giving out horses, mules, and perhaps other goods to the assembled dancers. By redistributing stolen horses to young women who usually
had few other opportunities to acquire the animals, prominent men also used
the so-called shakedown dance as an opportunity to increase their public stature and personal followings. Deaths in the family presented other occasions for
conspicuous generosity and the reaffirmation of client allegiance. When close
kin of a wealthy Comanche died, mourners wailed and wept in fantastic dis-
plays of exaggerated grief. Only through distributing gifts could kin of the dead
silence these public mourners. The public grieving and the requisite number of
silencing gifts became all the greater if the deceased had been a warrior killed
on campaign. Should there be a body to dispose of, pallbearers received gifts as
well.[19]

Through a variety of channels, then, horses taken from Mexico trotted off
to different households throughout la comanchería, and with their hoofprints
laid down a community schematic of patronage and obligation that testified to
raiding's political dividends. War, especially so lucrative a war as the one waged
against Mexican ranchers and hacendados, offered juniors opportunities for
economic and social advancement that simply did not exist in times of peace.
More details survive about the Hois in this regard than about other Comanche
divisions because of their interactions with Texans during these years. With so
many prominent men killed in 1840 during the Council House Massacre in San
Antonio, emerging Hois leaders found a mournful opportunity to distinguish

themselves. After 1840 a handful of warriors appear often enough to indicate the rise of certain individuals through raiding in Mexico, but only two emerge in any kind of detail: Pia Kusa and Potsanaquahip.[20]

Almost nothing is recorded about Pia Kusa's (Big Leggins') life before 1840, though he surely cut his teeth in conflicts with other native peoples in the 1820s and early 1830s. Mexicans, Texans, and Americans came to know him as Santa Anna. He likely acquired this second name in manhood, perhaps because it was one he or his people thought Texans held in dread. After the Council House Massacre he became a key leader in the resistance against Lamar's Texas. Few Hois rivaled Pia Kusa in raw hatred for Texans, and he long remained a bitter holdout while older leaders tried to reestablish peace during Houston's second term. But Comanches faired poorly against Texas, and few war leaders seem to have obtained much honor, wealth, or prestige from that lopsided contest. Like many of his contemporaries, Pia Kusa made his reputation on campaigns against Mexicans. He led scores of expeditions throughout the northeast and possibly into Chihuahua, and "Santa Anna" became well known and much feared by the people of the lower Rio Grande. George Wilkins Kendall, cofounder of the influential newspaper the *New Orleans Picayune*, met Pia Kusa in 1846 and described him as "a fine, portly looking fellow, weighing over two hundred pounds and with a countenance expressive of both good humor and good nature. They say, however, that he is one of their fiercest and most relentless warriors." A German visitor to Texas described him simply as "a powerfully-built man with a benevolent and lively countenance."[21]

The most prominent Hois raider to emerge from the campaigns of the 1830s and 1840s was a man named Potsanaquahip ("male buffalo," commonly called Buffalo Hump). Potsanaquahip seems to have been considerably younger than Pia Kusa, likely only in his midtwenties by the time of the Texas rebellion. He enjoyed a reputation for bravery and sound leadership even before Comanches started sending huge campaigns below the river. Potsanaquahip distinguished himself in a number of these raids, organized some of his own, and after the Council House Massacre quickly emerged as the Hois' most influential war leader. Potsanaquahip also earned the trust and esteem of older Comanches and was said to be a "great favorite" of the prominent Hois paraibo Pahayuco. Like Pia Kusa he initially resisted peace with the Texans. When he finally agreed to attend talks Potsanaquahip became an eloquent and strident advocate of Comanche territorial rights. His reputation and his knowledge of northern Mexico helped him organize many hundreds of men for campaigns, and his exploits below the river found their way into the occasional Texan and U.S. newspaper. Writers who met Potsanaquahip described a paragon of Indian manhood. The German traveler characterized him as "the genuine, unadulterated picture of a North American Indian." Unlike his companions he wore no Euro-American textiles and sat naked above the waist with a bison hide around his hips. He had yellow copper rings around his arms, beads around his neck, long black hair hanging down, and "sat there with the earnest (to the European almost apathetic) expression of the North American savage." The artist John Mix Stanley accompanied a U.S. delegation onto the southern plains in 1844 and painted Potsanaquahip's portrait, but the work was destroyed along with another 199 of Stanley's paintings in the Smithsonian fire of 1865.[22]

Pia Kusa and Potsanaquahip probably did as much as any other individuals to shape the War of a Thousand Deserts. These men and their lesser-known Hois, Kotsoteka, Tenewa, Yamparika, Kiowa, and Kiowa Apache counterparts obviously had privileged access to animals, captives, and plunder that they could redistribute to kin and clients upon returning from Mexico. Prior to this, war leaders had to oversee the division of booty among the campaigners. In the end the leaders usually ended up with a minor share. To take too much would be miserly and suggestive that he was pessimistic about acquiring more at a later date; that his prowess was waning. Leaders of raiding campaigns "gave" shares of spoils to the men under their command. Giving booty to the men who helped take it did not create the same kinds of political obligations as would giving gifts to poor families, but war leaders developed reputations and followings based in large part on how liberal they were in splitting the spoils. Given that the size of war parties correlated with the prestige of the man leading the campaign, the many large parties that rode south of the Rio Grande in the 1830s and 1840s testify to the political careers forged during the war against Mexico.[23]

Older Hois paraibos such as Muguara, Pahayuco, and Mopechucope seem not to have gone on campaign below the river in the 1830s and 1840s, but they nonetheless reaped significant political dividends from raids into Mexico. Elder leaders were critical figures in the raiding economy because they generally negotiated trade and relations with outsiders. Unlike marketplace bargaining, exchanges within the gift economy on the plains were not structured by competition between customers for producers. Traders in Comanche villages did not find Comanches undercutting each other, for example, in the number of mules or horses they would part with for a trade bundle. Instead, traders negotiated first with the resident authority, gave gifts, established or renewed friendships or even fictive kinships, and then arrived at an understanding with the paraibo about a set price for hides, horses, or mules. The diversity of the trade bundle allowed for minute adjustments based on availability of supplies and also on the quality of the relationship the trader enjoyed with the paraibo. Once trading commenced, everyone in the village more or less proceeded with the agreed-upon price. This mediating position gave leaders access to special prestige gifts and, more important, to the very political power that was itself the final aim of material wealth.[24]

Just as the material benefits of increased raiding into Mexico helped native leaders on the plains build their reputations and their personal followings, increased raiding also enabled Comanches and Kiowas to recreate a dominant position in regional trade that had eroded in the 1820s and early 1830s. During the eighteenth and early nineteenth centuries Comanches had enjoyed a privileged market position on the southern plains, with multiple trading partners on the fringes of la comanchería. Comanche families to the east enjoyed access to French, British, and finally U.S. traders from Louisiana. They also maintained close commercial relationships with several Wichita villages, which both provided necessary foodstuffs and acted as middlemen between Comanches and representatives of Euro-American markets east of the Mississippi. Families in the north and west of la comanchería did considerable business with New Mexican traders and towns, especially after the Spanish peace in the 1780s. More important, Comanches in this region interacted with a great variety of native peoples who came to trade with them seasonally on the upper Arkansas River. Peace with the Kiowas and Kiowa Apaches had connected Comanches to British merchants via the Mandans and Hidatsas on the upper Missouri, and for a time in the early nineteenth century representatives of the newly arrived Cheyennes and especially Arapahos participated peacefully in the Comanche trade.[25]

These diverse commercial relationships went into sharp decline in the 1820s and 1830s, thanks in large part to escalating violence in the region. Moreover, the Wichitas had been experiencing severe population losses from disease and warfare from the late eighteenth century onward, and as they lost their commercial position Comanches lost a critical trade outlet. But just as peace and steady trade with Mexico had been a consequence of war and closed markets with other communities, after 1834 war with Mexico was both a consequence of and a reason for peace and expanded commerce between Comanches and their former enemies. By the mid-1830s Comanches started recreating a diverse commercial network out from the southern plains, based in large part upon the spoils they wrested from Mexico. Southern plains raiders sought a variety of external market outlets through which they could dispose of human and animal plunder. By 1840 they enjoyed commercial relationships with *contrabandistas* and trading companies from the United States and the Republic of Texas, with a host of indigenous peoples and individual native traders, with New Mexican towns, traveling Pueblos and comancheros, and even with northern Mexicans below the river. The sound of opportunity rang like a bell and called ambitious men from all of these societies into the southern plains.[26]

SUNDRY ORNAMENTS: ANGLO-AMERICAN TRADERS

Compared to other peoples active on the southern plains, Anglo-American traders are the easiest to trace through the records. With the opening of commerce along the Santa Fe Trail in the early 1820s, some traders, Josiah Gregg among them, engaged in incidental commerce with Plains Indians along the way. But this rarely became more than distraction along the trail. Americans eager to trade with Comanches were much more likely to venture into Texas. Intrepid merchants had been traveling from Louisiana since the late eighteenth century to barter for Comanche horses and mules, but by the 1820s found the southern plains market difficult to work with. With justifiably suspicious Mexican officials on watch and amidst mounting conflicts between southern plains Indians and their indigenous neighbors, Anglo-American traders who would do business in la comanchería did so quietly, usually in small parties, and with the utmost caution. They also had to adjust their market economy expectations to the social realities of the gift economy. While commerce would benefit both parties involved, alien traders first had to open the relationship with presents for local leaders. Gifts had the power to tentatively eliminate the social distance that would otherwise produce relations of suspicion or even hostility. This was deadly serious business. Traders who bungled the established protocols of gift exchange ran the risk of making enemies rather than friends. Berlandier commented that while U.S. traders had taken advantage of growing Comanche–Mexican hostility to tap the southern plains market in the 1820s, business had cooled by the time of his visit to Texas because Indians had killed several Anglo-American traders. In 1832 a trading party was attacked and the traders killed in the Texas panhandle. On another occasion, a redeemed Mexican prisoner recalled seeing the body of an Anglo-American trader whom Comanches had killed for *desconfianza*, for being untrustworthy.[27]

Holland Coffee negotiated the trade's dangers better than most. Coffee probably came from Kentucky, grew up parentless in Tennessee, and moved to Arkansas as a young man to participate in the Indian trade. In 1833 he established his first posts in the Red River region of northeastern Texas and southeastern Oklahoma. Coffee assisted U.S. negotiators in the Camp Holmes Treaty with peoples of the southern plains in 1835. That same year alarmed Mexican officials learned that Comanches, Wichitas, and others had been frequenting one of his trading posts, a fort guarded by several Indians and twenty-five well-armed norteamericanos. The officials reported that Coffee had told Indians "to go to the interior and kill Mexicans and bring their horses and mules to him and he would give them a fair price." Authorities in east Texas were just organizing to march on Coffee's establishment when the Texan rebellion intervened. Anglo-Texan authorities likewise accused him of arming enemy Indians, but he some-how allayed these concerns and even served as a member of the Texan congress. Coffee apparently continued to provide an important outlet for stolen animals until 1846, when, in a confrontation over an insult to his wife, a rival merchant stabbed him to death with a bowie knife.[28]

Coffee had his competitors. Following the watershed peace agreements with the prairies and eastern Indians in 1834, with Southern Cheyennes and Arapa-hos in 1840, and with the Republic of Texas a few years later, Anglo-American trade increased considerably. Merchants approached la comanchería from a greater position of strength, building permanent trading establishments on its fringes, and operating with formal or informal backing from nation-states. Three merchant families dominated this establishment trade: the Chouteaus, Bents, and Torreys.

Auguste Pierre Chouteau established a trading post at Camp Holmes after the peace brought about by the dragoon expedition of 1834 and quickly began doing a brisk business with southern plains peoples. Chouteau, or Soto as Kiowas called him, had pedigree. He came from the founding family of St. Louis, dabbled in the Rocky Mountain fur trade during the 1810s, and maintained strong connec-tions to the Osages. He seems even to have been one of the traders in la coman-chería during the 1820s. Many observers thought he had a better understanding of western Indians and the protocols for interacting with them than any other American of his time. Chouteau forged profitable relationships with the Tenewa paraibos Isacony and Tabequena, and he regularly sent skilled family members onto the plains looking for more Kiowas and Comanches to trade with.[29]

In contrast to the Chouteaus, the Bent brothers failed to establish regular commercial connections with the southern plains during the 1830s. Chouteau's operation represented the brothers' main competition and was a market outlet that disinclined Comanches and Kiowas from dealing with Bent's Fort. Chou-teau's death in 1838 and the consequent shuttering of his post may have influ-enced the pace of peace negotiations with Cheyennes and Arapahos because such a peace was very obviously a prerequisite to opening up Bent's operation to the southern plains. The brothers started planning for a dramatic expansion in business immediately after the Great Peace in the summer of 1840. In Janu-ary of 1841, while a massive Comanche raiding campaign was making its way through three northern Mexican states, Charles Bent wrote an associate to say he expected fifteen hundred Comanche lodges at the fort in the spring. Thirty-one Kiowa and Comanche headmen arrived to formally "make peas" at the fort in March, and Bent sent his traders into la comanchería that summer. In 1842 the Bents built a log post on the south fork of the Canadian River in the Texas panhandle specifically catering to southern plains customers. They built another post in the panhandle in 1845. Traders attached to the company also seem to have ventured south onto the plains to visit the Indians in their rancherías. Given the booming hide market, the Bents were especially interested in the skins and robes processed by women throughout la comanchería and would more than double the number of robes they sent back east after 1840.[30]

Hois and Tenewas had another major firm to do business with. Sam Houston cautiously tried to secure a negotiated settlement with the Hois soon after he reassumed the presidency of Texas in late 1841, though formal peace would take years to materialize. As part of the gradual thaw in relations, Houston encouraged the firm of Torrey and Brothers to establish several trading posts. John Torrey and his brothers established posts at Austin, San Antonio, New Braunfels, and elsewhere in the early 1840s. In 1843 they received a license from the Texan government authorizing a major trading house on Tehuacana Creek, near the Brazos Falls, just on the edge of Comanche territory. This post was critical to Houston's Indian policy and came to have a virtual monopoly on the licensed Indian trade in Texas.[31]

All of these firms had the same material interests: hides, horses, mules, and, occasionally, captives. Traders could dispose of horses and mules that Comanches and their allies had seized from northern Mexico in a number of ways. As early as 1827 Anglo-American traders reported that they could buy mules for six dollars in northern Mexico and sell them in Missouri for sixty. The Bents drove their herds to eastern Missouri, where, by the early 1840s, thousands of immigrants were buying tens of thousands of animals to pull, pack, and carry them and their families to Oregon. The growing U.S. Army presence in the western states was another important market for horses and mules. And exponential population growth in Texas during the 1830s and 1840s meant that many thousands of Anglo farmers would need horses and mules to clear land, haul plows, and transport goods to market. Most brought animals with them to Texas, but those who did not and those who needed more would have had little compunction about buying animals with Mexican brands via traders such as the Torreys. It is also possible that many horses and mules stolen from Mexican settlements made their way east of the Mississippi to help with the enormous project of clearing and working the millions of acres of tribal land opened up to Americans following Indian removal.[32]

What did Texans and Americans give Comanches and Kiowas in return for their hides, horses, mules, and captives? Most Mexican observers understandably focused on two commodities in particular: guns and ammunition. Mexico had been lodging formal complaints with U.S. officials over the weapons trade since the 1820s, and even in the midst of the Texas revolt Santa Anna accused Anglo-Texans of arming Indian raiders. Later historians have followed the Mexican sources and focused on the animals-for-arms trade between Comanches and Anglos as well, suggesting that it was perhaps the key dynamic propelling the violence of the 1830s and 1840s. Some Anglo-American traders did indeed supply Comanches and their allies with guns and ammunition. Coffee did. A Mexican man who had been held among Comanches between 1820 and 1830 insisted that Americans came to his ranchería every year to trade weapons and powder, and these were probably Coffee's men. Sometimes the trade proceeded informally: the Texan commissioner for Indian affairs lamented the fact that Anglo-Texan settlers provided Comanches with arms and ammunition. Torrey's establishments sometimes distributed powder and lead to men from the southern plains, though ostensibly in modest amounts for hunting purposes only. By the mid-1840s Hois openly approached the fort and interior towns in an attempt to acquire the ammunition they needed "to carry on the war with Mexico."[33]

These examples notwithstanding, Mexican observers exaggerated the scope, the conspiratorial character, and the significance of the trade between Comanches and Americans for animals and guns. Most commerce that southern plains Indians carried on with Anglo-American traders went through the large commercial outfits. After 1836 Coffee came under pressure from the Republic of Texas to stop selling weapons to Indians. And Chouteau and Torrey both enjoyed the support of governments that for defensive, political, and sometimes diplomatic reasons felt disinclined to see la comanchería flooded with firearms and ammunition. Similarly, the Bents had much of their resources, personnel, and capital in New Mexico, where relations could have been greatly complicated if proof emerged that significant numbers of weapons went out from Bent's Fort onto the southern plains. Though the Bents had important adversaries in New Mexico who, given the chance, would have gladly discredited and undermined their operations, no credible evidence arose that guns or ammunition made for particularly important items in the brothers' trade.[34]

Comanches in fact demanded a very mixed assortment of goods for the horses, mules, hides, and captives they sold to Anglo-American traders. Abel Warren, on-and-off proprietor of small trading posts on the Red River during the 1830s and 1840s, stocked a variety of wares, including red and blue blankets, wampum, ochre, gingham handkerchiefs, iron for arrow and lance heads, calico, and brass wire (which his customers fashioned into armguards). Josiah Gregg found that Comanches wanted looking glasses, awls and other metal tools, flints, vermilion, beads, tobacco, and blankets. The account receipts from Torrey's establishment reveal even greater diversity, with an emphasis on textiles, clothing, and metal tools, and space left over for Jew's harps, shaving boxes, and "sundry ornaments." Comanches and Kiowas could go elsewhere for guns.[35]

ABUNDANTLY SUPPLIED WITH FIREARMS: INDIAN TRADERS

Southern plains Indians almost certainly obtained more weapons through other native peoples than through all of the Anglo-American traders combined. Indeed, Comanches had always gotten the bulk of their firearms from other Indians. During the late eighteenth and early nineteenth centuries, consumers on the southern plains turned to the French in Louisiana for guns, usually working through Caddo and Wichita intermediaries. British sources were probably even more important. British traders in Canada and the upper Missouri sent guns onto the plains via Mandans, Arikaras, and Hidatsas, who traded the weapons to groups on the prairies and central plains who in turn exchanged them for horses and mules from Comanches and their allies. Mexican General Manuel Mier y Terán observed that "the majority of this commerce is mediated by other barbarians on the frontiers of the United States." Berlandier agreed, noting that Comanches were "abundantly supplied with firearms" in the late 1820s, thanks in large part to the Skiri Pawnees, who brought them British guns from Canada. Skiri Pawnees seem to have been one of the few links Comanches and their allies had to non-Mexican markets in the late 1820s and early 1830s, however, and even this relationship seemed threatened. According to one account, the Osages who attacked Kiowas in the summer of 1833 stuffed the severed heads of their victims into brass buckets because they resented the fact that the Kiowas had obtained the buckets from enemy Pawnees.[36]

When the Mandan, Arikara, and Hidatsa villages saw their positions erode because of warfare with the Western Sioux and, especially, from epidemic disease in the 1830s, other indigenous traders stepped in. Relocated eastern Indians and tribes native to lands bordering the Mississippi River received annuities from the U.S. government for surrendered lands. These peoples had mature connections to the U.S. market economy and hence ready access to manufactured items from American merchants. There is even some evidence that Mexican authorities in Matamoros, eager to secure native allies against their Texan and native enemies, supplied Delawares, Shawnees, and others with firearms. These easily could have made their way into Comanche and Kiowa hands. Once they had established peace with southern plains Indians, Osages, Cherokees, Choctaws, Creeks, Delawares, Shawnees, and others would have had none of the Americans' ambivalence about arming Comanches and Kiowas. In 1840, for example, officials from the Republic of Texas complained to their U.S. counterparts that Caddos receiving pensions from the U.S. government were selling arms and ammunition to hostile Comanches. That same year the *Arkansas Gazette* reported that Creeks had sold Comanches many of the three thousand rifles they had obtained from U.S. officials. In 1842 Ethan Allen Hitchcock, a career army officer and an insightful observer of Indians, noted that Shawnees, some of whom "probably fought by the side of Tecumseh," carried on an "extensive intercourse" in ammunition and other supplies with Comanches. In 1843 a party of Omahas in la comanchería disposed not only of all their trade goods, but even the rifles and ammunition they had brought for their own hunting and defense. Testimony from captives also suggests that Indians were the key figures in the regional weapons trade. Comanches captured Francisco Treviño in 1841, and throughout his three years with the Indians he often saw Cherokee and Shawnee traders arrive with arms and ammunition.[37]

The native peoples surrounding la comanchería had good reason to engage the southern plains market. As thousands of eastern Indians moved into what had traditionally been Osage territory, for example, pressures upon land and hunting resources multiplied along with conflicts. Peace agreements with their neighbors provided Osages with a new economic opportunity to offset wartime losses, and trade on the southern plains became critical to the relative stability and prosperity they enjoyed through the 1840s. Native peoples forced west of the Mississippi through the U.S. policy of Indian removal demanded even more horses and mules than their Osage neighbors. Choctaws, for example, had integrated horses into their culture and economy as early as the end of the seventeenth century. Horses became indispensable to the burgeoning deerskin trade in the Southeast, and the animals retained their economic and cultural significance into the nineteenth century even as the deerskin trade collapsed. Estimates from a missionary census suggest that the Choctaws owned nearly fifteen thousand horses in 1829, collectively worth almost half a million dollars. Nearly one out of every seven Choctaw horses either died or was stolen during removal. Families had to restock herds, in part to work new lands in Indian Territory. Moreover, cattle quickly became critical to the reviving Choctaw economy after 1830 and demand for horses increased as a result. After they concluded peace with native emigrants from the East in 1834 and 1835, Comanches supplied Choctaws and the many other indigenous communities in similar situations with horses and mules taken from Mexico.[38]

11. Comanche powder horn. Cattle horn, brass tacks, and leather plug.
Collected by Jean Louis Berlandier, c. 1828–51. Courtesy of the Department
of Anthropology, Smithsonian Institution, E1472–0.

Sometimes eastern Indians traded with Comanches and their allies directly,
by venturing out on the plains and forging lasting relationships. Jesse Chisholm,
a Cherokee most famous for pioneering the so-called Chisholm Trail, was one
such trader. Chisholm had served as an interpreter to Dodge's dragoon expedition in 1834 and soon after began doing business on his own. Chisholm most
likely learned the Comanche language and became enough of a trusted figure
that he often served them as a go-between with outsiders. These diplomatic services enhanced his carefully cultivated trading position, allowing him to channel horses, mules, and skins east to Cherokees and others and manufactured
goods west to Kiowas and Comanches.[39]

Chisholm was unusual. Most eastern Indians obtained Comanche horses,
mules, hides, and captives through other native intermediaries. Comanches had
long relied upon Wichitas and Caddos to be their middlemen with eastern markets, but both groups suffered demographic and territorial losses in the early
nineteenth century that compromised their market position. New arrivals, especially Shawnees, Kickapoos, and Delawares, took their place in the trade. In the

early 1830s members of these communities settled on the Canadian River, took to hunting on the plains for part of the year, and quickly became vital players in the Comanche trade. Some imitated Chisholm and became important figures in diplomacy as well as commerce. The Delaware Jim Shaw, for example, emerged as the key guide and interpreter for Texan officials seeking to reestablish peaceful relations with Comanches in the early 1840s.[40]

Traffic between Indians is the most elusive sort of commerce to track through surviving documents, but the scattered references that do exist suggest myriad participants collectively doing an enormous volume of trade. In 1838, for example, while Houston tried to secure a stable peace with Comanches during his first term, his alarmed subordinates informed him that Shawnee traders were attempting to turn plains peoples against Texas by disposing of goods at artificially low prices. A Mexican taken captive in 1838 recalled in later testimony that in eight years he never saw norteamericano traders visit Comanches; his captors always traded with northern Indian intermediaries. Another freed captive reported that Cherokees and Shawnees were by far the most familiar traders among his band. In 1841, a letter writer from Santa Fe informed correspondents in Missouri that a recent expedition had encountered no Indians "except a few Delawares bound on a trading expedition to the Comanches."[41]

In 1843 one of Houston's emissaries got a glimpse into the burgeoning commerce on the southern plains. As the Texan made his way through Comanche territory he saw evidence of native traders nearly everywhere he went. At one village he learned that a hundred Pawnees had lately visited the Wichitas and that they hoped to continue into la comanchería to trade with "the wild Indians." The Comanches he met with were also expecting a party of Osage traders. When the agent reached the paraibo Pahayuco's village he learned that Cheyenne and Kickapoo parties had just left with most of the Comanches' disposable skins and mules. And as he made his way to a meeting with another band he became greatly inconvenienced when his Delaware interpreter and guide, the indefatigable Jim Shaw, made a lengthy and unscheduled stop to trade for mules with a Comanche paraibo they met on the road.[42]

Hois and Tenewas benefited most directly from connections to prairies and Eastern Indian traders. More northern and easterly Kiowas, Kotsotekas, and Yamparikas had access to other markets. Cheyennes and Arapahos who had long raided Comanche and Kiowa herds sought to satisfy their needs through trade after 1840. Moreover, Cheyennes and Arapahos had a strategic position on the central plains that enabled them to channel horses and mules from the southern plains northward to meet the demands of the massive market on the northern plains, dominated by the Western Sioux. The harder winters of the northern plains forced Western Sioux and others to replenish their herds annually, either by raiding or by trading manufactured goods acquired from Canada and the Missouri traders to southern allies such as Cheyennes and Arapahos. In other words, the central plains market had a demand for animals that even the most industrious raiders among the Kiowas, Kotsotekas, and Yamparikas were unlikely to satiate, and central plains traders sometimes traveled farther south to trade with Hois as well.[43]

By the 1840s, then, native peoples came from far and wide seeking deals in the plunderer's bazaar that was la comanchería. While their activities left a much smaller mark in the documentary record, indigenous entrepreneurs almost certainly did more to enliven the southern plains economy than Americans or Texans. In so doing native traders from the central plains and prairies played an indirect but crucial role in northern Mexico's despoliation—a supporting role they shared not only with avid Americans and Texas, but with many Mexicans as well.

THEY LEARNED FROM THESE FRIENDS: MEXICAN ACCOMPLICES

Nowhere did Comanches find a warmer welcome than in New Mexico. New Mexican officials had been key figures in forging the peace of the late eighteenth century, and the alliance endured in New Mexico long after it had collapsed elsewhere in the Mexican republic. There were several reasons for this. For one, Comanches and New Mexicans enjoyed a profitable and generally reliable trade with each other. Just as important, proximity gave both peoples a healthy appreciation for the dangers of war—none wanted to revisit the mutual destruction of the mid-eighteenth century. Finally, New Mexico's animal wealth was in sheep and goats, and Comanches were not shepherds. New Mexicans owned perhaps 3 million sheep in the 1820s, but another survey a few years later reported only a paltry 3,000 horses and mules.[44] By comparison, a careful observer estimated that Durango possessed more than 150,000 horses and mules in 1849—despite having been plundered by Comanches, Kiowas, and Apaches for nearly a decade. The benefits of peace and the dangers of war with New Mexico were hardly worth risking when in comparison to other states New Mexico remained so horse-poor. Confident of peace with their western neighbors, Comanches felt secure launching annual raiding campaigns against other Mexicans during the 1830s and 1840s. Confident of continued peace with Comanches, New Mexicans steadily expanded the ranges of their burgeoning flocks east of the Rio Grande during these same decades.[45]

Anglo-American captives often reported encounters between Comanche bands and traveling comancheros. These traders seem to have been interested in basically the same commodities as Americans and Texans, though what New Mexicans offered southern plains families in return was somewhat different. Comanches and Kiowas had a diet rich in protein but poor in carbohydrates, and comancheros from New Mexico regularly hauled bags of baked bread, flour, and cornmeal onto the plains to trade. New Mexicans also offered Comanches sugar, saddles and other riding equipment, onions, tobacco, dried pumpkins, lances, tomahawks, and iron for blades and projectile points. Josiah Gregg claimed that comancheros traded arms and munitions to Plains Indians as well.[46]

Mexicans in Texas, along the Rio Grande, and even below the river also participated in the trading network fed by Comanche raids upon their countrymen. In 1837, authorities in Tamaulipas learned from a captured Comanche warrior that the "ingrate" José Francisco Ruiz, only a few years before the key tejano ambassador to southern plains Indians, had been buying horses stolen from northern Mexico and encouraging raids. Hois regularly sought trade in San Antonio and possibly in other tejano villages and ranches. Most of the friendly visits Comanches made to settlements along or below the river went unrecorded, though there are scattered references to trading sessions in northern Coahuila in the late 1830s. Even into the 1840s, commerce between northern Mexicans and Comanches remained sufficiently widespread that frontier officials criminalized it and imposed severe penalties upon offenders.[47]

Northern Mexicans found another, still more important way to contribute to the Comanches' Mexico campaigns, by providing raiders with information rather than markets. The unprecedented expansion of raiding below the Rio Grande would in fact have been impossible without help from Mexicans familiar with the territory, its defenses, and its resources. The Cheyenne mixed-blood George Bent wrote that Comanches maintained close ties with Mexicans in towns and villages throughout northern Mexico, even in times of war, through the medium of acculturated Mexican captives who stayed in contact with kin and friends below the river. "They learned from these friends where the finest herds of horses and mules were to be found, and the movements of the Mexican troops. By making use of this information the peons [acculturated Mexican captives] often led their war parties into the heart of the Mexican settlements and made big hauls of plunder."[48]

Sometimes, of course, Mexicans rendered these services unwillingly. Comanches often granted Mexican men temporary reprieve in order to extract information. Sarah Ann Horn recalled that Comanches captured a Mexican man soon after her own party had been attacked. She watched as they stripped him of his clothes. This done, the raiders began to "protest the utmost friendship for him" and tried to calm his fears, speaking kindly to him and inquiring about the surrounding country: where his neighbors' houses were, what the terrain was like, how large was his family. The terrified Mexican answered the questions and somehow calmed down enough to fall asleep, whereupon his captors shot him dead. Following his directions, they found and plundered his house the next day, killing his wife and children.[49]

As useful as both raw and seasoned captives were in this regard, free Mexicans may have been more helpful still. Mexican authorities had tried to exploit the local, interethnic community bonds some residents of Mexican ranches and towns enjoyed with Plains Indians during their struggle to maintain peace in the early 1830s. But these relationships remained outside of government control. Once the peace between la comanchería and the northern Mexican states collapsed, some frontier Mexicans chose to profit from the connection and assist Comanches in their raids. The phenomenon was widespread enough that in the winter of 1840 Mariano Arista, the ranking general in northeastern Mexico, decreed that any Mexican found talking with a Comanche was to be summarily executed. In 1841 Arista ordered the arrest of an indigenous resident of the lower Rio Grande (presumably one of the mixed-blood descendants of Coahuiltecan speakers who lived peacefully among Mexicans) because he was spying for Comanches. And talking was not the worst of the offenses: many free Mexicans rode and raided alongside Comanche war parties below the Rio Grande and guided them from place to place in person. In 1845, for example, a Durango newspaper article mentioned in an almost offhand way that Comanches relied on Mexican guides "so that they will be more assured of success."[50]

Mexicans had several reasons to provide such assistance. Most obviously there were material incentives for cooperating. Mexicans raiders could expect a share of the same plunder and animals that Comanches took and would likely have had trading networks through which to dispose of suspect commodities like branded horses. There may also have been an element of personal politics involved. The opportunity to guide and assist Indian raiders put an individual Mexican in a position of considerable, if temporary, power, which he could turn against enemies or rivals by directing the raiders toward certain targets and away from others. Finally, it is likely that Indians compelled many free Mexicans to cooperate. Given the Comanche practice of manipulating new captives into helping them, even against their own families, it is easy to imagine raiders presenting local people with stark choices. In the spring of 1842, for example, Comanches killed six muleteers in Nuevo León. Survivors reported that a man named Jesús Najar had been seen with the mule train before the attack and noted that Najar's son had recently been captured by Indians. Locals denounced Najar and assumed he had guided the raiders to the mule train. Perhaps he did so as part of a deal to recover his son.[51]

Sometimes unlikely acts of mercy suggest the presence of reluctant or at least ambivalent Mexicans in raiding parties. In the fall of 1840 a large party of Comanches attacked a ranch in northern Nuevo León and captured a young woman and her daughter. The two were soon separated. Two days later a bearded raider whispering that he was not an indio but "a Christian" reunited the woman and her daughter and helped them escape to a nearby town. During a major campaign in 1844 Comanches captured a Mexican prelate and, extraordinarily, forced him to give confession to a wounded captive. There must have been someone with them who felt strongly about the power and necessity of this rite. In 1846 two young boys were captured by seven individuals, six of whom were obviously natives because they spoke no Spanish, and a seventh who was merely "disguised" as an Indian. This last man stopped the others from harming the boys and helped the pair escape at the first opportunity.[52]

More often free Mexican raiders became implicated in the same robberies, cruelties, and killings as their native companions. Northern officials reserved a special hatred for such men, the "thieves and contrabandists of the frontier," and came to associate them with the worst excesses of the Comanche war. In the fall of 1840, for example, four hundred raiders attacked the town of Bustamante in Nuevo León, killing eleven people, taking thirteen more captive, and stealing some eight hundred horses. Survivors claimed that many "Christians" accompanied the attackers, including two men from Rio Grande whom witnesses identified as Juan Jiroa and José María Ramos. Sometimes the presence of Mexicans riding with Comanches lulled isolated communities into naïve hospitality. In 1838 residents of Cuatro Ciénegas in Coahuila opened their town to a party of Comanches led by Mexicans from San Antonio, presumably under the pretext of trade. Once inside, the Indian and tejano party fell on their hosts, killing several, kidnapping more, and stealing over one thousand horses and mules. Four years later, Indians plundered two tiny ranches in Coahuila under similar circumstances after the raiders had deceived the "careless vecinos" with "the stratagem of presenting a white flag."[53]

On rare occasions authorities captured free Mexicans while they raided alongside Indians. In 1838, for example, Mexican forces apprehended Agustín Garza, a resident of Matamoros, who had been raiding in Tamaulipas with los bárbaros. Mexican officials hanged his native companions immediately, but delayed Garza's execution until someone could come and give him last rites. As the ranking official on the scene put it, "This wretch will pay for his crimes within two days, since the war of extermination waged by the savages with whom he came admits no prisoners whatever." In 1842 soldiers caught a Mexican named Estéban Montelongo plundering corpses in the wake of a Comanche raid into Durango. The soldiers had delayed their pursuit of the Indians and gone to much trouble to catch Montelongo because he had earlier been seen riding and raiding alongside Comanches. Three years later authorities in the state captured an unnamed Mexican identified only as an "old thief." The man said he had ridden with the Comanches for more than a year, and he took such satisfaction in recounting their exploits that his captors decided not to hold him in a regular jail for fear he would convince other prisoners to escape with him and rejoin the Indians.[54]

Mexicans like Garza, Montelongo, and the unrepentant old thief were indispensable to the massive expansion of Comanche raiding that took place in the 1840s. Without the knowledge and guidance of people such as these, plains casualties would have undoubtedly been far higher, and the sufferings and defeats of Mexicans fewer. But apart from epitomizing this specific, tactical contribution, these three Mexican entrepreneurs are equally illustrative as representatives of what was by 1840 a highly competitive, diverse, and rapidly expanding borderland economy that fed off northern Mexico. Comanches and Kiowas were the face of aggression and the key producers in this economy, but many other peoples—American, Texan, Mexican, and, especially, Indian—rushed to the southern plains in the 1830s and 1840s to profit from Mexico's losses. Comanches and their close allies cultivated these connections and used them to rebuild their lucrative trading position on the plains. This good fortune and success had a momentum of its own. The market opportunities and pressures were such that by 1840 raiding below the Rio Grande began to compete with bison hunting and hide processing as the activity of first importance to the Comanche economy. But Comanches and their allies wanted something more from Mexicans than cotton bedspreads, obedient captives, and sturdy horses. Plains warriors saw their Mexican neighbors not as victims, but as enemies. This distinction multiplied the grief and suffering of these years many times over and had political implications for Comanches and Mexicans alike.

4

THE POLITICS OF VENGEANCE

In early December 1840, Comanche raiders crossed the Rio Grande into Coahuila and embarked on a remarkable journey. The men began by following the Rio Sabinas nearly to the border of Nuevo León, striking settlements along the way—San Juan de Sabinas, Soledad, Berroteran, Oballos, and others. Desperate reports poured out of ranches and towns as the attackers changed course and raced south. Officials described houses sacked and women stolen in Santa Gertrudis, terrified, weeping families cowering on rooftops at San Buenaventura, wild-eyed Indian runners screaming through the streets of Nadadores, homes aflame in town after town, and piles of reeking, slaughtered animals inside Don Vicente Arreola's fattening pen.[1] Gathering horses, mules, and captives as they went, the raiders traversed the length of Coahuila, cut across the north of Zacatecas, and burst into northern San Luis Potosí, whose residents had not seen men like these in more than a century. After setting fire to the Hacienda de Salado, the raiders stopped, turned their horses around, and began the return journey north. Anxious and enraged authorities in Coahuila organized to intercept them, assuming they would head for the hacienda of San Francisco de los Patos, the richest and most magnificent in Coahuila, forty kilometers west of the state capital, Saltillo. Soldiers and civilians streamed out of Saltillo and its nearby towns to reinforce Patos and await the enemy.[2]

These Comanches had confounded Mexican expectations more than once, but the audacity of their next move left even the most chastened observers shaking their heads. Forgoing the hacienda's temptations, they attacked greater Saltillo itself. With most of their fellow soldiers and armed neighbors massing at Patos, Saltillo's few remaining armed men shook off their disbelief at the raiders' "inconceivable boldness" and rallied around Don José María Goribar, former governor, scion of one the region's preeminent families, and now magistrate of the Superior Justice Tribunal. Goribar and his volunteers probably said prayers before they rode out of the city. And at first it looked like their prayers might be answered: the Comanches seemed to hesitate, fall into confusion, and then retreat upon seeing Goribar's force. Mexicans often flattered themselves that salvajes were cowards when pressed, and, heartened, the defenders dismounted and prepared to block the road. But the enemy's hesitation had been a ruse—the Indians organized in an instant and raced at the Mexicans "with extraordinary violence." Sick with the realization that they had been fooled into dismounting, the Mexicans panicked and dashed for their horses. Comanches killed Goribar and several of his companions before they could climb into their saddles.[3]

The capital of Coahuila and its surrounding ranches and towns now had virtually no defenders. The attackers could have concentrated their formidable energies on rounding up the largest haul of captives, animals, and plunder ever taken by a plains raiding campaign and then driven it all to safety before the inevitable defenders arrived. And, indeed, they made captives of twenty-six people. But instead of finding more or fleeing with those they had, the attackers spent the precious time available to them searching for and killing more than one hundred other Mexicans. And while some raiders rounded up nearly seventeen hundred horses and mules, others rode through the fields, broke into pens, and slaughtered more than eleven hundred cows, sheep, goats, and pigs.[4]

The men who attacked Saltillo were remarkable for their "inconceivable boldness" but not for their determined cruelty. Other raiding parties likewise spent precious energy and took tremendous risks to kill or injure Mexicans, slaughter domestic animals, and destroy property. Any interpretation of Comanche and Kiowa raiding has to confront and explain the fact that plains warriors crossed the river to hurt as well as steal.

INTERPRETATIONS OF COMANCHE RAIDING

The current scholarly consensus about raiding does a better job explaining theft than destruction. Refuting older interpretations that stressed cultural and ecological explanations and often trivialized plains Indian raiding and warfare, the last generation of historians and anthropologists has demonstrated convincingly that economic considerations were central to conflicts between Indians and between natives and nonnatives. One of the most fruitful directions this argument has taken emphasizes inequalities of wealth and status within individual indigenous groups. Ambitious men on the southern plains, for example, robbed horses, mules, and people in part to better their social and economic positions

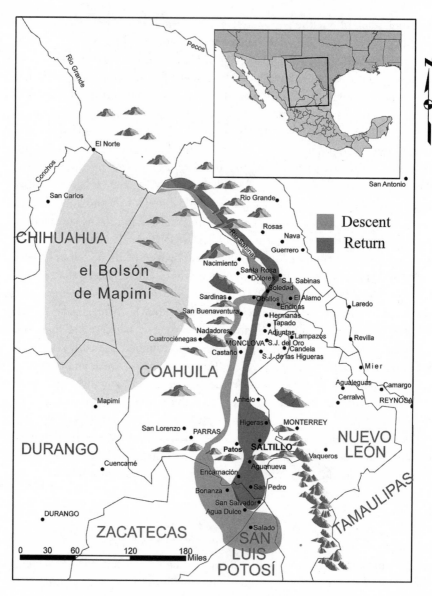

Pecos

N

El Norte

Rio Grande

Conchos

San Carlos

San Antonio

Rio Grande

Rosas

Nava

Descent

CHIHUAHUA

Guerrero

Return

Nacimiento

Santa Rosa

Rio Sabinas

el Bolsón

Dolores

S.J. Sabinas

de Mapimí

Soledad

Sardinas

Oballos

El Álamo

Laredo

San Buenaventura

Encinas

Hermanas

Tapado

Nadadores

Adjuntas

Cuatrociénegas

MONCLOVA

S.J. del Oro

Lampazos

Revilla

Castaño

Candela

S.J. de las Higueras

COAHUILA

Mier

Agualeguas

Camargo

Mapimí

Anhelo

Cerralvo

REYNOSA

Higeras

MONTERREY

San Lorenzo

PARRAS

DURANGO

Patos

SALTILLO

NUEVO

Cuencamé

Aguanueva

Vaqueros

LEÓN

Encarnación

Bonanza

San Pedro

San Salvador

TAMAULIPAS

DURANGO

Agua Dulce

ZACATECAS

Salado

SAN

0   30   60   120   180

LUIS

Miles

POTOSÍ

4. The raiding campaign of December 1840–January 1841

relative to kinsmen.[5] This perspective has recently been expanded upon and presented as an explanation for the dramatic increase in Comanche and Kiowa raiding during the 1830s and 1840s. Poor men of low rank had either to accept permanent subordinate status or else "strike out on their own with others of their cohort," often in defiance of their leaders, and acquire through raiding the things they desired. Such individualistic struggles were, according to one historian, "the internal force behind the expansion of the plains raiding economy in the nineteenth century."[6] That argument fits nicely with another recent study that associates increased raiding with Comanche political decline. By the early 1830s, influential leaders were few compared to prior decades, and raiding had supposedly become an uncoordinated, unregulated activity in which small parties of young men engaged, slinking off into the night with little or no sanction from elders.[7]

This individualistic and materialistic framework has yielded important insights into social tensions and highlighted the centrality of markets and material interests in fueling raids. But the interpretation reinforces a tendency among historians and anthropologists to focus on raiding as an ongoing economic activity instead of on individual raids as historical events. Thus while raiding merits study, particular raids generally do not. This tendency helps explain why scholars of southern plains Indians have not done research in present-day Mexico to determine what exactly Comanches and Kiowas did below the river. However, if we historicize raiding by collecting the details of individual encounters and then seeking patterns in the aggregate data, two insights emerge to complicate the prevailing individualistic and materialistic consensus.[8]

First, if Comanche politics was in tatters or otherwise marginal to raiding activity by the 1830s, the remarkable coordination that characterized campaigns below the river would have been impossible. The fact that the scale and intensity of raiding in the 1830s and 1840s expanded in sharply defined stages, stages corresponding to geopolitical events on and around the southern plains, reflects coordination of policy more than coincidence of ambition. Just as important, individual raiding campaigns were often huge, tightly organized endeavors. Between the fall of 1834 and the winter of 1847, Comanches and Kiowas sent at least forty-four major raiding campaigns south into Mexican territory, each involving one hundred men or more. Nearly half of these campaigns, including the one that struck Saltillo, included four hundred men or more, and on at least four occasions Mexican officials reported expeditions of eight hundred to a thousand men. Assuming that warriors accounted for one out of every five people in a total southern plains population of ten to twelve thousand, these largest endeavors involved upward of half of the region's total fighting force.[9]

Second, if men on these campaigns were motivated only or even mostly by
material ambitions, then the breathtaking, systematic carnage they inflicted
on Mexicans below the river makes little sense. A certain amount of violence
would have been inevitable, not least because Mexicans used force to resist
their would-be despoilers. Moreover, southern plains Indians themselves lived
in a phenomenally insecure and violent world and perhaps could be expected
to subject their Mexican adversaries to the same cruelties their own enemies
had visited upon them.[10] But the character and scale of the damage inflicted
on Mexicans suggest that violence was less an inevitable by-product of raiding
than an important goal in its own right. Indeed, the violence was so frequent,
determined, and severe that it often deprived the raiders of some or all of their
spoils and put their own men at grave risk. The force that struck greater Saltillo
in early 1841, for example, became so engrossed in what were obviously the twin
priorities of taking what they wanted and destroying what they did not that they
tarried too long around the capital. Mexican reinforcements arrived from Parras
and merged with an impromptu militia raised by the sitting governor. After a
bitter fight the defenders forced the Comanches to flee with scores of dead and
wounded comrades. The raiders left eleven Mexican captives, three thousand
horses and mules, and nine of their own dead on the field.[11] A few weeks later emboldened Mexican defenders intercepted the wounded, weary, and burdened
Comanche force near the Rio Grande, killed many, and deprived the survivors
of most of their remaining animals and captives. If Comanches and Kiowas conceived of their raids primarily in terms of material wealth, why then risk coming
home with fewer horses, mules, captives, and, most important, fellow warriors
just so they could hurt Mexicans?[12]

HATEFUL TO THE EYES OF THEIR WOMEN:
DISCIPLINING WARRIORS

Explaining the size and destructive malice of the raids means paying as much
attention to how Comanches and Kiowas organized their campaigns as to the
material and social rewards they hoped to reap through them. It means paying
as much attention to political process as to economic calculation. There are no
written sources to tell us exactly how Comanches and Kiowas organized their
policies and activities in these years, and it is doubtful that the full workings of
what was a very complicated, informal, and fluid political tradition can ever
be recovered. But it is clear that order cannot have been imposed from the top
down. Comanche and Kiowa paraibos had little prescribed coercive power, except in the midst of dangerous expeditions, when war leaders enjoyed strict com-

mand. Before men took to the trail, no individual had the authority to compel widespread cooperation.[13]

Mexican, Texan, and American observers from the period often saw the inability of Comanche leaders to dictate and enforce policy as evidence of a political vacuum. But as anthropologists have long recognized, most societies in world history organized themselves without the sorts of formal roles and codified institutions associated with nation-states. The all-too-common notion that nation-states are normative and that polities deviating from that norm are somehow politically incomplete necessarily misrepresents the workings of nonstate societies. It is more illuminating to pay closer attention to process than to form and to define politics broadly, as the process whereby public goals are discussed, established, and acted upon. A public goal is a desired outcome that a considerable portion of a community is directly or indirectly invested in. If, to choose a relevant example, a few prominent warriors from a village announce their intention to attack and plunder an enemy and then proceed to recruit young men to their cause—that would be an eminently political act. While private aspirations obviously play a key role in this scenario, such aspirations were bound up in concerns of wealth and poverty, honor and shame, and life and death that almost always transcended the individual. On many levels the fate of the men setting off together would be a matter of great public import, and communities employed an array of subtle but potent political tools to make that known.[14]

Comanches and Kiowas relied upon several established mechanisms to harmonize the activities of their warriors with the consensus policies and interests of the larger community. These mechanisms helped turn individual interest to communal ends. Conversely, they encouraged and promoted a value system that bestowed communal legitimacy and honor upon men's pursuit of glory and wealth. Communities on the southern plains nurtured cultures of honor, bravery, and martial prowess not simply to turn boys into warriors, but also to co-opt personal desires and safeguard communities—families, extended families, and residence bands—against the potentially disruptive effects of individual ambition.

Military societies were one of the mechanisms through which southern plains Indians imposed communal responsibilities upon men and their personal goals. Kiowas had several active military societies by the 1830s, one of which served to educate and socialize male children. Men held membership in different societies according to their age, accomplishments, and social status. By bringing together men from multiple bands, Kiowa military societies contributed to the integration of the tribe and the perpetuation of shared notions of honor, valor, and appropriate behavior. While Kiowas and other native peoples on the north-

ern and central plains had long traditions of organizing warriors into associations that cut across residence groups, Comanches seem to have had no such
organizations until the 1810s or 1820s, and they developed unevenly thereafter.
In the 1820s Jean Louis Berlandier, probably drawing on conversations with
José Francisco Ruiz, described the existence of a "society of elite fighting men"
called *lobos* (wolves) who went into battle with a long strap of wolf skin trailing
behind them. These men—older, experienced warriors—pledged never to flee
from the enemy unless their leader called retreat. So long as they observed the
highest standards of bravery, the men in this organization enjoyed great prestige
among their people; and the granting of conditional prestige is an extraordinarily effective means of social control. In other words, lobos became bound by
their social positions to always put concern for maintaining "face" among their
peers and their broader community above the pursuit of individual economic
interests.[15]

The typical Comanche man may not have felt bound by the lobos' standards,
but he nonetheless had to reconcile his personal ambitions with the norms of a
community perpetually reevaluating his social worth. This reconciliation often
took place at a dance. Dances were among the most important tools Comanches
and their allies used to imbed personal ambition into a matrix of communal
values. Ceremonial dances held on the nights before warriors departed on expeditions gave the men an opportunity, and an obligation, to assert their regard for
their community's values. Just as important, dances allowed the community and
its leaders to legitimate the undertaking and thereby exert some control over it.

Ceremonial dances connected with raiding and warfare could be held in a
number of social contexts. Some were very small and simple, nearly informal, in
which a group of young men in war regalia danced or pranced their horses before some of their leaders and kinspeople prior to departing on an excursion. An
observer in Texas during the 1840s reported seeing "some young men on parade
just about to start to war against the Mexicans." Another described a different
group with red face paint, most with bison headdresses, decorated shields, and
horses whose heads and tails had been painted carmine red. The men paraded
several times and then disappeared into the darkness. Other observers saw more
elaborate dances, often held for several consecutive nights prior to an expedition. Whatever their form or size, dances helped integrate the activities of individual warriors into a sensitive system of shared values and expectations. In this
way nonwarriors participated indirectly in a raid by helping to shape the social
identity of those executing it.[16]

Sometimes nonwarrior Comanches participated more directly. Women in
particular made vital contributions to raiding and to the imposition of social

rules upon raiding activities. Most concretely, Comanche campaigns often included a small number of women who helped manage and guard camp, assisted in carrying off spoils, and, according to Berlandier, served to "accommodate their husbands' relations and friends."[17] Very occasionally women also participated in the action of individual raids. In 1844 several Comanches captured three women who had been fetching water at a ranch outside Matamoros. According to Mexican sources, the warriors raped two of the captives, but a native woman present in the party intervened on behalf of the third. The intervention secured a momentary reprieve, though it may have angered the men somehow because a search party soon found the corpse of the Mexican woman a few leagues from her family's ranch.[18] In 1844 another Indian woman was seen in the midst of a large Comanche force campaigning through Durango. She wore elaborate dress and sat mounted on a large horse which was also much adorned, and she apparently served to inspire her warrior kinsmen in battle. A year later Mexican forces in the state killed a female warrior, whom they referred to as a "captain."[19]

Still, female raiders were the exception. Women performed a more regular and more fundamental task in cultivating and maintaining the value system that made raiding and warfare such important and such communal elements of Comanche life. Despite their notoriously subservient economic and political position by the nineteenth century, it nonetheless fell to Comanche women to police the landscape of martial honor in their communities. Once a raiding expedition had been announced, for example, scores of young women often gathered in public to chant the names and reputations of male kin and neighbors. Josiah Gregg said that these informal ceremonies could continue for several nights and that "all those designated by the serenading band are held as drafted for the campaign."[20]

More often women performed the critical task of policing male honor after the campaign ended. Families across la comanchería passed the weeks that brothers, husbands, sons, and fathers were away on campaign anxiously waiting for news. That news could come one of two ways. A herald might ride boldly into camp, announcing the men's imminent return. Such was the protocol if the endeavor had been successful. The relieved community would send a respected older woman to escort the party back into camp. Soon she returned chanting and carrying a long, decorated pole to which she had affixed whatever scalps the men had taken. Before long other women young and old joined the matron, each chanting, dancing, and celebrating acts of daring that had taken place during the expedition. Berlandier's informants told him that young women also rewarded victorious warriors with sex. Ruiz noted that women who refused would be "subdued by force." Upon the return of a lobo from a successful raid, unmarried girls in the camp danced for him and supposedly complied with his "every desire." Kiowa women likewise celebrated victorious men, singing, dancing, and carrying scalps through camp on long poles. The successes of warriors on campaign gave mothers, daughters, and sisters prestige of their own. Kiowa women, for example, put stripes upon their leggings for every scalp or coup won by some intrepid kinsmen.[21]

If, however, the party had been unsuccessful and lost men, communities learned the news in a very different way. Without notice individual men would begin slinking back into camp, often with their faces painted black, their ponies' tails shorn down to the nub. News of ill tidings sped through the ranchería, and lamentations went up from all quarters. Women made frantic inquiries about kin, and once the names of the dead became known grieving families sobbed inconsolably and slashed at their arms and legs with knives. Kin demanded to know the circumstances of the deaths, probing survivors for their own roles in the event. Lobos came under special scrutiny. If a lobo had been among the party and had acted cowardly in defeat, the women ran to "to break and burn his belongings," to taunt and insult him, and to say he was "nothing more than a woman like themselves." Shunned lobos sometimes fled their rancherías entirely, amid the taunts of children. "Often the very women who were so eager to offer their favors as rewards for the Wolves' mighty deeds try to kill them as the only way to slake the fury and disgust they have aroused."[22]

Policing honor and martial prowess in these ways, Comanche women served their community by demanding the highest standards of bravery and competence from all of the men, by rewarding success, and by imposing severe social sanctions for failure and weakness. Comanche leaders depended heavily upon women in this capacity. Old men would rush through the camp before an expedition got under way, admonishing unmarried girls "to satisfy all the desires of those warriors who distinguish themselves in battle, and not to forget to heap scorn and opprobrium on those who show cowardice." Berlandier recalled that the old paraibo Paruakevitsi "could rouse the women of his tribe to fury against the leader of a minor foray against the Spanish in which one of the chief's nephews had been lost." Comanche women possessed immense influence over the apportioning of male honor. It was said even that permanently crippled warriors would kill themselves "rather than be hateful to the eyes of their women, who mock them."[23]

Raiders would have been able to extricate themselves from these coercive webs of collective values and community oversight only with great difficulty. Few would have wanted to. But these mechanisms promoted conformity and cooperation at the local level. Few residence bands could have mustered one hundred warriors for a campaign into Mexico, let alone five hundred or a thousand. Organization above the band level required different political tools.

TO SUMMON THE TRIBES OF THEIR PEOPLE: COOPERATION IN REVENGE

In Comanche society extended families collected into bands, and bands collected into one of the four Comanche divisions active in the 1830s and 1840s. Little existed in the way of formal obligations between distinct units, but families from different bands and divisions forged relationships in a variety of ways. These obviously included marriage, but also exchange and cooperation in ceremonies, hunts, and warfare. It has been argued that in order to realize the widespread political coordination latent in such a system, the many segments had to be confronted with either a serious threat or an especially compelling opportunity. Physical threats from enemies were more obviously situations demanding cooperation. It is less clear in such a social system how one leader or group convinces other leaders or groups that an opportunity requires widespread cooperation. Opportunities such as those presented by Mexican ranches and haciendas required something more than simple material incentive to elevate them above the realm of band politics.[24]

For Comanches and Kiowas, vengeance was the principal political idiom used to invoke collective responsibilities and mobilize broad cooperation. Like many other plains peoples, Comanches traditionally thought of raiding for plunder, animals, or captives and waging war for revenge as separate activities. Ideally, horse-raiding parties included a handful of men and generally avoided violence. Revenge or war parties could exceed one thousand men but were supposed to last only a brief time and culminate in a single enemy's death and scalping.[25] This notional distinction may have held for most of their history, but the dichotomy does little to illuminate periods of intense warfare against Spaniards and Mexicans. Amid the conflicts with New Mexico and Texas in the eighteenth century and, less so, the bouts of destructive raiding in the 1810s and 1820s, raiders plundered horses and seized captives but also went out of their way to kill Spaniards and Mexicans. The idealized separation of raiding and warfare meant even less in the 1830s and 1840s, when these supposedly distinct endeavors collapsed into one. Vengeance helped Comanches raise enough men to travel with confidence throughout northern Mexico and plunder the region's richest properties. In addition to championing the individualistic, economic benefits of raiding Mexican settlements, therefore, Comanches and Kiowas united their broader communities in the enterprise through a discourse of honor, pity, and, above all, revenge. One Mexican observer listed vengeance as the Comanches' "most common vice." Berlandier wrote that "their fathers inculcate the idea of vengeance in them from their tenderest infancy. They are so thoroughly accustomed to the violence of this passion that they constantly invoke it to incite their compatriots to arms. It is invariably the desire for vengeance that incites them to make the raids which occupy most of their days."[26]

In some tribal societies revenge made demands on a relatively small number of people—for the most part immediate and perhaps extended family members. But many peoples on the plains could enlist help from a massive network. Comanche mourners visited extended family, naturally, but also approached respected warriors and paraibos within their own band. The injured party came before these influential men as supplicants, wept, appealed to their honor to show pity and to help them assuage their grief and their responsibility to dead kin. Then the seekers would widen the circle. Once the grieving relative had convinced a paraibo in his own community to sponsor his quest, according to Berlandier, the pair then journeyed to other neighboring bands, "weeping and calling for help in defeating the enemy." This more distant paraibo received the two "afflicted ones" graciously, gathering warriors and old men to listen to the guests explain "why they have come and the reasons which impel them to summon the tribes of their people." The social context pressured the resident paraibo to grant the request. If the leader were inclined to refuse, he had to justify himself before the assembly and "set forth the reasons why he cannot accept the invitation that has been extended." More commonly the paraibo accepted the summons, in which case, according to Ruiz, "his decision is then communicated to the entire ranchería by an old man who loudly announces the results of the meeting." The recruited paraibo thus drew upon his political capital to raise volunteers and perhaps send runners to other resident groups. The soliciting pair would "explain who the enemies are," set a time and a place for a general rendezvous, and then move on to visit still another paraibo. This process could continue for weeks or even months.[27]

Mourners and their sponsors also sought volunteers for revenge campaigns at tribal and pantribal meetings. Divisional gatherings seem to have happened during most summers. There is also evidence of enormous, multidivisional gatherings in the 1830s and 1840s, which might also be attended by Kiowas, Kiowa Apaches, Shoshones, Wichitas, and others. The Kiowas held annual Sun Dance ceremonies, and mourners regularly saw these tribal gatherings as opportunities to raise men for revenge expeditions against Mexican settlements.[28]

Once parties of warriors began to arrive at the prearranged meeting place, they held ceremonies and dances to integrate this new, temporary community, establish standards for behavior, and serve as a forum for the public evaluation of personal worth in advance of the campaign. Berlandier has left us a remarkable description of a ceremony held on such occasions, something he called the "little war" and that Comanches call the *Na'wapina'r*, or "stirring up." A parade took place in the morning, wherein fighting men in their regalia marched in double file amid their paraibos and renowned warriors, followed by the women and children in their "choicest finery" to the sounds of drums, chants, whistles, and pebble-filled gourds. Old men past their fighting prime stood at the margins recounting their own brave deeds and exhorting the young men to acts of valor: "The homilies are delivered with such fervor and energy that they inspire almost all who are present."[29]

Then, at twilight, a great fire would be lit. Men dressed for war formed a huge circle around the bonfire, leaving an opening in the direction of the enemy's territory. Paraibos and the bravest warriors entered the circle, gave public recitations of their own daring careers, and implored their comrades to shoot them down if they acted cowardly in the impending campaign. Outside the circle warriors were grouped together in three flanks. First, the right flank entered through the opening and began chanting and dancing around the fire. The warriors pretended to attack those in the circle and fired their weapons into the night while aged warriors urged them on. Then the dancing stopped and all of the men gave "a horrible, piercing cry, which seems to voice their thirst for vengeance." The warriors fired their guns above the head of their leader and then exited the circle. Next, the leader himself entered, galloped right up to the fire, "whose flames, whipped by the desert winds, lights this scene at once wild and impressive," and thanked the warriors for their bravery and coolness. The men of the left and then the middle flanks repeated the sequence, and then everyone dispersed to sleep before embarking in the morning.[30]

Men's societies, pre- and postraid dances, the powers of women to police male honor, rituals and obligations regarding revenge, integrative ceremonies at divisional and pandivisional meetings, and the Na'wapina'r were all pieces of an informal political tradition. This tradition generated impressive coordination of policies and people without relying on formally coercive political structures. Shared notions of honor and obligation served to activate the remarkable potential for cooperation always inherent in the superficially fragmented social organization that characterized the Comanche people. Individual warriors came under enormous pressure to adhere to group norms and to act as responsible members of their societies. Thus a seemingly individualistic activity like raiding for animals and captives became subsumed into a group endeavor that communities supported and invested themselves in. Finally, traditional protocols for seeking

revenge, and pressures upon plains leaders to assist in such undertakings, provided the centripetal force to pull these disciplined men from separate local
communities together into a single, focused, aggressive unit. All of these elements converged to empower the Comanche war against Mexico in the 1830s
and 1840s.

BEASTS THEY HAVE DEVOURED: WHY MEXICO?

Comanches and Kiowas obviously had other, more dangerous enemies than
Mexicans during these years. For a variety of reasons Mexico almost never managed to send forces into la comanchería to kill Comanche and Kiowa families
and plunder their herds. In contrast, Texans and Lipanes killed hundreds of
Comanche men, women, and children, and other Indians killed hundreds more.
If vengeance structured acts of collective violence, southern plains communities might have focused on these more threatening groups. And yet Comanches
and Kiowas seem to have organized large revenge campaigns against these enemies only rarely between 1834 and 1846. In contrast there were, as noted, more
than forty such campaigns below the Rio Grande during these same years. Why
would they turn the formidable power generated by the politics of vengeance
against Mexicans when other enemies seemingly did them more harm?

The question contains part of the answer. Because Texans, Lipanes, and other
native peoples had it in their power to attack Comanches and Kiowas where they
lived, the costs of escalating the conflict could be grievous, as those who tried
to avenge the Council House Massacre learned to their sorrow. Moreover, as
long as southern plains families had multiple enemies, men had to think twice
about leaving on revenge campaigns. Finally, groups several hundred strong
often had difficulty finding enough food for themselves and their mounts on the
plains if they stayed together for long. Consider the massive revenge expedition
against the Osages that Ruiz witnessed in 1824, involving two thousand men and
a vast, guarded camp of women, children, and animals. "This campaign, which,
by all appearances, was to decide the destinies of two mighty peoples," ended
instead with a modest skirmish and two Comanche deaths. Groups that large
simply could not travel together for very long on the plains, unless they had a
reliable supply service. This is surely one reason so many plains peoples put strict
notional limits on what large revenge campaigns were meant to accomplish. It
was important for the broader community to have a part in avenging deaths, and
yet it was dangerous and often impossible for hundreds, let alone thousands, of
men seeking revenge to stay together on the plains for extended campaigns. But
conditions below the Rio Grande were different.[31]

When plains warriors embarked on their huge Mexican expeditions they usually descended down a compact system of trails that itself testified to the collective nature of Comanche raiding. A visitor to Texas in 1837 reported seeing "an immense trail of the Comanches who have recently returned from their expedition into Mexican territory" and estimated that the raiders must have been leading a thousand animals back to their camps. An officer in the U.S. Army noted "deep trails worn into solid limestone rock by the unshod feet of the ponies." At one point the trail "was at least two miles wide and there was no more grass on it than there would be in any well-beaten road . . . small trails were cut into the ground in every direction. None of us had ever seen anything like it before." Warriors following this system eventually arrived at a ford, often one near the Big Bend of the Rio Grande known as el Vado de los Chisos, or el Gran Paso de los Indios. From there, as one Mexican frontier official put it, riders crossed over from "the great desert where our enemies live [to] the other desert, the Bolsón de Mapimí."[32]

The Bolsón de Mapimí is a huge, vaguely bordered region extending perhaps four hundred kilometers from the Big Bend south to the Rio Nazas, and two hundred and fifty kilometers east from Parral in Chihuahua to Cuatro Ciénegas in central Coahuila. The Bolsón (literally "lagoon") is in fact a region of varied topography, cut by seasonal rivers and streams and broken by scattered mountains, canyons, and several individual lagoons. During one of their intermittent peace agreements, Apaches taught Comanches about the topography and resources of the Bolsón and also about the best routes out to the exposed ranches, farms, and haciendas to the west, south, and east. By the 1830s the Apache–Comanche alliance had long since collapsed, and Comanches had come to dominate the Bolsón de Mapimí for their own purposes.[33]

Because the terrain is so arid, varied, and difficult, Mexican officials in the early nineteenth century found it impossible to patrol the Bolsón regularly and had to content themselves with the occasional costly reconnaissance expedition. During one particularly ambitious and typically fruitless tour in 1843, Mexican forces marched throughout the area and never found the Indians, though they saw signs of them everywhere they went. At one abandoned camp they found a system of barricades and trenches that Comanches had constructed for defense against Mexican forces. They also discovered "a multitude of skulls and bones of the beasts that they have devoured" and a camp crisscrossed with children's footprints. Entire rancherías would sometimes establish themselves in the Bolsón. This enabled raiders to ride almost to the point of collapse, knowing that if they could only return to their people in the Bolsón they could "surrender to fatigue for many days, leaving their arms and handing their animals over to other

Indians." The region offered more than safety and sustenance to Comanches. Most important, it presented a series of portals into Coahuila, Chihuahua, and Durango. Raiders could enter these states at any number of points, slip quickly out of one into another, and elude the most determined pursuers inside the Bolsón's rough, irregular geography.[34]

When raiders did emerge into the settled regions of northern Mexico, they commonly split into smaller parties only to regroup at prearranged times and places. As they moved across the land in these shifting cohorts, parties small and large enjoyed a virtually inexhaustible supply of food for men and animals. In contrast to the plains, where enemy peoples and game animals moved constantly and were rarely in the same place, below the river the targets were fixed settlements where people and animals lived together. Raiders easily found and caught livestock, and they simply killed and ate what they wanted when they wanted it. In contrast to bison, deer, or antelope, spooked cows, oxen, pigs, and sheep on Mexican ranches could only go so far, so fast. Mexican forces on patrol often found the remains of dozens or even hundreds of animals where Comanches had made camp. Some Mexicans such as the unfortunate Don Arreola even kept their livestock in fattening pens—a delicious change for men accustomed to tiring hunts. Most animals were not even eaten but simply destroyed, like so much other Mexican property. Thousands of dead animals unused for food and scattered in rotting heaps across northern Mexico offered graphic testimony to the superabundance of protein available to Comanches and Kiowas on campaign below the river.[35]

Moreover, raiders found it easier to feed their horses below the river. Killing frosts generally came later south of the Rio Grande than in la comanchería, and in some places they did not come at all, so mounts had more reliable pasturage. Indian raiders also took advantage of the mountain environments scattered through much of northern Mexico, using the rough terrain and cover to travel undetected and elude pursuers. The low mountain forests in Coahuila and Nuevo León had significantly higher precipitation than the lowlands and consequently copious grass cover for grazing horses. Once actively raiding haciendas and ranches, plains warriors again found fodder for animals. The Mexicans' own grazing lands were obviously available in the comparatively warmer climate, and native raiders would also have occasional access to grain stores they could distribute to hungry animals.[36]

These dependable resources help explain why two-thirds of all campaigns in the 1830s and 1840s happened in fall and winter. Large expeditions did sometimes embark in summer, though doing so left less time for other important activities—hunting, especially, but also extensive trading and participation in integrative summer ceremonies. Comanche women spent the winter months processing hides and tending to innumerable domestic tasks, but, relative to their busy summers, men remained comparatively idle in winter. Winter raiding thus had the incidental advantage of making Comanche men economically productive during months when they often did little more than guard camp and hunt casually. Moreover, fall and early winter were the best seasons to traverse much of northern Mexico. The rainy season (such as it is) on the lower Rio Grande begins by around September to fill up the watering holes that men and animals depend upon while traveling. Winter campaigns also brought men from different bands and divisions together at a time when peoples on the plains generally separated out of necessity and thereby presented another opportunity to deepen connections.[37]

Comanches and Kiowas therefore had many practical reasons to raid Mexicans rather than Texans or other Indians, apart from the obvious fact that Mexicans had far more horses and mules than anyone else. But safety, convenience, and profit are not enough to explain the terrific violence of the campaigns below the Rio Grande. The question remains how Mexicans attracted such wrath if they posed no threat to families and fortunes on the southern plains. The answer reveals northern Mexico's unhappy predicament. Comanches and their allies sought revenge for dead raiders — for men killed while attacking Mexican towns, ranches, and haciendas.

THEY ARE IN FACT BUT ONE PEOPLE: THE GALVANIZING DEAD

Comanche and Kiowa families presumably would have expected warriors to die this way, given that their sons, husbands, and brothers were, after all, trying to kidnap and rob the Mexicans they encountered. And yet Comanches and Kiowas viewed the battleground death of a warrior as simultaneously glorious and shattering, wherever it happened. Kiowas often chose the deaths of prominent men as the defining incidents of the year. The winter of 1834–35, for example, was "winter that Pa'to'n was killed"; 1835–36 was "winter Tó'edalte was killed"; and 1836–37 was "winter that K'íñähíate was killed." Mexicans shot each of these warriors to death below the Rio Grande. These kinds of deaths produced mourners and calls for revenge, and the complicated machinery on the southern plains for provoking pity, invoking obligations, and organizing retaliatory campaigns would begin its work.

In the winter of 1844–45, for example, a Kiowa man named Zépkoeéte organized a campaign to avenge the death of his brother, killed while raiding in

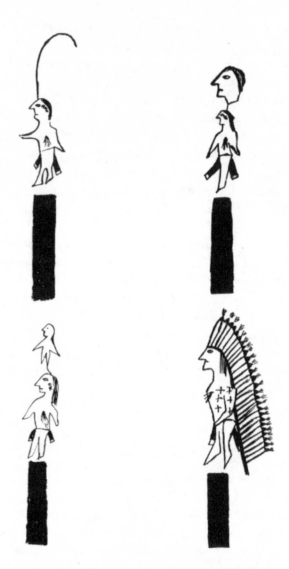

12. Prominent Kiowa casualties in Mexico. The black
bars indicate winter. Each figure has something peculiar
to identify him. Pa′to′n, "Bull Tail," is indicated by the tail
above his head. Tó‘edalte, or "Big Face," has an obvious
symbol. K′íñähíate, "Man," is identified by the small
human figure above the head. Ä′taháik′í, "War-bonnet-
man," wears his identifying headdress. Each of the
four figures bears a fatal wound. From Mooney,
Calendar, 269–71, 282.

Tamaulipas the year before. More than two hundred warriors, Kiowas, Kiowa Apaches, and Comanches, followed Zépkoeéte into Tamaulipas. Ä´taháik'í, one of the more prominent Kiowa participants, was himself killed in a siege of a Mexican ranch, and Kiowas thereafter memorialized the season as "winter that Ä´taháik'í was killed." Euro-American sources occasionally detected the revenge component of major raids as well. In 1840, following the deaths of thirty warriors in a disastrous Mexican campaign, men in Dolly Webster's Comanche camp began organizing themselves to seek revenge. Twice in 1845, large parties of Hois preparing to descend upon Mexico told Texan envoys that vengeance was their goal. The first sought to redress an "unfortunate expedition to Mexico," and the second to avenge the deaths of many men in one of Potsanaquahip's campaigns the year before.[38]

It is difficult to know who exactly Comanches and Kiowas sought to avenge themselves upon. Neither people's notions of justice demanded that revenge be exacted upon a particular person, family, or settlement. That does not mean, however, that these peoples viewed "Mexicans" as equally culpable or even that they thought of Mexicans as a distinct and meaningfully coherent political community. For example, the root element in the compound terms Kiowas used to refer to particular groups of Mexicans, t'a'ka´i, is also present in the term they used to refer to Americans (T'o´t'a'ka´i, "cold [northern] whitemen"). There is a certain rhythm to the shifting geography of raiding campaigns below the river that indicates warriors leveled their wrath not at Mexicans per se but at the residents of particular regions. Campaigns focused on Chihuahua during the early and mid-1830s, shifted to the northeast and especially Nuevo León from 1837 through the early 1840s, and concentrated on Chihuahua, Durango, and Zacatecas by mid-decade. Warriors killed in these regions would help explain why campaigns returned there year after year.[39]

At the same time vengeance was a flexible tool. Calls for revenge accommodated shifting judgments about the most lucrative regions to strike; raiders constantly probed new areas and need not have visited a place previously to kill and impoverish people they found there. Indeed, Kiowas apparently thought it acceptable to avenge themselves upon an enemy who had no connection whatever to the one that first brought them to grief. If so, the losses they endured at the hands of Osages, Cheyennes, Arapahos, and others might have helped fuel revenge campaigns below the Rio Grande. And whatever distinctions Kiowas and Comanches made among different Mexicans, the fact remains that they sent huge campaigns everywhere in the north except for New Mexico and distant Sonora and California in the 1830s and 1840s.[40]

Collective revenge excursions became folded into the ongoing economic program of animal and captive raiding, resulting in dozens of focused, coordinated, large-scale campaigns in the 1830s and 1840s. Once a formidable force had been organized, it proceeded down to the Mexican settlements with vengeance as a shared goal, though this formal and sacred purpose in no way precluded the plundering of Mexican ranches—on the contrary. A single Comanche death at the hands of a Mexican defending his family or ranch or town could provide occasion for hundreds of raiders to unite in a later revenge campaign. Revenge helped organize and motivate the second campaign, but in practical terms vengeance gave momentum to and imposed political coherence on the widespread desire for the same animals, captives, and war honors that had motivated the first raid. More Comanche or Kiowa deaths during the revenge campaign led to still more calls for vengeance and to a steady stream of large raiding parties heading south every fall and winter. As a knowledgeable Mexican observer put it, Comanche leaders impress upon their men "the necessity of opening a campaign, both to provide the plunder that the tribe needs and to avenge some outrage or offense."[41]

The raiding–revenge cycle therefore became a self-reinforcing phenomenon, and increased raiding in northern Mexico following the eastern peace in 1834 provided ample human material. There is documentary evidence of 622 Comanches and Kiowas killed in conflicts with Mexicans from 1831 through 1846. Fighting men accounted for nearly all of these casualties because nearly all of the violence in these years took place while warriors campaigned below the river.[42]

Six hundred twenty-two dead is in fact a significant underestimate. Many smaller raids were likely never documented, or the documentation has been lost or destroyed or else has yet to be found. Comanches often left their confrontations with Mexicans bearing serious wounds, and undoubtedly many of these men died without their adversaries knowing.[43] Finally and most important, Comanches and Kiowas put the highest priority on recovering the bodies of their slain warriors and carrying them off the field before a retreat. They thought the fulfillment of this duty one of the most laudable and honored deeds a warrior could perform, and they took extraordinary risks to ensure that their companions would not be defiled in death. Mexicans reinforced this imperative by regularly dismembering dead Indian enemies, by displaying Comanche scalps, ears, hands, and heads in Mexican settlements as trophies. Because plains raiders usually absconded with their dead, Mexican authorities often had no definite number of enemy casualties to record, even in the aftermath of the largest battles, and could only gesture at the blood the attackers left behind to suggest the scale of their loss. If there were no such silences the known Comanche death toll would be far higher. Still, even with the very low estimate of 622 killed, on average every extended family in la comanchería could have mourned a slain male relative at some time during these fifteen years.[44] Ambitious war leaders began attaching their political fortunes to this potent revenge cycle as early as 1834. Mourning kin appealed to the honor and pity of such men to organize revenge campaigns. The mourner traditionally led the campaign himself. But with all the violence and death of the 1830s and 1840s, any single campaign could include a crowd of mourning kin, with many deaths to be avenged. Under such circumstances, men like Zépkoeéte, Potsanaquahip, and Pia Kusa, proven leaders with experience below the Rio Grande, assumed leadership of the endeavor. Such men had the skills and the political capital to attract a huge and diverse following of raiders.[45]

The lure of animals, the growing expertise and prominence of young war leaders, the mounting casualties of the war, and the established practice of soliciting help in seeking revenge combined to bring together men from across the southern plains. It is clear from the Kiowas' calendar, for example, that they included Kiowa Apaches and Comanches in their revenge campaigns. In 1844 Pierce M. Butler, former governor of South Carolina, journeyed to the southern plains as a representative of the U.S. government. He learned from a "very reputable and intelligent Delaware" that Tenewa and Hois warriors had recently formed a joint campaign into Chihuahua that resulted in the "destruction" of two towns. A year later an observer in Texas reported that "several of the northern bands of the Comanches, and a portion of the tribes of the Towaccanies, Kioways, and Wacos had mustered about 1000 warriors under a chief named Santa Anna" (presumably the Hois Pia Kusa) to campaign below the river. Robert S. Neighbors, the most skilled Anglo-American intermediary between Texans and Hois, wrote that although Comanches were separated into several divisions, "they keep up continual intercourse with each other, and are equally engaged in their depredations and war parties. Whenever a chief from one of the upper [divisions] starts to Mexico or to any point on our frontier, they send runners to the lower [divisions], and all their warriors join him, so they are in fact but one people." On another occasion Neighbors reported that Kiowas, Apaches, and Yamparikas were endeavoring to recruit Hois warriors for a joint campaign into Mexico, "proposing to unite and send several thousand warriors." When invoked by skilled, experienced leaders, the politics of vengeance therefore attracted acquisitive men from different families, bands, divisions, and even different linguistic groups to pursue their economic interests collectively. Vengeance thus made it possible for war leaders to organize armies and go places that a few dozen raiders could not, plundering richer and richer areas of Mexico's north.[46]

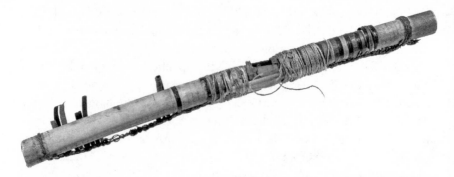

13. Comanche war whistle. Bird bone, plug of gum and pitch, buckskin cord, painted
quill. This whistle testifies to the collective nature of Comanche raiding in more
ways than one. First, southern plains war leaders used whistles such as these to give
signals to their men during combat. Second, the precise decorations of black and red
quillwork, which once covered the entire bone and were almost certainly put there by
a Comanche woman, reflect the fact that the performance and the fate of the whistle's
owner was a matter of profound importance to the broader community. The whistle
broke at some point and was enough valued to be carefully repaired with twisted cord
and a bone splint. Collected by Jean Louis Berlandier, c. 1828–51. Courtesy of the
Department of Anthropology, Smithsonian Institution, E5964-0.

Despite its obvious utility, vengeance did more than impose a superficial or
merely ceremonial coherence upon individual economic ambitions. Vengeance
was such a devastatingly effective organizational tool because it had genuine
meaning. Conditions were such on the southern plains and in northern Mexico
during the 1830s and 1840s that vengeance helped embed individual ambition
into a profound collective purpose: it folded plunder into war. Indeed, in those
rare moments when literate observers recorded conversations with Comanches
about their activities below the river, the word *war* appeared again and again.
Such references became especially common once Hois began interacting regularly with Texans during Houston's second term. In the spring of 1844, for example, two Comanches told a tejano that the Hois paraibo Pahayuco had lost a
son in the "Spanish war." In 1845 Pia Kusa requested a passport from Houston
so that Texan soldiers would not harass him and his men when they "went to
make war on the Mexicans." He went on to say that the cause of "the war with
Mexico" was the bad faith of the "Spaniards." That same year, Texan authorities
reported that one thousand Comanches were readying a "war expedition on the
other side of the Rio Grande" to avenge the casualties of a previous expedition.
Texan representatives were repeatedly told that Hois men were "going to war

against the Mexicans" or "to make war upon the Mexican towns of the Rio Grande."[47]

Still, it was common enough for Texans, Mexicans, or Americans to put words in native mouths; *war* certainly meant something different to Comanches and Kiowas than it did to their non-Indian counterparts, and, after all, words usually tell us less than deeds. The most important evidence that vengeance was something greater than a convenient excuse for organized plunder is that Comanches and Kiowas spent much energy and took tremendous risks to hurt Mexicans as well as steal from them. Revenge helps explain not only why the campaigns of the 1830s and 1840s were so large, but also why they were so destructive.[48]

THE LAW OF RETALIATION: HURTING MEXICANS

One of the usual ways raiders inflicted pain on their Mexican enemies was to destroy the animals they depended upon for their livelihoods. Animals have no clear place in Comanche and Kiowa notions of revenge, but slaughtering cows, goats, pigs, and sheep seems to have been part of a broader program of inflicting damage on Mexican enemies. In the aftermath of a raid in February 1837, for example, Mexican soldiers on the lower Rio Grande counted more than fourteen hundred dead horses and cattle and seemingly innumerable goats and sheep "piled up in heaps in every direction." Comanches killed more than a thousand animals in a single afternoon in greater Saltillo in January of 1841. Following a particularly destructive campaign into Durango in 1845, a local official reported there were so many dead sheep "littering the fields that they cannot be counted, though it is certain that I have lost more than two thousand." That same year, residents of El Paso suffered a typhoid epidemic, and many blamed the illness on bad air drifting in from the countryside, where Comanches had lately slaughtered large numbers of animals.[49]

Southern plains warriors also regularly set fire to huts and houses in raids across northern Mexico, leaving survivors bereft of homes as well as animal property and missing or dead kin. Sometimes the consequences were more dire still, as when in the autumn of 1845 Comanches killed thirty residents of La Pilla, Durango, and set a fire that consumed ten thousand bushels of maize, likely all of the stores the residents had saved for winter. Setting fire to buildings and chasing after and killing thousands of animals took a considerable amount of time and therefore exposed native men to increased risks in an already dangerous endeavor. There were no material incentives to slaughter livestock and torch buildings; rather a desire to hurt people Comanches and Kiowas evidently considered hated enemies instead of incidental victims.[50]

Raiders took the horses and mules they wanted and destroyed other animals as well as fixed property. One of these activities could delay or temporarily interfere with the other, but even greater complications arose over Mexican bodies. Captives had value as marketable chattels, as laborers in every dimension of the southern plains economy, and, for many, as eventual full-right Comanches or Kiowas. But just as their humanity made them more than simple commodities, so too did their humanity mark them initially as enemies subject to a terrible wrath. Plains warriors sometimes killed Mexicans soon after capturing them. Documents often make reference to bodies discovered in the aftermath of campaigns, sometimes mutilated and scattered in fields distant from population centers. Many of these had likely been temporary captives. When the Indian fighter Galán dispersed the huge Comanche encampment at the end of the great campaign in 1840–41, redeemed Mexican prisoners told him that the raiders had been "immolating" three or four captives each day as they traversed the Mexican countryside. Comanches and their allies plainly believed that many Mexican captives were worth more as corpses than cousins.[51]

Nonetheless, most Mexicans killed during these years were not people Comanches had taken captive, even temporarily. Plains Indians killed three Mexicans for every one they captured. The sources consulted for this book contained notice of nearly two thousand Mexicans killed by Comanches and Kiowas in the fifteen years before the U.S. invasion. Like the number of Comanche dead, this is an underestimate. The figure derives from what scholars of public health call passive surveillance, that is, from counting figures in reports that come in from local officials, military personnel, and the like. Studies of modern wars have shown that in conflict situations passive surveillance methods (as opposed to active surveillance, where researchers go out and seek information from a representative sample of the population) reveal only a fraction of total casualties. Indeed, the occasional state estimate from nineteenth-century northern Mexico suggests that Comanches took many more than two thousand lives in these years. A report from Coahuila, for example, insisted that twelve hundred Mexicans had been killed in that state alone between 1835 and 1845. The violence in Coahuila seems to have been roughly equal to that in Nuevo León and Tamaulipas and was probably less than in Durango and Chihuahua. In other words, if Coahuila lost twelve hundred people in ten years, then the total figure of northern Mexicans killed by Comanches in the same period would have been several times that many.[52]

The majority of Mexican victims were not soldiers or even organized, armed defenders. Mexican military and militia engaged in numerous battles with raiders, but most Mexican casualties were noncombatants: lone herders, travelers, and field hands, especially; but also women and children washing clothes or fetching water, adolescents racing to fetch the animals no one could afford to lose, terrified men lined up together with lassos, slings, and farm tools for weapons, families burned alive inside their homes. Plains Indians inscribed their grief and their rage upon Mexican bodies, sometimes to the point of taking identity as well as life. In October of 1845 the heartsick mayor of San Juan del Río, Durango, reported sixty-eight deaths in the wake of a Comanche raid but could identify only fifty-six by name because twelve of the dead had been "torn to pieces." Such were the consequences of the politics of vengeance. David G. Burnet once asked his Comanche hosts why they occasionally killed women and children: "When reproved on this awful subject, these undisciplined warriors justify their deeds of horror, as more enlightened nations have attempted to justify theirs, by the law of retaliation."[53]

Some of the Mexican reports describe scenes almost too brutal to be believed. In 1844, for example, Mexican officials corresponded furiously about hundreds of Kiowas and Comanches attacking ranches and towns in northern Tamaulipas. At Rancho de la Palmita alone the raiders were said to have killed around one hundred people. When the raiders arrived at nearby Rancho de los Moros they found the settlement nearly abandoned, save for one building where more than twenty men, women, and children had crowded together for protection. According to the Mexicans, the raiders set the building on fire and burned everyone inside alive. Expecting raids motivated by strictly material objectives, modern-day readers might be tempted to dismiss such an account as wild exaggeration.[54]

But the burning of los Moros is one of those rare events confirmed by a native source. In the campaign into Tamaulipas that the Kiowa Zépkoeéte organized to avenge his brother's death, his was the force that rode into los Moros in the fall of 1844. According to the history associated with the Kiowa calendar, Zépkoeéte's warriors discovered that a small number of Mexican men, "not soldiers," had taken refuge with their families in a fort. The Indians attacked the building and someone inside fired a gun, killing the warrior Ä'taháik'í. The besiegers reacted by stacking wood against the log walls of the fort and setting the building on fire. Everyone inside either died in the smoke and flames or was killed while trying to escape. The list of the dead reveals that what had started with family grief ended with family grief. Don Manuel Benavides, Don Trinidad Benavides, Nepomuceno Benavides, Angela Benavides, Faustino Benavides, Doña María Francisca Juárez, Marta Garza, Margarita Garza, José María Garza, Juan Garza, Ventura Garza, Justo Rodríguez, Salome Ortiz, Nepomuceno Ortiz, Josefa Herrera, Refugio Pérez, Espiridion Pérez, Antonio Botello, Francisco Botello, Margarita Botello, Natividad Botello, and Sabrino Botello all died at los Moros that day, cowering inside their little fort.[55]

Nineteenth-century Mexico was part of the modern Western world, where wars were supposed to be fought by armies against other armies and where independent indigenous peoples were supposed to be too weak to effect more than the occasional "outrage" against civilians. This was an ideal, of course, and yet dozens of massive and destructive Comanche campaigns might have wrecked the foundations of that illusion but for the related Western notion that Indians were holdovers from an ancient past, from a time when people acted more like animals than humans. Indian raiders did what they did because they were savages. Modern historians have to think harder about the problem. Today, scholars usually situate indigenous violence against colonial populations within a framework of resistance.[56] An older scholarship had recounted native North American history in stark and bloody detail, invoking purported acts of Indian atrocities against non-Indians by way of justifying the wars that drove native peoples from their lands. Work over the past generation has shown that later chroniclers often exaggerated Indian aggressions and that native peoples generally resorted to collective violence against their dangerous neighbors only in order to resist dispossession.

This resistance model explains much, but not what Comanches and Kiowas did to Mexicans in the 1830s and 1840s. By 1834 most southern plains Indians had stopped trying to adjust their relationship with Mexico. Comanche and Kiowa men were not fighting to change Mexican behavior. They were not fighting for their land or for the safety of their families or in defense of their culture. They were not avenging Mexican attacks on their villages or resisting Mexican economic and territorial colonialism. At bottom they were fighting to win honor, avenge fallen comrades, and grow rich. But to say that Comanches and Kiowas waged an extraordinarily cruel war for revenge, personal prestige, and material gain and that they justified it with arguments that might sound unpersuasive today is not to revive the discredited stereotype of the subhuman "savage." Just the opposite: it is to say that these people were fully human. Comanches were obviously not the only group in history, or even in nineteenth-century North America, to butcher, enslave, and impoverish people who had done them little harm. And, as any atlas will attest, Comanches were not the only people to exaggerate their grievances with Mexicans in order to take from them what they wanted during the 1830s and 1840s.

Part Two

NATIONS

5

INDIANS DON'T UNMAKE PRESIDENTS

Writing about Comanches during the relative calm of the late 1820s, Jean Louis Berlandier insisted that "it is still a very difficult matter to live in peace with the whole people. Divided into a multiplicity of independent tribes, they do not realize that all the people on the Mexican border belong to the same nation, and that they cannot perfectly well live in peace in Texas while they make war beyond the Rio Grande." Here, unusually, this inexhaustibly curious reporter had it wrong. Comanches could and did maintain an imperfect peace with Texas from the late 1820s to the Texas rebellion and with New Mexico for much longer while warring below the Rio Grande. They enjoyed trading relationships and occasionally made treaties with individual Mexican settlements and even found free Mexicans to ride alongside them, men who helped rob, murder, and enslave their own countrymen and women. Indians on the southern plains enjoyed far more political coherence than Berlandier realized, and Mexicans evidently had much less.[1]

Understanding why is a prerequisite to grasping the national and international consequences of the War of a Thousand Deserts. Northern Mexicans faced mounting terrors and tragedies in the fifteen years before the U.S. invasion, when they stumbled into bloody conflicts with Navajos, Utes, and several different tribes of Apaches as well as Comanches and Kiowas. As interethnic violence escalated in all quarters, northerners struggled with one another, with local and state authorities, and with a succession of national administrations over resources to protect themselves, their families, and their property. They also engaged in bitter debates with their countrymen about the nature of the enemy and, inevitably, about the nature of the nation-state. The questions arising from these debates were practical, aimed at wresting money, weapons, and horses from government, but they also shed light on fundamental ambiguities in the Mexican national project. What were the rightful obligations and expectations of mexicanos? What constituted a *national* crisis? or a *national* enemy? What was the proper relationship of the national government to the states? And what was government for, if not to protect its people? In other words, when raiders came and attacked a family in northern Mexico, what good was Mexican citizenship?

It is easy to be skeptical about such questions and the claims northerners made regarding their rights and obligations as Mexicans. Obviously they wanted help from the central government, but whether or not northern Mexicans really thought about their predicament in national terms is another question. Most scholars agree that states preceded nations in Latin America, in contrast to emerging states in Europe, which generally grew up around preexisting "nations" with shared ethnic and historic identities. Independent Mexico, like most postcolonial countries, had a fledgling state apparatus long before the people inside its territorial boundaries subscribed to a common national identity. Village, local, or ethnic identification mattered far more to the great majority of nineteenth-century Mexicans than did the abstraction that was Mexico. Hence one could dismiss northern talk about the nation and about national rights and obligations as the predictable and ultimately meaningless jargon of supplicants kneeling before the state treasury.[2]

In fact there was something more complex and more interesting going on. After 1821 Mexican governments worked earnestly to inculcate the symbols, stories, and values of Mexican nationalism within the broader public. They strove to integrate populations at the margins of the country through a variety of religious and civic rituals, political and economic bureaucracies, and patronage networks that cut across several sectors of society. While these efforts were halting and incomplete even into the early twentieth century, nonetheless, in the words of one scholar, they "engaged the emerging loyalties of frontier society" in the years after independence. Once Indian raiding became a systemic problem in the 1830s, northerners returned to the same rhetoric of nationalism they had encountered over the previous decade and turned it to their own purposes. They called Mexico City's bluff. Northern officials and commentators insisted that the nation-state was indeed a reality, that northerners were Mexicans, and that they therefore had a right to expect national help. In the process they took the idea of the nation-state away from administration officials and nationalist thinkers in the capital and fashioned their own vision of what it meant to be mexicano—one they would risk much to defend. This vision of rights and responsibilities was not without its internal contradictions, exaggeration, and hypocrisy. But the War of a Thousand Deserts nonetheless compelled many northern Mexicans to talk about the nation-state and their place in it in an authentic and urgent way. In this sense their long struggle to nationalize the war against los bárbaros gives insight not only into a failure and a missed opportunity, but also into the contested and often regional nature of nation making in the postcolonial world.[3]

At bottom northern Mexico's struggles were not so different from those that independent Indian communities grappled with during these same years as they tried to secure unanimity of purpose in their conflicts with Mexicans. The most practical difference was that, unlike Comanches, Kiowas, Navajos, and Apaches, Mexicans recorded their conversations in books, newspapers, political and military correspondence, memoirs, public pronouncements, laws, and congressional records. What emerges from these sources is the parallel story of Mexicans struggling against Indian raiders and struggling with each other about Indian raiders, from the start of the security crisis in 1831 to the eve of the American invasion in 1846. Each contest had consequences for the other and ultimately for the shape of North America.

THE CRUEL AND INDOMITABLE APACHES: THE NEW WAR BEGINS

In early 1831 authorities in Chihuahua and Sonora made history by refusing to feed Apaches. Though this proved to be a catastrophic error, at the time the decision seemed sensible. Mexicans had been supporting the Indians at peace establishments for nearly two generations—ever since the nightmarish interethnic wars of the late eighteenth century. Officials argued that it was finally time for Apaches to start raising their own crops and their own cattle, settling down and caring for their families in the same way that humble Mexicans did. And while the ration program amounted to only a small fraction of the frontier's overall military budget, it nonetheless cost nearly as much to keep an Apache in blankets, corn, salt, cigarettes, and beef throughout the year as most neighboring Mexicans made in annual wages. That was unseemly. So was the fact that Apaches kept getting handouts while dwindling revenues meant salary cuts for soldiers on the frontier. Things needed to change, the thinking went, and authorities began cautiously, starting in the 1820s, by eliminating salt, tobacco, even beef from the program. They also stopped distributing food in absentia, an old practice that had allowed Apaches to have kin collect rations for them while they hunted or gathered food elsewhere. By 1831 even the vestigial remnant of the ration program, allotments of corn for individuals who came in person to collect them, was more than the states were willing to bear. The time had come for the Indians to fend for themselves.[4]

Apaches rose to the challenge. Most who were hanging on at the old peace establishments evacuated en masse, and within months Apache raiding parties were stealing animals, waylaying travelers, and killing and kidnapping Mexicans across Sonora and Chihuahua. Before long the raids spread to southern New Mexico, northern Durango, and western Coahuila as well.[5] The sudden and widespread collapse of peace testifies to a shared sense of identity and to political mechanisms that promoted informal coordination of activity. Apaches living to the north of Sonora and Chihuahua were divided into three tribal groups—Mescaleros, Chiricahuas, and Western Apaches—but decisions about raiding and warfare fell to the bands that comprised the three tribes or, more narrowly, to the local groups of extended families that comprised the bands. Despite the fragmentation of political power, kinship networks ensured communication and a shared sense of obligation between members of different local groups and bands. Consequently, informal political mechanisms fostered patterns of coordinated action in both peace and war that could transcend the local nature of regular political activity. For example, while only a fraction of the ten thousand or so Apaches in north-central and northwestern Mexico had ever lived at the peace establishments at any one time, Mexican rations had provided certain older, conciliatory leaders with resources they could redistribute to kin and clients in the interior. So long as these resources had been steady and regular, an influential cohort could argue persuasively that their people had more to gain through peace with Mexico than through raiding. Once rations dwindled and then disappeared, advocates of more confrontational policies became ascendant and drew on the same far-flung networks to galvanize support for raids. Older leaders with a militant bent like Pisago Cabezón sent runners out to other Apache bands and even to other Apache tribes, seeking solidarity in war. Although sometimes setting forth in war parties one or two hundred strong, more commonly Apache raiders moved in small groups. Nonetheless, the raids were frequent and widespread enough to inflict tremendous damage across the northwest.[6]

However burdensome the ration program might have been to Mexican pockets or sensibilities, by late 1831 a little tobacco, salt, beef, and corn seemed mercifully reasonable compared to the gathering catastrophe. Indeed, Mexicans would later urge their leaders to reinstate the ration program in return for peace—but the genie could not be put back into the bottle. Newly influential Apache leaders such as the famed Mangas Coloradas (Red Sleeves) could better provide for their people on plunder than on Mexico's parsimonious handouts, and knew well that Mexican defenses had deteriorated since the Bourbon era.

More elementally, once Mexicans and the "cruel and indomitable Apaches" started killing, enslaving, and stealing from each other, hatreds, reprisals, and calls for revenge acquired a fierce and ultimately irresistible momentum. And in November of 1831, just as Chihuahuans began to come to terms with the gravity of the Apache breach, one hundred Comanche warriors arrived from the plains to herald another long-term threat. Desperate residents of northwestern Mexico started to fear, correctly, that they were entering a terrible new war, a war like the one their grandparents had suffered through in the 1770s and 1780s. But the Republic of Mexico was not New Spain, and this war would be worse.[7]

HAPPY WILL BE THE DAY: APPEALS FOR HELP

Poorly armed, often isolated from each other on scattered ranches and settlements, and unaccustomed to war after decades of usually peaceful interaction with independent Indians, northwestern Mexicans looked to different levels of government for help against raiders. At the first sign of trouble, local leaders would dispatch a rider or two to summon men from nearby settlements. Once the original report had been received, hasty letters would be written to minor officials, alcaldes and subprefects, who would try to organize men and supplies and then write more letters that worked their way up the political chain from prefects to the governor or the state's military commander or both. Ideally all of this correspondence would result in a sufficient force intercepting the raiders, defeating them in battle, and recovering Mexican captives or stolen animals. Northerners had only too many opportunities to practice this drill in the early 1830s, but the results left much to be desired. Reaction made for a losing strategy. Government could deliver important services in coordinating men and resources while raids were under way, but, more than this, northerners understandably wanted their officials to be proactive. Government needed to take the war to los bárbaros, to force them into treaties, to fortify defenses along the frontier, to stop raids from happening in the first place. Justices of the peace, alcaldes, subprefects, and prefects coordinated with militia and military authorities to respond to raids once they began, but for more systematic steps at improving overall security most people looked to the governor.

Governors did three sorts of things in response to the renewed security crisis. First, they ordered frontier settlements to take practical steps in preparation for war. Once the Apache peace collapsed in Chihuahua and Sonora, for example, authorities in both states moved aggressively to reform relaxed behaviors that had become habitual during the long peace.[8] Governor José Isidro Madero of Chihuahua lamented the "apathy and carelessness" rife in his state and ordered local officials to arm all the people, if not with guns then at least with bows and lances. Those unfamiliar with such weapons were to be instructed in their use, on Sundays. Towns, ranches, and haciendas were to be fortified, lookouts posted, and patrols organized. No one was to travel in the countryside in parties of fewer than three armed men. Chihuahua decreed that those who refused to fight los bárbaros or even hung back under the pretext of fighting defensively were to be executed on the spot.[9]

Second, state authorities attempted to unify and rally their people against the Indian enemy. They ordered reports of hostilities reprinted verbatim in official state newspapers and published fiery circulars meant to galvanize the population. Governor Manuel Escalante y Arvizu of Sonora urged his state on, insisting that Apaches, that "most barbarous and cruel" of peoples, had committed such heinous acts against Sonora's population, sparing not even the most innocent, as to place themselves entirely outside the law. He thus authorized all the state's residents to pursue and exterminate Apaches "like bloodthirsty animals." Governors also tried to police ambivalent loyalties. Mexicans had forged many social and economic connections with los bárbaros during the generations of peace — connections that persisted despite renewed war. Authorities learned that certain Mexicans had been trading liquor and foodstuffs to Apaches in return for animals the Indians had taken from Mexican settlements. Others, known as *entregadores* (deliverers), were acting as spies for the raiders and "delivering" them to vulnerable settlements, just as Mexicans in Nuevo León, Coahuila, Durango, and elsewhere would do for Comanches in years to come. Governor José Joaquín Calvo of Chihuahua decreed in 1834 that all such persons were to be surrendered to military authorities upon discovery of their crimes, tried, and if found guilty immediately put to death. Sonora passed a similar measure in 1835.[10]

The third and most important thing governors could do to improve security was to spend money. Terrorized, impoverished families, whether they had experienced Indian raiding directly or not, began abandoning certain frontier areas as soon as attacks intensified in the early 1830s. Population flight only compounded the security problem because it reduced the number of frontier settlements and left those remaining shrunken and less capable of repelling raiders before they reached the interior of the state. So authorities labored to keep people where they were. Governor Calvo tried to stem the exodus by excusing the "neediest classes" from contributing funds to the war and by making conspicuous rewards to certain communities who stayed and fought. The town of Coyame, for instance, which, "notwithstanding its small population mounted a vigorous defense against more than five hundred enemy Comanches" in the summer of 1835, was exempted from all contributions and taxes for the duration of the bárbaro war. The governor also abolished all duties on domestic produce and manufactured goods shipped north to the state's frontier settlements. While necessary and popular, these sorts of concessions deprived desperate state administrators of precious funds.[11]

More important, state administrators found themselves flooded by local requests for security investments of various kinds. Local officials always needed more guns, more ammunition, and more horses. Above all, they clamored to have the presidio (military garrison) system revived. This most common suggestion also happened to be the most expensive. Presidios had been critical institutions in northern New Spain since the late sixteenth century and were a vital component of Bourbon frontier policy in the late eighteenth century. By the close of the colonial era there were more than a dozen presidios in Sonora and Nueva Vizcaya, one in New Mexico, one in Texas, and several others in the northeast. Presidios were military institutions, but perhaps more to the point they served as centers of commerce and diplomacy with independent Indians. Presidios also encouraged regional development along the thinly populated northern frontier. Soldiers often lived at or near the bases with their families, and they attracted other settlers, who established nearby farms, ranches, and towns. New mines were frequently opened up nearby, and commerce and communication developed in lines radiating out from the garrisons. In this way well-integrated, fully funded presidios enabled growth where it would otherwise have been impossible.[12]

Conversely, threats to the presidios were also threats to the prosperity and growth they encouraged and protected. Funding diminished and soldiers drifted away during the War of Independence, and frontier defenses went into a sharp decline during the 1810s and early 1820s. In 1826 the independent Mexican government seemed poised to remedy the situation, outlining a plan for reviving existing presidios and even creating several new ones. The project never received adequate resources or attention, however, and individual states bore the burden of financing frontier defense. According to José María Sánchez, the draftsman on Manuel Mier y Terán's border commission of 1828, miserable presidial soldiers in Texas endured months, even years, "without wages, without uniforms, engaged in continuous warfare with the savages in the desert, sustaining themselves on buffalo meat, venison, etc." Venal officers preyed upon the isolation and vulnerability of their men by charging exorbitant prices for basic goods and by dispensing pay in credit or with certificates called *pagarés* instead of coin. Demoralized soldiers sank into debt and understandably focused less and less on the public good and more and more on simple survival. Many sold their weapons and animals out of desperation, and others fled—some becoming bandits. By the 1830s service at the frontier had become synonymous with poverty, misery, and danger, not only for the men but for their families as well. When in 1834 Governor Calvo wanted to persuade local officials to take seriously the unpopular task of arresting Mexicans who collaborated with Apaches, he threatened anyone who failed to perform this duty with five years' presidial service.[13]

Reviving the presidio system would mean having to pay soldiers regularly and in cash; give them the horses, weapons, and supplies they required; reform abuses in command; attract more honest and able men, especially in the upper ranks; and repair or reconstruct the buildings and infrastructure of the presidios themselves. To do all of this and also supply resources for local defense and the occasional offensive campaign would require an enormous sum of money. A writer from Chihuahua estimated in 1834 that it would take at least half a million pesos a year to save his state from ruin. No governor in northern Mexico had access to anywhere near this kind of money, though all of them spent a good deal of their time trying to raise as much as they could. Authorities in Chihuahua and Sonora issued numerous pleas for donations, arranged for voluntary and forced loans, neglected "nonessential" public services, and slashed the salaries of government employees. Deputies in the state congress would take a one-third pay cut, while other state employees would lose either one-fourth or one-tenth of their salary, depending on their income. But none of these measures generated enough revenue even to provide arms and ammunition to all the settlements that requested them, let alone revive their state presidios.[14]

Inevitably, then, people and politicians in the north turned to the national government. This seemed obvious and necessary to most because no state could cope with the deepening crisis on its own. Appeals to Mexico City also seemed just: northerners believed they were doing the republic's work by protecting the frontier against barbarians. Moreover they paid taxes into the national treasury and understandably expected some measure of assistance in return. But in effect the obligations and the rightful expectations of mexicanos differed in important ways from those of *nuevomexicanos, chihuahuenses,* and *sonorenses.* Governors reflexively devoted time and resources to combating Indian raids upon settlements in their states. Distracted national leaders needed convincing.

Though northern Mexicans requested national aid through a variety of channels in the early 1830s, the most detailed and comprehensive appeals came from three politicians: José Agustín de Escudero, Antonio Barreiro, and Ignacio Zúñiga. Escudero was a native of Chihuahua. He practiced law in his home state and served in several capacities in municipal, state, and national government, including two terms as congressional deputy and five as senator. A scholar of considerable talent and energy, Escudero took inspiration from Baron Alexander von Humboldt's monumental work on New Spain. He belonged to several learned societies, including the Mexican Society of Geography and Statistics, and wrote a number of careful books on northwestern Mexico, the first being *Statistical News from the State of Chihuahua* (1834). Like Escudero, Barreiro was a lawyer and politician, though he did not hail from the north. Sent from Mexico City to New Mexico in 1831 to serve as *asesor* (legal advisor) to terri-torial authorities, Barreiro acquired a quick passion for his new home, raising a family there and doing his utmost to champion its development. He printed New Mexico's first newspaper, *The Twilight of Liberty*, and twice won election as New Mexico's representative in the national assembly. His work *Glance over New Mexico* (1832) reflected both his belief in the territory's potential and his anxieties about what threatened it. Finally, Zúñiga understood the frontier with his hands as well as his head and evoked its hard sadness more fervently than his restrained contemporaries. His father had been a frontier officer and a com-mander at Tucson, and Zúñiga himself entered military service around age fif-teen. He spent a decade serving at frontier presidios before becoming a mer-chant and politician, first in the state legislature and, after 1832, as a deputy in the National Congress. He published his *Quick Glance at the State of Sonora* (1835) while in Mexico City.[15]

The authors spoke for an economic and political class with much to lose in the war against los bárbaros. They wrote their books to educate officials in Mexico City, officials the authors believed to be dangerously ignorant of the northern territories. Zúñiga complained, for example, that he had "heard people very close to the government speak with more ignorance about remote Sonora than they would about Tunkin or Biledulgerid." All three works pivot on the same theme: their states could be enormously productive if only Indian raiders could be kept in check. Barreiro detailed New Mexico's vast wealth in wild ani-mals, whose skins and meat could make the state rich, especially if bison were domesticated. Sheep in New Mexico multiplied "in an almost incredible man-ner," and the state abounded in uncultivated but "delicious" lands that could blossom into productive farms if only the people did not fear los indios bárbaros. "Happy will be the day," Barreiro wrote, "when the government extends a pro-tective hand over this land, for then the countryside, now wilderness and desert, will be transformed into rich and cheerful pastures!"[16]

During the long Apache peace, Chihuahua reveled in the kind of growth Ba-rreiro dreamed of. Escudero observed that Chihuahuans had founded hundreds of ranches and haciendas in the late eighteenth and early nineteenth centuries. These flourishing enterprises had produced nearly one million pesos in crops and in animal increase annually. Zúñiga likewise recalled a remarkable transformation in Sonora following the Apache peace: "What had been for a hundred years a theatre bloody with war, became in little more than thirty years of peace a place where one found ranches and haciendas." During its heyday, he claimed, Sonora had exported eighteen to twenty thousand animals to neighboring states each year. And, ever attentive to his audience, Zúñiga hastened to add that new, productive mines established in times of peace had enabled his state to send two hundred thousand pesos in gold as tax to the central government each year.[17]

By the early 1830s, however, all of this prosperity and productivity was turning to ash. Escudero offered the Hacienda del Carmen as an example. Once home to a thousand people, by 1834 del Carmen had half that many. Raiders had depopulated other haciendas and many more ranches. Those that remained were producing only one-eighth of what they had previously. Animals had been driven off or slaughtered, and laborers had fled their jobs. There was consequently a crisis in provisioning urban areas, and even residents of major cities feared starvation.[18] Zúñiga used more evocative language, insisting that terrified families were fleeing the region in huge numbers. Most of the new settlements that had sprung up under cover of peace had disappeared by 1835. All that remained was "the memory evoked by the rubble and by the embers that steam even now with the blood of more than five thousand citizens or friendly Indians who have been sacrificed to the ferocity of these barbarians." Zúñiga's claim of five thousand killed in Sonora was a gross exaggeration. Less than two years earlier Governor Escalante, anxious for help and unlikely to understate his problems, had insisted that Apaches had killed two hundred Sonorans since the start of the conflict. Zúñiga's hyperbole exploited the very ignorance he deplored in hopes of shocking and perhaps shaming national officials into taking action. Escudero, though soberer than Zúñiga, went so far as to predict the "disappearance of the state of Chihuahua. Its people want to emigrate, and this they will do unless they receive the guarantees that society owes them."[19]

And there was something Mexico City had to fear even more than the "total ruin" of the region. Zúñiga gingerly reminded officials there that Sonora could find other protectors, close as it was to "two powerful peoples," Russia and the United States. Barreiro more subtly asked his readers to consider what would happen if three or four thousand armed men from the United States invaded defenseless New Mexico, home to only one hundred permanent soldiers? Editors in Chihuahua went into more detail, insisting that northwesterners had but two options. They could either "flee those places wet with the blood of our children and wives, of our fathers and brothers," abandon the land "to the authors of our misfortunes," and, in flight, destroy "those conventions necessary for political society"; or else they could court a foreign power. The authors offered several precedents from Europe, where cities or regions had been forced to break bonds with a weak lord or empire and seek protection from an abler champion. If such things had been done in Europe, "then what reason could stop the chihuahuenses, sonorenses, and nuevomexicanos from doing as much with any other nation, feeling absolutely undervalued or poorly attended in their just complaints sent by different means to the supreme powers of the federation?" Another editorial put a finer point on the proposition, insisting that given federal indifference Chihuahua had a right to "break the bonds that unite it to the Mexican nation and join the republic of the north."[20]

EMPTY COFFERS: MEXICO'S FINANCES

Mexico's leaders had little reason to worry over such threats. It is doubtful that Sonorans, Chihuahuans, or even isolated New Mexicans seriously contemplated secession. Even if they did, they really had nowhere to go in the early 1830s. But the threats reflected deepening despair that national leaders could ever be convinced to treat attacks on northern states as attacks on the republic. Appeals from Barreiro, Zúñiga, Escudero, scores of newspaper editors, and government functionaries from across the north met with little success for a variety of reasons, but none mattered more than money.[21]

By the early 1830s the Mexican government had become mired in fiscal crisis, with revenues consistently falling short of expenses. The reigning assumptions for more than a decade among Mexico's political elites were that government could be financed primarily by taxing foreign trade, that foreign trade would grow steadily, that internal trade would likewise expand if not taxed, that foreign investment would revive the all-important mining sector (which the war had left in tatters), and that these happy developments would encourage wealthy Mexicans to make loans and invest. None of this happened. Import tax policy quickly became complicated and iniquitous, which encouraged smuggling and corruption and depressed foreign trade overall. Political instability discouraged foreign and domestic investment, and the mining sector did not rebound as expected.[22]

Meanwhile, expenses soared. Three mouths consumed most of Mexico's budget in the ten years after independence. Twelve percent went to tax collection and another 21 percent serviced loans, but above all it was the voracious war department that devoured the treasury. Throughout the decade an average of 58 percent of Mexico's annual budget went to the military.[23] Mexico's bloated army exited the independence war with enormous political power—anyone who would be president had to secure and maintain the support of the military. Indeed, military men occupied the presidency for all but two and a half years of Mexico's first three decades of independence. National politicians therefore came under mighty pressure to maintain high levels of funding for the army, pressures exacerbated throughout the 1820s by constant fears, justified to some extent though exaggerated for temporary political advantage, that Spain would try to reestablish its control over Mexico. Thus while most politicians understood that their treasury would remain as empty as a drum until the war department was disciplined, it seemed politically impossible to do so.[24]

With so much money going to the army one might expect secure frontiers, but massive military spending had not translated into significant support for northerners fighting independent Indians. The permanent army consisted of more than twenty thousand men serving in artillery brigades, infantry battalions, cavalry regiments, mobile companies, and presidial companies around the republic. Excepting the presidial companies, the great majority of these units were based in central Mexico or on the coasts.[25] It would have been extremely difficult for any president to convince a commander general to abandon his own regional interests and move to the relative poverty of the frontier. Moreover, Mexican elites of all political stripes, like their counterparts elsewhere in postindependence Latin America, obsessed over internal instability and the specter of class or race war. In reality, therefore, the primary function of most Latin American armies was not to fight independent Indians or resist foreign invasion, but to suppress social unrest. In any case few northerners expressed much enthusiasm for an increased national military presence. Despite its ravenous consumption of national funds, the sheer size of the army left individual soldiers impoverished and their commanders desperate for resources. Like presidial troops, regular soldiers often went without adequate pay, weapons, and supplies, and their ranks were filled through a despised system of conscription and by rounding up criminals and vagrants. Desertion became a chronic problem. Generals often had to resort to using their personal credit or to confiscations and forced loans to provision their men. Regular army units would therefore more likely be a draining, destabilizing burden to struggling frontier states than an effective barrier against raiders. Hence the northern fixation on presidios, which, while nominally overseen by the war department, were staffed by governors and state military commanders with locals or with men who would become locals. In other words, few in northern Mexico wanted army units; they wanted national money to pay for state defenses.[26]

They would get neither. Anastacio Bustamante occupied the presidency when raiding began to surge in the early 1830s and, with the fiscal crisis worsening around him, did little to help the frontier. Bustamante had in fact managed to increase revenue through more rigorous enforcement of existing taxes and

14. Anastacio Bustamante. Courtesy of the Benson Latin
American Collection, University of Texas, Austin.

tariffs, but his slavish devotion to and profligate spending on the military more
than offset gains in collection. Major international loans would have given his
administration more room to maneuver, but here too the earnest president ran
into complications. In the mid-1820s President Guadalupe Victoria's government had negotiated two huge loans from British firms for seventeen million
dollars. Within a few years the money had been spent, and financial problems
at home discouraged the British from lending more. With revenues from foreign
trade falling sharply, the Mexican government defaulted on the loan—leaving
its international credit in shambles. Like his predecessors, therefore, Bustamante
turned to short-term loans from lenders inside Mexico, who usually charged exorbitant interest rates—sometimes exceeding 300 percent.[27]

These entrenched fiscal problems fueled such political instability that northerners had difficulty keeping pace. Barreiro had dedicated his book on New Mexico to Bustamante, only to have Bustamante driven from office months after it was published. Escudero dedicated his book on Chihuahua to the man who took Bustamante's place, the federalist Valentín Gómez Farías. Gómez Farías was ousted by Santa Anna and a coalition of centralists soon after the book went to press. Worried perhaps that no one in Mexico City was any longer reading works dedicated to fallen leaders and sensibly uncertain about how long Santa Anna would last, Zúñiga prudently if blandly dedicated his book on Sonora to "the Supreme Government."

APACHES ARE MEN SIMILAR TO US: KNOWING THE ENEMY

If Santa Anna felt slighted it did not show because he paid more attention to the frontier than either of his predecessors. For example, he authorized the governor of Nuevo León to spend the funds necessary to relocate certain presidios as a barrier against Lipán Apaches and increasingly belligerent Comanches and Kiowas. The president also expressed alarm over New Mexico's wretched defenses, sending a new governor to Santa Fe and urging him to move vigorously against the Navajo raiders, lest New Mexico's "fertile lands become deserts, and everything [turn] into devastation and horror." Santa Anna ordered four hundred carbines, four light cannon, and fifty cases of ammunition sent to Santa Fe. He even acknowledged the fact that the presidios needed rebuilding. While Mexico City's "empty coffers" prevented the central government from immediately financing the whole project, some money, arms, munitions, and technical advisors were to be supplied to presidial commanders in long-suffering Chihuahua and Sonora. Congress also seemed more attuned to the mounting interethnic violence, calling for increased frontier security. Despite the ongoing fiscal crisis, then, by mid-decade it seemed that the central government had finally begun to take *los salvajes* more seriously.[28]

Effective defense required more than money, weapons, and advice, however. Santa Anna went a step farther and told northerners something they needed to hear, namely, that since Apaches and Comanches threatened multiple states, those states needed to cooperate. "The lack of a combined plan of operation has for many years made the tribes insolent," the president observed. Want of coordination had "deteriorated the presidial companies and placed the peaceful inhabitants at the mercy of the aggressors." For their own security, in other words, those threatened by Indian raids had to respond not as residents of this or that town or simply as New Mexicans, Chihuahuans, or Sonorans, but as Mexicans.[29]

Northerners seemed to understand this, in principle. In the early days of the conflict Sonora's governor ignored protests from his subordinates and agreed to supply Chihuahua with sedentary Opata Indian auxiliaries to fight Apaches, arguing that the sacrifice would be "beneficial not only to that state but to this." Escudero observed that broad cooperation had been vital to Spain's success on the northern frontier during the late eighteenth century. Despite Bourbon willingness to pour resources into northern defense, raiding continued until the flexible, comprehensive strategies outlined in Gálvez's *Instructions of 1786* had been implemented across the frontier. In other words, Bourbon New Spain enjoyed peace in the north not only because it had spent more money than independent Mexico, but also because it offered creative, responsive leadership that resulted in cooperative policies across the region. While many northerners remained dedicated federalists when centralists became ascendant in Mexico City, there was nonetheless a growing realization among some in the north that their salvation would hinge on coordinated defense and centralized leadership. "God grant that the president of the republic will realize the need to take such a step," insisted an editor from Chihuahua, "because this portion of the republic would, under the auspices of peace, come to occupy a very distinguished place in the world."[30]

While cooperation seemed sensible in the abstract, however, in practice northern states were usually loath to coordinate policy with each other or relinquish command of the bárbaro war to national officials. Despite tentative cooperation early on, Sonora and Chihuahua illustrate this point well. In the mid-1830s Chihuahuan policy still revolved around the Bourbon principle that Apaches could not be permanently defeated through force. Warfare helped only insofar as it compelled native leaders to renew and respect the peace. Chihuahua's strategy therefore focused on reestablishing even an imperfect peace as quickly as possible, and while the state pursued war aggressively and even treacherously, it also seized upon opportunities to negotiate. Escudero reminded his contemporaries that the sage Bourbons had never refused to enter into peace agreements with Apaches, even though they took it as a given that the Indians negotiated in bad faith. Part of the genius of late colonial policy was tolerating ambiguity—negotiations need not achieve perfect peace to be useful. Sonoran authorities, on the other hand, disliked the subtleties of Chihuahuan policy. They maintained that their neighbors dealt too mildly with Apaches and were convinced that los bárbaros had to be soundly defeated before genuine peace would be possible. There was more to this stance than dispassionate policy. The Sonoran government publicly committed itself to exacting vengeance upon Apaches for the many Sonorans they had killed since 1831, and the heated public rhetoric made negotiations all the less likely.[31]

The strategic divide had important consequences. In 1834 Sonora's governor personally led an ambitious and costly offensive against Apaches but withheld information about the campaign from his counterparts in Chihuahua for fear that in their shortsighted quest for peace they would alert the enemy. Sonoran militia and allied Opatas attacked a relatively small Apache party in the Mogollon Mountains in October and captured the prominent Chiricahua war leader Tutije. By jurisdiction, Tutije ought to have been delivered to authorities in Chihuahua City. Instead he was marched to the Sonoran capital of Arizpe, paraded before jeering crowds, and then strung up and executed in the street. Aside from the gratification coming from this spectacle, the expensive campaign had been a conspicuous failure. Apaches were expert at eluding hostile Mexican forces in their homeland and disinclined to engage in set battles. Moreover, revenge was at least as potent a political tool among Apaches as among Sonorans, and Tutije's execution predictably put wind at the backs of Chiricahua leaders such as Mangas Coloradas and Pisago Cabezón, who argued for escalation. Raiding intensified.[32]

The disagreements between Chihuahua and Sonora obviously complicated an effective response to Apache hostilities, and, in theory, this was precisely the type of unproductive factionalism that centralism was supposed to overcome. Accordingly, in February 1835 the commander general of northwestern Mexico, Colonel Ignacio Mora, who had jurisdiction over Chihuahua and Sonora, ordered the governors of both states to send representatives to meet with certain Apache leaders willing to negotiate peace. Any settlement had to be comprehensive, or else Apaches would continue raiding in one state while trading in another. Mora's directive represented a triumph for the Chihuahuan view, and Sonora's officials now had to decide whether to bow to national authority.[33]

In his first response to Mora, Sonora's Lieutenant Governor Ignacio de Bustamante (no relation to Anastacio) insisted that while the intentions behind the order were good, the commander general misunderstood barbarians. Apaches did not live under Mexico's government, Bustamante explained, nor did they live even under their own government. They had no principal chief or king—every Apache was a chief (an interesting argument, given that Bustamante employed it to justify defying a national authority). "They do not live in a society whose aim is peace, like the one you know, they live free, and consequently their natural vocation is war and hunting . . . they only want peace as a means to improve their war." Sonora would not send negotiators to talk with Apaches. Mora responded patiently but firmly, insisting that Sonora follow his instructions: "The Apaches are men similar to us, though their ferocity is equal to that of the Beduins." He explained that Apaches were fierce because they lived in a state of nature, because their society had not been constituted and regularized by social and civil rights. Most of all, they were fierce because the Spaniards made them so when in their brutal way they tried to conquer North America. Mexicans were different. In a nation as wise and illustrious as Mexico, "should we entirely shut our ears when the indigenes of the American continent make a request for peace?"[34]

Bustamante's modest reserve of patience ran dry. He bitterly resented Mora's characterization of Spanish cruelties and mocked his estimation of Apaches: "The Apaches are not similar to us, except in their human shape." Apaches were perhaps like Beduins or like the barbarians who overran Europe ages ago: "They may be similar to them, in a good hour, but you will never convince me that they are like us who profess religion, live in society, and recognize all the rights established in it." Bustamante offered proof. Within the last year Apaches had murdered one of Sonora's bravest presidial soldiers while he was unarmed, then danced for three nights around his severed head. They had killed twenty-eight people in the previous month in a single section of the state and recently had murdered a priest of great virtue, someone who had in fact performed many services for them. "And still the general insists that these barbarians must have their rights protected and must be shown mercy?" Apaches had broken innumerable treaties and were patently incapable of negotiating an honest peace. They were "a nation always wandering, always barbarous, that knows no society, that is morally impotent to celebrate treaties, to make agreements, or to promise a political loyalty that they do not possess." Under no circumstances would Sonora talk to Apaches. Bustamante ended acidly, suggesting that Mora would not hold such irresponsible views if he kept his headquarters at the frontier instead of hundreds of leagues away on the Pacific coast.[35]

So the state sent no commissioners, and Chihuahua negotiated a treaty with Apaches on its own. The agreement did not eliminate Apache raids in the state, but frontier officials believed that overall violence decreased—in Chihuahua, at least. The treaty explicitly exempted Sonora from all of the agreement's provisions, and raids there did not diminish. Sonoran legislators lambasted Chihuahua for the negotiations, insisting correctly that the treaty granted safe haven to Indians who robbed and killed in Sonora. They defiantly swore that "destruction and eternal war against these barbarians will be the standard that ennobles the Sonorans," implying that they needed no greater banner to rally around than that of revenge.[36]

Northern Mexican opinion therefore diverged, sometimes cavernously, about how to respond to Indian violence. Nonetheless, the correspondence between Mora and Bustamante reflected a tension that to varying degrees characterized all of the northern states. While northern authorities all clamored for national assistance against los indios by the mid-1830s, they nearly always wanted money rather than leadership. State oligarchs remained intensely protective of their autonomy and often genuinely convinced that national authorities misunderstood los salvajes. Occasionally representatives of the central government proposed policies that resonated with this or that state leader and would therefore be met with enthusiasm, as with Mora's reception by Chihuahua. But this enthusiasm should not be confused with a willingness to subordinate the immediate concerns of one's administration or one's state to national leadership in order to coordinate frontier policy and work toward long-term security for all of northern Mexico. That kind of sentiment was conspicuously absent throughout the 1830s and 1840s. Whereas the viceroy or the old commander generals in northern New Spain could usually command policy coordination across the region, officials in the republic lacked such legitimacy. So it was that Sonoran authorities could be openly contemptuous of multiple direct orders from a national official.[37]

And yet Sonora suffered no official censure for its insubordination. The president might gesture at the obvious need for cooperation, and the minister of war might occasionally encourage low-profile national authorities like Mora (a colonel) to arrange for such cooperation. But national leaders were reluctant to dedicate significant attention or political resources to the project. This reluctance had much to do with how they understood the problem. In addition to the entrenched tendency toward factionalism in the north, the argument between Mora and Bustamante also illuminates a basic disagreement between national and state officials over the nature of the Indian enemy. This disagreement would have fateful consequences for Sonora and Chihuahua, and eventually for the whole of northern Mexico.

According to the constitution of 1824, everyone born in Mexican territory was Mexican, including los bárbaros such as Apaches, Comanches, and Navajos. National authorities reiterated this view to the first minister from the United States, Joel Poinsett. Poinsett told Secretary of State Henry Clay in 1827 that "the government of Mexico does not regard the Indians living within their territory as an independent people in any perspective whatsoever but as a component part of the population of their states, and subject to the laws of Mexico." Therefore Comanches who sometimes attacked Mexicans and U.S. traders "can be regarded only in the light of a lawless banditti." Most northerners disagreed with the inclusive interpretation, insisting it was not birth, but rather a willingness to live under the nation's "pact," that made one Mexican.[38]

Still, there was some ambiguity here. Apaches had lived so long at Mexican-administered peace establishments that they came to occupy something of an intermediary position between manifestly autonomous peoples such as Comanches and groups like the Yaquis, Mayos, and Opatas in Sonora—sedentary, Christianized Indians who lived separately on their own lands from other Mexicans. When these three groups fought Mexican authorities in the decades after independence to protest taxes or land policies they were branded *sublevados*, rebels. This is the same term Mexican officials initially applied to Apaches in the early 1830s.[39] But by 1835, after nearly four years of destructive raiding, Chihuahua's officials wrote the president and asked him to clarify the Apaches' status. The president replied that "the rebellious Apaches and those individuals belonging to groups known by the name of barbarian nations who live in our territory are Mexicans, because they were born and live in the republic, and they do not and cannot have a government independent of the general government." These unlucky "groups of forest men . . . demand the attention of all friends of humanity" and had to be reduced to a state of culture and civilization.[40]

National leaders struggling to promote a clear sense of Mexican identity throughout the republic stressed the idea of Mexico as inclusive, in sharp contrast to the Jacksonian-era United States, for example, which exterminated Indians or forced them from their lands. More important in regard to the 1820s and early 1830s, they conceived of Mexican liberality in opposition to Spanish cruelty. There was irony in this. While metropolitan rhetoric often blamed native hostility on the memory of Spanish excesses, national leaders advocated a moderate and relatively enlightened approach to Indian affairs that resonated with Bourbon practice and indeed owed much to it. In contrast, northern writers and officials commonly idealized and extolled Spain's wise frontier policy. In practice, however, they often adopted brutal, shortsighted war plans that gratified public desire for vengeance and indigenous slaves but usually exacerbated conflicts with native communities.[41]

The debate between national and state officials over whether or not to call los bárbaros mexicanos was about more than names. Presidents would reiterate the view that Comanches, Apaches, Navajos, and others could indeed be civilized into good Mexicans even into the 1840s, when the country witnessed an appalling expansion in the scope and violence of Indian raiding. These optimistic views inevitably clashed with the hard and often murderous policies embraced by desperate northern policymakers. Elected officials and businessmen in Chihuahua and Sonora, for example, encouraged scalp hunting. A Chihuahuan plan promised one hundred pesos for the scalp of an Apache man, fifty for the scalp of a woman, and twenty-five for captured Apache children eleven years old and younger (apparently twelve-year-olds were fit for scalping). Northwesterners therefore looked to the market to do what government could not or would not do. Indeed, bounty hunting had much to offer poor Mexicans. By way of context, a government survey done in 1848 found in the district of Guerrero, Chihuahua, more than 85 percent of the population earned less than twenty pesos per month.[42]

Yet it was foreigners, especially traders and trappers from the United States, who dominated the scalp business. Two in particular became regional celebrities. In 1837 John James Johnson lured several prominent Apache leaders into a trading session and, while they inspected a sack of pinole, blew them to pieces with a swivel gun. Soon after, he triumphantly presented the scalps of his victims to Sonora's commander general. While Johnson's fame derived from that one stunning act, James "Santiago" Kirker made a career of killing Apaches. A surviving daguerreotype in Missouri shows him in a suit and tie, mouth barely open as if he were listening intently, weathered face cocked at a defensive angle, and large, clear eyes locked upon the lens. His arms are folded across his chest, and while everything else is still, the left hand is blurred with movement, as if he were about to pounce upon the fool behind the camera. Kirker frightened people. A Scotch-Irishman who immigrated first to New York, then to Missouri, and finally to New Mexico and Chihuahua, Kirker became a prospector, trapper, and trader in Apache territory. He probably sold more guns and ammunition to Apaches during the 1830s than anyone else. In 1838 a Mexican boy who escaped from Apaches reported that his captors were well armed with guns and ammunition obtained from an American named Santiago. Starting that same year, however, officials in New Mexico and Chihuahua began employing Kirker and his men to hunt his erstwhile customers like animals. Together with a shifting band of Mexicans, Anglo-Americans, Delawares, and Shawnees, Kirker hunted Apaches throughout Chihuahua and New Mexico and, like Johnson, secured his most celebrated triumphs through treachery and massacre.[43]

All of this was too much for the national government to bear, initially at least. Authorities in Mexico City canceled Chihuahua's elaborate proposal for a permanent, state-funded company of scalp hunters under Kirker's direction, branding it immoral, unconstitutional, dangerous, and repugnant to Mexico's civilization. Nonetheless, scalp hunting continued apace, and eventually national authorities would simply stop complaining. But the viewpoint behind the original protest, that Comanches, Apaches, and other bárbaros were Mexicans, fundamentally shaped the way national authorities perceived and reacted to the problem of Indian raiding. In short, indigenous raiders could not attack "Mexico" because they themselves were part of Mexico. This was not to say they should not be resisted—obviously they should. If peace proved impossible with certain groups, then they should be attacked vigorously, even destroyed. The

15. James Kirker. Thomas M. Easterly, 1847.
Courtesy Missouri Historical Society, St. Louis.

priority of and the responsibility for this resistance, however, had nothing particularly *national* about it.[44]

THE IMMEDIATE DESTRUCTION
OF THE REPUBLIC: PRIORITIES

From Mexico City's distracted perspective the war against los bárbaros was
therefore more of a long-term project than an immediate priority. National
leaders reflexively privileged a variety of issues over frontier defense. Unsurprisingly, administrators spent more time worrying about Mexico's abysmal finances
than about Apaches or Comanches. Since independence, states had been slow,
irregular, and miserly in contributing to the national tax base, and this is one rea-

son centralists wanted a concentration of political power in Mexico City. This project went forward even after Santa Anna's defeat and imprisonment in Texas and culminated in a new constitution in 1836. Among other things, the centralist constitution eliminated state assemblies and replaced them with seven-member juntas (committees) without legislative powers, transformed states into less autonomous administrative units called departments, and made governors appointed rather than elected.[45]

These reforms laid the groundwork for changes in the all-important realm of tax policy. Under the federalist system individual states had been required to send a predetermined cut of their revenues to the national government—a payment called the *contingente*. In theory money left over could be used at the state's discretion, but in practice the states usually took care of their own priorities first—which is why contingente payments amounted to less than 20 percent of scheduled funds on the eve of the centralist takeover. Thus, as cash-strapped as northwestern states were during the early years of the War of a Thousand Deserts, governors and state legislators nonetheless had the power to stretch their budgets. In early 1833, for example, Chihuahuan officials had unilaterally declared that the war would be the state's fiscal priority, with a minimum of nine thousand pesos going to support frontier troops each month.[46]

Centralists set out to change all this. As early as December 1834 Mexico City asserted its right to dispatch the army to confiscate state funds in order to guarantee that the contingente was paid in full. In late 1835 it ordered states to surrender one-half of all their monthly revenues to national treasury officials. These funds would go directly toward supporting the army unit inside or nearest to that state. The measure still left states some room for creative bookkeeping, but in December they were ordered to turn over *all* revenues directly to national authorities. Military funding would take precedence, and whatever remained would go toward paying state salaries and legal credits. With his rival Santa Anna discredited in Texas, Anastacio Bustamante was again elected president in 1837. Under Bustamante's leadership the central government circumvented departmental fiscal structures entirely, sending its own representatives to do the tax collecting.[47]

Because Mexico City now controlled nearly all state revenues, northerners understandably expected more help with defense. And officials in Mexico City did occasionally provide targeted resources to the northern frontier, as in late 1836 when several hundred British shotguns were apparently shipped to Chihuahua. But tax reforms had not solved Mexico's overall fiscal crisis. Deficits went even higher after 1834 than they had been during the federalist period, and though spending on the army dipped modestly it remained wildly inefficient and ruinous to the budget. Most important, by the mid-1830s debt repayment had become the single greatest expense for the Mexican government, outdoing even the insatiable military. The strain convinced Bustamante to make some cautious attempts at imposing new taxes, but mostly he continued funding the government through burdensome short-term loans that drove the government deeper into the red year after year.[48]

Given Mexico's perpetual fiscal crisis, the frontier would receive national attention and funding only in proportion to the relative absence of events that *were* considered national crises. Two phenomena fell into the category of national crisis: internal rebellions that threatened the sitting administration and conflicts with foreign nation-states. Mexico suffered from both afflictions. The centralists faced hundreds of minor plots to restore the constitution of 1824, and some evolved into formidable uprisings. In June of 1836, for example, federalists in Guadalajara and Oaxaca attempted rebellion, in December a federalist conspiracy came to light in Mexico City, and a significant revolt began the following April in San Luis Potosí.[49] All the while the government railed against Texas and insisted that its reconquest was imminent. With the republic's arms, money, and imagination monopolized by federalists and Texans, Mexico City paid even less attention than before to Apaches, Comanches, and Navajos. Northerners complained passionately, but administration supporters defended centralist priorities, refusing to see national implications in Indian raiding. "If the government has not sent a large army under the General and President to the frontiers of Chihuahua, as it did in Zacatecas," one insisted, "it is because the war with the rebellious tribes does not threaten the immediate destruction of the Republic as the rebellion in Zacatecas did."[50]

More worrying even than federalists was the fact that the republic's political instability, its mercurial and often corrupt policies on tariffs and trade, and the desperate efforts of its administrators to raise money wherever they could, even from foreign merchants, had by the mid-1830s provoked a number of diplomatic crises. Relations with the United States, already sinking because of unsatisfied claims of U.S. citizens against the Mexican government, sounded new depths when Mexico's minister denounced President Andrew Jackson's administration for recognizing Texan independence. Characteristically enraged, Jackson told the Senate in 1837 that the grievances of U.S. merchants, along with other perceived insults, "would justify, in the eyes of all nations, immediate war." He toyed with the idea of sending warships to Mexico, but did not. France did. In early 1838 the French government demanded that Mexico pay over a half-million pesos toward the claims of French citizens who had through various means been deprived of income and property in the country since independence. When Mexico refused, a French squadron blockaded the vital port at Veracruz and, by November, had begun bombarding the city. Bustamante sounded frantic alarms about an imminent invasion, expanded military conscription, and made the situation as frightening as possible in hopes that the impatient republic would rally around him. The two powers finally arrived at a negotiated settlement in early 1839, but for nearly a year the dispute monopolized the administration's attention.[51]

All the while violence wrecked more and more lives in the north. New Mexicans had observed an uneasy peace with Navajos through the late 1820s and early 1830s, but war had resumed just before Santa Anna and the centralists took power in Mexico City and would continue with little interruption through the 1830s. Apaches meanwhile steadily intensified their raiding in northwestern Mexico and killed more chihuahuenses in 1838 than they had in the previous two years combined.[52] And by 1836 frantic local and state officials in Tamaulipas, Nuevo León, and Coahuila were all bemoaning destructive Comanche raids upon their northern settlements, predicting—correctly—that the worst was still to come.

In the meantime northerners had cause to think about what exactly it meant to be mexicanos fighting a war against los bárbaros. Weary officials from Tamaulipas, Nuevo León, Coahuila, Chihuahua, Sonora, and New Mexico continued writing letters to a seemingly indifferent audience in Mexico City, begging their superiors for protection. The minister of war gave a short, candid reply to one such entreaty from Chihuahua that identified precisely why raiding remained such a low priority for the centralists: "Indians don't unmake presidents." Over the next few years exasperated Mexicans across the north would take up arms and try to prove him wrong.[53]

6

BARBARIANS AND DEARER ENEMIES

Antonio Zapata and Albino Pérez never met and undoubtedly would have disliked each other if they had. Zapata hailed from Tamaulipas's hardscrabble frontier town of Guerrero. He spent his youth herding sheep and, through determined work, regional connections, and luck, accumulated enough land and animals to join the ranks of the local elite. He served in various political capacities in Guerrero and by his early thirties had become an esteemed champion of local interests and local autonomy. Like most of his neighbors, Zapata thought the national government should fund frontier defense but otherwise stay out of people's lives. In contrast, Albino Pérez was a creature of metropolitan politics. An energetic and ambitious career army officer with a taste for hot chocolate, elegant clothes, and the finer things in life, Pérez worked assiduously to cultivate powerful friends and curry favor with this or that rising star. Unlike Zapata, Pérez saw nothing wrong with centralized government—so long as he had a place in it.[1]

Despite their differences, these men had at least two important things in common. First, both were intrepid Indian fighters. Zapata's local renown derived as much from his battlefield prowess as his business acumen. He rallied the people of the lower Rio Grande against Comanches, Kiowas, and Lipanes and seemed to relish the thrill of combat. Raiders became so accustomed to seeing Zapata at the front of Mexican defenders that they gave him a nickname: Sombrero de Manteca—Grease Hat—on account of a hair tonic that made his head shine in the sun. Pérez likewise gave enemy Indians reason to remember him. Sent north by Santa Anna in 1835 to become governor of faraway New Mexico, he campaigned tirelessly against Navajos and struck deep into their country on multiple occasions.

The second and rather more important thing Zapata and Pérez had in common is that they both lost their heads—literally—on opposite sides of federalist
uprisings that swept the north in the late 1830s. Like federalist rebellions elsewhere in Mexico, uprisings in New Mexico, Sonora, and the northeast championed a responsive union of state and local governments instead of the centralization of power in Mexico City. What made the northern rebellions different
was that here autonomous Indians became vital components of the argument
over government and nationhood. Indian raiding had become the dominant political issue in all of northern Mexico by the late 1830s. Widespread discontent
that the centralists had taken political and fiscal power away from the states,
while doing nothing about raiding, provided federalist leaders in the north with
their most resonant arguments. The uprisings therefore opened a window onto
the problems of nation building in the north and onto the complicated place of
independent Indians in the charged discourse surrounding that process. Most
important, the rebellions reveal the mounting political consequences of the War
of a Thousand Deserts, a war which in the late 1830s led northern Mexicans to
turn away from their Comanche, Apache, and Navajo enemies and kill their
own champions instead.

GOVERNMENT HAS NOT GIVEN ASSISTANCE:
NEW MEXICO

The first of the three uprisings, the so-called Chimayó Rebellion, took place
in New Mexico and intersected in complex ways with concerns about Navajos. In the 1830s there were probably seven thousand Navajos living in foothills,
valleys, and canyonlands across a huge region west of New Mexico's settlements.
They led a semisedentary life, subsisting on agriculture and herding to a far
greater degree than most of their Apache cousins. Like Comanches, Kiowas,
and Apaches, Navajos recognized different and interlocking levels of social and
political organization. Most decisions were made by individual families or by
collections of families within residence groups. But on important matters such
as war and peace they relied on a complex and far-flung kinship system to help
them access higher levels of organization. Occasionally Navajos even held an
elaborate tribal council known as *naach'id*, for which nearly all of their people
would come together to listen to speeches, negotiate, and seek unanimity in
their policies toward outsiders. Such political mechanisms helped make Navajos
formidable enemies when they came into conflict with New Mexicans.[2]
    In fact peace was the norm for most of the eighteenth century, despite inter-
mittent theft of animals on both sides, until territorial disputes led to war in the

mid-1770s and again in 1804–05. In these as in later conflicts, a discrete period of violence culminated in treaty talks wherein Navajo negotiators spoke for most of their people in an attempt to wring concessions from New Mexicans. Despite the treaties, conflicts resumed near the end of Spanish rule, from the late 1810s through the mid-1820s, though for increasingly complicated reasons. Mexicans had always captured Navajos in wartime, baptized them, and put them to work as household servants. But the practice became far more common after independence. Whereas there were only 14 Navajo baptisms recorded for the last thirty years of Spanish rule (1790–1819), there were 408 for the first thirty years of independence (1820–49). Moreover, in contrast to previous conflicts, after 1820 New Mexicans almost always refused to release these captives even after the two sides had negotiated peace. Though Navajo complaints over captive taking never seemed far from the surface, the parties observed an exhausted truce in the late 1820s and early 1830s. Navajos had reason to be cautious. Thanks to their fields, orchards, and flocks they were far more vulnerable to their Mexican enemies than Comanches or even Apaches. During wartime New Mexicans and their subordinated Pueblo allies marched into Navajo country in parties several hundred or even a thousand strong, attacking or enslaving whomever they could find and plundering sheep and horses. Though Navajos usually suffered far more casualties in these conflicts than their adversaries, nonetheless grievances sometimes became so intensely felt that a majority advocated conflict in hopes they could force Mexicans into making concessions on land and, especially, captives. In such times Navajos could temporarily drive Mexicans from their western settlements, sow fear throughout the province, and place tremendous stress on New Mexico's militias, politicians, and modest public treasury.[3]

This is precisely what happened once killings resumed in 1834. Albino Chacón, patriarch of one of the territory's elite families and a member of Pérez's administration, recalled widespread public frustration: "The geographical situation of New Mexico, separated from the rest of the republic by great distances . . . was subject to furious attacks from its barbaric neighbors which patriotic love and national honor have made it resist." New Mexico had always waged its wars "at the expense and fatigue of its own inhabitants, and certainly the general government has not given assistance, not even one time, of arms and ammunition." When it became known in 1835 that the central government would be sending Pérez north as New Mexico's first outsider governor in a decade, some *ricos* (wealthy and influential New Mexicans) expressed outrage. Other nuevomexicanos, however, hoped Pérez's "important connections" in Mexico City "would enable him to obtain from the supreme government the aid that New Mexico needed so keenly."[4]

Pérez's welcome therefore consisted of suspicion and optimism both. The new governor understood that his political credibility would hinge on reducing Indian raiding, and, according to Chacón, the people did indeed warm to Pérez when early in his term he announced his intention to "annihilate the Navajo Indians." It is not clear whether the governor actually expected significant help from Mexico City, but in any event none came. He therefore organized several campaigns in the usual way, by ordering subordinates to conscript locals, men who had no choice but to outfit themselves and pray that they would come away with spoils enough to compensate them for their time and expense. To his conscripts' frustration and his own chagrin, none of Pérez's incursions into Navajo country was decisive or even very profitable. Against advice the governor pushed on by launching an unusual winter campaign in 1836–37 that left hundreds of the militia's animals frozen dead on the trail and 140 men with toes or ears lost to frostbite. Though the endeavor resulted in "the ruin of many unhappy farmers," Pérez did finally secure peace talks. This would have been the moment to make good on the militia's sacrifices, but the governor underestimated the gentlemen across the table. A prominent New Mexican later claimed that Pérez had been a "toy of the Navajo negotiators," who "diverted him with beautiful promises and distracted him with lengthy discussions about the time and place of the next meeting until they gained with no difficulty the objectives they sought." Thus many New Mexicans had endured "great financial losses" with little or nothing to show for them.[5]

The festering complaints against Pérez began morphing into widespread disgust with the national government once the new centralist constitution arrived in 1836. The document made New Mexico a full-fledged department. That, many nuevomexicanos assumed, would expose it to taxes from which it had long been immune as a territory. Far from compensating the militiamen who had sacrificed so much in their "patriotic" campaigns against Navajos, the centralists were apparently demanding that nuevomexicanos pay for the privilege of membership in the republic. Outrage grew as news spread of the new constitution and its likely implications. Pérez made matters worse in the summer of 1837 when he tried to implement certain of the new constitution's provisions by restricting local governance. Finally, in early August, a group from the town of Santa Cruz de la Cañada declared themselves in opposition to centralism and to the governor. They put themselves at the head of an incipient coalition of vecinos and Pueblo Indians united behind assumptions about their rights and obligations as Mexicans. This sense of rights and obligations had been tested and illuminated by the ongoing Navajo war, and it seemed increasingly threatened by the centralist program.[6]

The rebels took to the streets. When Pérez and his men marched out to restore order they found themselves vastly outmatched, facing upward of two thousand men (even this force would soon double or triple). These angry people routed the governor and his small escort. The rebels apprehended Pérez a short time later, and crowds were soon shouting insults at his severed head, set on high near the church of Nuestra Señora del Rosario in Santa Fe. Flush with victory, the movement's leaders issued a proclamation articulating five goals. The first was "to sustain God and the nation and the faith of Jesus Christ." The second was to "defend our country until the last drop of blood is shed to achieve the desired victory," possibly a statement of determination to continue the rebellion or, just as likely, a reference to the honorable national service New Mexicans had always provided against hostile Indians. The last three goals simply expressed opposition to the new constitution and national taxation and to anyone who would try to impose them. The participants in the rebellion spoke to the national government from a position of relative weakness and used violence to force a conversation that would not otherwise have taken place, a conversation about what it meant for them to be Mexican.[7]

With Pérez gone, however, the movement had secured its most immediate goal and began to lose focus. One of the rebellion's putative leaders and suddenly the new governor of New Mexico, José Gonzáles felt ambivalent about how to proceed. A mixed-blood bison hunter and militia captain in Pérez's ill-advised winter campaign against Navajos, Gonzáles proved to be an honest, naïve, and ineffective leader. He initially tried to moderate between those demanding a return to the federal constitution of 1824, those content to have rid themselves of Pérez, and ricos, who, like most elites in Mexico, obsessed about "social stability"—in other words, avoiding a race or class war. Gonzáles had neither the support nor the skill to placate these factions, let alone unite them. Just as important, the new governor had few options for improving relations with Navajos. New Mexico could have freed all captives and compromised on long-running land disputes, but neither Gonzáles nor other rebels seemed to have advocated such sacrifices. Thus what the department apparently needed was cash to wage the war without impoverishing the citizenry. Given the movement's bloody execution of its appointee, there was little reason to expect that Mexico City would suddenly start funding the war. The rebel government therefore had little hope of improving long-term security.[8]

This fact emboldened centralists among the ricos, the clergy, and certain military men aghast at what they saw as the revolt's excesses. They set about to restore centralist rule by demonizing and dividing the rebels, in part through skillful manipulation of the same concerns over Indians and identity that had helped fuel the uprising in the first place. The reaction began by insisting that Navajos would attack the divided territory with the help of allied Apaches and disaffected Pueblo warriors, some of whom had fled to Navajo country over the last few years to avoid being conscripted into the government's unending campaigns. Indeed, the western Pueblos of Zuni, Acoma, and Laguna had close if complex relations with Navajos and had refused orders to move against them in the months before the uprising. If anyone wondered what such an alliance could mean to New Mexico's non-Indian population, ricos suggested, they need only look around them. Indigenous rebels had supposedly kicked the governor's head around like a football. They had also captured a hated former governor (Santiago Abreu) and "cut off his hands, pulled out his eyes and tongue, and otherwise mutilated his body, taunting him all the while with the crimes he was accused of, by shaking the shorn members in his face." These grisly doings stirred fears of a reprise of 1680, when during the famous Pueblo Revolt Indians cooperated across ethnic divides to kill hundreds of Spaniards and drive survivors from New Mexico altogether.[9]

Those opposed to the rebellion insisted that everyone's safety was at risk. The first major proclamation from the counterrevolt warned local officials that New Mexico had to "reestablish order at all costs. Seeing our weakness, the Navajos will continue with the Pueblos to wage war on us." No one pushed this line of argument more effectively than Manuel Armijo. Born into two of New Mexico's great landholding families, Armijo parlayed his privileged start into considerable holdings of land, animals, and political capital. He served as territorial governor in the late 1820s and in 1836 used his many connections to the overland trade with Missouri to help win him the lucrative position of New Mexico's chief customs officer. Armijo lost the job once Pérez assumed his governorship, a fact that led some to whisper that Armijo himself had helped organize the revolt. True or not, he offered himself as a sober champion of centralism and of security against barbarians once Pérez lost his head. Armijo wrote an open letter to the department's residents, warning that "the Navajos, reassured by the deplorable condition in which we find ourselves, and in combination with the Pueblos of the frontier, wage a disastrous war that reaches even into the very bosom of our families."[10]

Losing ground, Gonzáles took a radical and ultimately fateful step. In light of the worsening security situation and of the futility of asking Mexico City for help, the governor suggested that New Mexico sever its allegiance to the republic and arrange for annexation to the United States. The proposal certainly set off alarms. A panicked President Bustamante had church authorities instruct New Mexican clergy to convince their parishioners of the "evils that would befall

16. Manuel Armijo. Alfred S. Waugh, 1846. Courtesy
Palace of the Governors (MNM/DCA), neg. 050809.

them if they were to become part of a foreign nation with a different religion
and customs so incompatible with the Mexican character." But union with the
United States was never much more than a notion in the governor's head. Indeed, Gonzáles's proposal proved to be a boon for his enemies. Talk of secession
gave his opponents a powerful weapon, one they used to pound away at the complexity of the movement's message. Rather than engage that initial protest by
debating the relative merits of federalism and centralism for New Mexico's security or by arguing about the sorts of things Mexican citizens owed one another,
Armijo and his allies exploited Gonzáles's gambit to force a simpler conversation
about patriotism and treason. In the end a relatively subtle question about the
rights and obligations of being Mexican was battered simply and unimagina-
tively into "Mexican or no?"[11]

With the rebel government in disarray, mounting fears over raiding, and the essence of the movement perverted into a question with only one realistic answer, nearly everyone, even most of the Pueblo warriors, responded yes, Mexican. Armijo was made governor (with Mexico City's blessing), and New Mexicans lost yet another skilled Indian fighter when they executed Gonzáles as a traitor. The triumphant conservative coalition thereafter saturated New Mexicans with nationalistic rhetoric and ceremony that would make violent protest against the central government's indifference to raiding or to anything else synonymous with treason. The rebellion had done nothing to improve New Mexico's situation vis-à-vis Navajos. Yet it had changed New Mexico's situation vis-à-vis Mexico City. A few months after the movement collapsed, the president decreed New Mexicans exempt from all national taxes for seven years. In this regard the Chimayó Rebellion stands out among its counterparts elsewhere in the north insofar as it actually secured a change in national policy that improved life for frontier settlers fighting Indians—it effectively returned New Mexico to the fiscal status quo pre-1836. The course of the rebellion was typical, however, in the way that local critiques of centralism's fiscal policies regarding frontier defense were quickly smothered in a facile discourse of patriotism vs. treason.[12]

BY THIS AND NO OTHER THING: SONORA

Just weeks after the start of the uprising in New Mexico, federalists in Sonora began agitating for changes in the department's national tax burden so that it could more effectively wage war against Apaches. Federalists suggested that departmental officials should retake control of all revenues and devote them exclusively to the bárbaro war, ignoring any orders from the national government that interfered with this priority. Ignacio Zúñiga supported the idea and later explained that Sonora's actions could be condemned "only by those who do not know what it is to be forced to have recourse at a distance of more than fifteen hundred miles for aid in exterminating the Apaches."[13]

Sonorans found the federalist plan immensely attractive. Leading residents and departmental officials held a meeting in the capital, Arizpe, in September 1837, after which they petitioned the national government for autonomy, given that Mexico City had done nothing to remedy Sonora's problems with Apaches. Practically speaking autonomy meant only securing control over tax revenues, since the central government did little else in northern Mexico save collect taxes. The official newspaper reprinted the petition in Mexico City, and President Bustamante intemperately branded the movement treasonous, which only radicalized moderates and galvanized support for the plan across Sonora.

In December General José Urrea, commander general of the department and a man with a personal grudge against Bustamante, publicly declared himself in open revolt against the centralist constitution. Representatives from across the department gave him nearly unanimous support. Urrea came from a long line of Sonoran presidial commanders and Indian fighters. He himself had fought Apaches and had been one of the few senior officers to perform with genuine distinction in the Texas war. Sonorans therefore had much hope that they would finally get the necessary resources and leadership to defeat their native enemies. The newly optimistic departmental assembly authorized Urrea (now governor) to cooperate with nearby departments in formulating Indian policy. It also turned its attention to the miserable plight of presidial soldiers who in their desperation had been selling their weapons to survive, and it approved the establishment of costly military colonies along the northern frontier.[14]

And yet the movement was already changing. At the start Sonora's protest had been driven entirely by concerns over Indian raiding: "By this and no other thing have the change of government and the unfortunate position in which Sonora [finds] itself generalized these principles." When the department embraced Urrea's pronouncement, however, it wedded this primary concern to the larger project of reforming the constitution for the whole republic. Indeed, Urrea's first significant campaign was not northward against Apaches, but southward into the department of Sinaloa, where he hoped to export the rebellion and gain control of customhouse revenues at the wealthy port of Mazatlán. Progovernment forces in Sinaloa drove Urrea back home, however, and upon his return he found that Sonora's own centralists had organized a formidable counterrevolt. They had even enlisted sedentary Opatas, Yaquis, Mayos, and Papagos, who fought terrifically because they had been promised concessions in long-standing land disputes. For his part, Urrea incorporated allied Apaches into his federalist force, Indians who had resisted the entreaties of kin and remained at peace at Tucson throughout the 1830s.[15]

There followed a destructive civil war that for six months sucked resources and attention away from the frontier, until finally the French blockade of Veracruz gave Bustamante the arguments he needed to recast the rebellion in strictly nationalist terms. Support for the movement had already cooled after months of violence, and, weary of the conflict, supporters began abandoning the cause following President Bustamante's call for patriotism and unity in time of foreign invasion. Even the influential governor of Chihuahua, who sympathized with the federalists' concerns and had remained neutral throughout the rebellion, finally acquiesced to the president's appeals and called for an end to the revolt. Urrea's federalist base crumbled away, and he soon abandoned the department, leaving Sonora in an even worse position relative to Apaches than it had been prior to the rebellion.[16]

A COLD INDIFFERENCE: THE NORTHEAST, FIRST PHASE

The Chimayó Rebellion never expanded beyond New Mexico, and, Urrea's best efforts notwithstanding, Sonorans failed to enlist neighboring departments in their struggle. But in 1838 a movement that began in Tamaulipas spread quickly throughout Nuevo León and Coahuila. Like the previous two revolts, the rebellion in the northeast fed off of popular resentment over the central government's indifference to frontier security. But this time the movement was larger, more complicated, longer lasting, and considerably more threatening to Mexico City.

Life had gotten much worse for northeasterners after 1836. The editors of *El Mercurio de Matamoros* insisted in 1837 that within one year Comanches had "wrecked the fortunes of the ranchers and the people. Those who yesterday had ten to fifteen thousand pesos, today count but a quarter of that." A more minor and localized, if still troublesome, threat came from gangs of Texans stealing animals and robbing travelers in the area between the Rio Grande and the Nueces River. Neither the underfunded presidios nor the regular army in the northeast had been effective against these threats. General Nicolás Bravo, a hero of Mexican independence and at various times interim president of the republic, observed in 1837 that the men remaining at the northeastern presidios were "starving to death, along with their families" and that they were reduced to running after mounted raiders on foot.[17] A coauthored letter by "the Sufferers" that appeared in *El Mercurio* remarked that recent Comanche raids had "not aroused the courage that the Mexican soldier is said to possess, when he sees the property and security of his fellow citizens insulted, those for whom he takes up arms, and at whose cost he is maintained." In effect, "the present government provides no protection but watches the barbarians annihilate the interests and inhabitants who cover the frontier all down the length of the Rio Bravo. . . . God contain them, for our soldiers cannot!" Letters and editorials such as these appeared more and more often, alternately imploring the government to revive the presidios and castigating leaders, who viewed the "robberies and horrible killings . . . with a cold indifference."[18]

By early 1838 officials in the region began to realize that popular anger over the unending demands of the military and the government's failure to do anything effective against the worsening Indian problem could lead to rebellion. The top officers of the Army of the North issued a joint statement in March.

The document praised the "heroic resignation" with which northeasterners had borne the "depredations and cruelties of the ferocious hordes of barbarians" and acknowledged that patience was wearing thin. The officers insisted that the government would soon be rebuilding the presidios, equipping them properly, and "exterminating the bloody barbarians as well as the bandits and pirates that style themselves volunteers of Texas." But this longed-for outcome would only materialize if the people remained quiet and obeyed the laws. In other words, if the people rebelled los salvajes would win.[19]

The logic failed to convince. In October federalist leaders began an uprising in Tampico, Tamaulipas, which quickly attracted sympathy and support from settlements across the northeast. Having fled Sonora but still unbowed, General Urrea arrived in Tampico to help lead the effort. Other prominent generals, officers, and officials sided with the rebellion. A parallel and cooperative movement emerged from the towns on the lower Rio Grande led by Antonio Canales Rosillo, who issued a proclamation from the town of Guerrero, Tamaulipas, in November calling for a return to the constitution of 1824. Several other frontier towns that had likewise suffered the brunt of the Comanche raids quickly issued similar declarations. Federalists won a major victory against centralists at the end of the month and decided to split their forces into three units. The first would proceed to Mexico City, the second to Zacatecas and San Luis Potosí, and the third would remain in the northeast and take the departmental capitals, Monterrey and Saltillo. By May 1839 this northern force had control of both cities. Mexican traders journeying north to San Antonio, Texas, enthusiastically reported that all northern Mexicans were now federalists and that "they wish to make common cause with [Texans] against the savages."[20]

Urrea, Canales, and the movement's other leaders acted out of a variety of personal and ideological motives, but their early successes depended in large part on their ability to tap into popular anger at the centralist government. A closer look at correspondence between officials from a single department and their superiors in Mexico City, correspondence that was very often reprinted in regional newspapers, hints at the frustrated expectations that helped fuel the rebellion. Like all authorities in northern Mexico, officials in Nuevo León had started pressing the central government for defensive resources as soon as raiding escalated in the 1830s. While Urrea was still leading federalists through Sonora in late 1837, Nuevo León's impoverished presidial commanders were warning departmental authorities that they could not contain the Comanches. One declared that the raiders "make their appearance almost daily, with perhaps three *gandules* [warriors], and when they number more than twenty, they don't hesitate to walk the streets at night, and the rural roads at all hours of the day, as if laughing in our faces." Responding to these kinds of reports, the governor of Nuevo León frequently implored Mexico City for funds to reestablish the presidios. In April of 1838 the minister of war finally agreed to provide two thousand pesos for the reorganization of the presidios. The governor wrote back in disbelief, explaining that it would take more than ten times that amount just to revive three presidios in his own department. He concluded by saying that the inhabitants sustained themselves with the hope that the central government will save them; if it did not, they would emigrate to "somewhere that they may enjoy the guarantees of mankind."[21]

By December 1838, in the thick of the northeastern rebellion, Governor Joaquín García was still trying to convince Mexico City to rebuild the department's presidios, especially the one at Lampazos. Otherwise, he cautioned, the frontier would become totally depopulated "both through the murders of the barbarians, and through the flight of the inhabitants, which this government could not prevent without trampling over the natural right of these unlucky people to preserve their lives." The minister of war replied cryptically that he had "ordered" the presidio at Lampazos to contain the barbarians. One can only guess what the governor thought of the letter since the garrison lacked resources, not orders. In his extensive annual report to Congress in early January, the secretary devoted only one sentence to the plight of the presidios, declaring that it was "indispensable" that the frontier be fortified against hostile Indians. The following day the governor told a prominent general that a recent Comanche raid had just claimed the lives of more than eighty people in his department, that the raiders came within fourteen leagues of the capital, and that the settlements would soon disappear unless the government provided help.[22]

In his mounting desperation, the governor stumbled. On January 12, 1839, his administration issued a circular ordering the residents of Nuevo León to provide exact information on the number, type, and quality of firearms they possessed. García probably wanted to use this information to force national authorities into recognizing the miserable condition of northern defense. Perhaps the arithmetic of frontier helplessness would move the nation's decision makers in a way that generalities and adjectives had not. But the residents of Nuevo León had reason to see something sinister in García's request. Weapons had been confiscated in Mexico before, and despite assurances that he regarded the peoples' arms as "sacred," the order likely fueled suspicion over centralist motives. In February 1839 García wrote the secretary of war in near panic, insisting that the department's residents were enraged by Comanche raids and that they had come to see the "poor government" as abhorrent and detestable: "Tell the president that the attention of this government is very divided, and that it is impossible to cover everything without a large force that is regularly paid and supplied." The secretary gave a typically maddening and meaningless reply, that the president trusted the governor to do everything necessary to "pursue implacably the barbarians." Days later the federalists seized Monterrey and replaced García with the former governor and local liberal icon Manuel María de Llano.[23]

With so little else to console him in the late 1830s, Nuevo León's beleaguered Governor García would at least have known that his counterparts in Coahuila and Tamaulipas had identical problems. The northeastern revolt would have been impossible but for the widespread discontent over the central government's indifference to Indian raiding, a fact federalist leaders understood very well. As soon as María de Llano took office, for example, he publicly blamed the centralists for "unleashing the savage tribes that threaten us." Antonio Canales put a finer point on the governor's claim by arguing that in conscripting soldiers for the interminable and disastrous war on Texas, the central government had left the towns and villages along the lower Rio Grande without the men and resources necessary for fighting barbarians.[24]

But whatever sympathy federalists mobilized with this kind of rhetoric, the actual support they could attract would largely depend upon military victories. The rebellion's successes in late 1838 and early 1839 likely fueled hopes that the centralist administration could indeed be overthrown, yet these initial successes depended upon the distraction of the French blockade and bombardment of Veracruz. Once the French had been placated, the administration turned its full attention to the rebellion. President Bustamante marched north from Mexico City himself to lead an army against Urrea. The rebel general countered by moving south, but his forces were defeated while trying to take the city of Puebla. Authorities locked Urrea in prison, and the larger movement began to unravel. Many of its leaders surrendered. Most were forgiven and reinstated into the army, and by the summer of 1839 the remnants of the opposition, now confined to the lower Rio Grande, had evacuated north across the river.[25]

THAT WE ARE MEXICANS:
THE NORTHEAST, SECOND PHASE

The rebellion had not ended, however. With Urrea gone, Canales emerged as the leader of a less ambitious though more focused movement centered on the lower Rio Grande, among the towns and ranches that had lost the most to raiding. Antonio Canales Rosillo was a native of Monterrey, a lawyer by training, and a onetime member of the house of deputies in Tamaulipas. During the early 1830s he served as a militia captain guarding the lower Rio Grande against raiders. Like most in the northeast, and especially along the river, Canales deplored the shift to centralism in the mid-1830s, and he helped coordinate northeastern resistance against Santa Anna's new government. But once Texans proclaimed independence Canales withdrew from the contest. He remained committed to federalism and may have toyed with the idea of separatism, but Canales also saw himself as a Mexican patriot. This ambivalence haunted his career. Canales was neither a coward nor an incompetent, as Anglo-American historians have claimed, but he could be indecisive in battle. While a mediocre general, he had a genius for raising men, and he seemed immune to long odds or bad news. Despite the defeats of early 1839 he quickly turned around, raised more than one thousand men, and began driving centralist leaders and forces from the river towns. The federalists had less success taking large cities such as Matamoros and Monterrey, however, and by the end of the year the centralist General Mariano Arista had driven them back to their base of support along the Rio Grande. As before, Canales started over and began organizing another campaign.[26]

In the meantime the central government tried harder to court local opinion. For example, the minister of war authorized Nuevo León's governor to divert about four thousand pesos to defense expenses, and he ordered Arista to ship a quantity of arms and munitions to the department so that the people could defend themselves against los bárbaros. He even agreed with the governor and Arista that the military draft should be temporarily suspended in Nuevo León as a "political measure" to avoid driving the "disgusted" vecinos into rebellion.[27] Admitting that the presidio system had become "very sad—its force is so insignificant, that it may be said to have been reduced to nothing," the minister promised presidial soldiers English rifles so that they might finally be armed as well as the raiders. And yet every such promising sign was offset by another indicating that Mexico City still saw raiding as a grim and somewhat anachronistic curiosity instead of a national emergency. In late 1839, for example, Minister of War Juan N. Almonte informed northern governors that the "commission for military statistics" had decided to establish a museum and therefore ordered them to send him whatever native weapons they could acquire. The governor of Nuevo León responded dryly that he had no such objects on hand but would instruct his subordinates to save what they could.[28]

Officials in Mexico City therefore made token efforts to improve defense in the northeast during the late 1830s, but their financial problems and their fundamental attitude about independent Indians remained unchanged. Centralist officials on the frontier did better. In January 1840, six hundred Comanches crossed into Nuevo León, and Arista sent one hundred well-armed dragoons and twenty-five vecinos to intercept them. Near Marín in the center of the department the Mexican force engaged the Comanches in a great battle. Arista lost nearly one quarter of his men (he claimed that "the blood flowed in torrents"), but the Mexicans cut down a large number of raiders. The defeated Comanches finally gathered up their dead and fled north across the river, "terrified by the slaughter they had suffered." Dolly Webster, captive in a Comanche village at the time, reported that in February 1840 a group of warriors returned from an expedition to Mexico. Of the forty-five who had gone out, only fifteen returned. Even if this one village bore the brunt of Arista's slaughter, it had been a disastrous encounter for the raiders—and a triumph for Mexicans. This was one of the few instances in the 1830s and 1840s when the military managed to turn back a Comanche campaign in its initial stages, and the central government made much of it in the official newspaper.[29]

Meanwhile progovernment editors and officials in the north concentrated on demonizing their opponents. The federalists themselves made this task far easier by enlisting Texans to fight alongside them. Canales had repeatedly sought safe haven in Texas, and he seems to have viewed Texans as natural and uncomplicated allies in his struggle against centralism. This was an astonishing miscalculation. Though they often amounted to less than 10 percent of the total federalist force, the Texans, or "those bloodthirsty enemies of our country" recruited from "the most filthy scum of the demoralized people of that country," as Arista called them, were, to say the least, a public relations liability. The general exploited it ably. Arista described Texans as "naked bandits," who "with their rifles in their hands . . . insult our countrymen, saying they wish to discharge it into a Mexican Comanche Indian, as they call us." Apart from the negative reputation they had acquired in Mexico since 1836, Texan volunteers became notorious for looting towns and ranches that had been "liberated" from centralist control. For his part Arista demanded of his men absolute respect for private property, which facilitated his project of equating federalism not only with Texans, but more generally with chaos, lawlessness, immorality, and banditry.[30]

The centralists also worked to associate the rebellion with Indian raiding. Again the federalists themselves provided the raw material for the charge. Canales had attracted the loyalty of perhaps one hundred or more Carrizo Indians who fought alongside him. These were mostly mixed-blood descendants of Coahuiltecan speakers who had in previous centuries been caught between northward-moving Spaniards and southward-moving Apaches. Many had been baptized at area missions during the colonial era, and by the early nineteenth century survivors worked in towns and haciendas or else ranged in small family groups along the lower Rio Grande. Berlandier reported that Carrizos had fought in the

17. Carrizos. Watercolor by Lino Sánchez y Tapia after a sketch by Jean Louis
Berlandier. Courtesy of the Gilcrease Museum, Tulsa, Oklahoma.

War of Independence against Spain, that they all spoke Spanish, and that many
had in fact forgotten their native tongue. He also said they and other remaining
groups like them along the river "preserve an implacable hatred of the Comanches, against whom they have sometimes waged war in favor of Mexican towns."
The Carrizos were thus low-status residents of the lower Rio Grande who lived
in peace with, often worked and fought beside, and sometimes even married the
Mexican villagers who comprised the majority of Canales's supporters. The centralists referred to these people not as *los carrizos*, but as los bárbaros or los salvajes, the epithets used for Comanches and other raiders. This cultivated ambiguity helped spawn wild reports about several hundred of these generic savages
riding alongside Canales and his federalists.[31]

In other words, centralists constructed a caricature of the federalist movement
that both equated and directly associated the rebellion with treason and with the
scourge of Indian raiding. A prominent centralist in Nuevo León, for example,
asked the inhabitants of his department, "have we not seen losses to our properties as if we had been invaded by one of the savage tribes of our frontier?" Arista
went further, amalgamating the most resonant images of a typical Comanche

raid with the specter of Texan imperialism. The general implored northeastern Mexicans "to save the country from the traitors, pirates, rebels, and savages" who intended to "rob you of your wives, your children, lay waste to your farms, burn and destroy your property, change your laws, in fine enslave you like they would the black man." Arista warned northeasterners against joining the rebellion: "Those that the traitor Canales leads are not federalists. They are thieves! They are barbarian Indians!" Centralists reported even that the federalists disarmed the frontier towns, leaving them helpless before native raiding parties.[32]

These claims may have been even more cynical than meets the eye. In 1840, while trying to escape her captors, Dolly Webster stumbled upon a small group of men that included Africans, Caddos, and a solicitous Mexican: "He was an intelligent smart looking Spaniard [Mexican], who had been sent to Matamoros by the Centralists as an emissary among the Indians, to procure their aid in their war with the Federalists in Mexico." Whether or not centralists really tried to recruit Caddos and other independent Indians, their attempts to link federalists with los bárbaros inverted the federalists' true interests. Most of the movement's key leaders came from the harried towns along the lower Rio Grande, and the inhabitants of these places constituted the federalists' popular base. Core leaders of the rebellion such as Antonio "Sombrero de Manteca" Zapata (Canales's most able lieutenant) and Juan Ramos were well known as accomplished Indian fighters, and the rebels went to great lengths to promote the notion that they would protect the residents of northeastern Mexico from Comanches and their allies. Canales issued proclamations promising to contain raiding on the lower Rio Grande, and to establish mounted patrols to guard the frontier. He apparently sent out emissaries offering assistance to towns and ranches threatened by Indians, and federalist commanders sometimes divided their forces and compromised their plans to provide that assistance. In early 1840, for example, Zapata led a federalist detachment to the river town of Morelos, where he was to be absent from the main body of rebel troops one day only. Despite news of approaching centralist forces, Grease Hat instead stayed for five days to protect the town against an anticipated Comanche attack. Consequently, troops under the famed Indian fighter Juan José Galán attacked Morelos and took Zapata captive. Canales mobilized his men to try to attempt a rescue, but his own forces were diminished because only days before he had sent two of his mounted squadrons to pursue Comanches. In March, Arista's troops attacked the now muchdiminished federalist force and killed half, about two hundred men, including most of the Carrizos, depriving the lower Rio Grande of some of its preeminent warriors and leaving the survivors to flee north across the river.[33]

Arista had Zapata executed as a traitor. The general arranged for the rebel's severed head to be soaked in a cask of brandy and then erected atop a pole in front of Zapata's house in Guerrero. Somehow Canales regrouped yet again in late 1840 and managed to retake many of the river towns and even the capital of Tamaulipas for a brief time. But everywhere he went the centralists branded him and his men traitors and confederates to barbarians. Texan volunteers continued to loot whatever they could, and the public finally abandoned the cause. By October federalist leaders had opened negotiations with Arista, and the armistice they finally signed reflected the degree to which the centralists had managed to distort the identity of the movement and obscure its intent. "That we are Mexicans," the first clause read, "decided lovers of our countrymen, that we have never thought to rebel against the nation, nor much less acknowledge the independence of Texas." The only concession to the rebellion's core complaint lay buried in a clause calling for the creation of a regiment dedicated to protecting the towns of the lower Rio Grande.[34]

Together with the superior force they mobilized, the centralists' exercises in politicizing identity allowed them to do what Armijo and other ricos had done in New Mexico: set boundaries around the conversation over Indian raiders. Zapata's besotted head was meant as a warning to would-be rebels, but it was also a graphic signpost marking the limits of protest against the central government's incompetent frontier defense. Complaints over government inaction would henceforth be confined to desperate letters, indignant editorials, and the occasional jeremiad from northern congressmen. Northerners had attracted far more government attention in their revolts than they ever had with their alarms about los bárbaros, a sour irony for everyone in the north. In late 1840 a congressional delegate from Chihuahua announced with biting sarcasm that the exasperated frontier settlements in his department had decided to "unite with the Apaches and declare a federation in hopes of attracting the attention of the federal government, which notoriously confines itself to pursuing federalists." But neither his desperate constituents nor anyone else would manage another significant armed protest against the government's Indian policies in the bloody decade to come.[35]

WE MARCH TO DEFEAT A COMMON ENEMY: ARISTA'S COMANCHE CAMPAIGN

While Mexicans were busy killing each other on the lower Rio Grande, Comanches and Kiowas made peace with their dread Cheyenne and Arapaho enemies near Bent's Fort. Mexicans below the river seemed unaware of this momentous event, but they soon felt its consequences. The Great Peace paved the way for renewed campaigns into Chihuahua after a long hiatus, more furious attacks upon the northeastern departments, and, for the first time, huge and devastating campaigns into Durango, Zacatecas, and San Luis Potosí. Combined with ongoing, intensifying conflicts with Apaches in the northwest and with alarms from New Mexico over Navajos and, for the first time, Arapahos, Indian raiding had become a serious, even desperate problem across nearly a third of Mexico's settled territory.[36]

Los bárbaros suddenly became a matter of national interest. This change is reflected in an exponential growth in the number of stories about northern Indians published in the capital's newspapers, which soared from just over one hundred in the period 1839–40 to more than six hundred during the next two years. Even genteel Fanny Calderón de la Barca, the wife of Spain's minister in Mexico, thrilled to stories about Comanches circulating in the capital in 1841. She met a colonel who regaled her and her companions with "an account of his warfare against the Comanches, in which service he has been terribly wounded." Calderón learned more from an old soldier covered in scars from Santa Anna's ill-fated Texas campaign. The veteran evinced a "devout horror" of Comanches and stated "his firm conviction that we should see [them] on the streets of Mexico [City] one of these days."[37]

The unnamed Comanche war leader who led the bold attack on Saltillo and its environs in early 1841 probably did more than any other individual to force the subject of Indian raiding upon the national consciousness. Northern officials justly billed the raid as a national disgrace, evidence that even the capital cities of the Mexican north had been abandoned to the Comanche scourge. Coahuila's governor complained bitterly to the minister of war, insisting that the people of his department paid federal taxes like all Mexicans, and yet they were entirely without protection when Comanches arrived: "By the morning there was hardly a family not weeping for dead parents or loved ones." The department's official newspaper demanded to know whether the national government was "totally indifferent to the picture of our agriculture destroyed, our commerce paralyzed, our brothers assassinated and our women and children dragged into horrible slavery in the lands of Texas?" The editors blamed their leaders in Mexico City for not reviving the presidios: "They and only they will be held responsible before God and man for the calamity these Pueblos suffer thanks to their criminal abandonment; held responsible for the blood of the victims, and for those who are daily sacrificed to the furor of the barbarian Indians."[38]

Coahuila and the other northern departments had, of course, been complaining like this for years, to no avail. But now the richer departments farther south started complaining too. The same Comanches who had attacked Saltillo had also struck points in northern San Luis Potosí, and editors there penned angry articles demanding federal assistance. San Luis Potosí was home to powerful generals and politicians, and officials in Mexico City apparently sent some kind of aid as soon as it was requested. This left editors in Chihuahua dumbstruck: "It has been ten years that Chihuahua has suffered and lamented this same evil that San Luis Potosí experienced for a few days," and yet, like Coahuila, Chihuahua was still waiting for Mexico City to act. The editors reiterated their position that raiding in Chihuahua was a *Mexican* problem, "both because Chihuahua forms part of that nation, and because [Indian invasions] amount to a cancer that spreads and replicates itself."[39]

With newspapers reprinting livid editorials and astonishing correspondence from northern officials concerning raids, centralists in Mexico City came under mounting pressure. In early February 1841, for example, Congress summoned the minister of war to explain how a few hundred Comanches could have done what they did in Coahuila, Zacatecas, and San Luis Potosí in December and January. The minister answered defensively, blaming the debacle on the "egotism" of the region's landowners and their failure to cooperate properly. A deputy from Zacatecas rose in a rage, denouncing the government for abandoning the frontier and insisting that Mexico City had disarmed even the haciendas in 1835, leaving everyone in his department helpless before los bárbaros.[40]

Indian raiding became an important topic in Congress, for the moment. The Mexican house and senate debated the issue through February and finally agreed on a vague bill calling for the establishment of the "necessary" forces to protect the frontier within forty days. The president approved the measure, and the minister of war told the northern governors they could expect help soon. Promises such as these were cheap in the 1830s, but this time it seemed Bustamante intended to deliver. The antitax candidate of the mid-1830s now decreed that all Mexicans over eighteen had to pay between one *real* and two pesos each month, depending on income. One-half of the new tax was to be sent north to fund presidios and the war against los bárbaros. All of this would naturally take time to organize. In the interim the administration assured northerners that General Mariano Arista was just then organizing a bold campaign to destroy the Comanches, or at least "teach them a lesson such that they will not return to threaten the frontier pueblos for many years."[41]

While gears turned slowly but auspiciously in Mexico City, the northeast looked to its would-be champion. Arista was an honorable, intelligent, and able man, ambitious but willing to sacrifice personally and professionally for principle and for the good of his country, or at least for what he believed the good to be. He had enlisted in the army near the end of the War of Independence and moved

18. Mariano Arista. Courtesy of the Benson Latin
American Collection, University of Texas, Austin.

quickly through the officer ranks. Arista supported Bustamante in the coup
against then-president Vicente Guerrero in 1829 and, once Bustamante became
president, rose to the rank of general. During Bustamante's second administration he became commander general of Tamaulipas and then commander-in-
chief of the Army of the North. Arista was charming, witty, personally brave, and
well liked by most people in the northeast. He wanted and probably deserved
to be great as well as popular, and yet the man's luck always left him when he
needed it most. But at the end of 1840 his greatest failures had yet to find him.
Throughout the rebellions he and others in the military had assured the northeast they would deal once and for all with the Comanches as soon as they had
"embarrassed the revolutionaries." Now that the rebellion had been defeated,
Arista turned with energy and optimism to fulfilling his promise.[42]

The general first had to decide how best to employ his limited resources. The huge, empty expanse of the frontier meant that only a small minority of Indian campaigns could ever be prevented from entering the northern departments, and in the early days of a campaign below the river Comanches and Kiowas were almost impossible to catch. They crossed the Rio Grande on strong horses, often traveled with the help of Mexican "deliverers" who knew the terrain, and even Arista expressed awe at the distances the raiders could cover in a day. One experienced frontier commander estimated they could travel an astonishing forty to fifty leagues (100 to 125 miles) in twenty-four hours, twice as far as typical Mexican forces. And because Comanches often moved in such huge numbers Mexicans had to coordinate men from multiple towns, ranches, and haciendas simply to give chase. By the time sufficient men had organized themselves the attackers might be far, far away.[43]

Even when militia units went out after the raiders they typically had to rely on weak horses and mules to move men and supplies. There are innumerable reports from the 1830s and 1840s of Mexican parties quitting the chase because their animals were too tired to continue. The only way to compensate for the problem was to bring along large numbers of replacement mounts. This created more logistical challenges and more worries about pasturage and water, and it also meant that the size of the expedition and the dust it produced was much increased, nearly eliminating any chance of catching the enemy by surprise. And if Mexicans somehow managed to raise a swift, formidable unit the raiders could disappear into the mountains, riding from one lonely water source to the next. Mexican forces sometimes braved this kind of challenge, following Comanche example and pushing themselves and their animals to the point of collapse in order to reach the next water hole, only to find it poisoned: "infested with dead horses, killed intentionally by the Comanches." Even if all these obstacles were overcome and Mexican forces caught and bested their adversaries, which they sometimes did, by then the raiders had already caused enormous damage in their time below the river.[44]

Most northern observers realized all of this and believed, like the Spanish, that the raiders would be stopped only by a "pitiless campaign that brings blood and fire to their homes." During the eighteenth century, as one commentator explained in 1841, "the only way to keep the Indians in peace was to threaten them from time to time in their rancherías, because the Spanish knew well that the Indian men were capable of making the greatest sacrifices to save their families." And the remarkable peace Comanches and Spaniards made in the late eighteenth century did indeed come on the heels of some exceedingly violent Spanish campaigns into la comanchería. But things were quite different by the

1830s and 1840s. So long as fighting men were the only Comanches and Kiowas who died in the war, plains peoples felt little pressure to reestablish the peace. Quite the reverse: the deaths of fighting men prompted calls for revenge and helped Comanche war leaders organize their huge campaigns. "The purely defensive war," observed an experienced frontier fighter, "is one that we have lost." Mexicans therefore had to do what Texans, Lipanes, Osages, Cheyennes, and Arapahos did: attack Comanche women and children. As an official in Coahuila once put it, "Pursue them as they pursue us. Threaten them as they threaten us. Rob them as they rob us. Capture them as they capture us. Frighten them as they frighten us. Alarm them as they alarm us."[45]

Still, campaigns against independent Indians were difficult endeavors. Sonorans learned Apaches were exceedingly hard to find and attack in their rugged homelands and had not put an end to raids despite numerous costly campaigns. New Mexico's state-run expeditions against Navajos were likewise militarily dangerous, enormously costly, and often unpopular, as the refined Pérez discovered to his sorrow. Campaigns could be worse than ineffective—they could be financially and politically ruinous. In 1838, for example, Simón Elías González, the powerful governor of Chihuahua, launched a drive to raise one hundred thousand pesos for a particularly ambitious offensive against Apaches. Convinced that the status quo would bring Chihuahua "ruins, deserts: dishonor for its people," González worked tirelessly throughout spring and summer to raise funds for his campaign. In October, with the weather already turning colder, he finally put five hundred men into the field for what was supposed to be a decisive, four-month slaughter across la apachería. The exhausted and freezing men returned less than three months later, having done little more than attack a handful of Apache families and capture two women and five children. For this the governor had emptied the departmental treasury and mortgaged his political career. In the aftermath of the debacle certain public officials had their pay suspended, including the magistrate of the supreme tribunal and the employees of the official newspaper, which had to close down. The assayer of the *casa de la moneda* and the professors of the institute of science and literature resigned for lack of salary, and within a few months the disgraced governor resigned as well.[46]

The lesson was not lost on other northern governors, most of whom understandably thought better of following in González's footsteps. But unlike the governors, Arista was in the unique position of commanding significant national resources as well as authority that transcended the boundaries of individual departments. If anyone could defeat Comanches in their homeland it would be someone of Arista's stature, and the general became obsessed with the project. Though Comanches enjoyed more political unity than Apaches and though their home ranges were more distant from Mexican settlements, in theory they would be easier to locate because they inhabited plains and prairies rather than inaccessible mountain ranges and canyons. The general therefore had reason to think his plan could work, and just weeks after the armistice with the federalists he disclosed its details to the northeastern governors. He would outfit six hundred of his own mounted soldiers with enough supplies for an extended campaign onto the plains. In return, he requested that the departments provide their own men with mounts and provisions. In Tamaulipas, the settlers on the lower Rio Grande had already promised seven hundred—likely many of the same hardened men who had fought alongside Canales. Another three hundred would be needed from Nuevo León, and four hundred from Coahuila. Arista himself would lead the two-thousand-man force into la comanchería, and he insisted, plausibly, that the expense of the campaign would be more than offset by the multitude of animals that would be plundered from Comanche camps.[47]

The question now was whether the governors would subordinate themselves to the general and supply the men and resources he needed. They were not under any obligation to do so. Even the minister of war qualified his optimism about the campaign by saying its success depended upon the voluntary cooperation of the departments. Arista made anxious appeals to each of the governors in early 1841, especially to Coahuila's governor, who had been highly critical of the general following the Comanche raid on Saltillo. Arista also took his case to the people, insisting that the shocking attack on Coahuila's capital only underscored the need for a decisive campaign. As the general had demonstrated during the federalist uprising, he understood the power of connections, real or imagined. He sent letters to departmental newspapers and shipped hundreds of copies of circulars to governors, ordering that they be distributed throughout the cities, towns, and ranches. These letters articulated a rationale for the campaign that connected los bárbaros to two of Mexico's most elemental problems.[48]

The first problem was unity, or lack thereof. Arista insisted that while the scandal of raiding demanded "the attention of the entire republic," the interminable series of uprisings or civil wars had made it impossible for Mexico to cope with its native enemies. But now all northern Mexicans needed to come together: "Having set aside our disastrous disagreements, and united in the double bond of our true interests and love of country, we march to defeat a common enemy, who, intoxicated with the blood of our unfortunate kinsmen, has razed our countryside, and left our tender and innocent children wailing in captivity." Unity was a prerequisite for the campaign, but Arista believed it could also be a dividend of the war against los bárbaros. "While most of the civil conflicts have passed," Arista wrote in one of his circulars, "we have not redirected those who fought toward a new aim." The people lacked "an object that can distract the ardor and love of war," something to help "forge a public spirit and establish in the region the healthy idea that civil wars lead nations into impotence and misery." Arista believed that independent Indians could be the key, "an irreconcilable and ferocious enemy" that could unite northeastern Mexicans across their divisions.[49]

Second, the general associated the bárbaro war with Texas. So long as Indian raiders enjoyed safe haven and trading opportunities in Texas, the north would never know peace. Along with the reestablishment of the presidios and the population of the frontier, the reconquest of Texas was a prerequisite to reestablishing peaceful relations with Plains Indians. And yet Arista insisted that the Indians' constant raids throughout the north had complicated, even prevented, the concentration of men and resources that would be necessary to retake the territory. Thus the campaign against the Comanches, even if it produced only a temporary suspension of raiding, would hasten "that blessed day when we will march to reconquer our usurped territory and avenge our national honor."[50]

Arista's campaign would be glorious: a vehicle for revenge against the hated savages, a guarantee against future attacks, a trumpet call to Mexicans to put aside their calamitous disagreements, and the first step toward erasing the obscene Texan stain from the republic's dignity. He urged the people on: "Peace! Peace! Eternal peace between Mexicans! War! War! Eternal war against the Texans and the barbarian Comanches!" The campaign would avenge all of humanity for the outrages that Indians had forced upon the people of northern Mexico. "To arms! Terrify the barbarous Comanche race: Send their black blood into the rivers and may it nourish the fields of Tamaulipas, Nuevo León, and Coahuila."[51]

It was a powerful image—but not powerful enough. Arista's graphic ambitions ran into the same barriers that had stymied effective Indian policy in Mexico since the early 1830s: lack of resources, Mexico City's stubborn calculation that indios bárbaros always mattered less than rebels, and the unwillingness of governors to subordinate themselves to national officials in matters of frontier defense. The central government had originally promised to send money so Arista could purchase a thousand horses in Durango but then decided instead to give the funds to army units fighting rebels at the other end of Mexico, in the department of Tabasco. According to schedule, the campaign against Comanches should have begun in early March. But it was mid-April by the time the general had gotten his six hundred soldiers to the rendezvous at the derelict presidio of Lampazos. Once he arrived he found that Tamaulipas and Nuevo León had both sent fewer than half of their expected men. Coahuila's governor revealed the depth of his contempt for the general by sending a mere nineteen out of four hundred requested. The troops that had come from the three departments arrived "exhausted, on horses near death" because of a regional drought that had dried up water holes along the route.[52]

Enraged, humiliated, and quite certain that the campaign would fail under such circumstances, the general hastily convened a panel of local experts, including Canales, the ex-rebel, and several Mexicans who had been long-term captives among Comanches. The panel soberly agreed that while the offensive might have succeeded in early March, by mid-April Comanches were moving north in pursuit of bison. The distance would make it exceedingly difficult to find them, and, in any case, the regional drought would make it impossible to get there, especially given the quality of the horses. The campaign would have to be postponed. Newspapers across the northeast reprinted the panel's conclusions, and the general released a tortured statement defending himself and the government against the inevitable recriminations. Besides the troubles with men, horses, and the drought, "the Indians enter through vast deserts and rough mountains in a manner that cannot be prevented," he insisted. *"It is not the supreme government's fault nor mine,* because the government sends all the resources its great distractions and depleted treasury allow, and I duly endeavor to apply the force at my command to support and protect these departments as much as possible. *We have fulfilled our duty."* Arista swore, however, that he would march against Comanches later in the year. He even resorted to writing President Mirabeau Lamar of Texas, proposing a temporary armistice since Mexican forces would have to march into Texas to reach la comanchería.[53]

Though testimony to his seriousness, the letter was an unnecessary humiliation. The general had suffered permanent damage to his credibility in the north, and in any event Mexico City's predictable unpredictability would soon redefine the possible. Bustamante's government had withdrawn vital funds from Arista's campaign at the last minute, but it had at least given lip service to its importance and wisdom, approving the use of national troops and effectively (if temporarily) privileging the war against los bárbaros over the Texas war. This understated but significant shift in attitude was a consequence of the dramatic, well-publicized surge in Indian raiding that followed the Great Peace on the Arkansas, and it was this window of opportunity, together with the end of the federalist uprising, that Arista had rushed to take advantage of in the spring.[54]

That window slammed shut in August when a trio of powerful generals moved against Bustamante's administration, condemning the beleaguered president for, among other things, his failure to do anything about Texas and his imposition of new taxes. This presumably meant that the authors disapproved of the tax to bolster frontier defense, though one of the three accused Bustamante's gov-

19. Antonio López de Santa Anna. A. Hoffy, ca. 1847.
Library of Congress, Prints and Photographs Division.

ernment of "entirely forgetting" the exhausted northerners and the handfuls of
soldiers struggling against raiders. The coup had adherents in the north as well:
prominent figures in Nuevo León signed on and, among other things, blamed
Bustamante for abandoning the frontier to the "bloody and barbaric depredations of the savages." After some jockeying among the three conspirators, the
irrepressible Santa Anna won out, yet again. His reputation destroyed in Texas,
this master opportunist had managed to resurrect himself by leading Mexican
forces against the French at Veracruz in 1838, heroically losing a leg in the process. Calderón de la Barca paid him a visit at the end of 1839 and came away
struck by the man's languid and melancholic demeanor. "Knowing nothing of
his past history," she observed, one would believe that he was wearily "above the
world," that he deigned to "engage in its toils only to benefit others. . . . Yet here
sat with this *air de philosophe* perhaps one of the worst men in the world—ambitious of power—greedy of money—and unprincipled—having feathered his
nest at the expense of the republic—and waiting in a dignified retreat only till'
the moment comes for putting himself at the head of another revolution."[55]

Once that moment came, Santa Anna moved forcefully to consolidate his
gain. He was temporarily given autocratic powers while a new congress could
be convened and a new constitution drafted. Finally in 1843, having dismissed

an unexpectedly independent congress that had drafted an unacceptably liberal constitution, he became president with near dictatorial privileges under a new constitution that centralized power as never before. A statue of the great leader went up in the central plaza, one hand pointing due north; but of course it was not gesturing toward Navajos, Apaches, or Comanches. The president swore he would retake Texas, and he directed Arista and the northern army to refocus their energies upon that project. Many in the north continued to dream of an offensive campaign, but national officials stopped talking about killing Comanches where they lived.[56]

When northern Mexicans decided to rebel against centralism they understood they were taking grave risks. They obviously risked the wrath of the central government, which in its brutal suppression of federalism in Zacatecas and in its cruel massacres in Texas had set threatening precedents. More fundamentally, the people of northern Mexico were already fighting a war against independent Indians. They had to calculate whether in the short and medium term it was worth diverting people and resources away from that desperate struggle to indulge the uncertain hope that victory in a civil war would improve security in the long run. This is surely one important reason that bloody Chihuahua, where overlapping Apache and Comanche campaigns made for unparalleled destruction, was the only department in the far north without a major rebellion in the late 1830s.

That so many people did decide to rebel speaks to a profound concern with and ultimately an optimism about their place within the larger Mexican national community. A few rebels spoke about secession, about forming a new republic or joining with the United States, but talk like this was on the margins.[57] The vast majority of northern federalists sought to institutionalize a different vision of what it meant to be Mexican, one that would preserve the republic but reform its organization to better protect their families and fortunes from Indian enemies. They failed, and lost much. Apart from years of distraction and cost, the uprisings robbed the north of hundreds of men like Antonio Zapata and Albino Pérez who had been leaders in the fight against independent Indians. More broadly, rebellions left northern communities smaller, weaker, poorer, divided by new enmities, and, as before, begging the distracted central government to deliver them from los bárbaros. For a moment in early 1841 it seemed as if the central government's views were changing, that something positive had come from so much fighting and loss, that the Indian war had finally become Mexico's war. But Arista failed to keep his promise of protection, Santa Anna and his Texas obsession resumed a presidency ever more jealous of power and resources, and raids became more audacious and ambitious than ever before.

Northerners continued talking about the nation's obligations and demanding weapons, money, and reforms from Mexico City through the early 1840s. But mostly they focused on protecting themselves and their interests. Lacking meaningful support from Mexico City and now without realistic hope of forcing reform through rebellion, northern community at nearly every level became increasingly fragmented. Northerners still spoke of unity but more and more they acted in isolation. And independent Indians continued to mean different things to different people, until by mid-decade another enemy arrived from the north and national officials realized too late what northerners knew all along—that the war against los bárbaros had indeed been Mexico's war, whether Mexico recognized it or not.

7

An Eminently National War?

THE CLOUDBURST: COSTS

By the time Santa Anna orchestrated his resurrection the War of a Thousand Deserts had raged for more than a decade, directly or indirectly touching almost everyone in northern Mexico—Mexicans and independent Indians alike. Think of a cloudburst over the surface of a pond. The direct effects of individual acts of violence generated secondary effects that rippled outward, consequences colliding into, reshaping, and amplifying other consequences, changing the lives of an ever-larger portion of northern Mexico. Though in practice they were profoundly interrelated, it is useful to consider the effects of the war upon northern Mexicans as falling into three separate realms: population, economy, and community.

Most immediately, raiding led to the depopulation of much of the rural north and to a sharp decline in the annual growth rate of northern Mexico's population overall. Apaches, Kiowas, Comanches, Navajos, and others killed or captured several thousand northern Mexicans between 1831 and 1846, tearing holes in families and communities throughout the region. It is difficult to know how many northern Mexicans suffered serious injuries in raids, though the injured likely outnumbered those killed or captured. Oftentimes such wounds were severe, and the victim had no access to quality medical treatment (ranchers in Coahuila, for example, tended arrow wounds with a poultice of maguey pulp and cobwebs). By physically and mentally scarring and crippling so many in the north, the violence inflicted a different sort of damage on families and communities. Finally, in addition to killing, capturing, and wounding Mexicans, independent Indians could break families apart or unmoor them from their communities by stealing or slaughtering indispensable animals, robbing houses, and destroying buildings. Picture all of these deeds as raindrops hitting the water.[1]

Notwithstanding the searing but now irretrievable pain and grief, fear and heartbreak caused by impact, the waves of indirect consequences that radiated outward from direct attacks ultimately mattered more for northern Mexico's demography. For every immediate victim there were hundreds more who knew that they, their kin, or their property could be next. Many of these people simply decided to leave. Sometimes losses of family members, property, and even homes turned such Mexicans into refugees, desperate people with little choice but to move. More often decisions were gradual, as months or years of insecurity and deepening poverty convinced many they could have better lives elsewhere, perhaps near kin who lived somewhere safer. The result was an exodus from many of northern Mexico's smaller towns and rural settlements into larger northern cities or else southward, out of the region altogether.

Officials and commentators from the northwest had long lamented the abandonment of settlements and the depopulation of the countryside. As early as the mid-1830s, Sonoran officials warned that emigration would ruin their state. Within a decade there seems to have been an absolute decrease in population in northern Sonora, while major cities such as Thermopile, Ures, and Guaymas became swollen havens for refugees. A report from 1848 insisted that Apaches had provoked the abandonment of ninety ranches, thirty haciendas, and twenty-six mines in the state. Anecdotal evidence suggests that other northern states experienced similar losses. A prominent American journalist taken through Chihuahua in 1841 and 1842 described depressed trade, an idle canal system, and a once-prosperous hacienda near Carrizal abandoned because of Apaches. The man insisted that its owner dared not visit without a sizable guard. Half a decade later editors of the *Registro Oficial* wrote that "for a number of years Durango has contemplated the strange and impassive ruin of Chihuahua. This state possessed many peculiar means of resistance, means that neither Durango nor Zacatecas have, and yet in ten years Chihuahua has disappeared."[2]

In Coahuila raids forced the powerful Sánchez Navarro family, the largest landholder in all of Mexico, to abandon its Hacienda de Nacimiento in the early 1840s. Within a few years matters became desperate enough that the prefect of Monclova urged his superiors to give northern Lipanes land titles if they resettled the many abandoned places along Coahuila's northern frontier. Officials in northern Tamaulipas likewise reported widespread talk of emigration, and not only in the isolated ranches. Even some moderate-sized towns on the frontier lost population during these years. Between 1835 and 1837 massive theft and destruction of animal property helped convince one out of every eight people living in Laredo to move away. Comparatively tranquil New Mexico was the exception to the overall pattern of population stagnation in the north during the 1830s and 1840s. Yet even here population flight became a troubling if localized problem. On several occasions officials imposed fines and threatened to nullify land titles in hopes of dissuading settlers in the far north and far west from leaving their properties for fear of Utes and Navajos.[3]

Changes in rural areas had a striking effect on northern Mexico's demography overall. One study suggests that the north experienced nearly triple the growth rate of the rest of Mexico during the period 1800–30, with population increasing at nearly 3 percent a year. Over the next thirty years, however, its average growth rate plunged to the level of the rest of the republic, an abysmal .15 percent. These are very rough estimates, and obviously many factors influenced population change in northern Mexico, especially after 1848. But the trend is unmistakable. After 1830 raiding did much to extinguish a period of impressive population growth and settlement expansion begun during the late colonial era, and it shifted much of what became a nearly static population from the countryside into towns and cities.[4]

Population loss was both influenced by and influencing changes in the regional economy. Again, the direct effects of raiding were the most obvious. In 1842 officials in Chihuahua estimated they had already lost more than ten million pesos' worth of property in raids and believed the figure would be three times as high if it included lost revenues. In an economic context in which most people lived on the edge of poverty and even children made important contributions to family sustenance and income, killings and kidnappings could easily reduce survivors to destitution. Poorer families depended on a small number of mules and horses to transport themselves and any marketable goods they produced, to provide field labor, and for fighting and communication in times of crisis. The loss of a few animals could ruin a family and provoke flight.[5]

Raiding indirectly created different problems for larger ranchers and hacendados, one of the most serious being a scarcity of labor. Rural laborers were more likely to be killed by independent Indians than anyone else in northern Mexico for the simple reason that they were more exposed, working alone or in small parties tending to animals and crops. Cowboys, field hands, and shepherds understandably feared working when los indios were about, which they often were, and in times of alarm many refused to leave their homes. This created numerous problems. Someone had to go out and bring animals in nearer to the settlement if they were to be protected from raiders. Untended stock was also more exposed to wolves and other predators, more liable to wander away and become lost, more tempting to Mexican thieves, and more vulnerable to disease since no one was there to separate sick animals from healthy ones. Frightened laborers and tenants also abandoned fieldwork on ranches and haciendas, "leaving our agriculture paralyzed," in the words of an editor from Coahuila. A traveler to northern Chihuahua remarked in the early 1830s that Apache hostilities had made it a practical impossibility to grow wheat, and thus settlers and mine operators had to import costly grain from elsewhere. One commentator went so far as to say that whole towns experienced shortages because los bárbaros had frightened workers from the land and that Chihuahua's capital faced famine.[6]

Fear of Indians could therefore cripple ranching and farming economies in the north, and if determined hacendados pressured laborers to do their jobs despite the risks, then workers were liable to quit and look elsewhere for wages. This became enough of a concern in Chihuahua that the government ordered workers to give hacienda and ranch owners at least two months' notice and settle all outstanding debts before quitting. Mostly symbolic, such laws meant little to those determined to leave. Labor shortages sometimes drove regional elites to take measures that compounded the security crisis. Certain hacendados, the Sánchez Navarros included, resisted orders to arm laborers in part because, when armed, workers may have felt enough protected against Indians to flee the hacienda—and any debts they had accumulated there—for relative freedom and security farther south.[7]

The concern over personal safety had obvious economic implications. Indian raids interfered with the transportation of people and goods across northern Mexico, which among other things meant that farmers, ranchers, and hacendados had trouble getting animals and goods to market. Individual producers usually lacked the manpower and weapons necessary to travel from one city or town to the next during the bárbaro war. They might hire freighters, but raiders often intercepted pack trains, took the animals, killed the drivers, and seized or destroyed the wagons and their goods. Consequently, freighters charged much more for their services and sometimes refused to move goods at any price. In 1842, for example, the governor of Tamaulipas complained that producers had been unable to get their products to market, and as a result the total departmental sales of all types of *productos del campo* plummeted. The governor had special reason to worry because sales of such products were one of the only tax domains he and his counterparts in other departments still controlled after constitutional reforms in the mid-1830s. Therefore, by putting a chill on overland travel Indian raiders did more than simply damage the rural economy. They also inhibited communication between and thus cooperation among regional officials, and they indirectly denied tax revenues to departmental authorities try-

ing desperately to finance an effective defense against los bárbaros. The economic implications of raiding are especially striking given that much of northern
Mexico enjoyed higher than average rainfall from 1830 to 1846, rainfall that but
for Indian raids would have initiated a significant expansion in ranching and
agriculture and thus helped enliven the regional economy as a whole.[8]

Finally, the War of a Thousand Deserts had by 1846 undermined Mexican
community at nearly every level. Northern Mexico had a Spanish-speaking
population roughly thirty times as large as the Comanche, Apache, and Navajo
populations combined. If more northern Mexicans had cooperated against their
common Indian enemies they might have ended the raiding or at least saved
themselves much anguish and loss. Yet at nearly every level of community integration the war presented Mexicans with compelling reasons not to cooperate.[9]

UNWORTHY OF THE NAME MEXICANO:
DEPARTMENTS AT ODDS

The northern departments never came so near to cooperating offensively
against their shared Indian enemies during the 1830s and 1840s as they did in the
buildup to Arista's failed campaign. Despite the pretension of centralism, the
Mexican republic as a whole remained profoundly fragmented. Elite families
dominated internal departmental policy, and while the centralists demanded
docile governors, conscripts for the army, and reliable access to tax revenues,
they had neither the desire nor the ability to manage politics within departments.
Consequently, there were often incongruities in policy, and nowhere was such
incongruity more costly and self-defeating than in the domain of Indian policy.

Consider isolated New Mexico. Despite its small population, fragile economy,
and the independent Indians who surrounded it, Mexicans and their property
were safer there than anywhere else in the north during the 1830s and 1840s —
excepting perhaps Alta California. Navajos provoked panic in western villages
and created serious political and fiscal problems in Santa Fe. But their activities
paled in comparison to the things Apaches and Comanches did elsewhere in the
north, and New Mexicans enjoyed profitable working relationships with these
more far-ranging and dangerous peoples. While Chiricahua Apaches raided
points in southern New Mexico in the earliest days of the war, these attacks
stopped by the mid-1830s and did not become serious again for at least a decade.
Chiricahuas cultivated markets in New Mexico, sometimes made diplomatic
visits to Santa Fe, and clearly wanted to avoid fighting Mexicans to the north as
well as the south. This "singular and most unrighteous compact," as one observer

called New Mexican relations with Apaches, endured despite complaints from other departments.[10]

The compact might have been unrighteous, but not singular. Authorities throughout Mexico knew that Comanches, too, traded with New Mexicans and even visited Santa Fe to receive the governor's presents. Worried about their isolated northern outpost, national authorities nonetheless bit their tongues—until 1841 when Mariano Arista asked Armijo to cooperate in his ill-fated offensive campaign. Armijo called for a conference at Santa Fe to discuss the possibility of going to war with Comanches. He even received some unsolicited advice from the trader Charles Bent: "Theas people by all means should not be drawn into war with any Indians of the planes, they are too numerias and well armed, they will be found a very different enime from the Apachies and Nabijos."[11]

The council apparently concurred because Armijo refused Arista's request, insisting to the minister of war that "to declare war on the Comanches would bring complete ruin to the Department." In the end of course it mattered not, but had Arista gotten his men across the Rio Grande an additional force from New Mexico could have been the key to success. No other Mexicans knew Comanches and their homeland so well, and, thanks in large part to formidable Pueblo warriors, New Mexico excelled all other departments in offensive campaigning against independent Indians. Indeed, at precisely the time when Arista was trying to generate support for his plan, Armijo informed Mexico City that he could raise seventeen hundred volunteers to fight Texans if necessary. Combined with a large, well-provisioned force from below the river such a New Mexican army could have devastated la comanchería, just as New Mexicans had during the wars of the late eighteenth century. In just two campaigns in 1774, for instance, New Mexican forces killed nearly five hundred Comanche men, women, and children. New Mexico's refusal to cooperate with Arista therefore bred understandable resentment elsewhere in the north. Editors in Tamaulipas, for example, wrote that "we like to think that the Comanches and all the races of ferocious Indians are not enemies of New Mexico in particular, but of all the republic in common." Some barbarians "threaten New Mexico, others Sonora and Sinaloa; these threaten Chihuahua, those Durango, and still others Coahuila, Nuevo León, and Tamaulipas. Does it not follow that the security of the entire republic demands that we make war upon all of them, wherever they strike?"[12]

New Mexico's isolation made its dilemma extreme, but none of the other departments cooperated in offensive actions against Indian raiders either. More surprisingly, departments rarely even coordinated defenses against their mutual enemies. Faced with attackers who knew the territory well and paid no attention whatever to district or departmental boundaries, fragmented defenses were doomed to fail. A single example illustrates the problem. In the fall of 1842, in anticipation of what had become annual Comanche raids, Nuevo León's energetic governor, José María Ortega, established two effective lines of defense on his northern frontier involving hundreds of men each. He would reward service with animals taken from los bárbaros or else with cash bounties paid out by the owners of returned livestock. In late October the governor proudly wrote the minister of war that the defensive lines had kept raiders out of the department. But his diligence had only increased the likelihood that Comanches and Kiowas would invade Tamaulipas or Coahuila instead, where defenses were less organized. Moreover, shared borders meant that such an invasion could easily spill over into the governor's own department. So it was that only three days later Ortega had to write the minister again, ruefully admitting that Comanches had entered Nuevo León through the unguarded frontiers of neighboring departments and that they now threatened his unprotected interior.[13]

The exasperated minister of war ordered all the northeastern governors to coordinate their defenses. Indeed, Mexicans from across the north issued passionate calls for cooperative defensive policies and for wealthier states such as Zacatecas and San Luis Potosí to help finance northern defense. But never knowing when or where the next invasion would materialize, governors were loathe to send their few armed men or their scarce resources outside of their own borders. When forces did unite it was often without explicit orders to do so. In 1844, for example, men from Durango pursued Comanches through the Bolsón de Mapimí into Chihuahua and, in spontaneous cooperation with Chihuahuan forces, managed to rout the invaders, killing dozens and recovering more than thirty captives and two thousand horses.[14]

It was an exceptional moment. More typically Mexican pursuers quit the chase once they reached the borders of the next department. A year after their fortuitous collaboration with the duranguéños, for example, Chihuahuan forces positioned themselves at points along the border between the two departments and stayed there while Comanches laid waste to settlements across Durango. Even if a governor was prepared risk his own department's safety by sending men across a border, protocol demanded that he do so only at the request of his counterpart. In 1842 the governor of Durango had a force poised to enter Coahuila and attack Comanches there, but he eventually disbanded the men because authorities in Coahuila never requested assistance. Interdepartmental offers of or requests for military aid against Indians were rare. Governors only expected that information would be shared, and even for so simple a thing they felt compelled to remind each other often that they would be grateful for the service. Moreover because raiding had made interdepartmental travel extremely dangerous and costly, even when officials were determined to coordinate and share intelligence they often found it difficult or impossible to do so.[15]

While the norm was polite interest but effective disregard for the security of neighboring departments, sometimes the Indian policy of one department directly promoted raiding in another. Northwestern Mexico provides the best example of this glaring defect in the façade of national unity. The ruinous feud between Sonora and Chihuahua over Indian policy continued into the early 1840s, when Chihuahua signed a number of peace agreements with Mescaleros and Chiricahuas. Apaches receiving rations in Chihuahua continued raiding neighboring departments, and editors in Durango denounced the agreements. "Chihuahua would make itself unworthy of the name *mexicano* if in treating [with the Apaches] it did so only to its own benefit." Sonora went farther, actually invading Chihuahua on different occasions in pursuit of Apaches, which predictably threatened Chihuahua's precarious peace and left frontier officials there sputtering with rage. Whether Sonorans, Chihuahuans, or New Mexicans, they were all *mexicanos*. But this common national identity implied no effective obligations for mutual defense against raiders beyond the departmental level.[16]

INSUBORDINATE AND IRRESPONSIBLE CONDUCT: INDIVIDUALS AT ODDS

People within departments disagreed about Indian policy as well, and authorities often found it impossible to unify their constituents against the enemy. Since the early 1830s northern officials had been worrying that *los bárbaros* undermined Mexican unity. As one observer put it, the war had not only consumed the treasury and hindered the administration of government, but also divided opinion and "numbed the spirit of civic responsibility." Governors appealed to their constituents' sense of "civic virtue" and denounced the "scandalous egotism" that led too many to neglect the common good. In a pamphlet from 1839 José Agustín Escudero insisted that a "national spirit" had to be awakened within the populace before defense against *los salvajes* would become coordinated and Mexicans would together wage what he called "the national war, by all and for all against the infidel."[17]

Here lies a fundamental difference between Mexicans and their native adversaries. Whereas among Comanches and Kiowas, for example, individual ambitions and interest were compatible with and even served by broad cooperation in war, the reverse was often the case for northern Mexicans. A variety of competing interests and identities took precedence over cooperation with departmental authorities. Individual towns, cities, or regions might harbor intense rivalries with each other, rivalries fueled by bitter competition between elite families over economic and political preeminence. Sonora is the extreme case: civil wars there between northern and southern factions sabotaged any hope of a unified and effective Apache policy. Usually rivalries had subtler effects. During the early and mid-1830s, for instance, Monclova and Saltillo had been in brutal competition for political dominance in Coahuila. The residual tension was still visible in 1842, in charges that the prefect of Monclova had deliberately neglected frontier defense so that raiders could reach Saltillo.[18]

Departmental authorities also had to cope with what editors in Durango described as "the repugnance that the owners of haciendas generally effect" when asked to cooperate in the defense of the department. Authorities in Coahuila, for example, set quotas for the number of men different haciendas were required to contribute for the common defense. The Sánchez Navarros, the largest landholders in the department, refused to provide any men at all, insisting that their own properties needed protecting. Divisions over wealth and status also inhibited cooperative defense. Chihuahuan authorities had difficulty convincing ranchers and laborers to risk their lives to defend the horses of wealthy hacendados, and Pueblo Indians and poor New Mexicans complained that they were required to campaign against Navajos only to protect rich men's sheep.[19]

These sorts of attitudes helped fuel a species of profiteering whereby men from certain communities pursued bárbaros primarily to recover booty for themselves. Mexican newspapers and archives abound in references to small- and medium-sized parties of Mexicans giving up after recovering a handful of animals or other spoils. Raiders regularly cut some of their mules and horses loose if they found themselves too closely pursued. Large Mexican forces took no part in this tacit agreement between raiders and their pursuers, and smaller, local groups often performed with great valor and tenacity, especially if attempting to redeem captive kin. But when frontier militia pursued Indians who had plundered properties elsewhere in the republic, they faced considerable temptation to quit the chase (and thus the hazard) once some prize had been won. Mexican officials decried this sort of "insubordinate and irresponsible conduct," correctly insisting that it prolonged the war and led to more Mexican casualties. But slack passion in pursuit of raiders was difficult to prove or punish.[20] Much less representative but more disturbing for northerners were those Mexicans profiting directly from Indian raiding. In addition to los entregadores who facilitated raiding campaigns, some stood accused of falsely reporting indio sightings so that they might rob their neighbors once local men raced off to chase phantoms. Others disguised themselves as Comanches or Apaches in hopes of committing their crimes with impunity.[21]

But personal venality was not the most important impediment to a successful defense against los bárbaros. Northerners—most notably poor northerners—often sacrificed from what little they had to help kin and neighbors affected by raids and to support local governments' efforts at defense. In 1838, for example, Coahuila established a coordinated system for collecting grain, animals, cloth, currency, and other donations to sustain operations against raiders. Families of modest means from across the department gave what they could—maize, beans, meat, horses, coins, saddles, blankets, cows, pigs, and goats—testimony to a shared willingness to sacrifice. Moreover, energetic leaders did sometimes manage to rally northerners at the local, district, and departmental level, pursue Indian raiders, and secure remarkable victories. On October 17, 1845, for example, Don Francisco de Paula López led forces from Durango in an attack on hundreds of Comanches who had been causing massive destruction throughout the department. Paula López and his hardy duranguenos routed the Indians and freed seventy traumatized but grateful Mexican women and children who had been taken captive over the previous weeks. Remarkably, this victory and a few others like it ensured that over the course of the 1830s and 1840s Mexican forces redeemed most of the people that Comanches and Kiowas captured before the raiders got them back across the river. But the carnage continued despite the occasional triumph. Just days after losing their seventy captives the same Comanches killed nearly seventy people in one of Durango's towns; and while the hero Paula López had given Mexicans hope, he himself would be slain by the raiders one year later in their next campaign.[22]

The most elemental and consequential division among northern Mexicans therefore arose not from selfish indifference but from conflicting loyalties—when men had to decide whether to heed the authorities' call and join a company in pursuit of Indians or stay behind and protect their own families and property. People understood that cooperation was the key to genuine security. Individual towns sometimes made security arrangements with one another and held public forums to discuss the overall problem of collective frontier defense. But by contributing to the common good a man could lose everything because he had not been home to defend his own. Mexicans therefore faced a kind of prisoner's dilemma that played out over and over again across the northern third of Mexico by the 1840s. *If* everyone cooperated as authorities asked them to and *if* government provided the necessary resources and leadership, then the raiders *might* be driven out of the department before they did much damage.[23]

Absent sufficient resources and leadership, the different sorts of factional-ism—between rival departments, competing towns or regions, hacendados and departmental officials, the poor majority and the elite, the personal and the pub-lic—intersected and bled into one another, sometimes hopelessly complicating defense. On June 9, 1844, for example, news arrived in Matamoros that a party of Comanches had crossed the Rio Grande and was stealing horses from nearby ranches. Matamoros's mayor, Francisco Lofero, sent an order out to the heads of all surrounding ranches and haciendas to send armed, mounted men for a coordinated, collective defense. Most equivocated or refused. One not only re-fused but unceremoniously scrawled the words, "I also demand you send me arms and flints" on the bottom of his reply. By the fifteenth, with little left to do, Lofero somewhat pathetically imposed fines upon those who refused to pursue the raiders. He next became embroiled in a dispute between a military com-mander and a rancher who would not lend horses for the chase. Soon after, fifty Comanches attacked a settlement three leagues from Matamoros, and Lofero again harangued nearby officials, imploring them to take up the defense. Again, most refused. Defeated, the mayor sent out bitter letters damning locals for self-ishness and promising more fines. By the end of the month the Comanches finally withdrew after nearly three weeks in the city's hinterland, never having had a significant engagement with Mexican defenders.[24]

Some of Lofero's antagonists may have been cowards—there was obviously much to be terrified of, and it is difficult to imagine the cumulative strain of so many years of uncertainty, vulnerability, and loss. More likely, though, they were men who had decided not to risk their families and fortunes on the uncertain virtues of cooperation. Nevertheless, northerners constantly risked their lives to protect their families, their close neighbors, and even their departments. Some-times Mexicans were in fact irrationally courageous, as on the "disastrous day" in 1845 when Comanches arrived at San Juan del Río, Durango. The town's inhabitants "enthusiastically" poured out of their homes to fight the invaders with little more than bare hands and rawhide slings. The hapless mayor stood by horror-struck as the bemused raiders set about slaughtering his townspeople. By the end of the day nearly 120 Mexicans had been killed or wounded at San Juan del Río. Most northerners had a healthier fear of Comanches. But they fought them all the same, because they had to. Northern Mexico did not want for cour-age. It lacked the resources and leadership necessary to convince people that their more personal identities and interests would be best protected through sustained, public cooperation as mexicanos. Weary departmental officials some-times inadvertently reinforced the collective sense of despair. In 1845, for ex-ample, in the aftermath of a terrifically violent Comanche campaign, Durango's assembly met and decided to establish a celebration in honor of Saint Francis Xavier because of the public calamities caused by los bárbaros. In honoring this greatest of Catholic missionaries the assembly seemed to be saying that if Mexico was unable to stop Comanches and Kiowas, then perhaps God could be convinced to change them into something else.[25]

BARBAROUS CRUELTY THAT I CANNOT EVEN SPEAK OF: THE DISCOURSE OF WAR

Indeed, Mexicans dearly needed to turn Comanches, Apaches, and Navajos into something else—but not Christians. After more than a decade of spiraling violence, Mexicans still had not found the ideas and the language necessary to portray their enemies as irredeemably alien. On other nineteenth-century North American frontiers, racial dichotomies provided that distinction. In Texas and the United States, the habit of thinking in binary racial categories made it easier for European Americans to ignore the differences and complexities of regionally diverse native populations. Racism helped them to overlook the way in which their own behavior provoked native hostility and to countenance their own spectacular and indiscriminate acts of wartime violence. More important, since at least the late eighteenth century hard distinctions pitting "Indians" vs. "whites" had enabled fractious and diverse frontier communities to surmount their internal differences and cooperate in war. Bloody, oft-told tales of massacres and treacheries, a shared sense of outraged victimhood, and perpetual alarms over supposedly imminent attacks helped people discover their common "white" identity and work together against nonwhites. Especially as wars progressed, the language of Indian hating often allowed the most confrontational elements in American or Texan frontier society to silence voices of caution and conciliation and increase pressure on local political and military leaders to coordinate vigorous and vicious action against native families.[26]

Racist Indian hating helped Americans and Texans do things that northern Mexicans dearly wanted to do. If all of Mexico's indigenous enemies could have been homogenized as uncomplicated racial others, the project of drawing clear boundaries, overcoming internal divisions, and focusing energy and malice cooperatively would have been simpler. But while most northerners feared and hated their attackers, this fear and hatred was rarely conceived of or expressed in terms of a racial divide. This is not to say that the region's inhabitants rejected the concept of race. On the contrary, shifting concerns over forebears, bodies, and blood had helped structure power and social relations in the north ever since the region's initial colonization in the sixteenth century. Even in the officially (and superficially) race-blind atmosphere after independence, northern authorities occasionally toyed with racist formulations during the war against independent Indians. Yet outbursts like Arista's screeds against the Comanche "race" or his injunction to northerners to nourish their fields with the raiders' "black blood" were striking precisely because they were so unusual. Race could never have the same discursive potency for Mexicans that it did for Texans and Americans, for the simple reason that Mexico was a republic comprised mostly of Indians and mestizos. Northern politicians and commentators certainly conceived of themselves as racial superiors to raiding Apaches and Comanches. But they could hardly hope to inspire passionate unity and focused cooperation by talking about the degenerate evils of the Indian race when most of the people they hoped to enlist had native ancestry themselves. Like other postindependence Latin American republics, moreover, Mexico's long-term hopes for stability, productivity, and reform hinged on integrating native and mixed-race peoples into the republic as productive citizens. Hence the reflexive insistence that everyone born inside the republic was mexicano.[27]

Northerners endeavored to contrast Apaches, Comanches, and Navajos with indigenous ranchers, farmers, and laborers by continually referring to raiders with words such as *barbarian, savage,* or even *caribe* — a retreat to the very oldest of Spanish epithets for enemy indigenes. But northern authorities and commentators were surprisingly reluctant to describe the acts of these caribes in detail. This may be attributed partly to sensibilities about propriety and privacy. But to denounce the raiders' tactics in great detail would also have invited uncomfortable comparisons, given that Mexicans regularly employed heinous tactics themselves. Like their Spanish grandfathers, Mexicans surprised and attacked Apache and Navajo families in their homelands, employed treachery to better kill their enemies, massacred them and dragged them off as slaves, burned their homes and crops, stole the animals they depended upon to live. Mexicans of every station continued to pay, support, and celebrate men like James Kirker who killed Indians for money. Mexicans nailed Navajo ears to the walls of the governor's palace in Santa Fe, displayed severed Comanche heads in provincial capitals, and jammed the streets of Chihuahua City for a glimpse of withered Apache scalps.[28]

Americans and Texans obviously did comparable things to Indians. But nothing masks the hypocrisy and logical inconsistency of savaging enemies for their supposed savagery as well as racial absolutes. This helps explain why Americans and Texans could go so much farther with the rhetoric of barbarism than their Mexican counterparts. English-speaking writers on diverse American frontiers often thought intimate descriptions of bodily harm indispensable to communicating the meaning and horror of Indian war. Children with their heads smashed in, pregnant mothers with their bellies ripped open, scalped and tortured men awash in gore, bellowing farm animals dragging their guts behind them—these had been stock images on successive American frontiers since the late seventeenth century. Sometimes even shocking words seemed insufficient, so settlers hauled the very bodies of their mutilated kin and neighbors to towns and cities, setting the corpses on display in order to shame officials into action. Nothing like that happened in northern Mexico during the 1830s and 1840s, and regional authorities were loathe even to include graphic details in their reports. Occasionally northern correspondents trespassed sensibilities, as when Raphael de la Fuente from Monclova reported that Comanches had slain seven freighters, "pulled some of the dead from their horses, slit their throats, cut them open, dismembered them." But even this atypical author had his limits, concluding that the raiders had "committed other acts of barbarous cruelty that I cannot even speak of."[29]

Therefore, because their constitutional assumptions, their history, and the very bodies of their constituents made it impossible for northern politicians and writers to deal in racial absolutes, and because they generally avoided a vivid discourse of savagery, they had to rely on feebler rhetorical tools. Above all, northern authorities and writers deployed a discourse of honor and shame, but one that sent decidedly mixed messages. On the one hand they tried consistently to shame national leaders into action. They demanded that authorities in Mexico City "save the tarnished national honor;" warned that if they did not "cover the frontier the sad result will be desolation and terror"; prayed that "these enormous evils will draw the attention of the supreme government"; and compared los salvajes to other threats: "We see that the entire nation cries out with one voice: war upon the Texans. Why do we not do the same with respect to the barbarian nations, who are another domestic enemy?" Such calls implicitly acknowledged the might of independent Indians—Mexico City had to help because los bárbaros were too formidable for northerners to defeat on their own.[30]

But northern commentators and officials seemed to say precisely the opposite when they turned the same discourse of honor and humiliation on their own constituents. In the face of disunity and insubordination they sought to shame northerners by rhetorically stripping independent Indians of organization, politics, and meaningful society and then pointing at the pathetic remnant and demanding that Mexicans account for their prostration before such a contemptible enemy. The most provocative questions came from Chihuahua, the sorry, brutal heartland of the War of a Thousand Deserts. "What?!" Escudero asked. "One hundred fifty thousand inhabitants fall back before a handful of enemies who neither carry the sign of the cross nor know civilization nor even recognize any other human symbol than do the animals of the desert?" Another author demanded to know whether a part of the brave people who only a generation before had united to overthrow one of Europe's great powers would now consent to become "slaves to some wandering barbarian tribes, who have no more policy than robbery and assassination, and no greater force than the caprice of their temerity, nor more moral authority than terror and menace?!!" What were Mexicans if they could not cope with foes such as these? "What is a miserable handful of fearful cannibals that they should keep an organized society in constant anxiety?"[31]

The fact that despairing authorities found it necessary to ask such questions speaks both to systemic disunity in the north and to the inability of existing discourse to do much about it. The complexities of northern factionalism at the regional, departmental, and local levels therefore derived not only from insufficient resources and leadership—ideas and rhetoric mattered as well. And if after more than ten years of terror and grief northerners had yet to rally themselves around a sufficiently useful caricature of their enemies, it is unsurprising that national officials in Mexico City still clung to the same patronizing fiction that independent Indians were wayward Mexicans yearning to be brought into the fold.

Consider President Santa Anna's response to a curious development in 1843. In January of that year word reached the capital that the paraibo Pia Kusa and several other Hois Comanches had signed a peace treaty in Coahuila, with Juan José Galán—the man who had captured Antonio "Sombrero de Manteca" Zapata and bested Comanches after their bold raid on Saltillo in early 1841. The intrepid Galán commanded respect among his adversaries, but he owed the diplomatic coup to a broader policy disagreement among the Hois concerning Texas. While Hois leaders eventually agreed to formal peace with Texas once Sam Houston replaced the hated Mirabeau Lamar in 1841, it took more than two years of agonizing internal debate and political maneuvering to get there. Older paraibos like Mopechucope and Pahayuco urged their people to formalize peace with the new president, who earnestly insisted that he had not been "chief" of Texas during the Council House Massacre and the slaughters of Comanche women and children in camp. Peace would put an end to a ruinous conflict, would open up valuable new commercial outlets (Houston's promised trading houses), and would also afford Hois men the security necessary to expand their raiding in Mexico. But Texan expansion threatened Comanche hunting territory, a matter that the young war leader Potsanaquahip, in particular, expressed alarm over. Just as important, Texans had done much to earn Comanche hatred.

An election could not change that. While conflict decreased dramatically after Houston's reelection, Potsanaquahip, Pia Kusa, and other young Hois leaders refused to come in and talk peace. As one of Houston's emissaries was told, "The bones of their brothers that had been massacred at San Antonio had appeared in the Road and obstructed their passage."[32]

The Mexican treaty suggests that Pia Kusa and others were trying to scuttle the emerging Texan peace. The paraibo confided to his Mexican counterparts that he and his followers opposed Texans because of their treacheries and massacres, especially because of what they had done at the Council House, and argued that Comanches and Mexicans should align against them. To cultivate such an alliance, Pia Kusa and his men were willing, at least temporarily, to defy elder leaders, forgo the spoils of raiding below the river, and make grandiose, impossible promises. The treaty committed "the Comanche nation" to peace with Mexico. Pia Kusa agreed to aid Mexico in wartime, promised to mediate between his new allies and the other Comanche divisions, and, unbelievably—literally unbelievably, given how extraordinarily rare it was for one Comanche to kill another—pledged to wage war upon any who refused to embrace the Mexican peace.[33]

The signatories lacked standing even to speak for the Hois, let alone other Comanches. Authorities in Coahuila seem to have treated the agreement with healthy skepticism, expecting little more than a local reduction in raiding. Nonetheless the treaty gave a bit of hope to exhausted families in the northeast and to Mariano Arista, who was desperate for good news and quick to take credit for the treaty. The general boasted that his "toil on the frontier had not been without success" and temporarily abandoned his vivid descriptors of Comanches in favor of the gentler epithet "children of the desert." He promptly sent the treaty to President Santa Anna for ratification. Santa Anna approved the agreement but insisted on one change. The amendment did not concern terms, enforcement, or the addition of new national resources in hopes of fortifying the truce—all things that would have indicated a realistic engagement with the situation. What bothered the president was that the document referred to Comanches as a *nation*. That term would have to be dropped. Comanches depended upon and lived in the territory of the Mexican republic, Santa Anna insisted, and therefore could in no way be considered a nation. Mexico was a nation—Comanches were a *tribe*, something internal to the republic.[34]

Soon after correcting Galán's vocabulary, Santa Anna's government took other steps confirming its willful misunderstanding of independent Indians and the threats they posed. "Considering that the use of force has failed in three hundred years to introduce the uses of civilization among the barbarian tribes," the

president invited the Jesuits back to Mexico to proselytize in the northern frontier for the first time since their expulsion in the eighteenth century. It was an
inexpensive way to both flatter the church and indulge the notion that Comanches, Kiowas, Navajos, and Apaches had only to be taught to be good Mexicans.
In late 1844 the central government exhorted frontier officials and presidial officers not to wait for the Jesuits but to civilize los bárbaros themselves. Presidial
commanders were to begin with any barbarians they captured, to treat them
well and provide them with moral and religious instruction in hopes of gradually
making them and their people "if not friends, then at least enemies who understand us, and whom we can understand." The rewards seemed obvious: "This
work is slow, but it will cover you in glory, placing you among the benefactors of
humanity."[35]

Occasional gestures at improving defense—stillborn colonization plans, edicts
on the education of select presidial soldiers, insincere promises to prioritize presidio funding above all else—did nothing to address fundamental problems. Despite modest increases in personnel at select garrisons in the early 1840s, no
presidios had even half of the men they were required to have by a law passed in
1826, to say nothing of the number they realistically needed following the surge
in raiding after 1831. Chihuahua's presidios apparently operated at less than one-
third of their requisite strength. Horses posed an even bigger problem. The five
departments that provided data on horses in 1840 reported herds less than 10
percent as large as they were supposed to be. And as raids escalated and Indians
stole more and more animals, mounts inevitably became harder and harder to
come by. Six years later reporting departments had on average less than 3 percent of their required horses. Even if there had been more men at the presidios,
they would have had to chase raiders on foot. The report of the minister of war in
1844 makes it clear that los bárbaros attracted as little national attention as they
did resources. In a section entitled "barbarian Indians" the minister bemoaned
the decline of the presidios and expounded on the necessity of their revival.
The section was less than one page long. By comparison the minister devoted
a page and a half to a farcical attempt by Texas to seize New Mexico (the so-
called Santa Fe expedition), five pages to Texas generally, and more than twenty
pages to an ongoing rebellion in the Yucatán. For Santa Anna's administration,
los indios bárbaros were, as always, a local or a regional problem, a persistent
social ill—unlike Texans and rebels in the Yucatán, who manifestly threatened
the nation-state.[36]

Frustrated northerners may have taken comfort in the knowledge that others
of their countrymen had grown equally weary of Santa Anna. Saddled with the
same dismal finances that had facilitated his overthrow of Bustamante in 1841

20. Presidial Soldier. Watercolor by Lino Sánchez y Tapia.
Courtesy of the Gilcrease Museum, Tulsa, Oklahoma.

and obsessed with the unrealistic and increasingly unpopular notion of reconquering Texas, the great leader pushed through huge increases in taxes and demanded millions of pesos to raise a larger army. By mid-1844 his political base
began to collapse. In November he marched out of Mexico City to put down a
challenge from a prominent general. The city turned against him in his absence,
pulling down his statue and installing the moderate José Joaquín de Herrera as
president. Santa Anna was arrested in January of 1845 and sentenced to exile in
Havana.[37]

Santa Anna's latest defeat came at a propitious time for the broken and harried Mexican north. The general's ouster made room for one of the most conscientious and responsible governments in Mexico's history, one whose leaders
took power at precisely the moment when weary ideas and ineffective discourse
about the war were giving way to something more promising. By the mid-1840s
a new consensus began taking shape across the republic that would at last pro-

duce a useful caricature of independent Indians, one based not on race, savagery, honor, or shame, but on an imagined alliance between the raiders and enemies more sinister still.[38]

MEDALLIONS OF SILVER: RAIDERS START MAKING SENSE

The notion that Texans or Americans fomented Indian raids had been lurking on the margins of the conversation about raiding from the very start, but moved to its center only in the 1840s.[39] As Texas adopted a more provocative stance toward Mexico early in the decade, northern officials observed with interest that hostile Texans could generate both interdepartmental cooperation and help from the central government, whereas Comanches, Kiowas, and Apaches provoked neither. In 1843, for example, more than a thousand men from Chihuahua and Durango marched to New Mexico to head off a rumored invasion from Texas (one that never materialized). Departmental authorities and editors shrewdly started peppering their laments and appeals for federal assistance with the word *Texan*. A typical editorial from Tamaulipas in 1844 noted that "the proud and triumphant Indians, certainly allied with the thieves and contrabandistas of the frontier and with the Texans, kill without pity, attack the countryside, rob the horses, and take them to sell or trade for arms in the markets of the United States."[40]

Independent Indians were made to be associates or even servants of Texans and norteamericanos. Northerners stopped talking simply about foreign markets fueling raids and began speaking more openly about agreements, alliances, and conspiracies. The governor of Durango, for example, tried to galvanize public opinion by insisting that Indian invasions were "directed by the Texans." The governor of Tamaulipas explained to President Herrera in 1845 that los bárbaros had forged an alliance with the Texans, who supplied the raiders with guns and ammunition in order to destabilize the frontier. Later in the year Nuevo León's governor drafted another of his perennial appeals for arms and ammunition, but this time he insisted that the resources were needed "against the frequent and bloody incursions of the barbarians, and above all to protect [the department] against a blow from the Texans." Two weeks later the ministry of war promised to send all of the weapons and munitions the governor had requested.[41]

Mexico City felt comfortable with the connection between Texans and Indian raiders. The problem of Anglo-American traders arming northern Indians had long been recognized in the capital, and the foreign ministry made a number of formal complaints about the practice to their U.S. counterparts during the 1830s.[42] By the 1840s national officials were prepared to see more systematic connections between norteamericanos and los bárbaros, in part because such connections helped explain native triumphs. While most of the republic's top administrators held more inclusive and in many ways less realistic views about independent Indians than northerners did, opinions converged on the matter of Indian politics.

Despite abundant evidence that Apaches, Navajos, and especially Comanches and Kiowas were able to mobilize their communities to an astonishing degree in pursuit of shared goals, most northern observers portrayed these Indians as thoroughly apolitical—as disorganized animals killing just to kill. Part of this has to do with the silence of the enemy. One of the most frightening and maddening aspects of the bárbaro war was its lack of words. Nearly all of the other organized violence that touched Mexicans' lives in the first half of the nineteenth century, and there was much of it, came with masses of words: declarations, plans, and pronouncements defending actions and defining goals. Even the uprisings of sedentary indigenous peoples in Sonora and elsewhere across the republic had goals accessible to other Mexicans through language. In contrast, northern Mexicans usually experienced and nearly always described barbarians as inscrutable. They thought that los indios bárbaros had no organized goals beyond assassination and plunder. They had no politics, no overall plan, only foul hearts that took pleasure in the murder and ruination of helpless Mexican families.

Most national leaders rejected so harsh a characterization and usually thought of these peoples instead as wayward Mexicans. Raiders were not members of coherent communities working toward shared goals; they were ignorant children in need of punishment and instruction. An exception to this apolitical interpretation helps prove the rule. In the aftermath of the Comanche attack on Saltillo in 1841, an author in Mexico City named M. Paino took it upon himself to disabuse his countrymen of their misconceptions. Drawing primarily on information from former captives, Paino observed that "those who have not traveled to the frontier believe that the war waged by the Indians has no plan or scheme whatever and is consequently insignificant. Unfortunately, this is not the case." The author went on to describe the councils that preceded Comanche campaigns, the "eloquent and logical" speeches of leaders, the ceremonies and songs that helped fix collective purpose, the common material and nonmaterial goals that bound raiders together, and the manner in which they embarked on their assaults. Northerners and national leaders recognized that raiders acted in concert but generally refused to do what Paino did, that is, understand that cooperation as something that emerged in their camps and councils as part of an indigenous political tradition. Instead Mexican observers simply tended to ignore the cooperative dimension to Indian raiding and portray raiders themselves as mindless animals or wayward children. Either way the political implications were the same: independent indigenous peoples were not mature political communities in pursuit of coherent policies. Thus the idea that foreign agents somehow directed their movements helped northerners and national officials alike explain how these nonpolitical beings could be so united and formidable.[43]

Early in the decade, then, editors and politicians in Mexico City began making the connection. In 1841, for example, with Lamar boasting of plans to make the Sierra Madre the southern boundary of Texas, the editors of Mexico's official newspaper insisted that Texans were inciting Indian raiders to prepare the way for a planned invasion. In 1842 the central government decided to reward the northern town of Reynosa, Tamaulipas, for its participation in a successful battle against Comanches. The militiamen and their leaders, including the ex-rebel Antonio Canales, received a coat of arms with a sun on a blue background and a title that had nothing at all to do with Comanches: "Valiant defender of Texas, of the integrity of the Mexican territory." In 1844 the Mexican Congress urged the president to send resources to frontier populations because "their loyal breasts are the walls that contain the barbarians beyond San Luis [Potosí], Zacatecas, and other departments" and because "the national honor and dignity want not to submit to the disloyal Texan."[44]

As soon as the purported Indian–Texan connection started coming into focus, two things happened that would finally produce something approaching national consensus on Indian raiding. First, U.S. president John Tyler presented Congress with a plan for the annexation of Texas in the spring of 1844. Tyler's scheme failed, but most observers realized that annexation was now only a matter of time, and commentators throughout Mexico began discussing the likelihood of war with the United States. While officials in Mexico City struggled over whether and how to prepare for such a war, the second change took place: independent Indians dramatically escalated their raiding activities across the whole of northern Mexico. In Chihuahua a series of agreements that had secured peace with Apaches in 1842 and 1843 started unraveling in 1844 and came entirely undone in 1845. In New Mexico the deepening conflict with Navajos seemed every month less comprehensible, and as of September 1844 well-armed Utes had declared war against the department as well.[45]

Most disastrously, after a relatively uneventful 1843 Comanches and Kiowas launched several huge campaigns into Tamaulipas, Nuevo León, Coahuila, Chihuahua, Durango, and Zacatecas in 1844 and 1845. The renewed, indeed unprecedented, energy behind the assaults seems to have been connected to the long-delayed consummation of peace between the Hois and Houston's Texas.

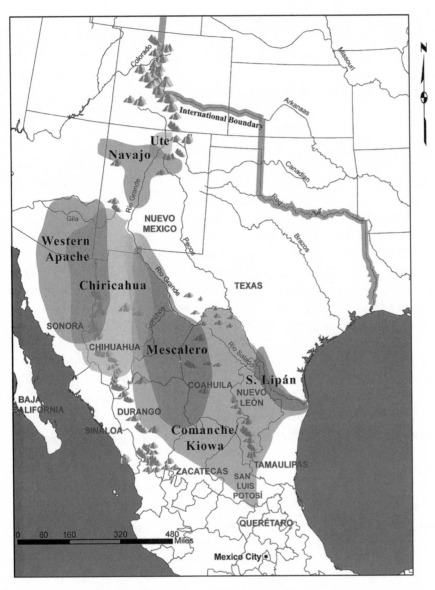

5. Zones of interethnic violence in northern Mexico, c. 1844

No matter the treaty Pia Kusa made with Galán, the potential threats of Texan expansion, or Lamar's treacheries and massacres, there remained the hard logic that seasoned leaders such as Pahayuco and Mopechucope evidently subscribed to. War with Texas had been ruinous and peace with them could be profitable, whereas the reverse seemed to be true with Mexico. By mid-1844, Comanche elders had convinced a critical mass of young warriors that a Texas treaty would be in their interest. The matter was effectively settled in October, when Potsanaquahip, the most influential of all Hois warriors, reluctantly and somewhat sullenly joined with his elder Mopechucope in signing a peace treaty with Houston. Texan authorities obligingly agreed to issue passports to prominent warriors should they need to approach San Antonio while en route to Mexico.[46]

Potsanaquahip's move left Pia Kusa as the only Hois of first importance refusing to make peace with Texas. It would be another year before he could bring himself to formally reconcile with Texan authorities, but reconcile he did. Whereas he made Mexicans grandiose and impossible promises on behalf of his people, Pia Kusa approached Texan negotiators humbly, insisting that he did not "talk," that he lacked the authority to engage in diplomatic conversation. He promised to abide by the peace all the same. Meanwhile, he had long since abandoned his now-irrelevant Mexican treaty. Pia Kusa seems to have paid his last peaceful visit to the Mexican settlements in spring of 1844. By summer, Texan agents observed parties of young men who claimed to belong to his ranchería preparing for raids into Mexico, and a few months later a Texan newspaper reported that Pia Kusa and his men had killed sixty people at a ranch near Guerrero. The Mexican peace was dead. Whatever the paraibo thought of the Texas treaty, he was quick to exploit the improved security and the market opportunities it offered to raise men for campaigns below the Rio Grande.[47]

The increased campaigning probably also reflects a change felt more broadly throughout the southern plains: a decline in bison. Decades of overhunting for the hide trade lay at the root of the problem. Moreover, the huge herds of horses and mules Comanches and Kiowas kept on the southern plains made it harder for bison to feed themselves. The diets of horses and buffalo overlap by 80 percent, and competition became deadly during winter, when Indians sustained their herds on the same riverine resources that bison depended on for survival. Thus, an ironic cycle: the massive increase in raiding after 1840 hastened the decline of bison populations by vastly increasing the number of horses and mules on the plains, while scarcity of bison gave Comanches and Kiowas another reason to organize raiding campaigns. A few non-Indian observers commented on the situation. In 1843, for example, Padre Antonio Martínez of Taos insisted that Indians raided into Mexico in large part because the animals they depended upon were vanishing. A year later an observer at the eastern edge of the southern plains remarked on the "extreme destitution" of the region's peoples, who supposedly told him that "our bows and arrows can no longer reach the buffalo, they are getting too far off." Comanches consumed herd animals in times of such shortages, and the extraordinary campaigns of 1844 and 1845 may well have been driven partly by a need to obtain meat and rebuild herds.[48]

Whatever the impetus, the campaigns were tremendously destructive. They began in October of 1844 when two groups of several hundred warriors each crossed the river, one heading east along the lower Rio Grande and the other riding west into Chihuahua. The timing of the twin campaigns itself fueled speculation about norteamericano collusion, and small but significant details about the raids only deepened these suspicions. The eastern group attacked and set fire to ranches in northern Tamaulipas and then killed nearly fifty Mexican men from Guerrero who had been sent to pursue them. Several days later a larger Mexican force attacked the raiders again, this time driving them off and rescuing fifty-five captive women and children. The plains warriors fled weeping, shamed, and grief-stricken at having to leave scores of fallen comrades behind. Mexicans reported that "on some of the dead barbarians were found medallions of silver, a bust of President Van Buren, dated 1837, and the emblem of the US on the reverse."[49]

Mexican defenders also had unusual success against the group that had gone into Chihuahua, killing a remarkable four dozen Comanches during a pitched battle in the district of Jiménez. Here too Mexicans found confirmation for their mounting suspicions. Among the Comanche dead were two norteamericanos. The Mexican commander went so far as to claim that the majority of the attacking Indians were in fact "not Comanches, because of their countenances, dress, etc. This affirms more the idea that the Texans foment them to make war upon us." The next year while Comanches were campaigning through Durango, authorities captured a Mexican who had been riding with them. The man reported that four "men of reason"—Christians—traveled with the raiders and tried to guide their movements with information they extracted from a Mexican whom they kept imprisoned: "They are from distant lands and are the most vicious murderers."[50]

MORE ADVANCED OBJECTIVES: THE NEW CONSENSUS

These sorts of intriguing details, combined with the fact that the surge in raids coincided with U.S. preparations to expand into Texas, convinced most Mexican observers that Indians, Texans, and the U.S. government were all connected.

It appeared that Indian raiding suddenly had, in the words of a writer from Tamaulipas, "more advanced objectives than killing and robbing." Mexicans had long assumed that residents of Texas and the United States profited indirectly from raiding through trade. But now editors and politicians were describing a more ambitious and integrated arrangement wherein los bárbaros were an essential component of a norteamericano plan to despoil Mexico of its northern territories. Durango's *Registro Oficial,* for example, observed that "the barbarians have never been so formidable as in the last years" and attributed the change to U.S. machinations. Some version of this basic hypothesis quickly found adherents across the republic. Newspapers throughout the north made the connection, as did papers in Mexico City and even in departments far south of the frontier. Carlos María Bustamante, the great Mexican chronicler of the period, wrote in one of his histories about norteamericanos providing los bárbaros with guns and ammunition and then pushing them into Mexico.[51]

The Mexican position became far more desperate thanks to the caprice of American electoral politics. In early 1844 political observers in Washington had reason to expect the Whig candidate Henry Clay would win the general election in November. Clay and his supporters assumed he would face former president Martin Van Buren as the Democratic candidate and that insofar as Van Buren's name was still shackled to the depression that had cost him reelection in 1840, the Whigs could prevail by focusing on economic issues. But matters soon grew more complex. Tyler's annexation ploy and John C. Calhoun's championing of annexation as critical to the survival of slavery refocused the election around divisive sectional issues. Van Buren insisted publicly that annexation would be tantamount to an act of war against Mexico; born of "lust for power, with fraud and violence in the train." It was a principled stance—and an expensive one. Proannexation Democrats managed to block his nomination at the convention and, after fisticuffs, recriminations, teary speeches, and round after round of inconclusive voting, James K. Polk emerged as the consensus candidate.[52]

John Quincy Adams once described Polk (to his face) as "an Anglo-Saxon, slave-holding exterminator of Indians." Polk was indeed a Jackson man. Elected to Congress in 1824, he became Jackson's key lieutenant in the House once Old Hickory became president, and through loyal and effective championing of Jackson's agenda he earned the sobriquet "Young Hickory." Polk was an intense, hardworking, and somewhat retiring figure, with little of his patron's combustive personality. He skillfully filled the position of Speaker of the House from 1835 to 1839, when he became governor of Tennessee. A failed reelection bid in 1841 and another in 1843 might have put an end to Polk's political career had not an

21. James K. Polk, Freedom's Champion.
Napoleon Sarony, 1846. Library of Congress,
Prints and Photographs Division.

ailing Jackson personally endorsed his candidacy during the tortured negotiations at the Democratic convention. Whigs reacted with glee to the nomination of a figure with so thin a national reputation, chanting derisively "Who is
James K. Polk?"[53]

It soon became clear who James K. Polk was—a committed, even zealous
expansionist. He championed an advantageous settlement with Britain over the
disputed boundary of Oregon and the reannexation of Texas; *re*annexation because, like Jefferson and Jackson before him, Polk claimed Texas had been part
of the Louisiana Purchase. Thus the election of 1844 presented voters with a

stark choice. Like Van Buren, the Whig candidate Clay equated annexation with a dishonorable war against Mexico. Clay insisted he was unwilling "to involve this country in a foreign war for the object of acquiring Texas." In the end the contest was phenomenally close and could not have been more important for the United States or for Mexico. Had Clay won just 5,107 more votes in New York State from the nearly one million cast, he would have become president and there almost certainly would have been no annexation of Texas, no war with Mexico, no U.S. Civil War, and a vastly different continental story. But by the narrowest of margins Polk's vision took the day. Outgoing President Tyler interpreted the election as a mandate to try again, and he pressed Congress to pass a joint resolution in favor of annexation. This time Congress obliged, barely—the resolution passed the Senate with one vote to spare. Tyler signed the measure into law three days before leaving office. All that remained was for Texas to accept the invitation.[54]

These events provoked a diplomatic crisis in U.S.–Mexican relations, one that began to converge with the war against los bárbaros. For nearly fifteen years northern Mexicans had labored in vain to convince their leaders in Mexico City that Indian raiding was a national crisis. Now, just weeks after annexation had finally been approved in Washington, no less a figure than the Mexican minister of war was arguing the case for them. Minister Pedro García Conde belonged to an old Sonoran family and had himself fought los bárbaros with distinction in the 1830s. Now in a position of power and emboldened by events in the United States, García Conde put all the pieces together. He confidently explained to the house and senate that the "hordes of barbarians" were "sent out every time by the usurpers of our territory, in order to desolate the terrain they desire to occupy without risk and without honor." García Conde described an agreement whereby the United States provided the Indian raiders not only with arms and ammunition, but also with a political education, with "the necessary instruction they need to understand the power they can wield when united in great masses, which cannot be resisted in the desert without enormous difficulties."[55]

As spring turned to summer, Mexico's administrators had more and more reason to worry about the deserts in the north. On July 4, 1845, Texans overwhelmingly voted to accept the U.S. annexation offer. Some in Mexico cried for war. The influential newspaper *El Siglo XIX* understood that the republic was ill-prepared for a war against the United States, but, perhaps assuming that defeat would mean little more than the permanent loss of Texas, advocated conflict anyway: "Defeat and death on the banks of the Sabine would be glorious and beautiful; a peace treaty signed in Mexico's National Palace would be infamous and execrable." While President Herrera had taken a conciliatory view of the

Texan situation and continued to hope for a negotiated solution, he now felt
compelled to prepare for war. Congress authorized a loan of three million pesos
to fund the defense, and Herrera ordered troops to march north to the lower Rio
Grande. Meanwhile, more alarms were coming in from the frontier. A prominent northern general reported in August that Comanche raids had created
vast, unguarded wastelands that the United States was preparing to exploit in its
planned invasion.[56]

   This claim seemed all the more believable given some of the things norteamericanos were writing in their newspapers. In September, the *New Orleans
Tropic* reported that four hundred Comanches had left on a campaign into
Mexico: "It is to be inferred, therefore, that should it be necessary to increase
the force of Uncle Sam and Texas combined, to whip our *blanketed* neighbors
(than which, however, nothing is more absurd), the aid of the brave Comanches
could be secured." The *New Orleans Commercial Bulletin* went farther, reporting in late summer that thousands of Comanches were preparing for a major
campaign below the river. The editors thought this intelligence might make
Mexico less bellicose in its dealings with the United States: "It is probable that
the government of that nation will very soon have enough fighting within its borders without any need to look without in search of enemies." Given "the extraordinary magnitude of the indigenous force that has united along the line of the
Rio Grande, the temptations that the rich but weakened population of northern
Mexico present to the . . . savage, and the irresistible impulse that will carry
[American] immigration to the Pacific," the editors reasoned, all of northern
Mexico would soon be "engulfed in a terrible Indian war." Such an event would
"powerfully influence political relations" as well as Mexico's foreign policy and
"would have to be considered as a new element in diplomatic calculations."[57]

   A newspaper in Veracruz reprinted the *Bulletin* article, and Durango's *Registro Oficial* published the Veracruz translation with comments in August. While
the Durango editors admitted the gravity of the Comanche threat, they insisted
that the *Bulletin* exaggerated the situation "to no other end than to justify the
treachery with which our northern brothers conduct themselves." They rejected
the implication that the war against los bárbaros would necessarily prevent
Mexico from defending its territory against the "longing gaze" of the United
States. The *Registro* argued that Mexico had the resources necessary to cope
with both threats but added that everything hinged on Mexico City's willingness to take Comanches seriously and fortify the frontier. If the government did
so, Mexicans would soon have the opportunity "to teach a lesson to those who
call themselves civilized and fathers of American liberty, and in certain regards
exhibit more barbarism than those others who have not given up the state of

nature into which they were born and raised." A month later the newspaper repeated rumors that thousands of Texan and U.S. soldiers were massing outside
Corpus Christi, Texas, and that this force would be preceded by Indians. "The
war against the barbarians cannot be considered isolated and like the one our
fathers suffered through," the editors insisted, "but rather intimately linked to
the Texas war [by which they meant the looming conflict with the United States
over Texas], to which it is auxiliary and cooperative."[58]

By autumn there were some scattered indications that Indian raiding was
finally becoming a national priority. In October alone the central government
took several steps to improve security. It ordered regular troops to march into
Zacatecas and protect haciendas from raiders. The gunpowder factory in Zacatecas was ordered to ship to Durango all the powder the people of that department
needed to resist los bárbaros. The president also promised to send the residents
of Tamaulipas several hundred firearms and forty thousand rounds of ammunition. He authorized the shipment of one thousand guns to Arista in Nuevo León
so that frontier populations there could be equipped to mount a defense against
los indios and foreigners. And when Comanches campaigned through Durango
kidnapping dozens of children, the government sent a regiment of cavalry north
to pursue them, at the expense of the national treasury.[59]

Such measures hardly amounted to a coordinated plan to fortify the frontier,
but they were a start. And in fact a coordinated plan was in the works. Near the
end of October, Herrera recruited several prominent men with experience on
the northern frontier, including former president Anastacio Bustamante, General Vicente Filisola, and governors of northern states, to review the problem of
frontier defense and suggest systematic, structural reforms. Considering the government's perpetual fiscal crisis and the atmosphere of alarm brought on by the
standoff with the United States, the attention and resources devoted to defense
against Indians in these weeks reflected new thinking in the capital. At long last
a national response to the interminable bárbaro war seemed to be emerging.[60]

Given several years of relative peace, García Conde and Herrera may well
have reformed the frontier's defensive infrastructure, concentrating the republic's talent and resources upon what they and others were finally coming to see
as a project vital to national security. But Herrera's government had run out of
months and even weeks, let alone years. It made many enemies through an ambitious and long-overdue program of military reform that threatened the power
and prestige of important generals. Moreover, the administration suffered intense criticism over constitutional issues. Powerful voices throughout the republic insisted on a return to the federalist constitution of 1824, but Herrera insisted
instead on reforming the existing Bases Orgánicas, the conservative constitution

pushed through by Santa Anna in 1843. Finally, the administration's conciliatory policy toward Texas had left it open to easy attack. Herrera had argued that
Mexico ought to recognize Texan independence so that Texas would have no
need to annex itself to the United States. But Texans went ahead with annexation anyway, after the administration had expended much political capital convincing Congress that recognition made sense.[61]

The president still had room for hope. Mexico had severed diplomatic relations with the United States following its annexation offer to Texas, and in
November of 1845 Polk sent his envoy John Slidell to try and reopen talks.
Herrera risked even more of his dwindling credibility by initially agreeing to receive the envoy, but, expecting the message and the messenger to be conciliatory, hoped to win concessions and defuse the crisis. The president would have
found it extraordinarily difficult to achieve a compromise on the Texas issue,
but, to his chagrin, he soon learned that Slidell wanted even more. The envoy
demanded to be received as a formal minister, which would have meant de facto
restoration of diplomatic relations and therefore would have denied Mexico one
of its few points of leverage. Rather than offering apologies and face-saving com-
promises, Polk had instructed Slidell to insist that the Mexicans recognize annexation as a fait accompli. Most surprisingly, Slidell had also been told to purchase Upper California and New Mexico and to use the perennial complaint of
unpaid American claims against Mexico to pressure and facilitate the sale. The
envoy had been ordered to be discreet, but by the time he arrived in Veracruz
the press knew of his mission. One headline screamed "HORRIBLE BETRAYAL!"
Another paper proclaimed, "A few months more and we shall have no country
at all!" The government refused to receive Slidell in his formal capacity, but the
mere suggestion of selling national territory undermined the tottering administration all the more.[62]

By late 1845 every paper in Mexico City had turned against Herrera except
for the administration's mouthpiece, the *Diario del Gobierno*. His detractors had
many complaints. Ironically they turned the Comanche raids of 1845 into one of
the most visceral illustrations of the administration's failures. The prolific writer
Carlos María de Bustamante recalled that the papers were full of reports of los
bárbaros in late 1845: "The blood, the carnage, the bodies of many thousands of
animals and no small number of skewered people marked their passage. Everyone was clamoring for the government to supply troops and arms—just requests,
because they had neither, and this was a long-standing evil." Herrera's enemies
blamed the devastation on the government's ineptitude.[63]

In December General Mariano Paredes y Arrillaga led a coup that finally
ousted the embattled president. There was understandable consternation in

much of the northern press, which noted correctly that the coup had directed resources away from the frontier at the moment of its greatest vulnerability. Paredes tried to placate northern opinion. He immediately expressed his concern for the frontier and "ordered" the northern departments to reestablish the presidios, promising that the central treasury would send all the money it could. Like Santa Anna before him, however, Paredes was too preoccupied with Texas, with the conservative program, and with his own political fortunes to deliver the money he promised or to devote any real thought to independent Indians.[64]

Mexican history might have been different had Herrera retained power, but in truth he could have done little in the short term to reduce raiding on the northern frontier. Even in the waning days of his relatively solicitous administration, the north's commentators sounded increasingly pessimistic. A prominent hacendado in Zacatecas predicted that los bárbaros would inevitably continue pushing south, even into the department of Mexico, "taking advantage of our apathy and disorder." Editors in Durango likewise denounced the "horrible status quo" that existed in the defenseless, impoverished north, insisting that it was "without a doubt a precursor of a catastrophe that will strip us of our nationality." After years of complaints the frontier was still prostrate before Comanches, Kiowas, Navajos, and Apaches. And now, with U.S. troops massing in Texas, northerners were about to face "an enemy even more terrible who has planned to rob the Mexican republic of its richest and most fertile lands." The official paper in Coahuila seemed to speak for the entire north: "Mexico, cut, defeated, insulted by some gangs of barbarians! . . . Why have we no warriors to halt the devastation and ruin of the country? . . . Will it be necessary to prove, or even to write, that the war with the barbarians is eminently national? All of this has been done a thousand times."[65]

Indeed it had been done a thousand times. From the conflict's beginning in the early 1830s through the eve of the U.S. invasion, commentators such as Barreiro, Escudero, and Zúñiga, dozens of governors and military authorities, congressmen, editors, hacendados, mayors, businessmen, and citizens' councils had insisted that the war against los bárbaros was eminently national—that it was Mexico's war. Not until much too late, until the mid-1840s, did a paradigm emerge that situated Indian raiders in an unambiguously national context. Even then the new consensus relied upon a caricature that made independent Indians into norteamericano puppets. There is no evidence of systematic attempts in Texas or the United States to direct raids against northern Mexico. And there is no reason to believe Texans and Americans could have do so even if they had tried. In any case they never found it necessary. Independent Indian communities did not lack incentives to kill and kidnap Mexicans and to steal and destroy Mexican property.

But the emerging consensus on Indian raiding did contain a vital truth: the War of a Thousand Deserts would have implications for the looming conflict between Mexico and the United States. The war had done much to turn northern Mexico into a fragmented landscape of deserts, into the picture of poverty, exhaustion, fear, and rural desolation that the U.S. Army was preparing to march through. And there was one more basic consequence of Indian raiding, something that had less to do with what norteamericanos would find when they arrived than with the attitudes, ideas, and expectations they would bring with them. Padre Antonio Martínez from Taos was one of the few Mexicans to recognize it. He argued that in addition to wasting Mexico's wealth and population, the disastrous war against los bárbaros had also "degraded it and made it look ridiculous before other cultivated nations when they contemplate the evils with which these rabble overwhelm us, evils we neither prevent nor punish."[66]

In fact independent Indians were far more important for how Americans thought about Mexicans than even Martínez may have realized. Just as Mexicans of different ideological persuasions had invoked los bárbaros to create politically useful caricatures of their opponents, politicians in Texas and the United States during the 1830s and early 1840s invoked Apaches, Navajos, and especially Comanches to demean Mexicans. In so doing they articulated an image of northern Mexico, its inhabitants, and their leaders that would do much to shape the coming war.

8

HOW TO MAKE A DESERT SMILE

Nineteenth-century Matamoros was a city with two faces. One looked north and west into the high grasses and humidity of the lower Rio Grande, out across small farms and fields of corn watered by the river, and farther away to dry, scattered ranches covered in twisted mesquite and knots of sheep, mules, horses, and cattle. Many of the city's families had their fortunes in nearby farms and ranches. These places moved cattle, hides, and salt through the city, and in return they asked for cotton cloth, metal tools, sugar, and other goods. They also asked for protection and sent officials in Matamoros desperate letters about Indian raiders, begging for men and weapons, asking that the federal government be informed, bewailing the lives and animals and property they lost to raids.

The city's other face looked northeast, to busy sloops and steamships, across the Gulf of Mexico and over the old wooden docks in New Orleans where Americans and their slaves unloaded hides, mules, wool, and Mexican silver. In return the ships brought Matamoros a variety of European and American goods, including clothes, shoes, cotton, sugar, wheat, rice, and tobacco. By the 1840s several hundred foreign merchants lived in Matamoros, then the principal port in northeastern Mexico. As a rule these men paid little attention to the city's hinterland and its complaints about Indians. Richard Belt was an exception. A merchant and the U.S. consul in the city, Belt's duties had him facing squarely east, protecting and promoting U.S. commerce. But Mexican officials would have been dismayed had they known how keen his interest was in their troubles with Indians.[1]

On July 4, 1844, Mayor Francisco Lofero received news in Matamoros that los bárbaros had entered the district and were threatening nearby ranches. Again. The beleaguered mayor had tried and failed only the month before to mobilize an effective defense against Comanche raiders. Understandably skeptical about the likelihood of having better success this time, Lofero and the city's military commander scrawled out dozens of circulars warning residents that Comanches had returned and, resignedly, urging everyone to get into a defensive posture however they could. Belt obtained one of these notices, put it into an envelope, and mailed it to perhaps the last person in the world Mexican officials wanted eavesdropping on their Indian problems: U.S. Secretary of State John C. Calhoun. Belt introduced the circular by noting that "the Comanche Indians have become very troublesome in this neighborhood" and alerting the secretary to a curious passivity on the part of the Mexican government. "Although there are between five hundred and one thousand troops quartered here," Belt observed, "no effectual measures have been adopted to check their depredations. . . . The authorities have taken no notice of them, further than the publishing of the enclosed documents."[2]

After the Texas rebellion, U.S. officials started paying much closer attention to Texas and to northern Mexico more broadly. Between 1836 and 1846, Americans formed a mental picture of the Mexican north as a place of enormous potential that the Mexicans had patently failed to redeem from independent Indians. In fact, Indians seemed to be pushing Mexico backward and threatening even the center of the country as raids struck farther and farther south. These perceptions do much to explain why by 1846 so many Anglo-Americans felt entitled, even manifestly destined, to possess and redeem the region themselves. This supreme self-confidence began, appropriately, with Texas.

AN IMPORTANT PRELIMINARY: THE TEXAS CREATION MYTH

Before 1835 few Americans paid any attention to Texas. Those who did were mostly land speculators, adventurers, would-be emigrants out west, and a small cohort in Washington hoping to acquire the territory for the Union. John Quincy Adams had more to do with the region than most major politicians of the era, and he mentioned it only once in his diary during the period 1827 to 1836. Newspapers in the country ran very few articles on Texas during the same years, except in 1829, when Jackson's attempted purchase prompted a flurry of attention. But once news broke in the fall of 1835 that the American colonists had rebelled against Mexico and that a large Mexican army was marching to subdue them, everyone started talking about Texas. Supporters held public meetings all over the republic to express solidarity with the rebels and to send them men and materials. Texans needed to capitalize on this sentiment if they were to resist the approaching Mexican army. In December of 1835 they sent their most illustrious citizen, Stephen F. Austin, to tour the United States and promote the cause.[3]

Austin perfected a stump speech which he delivered in several states. His speech before an audience of twelve hundred in Louisville, Kentucky, was exemplary. He began by thanking the crowd. Everyone knew there was a war going on, he said. Texas was confident in her case, and he would now lay it before them. He began with a history lesson. "But a few years back Texas was a wilderness," he explained, "the home of the uncivilized and wandering Comanche and other tribes of Indians, who waged a constant warfare against the Spanish settlements." Austin said that Indians also desolated settlements south of the Rio Grande: "In order to restrain the savages and bring them into subjection, the government opened Texas for settlement. . . . American enterprise accepted the invitation and promptly responded to the call." He repeated this basic message in New Orleans, Lexington (Kentucky), Baltimore, Philadelphia, and New York.[4]

Austin's tour helped stoke American interest in and even passion for the rebellion, which in turn fueled a ready market for writing on Texas. During the 1830s and 1840s, newspapers and publishing houses in every region of the country rushed out articles, pamphlets, and books to meet the demand. Most authors felt compelled, as Austin had, to begin with history. "The leading object of the Mexican government in allowing the colonization of Texas," insisted Rev. Chester Newell in his *History of the Revolution in Texas*, "was undoubtedly the protection of her frontiers from the hostile incursions of the Indians." To support this argument, Newell and his contemporaries had to say something about Texas in the period prior to colonization—an era one dismissed as "little more than the history of the wandering tribes of savages." Before 1821, residents of San Antonio had been perpetually confounded by hostile Indians. "With much of the sloth and indolence, and without the courage that characterizes the savages of our continent," L. T. Pease explained, "almost everything without the walls of the town became prey to [Indian] depredations." William Wharton, another prominent Texan who had accompanied Austin on his fundraising trip through the United States, explained to his readers that Mexico's leaders had "ascertained that the savages could not be subdued by the arms of Mexico, nor could their friendship be purchased." It was likewise apparent to Mexico's political elite that it would be impossible to populate the region with their own people because Mexicans, "owing to their natural dread of Indians, could not be induced to venture into the wilderness of Texas."[5]

Other writers embarked on similar analyses. Dr. Joseph Field thought one of two deficiencies explained the sorry condition of the tejanos: "Either through a want of personal prowess or military skill, they were unable to repel the frequent incursions of their savage neighbors." William Kennedy, a British consul and the author of an influential book on Texas, explained that no substantial advances had been made there until 1821 because of the defects of the tejanos: "The Zamboes and other low castes who were detached to the north-eastern frontier of Mexico, were too lazy to cultivate the soil, and too cowardly to resist the aggressions of the northern Indians, by whom they were plundered at will." These terrified, shiftless settlers stood by while Indians "openly carried off herds of cattle and horses from the settlements east of the Rio Grande." Indeed, the raiders spared tejano lives, "not from motives of humanity, but because they deemed it impolitic to kill those who were so useful in raising horses and mules for the benefit of the Comanches."[6]

Surveying this dismal state of affairs officials in Mexico City became "more and more convinced from year to year, of the importance of interposing a barrier between themselves and their hostile neighbors, [and] at length acceded to the proposals of Austin and others to colonize the country with foreigners." And what became of Texas once the Americans got there? Within a few years of their arrival, boasted one author, the colonists "had given security to the Mexican frontiers from Indian depredations, and made the mountains the boundary of the savage." "Under the smiles of a benignant heaven," another proclaimed, "the untiring perseverance of the colonists triumphed over all natural obstacles, expelled the savages by whom the country was infested, reduced the forest to cultivation, and made the desert smile."[7]

Texas's own politicians, naturally, were the great proponents of their new Creation Myth.[8] The Texan minister to the United States expounded upon the story in detail in an early bid for annexation. In the fall of 1837 the minister wrote to the American secretary of state and begged leave to begin with an "exposition of the history of Texas," which he believed "to be an important preliminary to the due consideration of the subject of annexation." "Until the settlement of Austin's first colony in 1821," he explained, "Texas, for the most part was an unexplored wilderness. The Spaniards had endeavored, in vain, to rescue it from the wild tribes of the forest." True, the Spanish had established a few towns, but these were perpetually harassed and "surrounded by prowling parties of savage Indians." In a bid to "increase her political influence and resources by every means in her power, and prompted by a desire to repress the Indians on her northern frontiers," independent Mexico invited American colonists in. Once they came and established themselves, everything changed. Forests fell, prairies became corn and cotton fields, plantations were established, and villages sprang up "on the hunting ground of the savage." After nine short years in Texas, the minister concluded, the American pioneer had "redeemed it from the wilderness of the wild beast and the savage, covered it with a hearty and industrious population and intermixed his labor with its most valuable soils."[9]

Some Texans clearly believed that Americans had been invited to colonize Texas in order to save Mexicans from Indians. The canonization of this idea as the core of a Creation Myth, however, was a deliberate public relations move, and it obscured what seems to have been an even more widespread historical idea about Indians held by Texans themselves. When in 1836 Jackson's envoy Henry Morfit reported back to Washington on the principal causes for the rebellion, he listed "a refusal upon the part of Mexico to protect the Colonial settlements from the depredations of Indian tribes" as one of two or three complaints most commonly heard. Before he took his trip back east, Austin went farther. In a widely circulated letter he asked Jackson for protection because Mexicans were "exciting the Camanches and other Indians" against the colonists. Such grievances may have been heartfelt, but writers and politicians with interest in Texas soon abandoned them because they contradicted the Creation Myth that became so useful to the cause.[10]

The proponents of Texas were talking about a compact. American settlers had been invited to redeem Texas from Indians in return for land and the blessings of good government. Texans insisted that they had lived up to their end of the bargain. They had, through great sacrifices and hardship, expelled the Indians and "made the desert smile." Thus, as one writer put it, "the lands of Texas, although nominally given, were in fact really and dearly bought." Mexico, on the other hand, had not delivered good government. Morfit reported that the Texans' other most repeated grievances included Mexico's refusal to incorporate Texas into the federal system as provided for in the Constitution of 1824, the establishment in 1835 of a despotic centralist regime against the will of the people, and the passage of laws prohibiting further American immigration to Texas. As Texans themselves put it, Mexico "lost her right of sovereignty over Texas when she violated her compact."[11]

The Texas Creation Myth was thus an argument for the justice of taking part of Mexico away from Mexicans, and it operated on two distinct levels. The notion of the broken contract between Mexicans and the colonists was the first and most concrete level. The deeper and more far-reaching argument implicit in the Creation Myth was that Mexico had broken a contract with Texas itself— with the very land of Texas. Its forests and deserts bore mute witness to Mexico's failure to subdue the land. Texans argued that the initial invitation Mexico had extended to American colonists was itself born out of an inability to control Indians. Indeed, the two failures were one and the same. The logic of the Creation Myth made Indians into the great signifiers of, rather than the reasons for, Mexico's failures. Texas had been a land of forests and deserts not because Indians were strong, but because Mexicans were weak. Then Americans arrived, turned the forests and deserts into gardens, and gave "security to the Mexican frontiers from Indian depredations." In this sense the rebellion had despoiled Mexicans of nothing, because their own weaknesses had stopped them from ever really defending, cultivating, or improving Texas at all. If anything, Texas had been a liability. "Mexico, even under the government of old Spain," Newell wrote, "had been unable to subdue or restrain [the Indians], and she would have to abandon Texas altogether, if not other parts of her territory, had she not found a hardy people, willing, for the sake of a small portion of soil, to go in and subdue them."[12]

TO RECLAIM THE WILDERNESS:
TEXAS'S CONGRESSIONAL CHAMPIONS

The significance, appeal, and political utility of the Texas Creation Myth may be gauged in part by the frequency with which it was used in Washington during the 1830s and 1840s. The notion that Mexico had had trouble with Indians in Texas was not an entirely new one in the U.S. capital. Secretary of State Martin Van Buren had invoked it when Jackson tried to buy Texas in 1829, and Secretary of State Henry Clay had mentioned Comanches when President John Quincy Adams tried and failed to do the same four years earlier. But these were trial balloons. Only after 1836 did rampaging Indians become essential to U.S. political discourse about Texas.

Arguing for immediate recognition of Texan independence in April 1836, Senator Robert Walker understood from the start that the rhetorical fight over Texas hinged on history. "There were thousands of American citizens invited by Mexico to participate in the blessings of a Federal Government and of free institutions," he insisted to colleagues not yet familiar with the story, "invited to settle the wilderness, and defend the Mexicans against the then frequent incursions of a savage foe." Less than a month later, Representative E. W. Ripley echoed these sentiments in the House. The Mexicans had "made grants of lands to the early settlers of Texas for the double purpose of settling their wilderness, and, by creating a barrier against the Camanches and the Indians of Red River, to protect the inhabitants of the interior States." Given these facts, he angrily responded to the rebellion's critics, "the people of Texas hold their right of territory by a more just title than most of the States. They acquire it by the colonization of Mexico; by the Mexicans' plighted faith. [The Mexicans] have not conquered it from the savages, the native possessors."[13]

The Creation Myth received a more elaborate exposition as the recognition debate intensified, and Comanches increasingly came to stand for the entire native threat in Texas. As Representative Adam Huntsman explained it, "These hordes of barbarians would take possession" of the few tejano towns and "compel the inhabitants, who were large owners of stock, to go and drive up their own horses, mules, and cattle." Once all the animals were assembled, Comanches would "select all the most valuable of them, and drive them off, after committing acts of rapine and murder of the most atrocious character upon the inhabitants." In spite of all this suffering and outrage, "no help could be received from the Government at Mexico." Enter the Americans. "To stop those lawless excursions of plunder, murder, and robbery, to beat back those ferocious barbarians, and protect the Spanish citizens who were the annual victims of rapine and violence, the Mexican Government adopted the only practicable mode of affording that relief that she had in her power to render. It was to make large grants of land to citizens of the United States." Once Mexico took this step, Texas changed over-night. "Immediately upon these events, the savage roamed no longer in hostile array over the plains of Texas. They were beat back into their own boundaries," and, nodding to the clichés of eastern North America, "the tomahawk and scalping knife rested from their labors."[14]

The rhetorical and political stakes rose as the debates shifted from recognition to annexation. Mexico's broken covenant with the colonists receded, while its failure to populate and subdue Texas in the first place assumed central importance. John C. Calhoun thought he knew exactly what would have become of Texas had Americans not arrived: "They came there as invited guests; not invited for their own interests, but for those of Spain and Mexico, to protect a weak and helpless province from the ravages of wandering tribes of Indians;—to improve, cultivate and render productive wild and almost uninhabited wastes, and to make that valuable which was before worthless." The annexation debates thus called not so much for an exposition of the suffering and humiliation endured by early Spanish settlers in Texas as for descriptions of the vast, largely unrealized potential of the land itself. Texas as a neglected Eden thus became a hallmark of the congressional conversation. Consider the enthusiasm of South Carolina's William Preston. The territory of Texas, Preston insisted in 1838, "is one of the finest upon the whole earth." The commercial advantages of annexation were obvious: "Under a sun which ripens the sugar cane and coffee, the surface is as green as New England. . . . It is intersected at short distances by large rivers, which form bays and estuaries along the Gulf coast, eminently fitted for commerce." Preston came to his point: "Under the quickening influences of our policy and our people, this fine tract of country, doomed to be an eternal waste if possessed by the Mexicans or Camanches, will spring into a glorious and vigorous existence. Its fields will teem with the richest productions of the earth; its rivers will bear down to what should always be considered in the policy of this government as our sea (*mare nostrum*)."[15]

If the senators and representatives opposed to annexation had been better informed about Texas, they might have challenged the Creation Myth directly. The first half of the story, concerning the condition of Texas prior to 1821 and the rationale for allowing foreign colonization, was obviously oversimplified but essentially accurate. Spanish officials had indeed been frustrated by their attempts to increase the population and productivity of Texas, hence their willingness to entertain colonization. But the Texan version omitted something fundamental from this part of the story. Spain had never been very interested in Texas for the sake of Texas. The viceroys obviously would have been delighted to see the region become a populated and prosperous part of New Spain. The more realistic goal, however, was to establish and maintain enough of a presence there to keep other European powers away from more productive regions of the Mexican north. By 1800 the Spanish saw very clearly that the U.S. government was the principal external threat to New Spain's security. The Louisiana Purchase and Jefferson's subsequent attempts to acquire Texas magnified this threat many times over. To hear the congressional proponents of annexation tell it, American colonists had been invited solely to save Texas and Mexico from Indians. But the entire reason Spain felt so compelled to "conquer Texas from the savages," the reason it made the remarkable decision to differentiate between the American government and American colonists, was to strengthen its claim to Texas enough to protect it from U.S. expansion. The ultimate and ironic rationale for inviting American colonists into Texas, then, was not to save Texas from Indians but to save northern Mexico from Americans.[16]

Congressional enemies of annexation could have found still more to challenge in the argument that Texans had in fact been able "to beat back those ferocious barbarians, and protect the Spanish citizens." Undeniably, the American colonists had brought many times more land under cultivation in Texas than Spanish and Mexican settlers had. The great majority of these colonists had settled in the woodlands and well-watered bottomlands of east Texas, away from the bison range, where they could sustain themselves agriculturally in essentially the same way they had before immigrating. Plains Indians rarely ventured that far east. Indeed, the earnest general Manuel Mier y Terán observed that "the first advantage" of the lands chosen by the colonists was that they were "not frequented by the most powerful tribes of savages." More conscientious colonial leaders, Austin chief among them, had collaborated with Mexican authorities in campaigning against smaller indigenous groups that lived in the vicinity of the new settlements—Karankawas especially and Tonkawas and Wichitas to a lesser extent—all diminishing peoples whose lands excited Texan ambitions. But Congress had other Indians in mind. When senators and representatives took their turn at the Texas Creation Myth, the only native peoples they mentioned by name were Comanches, and the Texan colonists had done nothing of consequence to impede Comanche attacks south of the Rio Grande or even upon tejano settlements in Texas itself. Most Mexicans in fact believed that the Anglo-American colonies promoted raids on their settlements, either indirectly through trade or directly in a sinister bid to increase Mexico's miseries. And by the 1840s Mexicans were occasionally challenging aspects of the Texan Creation Myth directly, especially the oft-repeated notion that Americans had somehow redeemed Texas from independent Indians. In 1840, for example, Mexico City's official newspaper reprinted part of Kennedy's treatise and ridiculed his claim that the colonists had "liberated Texas from the savage tribes that devastate it."[17]

Anti-annexationists in the United States had little information about the native peoples of Texas and offered only an occasional, indirect challenge to the Texas Creation Myth. In a famous letter to Clay, for example, William E. Channing simply ignored Texans' inflated claims of conquest and warned that annexation would involve the United States in war with Comanche Indians, "described as more formidable than any in North America. Such foes are not to be coveted." But for the great majority of these dissenters, Channing included, Mexico's rights and Mexico's losses were distant secondary issues compared with what really mattered: African slavery. Anti-annexationists formulated this primary concern into a counterhistory of Texas sure to arouse even more passions than tales of rampaging Indians. "To introduce and perpetuate slavery was the original intention of many of the early immigrants," insisted Representative Archibald Linn while denouncing talk of annexation in 1842. The engine of colonization and of the rebellion itself had been a "strange combination of interests" between northern speculators and southern slave dealers united in a "grand ulterior object— the annexation of the territory to this government through the agency of slave holders." Champions of annexation rarely answered these kinds of accusations directly. They preferred to warn instead of the dangers of such divisive talk or, even better, to ignore it altogether. Through the late 1830s and 1840s, then, both sides talked history straight past each other, one side telling stories about Indians and the other about slaves. But when annexation went through in early 1845 it became clear that the hardy people who had been invited into Texas "to reclaim the wilderness from the Camanche and other tribes of Indians" had more friends than enemies in the U.S. Congress.[18]

The Texas Creation Myth is historically important for two reasons, only one of which concerns Texas itself. First, the myth facilitated annexation. U.S. politicians and officials who had known very little about Texas prior to 1836 seized on the Creation Myth, refined it, and made it foundational to whatever historical thinking informed the years-long debate over annexation. It is difficult to quantify the effect this crafted, historical argument had upon the debate. Nevertheless, its appeal to members of Congress suggests that American politicians saw the Indian history of Texas as central to the question of whether the United States had a right to annex territory Mexico still claimed as its own. The second and more far-reaching significance of the Texas Creation Myth is that it helped introduce a set of ideas about Mexicans and Indians into American political discourse at a moment when the republic started taking notice of the whole of northern Mexico for the first time. Beginning in 1836 U.S. officials had more information available to them about the Mexican north than ever before. They learned about the region and its conflicts with Indians through consular dispatches, public memorials, travel literature, and reports from various government departments. Moreover, newspapers across the country took an interest in northern Mexico and its security crisis. When raiders burned more than twenty people to death at Rancho de los Moros in Tamaulipas in the fall of 1844, for example, the *New Orleans Picayune* ran a story about the raid and the fierce battle that followed. The *Picayune* piece soon made its way into newspapers in other states, including Vermont, New York, Mississippi, Pennsylvania, Massachusetts, and Ohio. Finally, Kennedy's history of Texas and other books like it intersected with and informed this emerging body of writing and opinion about Mexico's vast northern territories. Americans increasingly came to see the Mexican north in the same way they saw the history of Texas before Austin and his colonists had arrived, complete with savage Indians, suffering Mexicans, and desolate wastes. The Texas Creation Myth explained why this was so. Most important, it provided a historical precedent for the belief that Anglo-Americans could do what Mexicans could not: make the desert smile.[19]

LAID THE WHOLE COUNTRY WASTE:
AMERICAN IMPRESSIONS OF THE MEXICAN NORTH

One of the first things U.S. readers learned was that Indians had been frustrating Mexico all across its northern territories. After Texas, Americans knew more about New Mexico than any other portion of the Mexican north thanks to the overland trade between Missouri and Santa Fe. As part of a memorial to Congress in 1839 concerning taxes on the trade, Missouri's assembly described New Mexico in stark and desperate terms. The broke, distracted central government of Mexico, the assembly explained, "has permitted their northern province of New Mexico to shift for themselves." Hence "the Camanches, Apaches, Narahoes, and other tribes, unawed and unrestrained, have swept everything before them. The plains and pastures of that province have now become waste and deserted, and her people impoverished." If only independent Indians could be kept in awe, the province would be a pastoral paradise: "New Mexico's flocks and herds would soon extend over the prairies to the waters of the Arkansas, for no country in the world is so well adapted to the raising of stock as the high, dry, and salubrious land of this neglected province." Moreover, the memorialists insisted, New Mexico's mountains contain vast, untapped mineral wealth. The few gold and silver mines that had already been put into operation had enormous potential, "but the hostile disposition of the Indians forbids their being worked."[20]

Other sources confirmed this picture of perpetual destructive warfare in New Mexico. The official journal of a U.S. military reconnaissance down the Santa Fe Trail in 1843 concluded with the observation that New Mexico "has been greatly impoverished, almost ruined in the last ten years" by hostile Indians. In 1844 Josiah Gregg informed his readers that Navajos had for several years "ravaged the country with impunity, murdering and destroying just as their humor happened to prompt them." When the Senate took up President Tyler's first Texas annexation proposal in early 1844, they requested information about Texas's boundaries. Tyler sent them a detailed report recently made by Lieutenant W. H. Emory, depicting a New Mexican population living "chiefly in walled towns, where they rally to dispel the warlike bands of savages that descend from the hills for plunder." Kennedy claimed that Comanches frequently raided settlements in New Mexico, stealing horses and other animals, and that their attacks had greatly complicated trade and travel between the province and other parts of Mexico. He explained that Albuquerque and El Paso, for example, "are still separated by a desert," where "travelers are obliged to move in armed companies, to secure themselves from the attacks of the Comanches."[21]

It was certainly the case that Navajos and occasionally other groups threatened New Mexican settlements. But Kennedy's book is typical of English-language sources from the period insofar as it exaggerated the territory's security problems and omitted the fact that New Mexicans enjoyed profitable relationships with Comanches. The situation below the Rio Grande was very different, and here Anglo-Americans came far nearer to the truth. In the summer of 1837, for example, the *Boston Courier* reported that five hundred Comanches had attacked Mexican residents on the lower Rio Grande, "killed about thirty of them and plundered and destroyed everything they could lay their hands on." On Chihuahua, Emory reported that "the Camanches still hold a large portion of this country, and keep its inhabitants in dread of their incursions." Gregg marveled at the "temerity" of Apaches and at the inability of Mexicans to stop them: "Small bands of three or four warriors have been known to make their appearance within a mile of the city of Chihuahua in open day, killing the laborers and driving off whole herds of mules and horses without the slightest opposition." The journalist George Wilkins Kendall wrote that Apaches were "gradually wresting their lands back from the Mexicans" and that they had pushed their raids even to the gates of Chihuahua City and "laid the whole country waste." In the summer of 1843 the *Boston Daily Atlas* informed its readers that Apaches were "spreading destruction and carrying dismay before them among the Mexicans along the whole line of the Rio Grande."[22]

Americans also knew that raiders went even farther, passing through what now is the northern tier of Mexican states to attack places where Spanish speakers had lived for centuries. For instance, Kennedy informed his readers that Indians had for many years "penetrated into the interior of Durango . . . plundering and destroying the villages, and driving off horses and cattle." Gregg described the Mexican north as a virtual wasteland. Indian depredations "have been of such long duration that, beyond the immediate purlieus of the towns, the whole country from New Mexico to the borders of Durango is almost entirely depopulated. The haciendas and ranchos have been mostly abandoned, and the people chiefly confined to towns and cities." In 1840, *Niles' National Register* reported that a raiding party of several hundred Indians had penetrated as far south as Real de Catorce, in San Luis Potosí. Geographically minded readers would have marveled at the distances involved. Had those same Comanches ridden east from their home ranges instead of south, they would have been in striking distance of Nashville or Atlanta.[23]

Occasionally Americans mentioned Apaches, Navajos, Utes, or Wichitas— but they saw Comanches as the great scourges of the Mexican north. Americans who paid attention believed that Comanches organized their huge "predatory incursions" with two goals in mind. First, they wanted horses and mules. In early 1841, for example, the *Pennsylvania Inquirer and Daily Courier* reported that Comanches had stolen ten thousand horses and mules from the vicinity of Saltillo. The second object of Comanche raids, as far as most American observers were concerned, was the characteristic that most made these Indians "unlike those who dwell on our borders, or within our territories." Comanches had seemingly made an industry of stealing people. The same official letters, newspapers, and books that reported Comanche raids for animals often included notice that the raiders had also "carried off several women," "made their escape with several captives," or "carried off a large number of women and children," "whom they invariably convert into servants."[24] Even northern Mexico's ruling class lost children. Thomas Farnham introduced his readers to a tale involving the fair daughter of the governor of "Chewawa," who had been kidnapped by Comanches. Her heartsick parents managed to locate her after much effort, only to hear that the girl refused to return home because her captors had covered her face with tattoos and because she had married a kindly Indian. In his memoir of 1846, the former U.S. minister to Mexico Waddy Thompson claimed there were "not less than five thousand Mexicans at this moment slaves of Comanches."[25]

By the 1840s, then, American officials believed that Comanches and other native peoples had long been desolating communities all across northern Mexico and beyond, ruining commerce, robbing or destroying herds and flocks, spoiling mines, stealing people, and, needless to say, causing untold suffering and destruction in the process. By the early 1840s congressmen could make casual reference to northern Mexico's sufferings, confident that their colleagues already knew the context. In a speech in 1842 concerning the U.S. ambassador to Mexico, for example, Representative Henry Wise of Virginia recklessly (if presciently) speculated about the United States seizing Mexican territory, insisting that "the Comanches should no longer hold the richest mines in Mexico." The reports that fed this pool of common knowledge sometimes exaggerated the situation in northern Mexico, especially when it came to captivity. Thompson's figure of five thousand slaves was wildly exaggerated—Comanches and Kiowas probably took fewer than eight hundred captives back across the river in the 1830s and 1840s, a remarkable figure in its own right but still far less than the minister and other captivity-obsessed Americans often imagined. Most American observers had considerably less to say about the far more common phenomenon of Indians killing people rather than stealing them. If anything, U.S. observers and officials significantly underestimated this dimension of the problem. They nonetheless knew enough to see Indian raiding as a major crisis for Mexico. In the midst of the astonishing Comanche invasions during the winter 1840–41, one Anglo-American writer saw a parallel to the invasion of Rome by northern barbarians, themselves forced south by still more powerful tribes: "This descent of the Comanches upon the Mexican provinces may likewise prove the harbinger of the downfall of the Mexican dynasty."[26]

CRAVEN WRETCHES: AMERICA'S COMANCHES

If American observers had such a dismal picture of the Mexican north, why did they think things were so bad? One sensible explanation would have been that Indians had been able to "overrun" northern Mexico because they were remarkably powerful. After all, from Jefferson on down, American administrations had worked hard (and failed, for the most part) to ingratiate themselves with the formidable Comanches. In 1805 General James Wilkinson had fretted that Comanches might prevent the United States from invading New Mexico one day, and officials in decades thereafter tried repeatedly to cultivate friendly ties with northern Mexico's native peoples, especially Comanches. The treaty that U.S. officials finally made with Comanches and other southern plains Indians in 1835 emerged from years of effort. And when that agreement proved inadequate in light of the Texas rebellion, Washington sent several parties out looking for Comanches in the early 1840s, each time loaded down with more and more gifts. Shifting and greatly exaggerated estimates of Comanche demography likewise betrayed official anxiety over their might. From 1838 to 1845 the commissioner of Indian affairs estimated the Comanche population at nearly twenty thousand, while the Indian agent Pierce M. Butler, who spent time on the plains negotiating with Comanches, initially reported a total population of fifty thousand.[27]

Sometimes nongovernmental observers also viewed Comanches with a measure of respect and even awe. Bitter about annexation, the editors of the *Barre Patriot (Massachusetts)* predicted in 1845 that Texas would suck the United States into a new Indian war, one worse than the Seminole quagmire in Florida: "This, indeed is an alarming threat—a war with the Comanches, the most formidable of all the savage tribes which have ever inhabited the new world, the only one which has not yet submitted to the yoke of civilization." Much of the travel literature from these years, especially that portion with no conspicuous axe to grind in defense of Texas, described Comanches as a massive, ubiquitous threat to everyone living in the vastness of northern Mexico. Comanches haunt the first half of Farnham's memoir *Travels in the Great Western Prairies* (1841) like wraiths: though the author never sees them, his breathless journey west toward the Rocky Mountains is propelled by stories of their bloodthirsty fury. Albert Gilliam painted a similar picture of Mexican territories south of the Rio Grande in his *Travels over the Tablelands and Cordilleras of Mexico* (1846). The author's trek took him by mule and foot across Zacatecas and Durango. In the midst of his journey, his guide and porters became greatly alarmed, along with everyone else in the region, at reports that Comanches had been raiding nearby, "killing and plundering the inhabitants to a considerable extent." As their journey progressed, Gilliam's men grew obsessed with the Comanche threat, stopping everyone they met to ask for news of "los indios" and threatening to abandon their increasingly anxious employer to his own devices.[28]

Some therefore admitted that Comanches were a formidable people. Nevertheless, Americans held highly contradictory and self-serving views about these Indians. By the 1840s, Texan and U.S. observers questioning Mexico's right and ability to retain its northern territories found it useful to denigrate the Indians that had "overrun" the Mexican north. To do so they took inspiration from stories that had filtered out of the southern plains during the 1820s and 1830s, tales that recounted the bloody encounters Comanches had had with Cherokees, Shawnees, Delawares, Creeks, and others before they came to terms (through U.S. mediation) in the mid-1830s. Comanches had suffered mightily in these attacks and battles, in large part because the eastern Indians they clashed with were far better armed. Indeed, for Comanches access to markets and to firearms was one of the dividends of making peace with these groups. But for Americans constructing a useful caricature of Comanches neither the early arms gap nor the eventual peace agreements mattered. The point was that Cherokees and others had gotten the best of their southern plains rivals. By dismissing Comanches in comparison to other North American Indians—Indians U.S. political leaders had for years been forcibly removing from eastern North America—Americans could slander the Mexicans who had succumbed to such a pathetic foe.

"These Indians [Comanches] are all in a very wretched and destitute condition," insisted Francis Moore in 1840. He claimed that Comanches were "despised and often insulted with impunity by the few roving Shawnees, Caddos, Cherokees, and other Indians from the United States, who often frequent the prairies of Texas for game." Gregg understood a hierarchy among independent Indians in northern Mexico. He wrote that Apaches would seem an especially brave people, given everything said about them: "But the Mexicans themselves call them cowards when compared with the Comanches; and we are wont to look upon the latter as perfect specimens of poltroonery when brought in conflict with the Shawnees, Delawares, and the rest of our border tribes." Thompson concurred: "Of all our Western tribes the Comanches are the most cowardly,—the Delawares frequently whip them five to one."[29]

Since Comanches did so poorly against other native peoples, it is unsurprising that most Americans thought they would do even worse against Americans. "The Indian saying," remarked a writer in the *Arkansas State Gazette*, "that one American can whip two Camanches, and that one Camanche can whip two Mexicans, is not far from the truth." This very notion was the heart of the Texas

Creation Myth. In 1836, a Philadelphia publishing house issued what it claimed was Davy Crockett's Texas journal, culminating in the very last entry the congressman and backwoods hero made before he was killed along with the other defenders of the Alamo. The bogus but popular account includes a sojourn Crockett made for several days among Comanches, who, naturally, recognized Davy's valor and twice offered to make him one of their own. But Crockett's fondness for Comanches went only so far. Once inside the Alamo, the doomed colonel delighted at hearing how nine Texans under the command of James Bowie, another soon-to-be martyr, had once defeated a party of Comanche warriors two hundred strong.[30]

In 1840 a published description of Texas included an even less believable tale that began with two merchants who had been fooled into thinking Comanches wanted to barter; one of the traders is stabbed to death and the other is wounded in the arm by their supposedly treacherous customers. The wounded man kept his wits, managed to raise his rifle up to his shoulder, "and sixty of the craven wretches were put to flight." In one of a series of articles in the popular *New Orleans Picayune*, Matt Field explained that Comanches "care little for the Spaniards, but they dread the Americans; and the first question these Indians asked of us was how many Americans were in our party." Kennedy, the great authority, dismissed the Comanches as "a nation of robbers." "Even a single American armed with the rifle has been known to keep large parties of them at bay," he explained. So it was that Comanches chose to attack Mexicans, "an enemy more cowardly than themselves, and who has been long accustomed to permit them to ravage the country with impunity." Moore's readers learned that Texans had "become so fully convinced of the weakness and cowardice of these Indians, that they now rather despise than fear them." Another author writing about Texas insisted that the "cowardly" Comanches posed no threat to white settlements, that in fact they "recede as fast as encroachments are made upon their territory." Gregg thought Comanches appeared "timid and cowardly" when they encountered Anglo-Americans, and the Texan commissioner of Indian affairs insisted that fifty armed men could probably ride through the whole of la comanchería unharmed.[31]

Given the nature of their enemies, then, it seemed all the more astonishing that Mexican authorities responded so passively. American observers were grimly fascinated by the inability or unwillingness of the Mexican state to protect its northern territories. Consular reports from Matamoros, for example, present a damning chronicle of governmental indifference and incompetence. In 1836 Consul D. W. Smith informed the secretary of state that "the frontier settlements have been exposed to these predatory incursions for many years past.

They have appealed to the government from time to time for protection but no vigorous measures have been yet adopted to repel them." In 1837 he described an Apache raid deep into Durango and added that they returned "without having met with a single soldier to oppose their aggressions." In early 1841 Smith noted with grudging respect that General Mariano Arista was finally poised to launch a decisive campaign against "the terrible plague of the barbarians" and sent his superior a copy of the general's fiery proclamation announcing his intention to annihilate the Comanches. Only three months later Smith forwarded Arista's tortured and defensive letter "in which he acknowledges his inability to make a campaign against the Indians this season." In one of the last dispatches Consul Richard Belt sent back from pestilent Matamoros before dying of a fever in 1844, he announced yet another Comanche invasion in the region and drew the secretary's attention to the outrages "which they are committing with perfect impunity."[32]

Americans, in contrast, could not simply stand by. Just as the Texas literature celebrated the American capacity to defend Mexican populations from Indians, the travel literature out of Mexico offered several examples of besieged Mexican populations desperately seeking Anglo-American protection against savages. James O. Pattie, who had traveled extensively through northwestern Mexico in the decade before the Texas rebellion, recounted an episode in which New Mexican authorities enlisted his party to rescue several captives from Comanche raiders. Once the mixed Mexican and American force overtook the Indians and the Comanches turned to attack, the Mexicans fired their weapons and fled the field. "Stand resolute, my boys," Pattie's American commander told his men, "although those ** Spaniards have deserted us, when we came to fight for them. We are enough for these ** devils alone." The American force defeated the Indians, and, naturally, Pattie himself rescued the beautiful Spanish daughter of New Mexico's ex-governor. Albert Pike narrated a similar episode in his (purportedly true) story "Inroad of the Nabajo." Pike's friend and informer recounted a night when alarms went off in the town of Taos in northern New Mexico because around one hundred Navajo warriors were stealing animals. The Americans resident in the town rushed out to join the Mexican men in confronting the raiders. As soon as the Navajo charged, however, the Mexican "heroes who had been chattering and boasting in front of the Americans, shrunk in behind them, and left them to bear the brunt of the battle." The Navajos eventually escaped with some of their booty, but they paid a high price thanks to the valor of the Anglo-Americans and Pueblo Indians who charged the enemy while the cowardly Mexicans hung back.[33]

Such stories must have been reassuring to Anglo-American readers, but these in particular were inventions. Aside from the fact that Pattie's story finds no support in Mexican sources, it flies in the face of the Comanches' long-standing alliance with New Mexico, a relationship they respected scrupulously according to Governor Manuel Armijo. And according to Pike's informant, the Navajo attack on Taos took place sometime in the mid-1820s. None of several careful students of Navajo–New Mexican conflict have located reference to such an event outside of Pike's account, and in any case it was exceedingly rare for Navajo raiding parties to contain dozens of men, let alone a hundred. In other words, Americans often obtained credible information about Indian raids, but they seem to have invented most of the stories they told about saving helpless Mexicans.[34]

While other Americans made idle boasts about defending Mexicans against Indians, James Kirker became a celebrity among these braggarts by making his living that way. The scalp hunter undoubtedly made life worse for Mexicans because his actions only fueled cries for vengeance within Apache communities. But unlike Pattie and Pike, Kirker never needed to invent. In an interview in 1847 he said that he and his mercenaries had killed 487 Apaches, losing only 3 men in the process—a claim his most careful biographer more or less accepts. American newspapers entertained their readers with reports of Kirker's scalp hunters, and the popular authors Kendall, Gregg, and Kennedy all recalled his deeds. Matt Field thought he was "brave as a lion," "a man of reckless and daring disposition." The scalp hunter even impressed Senator Thomas Hart Benton, the most powerful western politician of his day. The senator gladly wrote Kirker a letter of introduction in 1848, which read in part, "When the savages were overrunning the Department of Chihuahua, he raised a few Americans, never exceeding twenty-three, and with them protected the settlement and repulsed the savages until the fame brought upon him the persecution of the Mexican officers, to whose conduct his own was a reproach." Known as "the Terror of the Apaches," Kirker represented to his admirers the ferocious, bloody apex of what Americans could accomplish in the deserts of northern Mexico. Apaches, Comanches, and other groups may have reduced Mexicans to helpless terror, but U.S. observers thought they had all the proof they needed that these Indians were as nothing before their intrepid kinsmen.[35]

THE MOST POISONOUS COMPOUND:
AMERICA'S MEXICANS

Native military might or political coherence could not account for northern Mexico's condition, so other explanations were called for. American writers paid little attention and gave even less credence to Mexico's claim that traders and

provocateurs from Texas or the United States were to blame for the most destructive raids. On November 17, 1844, for instance, the *New Orleans Picayune*
reported ongoing Comanche raids below the river: "The Mexicans, as usual, attribute these collisions to the enmity of the Americans, foolishly supposing that
the Indians are supplied with their ammunition, etc., from the American trading
posts." Soon after, the *Picayune* reported that Mexican forces fought Comanches in Tamaulipas and "pretended" to find U.S. peace medals on fallen Indians: "This they imagine to be a sign of utmost significance of the hostile designs
of this country upon their own. How idle the supposition we need not say." In
1845 when a large party of Hois under Potsanaquahip informed Texan authorities
of their plans to strike northeastern Mexico, "to make reprisals for some losses
they have recently sustained in that quarter," the *Richmond Whig* took the high
ground: "[We] presume that the Indians will neither be encouraged to make war
upon the feeble frontier of Mexico, or permitted to come within the vicinity of
our own settlements. Had Texas been disposed to imitate the examples of some
older nations in the employment of Indians as soldiers, many calamities might
have been inflicted upon Mexico which have been prevented."[36]

While these commentators rejected Mexico's own explanation for its collisions with independent Indians, some few took the trouble to look for systemic,
national distractions to explain the security crisis. Falconer, an Englishman,
tried to put the situation in context by suggesting that New Spain's presidio system had kept independent Indians under control and allowed for the expansion
of Spanish-controlled territory. In the absence of funds to maintain the presidios,
however, the Mexican settlements had actually been driven backward. "This
state of things may not last[,]" Falconer stated, "but it has been the consequence
of an unsettled government, which has hitherto been compelled to concentrate
its forces in the interior to sustain itself, while its frontier has been commanded
by savages." Representative Adam Huntsman likewise saw Mexico's northern
problems as consequences of national misfortunes that had dogged the republic
since at least 1810: "Being torn to pieces by civil and central revolutions, which,
succeeding each other in rapid succession, their finances were exhausted, their
armies were wasting away in civil wars, their convulsions were so quick and
terrible that they could not spare either men or money to defend the frontiers
against the habitual attacks of the Camanche and other hostile Indian tribes."
Albert Gilliam added a bit of sinister agency to this view. He suggested that President Santa Anna had deliberately withdrawn Mexican forces from the northern
frontier "to sustain himself in power at home, and to make the northern provinces a wilderness, inhabited alone by barbarous Indians, to prevent Mexicans

from making settlements, and thus cut off the emigration of foreigners to those regions."[37]

Even Gilliam's conspiratorial analysis was generous compared to the usual interpretations of Mexico's Indian problems. Typical explanations focused on flaws inherent to the Mexican population—especially cowardice. The charge carried with it more than the usual dose of irony, given that the furor of Comanche and Kiowa attacks had much to do with Mexican successes at killing native warriors and that Apache leaders like Mangas Coloradas relied upon the memory of kin slain by Mexicans to help motivate their followers for war. Nonetheless, America's Mexicans were cowards through and through. Writing about Apache depredations in Chihuahua, for example, Gregg insisted that the occasional efforts at pursuing Indian attackers did nothing but "illustrate the imbecility" of Mexicans, who were "always sure to make a precipitate retreat, generally without even obtaining a glimpse of the enemy." Despite this, the newspapers in Chihuahua "always teem with flaming accounts of prodigious feats of valor performed by the 'army of operations' against los bárbaros." Another author noted that Mexicans were "braggadocios in security, but when in danger, generally appearing to be much more afraid of the Indians than the Indians are of them." Pike put the sounds of empty Mexican bravado to bad poetry in his "Song of the Nabajo:"

> Whose mouth is so big as a Spaniard's at home?
> But if *we* rush along like the cataract foam,
> And sweep off his cattle and herds from his stall,
> Oh then to the saints who so loudly can call?[38]

Along with cowardice, American observers blamed Mexico's Indian problem on Mexican sloth, physical weakness, and stupidity. More holistic thinkers gathered all of these condemnations together under the roof of racial theory, where U.S. perspectives on Mexico's Indian troubles intersected with a fateful realignment in American identity. By 1844, most of America's intellectual and political elites thought of themselves as belonging to a separate and superior Anglo-Saxon race destined to take possession of North America from other "retrograde" races. Senator Benton, for example, thought the Texas revolt had "illustrated the Anglo-Saxon character, and given it new titles to the respect and admiration of the world." Much of the intellectual nourishment this transformation depended upon came from Europe, and it matured during America's long experiences with African American slaves and with Indians. In both cases, controversies during the 1820s and 1830s ignited feverish attempts to shore up the intellectual foundations of racial science. Pseudoscientific monographs on the phenomenon and consequences of race mixing, the emerging fields of ethnological classification and phrenology (the study of character and mental capacity through close examination of skulls), and historical attempts to locate the genesis and developmental trajectory of the Anglo-Saxon race all lent legitimacy to hardening and self-serving racial values. Proponents of slavery defended their institution against abolitionist rhetoric with increasingly complicated racial logic. Likewise, the architects of Indian removal relied upon a growing body of literature heralding the inevitable extinction of inferior races before the God-ordained march of the Anglo-American millions. Once Mexico became a topic of interest, Mexicans themselves became a third group to define and demean as America's "new ruthlessness of racial confidence" neared its zenith during the years between the Texas revolt and the U.S.–Mexican War.[39]

The political use of the term *Anglo-Saxon* in a strictly racial sense was unusual in the early 1830s but commonplace by the 1840s. This rhetorical shift was paced by a steady increase in damning descriptions of "mongrel" Mexicans. Senator Robert Walker of Mississippi, always ahead of the pack in this kind of thinking, calculated as early as 1836 that only one Mexican in seven was "of the white race." The rest were "Africans, and Indians, Mettizoes, Mulattoes, and Zamboes, speaking twenty different languages, and constituting the most poisonous compound that could be amalgamated." Could such a people, he demanded, ever hope to or be allowed to populate Texas and the valley of Mississippi? "No," he thundered, "it never could, it never ought, it never would have been permitted by the people of the West."[40]

American eavesdropping on the bloody conversations between Mexicans and Indians in the decade after the Texas revolt had the effect of denigrating the Mexican stereotype even farther. In a fundamental, physical sense, Mexican blood was to blame for the Indian raids that had so retarded the development of northern Mexico. Descriptions of fantastically destructive raids and dismissals of the Indians involved as pathetic cowards translated into even more profound condemnations, implicit and explicit, of the "poisonous" mongrel race that allowed such things to happen. The Texas Creation Myth had depended upon tales of Mexican "Zamboes" who, from either "their dread of Indians" or their "want of personal prowess or military skill," had been "too lazy to cultivate the soil, and too cowardly to resist the aggressions of the northern Indians." Tales of raids from elsewhere in northern Mexico had the similar effect of rhetorically invalidating Mexico's claim to the land, only on a much larger scale. In 1845, for example, the *Boston Daily Atlas* reprinted an editorial from a Texas paper which noted that an Indian war raged all along the Rio Grande from its source to its mouth: "Indeed, it is not improbable that the whole province of Chihuahua and Santa Fe may be in the possession of Indian tribes in the course of five or ten years, unless the government of the United States interposes its authority. For this reason Mexico would derive an immense advantage from annexation."[41]

Ambassador Thompson, who had nothing but contempt for Comanches, also thought that the unending Indian raids presented the best proof against Mexico's future in North America: "I do not think that the Mexican men have much more physical strength than our women," he began. "They are generally of diminutive stature, wholly unaccustomed to labor or exercise of any sort, and as a conclusive proof of their inferiority to our own Indians, I will mention the fact that frequent incursions are made far into the interior of Mexico by marauding bands of Comanches, who levy black mail to an enormous extent upon the northern provinces of Mexico." When, near the end of his memoir, Thompson again linked Indian raids with Mexico's perceived inability or, more exactly, illegitimate and unrealistic aspiration to retain possession of its northern territories, he was expressing what most other American observers had also come to believe: "That the Indian race of Mexico must recede before us, is quite as certain as that that is the destiny of our own Indians, who in a military point of view, if in no other, are superior to them."[42]

Starting in 1845, the United States began to take decisive steps in its relations with Mexico. President James K. Polk would have much preferred to purchase New Mexico and California than go to war. He believed that his envoy John Slidell would convince the Mexicans to accept the Rio Grande as Texas's boundary and to part with the other territories for a reasonable price. Secretary of State James Buchanan had armed Slidell with familiar arguments, including the long-standing complaint that Mexico still owed U.S. merchants and firms several million dollars in outstanding claims. These might be eliminated through a transfer of land. Moreover, Mexico should be glad to rid itself of the difficulty and expense of protecting New Mexico against "tribes of fierce and warlike savages." And by ceding its northern territories Mexico would "purchase security against [Indian] attacks for her other provinces . . . as it would at once become the duty of the United States to restrain the savage tribes within their limits, and prevent them from making hostile incursions into Mexico."[43]

But if the Mexicans remained unconvinced there was never any doubt that Polk was willing to go to war to get what he wanted. In January 1846, shortly after the Mexican president José Joaquín de Herrera had refused to receive Slidell in his official capacity, but before the envoy finally abandoned his mission, Polk ordered General Zachary Taylor to march his forces to the Rio Grande. This extraordinarily provocative move made war all but inevitable.

Texans had claimed that their boundary extended to the Rio Grande ever since they captured Santa Anna in 1836 and the Mexican troops followed his orders and withdrew across the river. Mexicans refused to recognize Texan independence at all and thought the Rio Grande claim especially disagreeable. At the time of the rebellion Texas had been joined with Coahuila, and most of the region between the Nueces and the Rio Grande belonged to the state of Tamaulipas. Even if Mexico had acknowledged Texan independence, the Texan boundary would have been the Nueces. While Indian raids had forced many families to flee the region, Mexicans still had ranches, dwellings, and even a modest city, Laredo, north of the Rio Grande. Finally, the Texans insisted that their borders ran to the source of the Rio Grande, somewhere in present-day Colorado, and therefore that all of the New Mexican settlements east of the river, including Santa Fe, belonged to them. Some Spanish-speaking families had been in this region for two and a half centuries, and the wild notion that they had suddenly become Texans likely provoked as much laughter in Mexico as condemnation.[44]

Nonetheless, Polk became champion to these fictions, in large part as a way of pressuring Mexico into a deal. Taylor left his base near Corpus Christi and marched his troops through the high grass and humidity of the lower Rio Grande. In late March he established his forces within bombing range of Matamoros. Mexican authorities denied the right of the U.S. Army to be where it was and refused to accept Taylor's proposed armistice because that could strengthen his claim to the Rio Grande. In response Taylor constructed a fort, trained cannon upon Matamoros's town square, and soon ordered a blockade of the port to deny food and other supplies to soldiers (and civilians) inside the city. What for Mexican officers had been a very difficult situation now became an impossible one. Back in Washington the president received more discouraging news from Slidell and by mid-April began accommodating himself and his cabinet to the idea that it would indeed take a war to acquire California and New Mexico. Everyone agreed it would be much better if Mexico started open hostilities—a distinct possibility given Taylor's hostile moves—but by early May the president grew tired of waiting. He drafted a war message and decided, even in the absence of Mexican military provocation, to risk sending it to Congress.

He was spared the embarrassment. On May 9, 1846, Polk received the providential news that some of Taylor's men had been killed and others taken prisoner by a detachment of Mexican soldiers on the north side of the Rio Grande.

The president hastily rewrote his war message and sent it to Congress two days later. It detailed the innumerable injuries and insults Mexico had heaped upon the United States as well as America's extraordinary history of forbearance: "The grievous wrongs perpetrated by Mexico upon our citizens throughout a long period of years remain unredressed; and solemn treaties, pledging her public faith for this redress, have been disregarded." Now, with the killing of U.S. soldiers, he solemnly announced, "the cup of forbearance has been exhausted. . . . Mexico has passed the boundary of the United States, has invaded our territory, and shed American blood upon American soil." He demanded vengeance, asking Congress "to recognize the existence of war" and provide him with the funds and authority necessary to prosecute it.[45] The bill the Democrats produced fused recognition of the war, Polk's assertion that Mexico, not the United States, had instigated it, and funding for troops already in the field into a single question, yea or nay. Congressional opponents of Polk's scheme complained bitterly, yet, agonizing over what they saw as a choice between conscience and patriotism, between supporting a wrong and taking a major political risk, finally gave the president everything he asked for. The war was under way.[46]

More precisely, the second war was under way. Northern Mexico's first war was with independent Indians, and the U.S. leadership understood this very well. Over the previous ten years Americans had come to see and to describe the whole Mexican north as a vast theater for an unfolding race war between mongrel Mexicans and the most savage and politically undeveloped of American Indians. This observation informed U.S. expectations about Mexico's willingness to sell its northern territory, Mexico's ability to defend that territory, and the way in which northern civilians would receive the U.S. Army. However imperfectly they understood its causes and dynamics, Polk and his generals knew that Mexico's Indian war was real. They intended to make the most of it.

Part Three

CONVERGENCE

9

A TROPHY OF A NEW KIND IN WAR

The U.S.–Mexican War is remembered as the conflict that brought trium-phant American troops to Mexico City and "the halls of Montezuma," but President Polk and his advisors wanted and initially intended to wage the war entirely in northern Mexico. Their plans differentiated between the far north and the tier of more developed departments from Sonora to Tamaulipas. The far north included regions that the administration was determined to possess permanently: the vast, poorly defined territories of California and New Mexico and the disputed land between the Nueces and the Rio Grande. Polk ordered the military to immediately conquer and occupy key points in these three places. He also wanted the army to occupy the region stretching from northeastern Mexico to Chihuahua. Behind closed doors the president and some of his cabinet would advocate annexing this more southerly region to the United States as well as everything to the north, but official policy remained ambiguous in 1846. Therefore in the early months of the war the campaign below the Rio Grande was primarily intended to break Mexico's will, to force its leaders to negotiate and cede their far northern territories. Polk believed that the fighting would be quick and relatively easy and that Mexico's government would feel compelled to negotiate as soon as his army achieved its objectives in the north.[1]

In limiting combat to northern Mexico the president and his advisors knew well they would be imposing one war on top of another. They understood that the army would literally be marching in the footsteps of Comanches, Navajos, and Apaches, marching through places where Indians and Mexicans had been killing, capturing, and impoverishing one another for a decade or more. This knowledge shaped U.S. expectations about the feasibility, duration, and difficulty of the coming conflict, and it also influenced the administration's overall war and occupation strategy.

But the War of a Thousand Deserts was an ongoing reality as well as an idea. While Americans hoped to exploit the conflict, it was not something they could control. Northern Mexicans and independent Indians saw their own opportunities in the contest between the U.S. and Mexican governments. Many Mexicans hoped that their norteamericano invaders would act as champions or at least provide security against Indian raids. Comanches, Apaches, and Navajos hoped and initially expected that the U.S. Army might help them against Mexican enemies or at least distract Mexicans and thereby indirectly facilitate raiding campaigns. All of these things came to pass, to a degree; and yet very little played out according to expectations. As the U.S.–Mexican War and the War of a Thousand Deserts converged between 1846 and 1848, each influenced the other in ways that have been all but forgotten. Sometimes the result was frustration and distraction for the U.S. Army, sometimes difficulties and dangers for independent Indians. While it lasted, however, the often chaotic convergence helped them both get what they wanted from Mexico.

THE AMERICAN INVASION OF THE MEXICAN NORTH

Combat began for the U.S. Army when General Mariano Arista's troops killed and captured a number of U.S. soldiers north of the Rio Grande in late April 1846. Emboldened, the Mexican general crossed the river himself and led a full attack on U.S. positions on May 8. Arista hoped he could beat Taylor and end the war before it really began, but the Battle of Palo Alto would inaugurate a pattern of Mexican defeat that continued throughout the conflict. Though Arista had more men than his rival (thirty-three hundred vs. twenty-five hundred), Taylor took the day, in large part because of his light artillery—weapons that could be quickly relocated anywhere on the battlefield and were used to terrible effect against masses of Mexican soldiers. Arista withdrew his shocked and bloodied men at nightfall, only to suffer another, more decisive defeat at the Battle of Resaca de la Palma the following day. The Mexicans made a chaotic retreat across the river to Matamoros. Realizing he could not defend the city without bringing much suffering down upon its inhabitants, and probably not even then, Arista withdrew his army and left Matamoros to the invaders. His soldiers deserted in droves. The embattled, now-discredited general was removed from command, and his successor marched what remained of the Army of the North to Monterrey. Taylor stationed troops along the lower Rio Grande and in September, after three months of incorporating and training volunteers and new regulars, laid siege to the city. Following three days of fierce urban fighting, the Mexican commander proposed an armistice and evacuated his men from Monterrey. By October Taylor controlled most of northeastern Mexico.[2]

Meanwhile, the U.S. occupation of New Mexico had unfolded with more suspense but less drama. In July word reached Santa Fe that a norteamericano force was on the march from Missouri, and all eyes turned to Governor Manuel Armijo. By 1846 Armijo was more widely known in the United States than any other Mexican besides Santa Anna. His notoriously idiosyncratic (many would say corrupt) dealings with U.S. traders and, especially, his cruel treatment of the hapless Texan Santa Fe expedition in 1841, recounted ad nauseam for American readers, had helped put a sneering face on the worst anti-Mexican stereotypes. While many American business associates in New Mexico thought well of him, the governor was pilloried by the U.S. press throughout the early 1840s (the trader Charles Bent tormented Armijo by sending him copies of the *New Orleans Picayune* so that the governor could "see what is said of him.") In U.S. books and newspapers Armijo emerged as the very picture of dishonesty, depravity, and cowardice—that is, as America's archetypal Mexican man. Now everyone wanted to know what Armijo would do.[3]

The first thing he did was request help from Durango and Chihuahua. By August it became clear that none would come. Armijo came to terms with the fact that he would have to lead the defense himself, with only nuevomexicanos in his ranks. Caricatures aside, Armijo had always been adept at turning good fortune to maximum political advantage, and as governor he had competently organized a number of campaigns against Navajos. But he was no great military man, and certainly no hero. He decided to flee before the U.S. Army arrived. Other New Mexicans felt honor-bound to resist, however, and let their governor know in no uncertain terms that they required his services. By mid-August Armijo found himself the reluctant leader of a huge number of New Mexicans assembled with whatever weapons they could find in Apache Canyon north of Santa Fe. A committee of citizens reported after the fact that more than four thousand men had converged on the canyon, men willing to leave their families and properties "exposed to the incursions of the savages" in order to protect the fatherland. U.S. observers later said it would have been nearly impossible to take the canyon had the New Mexicans fought to keep it. But, reviewing the ragtag force assembled around him, Armijo apparently agreed with the analysis of another prominent nuevomexicano that, in the end, he was but "a dwarf against a giant." He sent everyone home. Armijo then mustered the department's few professional soldiers and unceremoniously decamped to Chihuahua. U.S. General Stephen Kearny entered Santa Fe on August 18, occupied New Mexico's

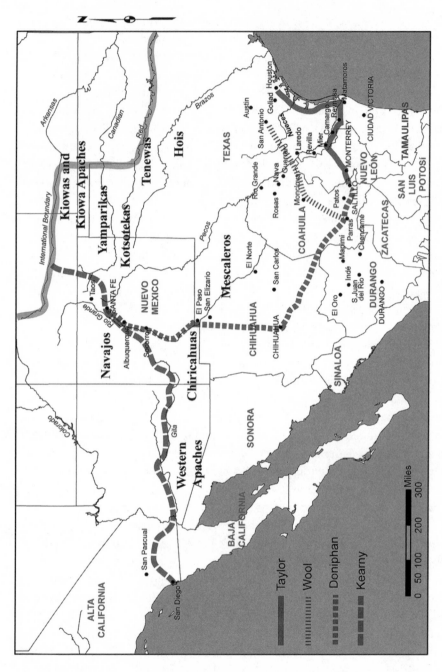

6. The northern theater of the U.S.–Mexican War. Routes based on Eisenhower, *So Far From God*, frontispiece

principal towns without violence, and informed the sullen inhabitants that New Mexico was now part of the United States.[4]

In short order Kearny installed the canny trader Bent as New Mexico's territorial governor, organized a small detachment, and marched south and then west through the Gila Valley to southern California, relying on the famous mountain man Kit Carson as guide. When Kearny reached California, he found that U.S. forces were about to lose what they had just won. As early as June of 1846 the U.S. explorer John C. Frémont had helped lead a revolt in California against the Mexican government, and in the summer U.S. warships arrived to occupy the coastal towns of San Francisco and Monterey. Together the navy and Frémont's forces had secured most of California's settlements, but by autumn a formidable resistance movement in the south put the U.S. victory in doubt. Kearny arrived in the midst of the struggle (nearly losing his life in it), and it took the combined U.S. forces until January to bring the resistance to an end.

Next came Chihuahua. Colonel Alexander Doniphan and his regiment, part of Kearny's force, had stayed behind in New Mexico, and in winter they marched south to expand the conquest. The colonel and his men emerged as the golden boys of the war. Editors compared Doniphan to Cortes and Xenophon, and the public hailed his motley volunteers from Missouri, who shunned the pomp and discipline of the regular army, braved any odds, and won some of the conflict's most lopsided victories. On Christmas they battled Mexicans from El Paso—locals accustomed to individual combat against Apaches. Doniphan easily drove them from the field in the so-called Battle of Brazito. Upon occupying El Paso the colonel gratefully accepted an offer of assistance from the fierce old scalp hunter James Kirker, who put his familiarity with Chihuahua's physical and political landscape at the colonel's disposal. Officials in Chihuahua City scrambled to cobble together an effective defense. By mid-February they had raised between fifteen hundred and two thousand men to be led by the generals José A. Heredia and Pedro García Conde, the former minister of war who had warned the republic of the sinister connections between Indian raiding and U.S. territorial ambitions. Kirker took Doniphan's Missourians through the dry country south out of El Paso to meet the Mexican force on February 28, just fifteen miles outside Chihuahua City at a place called Sacramento. After some pitched fighting the larger Mexican force broke and abandoned the field. Doniphan had taken both El Paso and Chihuahua City with only four of his men killed.[5]

Just days before the charmed Missourians celebrated their stunning victory Taylor nearly suffered a disastrous defeat at the hands of Mexico's phoenix, Santa Anna. In 1844, as an exile, he had taken refuge in Havana. As Mexico and the United States drifted into war, his agents convinced the Polk administration that if it could help get the disgraced president-general back into Mexico he would work to secure a negotiated settlement. The administration naively ordered the navy to let Santa Anna through its blockade and, once upon Mexican soil in August 1846, he immediately set to work preparing an army to drive U.S. forces from the republic. A coup begun early that month had forced Mariano Paredes from power in September and reinstituted the federalist constitution of 1824. By early December Santa Anna had been elected president under the newly revived federalist system (which, among other things, turned departments back into states), and by the end of January he started marching more than twenty thousand soldiers north from San Luis Potosí to engage Taylor's army.

Santa Anna's men endured terrible cold and fatigue, lacked proper clothing, food, and supplies, and died or drifted away by the hundreds as they traversed a barren country, noting along the way ghostly ranches and haciendas abandoned because of Comanche raids. By the time he reached Monterrey in late February the president had lost thousands of men. But still, he had three times the army Taylor did, and on the outskirts of an hacienda on the vast Sánchez Navarro latifundio he threw it at the norteamericanos with terrific force. Mexican troops came under withering fire and yet maintained their formations, nearly breaking U.S. lines on several occasions. By the end of the day the bloody battle can fairly be said to have been a draw, and by some accounts Taylor went to sleep that night expecting to be defeated in the morning. But by then more than a fifth of Santa Anna's men had been killed or wounded or had gone missing. Knowing that the republic would have little or no defense should his army be beaten decisively and, more important, beset by political anxieties over events in Mexico City, the president-general gathered up the wounded men likely to survive the trek and retreated in the night to San Luis Potosí. The Battle of Angostura (or the Battle of Buena Vista, as Americans called it) was the last major engagement in the north and the closest that Mexicans ever came to turning the tide of the war. At the end of February 1847 the United States had secure possession of most of northern Mexico.[6]

DELICATE MOVEMENTS:
COURTING MEXICANS AND INDEPENDENT INDIANS

Before and after these great confrontations, away from the din and the sick thrill of battle, U.S. officials quietly but persistently worked to ingratiate themselves with the diverse peoples of northern Mexico. The army not only had to defeat its counterparts on the field; it also had to sustain an occupation amid a long and bitter war between Mexicans and independent Indians. This presented challenges as well as opportunities because being friend to one might make enemies of the other. But Americans navigated the contradictions and ambiguities beautifully, at first.

Comanches received promises of American goodwill before anyone else. Authorities at the U.S. War Department had been trying to arrange a comprehensive peace agreement with the native peoples of Texas, especially Comanches, since the early 1840s. A treaty had been in effect since 1835, but given the Texas revolt and the likelihood of annexation, a new agreement seemed necessary. U.S. negotiators launched three expeditions to treat with Comanches during 1843 and 1844, the last led by Daniel Boone's youngest son, Nathan. While none produced a satisfactorily comprehensive treaty, the expedition led by Pierce M. Butler in 1843 had taught Comanches and Americans something about each other. Late in the year Butler held talks with Potsanaquahip, whom the elder paraibo Pahayuco had sent in his stead. Butler found the war leader forthright and amiable. Up to a point. The expedition's resident artist, John Mix Stanley, drew a picture for the Comanches showing two hands locked in friendship, with a calumet peace pipe set above. Potsanaquahip and his companions liked the drawing but asked Stanley to add a bulldog beneath, poised to bite either hand should it prove treacherous. The artist complied, "to their great amusement and gratification." In September 1845, with Taylor's troops already in Texas and war with Mexico looking increasingly likely, the U.S. government commissioned Butler to return to the plains and secure a comprehensive treaty. Congress eventually appropriated fifteen thousand dollars for the project. Polk met with Butler and the expedition's coleader, M. G. Lewis of Tennessee, to discuss the mission, which the president and his cabinet deemed "important at this time, especially if Mexico should declare war against the U.S. or invade Texas."[7]

Once the commissioners arrived in Texas their mission seemed all the more urgent. By November General Taylor was writing anxiously to the secretary of war, concerned that small misunderstandings with Comanches could be "the germ of serious difficulty on the Indian frontier." Butler and Lewis obtained direction, assistance, and supplies from men with long-standing connections to Texas's Indian communities, among them the merchants Holland Coffee and Thomas Torrey, the Cherokee trader Jesse Chisholm, and the ubiquitous Delaware scout and interpreter Jim Shaw. The diverse party also included assorted Mexicans, African slaves, and Indians, among them the famous Seminole war leader Coacoochee (Wild Cat), who at night amused the group (except perhaps the Americans) with tales of killing and confounding U.S. soldiers in Florida's swamps.[8]

The mission inched forward. March arrived before the commissioners had a preliminary meeting with Potsanaquahip and Mopechucope, and final treaty negotiations did not get under way until May. By then Butler and Lewis knew only that Taylor "was surrounded by an overwhelming body of Mexicans" and that his situation was "full of imminent peril." Taylor himself had expressed fears that Indians would either take advantage of his looming clash with Arista to attack frontier settlements in Texas or, worse, side with Mexican troops against the U.S. Army. The commissioners had to "make many promises and make many profuse presents and resort to unusual expenditures of money to secure both themselves and to divert and detain the Indians." After much negotiation the delegation finally signed a treaty with the most important paraibos in the south of la comanchería, including Pahayuco, Mopechucope, Potsanaquahip, Pia Kusa, and Saviah. The document called for perpetual peace between the United States and the tribes of Texas, and the Indians "acknowledged themselves to be under the protection of the United States . . . and no other sovereignty." The U.S. government would regulate trade, and there would be a mutual exchange of prisoners. The commissioners promised the native signatories biannual presents and assured Comanches they could send representatives to Washington whenever they wished. U.S. negotiators also included an ambiguous but crucial article that implied recognition of boundaries and Indian territorial claims.[9]

The U.S. Senate eventually struck out the all-important article on boundaries, rejected the promise of biannual gifts or annuities, providing instead for a one-time appropriation, and eliminated the article guaranteeing trips to Washington on demand—Comanches could have a single visit, no more. Once they learned about the changes native leaders would be furious, but for the time being Butler and Lewis had reassured Taylor that Comanches would not interfere with his war. As proof of their success, Lewis arrived in Washington in July with a delegation of indigenous men and women from Texas, headed by the Hois paraibo Pia Kusa. At 5:00 p.m. on July 1 President Polk received the party "in the Ladies Parlor above the stairs, in the presence of a few ladies and other persons." The Indians wore "American costume," listened politely while a Ms. Pleasanton played piano, delighted at full-length mirrors in the parlors, and quickly removed their shoes once they were taken to the lawn. According to one account, the president explained to his guests that the United States had gone to war because "Mexico owed his people a great sum of money, that she had killed and scalped some of his brave men, that she violated her treaties, and refused to make reparation for the murders she had committed." The nonplussed Indians were said to be unsurprised that the "treacherous and dishonest Mexicans" would do such things. Polk seemed impressed with Pia Kusa, "a fine looking man of good size and middle age . . . evidently a man of talents," and promised him that he and his people "might rely on the friendship and protection of the U.S. as long as they would remain peaceable and friendly."[10]

"Peaceable and friendly" might have been somewhat vague, but if there was any confusion the recent treaty explicitly bound Comanches to respect the lives and property of U.S. citizens. There had been no discussion whatever about the rights of Mexicans. Indeed, the Comanche delegates had every reason to believe that the great father would welcome their help against his Mexican enemies. George Wilkins Kendall, who attended the negotiations on the plains, believed that the commissioners had given tacit approval to, if not outright encouragement of, Comanche raids into Mexico.[11]

But Comanches soon found matters more complicated than first they seemed. Pia Kusa was back in Texas by the following September, presumably wearing more comfortable clothes and eager to capitalize on his newfound friendship with the United States. According to Samuel Chamberlain, at once the most brutally honest and maddeningly inventive chronicler of the war, several hundred Comanches rode up to meet an army convoy making its way from San Antonio to the Rio Grande. Pia Kusa, "an old wolfish greasy cuss," rode at the head of the Comanche party. He approached General John Wool with outstretched hand, exclaiming, "How de do, budder?" The paraibo squeezed Wool's hand until pain flashed across the face of the rather diminutive general, much to the delight of the other Indians, whereupon another, stronger officer stepped forward and gave Pia Kusa such a handshake that he "gave vent to his agony in a fearful howl." Moods more serious, the Comanches proceeded to explain their visit in Spanish, telling Wool that they were good friends to the United States (though enemies to the Texans) and that they would "kill a heap of Mexicans, and wanted arms [and] ammunition and pay for scalps." Wool supposedly replied that they would get no arms and that they would hang if he caught them attacking defenseless Mexicans. According to Chamberlain, the Comanches returned this unexpected insult with insults of their own, so a Texas ranger and two dragoons wrestled Pia Kusa from his horse, "tied him up to a Gun carriage and gave him a sound flogging with a mule whip!" When they finished, the shocked and humiliated paraibo remounted, and he and his men rode off in stunned silence.[12]

The encounter marks a jarring counterpoint to the treatment another, humbler member of the Washington delegation received from U.S. representatives around the same time. During the treaty negotiations Butler and Lewis had redeemed a Mexican boy from Comanches for $150, perhaps to retain him as a translator. The child eventually traveled east with Pia Kusa's party to visit the White House. The secretary of war and possibly the president himself took an interest in the boy and sent him first to the army quartermaster in New Orleans

and then to Taylor's headquarters in Mexico, ordering the busy general to return
the child to his home in Chihuahua. The secretary troubled Taylor with this
seemingly minor detail because he thought that "sending [the boy] to his parents would have a good effect upon the people of that province." Pia Kusa would
probably have found it incomprehensible that this child, who had only recently
been a slave tending Comanche horses, would receive such careful attention
while he himself had been treated with violence and contempt by another of
Polk's generals.[13]

The paraibo's wounded pride and the boy's unlikely salvation were both improvised details in a deliberate U.S. strategy for managing the occupation of
northern Mexico. On July 2, 1846, the day after the president met with Pia Kusa
and his Comanches, the powerful Missouri senator Thomas Hart Benton came
to the White House to discuss how best to pursue the war. Benton knew more
about Mexico, and particularly northern Mexico, than anyone else in Congress
except some of the Texans. Though he initially had profound misgivings about
the war and openly mocked Texas's claim to a Rio Grande boundary, the senator quickly fell in line to become one of Polk's great advocates and most trusted
advisors. In their meeting and in later correspondence Benton and Polk talked
generally about how the army ought to interact with Mexicans and specifically
about proclamations that the generals would read and distribute throughout the
north.[14]

The instructions that emerged from Polk's and Benton's conversations directed Taylor to ingratiate the United States to northern Mexicans and to play
upon the many divisions he was bound to discover, divisions between races,
castes, classes, between high and low priests, between regional rivals and local
adversaries. Most important, Taylor was to cultivate northern Mexicans' disaf-
fection with their leaders in Mexico City, thought to be even greater following
Paredes's coup. Much depended on the general's ability to exploit dissatisfaction
with the government and to win the friendship or at least the neutrality of the
occupied population. He had to worry about significant numbers of northern
men enlisting in the Mexican army or else forming guerrilla units, endangering
U.S. supply lines and making the occupation costly or impossible. More basically, Taylor's men could remain in northern Mexico only so long as they had
regular access to food and other supplies. If northerners felt truly determined to
resist, they could refuse to sell their products or even burn their fields and drive
off their animals, making nearly impossible any sustained march from Matamoros and the lower Rio Grande to points farther south.[15]

Taylor therefore needed to convince northern Mexicans that he could be their
friend, even their hero, and that incompetent villains controlled Mexico's na-

22. Major General Zachary Taylor. H. R. Robinson.
Library of Congress, Prints and Photographs Division.

tional government. The passive dimension to the occupation policy concerned what not to do—the army was not to insult Catholicism, or demean or brutalize Mexicans, or take supplies without paying for them. This naturally would have been sound policy anywhere. The more active and particular dimension of the strategy emerged out of what U.S. officials had learned about northern Mexico since 1836. The administration furnished Taylor with a proclamation to read wherever he went in northern Mexico, informing the people that their government was "in the hands of tyrants and usurpers." The general was to say that military strongmen had abolished state governments and left the people "defenseless, and easy prey to savage Cumanches, who not only destroy your lives and property, but drive into captivity more horrible than death itself your wives and children." The U.S. Army had come to northern Mexico more as a savior than conqueror: "It is our wish to see you liberated from despots, to drive back the savage Cumanches, to prevent the renewal of their assaults, and to compel them to restore to you from captivity your long lost wives and children." Taylor

was therefore to play upon Mexicans' fears of Indians as well as their exaspera-
tion with the central government's indifference to frontier defense. Managing
these and other "delicate movements" was not to detract from a vigorous military agenda, but the war planners believed skillful public relations would be
essential for victory: "Policy and force are to be combined; and the fruits of the
former will be prized as highly as those of the latter."[16]

A STRANGE STORY THIS TO TELL: AMERICANS AS SAVIORS

Once Taylor occupied Matamoros he found settlements throughout the
lower Rio Grande region eager for his help against raiders. An American soldier
recalled that "the great fear among all classes of Mexicans was not the American
occupation, but rather the extensive raids by warring bands of Indians from across
the Rio Grande. They were disgusted with the lack of protection from these raids
by their government far away in Mexico City." The residents of Mier, Reynosa,
Guerrero, and the little settlement of China (which Chamberlain described
with characteristic charity as "a place that would make a Comanche vomit")
all promised to cooperate with the general in return for security against Indians. Newly established American newspapers in Matamoros encouraged other
communities to follow suit. The *Matamoros Reveille* noted that while Mexico
City had lavished resources and attention upon the central states, those on the
frontier had been "spurned as bastards." The government taxed them ceaselessly
and yet denied them "arms necessary to the defense of their wives and children
against the incursions of the savages."[17]

Nonetheless, raids continued despite U.S. efforts. In early August, Kendall reported that "a large force of Comanche Indians is on this side of the Rio Grande,
committing depredations and murdering the inhabitants with impunity. Parties
of them have appeared at Guerrero, and have killed several of the principal citizens, among them one of the town council." Taylor began to worry. He anxiously
warned the secretary of war that the raiding, "taken in connexion with our recent treaty with those Indians, is calculated to give much embarrassment." More
attention and resources had to be devoted to protecting northerners: "Should
we exhibit any lukewarmness in this matter, the cry would instantly be raised
that the Indians are our allies—an impression already carefully disseminated by
the Mexican chiefs." The commander ordered one of his top generals to see
to the defense of Mier, and he instructed General Wool, then still in Texas, to
dissuade would-be raiders from the southern plains—hence Wool's severe encounter with Pia Kusa shortly thereafter.[18]

Wool's gallant protection of Mexicans even made the national news. *Niles* ran a letter from a soldier detailing the indignation he and his comrades felt when two old Lipán women arrived in camp trying to sell a pair of "dreadfully emaciated" Mexican girls. The women were apprehended, and Wool later arrested fifteen more Lipanes upon learning they had killed the girls' family several weeks earlier. Later in the war, Wool took steps to protect the town of Parras against Comanche raids. A starry-eyed chronicler asked his readers, "Was ever a war carried on, with as much humanity towards an enemy?" As proof, the author recounted the story of a Mexican colonel who supposedly admitted to Wool that he was "our greatest enemy, for you conquer us by your kindness and humanity. We cannot induce our people to take up arms against you." It seemed, to American readers at least, that the United States had indeed become champion to the long-suffering people of northeastern Mexico.[19]

In New Mexico, too, the invaders styled themselves saviors and liberators rather than conquerors. Before Kearny even arrived, the U.S. consul in Santa Fe tried to convince Governor Armijo to capitulate by invoking Mexico's sorry record on Indian affairs. "Far better to become a considerable portion of a powerful Republic," the consul argued, than to be part of "a nation continually engaged in revolutions . . . powerless to defend the citizens of this province from the thousands of hostile Indians who surround them, [who] have by a long course of murder, rapine, and plunder almost become the lords of the soil." Once Kearny made his triumphant entry, he presented a similar argument in a proclamation read throughout the territory. "From the Mexican government you have never received protection," he observed. "The Apaches and the Navajoes come down from the mountains and carry off your sheep, and even your women, whenever they please. My government will correct all this. It will keep off the Indians, protect you in your persons and property; and . . . protect you in your religion."[20]

The peace and apparent welcome Kearny found in New Mexico convinced him that keeping his promise would be the key task, that U.S. forces in the territory "will hereafter have nothing to attend to but to secure the inhabitants from further depredation from the Navajoe and Eutaw Indians." The need seemed manifest. As Kearny's officers fanned out through New Mexico exploring territory and explaining the new political situation to the inhabitants, they saw evidence of the Indian war nearly everywhere they went, especially in the south and west. Abandoned homes, deserted ranches, empty corrals, and mournful tales of missing wives and children only reinforced the conviction held by U.S. forces that New Mexicans needed them there. Kearny sent runners out to the surrounding independent Indian communities, and soon delegations of Utes and Jicarilla Apaches came in promising not to harm Mexicans or molest their property.[21]

Navajos, however, did not come in. Navajo raids apparently increased immediately before and after Kearny's arrival in New Mexico, and the general finally
dispatched Colonel Doniphan to secure a definitive peace. The colonel and his
men marched west and held parleys with different headmen until finally nearly
all the top Navajo leaders gathered for a peace conference in November. Like
Pia Kusa's encounter with Wool (though far more diplomatically), the negotiations revealed what for independent Indians were the maddening contradictions
of the Americans' quarrel with Mexico. Doniphan informed the Navajos that
their raids against Mexicans had to cease. The response came from Zarcillos
Largos, the brilliant headman who would be a central figure in his people's relationship with the United States for years to come: "Americans! You have a
strange cause of war against the Navajos. We have waged war against the New
Mexicans for several years. We have plundered their villages and killed many of
their people, and made many prisoners." Zarcillos Largos insisted that his people
had good reasons to do these things. "You have lately commenced a war against
the same people," he continued. "You now turn upon us for attempting to do
what you have done yourselves. . . . This is our war. We have more right to complain of you for interfering in our war, than you have to quarrel with us for continuing a war we had begun long before you got here." Doniphan replied that
it was his people's custom to treat defeated enemies with kindness. Everything
in New Mexico now belonged to the United States, he explained, including its
people. Thus when Navajos "stole property from the New Mexicans, they were
stealing from us; and when they killed them, they were killing our people, for
they had now become ours." Convinced or (more likely) not by these arguments,
Zarcillos Largos replied that Navajos did not want a war with the United States,
and his people agreed to a treaty calling for a cessation of raiding upon the New
Mexicans.[22]

The U.S. Army's active intervention in the War of a Thousand Deserts depended entirely upon goals and situations that varied over time and place, with
New Mexico representing the proactive extreme. Kearny had the political obligation to at least try to eliminate Indian raiding from New Mexico, given that
by his proclamation it had just become part of the United States. Taylor also
wanted to see an end to raiding along the lower Rio Grande, though he seems to
have dispensed protection on more of a settlement by settlement basis, as a tool
to both entice and reward local complicity in the occupation. When Doniphan
and his men left to conquer Chihuahua shortly after they concluded the Navajo
treaty, they too gave the people of El Paso and Chihuahua City the usual assurances about protection against raiders. But Doniphan was out of communication with his superiors and not at all sure what to do with Chihuahua. In the end

he and his men stayed only a few months before marching east to join Taylor. Perhaps because of this ambivalence about the occupation there, the colonel did little more than talk about Indian raiding in Chihuahua.[23]

The relativity of U.S. zeal for protecting Mexicans became especially obvious in the army's brief march through northwestern Mexico en route to California. Passing through northern Chihuahua and Sonora in October 1846, Kearny met with the famed Apache leader Mangas Coloradas. The general had no tolerance for Indian raiders in New Mexico, but he also had no intention of occupying northwestern Mexico. His only concern was obtaining sufficient animals and supplies for the trek to California. So Kearny traded with Apaches, gave them papers promising perpetual American friendship, and listened without protest as an old headman said much the same thing Pia Kusa and Zarcillos Largos had said before. "You have taken Santa Fe," the old man said, "let us go on and take Chihuahua and Sonora; we will go with you. You fight for the soul, we fight for plunder, so we will agree perfectly: their people are bad Christians, let us give them a good thrashing." A battalion of Mormon volunteers followed a few weeks behind Kearny, and they too sought to trade with Apaches. The commander of the battalion thought the Indians were afraid to come in and trade because of the "murderous treachery" of American scalp hunters like John James Johnson and Kirker. When he finally had an audience with an Apache headman he assured him that Johnson and Kirker were the worst his country had to offer and that true Americans wanted to help Apaches in their war against bounty hunters and Mexicans. The same commander wrote a letter to the governor of Sonora suggesting that "the unity of Sonora with the states of the north [the United States], now her neighbors, is necessary effectually to subdue these Parthian Apaches." U.S. military officials who crossed through the northwest therefore either remained neutral in the region's conflicts or feigned partiality to both sides.[24]

These were flexible champions. U.S. rhetoric notwithstanding, outside of New Mexico and, to a lesser extent, the lower Rio Grande and certain points in Coahuila, Mexicans had little success enlisting U.S. soldiers against Indians. It is therefore revealing that what for Americans became the most famous and archetypal salvation story of the war was a spontaneous and atypical event at an isolated hacienda away from the core areas of U.S. interest. When Doniphan left Chihuahua to join Taylor in the northeast, a small detachment led by Captain John Reid rode ahead. His group arrived at Parras in Coahuila in May 1847 to learn that a number of Indians, either Lipanes or Comanches, had just left the area after killing several people and taking scores of captives. The captain took an interest in large part because the inhabitants of Parras had tended wounded

American soldiers and endeared themselves to General Wool. So, upon learning that the raiders would have to pass near the Hacienda del Pozo on their way out of the region, Reid decided to intercept them. He and his men rushed to the scene in the company of a local hacendado, drew the Indians into a fight, and after two hours finally drove them away. The raiders left eight of their dead on the field, including one supposed to be a leader or "medicine man," and dragged still more of their fallen comrades away. Reid discovered seven more Indian corpses the following day. The captain and his men had managed to rescue eighteen captives and recover hundreds of horses and mules.[25]

Several men traveling with Doniphan's troops went on to write enthusiastically about the event in their letters and published books, materials that inspired and informed accounts in Niles' and other publications. The writings nearly all lionize Reid's bravery and magnanimity, but different authors focused on different details. The German scientist and traveler Frederick Wislizenus, for example, arrived at Hacienda del Pozo soon after the fight, and he was interested in the Indians themselves, what they wore and how they looked. He was so interested, in fact, that he took a "curiosity along for scientific purposes—to wit, the skull of the medicine man." He later gave it to the renowned professor Samuel George Morton, the author of the seminal text *Crania Americana*, proprietor of the world's largest collection of human skulls, and one of America's premier scientists of racial difference.[26]

A handful of Doniphan's soldiers also wrote about the event. John T. Hughes described Reid's "brilliant sortie" in breathless detail. Hughes admired Reid unabashedly, but he also despised Mexicans and somehow felt obliged to apologize for the captain's mercy: "Although they were considered enemies to the Americans, it did not become the magnanimity of the American soldiers to see them robbed and murdered by a lawless band of savages." Just as important, Hughes reminded his readers that Comanches were the enemies of Americans, too, as anyone familiar with the captivity narratives coming out of Texas would know: "Read the brutal treatment Mrs. [Sarah Ann] Horn and others received from them, and you can but justify Capt. Reid's conduct."[27]

The master chronicler of the Santa Fe trade, Josiah Gregg, also happened upon the scene shortly after the fight ended. While he apparently had no quarrel with Wislizenus decapitating the medicine man and boiling the flesh from his skull, Gregg had typically harsh words for locals: "It was disgusting to [see] the dastardly conduct of the Mexicans toward these dead Indians, whom they were too cowardly to fight while living—kicking and abusing them." Like Hughes, Gregg recognized some irony in Reid's actions: "This is certainly a novel warfare: fighting and defending the same people at the same time—and killing

those who would be our allies, if we would permit them." But Gregg was a practical man and did not need to invoke the unfortunate Mrs. Horn to justify what
he saw: "This display of a spirit to defend the people against their worst enemies,
the Indians, will, I hope, be attended with a good effect."[28]

By "good effect" Gregg obviously meant that the event might play well with
Mexicans. Yet the many stories about Reid's fight were all written for Anglo-
American audiences, composed in English, and (except for Gregg's unpublished
journal) printed in the United States. Beyond the grateful people of Parras, there
is no evidence the fight meant anything to Mexicans or was even talked about
in northern Mexico. But Americans clearly found something affirming in Reid's
"brilliant sortie." Newspapers across the United States reported the encounter,
regaling readers with the story of how "the Mexicans on a sudden beheld their
armed foes converted into friends and protectors, avenging their wrongs and
rescuing their wives and children out of the hands of the pitiless savage." The
tale deserved wide circulation, one letter writer insisted, because "it affords to
the public a better example of the indomitable spirit and gallant heroism of the
Missouri troops than either [the battles of] Brazito or Sacramento."[29]

No one would have agreed more than Senator Benton. Despite his decision
to support the war once it began, Benton remained anxious about the justice
of what his country was doing in Mexico and particularly worried about the
conflict's effect upon the international reputation of the United States. It must
have been with great pleasure, then, that he hurried home to St. Louis to greet
Doniphan, Reid, and the triumphant Missourians once they mustered out of
service in the summer of 1847. The senator felt smitten with his boys from Missouri. Their exploits seem to have represented for him the best of the war's meanings: bravery and military brilliance, the simplicity and stoic sacrifice of volunteer patriots, and, not least, Anglo-America's selfless intervention on behalf of a
helpless enemy.[30]

All of St. Louis turned out to toast Doniphan and his men when they returned. Church bells pealing, flags lolling in the heavy summer air, the enormous
crowd grew silent as Benton began his keynote address. The senator recounted
the bloodless triumph in New Mexico, Doniphan's journey into the mountains
wherein he bound Navajos to stop attacking Mexicans, the swift conquest of
Chihuahua, and the daring march east to join Taylor and his army. Benton dwelt
on all of these points but spent more time on Reid's fight at Hacienda del Pozo
than on anything else. "Here presents an episode of a novel, extraordinary, and
romantic kind," he began: "Americans chastising savages for plundering people
who they themselves came to conquer, and forcing the restitution of captives
and of plundered property. A strange story this to tell in Europe, where back-

woods character, western character, is not yet completely known." The senator recounted the terror and desperation at Parras, Reid's bold decision to pursue the raiders, the desperate fight that followed, and the redemption of the captive women and children. "Such noble conduct was not without its effect on the minds of the astonished Mexicans." The local mayor had presented Reid with an official letter of thanks that praised the captain's bravery, his "noble soul," and his determination to defend "Christians and civilized beings against the rage and brutality of savages." Benton held the document in his hand. "This is a trophy of a new kind in war," he told the huge crowd, "won by thirty Missourians, and worthy to be held up to the admiration of Christendom. The long march from Chihuahua to Monterrey, was made more in the character of protection and deliverance than of conquest and invasion."[31]

THREATENED AS NEVER BEFORE: COMANCHE CAMPAIGNS IN 1846

The Americans' tactic of selective intervention in Mexico's conflicts with independent Indians won some measure of Mexican gratitude and cooperation here and there, and it provided reassurance, or at least rhetorical ammunition, to Benton and others like him sensitive to the claim that the war was venal and unjust. But while the senator found heroic affirmation in Reid's exciting story, he could just as easily have taken it as evidence that Indian raids remained a serious problem for northerners, despite the self-congratulatory rhetoric of the American occupation. Anomalies like the confrontation at Hacienda del Pozo notwithstanding, the invasion and occupation probably encouraged and certainly facilitated Indian raids in the north, even in many places under the nominal control of U.S. authorities.

Comanches provoked the most anxiety, launching massive campaigns below the river throughout Mexico's war with the United States. Pia Kusa had learned firsthand that in certain areas it would be difficult to graft the Comanches' war directly on top of the U.S. occupation. But the occupiers were busy, easily distracted, and indifferent to most of northern Mexico. In other words, experienced war leaders had reason to believe they could exploit Mexico's new distraction so long as they focused their campaigns and paid attention to the shifting geography of the occupation. Along with the outbreak of the international conflict, other changes help explain the vigorous Comanche campaigns of 1846–47. The first was a major realignment of alliances on the southern plains that had been under way since 1844. After months of offering incentives, applying pressure, and interjecting themselves into the Lipán relationship with Texas, Hois leaders finally convinced hundreds of Southern Lipanes to leave the Bastrop area, where they had resided since aligning themselves with Lamar's Texans, and move to the Colorado River inside Comanche country. These Southern Lipanes apparently agreed to some diplomatic marriages, to live inside la comanchería as clients and allies, and to help rather than hinder Comanche raids into northeastern Mexico. By the summer of 1846 a similar agreement seems to have brought many Northern Lipanes onto the plains from their homes in Coahuila.[32]

More important even than the Lipán peace, Comanches in the southwest of la comanchería came to terms with their old enemies the Mescalero Apaches. There were perhaps three thousand Mescaleros in 1846 inhabiting land on both sides of the Rio Grande between El Paso and the Big Bend. Their territory included the principal crossing points for Comanche campaigns into the Bolsón de Mapimí. Mexican officials in Chihuahua had been adept at manipulating the long rivalry between the two peoples. Mescaleros occasionally joined Chihuahuan forces pursuing Comanche raiders, and they also fought Comanches independently in the Bolsón. Mexicans hardly ever heard of these kinds of clashes, but there is no doubt that plains raiders had to worry about Mescalero ambushes as they returned with animals and captives taken on campaign. Peace agreements with the various Apache communities eliminated these concerns. Peace also quite likely put the Lipanes' and Mescaleros' extensive knowledge about northern Mexico at Comanche disposal and probably led to joint campaigns. Indeed, in September of 1845 General Arista's spies informed him that Comanche raiders under Potsanaquahip and Pia Kusa were about to cross the Rio Grande with one hundred Lipanes under Ramón Castro, the son of the recently deceased Cuelgas Castro. Comanches therefore had much to gain, and the agreements made sense for Apaches for at least three reasons. First, they put an end to a long, bloody rivalry. Second, Comanches offered Apaches a refuge where they could escape those dangerous places occupied or traversed by the U.S. Army. Finally and most crucially, the alliances gave Lipanes and Mescaleros rights to peacefully hunt bison on the plains.[33]

Hunting rights would have been especially crucial starting in 1846 because that was the year that a long, stable period of unusual rainfall in the region suddenly came to an end. For nine of the next ten years annual rainfall dipped as low as 70 percent of the median, a disastrous drop for life on arid plains. The southern bison population had already been weakened by decades of overhunting for the hide trade and because of increasing competition with horses for winter resources. Moreover, the critical and steadily shrinking winter habitats along the Arkansas had come under mounting pressure with the opening of the Santa Fe Trail in the early 1820s, and traffic swelled with the onset of the U.S.–

Mexico War. Thus the punishing drought combined with other factors made life very difficult for hunters on the plains. By 1847 the U.S. Indian agent for Texas reported widespread consumption of horses and mules in Comanche camps, and the Kiowa calendar memorialized winter 1847–48 for its elaborate antelope drive, an activity resorted to only in times of great scarcity. Disappointing hunts in the summer made it all the more likely that experienced war leaders such as Pia Kusa and Potsanaquahip would find hundreds of men eager to offset their losses by spending part of the fall and winter on campaign in Mexico.[34]

Some of these campaigns likely moved through the northeast. Reports of raiding decreased dramatically across the region after the Battle of Buena Vista. Only scattered mention is made of Indians in Tamaulipas and Coahuila, and there is nothing at all about them in Nuevo León's archives for the entirety of the war. But observers within and around the U.S. Army reported that native peoples continued raiding in the region despite the occupation.[35] Still more raiders struck Chihuahua and Durango. In the issue for June 11, 1846, the editors of Durango's state newspaper led with Arista's letter describing his defeat at Resaca de la Palma. The next item was a letter from Durango's commander general notifying the public that Comanches had killed more than three dozen people in the district of Cuencamé. Southern plains Indians campaigned through Chihuahua and Durango every month for half a year, from August 1846 through January 1847. Comanches and Kiowas disposed of some of the fruits of their endeavors the following summer at a huge trade fair on the Great Salt Plains with Osages, Creeks, Delawares, Cherokees, Shawnees, Seminoles, and others. Osages alone traded twenty-four thousand dollars' worth of guns, ammunition, blankets, and other goods for fifteen hundred horses worth an estimated sixty thousand dollars.[36]

The largest, most devastating of the wartime campaigns got under way in early October, when eight hundred to a thousand warriors crossed the river, divided, and began attacking points throughout eastern Chihuahua and Durango. Durango's official newspaper, the only one in the north still covering Indian affairs with any consistency during the war, reprinted numerous letters about individual attacks during the October campaign. The state government implored local officials to work together for the people, "threatened as never before by the horrors of the savages' war, precursor to another of invasion and conquest." A large Mexican force engaged three to four hundred Comanches on October 20. Though they suffered eleven dead and twenty-eight wounded, the Mexicans killed nineteen raiders. A soldier decapitated one and resumed marching with the head on a pike. Five days later another, larger battle took place. The scene resembled what one would expect of formal armies, with Comanche warriors supposedly spread out across three leagues and fighting Durango's forces from three o'clock in the afternoon until nightfall. Duranguenos won some glory in this and other engagements, but in the course of their campaign the raiders killed at least one hundred people, captured dozens more, slaughtered animals, set fire to ranches, and disrupted communication across the state. Before they had even left the state the official paper was already calling the invasion the largest and most terrible ever, and the massive destruction gave northerners reason to dread the months ahead. Everyone in the Mexican north, it seemed, was at war with someone.[37]

10

POLK'S BLESSING

In July of 1846, the governor of Chihuahua wrote to his counterpart in Zacatecas lamenting his multitude of enemies. Sorry Chihuahua, he wrote, had to defend itself against the four divisions of Comanches, their Kiowa allies, the several tribes of Apaches, and now "the Anglo-American, rocked in the cradle of the Indian whom he abhors, and nurtured with the blood and sweat of the Negro whom he despises." Though Mexicans' experiences of the period 1846–48 depended on where they lived, most seem to have agreed that while their enemies were many, the war was one. In places farther south, such as Durango, where the U.S. Army engaged in no major operations, the people's enemies were almost exclusively Comanches and Apaches. But here, too, amid the smoke and ruin of empty homes and burned-out corrals, Mexicans thought they saw los norteamericanos lurking in the background. "And to think that we owe all this," the state's newspaper mused, "to those infamous North American enemies who push the bloody hordes of savages upon us and direct their operations with unparalleled astuteness and ferocity! Such are the methods through which a nation that styles itself enlightened and just wages war."[1]

THE THEME OF EVERY CONVERSATION: WITNESS TO WAR

While Comanche warriors traversed Durango and newspaper editors meditated on their misfortunes, a most able observer, George Ruxton, was happily surveying the carnage and panic. Ruxton was a precocious English adventurer. Before coming to Mexico he won a Spanish Cross medal from Queen Isabella II for his service in Spain's Carlist civil war, served the British army in Ireland and

Canada, spent a winter hunting with a Chippewa friend in Ontario's cold woods, traveled twice to Africa, and delivered papers before the British Ethnological and the Royal Geographic societies. He was twenty-six years old when he arrived in Mexico as a special representative sent to monitor British diplomatic and commercial interests during the U.S.–Mexican War. The young man quickly grew bored and decided to tour some of the northern states. Ruxton never missed an opportunity to criticize Mexicans. He generalized from the worst that he saw and considered all examples of charity, valor, and sophistication, of which he found many, exceptions. Yet his memoir captures wartime experiences in north-central Mexico better than any other source. By the fall of 1846 the war with the United States was well under way: Kearny had taken New Mexico, California had been occupied, Taylor had fought his bloody battle for Monterrey, and Santa Anna was assembling his army of resistance. Everywhere Ruxton went in the north he found people frantic for news about the enemy. But when these people spoke of the enemy they were talking about indios bárbaros rather than norteamericanos.[2]

The Englishman arrived in Zacatecas City in late September, and even this far south "'Los Indios! Los Indios!' was the theme of every conversation." He moved on to Fresnillo and then on the thirtieth headed north again into dry country, where every dwelling had fortifications to protect its inhabitants from Comanches. On the thirty-first he rode to Sombrerete, noting that the surrounding country looked "entirely depopulated, as much from fear of Indians as from its natural unproductiveness." Ruxton continued on through desolate country and crossed into the state of Durango, stopping at a ranch where a woman complained to him that the men went "hiding like rats" the last time Indian raiders appeared. He arrived at the state capital, Victoria de Durango, on October 4 and was still in the city days later when news arrived of the huge impending Comanche campaign. This information provoked panic and dismay. He found the populace in "dread and expectation" and remarked that Indians had "cut off all communication, and defeated in two pitched battles the regular troops sent against them." Ruxton heard that the raiders had already stolen upward of ten thousand animals, "and everywhere the people have been killed or captured. The roads are impassible, all traffic is stopped, the ranchos barricaded, and the inhabitants afraid to venture out of their doors. The posts and expresses travel at night, avoiding the roads, and intelligence is brought in daily of massacres and harryings."[3]

Three days out from Durango's capital the traveler came upon a caravan of teamsters accompanied by Manuel Armijo, the ex-governor of New Mexico, whom Ruxton characterized as "a mountain of fat." After abandoning his homeland to the U.S. Army, Armijo had spent some time in Chihuahua and then headed south to dispose of trade goods and travel to Mexico City, where he would have to justify his flight from Kearny. Armijo hailed Ruxton and nervously asked what durangueños were saying about New Mexico. The Englishman replied with evident pleasure that "there was but one opinion respecting it expressed all over the country—that General Armijo and the New Mexicans were a pack of arrant cowards." The distressed ex-governor muttered something about having only seventy-five men to fight three thousand, and he and Ruxton parted company. Eager no doubt for some sort of redemption, Armijo immediately offered to help the authorities in Victoria de Durango chastise Comanches who were desolating the state. The grateful officials put him in command of 188 men, but, for his own good or ill, he never found these Indians whom he had always refused to fight while governor of New Mexico.[4]

Ruxton pushed on. He arrived in La Noria on October 13 to find the inhabitants in "the greatest alarm and dismay." Comanches had just attacked a nearby ranch, and it was anyone's guess where they would go next: "The women were weeping and flying about in every direction, hiding their children and valuables, barricading the houses, and putting what few arms they could collect in the hands of the reluctant men." News came in that raiders had killed several Spanish bullfighters who had been headed for a regional fair and that there had been a battle with the Comanches at Rio Florido in which seventeen Mexican soldiers lost their lives. On the sixteenth Ruxton happened upon several vultures feasting on a roadside corpse with an arrow buried in its face. The traveler stopped for the night at El Gallo, where he stayed with a farmer who had lost three sons to the Indian war. The man's home was full of widows. The crowded household had corn ready to harvest but feared to go into the fields because of Comanches: "'Los Indios! Los Indios!' were on everybody's tongue."[5]

Before he left El Gallo an old woman gave Ruxton a medallion that would protect him from los bárbaros and also from the more dangerous weapons of the "enemy of the world, who, she said, was ever hunting after heretics." On October 21 he arrived at the frontier town of Mapimí, on the edge of the Bolsón, where "the people live in constant dread of the Indians." Ruxton learned that the surrounding country was "sterile and uninhabited; the villages and ranchos have been deserted, and the fields laid waste by the savages." He next traveled through what for him was a fascinating, haunted landscape of makeshift crosses, abandoned villages, fallow fields, and ruined homes, until he arrived in Chihuahua City in early November.[6]

Chihuahua had likely suffered as much as Durango during the October Comanche raids, but Ruxton nonetheless found people in the state's capital preoccupied with Apaches. The Englishman saw more than a hundred withered black scalps suspended over the portals of the city square. These were the scalps of Apaches who "had lately been most treacherously and inhumanely butchered by the Indian hunters in the pay of the state." In the spring of 1846, before Ruxton had arrived in Mexico, Chihuahuan authorities had had reason to hope that another imperfect but workable peace with Apaches might be within reach. Several prominent Chiricahua leaders had expressed interest in a negotiated truce and consented to a wary but promising period of regular communication. Within this optimistic context more than 100 Chiricahuas entered weaponless into the Chihuahuan town of Galeana in early July, whereupon they proceeded to gamble and to eat and drink copiously. Meanwhile, James Kirker, who had been commissioned by state authorities to hunt Apaches that remained at war, had found and killed 18 Chiricahuas at nearby Buenaventura. Hearing that more were drunk and unarmed at Galeana, Kirker hastened to the town, where on July 7 he, his party, and the town's Mexican residents fell upon the Indians and slaughtered at least 130 men, women, and children. Secondhand accounts portrayed the attackers as descending into grotesque revelries of mutilation.[7]

Kirker rode back to Chihuahua City carrying the scalps Ruxton would later see in the square. One observer of the scalp hunter's triumphant return recalled people shouting for joy, "throwing up their hats in wild exultation." Overcome with the happy news, normally tightfisted merchants rolled out barrels of tequila and mescal while onlookers poured into the city from near and far "to see and participate in the howling jollification, until the city was literally suffocated with the surging masses of humanity." Notwithstanding these spasms of joy, the massacres at Galeana and San Buenaventura may have constituted the most calamitous error the Mexicans ever made in their long war with Apaches. The murdered Indians had been some of the strongest advocates for peace, and their moderate voices would obviously never again be heard in debate. Indeed, the very position they represented had been suddenly and thoroughly discredited. Now Mangas Coloradas and other militants had all the arguments they needed, and they directed wave after wave of retributive violence upon the people of Chihuahua and Sonora. For the rest of the decade every one of the Chiricahua bands went to war against Mexicans.[8]

These developments would have been disastrous at any time, but they came at precisely the moment when authorities in the northwest had to begin diverting attention and resources away from fighting Indians in order to oppose to the U.S. invasion. When Ruxton arrived in Chihuahua in November Kearny had already occupied New Mexico, and officials in Chihuahua City were scrambling to put together a respectable army. And state authorities would become more distracted with the norteamericanos as the war dragged on, not less. The dearth of archival materials bearing on raiding from mid-1846 to mid-1848 therefore reflects not only the disruption of usual routines; it also reflects a general disengagement of government from the Indian war just as that conflict entered a terrible and intense new phase.

Once he left Chihuahua City, Ruxton stopped briefly at an estate owned by Governor Angel Trías. Raiders there had recently "destroyed the cattle of the hacienda, filling a well in the middle of the corral with the carcasses of slaughtered sheep and oxen. It was still bricked up." At El Paso he discovered that "as everywhere else in northern Mexico, the people are in constant fear of Indian attacks." Ruxton continued on to New Mexico, stopping for some time with Doniphan's men near Socorro as they prepared for their descent upon Chihuahua. Moving north through the Rio Grande Valley and out of the present story, the traveler concluded his Mexican diary with observations about the New Mexicans, whom he found terrified of and tyrannized by Navajos and Utes—this despite the presence of the U.S. Army. Doniphan had such confidence in his treaty with the Navajos that he neglected even to brief the territory's new governor, Charles Bent, on the document's contents, certain as he was that peace had been secured. Unlike Doniphan, Bent at least had an inkling of how complex and intractable the Navajo–New Mexican dispute really was. He doubted the treaty would be adhered to and wrote a long letter to Senator Benton, insisting that a significant military force would be needed to "bring into subjection" Navajos and other Indians whose raiding had virtually destroyed New Mexico's economy.[9]

Whatever the governor meant by "significant," he never got it. Mexican thieves took Navajo sheep, Navajos continued raiding Mexican settlements, Mexicans launched slaving expeditions into Navajo territory, and Navajos retaliated with still more killings and robberies. The *St. Louis Republican* ran a letter from Santa Fe insisting that the U.S. Army had kept none of the promises it made to the people of New Mexico, especially those regarding security: "During no one year, for the last twenty years, have the depredations of these Indians been so destructive to life and property. Upwards of fifty citizens have been killed or carried into captivity, and more than 60,000 head of horses, mules, and sheep have been carried off from the country called the Rio Abajo." U.S. authorities sent three more expeditions into Navajo country during the war with Mexico, but interethnic violence continued. Here, in the one place where U.S. officials unambiguously wanted to stop conflicts between Mexicans and independent Indians, the territory's new American administrators, like Mexican administrators before them, found that the problem required more thought and a good deal more financial, political, and military resources than their national government cared to expend.[10]

THE MARCH OF ATTILA:
AMERICAN CONQUEST AND INDIAN RAIDS

Indian raiding therefore remained a prominent and at times the dominant worry in northern Mexico during the period 1846–48, and the U.S. occupation exacerbated it in many ways. Initially this was only indirectly true—U.S. forces distracted Mexican resources and leadership from the Indian war, and native peoples seem to have recognized this fact as an opportunity. But by the winter of 1846–47 the character of the occupation had changed. In response to a rebellion and some minor guerrilla activity, U.S. forces started disarming towns and villages, terrorizing Mexicans, and destroying settlements. In short, they adopted tactics that left many northern Mexicans even more vulnerable to their Indian enemies than before.

When Doniphan took El Paso, for instance, his troops went door to door confiscating weapons. They collected twenty thousand pounds of "powder, lead, musket cartridge, cannon cartridge and grape canister shot; five hundred stands of small arms, four hundred lances, four pieces of cannon, [and] several swivels and culverins." The people of El Paso would have had little need for such things in the city, but without them they stood small chance of defending their kin and properties in the hinterland from Apaches or Comanches. Soon after this confiscation took place an insurgency erupted in New Mexico when Pueblos and vecinos at Taos killed several officials, including Governor Bent, whom they also scalped. It took U.S. forces several days to quell the rebellion, and once they did, according to a soldier chronicler, "no house was permitted to retain arms, or other munitions of war." In the northeast U.S. officials issued an order forbidding Mexicans from bearing arms in the Camargo area. There were surely other such orders and other confiscations, and, while prudent policy from the U.S. viewpoint, they obviously undercut the champion rhetoric that had been a hallmark of the occupation from the start. This sometimes put Americans in difficult positions. Doniphan disarmed the residents of Pelayo, in northern Durango, but after hearing their fearful complaints about Indians he grudgingly returned the weapons and made the Mexicans promise to use them only against raiders. Mexican officials in Chihuahua mocked the promises of safety and protection U.S. officers dispensed so lightly, "while with impunity the savages fall upon those of us whom the enemy has disarmed." A priest in Sonora complained not that U.S. forces were taking guns away, but that they were giving them away—to los bárbaros. Apaches had been sending well-armed raiding parties of several hundred men into the state, and the priest insisted they had gotten their weapons from the norteamericanos.[11]

Sometimes Anglo-American soldiers did worse than disarm Mexicans or arm Indians: sometimes they attacked Mexican civilians directly. In the northeast a handful of regional leaders organized guerrilla units dedicated to chipping away at the occupation. The most prominent local guerrilla leader was the former rebel chief Antonio Canales. Once he had surrendered to Arista in 1841, Canales resumed his position as a key political and military figure on the lower Rio Grande. He had helped organize defenses against native raiders and also distinguished himself in confrontations with Texans. On the eve of the war he had tried to convince Taylor not to cross over from the Nueces to the Rio Grande and, failing that, raised a company of men and fought beside Arista at Palo Alto and Resaca de la Palma. Taylor's decisive victory convinced Canales that Mexico had little chance of defeating the invasion through regular warfare, and he issued a call for guerrillas. "We will not win grand battles," he predicted, "but little by little we will finish with our conquerors." U.S. soldiers rarely captured guerrillas (they never captured Canales), and so they compensated by exacting arbitrary revenge upon northern communities. In September 1846, for example, Ohio volunteers burned sixty to eighty dwellings near Camargo in retaliation for guerrilla attacks in the region. Sometimes collective retaliation became so divorced from tactics or specific grievances that it seemed more like simple hatred and bloodlust. Following Taylor's victory at Monterrey, volunteer Texan rangers stormed through the city and murdered scores of civilians, more than one hundred according to a disgusted American regular.[12]

Taylor said he deeply regretted these "shameful atrocities." They kept happening. A group of Texans rode into the little Rancho de San Francisco, bound all of the thirty-six men they could find to posts, and calmly shot each of them through the head. In another instance soldiers arrived at a village near the scene of a particularly gruesome guerrilla attack on a party of teamsters and killed all the men they could find, twenty-four in all, amounting to nearly the entire adult male population of the village. Mexican men became reluctant to travel the roads, lest Americans punish them as proxies for guerrillas. Soldiers burned homes and fields in ranches and rural towns such as Marín, Cerralvo, Apodaca, and others, both as acts of revenge and to discourage people from supporting the resistance. Samuel Chamberlain thought Taylor intentionally "unleashed" such reprisals upon northeasterners, but by mid-1847 the general requested that the War Department send no more volunteers from Texas, given that they had "scarcely made one expedition without unwarrantably killing a Mexican." Ulysses S.

Grant, a lieutenant in the war, observed that some volunteers and nearly all Texans thought it "perfectly right to impose upon the people of a conquered City to any extent, and even to murder them where the act can be covered by the dark." Another U.S. observer noted that "American deserters had been guilty of many enormities: on their way from Saltillo to the Rio Grande they had not only plundered the inhabitants of horses, money, plate, jewelry, but ravished women, two of whom died in consequence of their brutality." Still another declared that "the march of Attila was not more withering and destructive."[13]

There was, of course, a nearer analogy than Attila the Hun. Descriptions of northeastern Mexico in 1847 read like Ruxton's descriptions of Durango and Chihuahua, and American atrocities begged the obvious comparison to Indian raids. Northeastern Mexicans took to calling the volunteers "Comanches of the North," or the "illustrious Comanches." A prominent Mexican general wrote Taylor protesting the "devastation, ruin, conflagration, death, and other depredations" committed by men under Taylor's command. He wanted to know whether the war was to be fought as between civilized nations or "as it is waged by savage tribes between each other." The author insisted that Mexican authorities had endeavored "to avoid that ferocity, that fury, proper only to the nomadic tribes of its frontiers" and demanded to know whether the United States would do the same. Taylor seems genuinely to have regretted the outrages and indeed feared they might turn the entire population against the occupiers. But he failed to prevent the crimes or to punish any but a handful of the perpetrators.[14]

All of this violence provoked population flight across the rural northeast, much as the Indian war had done over the previous fifteen years. Sometimes city-dwellers left places such as Monterrey and Chihuahua for fear of the "barbarous yankees," especially after tales of the atrocities committed by volunteers spread throughout the north. An American officer reported that illness and abuses by troops had compelled "nearly all" of the residents of Cerralvo, Nuevo León, to flee to outlying ranches, "where the Comanches killed many of them and the rest returned once more to suffer disease, insult, and outrage in Cerralvo." Others went the opposite way, abandoning ruined ranches and haciendas for what they hoped would be the safety of towns and cities. After he left Cerralvo, the U.S. officer happened upon a large ranch from which all but a dozen of the recent population of five hundred had fled. Some simply moved from one village to another, seeking safety in numbers or searching for shelter after their own homes had been destroyed. For instance, one of Doniphan's soldiers passing through the northeastern village of San Lorenzo noted that the place had "an over portion of inhabitants. Every house and hut was crowded with men, boys, women, and children." Still others felt that no settlement offered safety and took their chances in the mountains or the countryside. A veteran officer recalled that "from Saltillo to Mier, with the exception of the large towns, all is a desert, and there is scarcely a solitary house (if there be one) inhabited." He found that villages that had welcomed U.S. troops in the summer of 1846 were by 1847 "black and smoldering ruins, the gardens and orange groves destroyed, and the inhabitants, who administered to their necessities, have sought refuge in the mountains."[15]

Josiah Gregg, the well-known chronicler of the Santa Fe Trail, left behind a stark record of northern Mexico's ravaged landscape. Traveling from Chihuahua to the lower Rio Grande in the spring of 1847, Gregg kept a detailed geographic journal in hopes of eventually making an authoritative map of the Mexican north. His most striking landmarks were abandoned or depopulated ranches and villages. He saw them everywhere he went. On the western leg of the journey the settlements had been deserted because of Indian raids, but by the time his party got to eastern Coahuila Americans had created most of Gregg's cartographic monuments. As he moved past these dismal places, he made brief notes on the region's shifting demography. Gregg estimated that Marín had only one-half to one-quarter of its prewar population. The village of Ramos, once home to several hundred people, he found burned to the ground and entirely deserted. Puntiagudo once had two to three hundred residents, and it too had been abandoned by the time Gregg passed by.[16]

The ongoing Indian war made the prospect of homelessness and forced travel especially terrifying. Refugees risked being attacked while moving from place to place. They also had to worry about whatever property they had left behind. If refugees brought their animals with them, then they were more likely to attract Indian attention, but any animals left behind would almost certainly be taken or destroyed by Indians, soldiers, or thieves along with homes, crops, food stores, and anything else too difficult to carry off. Occasionally U.S. observers mentioned refugees being attacked by Comanches and other Indians, and accounts dribbled out into U.S. newspapers of Comanche raids in the northeast during 1847. In mid-May, for instance, an American officer wrote that a group rumored to be Mexican lancers harassing a ranch near Saltillo turned out to be nothing more than "forty-seven innocent Camanches who had been levying blackmail in the neighborhood." The raiders had "killed every Mexican man they met with, and had with them nine or ten very beautiful young Mexican girls as prisoners." When some of the men in his party suggested a rescue, the officer demurred: "We are at peace with them [the Comanches], and there's a bargain—'let me alone and I'll let you alone.'"[17]

To a great extent the occupying power does indeed seem to have disengaged from its promise to protect Mexicans from Indians, busy as it was with chasing guerrillas and punishing their alleged civilian supporters. Reading army accounts, one might conclude that raiding was minor or nonexistent in the occupied northeast late in the war. The occasional Mexican source from the period suggests otherwise. It is clear, for instance, that Coahuila suffered greatly from Indian raids in mid-1847. The problem was bad enough that a group of municipalities calling itself the "corporation of the Santa Rosa Valley" banded together and negotiated a plan for cooperative defense. The corporation's spokesman said that Indian raids were "never more frequent nor more serious than in these days."[18]

The international war intersected with the war against independent Indians even in places that American soldiers avoided. Confronted with potential threats from U.S. forces and periodic blockades of Pacific ports, in February 1848 the Sonoran government stopped sending the customary bimonthly wheat rations to the frontier town and presidio of Tucson. With the neediest families facing starvation, in May fifteen vecinos and presidials volunteered to march to the abandoned ranch of Babocómari sixty miles to the southeast, in hopes of rounding up feral cattle and driving them home. On May 10, a large group of Apaches surprised the fifteen men and killed every last one. The widows of the slain soldiers petitioned Sonora's commander general, pleading with him to reinstate the allotment of rations "and granting us a small donation so that we may clothe ourselves and our families. As it is now, we are forced to stay indoors to hide our nakedness."[19]

AN IDEAL THEATER:
INDIAN RAIDS AND AMERICAN CONQUEST

Just as Mexico's war with the United States complicated and aggravated its struggles with Indians in a variety of ways, the ongoing war against los salvajes made it extraordinarily difficult for northern Mexicans to cooperate with their countrymen against U.S. forces. Most fundamentally Americans found northern Mexico poorer and emptier, more insecure and divided in 1846 than it would have been but for the long war against independent Indians. The economic, defensive, and, to a lesser extent, the political and social realities U.S. forces encountered in the north had all been shaped by a decade or more of conflict with Comanches, Kiowas, Apaches, and Navajos. The cumulative effect of this history and of continuing Indian raids from 1846 to 1848 inhibited northern Mexican contributions to the multifaceted project of resisting the U.S. conquest and undermining its occupation.

Certain missed opportunities indicate the larger, systemic significance of the War of a Thousand Deserts to the northern theater of the U.S.–Mexican War. In the northeast, for instance, state authorities received orders from the minister of war that all males between the ages of sixteen and fifty were to take up arms against the American invasion. National authorities issued exemptions for those places most threatened by los bárbaros. But even so, many local authorities refused, insisting that their men were already occupied patrolling against raiders or else that they refused to leave their families and properties for fear that Indians would attack in their absence. Even when local authorities managed to raise men, few had firearms or ammunition, and fewer still had horses because raiders had run them off. Such situations became especially problematic for the Army of the North as it scrambled to enlist men in advance of the initial confrontation with Taylor and in preparation for the battle over Monterrey. More important, the threat of los bárbaros inhibited the emergence of a popular insurgency against the northern occupation. While northerners did organize against the invaders, most notably in New Mexico and California, guerrilla activity in the north never seriously threatened Taylor's position. Except for a few weeks in early 1847 when Santa Anna tried to encourage irregular attacks on Taylor's rear, guerrilla activity remained highly local, poorly coordinated, and apparently unattractive to most residents—much like the fighting against los bárbaros. Notwithstanding the brutal overreaction of Texas rangers and others to scattered acts of guerrilla violence, cooler heads recognized that the insurgency was but a shadow of what it could have been. Gregg thought that northeastern Mexico should have been able to field one hundred thousand men to wage an irregular war against U.S. forces, but that fewer than a thousand or even a hundred had joined General José Urrea, the determined federalist who had fomented rebellion in Sonora and the northeast, when he tried to raise a guerrilla army.[20]

Northern authorities outside of the zone of occupation faced similar problems when ordered to contribute to the war effort. The most important examples came from the fall of 1846. At that time Mexico's best hope of ending the war rested with Santa Anna's ability to amass a huge army at San Luis Potosí and march it north to defeat Taylor. Such a victory would have galvanized the population, emboldened war critics in the United States, and put Polk in a very precarious political position. In short, it could have redefined the dynamic of the entire war. The government issued an ambitious plan calling upon individual states to contribute a specific number of men. But, recognizing the troubles the north faced with los bárbaros and with the norteamericanos, the plan required contributions from only three northern states: Chihuahua, Durango, and Zacatecas.[21] None of the three sent Santa Anna any men. Chihuahua had to cope with Apache raiders and the anxiety of the eventual arrival of U.S. troops from New Mexico. More immediately, Chihuahua shared with Durango the crisis of several Comanche campaigns in the fall of 1846 that made parting with any manpower unthinkable. Officials in Zacatecas understandably harbored considerable ill will and suspicion for the man who devastated their state in 1835, and this resentment undoubtedly influenced their decision not to reinforce Santa Anna. But here, too, Indian raiders made for a legitimate if expedient excuse. In October and early November, exactly when Santa Anna was building his army, the commander general of Zacatecas had to march five hundred men and a precious artillery piece nearly to the edge of the Bolsón de Mapimí in an attempt to keep out the Comanches who were then devastating Durango. Between them Chihuahua, Durango, and Zacatecas had been asked to supply nearly three thousand men, a figure that would have increased Santa Anna's force at La Angostura/Buena Vista by almost a fifth. Given the tiny margin of victory Taylor enjoyed in that confrontation, the additional men from these states could have tipped the contest in Mexico's favor.[22]

Mexico's minister of internal and external relations believed that U.S. officials were directing the Comanches' movements and perceived a direct link between the war against Americans and the war against barbarians. In November 1846 he had told the governors they had to choose whether to bequeath to their children a strong, proud nation or "oblige them to curse our memory, and to soak with tears of desperation both the cities dominated by Americans, and the land desolated by the projects of savages." But when Santa Anna failed to defeat Taylor at Buena Vista, the minister of war and others in central Mexico castigated northern states and made little allowance for the distraction of Indian raiding. The editors of Durango's state newspaper responded to these kinds of criticisms with outrage: "After we have clamored in vain for many years for help in freeing ourselves from the barbarians who have destroyed the wealth of the state, after we have unceasingly requested arms and nearly always been denied for the most contemptible and miserable of reasons," still "there are those in the capital who have enough insolence to label us traitors! Why? Because we have not fielded armies that have been impossible to raise, because they need be composed of men paid in cash, and our brothers have been assassinated by the barbarians, or else fled far away from their fury?"[23]

Chihuahua's residents also had to defend themselves against charges of selfishness, cowardice, and treachery, especially after Doniphan and his men captured the state with such ease. The prolific Mexican writer Carlos María de Bustamante believed that "nearly a majority [of Chihuahuans] wanted the enemy to arrive; partly because they are oppressed by the department's continuous exactions and war with the barbarian Apaches, which has ruined them." Norte-americano occupation was attractive, Bustamante reasoned, because the U.S. would increase trade in the state and make Chihuahua "free from barbarians." Mexico's minister of war issued a scathing denunciation of Chihuahua's perfor-mance, which provoked a spirited response from some of the state's elite, in-cluding José Agustín de Escudero. The group insisted that Chihuahua had been forced to face the United States alone and that most of its men were trained in hand-to-hand combat against Apaches, not in formal battles with an organized army. A year later the state's representatives were still mocking the notion that Doniphan's forces had an easy victory simply because Chihuahua wanted them there: "Oh! It is a benign and hospitable state afflicted and desolated for fifteen years by the savages, drowned in the blood of the men and in the lamentations of the widows and the orphans, an ideal theater in which to showcase the power of the United States."[24]

This last barb was aimed both at critics in Mexico City and, perhaps most especially, at the norteamericanos. It was true that Polk and his advisors initially decided to wage the war in places such as Chihuahua that they knew had been ravaged by a decade or more of raiding.[25] But that did not mean the U.S. Army was incapable of fighting under more challenging conditions. When Mexico's leaders remained defiant even after Taylor took Monterrey, Polk began to ques-tion his assumptions about the war. Mexicans kept on, despite defeats, and, con-trary to expectations, the conquest and occupation of most of northern Mexico had not been enough to bring them to terms. By October 1846 the president reluctantly decided he would have to shift operations south and seize Veracruz. Then, after the Democrats took a drubbing in November's midterm elections, Benton convinced him that more troops would have to be called up in case the United States had to attack Mexico City as well. Democratic leaders worried that the war could become an unbearable political liability, and it had to be brought to a close.[26]

Polk put General Winfield Scott in charge of the new campaign. The gen-eral landed ten thousand men near Veracruz on March 9, 1847, just two weeks after the Mexican defeat at la Angostura, and bombarded the crowded city into submission. Santa Anna had hoped to preempt Scott's landing by defeating Tay-lor, and, having failed in that, he marched his exhausted men south to protect Mexico City. Santa Anna first confronted Scott at the Battle of Cerro Gordo on April 17, and U.S. forces drove defenders from three strategic points along the road to the capital. Both sides spent time regrouping while negotiators tried un-successfully to end the war. Finally in August Scott opened up his campaign to take the ancient metropolis, and by mid-September he had driven the Mexican army from the capital. Santa Anna still had nine thousand men and attempted to defeat his enemies at Puebla. His failure marked the last major battle of the U.S.–Mexican War.[27]

Mexico's interim government removed Santa Anna from command and the disgraced leader sailed into exile, again. Mexico now had to decide whether to fight on or sue for peace. The American negotiator Nicholas Trist had been in residence in Mexico for some time, ready to talk—though not on generous terms, especially now that Scott had taken the capital and left Mexico's army broken and demoralized. Some argued for continuing the war through guerrilla resistance, for wearing down the norteamericanos until they finally left the country or conceded more favorable terms. Others thought it would be futile or worse to fight any longer. The Mexican Congress elected the moderate Pedro María Anaya as interim president, and he convened a special council of state governors to help decide whether to pursue war or peace.[28]

The governor of San Luis Potosí argued passionately for war, perhaps because he did not know what Comanches were doing to his state while he was away. As a U.S. officer put it, "Whilst [the governor] was making most furious 'war to the knife' speeches at Querétaro, a handful of Comanches crossed the desert of San Luis Potosí and committed all sorts of depredations at the very gates of the Capital." There were in fact more than a handful. Several hundred Comanches came within seventeen leagues of the state capital and wreaked tremendous damage everywhere they went. A letter writer from the state claimed that "there are now known to be more than 400 unfortunates whom the Indians have killed in the countryside and at the watering places they have visited, committing a thousand iniquities and every class of cruelty as is their custom, sparing neither the decrepit nor children nor women." In between attacks on settlements, the raiders had a number of engagements with Mexican forces. In two pitched battles the Comanches killed 146 soldiers. Finally, on November 18 the Mexicans had better luck. A joint force of perhaps 1,400 men from San Luis Potosí and Zacatecas under General Francisco Avalos converged on about 350 Indians that he trapped at the Rancho de San Juan del Salado. Avalos claimed to have killed all but a handful of the raiders after a major battle and then a siege that lasted several days, and he reportedly recovered two hundred captives and two thousand horses. If the general did indeed kill more than three hundred raiders, it would have been the most calamitous defeat Comanches and Kiowas ever suffered below the Rio Grande. But even a victory of that magnitude would have underscored the fact that the people of San Luis Potosí had enough worries without spearheading Mexico's guerrilla war against the United States. Elsewhere Mexicans had several other kinds of major problems that made continued resistance seem impossible. The quixotic governor lost the argument. All of the other delegates voted to open negotiations, and representatives prepared to treat with the impatient Mr. Trist.[29]

ESSENTIAL TO US, USELESS TO HER:
THE MEXICAN CESSION

The representatives had an unenviable task. They knew going into the negotiations that the United States would make staggering demands. All along, Polk's primary goal in his dealings with Mexico had been the acquisition of the California coast. The president and his contemporaries considered California the jewel of northern Mexico for one simple reason: its spectacular harbors. Along with the settlement of the Oregon boundary that confirmed U.S. access to the Strait of Juan de Fuca, control of the California coast would position the republic to become perhaps the dominant power in the Pacific. Mexico had done little to exploit the commercial advantages of the California coast, and expansionists made a threatening case that some other world power, notably Britain, would surely acquire San Francisco if the United States did not. Even opponents of the war admitted the appeal of California's harbors. Recognizing that the Americans were fixed in their intention to possess the coast, Mexican negotiators had expressed willingness to part with much of California even before Scott took Mexico City.[30]

But Polk went farther, insisting that Mexico surrender not only greater Texas and coastal California, but also everything in between. Here the president had a harder case to make. This enormous, mostly uncharted region had as yet no commercial imperative to help justify expansion, little confirmed mineral wealth or agricultural potential, and even the most paranoid Anglophobe would have had trouble arguing that places like El Paso and Taos figured into British machinations. Moreover, the lower Rio Grande and New Mexico had a considerable population of Mexicans who had been there for generations and, in some cases, centuries. In 1846 there were some sixty-five thousand Mexicans and Pueblo Indians in New Mexico (as opposed to slightly more than seven thousand Mexicans in California). Except for "pure-blood Spaniards," all of these people were despised by the racist majority in the administration and Congress. As the Taos revolt demonstrated, moreover, many New Mexicans remained bitterly opposed to U.S. rule. Mexican negotiators initially refused to abandon these people, whom they started calling "the truest Mexicans, and most faithful patriots." But expansionists still had practical reasons for wanting the huge region between the California coast and the westernmost Texan settlements. Most important, they desired territory for a southern railway route to and from California, and if they were going to honor the Texans' wild claim over the Rio Grande to its source then they would have to acquire the most populous towns in New Mexico as well.[31]

Mexican negotiators, then, had to steel themselves for an almost incalculable loss. Apart from the greatly expanded state of Texas, the terms they finally resigned themselves to gave the United States all of present-day California, Nevada, and Utah, nearly all of New Mexico, most of Arizona and Colorado, and parts of Wyoming, Kansas, and Oklahoma. In return the United States would recall its army and halt its aggressive war. Of decidedly less importance, it would assume all of the outstanding claims that U.S. citizens had against Mexico and make a token payment of fifteen million dollars to "purchase" the territories it had seized. The U.S. Senate narrowly approved the treaty with amendments in March of 1848. The Mexican Congress ratified it in May. Including the loss of Texas, which Mexico had never formally recognized heretofore, the United States acquired half of the Mexican republic through the treaty of Guadalupe Hidalgo.[32]

This staggering transfer of territory is of course what was most significant about the U.S.–Mexican War. Much has been written about the diplomatic and political events that led to the conflict, about how these two nations finally came to blows. But the outbreak of the war is neither the most surprising nor the most important part of the story. Given Mexico's tense relationship with the United States after 1836, the inability of the parties to resolve the issue of unpaid claims and the status of Texas, and the strained ambiguity over Texas's proper boundaries, some sort of conflict seemed highly likely to observers in both countries. What is astonishing, though through familiarity Americans now rarely think it so, is that the conflict ended with Mexico surrendering half its territory to the United States.

The question, therefore, is how this incredible outcome seemed natural, sensible, just, inevitable, even overly generous to an American president, his cabinet, most of Congress, and much of the American public and the press in 1848. After all, thirteen years earlier Andrew Jackson had also attempted to buy Texas, most of New Mexico, the lower Rio Grande, and northern California, and, like Polk, had his offers rebuffed at a time of mounting diplomatic tension. Over the following months, as bad relations between the two governments grew considerably worse because of the Texas revolt, Jackson angrily told Congress that Mexico's many insults and injuries would "justify, in the eyes of all nations, immediate war." Yet his idea of war had been to send the U.S. Navy to demand satisfaction, probably by blockading Veracruz, as the Spanish had done and as the French would do only months after Jackson made his threat. In contrast, when Polk had his offer rebuffed he immediately sent a general to precipitate a land war and, as soon as one began, dispatched another general to conquer and claim the vast territories of New Mexico and California for the United States.[33]

How, then, had Americans in the 1840s come to think it legitimate and consistent with their sense of personal and national honor to seize half of a troubled neighboring republic through war? The answer brings to light the final major consequence of the convergence between Mexico's conflicts with Americans and independent Indians. Of the many things that had changed in the years separating Jackson and Polk, none was more significant than the shift in how Anglo-American leaders viewed Mexico's claims to its northern territories. And this shift had everything to do with the War of a Thousand Deserts.

By 1848 most in Washington took it as a given that Mexico's attempts at settling and developing its northern territories had been confirmed failures. That these attempts were considered failures was not so much because vast areas of the Mexican north remained undeveloped—the United States would have been vulnerable to that charge itself. For example, more than half a century elapsed before there were more than fifty Americans permanently resident in what is now central and eastern Colorado, territory acquired in 1803 as part of the Louisiana Purchase. The Mexicans had failed not because of what they had yet to do, but because the things they and their Spanish forebears had accomplished were being undone by Indians. In other words, between 1836 and 1848 stories about Indian raiding helped expansionists envision the Mexican north as a vast territory of man-made deserts—a place empty of meaningful Mexican history and increasingly empty of Mexicans themselves. As one prowar newspaper put it, "Our way lies not over trampled nations, but through desert wastes." Mexico retained its diplomatic claims upon the far north, but in light of the very old (and perennially useful) idea that possession, increase, and improvement constituted the only "true title" to land, the diplomatic claim seemed but a hollow pretense.[34]

This logic sounded familiar to anyone who had paid attention to the debates over Anglo-American title to Texas. And because the outbreak of war with Mexico hinged so much on the question of Texas's proper boundaries, Texans in Congress felt compelled to drag out the Texas Creation Myth and justify their title over and over again. At the onset of the war, for example, a representative from west Texas insisted that "any set of men, as has been justly asserted on this floor, have a natural right to take a territory" that is neither occupied nor cultivated. This, he declared, was how the Americans found Texas—they had come as invited guests to make it "a barrier to protect [Mexico] from the Indians, who are more than equal to the Mexicans in war." Months later Sam Houston, now a senator, reminded his esteemed colleagues that Texas had been a wasteland before Americans arrived: "The Indians had so pressed on the settlements of Mexico that towns which had been populous, towns which had consisted of fifteen or sixteen thousand souls, were reduced to mere hamlets. The Indians were pressing on, on every side. They had no frontier, for every village was a frontier, encircled and surrounded by savage tribes, from the seaboard to the interior."[35]

By 1846 expansionists had come to describe the rest of northern Mexico in nearly identical terms. An Indiana senator could thus defend the taking of so much Mexican land simply by characterizing it as empty, "essential to us, useless to her," a "wilderness uninhabited, save by bands of roving savages." Another from Virginia said he did not "believe it practicable to prevent our people from overspreading that country. The Mexican people [are] now receding before the Indian; and this affords a new argument in favor of our occupation of the territory, which would otherwise fall into the occupation of the savage."[36]

These kinds of perceptions have to be taken seriously. U.S. leaders invoked Indian violence against Mexicans not simply as rhetorical cover for naked territorial ambitions, though raiding certainly provided that. Congressmen, editors, and administration officials invoked Mexico's ruinous Indian war as compelling and, to their minds, honest evidence that Mexicans were incapable of developing their northern lands. This is not to say that everyone who thought Indians had reversed Mexican development in the north wanted to acquire Mexican territory. Politicians who felt ambivalent about or even opposed to the war also talked about raiding, but they incorporated Indians into arguments against the cession. For example, a Connecticut Whig who argued against acquiring the territory described it as worthless, home to little else than "savages and an impassible desert, where no man could travel with safety." A more common argument against territorial acquisition maintained that the U.S. polity would become debased if it were to absorb masses of Indians and mixed-race Mexicans. Along these lines one senator objected to talk of keeping the Mexican northeast by pointing to "the well-known fact, that in that quarter of Mexico the Indians have encroached upon and broken up many of the settlements of the Spaniards, that there is [therefore] a much larger population of Indians than in other parts of Mexico."[37]

In other words, if rhetoric about Mexico's Indian war was part of a calculated expansionist argument, it also opened a window onto fundamental assumptions that, by 1846, had become common across the political spectrum. Indeed, one of the men who invoked Indian raiding most regularly, John C. Calhoun, was often at odds with the expansionist program. Calhoun actually abstained from

23. "Indian Atrocities in New Mexico." From John Frost,
Pictorial History of Mexico and the Mexican War (1848).

the initial vote on the war, disliked the president's machinations, and thought
that the acquisition of significant territory below the Rio Grande, which is what
Polk and some on his cabinet privately wanted, would hurt the southern slave
states. So at two different moments when he feared that events might shift in
favor of a larger cession, Calhoun made passionate speeches in support of U.S.
forces pulling back to a defensive line on the Rio Grande and keeping everything
above, whether Mexico agreed to it or not. First, he justified taking New Mexico
and California in part by pointing to Mexico's singular failure with independent
Indians. "It was a remarkable fact in the history of this continent," he said in his
first speech, "that, for the first time, the aborigines had been pressing upon the

population of European extraction." Months later he again spoke about Indians, this time as part of his argument against a prolonged war and an increased cession: "Well, the whole of the country covered by that line is inhabited by Indian tribes, so powerful that there is no fear of Mexico invading. They invade Mexico! They are too powerful for her; and it will not require a single soldier to be stationed on its whole extent to protect us against Mexico." Nor would soldiers be needed to guard U.S. interests against Indian raiders, "as their hostility to Mexico, and their love of plunder, would direct their warfare exclusively against Mexico."[38]

No one rose to dispute Calhoun's characterizations. Many disagreed with his position certainly, but no one challenged the notion that Indians were dismantling Mexico's accomplishments in the north. That notion is surely why, with the exception of narrow debates about the land between the Nueces and the Rio Grande, opponents of the war and of the cession rarely spoke of Mexico's territorial rights, and even then only in generalities. Many in Congress thought the war unjust and made withering critiques of Polk's rationalization of the conflict. But when they spoke of Mexico's territorial rights they almost never ventured beyond the undisputed though sterile fact that Mexico retained legal title. It is striking that antiexpansionists, groping for ammunition against Polk's designs, failed to invoke more resonant and compelling arguments in defense of Mexico's claims. Were northern Mexicans not pioneers, warrior-farmers in difficult lands who had worked and bled for family, faith, monarch, and nation, just as the pioneer heroes of U.S. history had? Had not their recent sufferings underscored these sacrifices all the more? Was it not a perversion of basic American ideals to despoil Mexico of lands that its people and their ancestors had been fighting Indians for since the sixteenth century? The war's many opponents avoided these sorts of arguments. Antiexpansionists had a variety of reasons for opposing the president's war, and most of them may not have held Mexico's territorial claims in contempt. But neither did they care to dwell on the historical specifics of Mexico's northern endeavors because, like their opponents, they believed those endeavors had been either stalled or reversed by Indians.[39]

Northern Mexico's prostrate condition before Comanches, Kiowas, Navajos, and Apaches therefore became a component basic to how most U.S. politicians thought about the proposed cession—but that was only half of the story. The other half, fully realized in the Texas Creation Myth though as yet only latent in the ongoing war with Mexico, concerned the Anglo-American capacity, even destiny, to do what Mexico could not: redeem the desert, defeat the Indians, and provide security to the long-suffering people of the Mexican north. This was precisely what Polk had instructed his generals to tell Mexicans in the field, and, if Benton's St. Louis paean to Captain Reid is any guide, this is how many Americans in and out of power wanted to see the war.

Captive Mexican women and children gave mute but visceral reassurance to U.S. politicians that their demands on Mexico were just, even humane. Stories of hundreds or thousands of Mexican women and children living as slaves in Comanche camps had circulated widely in the ten years after the Texas revolt, and more emerged during the war debates. In his speech in early 1847, for example, Calhoun insisted that Comanches held no fewer than two thousand Mexicans captive. As the conflict progressed, expansionist rhetoric latched onto the captives' plight as perhaps the most urgent moral imperative behind the permanent occupation of New Mexico. In early 1848 another senator who, unlike Calhoun, wanted to include northeastern Mexican states in the cession, proclaimed that "the inhabitants of those provinces are assailed by Indians, and the women and children are daily falling into the hands of these roving bands, by whom they are made slaves for life. It would therefore be beneficial to Mexico to take this course." Here was a cry for help. Here was a compelling invitation into the deserts of northern Mexico, an unofficial version of the call that Austin and his colonists had answered in Texas a generation before.[40]

Fittingly, it was President Polk who made the most of this issue. In a careful speech before Congress in late 1847 he finally made explicit his territorial ambitions and explained how Mexico would actually benefit from his design. Polk said that the Mexican government should desire to place New Mexico "under the protection" of the United States because Mexico was too feeble to stop the bands of "warlike savages" from committing depredations not only upon New Mexico itself, but upon the other, more populous Mexican states farther south. Thus the cession would improve life for Mexicans north of the line, but, more important, it would be a boon for the much larger population below that had suffered so long from the raids. "It would be a blessing to all these northern states to have their citizens protected against [the Indians] by the power of the United States," he insisted. "At this moment many Mexicans, principally females and children, are in captivity among them. If New Mexico were held and governed by the United States, we could effectually prevent these tribes from committing such outrages, and compel them to release these captives, and restore them to their families and friends."[41]

Confident talk, but did anyone really believe it? Every senator had to decide for himself, because article 11 of the proposed treaty bound U.S. authorities to restrain Indians residing north of the new border from raiding into Mexico and to rescue any Mexican captives they learned were being held by Indians. The article had precedents. There had been a very similar mutual clause in an earlier treaty between Mexico and the United States, signed in 1831, that was itself based on an article in a treaty the United States and Spain ratified in 1795. But Indian raiding had obviously taken on new significance by the 1840s. Trist told Secretary of State James Buchanan that the northern states would never have approved the document were it not for article 11, and the Mexican negotiators held the article up before their countrymen as the bright spot in the otherwise disastrous agreement.[42]

The clause echoed Polk's own self-assured rhetoric about saving Mexicans from Indians, but, more important, it took such confidence to task. It forced senators to take a stand. All their talk about incompetent, cowardly Mexicans, contemptible Comanches, Americans easily defeating independent Indians and turning deserts into gardens—was this just talk? or did they really believe what they said? After more than a decade of eavesdropping on Mexico's Indian war, had U.S. politicians simply come away with fodder for expansionist discourse? Or had they actually come to believe that Indians had wrecked Mexico's northern experiment because Mexicans were weak and that Americans could and would succeed where Mexicans had failed? The arguments in the Senate over article 11 would have answered this question, but the treaty debates were held in secret and only scattered hints survive as to who said what. In the end, though, the votes went on record.

The people who understood Mexico's security problem best voted against article 11. Unlike nearly everyone else in Washington, the Texans appreciated how difficult it would be to prevent Indian raids into Mexico. They gladly talked in the abstract about saving Mexicans from their savage foes, but when it came time to vote they led the charge against the article. Houston opposed the treaty generally because he wanted more territory, and he argued against article 11 specifically because he thought it would leave the United States "encumbered by conditions relative to the Indians which would be worth more, in a pecuniary point of view, than all the vacant land acquired." Once it seemed clear the treaty would pass, Houston and his fellow Texan Thomas Jefferson Rusk enlisted Benton (also well informed about Mexican security), Jefferson Davis, commander of a regiment in northeastern Mexico during the war, Stephen A. Douglas, and a dozen others in an attempt to gut article 11 before the final vote. In the end they managed only to remove a prohibition against providing Indians with firearms and ammunition, something the secretary of state later explained was done on "a principle of humanity" since Indians had to live by hunting.[43]

The majority, senators versed more in the rhetoric than the reality of Mexico's Indian war, voted to assume responsibility for preventing Indian raids into Mexico. They apparently did so convinced of their own discourse: that the

Anglo-American people would indeed save northern Mexico simply by letting the energies of their historical trajectory flow into the new territories. They would defeat the Indians, would redeem the captives, and would rescue the vast, derelict garden of northern Mexico from Mexican neglect. The Mexican Congress accepted U.S. amendments to the treaty, and the two republics exchanged ratifications on May 30, 1848, remaking the continent with a handshake. Hundreds of miles away Comanche men hunted bison and made plans for autumn and winter.

Epilogue

ARTICLE 11

Article 11 of the Treaty of Guadalupe Hidalgo stands as a memorial to three things. First, it is a marker of Mexico's failure to respond as a nation to the security crisis posed by the War of a Thousand Deserts in the 1830s and 1840s. Faced with chronic fiscal problems, precarious national administrations spent their scarce political and financial capital placating allies and fighting rebellious countrymen. National figures out of power, those responsible for coups and rebellions, likewise viewed their own ideological and political ambitions as far more important to the republic's future than the seemingly apolitical project of fighting independent Indians and securing the frontier. Mexico's insufficient response to Indian raiding therefore emerged from both material and ideological causes. Northerners argued passionately that their war against los bárbaros could have consequences for the entire republic; that, like their Spanish predecessors, Mexico's leaders should invest in the frontier to safeguard the country as a whole. Not until the mid-1840s did this idea gain any powerful adherents in Mexico City, and by then the impoverished, divided, and exhausted north faced another kind of invasion. "How different the [U.S.–Mexican] war might have been," asked the editors of a national newspaper in the summer of 1848, "had the frontier states not been abandoned to their luck! Mexico would have been an impregnable barrier of patriotism among the inhabitants."[1]

After the war Mexico's leaders became more attuned to the idea that los bárbaros could threaten the republic's core interests. José Joaquín de Herrera, the moderate president who seemed poised to improve frontier defense in 1845 before losing office in a coup, resumed the presidency in 1848 and made Mariano Arista his secretary of war. Herrera and Arista used treaty payments from the United States to implement major reforms in frontier security. Two weeks after

the exchange of treaty ratifications, Mexico's Congress passed a law appropriat-
ing two hundred thousand pesos for defense against Indian raiders, to be divided
more or less equally among the governors of states exposed to attacks. More am-
bitiously, the government ordered the establishment of eighteen military colonies across the frontier. The plan allotted land and resources to Mexican men
willing to enlist for six-year terms, and it encouraged settlements around the
colonies. The government began stationing far more troops on the frontier than
it had before and introduced more elaborate measures for the coordination of
local militia. It also made grants of lands to Seminoles, Creeks, and eventually
Kickapoos who promised to help fight Indian raiders; forced defeated peasants
from the Sierra Gorda rebellion to serve at the frontier; and established a small
northern colony of French immigrants.[2]

Finally, northerners took steps of their own. Private organizations and public
officials created funds for head and scalp bounties, and soon scores of mercenary
outfits were doing across the north what James Kirker and others had done in
Chihuahua and Sonora. Just as important, representatives from northern states
met in council to talk about coordinating policy and defense across state lines.
Individual towns likewise made defensive compacts, governors reformed militia
procedures, and state treasuries boosted funding for frontier settlements. Eventually the reforms at the national, state, and local levels would help increase the
north's population and make the region more prosperous and secure than ever
before.[3]

But first, northern Mexicans would endure many more years of calamity.
The postwar period began with a prolonged regional drought, a crisis in the
food supply, and a cholera epidemic that burned through the north from 1849
through the early 1850s. In the midst these troubles, raids grew progressively
worse. Mexico's official newspaper ran just over 200 articles on northern Indians each year between 1849 and 1851, but it ran 452 in 1852 and 362 in 1853.
Apaches continued to attack points in Sonora, Chihuahua, and Durango, while
Comanches and Kiowas sent huge campaigns into Tamaulipas, Nuevo León,
Coahuila, Chihuahua, Durango, Zacatecas, San Luis Potosí, and, for the first
time, into the state of Jalisco. Lieutenant William Emory, charged with surveying the new border for the United States, encountered multiple parties of raiders
in the course of his labors and believed that the unceasing campaigns had driven
even the residents of Durango's capital city to an "unmanly despair." It is easy
to see why. In 1856, authorities in Durango would calculate that in two decades
Indian raiders in that state had killed nearly 6,000 people, seized 748 captives,
and forced the abandonment of 358 settlements. Emory himself indulged in a
little despair when he contemplated the U.S. commitments in article 11: "No

amount of force could have kept the Indians from crossing the line to commit depredations, and I think that one hundred millions of dollars would not repay the damages they have inflicted. Whole sections of country have been depopulated, and the stock driven off and killed; and in entire states the ranches have been deserted and the people driven into the towns."[4]

Mexico's gradual security reforms could not beat back this surge in raiding. And, as before, instability in the capital would drain any plans for the frontier of urgency and attention. The humiliation, despair, and recriminations occasioned by Mexico's defeat in *la intervención norteamericana*, as Mexicans came to call the war, brought renewed intensity to familiar ideological debates about how the country should be governed. Many agreed with the old conservative Lucas Alamán that the debacle of the war only proved Mexico unfit for republican government. Alamán and others insisted that the country needed a monarch if it was to recapture the security, stability, and prosperity of the late colonial era. These sentiments even gave rise to a failed coup against Herrera's government, one put down by an aging General Anastacio Bustamante. Despite mounting political instability, Herrera made Mexican history in 1851 when he peacefully surrendered power to his constitutionally elected successor, Mariano Arista.[5]

Arista would not get to do the same. Under Alamán's tutelage the conservatives worked diligently to exploit any weakness or misstep and bring the new president down. Faced with a diminishing treasury and envisioning some aggressive reforms, Arista inevitably made new enemies. When he tried to shrink the bloated Mexican military, conservatives rallied career officers against him. A coup forced Arista from office in early 1853, whereupon he went into exile in Europe and soon perished in a shipwreck near the Portuguese coast. His heart was eventually extracted from his body and reburied in Mexico. No president before him had understood better the hard reality of the war against los bárbaros or the political consequences of failure. Nonetheless, the movement that ousted Arista found early support in Chihuahua, where, among other things, the people accused him of failing to protect them against savages.[6]

The second thing that article 11 stands for is the paradox of Anglo-American racial confidence, which both facilitated U.S. expansion and blinded it to the limitations of its own power. In the decade after the Texan rebellion, many U.S. officials had come to believe that northern Mexico's security crisis amounted to a race war between two retrograde peoples. The conceit, supposedly born out in the Texan experience, was that Indians raided only because of Mexican weakness; that once Anglo-Americans possessed former Mexican territory, they would quickly subdue the raiders and make gardens out of deserts.

Polk and his generals skillfully capitalized on northern Mexico's misery in managing the occupation, and in the process commanders on the ground learned that raids could be more easily exploited than controlled. But back in Washington few questioned their country's ability to redeem captives and control Indians. Hence the vote in favor of article 11, and the later assurance from the U.S. secretary of state to his Mexican counterpart that Americans possessed "both the ability and the will to restrain the Indians within the extended limits of the United States from making incursions into the Mexican territories."[7]

Mexicans obviously had reason to doubt the secretary's sincerity in the late 1840s and early 1850s. As was true of Mexico in previous decades, U.S. neglect of the frontier derived partly from a sense of crisis in Washington. The vast Mexican cession had forced a divisive constitutional question upon the Union: did Congress have the right to regulate slavery in the new territories, and, if so, how? The question, and the attendant specter of sectional crisis, had been loosed upon the debate at the outset of the war when Representative David Wilmot of Pennsylvania attached an amendment to the first war spending bill that would have prohibited slavery in any territory acquired from Mexico. Though the Wilmot Proviso never passed the Senate (where southerners had more votes than they did in the House), it became a point of bitter dispute and haunted the election of 1848. To salve wounds after the bruising Democratic nominating convention of 1844, candidate Polk had promised to serve only one term. Thus the election of 1848 set the Democrat Lewis Cass against the Whig candidate and hero of the Mexican War, Zachary Taylor. The parties addressed the slavery question with spectacular dishonesty, assuring northerners that the territories would be free and southerners that the territories would have slaves. In the end Taylor won handily and assumed the presidency in early 1849. Polk left office an exhausted wreck and was dead by summer.[8]

General Taylor had earned his battlefield reputation, but President Taylor possessed little subtlety, nimbleness, or bargaining instinct with which to defuse the mounting constitutional crisis. In fact his bold but unrealistic reaction to the complex situation made matters considerably worse. Convinced that African slavery would never flourish in the west, Taylor proposed that the entire Mexican cession should bypass the territorial stage and be admitted to the Union as two vast states, California and New Mexico, and that slavery should be barred from both. Incredulous southerners denounced the president, and soon even mainstream politicians began talking about secession. The smoldering standoff nearly exploded in the southwest. Still insisting that their boundary followed the Rio Grande to its source and livid about being told they could not take their slaves west, Texans began trying to exert authority over eastern New Mexico (or, as they called it, west Texas). New Mexicans had little interest in adopting African slavery, partly because the climate made plantation agriculture impractical and partly because they had long relied on their own peculiar institution—Indian slavery—for labor. When Texan threats resulted in increased agitation for New Mexican statehood, some in the Texas state congress labeled New Mexicans traitors and insisted that an armed body be sent to "suppress the existing rebellion in Santa Fe." Taylor thought Texas's claim outrageous and ordered federal troops in New Mexico to prepare for hostilities. Sober observers began worrying about civil war; about federal troops, Texans, and volunteers from other southern states killing each other outside Santa Fe. Many began to see the sense in Ralph Waldo Emerson's prediction in 1846 that victory over Mexico would "poison us."[9]

The United States might have torn itself apart in 1850 had not a fateful bowl of iced milk and cherries on Independence Day given Taylor the gastroenteritis that killed him on July 9. Mild Vice President Millard Fillmore ascended to the presidency and embraced congressional efforts to defuse the crisis. By September, Henry Clay, Stephen Douglas, and others had pushed through a series of bills that admitted California as a free state, organized the rest of the cession into the territories of Utah and New Mexico without reference to slavery, and convinced Texas to surrender about half of its claim on New Mexico in return for federal assumption of ten million dollars in Texan debt. The legislation also outlawed the slave trade in the District of Columbia and enacted a tough new fugitive slave law, one bitterly resented by many in the north. The fruits of the U.S.–Mexican War had become inextricably connected to controversies over slavery, and, notwithstanding the profound relief and jubilation occasioned by the Compromise of 1850, Clay and Douglas had only quieted these controversies, not killed them.[10]

Meanwhile, the crisis had consumed Washington's attention for more than two years while Indian raids across the new border with Mexico had grown progressively worse. Since the signing of the treaty many Indian agents and military officers in New Mexico and Texas worked earnestly to prevent cross-border raids through force and diplomacy. Indian agents moved aggressively to build relationships with key native leaders, securing new treaties that included clauses about releasing Mexican prisoners and, in one case, prohibiting raids across the border. But agents found their influence undercut by aggressive civilians, by delays and parsimony on the part of Congress, and by the lack of a credible military deterrent to cross-border raids. The military did establish new forts in Texas and New Mexico and by the end of 1849 had stationed nearly two thousand troops in the region. But infantry were not going to intercept horse-borne raiders, and there were never more than six hundred U.S. cavalry within reach of the international border in the first four years following the treaty's ratification. Even this paltry figure overstated U.S. capabilities because none of these cavalry were stationed on the river between its mouth and El Paso. Without the requisite support from Congress, U.S. agents and soldiers managed to redeem only a handful of Mexican captives from the Indian peoples of the region, and they obviously failed to keep raiding parties from crossing into Mexico.[11]

The U.S. Army even had trouble protecting Mexican settlements above the border. Navajos and Mexicans continued to prey upon each other in New Mexico, and in early 1850 eight hundred Comanches attacked the city of Laredo and reached its main plaza before retreating. One hundred Mexican and Anglo-American men pursued the raiders, and in the resulting confrontation the Comanches reportedly killed them all. Many northern Mexicans continued to believe that only unrelenting military campaigns into la comanchería and la apachería would convince bárbaros to stop raiding Mexican settlements, and the increased resources and manpower on the frontier might have made such campaigns a possibility by the early 1850s. But the new border meant that Mexican forces could not pursue Indians where they lived, and thus northerners could only be reactive and hope the United States would start taking its obligations more seriously.[12]

And they could sue. In 1850 Robert Letcher, U.S. minister to Mexico, warned Secretary of State Daniel Webster that hacendados in Durango and elsewhere intended to file claims against the U.S. government for all damages committed by independent Indians since the end of the war. That claim could be enormous. Letcher sent astonished letters back to Washington detailing Comanche campaigns across the north, campaigns that left entire haciendas in ruins. Mexican cowardice and incompetence evidently had less to do with Indian raiding than many in Washington believed. Congressmen started talking openly about returning territory to Mexico, and the secretary of war raised the possibility of abandoning much of the southwest to native peoples and relocating Anglo-American settlers.[13]

Cooler heads suggested a less drastic solution. Webster wrote Letcher in the summer of 1851 to say that "the President deems it of the utmost importance that we should be released from the [treaty] stipulations in regard to Indians." Mexican authorities seemed open to the idea, though they initially insisted on twelve million dollars, which the United States rejected outright. But raiding only intensified and damages mounted. Letcher worried that unless the parties reached agreement on "that miserable 11th article" immediately, "G-d only knows, the consequences which our country must suffer hereafter." By mid-1853 the Mexican government claimed that it could reasonably insist on forty million dollars and that it would accept nothing less than half that sum to adjust the treaty. Letcher had previously mused that the Mexican Congress was the problem, and that if only Mexico had a dictator then the matter could be resolved amicably.[14]

The minister's wish came true in short order. The plotters in the coup that deposed Arista had difficulty agreeing on a figurehead to govern while they tried to find a European prince to establish a monarchy. Eventually they compromised by once more resurrecting the great political phoenix, Santa Anna. Recalled from exile, he inherited serious deficits from Arista's government and also had to cope with a vexing boundary dispute with the United States. Poor maps had produced confusion over the proper boundaries of southern New Mexico, and conflicts with Chihuahua threatened a diplomatic crisis. Moreover, the U.S. government had concluded that it wanted a stretch of land in northern Chihuahua and Sonora for a railway route. Given his fiscal problems Santa Anna looked kindly on a U.S. offer to pay ten million dollars to settle the boundary dispute, purchase land for the railroad, and obtain release from article 11.[15]

But when he willingly sold national territory through the Gadsden Purchase Santa Anna's star came crashing down for the last time. Another coup drove him from office in 1855 and he sailed into exile, not to return until nearly two decades later, when he came home to die in near-obscurity. For their part U.S. negotiators had expanded their republic at Mexico's expense, yet again, and eliminated an embarrassing reminder that in their potent, racist confidence the Anglo-Americans had badly underestimated Mexicans and Indians and overestimated themselves.[16]

Third and finally, article 11 testifies to the fact that indigenous polities continued to shape the international contest for North America even into the mid-nineteenth century. Comanche, Kiowa, Apache, and Navajo raids disrupted northern Mexico's economy, population, and community; provoked political crises throughout the Mexican north and set northerners against their central government; facilitated the U.S. conquest and occupation of northern Mexico; and helped shape Anglo-American confidence about the justice and inevitability of its aggressive territorial expansion. Indian raids mattered. But because these raids came with few or no declarations of purpose, because they unfolded in seemingly random places with little formal leadership, and because racism and hatred impeded understanding, Mexican and Anglo-American observers rarely acknowledged the fluid but sophisticated political accomplishments that made their Indian enemies so formidable.

This is not to deny that disagreements existed within indigenous communities, or to suggest that opinion or action ever approached unanimity. But it is

clear that Comanches, Kiowas, Apaches, and Navajos, albeit under very different circumstances, managed to coordinate the energies of their people in pursuit of shared goals. How else explain so many bands of Mescaleros, Chiricahuas,
and Western Apaches, for instance, abandoning peace with Mexico more or less
simultaneously; or so many Navajo families letting a handful of representatives
speak for them all to make coherent (if temporary) peace agreements with New
Mexicans? Distinct political mechanisms and traditions allowed considerable
factions of each people to forge broad consensus on policy and to execute policy
cooperatively. The fact that Indians raided for material gain hardly precluded
other, nonmaterial motivations or the significance of politics to the endeavor.
Economic ambitions have always motivated nation-states to make war on one
another, and none doubt the fact that politics has always been integral to their
pursuit of power.

Given evidence, then, of political organization behind raids, the relevant
question is how native communities used politics to pursue their goals. After all,
it is not simply the fact of organization, but the means and modes of organization, that determines the dynamics of conflict. Comanches illustrate this point
well. During the 1830s and 1840s, as they made peace with former enemies and
gained access to new markets, Comanches dramatically increased their thefts
of Mexican animals. Social pressures and political mechanisms at the family,
extended family, and residence band levels gave communities a stake in and also
a measure of control over personal quests for horses and prestige. As raiding intensified and more and more warriors died below the river, established protocols
for seeking revenge enabled paraibos to organize highly coordinated campaigns
of many hundreds of men from different Comanche bands, divisions, and allied
tribes. The huge campaigns empowered plains warriors to travel hundreds of
miles below the Rio Grande to attack ranches, haciendas, and even more populous towns and cities throughout the Mexican north. But because the politics
of these campaigns relied in part upon revenge for momentum and organization, Comanches spent nearly as much energy punishing Mexicans as they did
stealing from them. Hence the devastation in northern Mexico and its manifold
consequences must be understood with reference to the way Comanches and
Kiowas organized themselves to campaign below the river.

The escalating raids in the early 1850s, the threatened lawsuits, the frantic
efforts of U.S. officials to be released from article 11, and the quiet humiliation
embedded in the Gadsden Treaty all testify to the fact that decisions made by
Indian polities continued to influence international relations into the second
half of the century. And yet the Treaty of Guadalupe Hidalgo did represent the
apex of a distinct period of Comanche history, a period when a combination of

diplomatic, climatic, and economic factors empowered Comanches and their allies to act upon their remarkable potential for cooperation. Plains Indians continued and in certain years even intensified their large, long-distance campaigns through the mid-1850s. But thereafter most raiding parties became smaller, less coordinated, and less ambitious.[17]

In part this shift reflected a mounting demographic crisis. In 1849 cholera swept off hundreds, perhaps thousands of people from the southern plains. The Hois paraibos Mopechucope and Pia Kusa were among the dead, and Kiowas remembered the epidemic as the worst event in their history. Nonetheless, Comanches and Kiowas sent approximately nine hundred warriors to Chihuahua and Durango in the fall of 1850, thus committing more men in proportion to population than ever before to raiding campaigns. And yet the raids themselves had claimed several hundred warriors' lives in the 1830s and 1840s, and casualties continued to mount after 1848. Sometimes losses were staggering. In January 1854, for example, jubilant Mexican authorities reported that five hundred men from Durango had surprised a huge camp of raiders and killed more than one hundred.[18]

Reflecting on the cumulative costs of the war, southern plains peoples may have consoled themselves with the thought that captive Mexican women and children offset their own loses below the river. If so, they were mistaken. Overall, Comanches and Kiowas lost more than two men for every Mexican captive they managed to get across the Rio Grande during the 1830s and 1840s, and there is no reason to believe the ratio changed significantly afterward. Moreover, through regular contact with people across northern Mexico, raiders dramatically increased their exposure to disease. When returning home, they likely precipitated epidemics their communities might otherwise have avoided. While the 1849 cholera epidemic may have come from forty-niners traveling overland to California, for example, it is at least as likely that raiders acquired the sickness from their Mexican enemies, who were also ravaged by the disease. In other words, southern plains communities paid an enormous price for the spoils, war honors, and vengeance they obtained from Mexico. Their bold campaigns were self-consuming and ultimately unsustainable.[19]

Potsanaquahip and like-minded war leaders who survived the epidemic of 1849 faced other sorts of obstacles after the U.S.–Mexican War. Increased settlement and traffic on the margins of la comanchería, especially after the California gold rush, represented new market opportunities that probably fueled raids for a time. But these changes also brought new dangers. The huge campaigns of the 1830s and 1840s had depended in part upon security on the southern plains. By the 1850s Comanche and Kiowa men had to be more cautious about leaving their families and herds unprotected for weeks or months at a time, in large part because Anglo-American settlers continued to displace Indian communities from the prairies. More important, Texan rangers resumed their attacks on Comanche villages in the 1850s and 1860s, slaughtering men, women, and children by the hundreds. And while Mexican defenses developed unevenly, mounting Comanche and Kiowa casualties below the river make it clear that they had to be taken seriously. Would-be raiders seem to have adapted by traveling in smaller, more mobile parties to avoid the sort of attention their ill-fated kinsmen received in January 1854. These smaller parties increasingly sought cattle, in addition to horses, mules, and captives. Market demand for stolen cattle increased through the 1850s and into the 1860s. At the same time, the Comanches' and Kiowas' own voracious herds and increasing traffic through the southern plains devastated the grazing resources near rivers and streams that bison depended upon in winter. Starving and harried by more and more commercial hunting, bison populations collapsed. Southern plains Indians became increasingly dependent on other animals for food. It would have been exceedingly difficult for, say, eight hundred Comanches to round up thousands of cows from haciendas in Zacatecas or San Luis Potosí and get the plodding animals back across the Rio Grande without being attacked by Mexican forces. Smaller parties concentrating on herds in Texas and northernmost Mexico had better chance of success.[20]

Moreover, while the U.S. government managed with some embarrassment to extricate itself from article 11, it still sought to discourage Comanche raiding. It did so partly through violence, by gradually projecting more military force on the border and threatening Comanches where they lived; and partly through diplomacy, by offering inducements to Comanche leaders who compromised on land claims and stopped raiding activity of all kinds. At the Treaty of Fort Atkinson in 1853, for example, Comanches and Kiowas agreed to allow roads and posts in their territory and to remain at peace with both the United States and Mexico in return for a decade of eighteen-thousand-dollar annuities. The treaty certainly did not discourage determined raiders, but it did present yet another obstacle to the bold policy of collective warfare against Mexico that had characterized previous years.[21]

Finally, the civil wars that wracked Mexico and the United States in the 1850s and 1860s ultimately bequeathed upon both republics the military and political power to destroy Indian independence for good. Following Santa Anna's ouster in 1855, liberal politicians came to power in Mexico City. Convinced that archaic corporate entities had retarded Mexico's progress by inhibiting individual liberty, the liberals passed sweeping reforms culminating in a new constitution in 1857. Among other things, the constitution enshrined personal freedoms in a bill of rights, abolished corporate ownership of real estate (something dear to the church and critical to the autonomy of indigenous peasant communities), and eliminated age-old privileges for the clergy and military.[22]

Disgruntled officers mounted a coup at the end of the year, and this led to civil war. Liberal forces ultimately triumphed, thanks in part to the support of the United States, and the reformer Benito Juárez ascended to the presidency. In short order, however, he confronted yet another grave crisis when Emperor Napoleon III of France responded to the pleas of exiled Mexican monarchists and helped them find their longed-for European prince. Napoleon III suggested Archduke Maximilian of Austria, and Mexican conservatives enthusiastically agreed to make him king. In 1864 French troops helped conservatives drive Juárez from the capital and install Maximilian I as emperor of Mexico. By 1865 it seemed the new emperor had things well in hand; yet within a year's time, thanks in part to material and diplomatic support from the United States, liberals mounted a vigorous counteroffensive. In 1867, just as the fickle Napoleon III recalled his troops to France, liberal forces took the capital, captured Maximilian, and executed him along with some of his top Mexican allies. Juárez won reelection as president at the end of the year, and, after more than half a century of turmoil, Mexico at last entered an extended period of political stability. Juárez and, especially, his eventual successor Porfirio Díaz, moved forcefully to consolidate political power and promote economic growth. In the north this program included brutal campaigns against sedentary indigenous peoples like Yaquis and unprecedented financing and coordination of efforts against Indian raiders.[23]

In the United States, meanwhile, the sectional disputes that war with Mexico had done so much to energize soon overwhelmed the Compromise of 1850. By mid-decade proslavery and free-soil factions were killing each other in Kansas, armed Congressmen were menacing one another in the U.S. capital, and the national party system that had previously managed to defuse the slavery issue started coming apart. As the southern-dominated Democratic Party withered in the north, the Whigs lost all support in the south and even found their northern popularity collapsing as former supporters turned to new parties like the Republicans, which had less ambiguous stances on issues such as immigration and slavery. Abraham Lincoln's election provoked secession in 1861, and for the next four years the country was awash in blood. A civil war that left 620,000 soldiers dead and cost twenty billion dollars also saved the Union and freed four million slaves, though the full promise of that freedom would remain grossly unfulfilled for more than a century. The federal government emerged from the war far larger, more powerful, and obviously more united than ever before. As American settlers, politicians, and entrepreneurs began projecting new dreams onto the unconquered American west, that government and its army—now among the most effective and modern armed forces in the world—started moving decisively against independent Indians.[24]

Most Navajos had lost their freedom even in the midst of the Civil War. In 1864 New Mexican militia, initially organized for protection against confederate Texas, destroyed Navajo crops, orchards, and sheep and then marched more than nine thousand Navajos to a barren, impoverished reservation at Bosque Redondo east of the Rio Grande.[25] For many other independent native peoples the civil wars in the United States and Mexico were something of a reprieve, but a temporary one. In their aftermath independent Indians came under greater pressure from all directions. Authorities in Mexico City boosted funding for frontier defense and, critically, did more to intervene when squabbling state governments worked at cross-purposes. For their part, state and local officials in the north labored to coordinate defense and organize ambitious campaigns against Apaches in the northwest and against Apache and Comanche hideouts in the Bolsón de Mapimí. Meanwhile, officials at all levels urged northerners on, celebrating their intrepid valor and assuring them that in fighting barbarians they were doing the work of the nation and of civilization. Northern warriors agreed. Their profound conviction that they had nurtured the land and the nation with their own blood helped fuel a sense of outrage over their dispossession during the Porfirian era, one that would eventually contribute to northern mobilization in the Mexican Revolution in 1910.[26]

Above the border, U.S. officials accelerated efforts to confine Indians to reservations following the Civil War. Some Comanches had settled on reservations as early as the mid-1850s. Potsanaquahip, the most influential man among his people by then, could not bring himself to remain on a reservation but urged others to take advantage of the rations and security that agents offered. By the time the great paraibo died in 1867 U.S. agents and military officers had become more determined to withhold rations from those who refused to come in and stay. With bison scarcer and the U.S. military more threatening, thousands of southern plains Indians left Texas for reservation life in Indian Territory in 1867 and 1868. A minority refused, emboldened by a younger generation of warriors such as Quanah Parker, son of the paraibo Peta Nocona and the famous Texan captive Cynthia Ann Parker. By the early 1870s General of the Army William Tecumseh Sherman authorized punitive campaigns against "renegade" Comanches and Kiowas still raiding as before. The U.S. Army attacked native villages, killing many and capturing others. Officers also ordered all captured Indian horses round up and shot and gave encouragement and protection to commercial bison hunters who had all but destroyed the remaining herds by 1874. In the following spring, the last desperate, hungry holdouts surrendered to Sherman's officers and submitted to reservation life. In the coming decades Comanches would draw upon their remarkable cultural and political creativity to sustain themselves as a coherent people, but they underwent tremendous change and suffering in the process.[27]

By the mid-1880s, when Geronimo and his Apaches surrendered to U.S. authorities and cross-border Indian raids finally came to an end, the Comanche population had reportedly dwindled to fewer than two thousand people. Bison had become all but impossible to find, so reservation families relied on canvas to make tents and government handouts to feed their children. When the government decided southern plains Indians needed to be more self-sufficient, as it did on various occasions, it curtailed rations and used hunger to discipline the recalcitrant. With no game and few domestic animals, Comanches had little to trade, so many went without things they had come to take for granted in better days.

Some refused to live amidst the illness, despair, and deepening poverty of reservation life and so set out on a final trip to Mexico. One of the last stories that Mexican papers ran about plains raiders concerned a group of Comanches and Lipanes apprehended by federal troops below the border in 1879. Sick with smallpox, the Indians were dragged to Mexico City as dying showpieces from a bygone era. The irony is that Comanches themselves had helped usher in their new, diminished reality. And this is one way to compress their story: into a tidy, grim trajectory in which Indians inadvertently empower their most dangerous enemy and see their own power, prosperity, and freedom disappear as a consequence.[28]

But Comanches had reason to see it differently. They had not waged war against Mexicans to facilitate Anglo-American expansion, and few seem to have seriously considered suspending their campaigns even after it became plain that they served U.S. interests. Comanches had their own story, more important to them than American expansion. They made a history of their own below the Rio Grande, one that set the trajectory of the whole region in those years. If Mexicans found some of their ruin in its course and Americans some of their triumph, it was no less a native creation for that. No doubt Comanches saw their world shrunken and transformed in the second half of the nineteenth century. But on the bleak reservations many still lived who had come together to do things that few who had not witnessed them would have thought possible, reshaping the continent in the process. By the 1880s, aging warriors told stories their children and grandchildren could hardly imagine, of handsome men setting forth in armies; of freedom, hazard, and honors won in alien country; of slain friends, audacious plans, and rivers of horses rushing north—war stories, brought back from the deserts they had made of a thousand Mexican homes.

Appendix.

DATA ON COMANCHE–MEXICAN VIOLENCE, 1831–48

INTRODUCTION TO THE DATA

SOURCES

This appendix compiles information taken from two kinds of sources. Most of the data comes from documents written by Mexican officials reporting encounters with Indians to their superiors or to counterparts in nearby towns, ranches, and haciendas. Sometimes the citation is to the documents themselves (now in Mexican archives), but more often I have relied upon official newspapers, which reprinted such documents about Indians verbatim.

Second, I have extracted data from the work of other historians and anthropologists who themselves have relied upon Mexican sources. Each entry in the database is keyed to a source number that corresponds to an endnote citing the source. Work by three scholars in particular appears often in the notes. William Griffen's *Utmost Good Faith* provides excellent data on Chihuahua and serves as a model for quantifying Indian–Mexican violence. Isidro Vizcaya Canales's *La invasión de los indios bárbaros al noreste de Mexico en los años de 1840 y 1841* is a wonderful edited collection of official letters culled from Nuevo León's newspapers. Last, in 1959 and 1961 Ralph A. Smith wrote articles that used newspaper accounts from Chihuahua and, especially, Durango to reconstruct two particularly destructive Comanche campaigns. I have taken data from his careful narratives of these events.

SCOPE

This is by no means a comprehensive list of everything Comanches and their allies did in northern Mexico. More work needs to be done in provincial archives across the north, and historians know little about Comanche activities in San Luis Potosí, Zacatecas, and Querétaro, which the Indians were rumored to have reached. Kiowas also claimed to have raided as far east as Sonora, and evidence of this might be waiting in Sonoran archives. Interested readers can consult the bibliography for the collections I have consulted. Because of time constraints, the relative organization of archives, and occasional limitations to access I was able to make more thorough use of some collections than others. The data here are most complete for Coahuila, northern Tamaulipas, Chihuahua (thanks to Griffen's work), and Durango from 1842 to 1847. I have very little data for the activities of southern plains Indians in Mexico in 1848. In other words, much work remains to be done, and the figures here *understate* the scope and consequences of Comanche and Kiowa raiding into northern Mexico.

Related to the question of comprehensiveness is the question of reliability. Can one trust the Mexican documents to provide an accurate account of what independent Indians did below the Rio Grande? There is at least one reason to be suspicious. Because frontier residents and officials felt so desperate to attract state and national aid, there must have been temptation to exaggerate the numbers of Indians involved and the casualties Mexicans suffered.

Inflation undoubtedly crept into some correspondence. Nonetheless, ongoing warfare discouraged wild exaggeration about numbers of Indians, and the public nature of official correspondence (the fact that it was reprinted in widely distributed newspapers) discouraged exaggeration of all kinds. The great majority of documents used in this study came from one local or regional official to another or else from military authorities to state authorities. These were essentially military documents, usually written to apprise other officials of an imminent threat. In the midst of a raiding campaign, the proper distribution and coordination of scarce resources depended absolutely upon timely and accurate information. Therefore if one hundred Indians were reported as five hundred, then men, horses, and weapons would be sent after phantoms and hence be unavailable to cope with other dangers. Moreover, because official papers reprinted letters verbatim, liars ran the risk of public exposure. On occasion editors ran letters challenging a particular version of events, and in Mexico City rival newspapers accused one another of misrepresenting raids for political purposes. Furthermore, on extended campaigns for which substantial documentation exists, estimates of numbers of Indians usually remain approximately the same from one place to the next (so long as one allows for the Comanches' habit of breaking into smaller parties and regrouping later as they progressed). Finally, officials intent on exaggerating to attract national aid generally employed editorials, pamphlets, or books that purported to describe the overall condition of the frontier rather than specific encounters with Indians. Such sources do not figure into the data below.

CATEGORIES

Some important categories are absent from this appendix. I include no data on stolen animals. Though the acquisition of horses and mules was absolutely central to Comanche and Kiowa raids into Mexico, Mexican documents are so often imprecise on numbers of stolen animals that useful quantification is very difficult. Authors wrote about recovered animals in more detail, but because I exclude data on stolen animals I exclude data on recoveries as well. Mexican observers almost never reported numbers of wounded Indians with any precision, so I exclude this category, too. Finally, I include no data on the age or gender of Comanches or Kiowas killed and captured in their conflicts with Mexicans because, unlike Mexico's wars with Navajos or Apaches, fighting men accounted for nearly all of the Indian casualties in the Comanche theater. When I have positive information about the killings of Comanche women or children below the river I say so in the notes.

Date: The year is followed by the month and the day, so 18360718 is July 18, 1836. If unsure about the day or (rarely) the month, I have inserted "oo." Sometimes the best source available lumped multiple encounters together. I have tried to disentangle individual events in such cases but occasionally have had to follow the source and combine the results of more than one encounter in a single entry.

Place: D = Durango ; NL = Nuevo León ; *Tam* = Tamaulipas ; *Coa* = Coahuila ; *Chi* = Chihuahua ; *TX* = Texas; Z = Zacatecas; SLP = San Luis Potosí. Other abbreviations refer to common terms. R = Ranch; *H* = Hacienda; S = San. If multiple locations are separated by a semicolon, the place on the left is the partido, or district, within which the place on the right is located. So "D: Indé; H. de S. Salvador" refers to an encounter at the Hacienda de San Salvador, located in the district of Indé in Durango.

Indian name: Sometimes Mexicans referred to "los Comanches Caihuas," to distinguish Kiowas from Comanches, but because this was so rarely done and because the two groups cooperated in their campaigns, I refer to any event involving either with the abbreviation C for Comanches. Unless the source specifically identifies another group, I attribute all encounters in this appendix to Comanches/Kiowas, even if the source identifies the Indians only as bárbaros, indios, salvajes, etc. In contrast, Griffen attributed encounters to Comanches only if he had positive information or if other data clarified the identification, partly because Apaches and Comanches regularly attacked the same places in Chihuahua. As a result many events in his database are attributed to "unknown" Indians, and I have not included these in this appendix. Therefore Comanches and Kiowas were almost certainly more active in Chihuahua than the data below, drawn from Griffen's exhaustive work, suggest. The other abbreviations below are L for Lipanes; A for Apaches; T for Tahuacanos. For all other identifications I have inserted the abbreviation S under "Indian Name," directing the reader to see the note for that entry.

Number of Indians: Because effective defense depended upon accurate information, Mexican writers almost always gave an exact or approximate number of Indians if they could. In those instances when a writer provided a range, for example, estimating six or seven hundred, I give the smaller number. Sometimes writers lacked firm numbers and instead used adjectives like "a few," "several," "many," "a great many," "a considerable number," etc. I have simplified these labels into two abbreviations. "#" indicates a small group, and "##" a large one. The same applies to the other numeric categories: Mexicans captured, Mexicans wounded, Mexican animals killed, Indians killed, Indians captured, and Mexican captives retaken/esc(aped). (For the exception to this rule, see note on "Mexicans Killed," below.)

Mexicans Killed. In rare cases the best source on an encounter mentions deaths but gives no firm number. In such instances I have translated the words used ("a few," "several," "a great many," etc.) into what seems to me the lowest possible number and noted the alteration in the notes. I have not done the same with "Comanches Killed" and other categories simply because ignorance about specific numbers was much more common when it came to slain raiders, and guessing at figures would have introduced too much uncertainty into the data.

Age and gender of Mexicans killed/captured: M = man; W = woman; B = boy; G = girl; C = child; I = infant; P = person. Men account for almost all of the Mexican deaths in battles (see below for distinction between different types of encounters), the most common exception being when women or children captives were killed during the action. The fragmentary data indicate that Comanches and Kiowas killed more than one Mexican woman or child for every four Mexican men killed in raids. Partly this reflects the geography of gendered labor roles in northern Mexico. Indians found it relatively easy to attack laborers out working with animals in the fields, travelers in small parties, letter carriers, horse and mule drivers, and workers in the overland trade—all positions usually filled by males. The fact that raiders killed men more often than women and children also reflects the fact that Comanches and Kiowas almost never took grown Mexican men back to the southern plains as captives. But the ratio of men to women and children killed was probably closer than the data here suggest. Comanches and Kiowas were more likely to encounter women and children once they reached the outskirts or even the interior of ranches, haciendas, and towns. These were the times when Mexican casualties were the highest. But the likelihood that a writer would provide age and gender information about Mexican deaths decreased as the number of casualties increased. Hence the percentage of women and children among the dead would almost certainly be higher if there were more detailed casualty information from these more destructive encounters in or near settlements.

Mexican Captives Retaken/Esc(aped): Mexican sources often mention the redemption of captives for whom I found no evidence of their initial capture. In such cases I have compensated by adding the appropriate number of "Mexicans captured" to the same entry wherein the redemption took place and noting the change in the corresponding endnote. Even with this correction the data still produce the strikingly high ratio of more than two out of every three Mexicans captured by Comanches and Kiowas either escaping their captors or being redeemed by Mexican forces before the raiders could recross the Rio Grande. Considering that we know of many captures only because of later redemptions, there must surely have been many more less fortunate captives who never escaped and who would make the ratio lower if we knew about them. Still, the fact that 580 Mexicans were redeemed during the period 1831–48 might seem to indicate a remarkably effective defense. But in fact 401 of these redemptions came from just five engagements, when large Mexican forces fought weary, wounded, and overburdened Comanche parties on their way back to the Rio Grande.

Type of encounter: 1 = Indian raid upon Mexicans; 2 = Mexican raid upon an Indian family camp; 3 = Battle between organized Mexican forces and Indian forces; 4 = Sighting. In reality, encounters between Mexicans and Comanches often defied these tidy categories. For example, locals usually rallied to try to defend themselves against Comanche raiders and fierce battles often ensued, but I nonetheless refer to such events as raids. I reserve the term "battle" for those instances when organized Mexican forces already prepared for combat encountered and fought their Indian enemies, often after a pursuit. I include sightings only rarely, when no other information exists about Indian activities in a particular location.

TABLE AND FIGURES

Table A.1 lists all of the Comanche campaigns I know of involving 100+ men for the period 1831–47.

Figure A.1 breaks down the total reported human casualties of the Comanche–Mexican War by type, for the same period. I exclude casualties from encounters between Mexicans and those Indians positively identified as other than Comanches and Kiowas.

Figure A.2 breaks down the total casualties (killed and captured) by year, minus redeemed or escaped Mexican captives and minus casualties that I know were inflicted by Indians other than Comanches or Kiowas. Because Comanches and Kiowas embarked on most of their ambitious campaigns during winter, calendar years can be misleading. To minimize distortions I display the figures in years from July to June. By itself figure A.2 represents an important but incomplete picture of trends in the war. The numbers of actual dead and captured varied campaign to campaign, and the numbers of dead and captured we know about vary for a variety of reasons. Simply looking at human casualties over time, for example, one would have no idea that southern plains Indians dramatically expanded the range of their long-distance raids following the Texas rebellion. Consequently figure A.2 needs to be paired with map 2 showing changes in the range of Comanche raiding, and with table A.1 on campaigns by 100+ men.

Table A.1
Comanche Campaigns into Mexico involving 100 + Warriors, Oct. 1831–Nov. 1847

DATE	PLACE	# OF MEN
October 1831	Chihuahua	100
October 1834	Chihuahua	117
December 1834–January 1835	Chihuahua	100
March 1835	Chihuahua	100+
May–June 1835	Chihuahua	800
May 1836	Chihuahua	200+
August 1836	Chihuahua	200
February–March 1837	Tamaulipas, Nuevo León	500
July 1837	Tamaulipas	1000
March 1838	Coahuila	100
June 1838	Coahuila	400
October 1838	Nuevo León	150
December 1838–January 1839	Nuevo León	300
March 1839	Nuevo León	500+
November 1839	Nuevo León	300
January 1840	Nuevo León	600
April 1840	Nuevo León	150
September 1840	Nuevo León	200
October 1840	Nuevo León	400
December 1840–January 1841	Coahuila, Zacatecas, San Luis Potosí	400
December 1840–January 1841	Nuevo León	300
February 1841	Chihuahua	800
February–March 1841	Nuevo León	300
September 1841	Durango	200

DATE	PLACE	# OF MEN
January 1842	Tamaulipas	300
February 1842	Nuevo León	300
March 1842	Tamaulipas	500
August 1842	Durango	100
November–December 1842	Coahuila, Durango	500+
February 1844	Coahuila	200
May 1844	Coahuila	200
October 1844	Nuevo León, Tamaulipas	400
October–November 1844	Chihuahua, Durango	500
April 1845	Chihuahua	100+
July–August 1845	Coahuila, Nuevo León	600
September–October 1845	Chihuahua, Durango, Zacatecas	600
February 1846	Tamaulipas	150
June 1846	Durango	200
August, 1846	Durango	500
October, 1846	Chihuahua, Durango, Zacatecas	1000
January 1847	Durango, Chihuahua	300
August–September 1847	Durango	700
October 1847	Durango	500
November, 1847	Durango, Zacatecas, San Luis Potosí	500

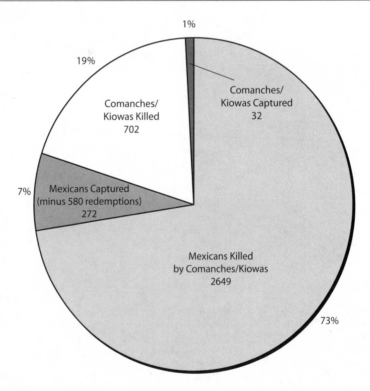

Figure A. 1. Total Casualties by Type, Comanche Theater, 1831–April 1848

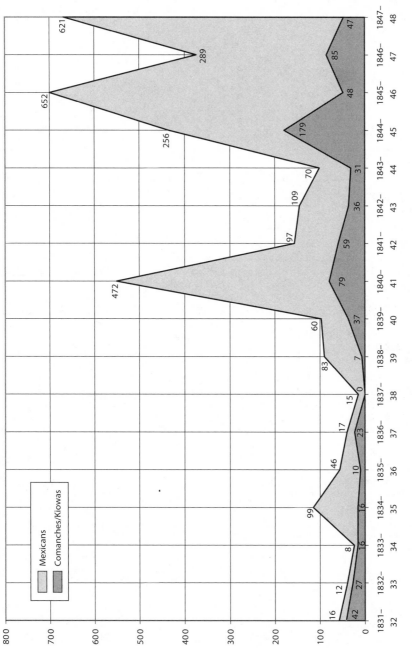

Figure A.2. Total Casualties (Killed and Captured, Combined), by Year

Date	Place	Indian Name	# of Indians	# Mexicans Killed	Age/Gender Mex. Killed	# Mexicans Wounded	# Mexican Captives Taken	Age/Gender of Captives	# Mexican Animals Killed	# Indians Killed	# Indians Captured	Mexican Captives Re-taken/Esc.	Type of Encounter
18310800	TX: Gonzales	C		2	m								I
18310816	TX: Goliad	C	30	4									I
18310831	NL: La Bahía area	C		2									I
18310902	NL: La Bahía area	C		3									I
18311013	Chi: Bado de Piedra	C	100	2	m								I
18320100	TX:	C								30			2
18320200	TX:	C								12			2
18320400	TX: Goliad	C		2			1	b					I
18321000	TX: San Saba River	C								9			2
18321000	TX:	C		4	m								I
18321013	TX:	C								5			3
18330000	NM: Río Pecos	C								5			2
18330100	Tam: Laredo	C		2			1						I
18330105	NL: Lampazos; el Puerto de Becerro	C	20	3	m		2	w, i					I
18330206	Chi: El Paso; S. Elizario area	C	1							1			3
18330400	TX:	C								7			2
18331022	TX: S. Antonio	C	20	8	m	1	1	m				1	I
18340500	Comanchería	C								2	14		2
18341015	Chi: Aldama; H. de Zanja	C	117							1			3
18341016	Chi: Cusihuiriáchic; Cerro Prieto	C					3	m					I
18341213	Chi: Corral Piedras; H. de Corral de Piedras	C	3	1	m								I
18341214	Chi: Aldama/Norte; Gallina, Tinaja	C	3										3
18341214	Chi: Corral Piedras; H. de Corral de Piedras	C	80+										3
18341215	Chi: S. Elizario	C											I
18341215	Chi: Satevó; Colegio, Sierra	C											3
18341216	Chi: Corral Piedras; Cerro Prieto	C	80+										3
18341217	Chi: Santo Toribio; Herrera	C	35										3
18341219	Chi: S. Borja; Sierra Durazno	C											3
18341219	Chi: S. Lorenzo; Cuevas	C											I

	Place	Indian Name	# of Indians	# Mexicans Killed	Age/Gender Mex. Killed	# Mexicans Wounded	# Mexican Captives Taken	Age/Gender of Captives	# Mexican Animals Killed	# Indians Killed	# Indians Captured	Mexican Captives Re-taken/Esc.	Type of Encounter	Source
222	Chi: Concepción?; H. de Laguna	C											4	30
104	Chi: Cusihuiriáchic; H. de Quemada	C	100										1	31
109	Chi: Chuvíscar; road to S. Andres	C	2										1	32
17	Chi: Encinillas; H. de Malanoche	C	14										3	33
119	Chi: Namiquipa; Santa Clara	C	##										4	34
203	Chi: Allende; Sierra de Todos Santos	C		1	m					4			3	35
329	Chi: Nombre de Dios; H. de Laborcita	C	5										1	36
331	Chi: Aldama; Colonia de S. Carlos	C	100+	1	m					2			3	37
409	Chi: Aldama; Colonia de S. Carlos	C	##										4	38
513	Chi: Aldama; Colonia de S. Carlos	C	##										4	39
517	Chi: Coyame; Presidio de Coyame	C	500	5	m		7	1m, 6b		6			3	40
518	Chi: Norte; Punto de la Cruz	C	800							1			3	41
521	Chi: Norte; Paraje Mesquite	C	300							#			3	42
523	Chi: Chi?; Ojo de S. Pedro	C	1							1			4	43
523	Chi: Conchos River; Campo de Cruz	C	800+							1			4	44
525	Chi: Norte; Río Puerco, la Mula	C	##										4	45
527	Chi: Encinillas; Sierra de Espía, Agua Nueva	C	12							#			3	46
527	Chi: Santa Rosalía	C	800+										4	47
529	Chi: Hidalgo; H. de S. Gregorío/Gomera	C		1	m								1	48
529	Chi: Santa Rosalía; La Cruz	C	500										4	49
531	Chi: Allende, H. de Corralejo	C	##										3	50

Date	Place	Indian Name	# of Indians	# Mexicans Killed	Age/Gender Mex. Killed	# Mexicans Wounded	# Mexican Captives Taken	Age/Gender of Captives	# Mexican Animals Killed	# Indians Killed	# Indians Captured	Mexican Captives Re-taken/Esc.	Type of Encounter
18350531	Chi: Jiménez; H. de Gomera	C					1	b					1
18350601	Chi: Chi; Hormigas	C											3
18350601	Chi: Norte; S. Aparicio, O/Ternera	C	##										4
18350603	Chi: Hidalgo; H. de Animas	C	##	6	m		39	17m, 22w					1
18350604	Chi: Hidalgo; R. de Cuevesillas	C		2	m								1
18350604	Chi: Minas Nuevas; R. de los Muñoces	C		5	2m, 3w		2	w					1
18350605	Chi: Hidalgo; Cuevesillas/Velázquez	C	800										4
18350607	Chi: Satevó; S. Javier	C	##										1
18350609	Chi: Chi; Torreón/Mesa & Cañada	C	##	12	m		2	g		#			3
18350610	Chi: Jiménez; Ojo de Barraza	C	60										3
18350610	Chi: Torreón/Satevó?; Potrero	C											1
18350610	Chi: Torreón; H. de Torreón	C											1
18350611	Chi: Aldama; R. Viejo/Pastor	C	70										4
18350611	Chi: H. de S. Cristóbal	C		2									1
18350611	Chi: S. Cristóbal, Animas, R. Maturana	C		2	w								1
18350613	Chi: Chi; H. de Tres Hermanas	C											1
18350614	Chi: Satevó; R. del Terrero	C	##										1
18350614	Chi: Satevó; Satevó (Cienega Ortiz?)	C		2	m		2	m					1
18350615	Chi: Allende; H. de Santa Cruz Nieras	C	##	1	m								1
18350616	Chi: Allende; Allenda (Parral Road)	C/A	20	1	m		1						1
18350616	Chi: Santa Isabel; Zarca, Agua	C	300+										4
18350708	Chi: Encinillas; H. de Torreón	C	##										1

	Place	Indian Name	# of Indians	# Mexicans Killed	Age/Gender Mex. Killed	# Mexicans Wounded	# Mexican Captives Taken	Age/Gender of Captives	# Mexican Animals Killed	# Indians Killed	# Indians Captured	Mexican Captives Re-taken/Esc.	Type of Encounter	Source
710	Chi: Carrizal; Carrizal/ Presidio	C	10										1	73
712	Chi: El Paso; El Paso	C	5										1	74
829	TX: Goliad	T											1	75
029	Chi: Aldama; S. Diego	C											1	76
000	Tam: Laredo	C		22									1	77
206	Chi: Aldama; Palomas, Laguna/Parrit	C	##										1	78
309	Tam: Laredo	C		4	m								3	79
329	Chi: Coyame/Carrizal; Tosesigua	C	##										1	80
400	NL: Tam frontier	C											4	81
400	Tam: Mat. Coast dist.	C		2									1	82
400	NL: Agualeguas; R. de Tanque area	L		1			1					1	3	83
400	NL: Lampazos area	C	50				1		##			1	3	84
404	Chi: Coyame; Movano/ Sierra Guadalupe	C	##										4	85
416	Tam: Laredo	C		4									1	86
419	Chi: El Paso; Ojo de la Punta	C	8										3	87
422	Chi: Coyame; Coyame area	C	8								8		3	88
428	Chi: Cusihuiriáchic; S. Juan Bautista Llanos	C											1	89
428	Chi: Cusihuiriáchic; Cerro Prieto	C											1	90
429	Chi: Cusihuiriáchic; Punto Miguel Chiquito	C		11	m								3	91
430	Chi: Cusihuiriáchic; H. de Rubio	C		1	b		1	b					1	92
500	NL: Carrizal area	C	9	1	m	2				2			3	93
508	Chi: Cusihuiriáchic; Caríchic	C	200+										1	94
508	Chi: Cusihuiriáchic; Sisoguichi/Temeichi	C	##										4	95
615	Chi: El Paso; Isleta (del Sur)	C	2										4	96
700	Tam: Matamoros area	C		11			#						1	97
806	Chi: Norte; Vado de Piedra area	C											3	98

Date	Place	Indian Name	# of Indians	# Mexicans Killed	Age/Gender Mex. Killed	# Mexicans Wounded	# Mexican Captives Taken	Age/Gender of Captives	# Mexican Animals Killed	# Indians Killed	# Indians Captured	Mexican Captives Re-taken/Esc.	Type of Encounter
18360807	Chi: El Paso-Chi road	C											1
18360807	Chi: Norte; Vado de Piedra area	C								2			3
18360813	Chi: Pilares area	C	200							2			3
18360826	D: Canutillo, Torreoncillo, Torreón	A	100				#			8		all	1
18360909	Tam: Reynosa dist.	L		7	m	#	5	w, g, 3i					1
18361200	Tam:	L											1
18370200	Tam: Reynosa dist.	C	500	1		14	##			10			1
18370228	Tam: Charco de los Becerros	C							1400				1
18370301	Tam: Mat dist.	C	200	5	m				100				1
18370305	Tam: S. Jaunito Area, Las Ahuajas	C	400										3
18370400	TX: Río Nueces	C								#	1		3
18370700	Tam: Matamoros dist.	C	1000	9	m								1
18371000	Coa: H. de S. Buenaventura	C											1
18371000	NL: Salinas Victoria; Sabinas Hidalgo y Vallencillo	C											1
18371204	Tam: Camargo, Chaco Verde	T								5			3
18380100	NL: Cerralvo, Agualeguas, Los Aldamas	C											1
18380204	NL: Cerralvo, Agualeguas, Los Aldamas	C		#			#						1
18380218	NL: Lampazos area	C											1
18380300	Coa: Cuatro Ciénegas	C	100				##	w and c				#	1
18380425	Coa: Cuatro Ciénegas	C		6									1
18380600	Coa: H. de Sardinas	C											3
18380607	Coa: Monclova area	C	400				9					9	3
18381020	NL: Laguna de Leche	C	150	3	m	#				7			3
18381200	NL	C	##	50					##				3
18381209	NL: Cañas, Agualeguas, Vallecito	C	300	30	m								3
18390108	NL: Laguna de Leche	C	150										1
18390322	NL: Cadereyta Jiménez; Agualeguas	C	500+				16					16	1

324

	Place	Indian Name	# of Indians	# Mexicans Killed	Age/Gender Mex. Killed	# Mexicans Wounded	# Mexican Captives Taken	Age/Gender of Captives	# Mexican Animals Killed	# Indians Killed	# Indians Captured	Mexican Captives Re-taken/Esc.	Type of Encounter	Source
800	Coa: Río Grande Dept.	C					2	m					1	126
100	NL: Marín area	C	300	12									1	127
108	NL: Cadereyta Jiménez; H. de Higueras	C	300				#						1	128
109	NL: Marín area	C	300	4									1	129
100	NL: Cadereyta Jiménez; Marín	C	600	23	m	10				30			3	130
118	Chi: Jiménez; Jiménez	C											1	131
119	Chi: Jiménez; Jiménez	C	30										4	132
200	Bolsón de Mapimí	A								15	20		2	133
319	Chi: Aldama; Colonia de S. Carlos	C	50	6			2						1	134
321	Chi: Aldama; Polvorilla, Ciénega	C	50							2			3	135
325	Chi: Aldama; Mesteño/ Colonia de S. Carlos	C		3	m					1			3	136
327	Chi: Encinillas; Tinaja de Santa Clara	C	7							4			3	137
400	NL: Cerralvo	C	150										3	138
400	NL: Cerralvo and Marín areas	C	150	4		1	2	w, g					1	139
411	Chi: Coyame; Cuchillo Parado	C	50										1	140
414	NL: Agualeguas	C		1		2	1						1	141
700	D	C	6							3			1	142
712	Chi: Jiménez; Zarca area	C	30	1	m								3	143
906	NL: Cadereyta Jiménez; R. de Botellos	C	200	1	m	11							1	144
906	NL: Cadereyta Jiménez; Agualeguas	C	200							1			1	145
906	NL: Cadereyta Jiménez; R. de Cochinitos	C	200	1	m								1	146
908	NL: Cadereyta Jiménez dist.	C		4	m, 2w, c		1		##				1	147
910	NL: Cadereyta Jiménez dist.	C	80	1	m				##				3	148
915	NL: Cadereyta Jiménez; Boca del Potrero	C		2									3	149
000	NL: Monterrey area; R. de Arco	C		4			5						1	150

Date	Place	Indian Name	# of Indians	# Mexicans Killed	Age/Gender Mex. Killed	# Mexicans Wounded	# Mexican Captives Taken	Age/Gender of Captives	# Mexican Animals Killed	# Indians Killed	# Indians Captured	Mexican Captives Re-taken/Esc.	Type of Encounter
18401000	NL: Monterrey area; S. José de la Popa	C		1	m	1	5	3m, 2b					1
18401000	NL: Monterrey area; near Ciénega de Flores	C		4									1
18401004	NL: Salinas Victoria; Lampazos	C	300	7	6p, 1w	2				4			3
18401005	NL: Salinas Victoria; Bustamante	C	400	11	10m, 1w		13	12b, 1m				3	1
18401005	NL: Salinas Victoria; Valenzuela	C	300	1	m		2					1	1
18401006	NL: Salinas Victoria; H. de Potrero	C		4			2	w, c		1		2	1
18401007	NL: Salinas Victoria; Palo Blanco	C	400						#				1
18401008	NL: Monterrey; Paraje de Delgadito	C		1	b	1							1
18401009	NL: S. Francisco de Cañas	C	150	4			2						1
18401010	NL: Salinas Victoria	C	5										3
18401010	NL: Salinas Victoria; H. de Mamulique	C								1			1
18401011	NL: Salinas Victoria; S. José de la Popa	C		1		1	2						1
18401025	NL: Cadereyta Jiménez; Ciénega de Flores	C	30	3	m, w, b		3	3c					1
18401026	NL: Monterrey; S. Nicolás de los Garza	C		2									1
18401026	NL: Monterrey; Santa Rosa	C				1	1	b					1
18401108	Chi: Jiménez; Jiménez	C	30										3
18401108	Chi: Norte; Punto de Mayjoma	C											3
18401109	Chi: Norte; Río Puerco	C	4										1
18401109	NL: Cadereyta Jiménez; Paraje de Comas	C		1									1
18401109	NL: Cadereyta Jiménez; Marín	C		1		1							1
18401111	NL: Cadereyta Jiménez	C										2	3

	Place	Indian Name	# of Indians	# Mexicans Killed	Age/Gender Mex. Killed	# Mexicans Wounded	# Mexican Captives Taken	Age/Gender of Captives	# Mexican Animals Killed	# Indians Killed	# Indians Captured	Mexican Captives Re-taken/Esc.	Type of Encounter	Source
112	NL: Cadereyta Jiménez; H. de Higueras	C								1		2	3	172
116	NL: Salinas Victoria; Sabinas Hidalgo	C								#			3	173
130	NL: Salinas Victoria; Los Pozos	C		1		2							3	174
200	Coa, Z, SLP	C	400	300			100		1386+	8		40	1	175
200	NL: Monterrey; Villadama	C								1			3	176
202	NL: Monterrey; Villadama	C		1									1	177
227	NL: Monterrey; Pesquería Grande	C		12		#				2			3	178
100	NL: Salinas Victoria; R. del Huizache	C	200			1				2			1	179
110	Coa: Saltillo	C								9			3	180
121	Coa: Los Horcados; Puerto de Macho	C	300	3						7		41	3	181
122	Coa: Guerrero area	C	7							2			3	182
122	NL: Cadereyta Jiménez; Agualeguas; R.Nuevo	C								1			3	183
123	Tam?: On Rio Grande	C	7							2			3	184
125	NL: Cadereyta Jiménez; n. of Agualeguas	C	30			3				3			3	185
200	Chi:	C	800							6			1	186
200	NL: Villadama	C		2	m								1	187
200	Chi: Coyame; Príncipe	C											4	188
209	NL: Cadereyta Jiménez; China area	C	5	2	m		1	b					1	189
212	NL: Salinas Victoria; R. de Iparraguirre	C	300	2	m								1	190
215	NL: Cadereyta Jiménez; Marín; Puerto del Aire	C		1	m								1	191
215	NL: Salinas Victoria; Vallecillo	C	70										1	192
220	NL: Salinas Victoria; H. del Alamo	C					1						1	193
223	NL: Salinas Victoria; Vallecillo	C		2					##				1	194

Date	Place	Indian Name	# of Indians	# Mexicans Killed	Age/Gender Mex. Killed	# Mexicans Wounded	# Mexican Captives Taken	Age/Gender of Captives	# Mexican Animals Killed	# Indians Killed	# Indians Captured	Mexican Captives Re-taken/Esc.	Type of Encounter
18410226	NL: Salinas Victoria; Sabinas Hidalgo, Lampazos	C	##	8	1m, 4c, 3p		#						1
18410226	NL: Salinas Victoria; Vallecillo	C		1									1
18410228	NL: Cadereyta Jiménez; Estancia de l. Pozos	C	100							2			3
18410301	NL: Ojo del Agua Nueva del Lantrisco	C								2			3
18410302	NL: Cadereyta Jiménez; Marín	C				2				2			3
18410313	NL: Salinas Victoria; Venadito	C	18	1									1
18410315	Chi: Satevó; Sierra de Vallecillo	C	5										3
18410319	Chi: Jiménez?; Parida	C		1	m								3
18410330	NL: Charcos del Macho	C	8							2			3
18410331	Coa: Paraje de los Ahorcados	C	23							1			3
18410410	Tam: Camargo	C	7							2			3
18410416	D: H. de la Zarca	C	40	9		6			9	3			1
18410430	Tam: Reynosa, Mier, Camargo	S		4	m								1
18410512	Chi: Agua Chili	C								9			3
18410528	Tam: Jur. de Carmargo, Jur. de Reynosa	C		4		1							1
18410530	NL: Cadereyta Jiménez	L		3									1
18410531	Tam: La Noria de las Escobas, Cuevitas	C		4									1
18410600	Chi?	C								1			3
18410604	NL: Salinas Victoria; Vallecillo	C	30										1
18410608	NL: Cadereyta Jiménez; Agualeguas	C	3							1	1		3
18410611	Tam: B/T Mier y Guerrero	L	##	1									1
18410613	NL: Punto de Chaco Dulce	C	6										1
18410619	NL: Cadereyta Jiménez; China	C					1						
18410700	Tam: R. de Santa Teresa	C	##										1

	Place	Indian Name	# of Indians	# Mexicans Killed	Age/Gender Mex. Killed	# Mexicans Wounded	# Mexican Captives Taken	Age/Gender of Captives	# Mexican Animals Killed	# Indians Killed	# Indians Captured	Mexican Captives Re-taken/Esc.	Type of Encounter	Source
705	Tam: Mier; R. de S. Antonio	C	50							1			3	219
712	Chi: Satevó; Arroyo de S. José	C		11									1	220
717	Chi: Satevó; Sierra de la Silla	C	25							1			3	221
724	NL: Salinas Victoria; Sabinas Hidalgo	C	9										3	222
731	NL: Cadereyta Jiménez; Puntiagudo	C					3			1			3	223
821	Chi: Príncipe; Cuchillo	C											4	224
924	NL: Cadereyta Jiménez; H. de la Escondida	C	30	1	m								1	225
924	D: Mapimí region	C	200	5			3						1	226
925	D: Mapimí region; Goma	C	150	24			6	c					1	227
927	Coa: Parras	C		4									1	228
015	Chi: Hidalgo; H. de Sapién	C	30+								1		1	229
016	Tam: Río Grande, Guerrero	C					1			4	5	1	2	230
020	Chi: Hidalgo; R. de Solices-Ampareño	C	30+										1	231
020	Chi: Hidalgo; S. Isidro de Cuevas	C	30+	6									1	232
021	Chi: Hidalgo; H. Corral de Piedras	C	30+										3	233
023	Chi: Jiménez; Paraje de Mula	C	35	1	b		1	b					3	234
023	Chi: Jiménez; Vara de S. Juan / Tinaja	C	35							##			3	235
024	Chi: Allende; H. de Concepción	C	30+	1	m								1	236
024	Chi: Allende; Vara de S. Juan	C	30+										3	237
100	NL: Eastern	C	40	7									1	238
200	Coa: Burgos	C		3									1	239
206	NL: La Loma del Huérfano	A?									4		3	240
121	Tam: Río Grande	C	300	7	m	19				14			3	241
121	Coa: Partido de Parras	A	150										1	242

Date	Place	Indian Name	# of Indians	# Mexicans Killed	Age/Gender Mex. Killed	# Mexicans Wounded	# Mexican Captives Taken	Age/Gender of Captives	# Mexican Animals Killed	# Indians Killed	# Indians Captured	Mexican Captives Re-taken/Esc.	Type of Encounter
18420200	TX: Goliad area	L	120										3
18420200	TX: Nueces River	S	300			15							3
18420201	NL: Vallecillo	C	300	5		3	1		#	5			3
18420215	Tam: Guerrero	C					1			3		1	3
18420303	Tam: Reynosa	C	500										4
18420323	Tam: Laredo	C	7				1					1	3
18420400	NL: Cadereyta Jiménez; el Ayancual	C		6									1
18420407	Tam: Distrito del Norte	C											1
18420423	Tam: R. de los Granjenos (n. of Rio Grande)	C		1			1					1	3
18420424	Tam: Paraje de Agua Negra (n. of Rio Grande)	C		4	m	11				24			3
18420500	Coa: Partidos de Parras and Monclova	C											1
18420700	Z: H. de Bonanza	C											1
18420800	Chi: S. Carlos	C	80										4
18420800	NL: Lampazos area	C				3	2			1		2	3
18420814	D: H. de Torreón	C	100	6	m	5	3	b		1			1
18420814	D: R. de Peinadar	C	100	2	m								1
18420814	D: Torreón area	C		6									1
18420815	D: Paraje Peñoles	C		6	m	1	1						1
18420815	D: R. de la Peña	C	40 (?)	3			7						1
18420816	D	C		4									1
18420817	D	C		1									1
18420818	D: H. de Cadena area	C	50										1
18420819	Chi: Jiménez; Sierra de Diablo	C	9			4				9			3
18420821	Coa: Parras; R. de Aguichila	C		21		5	4	w					1
18420822	Z: Pizolaya	C		5			2						1
18420826	D	C		7	m	##							3
18420900	NL: Lampazos area	C		4									1
18420904	Chi: Paso de los Chizos	C		3	m	4	6			18		6	3
18420923	Chi: Hidalgo; Arroyo de Partida/R. Florido	C		1	m								1
18421000	NL: Salinas Victoria; Mamulique	C	70	3	m	2				2			3
18421000	NL: Salinas area	C		2	m								1
18421000	NL: Santa Rosa area	C		1	m								1

	Place	Indian Name	# of Indians	# Mexicans Killed	Age/Gender Mex. Killed	# Mexicans Wounded	# Mexican Captives Taken	Age/Gender of Captives	# Mexican Animals Killed	# Indians Killed	# Indians Captured	Mexican Captives Re-taken/Esc.	Type of Encounter	Source
000	NL: Agua Fría	C		1	m								1	275
000	NL: Pesquería Chica area	C		2									1	276
006	NL: Marín; Loma de los Magueys	C								2			3	277
029	NL: Paso de los Rancherías del Río Salado	C	15							1			1	278
031	Coa: Cuatro Ciénegas	C											3	279
119	Coa: Saltillo dist	C	500+										1	280
121	Coa: H. de Hornos	C	400										1	281
124	D: H. de la Loma	C	400										1	282
206	D: Cerrogordo	C	150	1			2	3				3	3	283
209	D: H. de la Zarca	C	80+							1			1	284
0100	NL: Villadama area	C	15	3	m								1	285
0102	D: Mapimí	C											1	286
0200	Tam: Distrito del Norte	C		8	6m, 2c								1	287
0216	Coa: Partido de Río Grande	C	#										1	288
0223	NL: El Llano de Chueca	C					6					6	3	289
0223	NL: Salinas; Lomas Ballas	C								2			3	290
0300	D: Cerrogordo	C	20										3	291
0301	D: Boca de Santa Catorina	C		2									1	292
0304	Tam: R. de los Fresnos	C											1	293
0718	Coa: Canyon de Santa Rosa	C	#	3	m		1			1		1	1	294
0719	Coa: H. de Encinas	L	3	1	m								1	295
0800	NL	C?	60							12			3	296
0902	D: Torreón	C				1	1					1	1	297
0910	D: H. de Canutillo	C	##	8			2						1	298
0911	D: R. de la Peña	C		1		1	1	w			1		1	299
0917	D: Partido de Nazas; H. de Dolores	C											1	300
1004	Chi: Rosales; Santa Rosalía/S. Miguel	C								#?			1	301
1014	Chi: Norte; Los Alamos de S. Juan	C								1			3	302
1200	D: Santa Rosalita dist	C		31	m	14							3	303
1209	Coa: H. de Nacimiento	C	50	1	m	10				7			3	304
0120	D: Mapimí	C	20	1	m								1	305
0126	D	C					1			1		1	3	306

Date	Place	Indian Name	# of Indians	# Mexicans Killed	Age/Gender Mex. Killed	# Mexicans Wounded	# Mexican Captives Taken	Age/Gender of Captives	# Mexican Animals Killed	# Indians Killed	# Indians Captured	Mexican Captives Re-taken/Esc.	Type of Encounter
18440200	Coa: (center of dept)	C	200										4
18440200	D: NW; La Tinaja	C								3			3
18440200	D: Sierra del Rosario	C											1
18440300	D: R. de la Zarca	C		3	m		1	b					1
18440300	Tam: Mat dist	C											1
18440310	Chi: Allende; H. de la Noria	C											1
18440400	Chi: Balleza; Balesquillo	C		1			1	b					1
18440400	Chi: Hidalgo; Balleza	C		4			2						1
18440400	Chi: Hidalgo; S. Isidro de Cuevas	C					1	m					1
18440401	D: Estancia del Salgado	C	30	3	2w, 1m	2	5			5	1	4	1
18440415	Chi: Allende; H. de Santa María	C	##										4
18440416	Chi: Hidalgo; Valsequillos/Balleza	C		1	m		1	b					1
18440500	Coa: Parras	C	200										1
18440600	Tam: Mat dist	C		2	w	2	2	w, g	##				1
18440704	Tam: Mat dist	C											4
18440816	Chi: Norte/Príncipe; Presidio Viejo	C	60										4
18440826	D: R. de Sestin	C											1
18440910	Tam: Río Grande	C	30										1
18441000	NL: Cadereyta Jiménez; China	C	250	2		1							1
18441000	Coa: El Aguaje de S. Pedro	C				2				7			3
18441000	Tam: R. de la Alaja	C		1									1
18441000	Dur: Magistral	C		2	m		2						1
18441007	Tam: Guerrero dist	C	400	46	m	14							3
18441007	Tam: Guerrero dist; R. de los Moros	C	##	22	m, w, c								1
18441010	Chi: Rosales; La Cruz	C	##	1	w		10	c					1
18441012	Tam: R. de Palmito	C	300	100	m, w, c								1
18441015	Chi: La Cruz del Refugio	C		1	w		13	c					1
18441016	Chi: Santa Rosalia de Ciudad de Camargo	C					1	c					3
18441017	Tam: Paraje de Salado; R. de Ramírez	C/T	400	19	10m, 9c	41	59	w, c		29		59	3
18441018	Chi: Hidalgo; Casa Colorado	C	100	3	m								1

Date	Place	Indian Name	# of Indians	# Mexicans Killed	Age/Gender Mex. Killed	# Mexicans Wounded	# Mexican Captives Taken	Age/Gender of Captives	# Mexican Animals Killed	# Indians Killed	# Indians Captured	Mexican Captives Re-taken/Esc.	Type of Encounter	Source
1020	Chi: Oro Valley	C		3			3	w, 2b	#				I	337
1020	Chi: R. de Amadar (upper Rio del Oro Valley)	C		7	w, 2b, 4m	16							I	338
1021	Chi?: Los Sauces de Cardona	C	500				4		#				I	339
1021	D: Villages on El Corral de Piedra Ranch	C		4			7		#				I	340
1022	D: Indé dist	C	12							6	1		3	341
1026	Chi: Laguna de las Palomas	C								70		32	3	342
1027	Dur: Hidalgo; Hidalgo de Parral	C		3									I	343
1101	Tam: Guerrero area	C				3				2			3	344
1101	Tam: La Palmita area	C								2			3	345
1114	Chi: Jiménez; H. de la Ramada	C	400							48			3	346
1116	D: Cerro Gordo	C											I	347
1120	D	C	500	7	m					9		1	3	348
1122	Chi: Jiménez; Llanos del Encino	C											3	349
1126	Chi: Allende; H. de Valsequillos	C	200										4	350
1127	Chi: Hidalgo; Hidalgo	C		1	m								I	351
1128	Chi: Hidalgo; H. de Santa Rosa	C		1	m								I	352
0118	D: La Mesa de las Cruces	C	20+	4		5							I	353
0118	D: Oro; Punto de María de Torres	C								1			I	354
0129	D: Partido de Pandito	C	60										4	355
0200	D: H. de Ramos	C	12	2		2				4			I	356
0225	Chi: Aldama; Colonia de S. Carlos	C											4	357
0301	Chi: Aldama; S. Carlos/ Pena Blanca	C	##										4	358
0312	Coa: S. José	C	20+			3							I	359
0400	Coa: Partido de Parras	C	##										4	360
0400	NL: Northeast	C		2	m	2	4	b				3	I	361
0405	Chi: Aldama; Laguna de Jaco/S. Carlos	C	100+										4	362

333

Date	Place	Indian Name	# of Indians	# Mexicans Killed	Age/Gender Mex. Killed	# Mexicans Wounded	# Mexican Captives Taken	Age/Gender of Captives	# Mexican Animals Killed	# Indians Killed	# Indians Captured	Mexican Captives Re-taken/Esc.	Type of Encounter
18450416	D: Indé; La Mina de Caballo Creek	C		1									3
18450700	Coa: Partido de Río Grande	C	600										4
18450715	Coa: Monclova	C	##										4
18450731	D	C		1	m								1
18450800	NL	C	200				.						1
18450800	Coa	C	200	1	m	4							1
18450800	D: NE	C					#						1
18450900	D: NE of capital	C											1
18450900	D: Nazas; Gallo	C	150				6		10				1
18450906	Coa: Partido de Parras, Mapimí	A	##										4
18450913	D: H. de las Ovejas	C	80			2			#				1
18450913	D: La Puerta de la Huerta	C		1	m	2							1
18450913	D: Mapimí area; Lagualilas, El Palo Blanco	C	80	3		3			#				1
18450913	D: Torreón area; Laguna de Tlahualilo	C	##	1	b					1			1
18450914	Chi: Norte; Puliques	C	150+							6			3
18450916	D: Indé	C		3	m	2							1
18450916	D: Indé; La Mina de Caballo Creek	C	14	1	m								1
18450916	D: Road to Bolsón	C		1	w								1
18450917	D: S. Juan del Río; H. S. Salvador de Horta	C	200+	19		7	11		2000+				1
18450919	D: Pelayo	C					#	c					1
18450919	D: Pelayo Area	C	100	12		8						3	3
18450922	D: Laguna de Santiagoillo area	C											1
18450923	Chi: Chi; H. de Tres Hermanos	C											1
18450925	Chi: Chi; H. del Sitio	C					4	m, w, b, g					1
18450926	Chi: Río Florido; Conchos	C	50										4
18451000	Chi: Hidalgo; Balleza	C											1
18451000	D: Cuencamé; Peñón	C					2						1

	Place	Indian Name	# of Indians	# Mexicans Killed	Age/Gender Mex. Killed	# Mexicans Wounded	# Mexican Captives Taken	Age/Gender of Captives	# Mexican Animals Killed	# Indians Killed	# Indians Captured	Mexican Captives Re-taken/Esc.	Type of Encounter	Source
000	D: Cuencamé; Terrero	C					15						1	390
000	D: Mezquilal River	C		6									1	391
000	D: Muleros	C		8			1						1	392
000	D: Near Z; R. de la Ochoa	C		5	m		3						1	393
000	D: Near Z; R. de la Punta	C		2			1						1	394
000	D: Parilla	C	200	12		##	3			3			3	395
000	Z	C					10		##				1	396
000	Z: NE	C			m								3	397
000	Z: western	C					17						1	398
000	D: Cuencamé; R. de Atótoncillo	C		3					#				1	399
000	D: Cuencamé; Cerro de Santiago	C		26			2	b	#				1	400
001	D: El Oro; S. José de Ramos area	C	100	3	m	7						2	3	401
001	Chi: Hidalgo; Manga/Balleza	C	24?										3	402
001	Chi: Hidalgo; R. de Guages/Balleza	C											3	403
001	Coa: Distrito de Monclova	L?	40										4	404
003	Chi: Hidalgo; Agua Caliente/Balleza	C											3	405
004	D: Cuencamé; Santiago Pueblo	C	##	4	2m, 2c	#	1	g	##				1	406
004	D: Mapimí area	C	5										1	407
004	D: Cuencamé District	C		4	m	#							1	408
005	D: Cuencamé	C	150	3	m								1	409
006	D: Nombre de Dios; El Ojo de S. Juan	C		7		8	16		207				1	410
007	Tam?: [north of Rio Grande]	C	20							3			3	411
010	D: La Boquilla de S. Benito	C					5				#	70	3	412
010	Z	C	600	200									1	413
015	D: near Muleros	C		8									1	414
015	D: Graceros	C		2		1							1	415
015	D: La Parilla	C		12									1	416

Date	Place	Indian Name	# of Indians	# Mexicans Killed	Age/Gender Mex. Killed	# Mexicans Wounded	# Mexican Captives Taken	Age/Gender of Captives	# Mexican Animals Killed	# Indians Killed	# Indians Captured	Mexican Captives Re-taken/Esc.	Type of Encounter
18451015	D: Aranjuez	C		1		1							1
18451015	D: S. Quíntin	C	2			1							1
18451015	D: Ojo de S. Juan	C	6										1
18451016	D: R. de la Punta; Guadalupe	C	38			8							1
18451017	D: Cuencamé; Los Llanos	C				5	3b, 2g						1
18451017	D: Los Sauces	C		1	m		1	b					1
18451017	D: Porfias	C	200	7	m	5							3
18451018	D: S. Juan del Río	C		68		50				13			3
18451019	D: H. de Menores	C		1	m		3	2g, 1b	##				1
18451020	D: El Rodeo	C											1
18451020	D: El Rodeo	C		3	m	1	3		#	2		1	3
18451021	D: S. Gerónimo	C					2	b					1
18451021	D: Ticorica	C					1						1
18451022	D: H. de la Zarca area	C		8	m		3			12		28	3
18451024	Coa: Distrito de Monclova	C							32				1
18451029	Coa: Partido de Parras	C		11		3	1	w					1
18451030	Coa: Parras area	C		2									1
18451209	Coa: Partido de Parras	C	20	3	m, 2c								1
18451216	NL: Lampazos area	C								2			3
18451222	D: NW; el Cerro Prieto	C	42			3	1	b		1			1
18460106	D: Mapimí	C	7			2	b					2	1
18460111	Chi: Chi; H. de Corral de Piedras	C											1
18460111	Chi: Chi; Sierra de la Silla	C	5	1	m								3
18460115	Chi: Encinillas; H. de Torreón/Tinaja, Crucero	C	20										3
18460222	Tam: Laredo	C	150			2							3
18460225	D: H. de Guntimapé	C	40										4
18460302	D: Nazas; near Gallo	C		5	2m, 2c, w								1
18460302	D: Partido de Santiago Papasquiaro	C		11	4m, 3w, 4p		3	g					1
18460303	D: Estancia de Chinacates	C	18	4	2w, 2p	2	1	g					1
18460304	D: Durango	C	15	1	m	1						1	3

Date	Place	Indian Name	# of Indians	# Mexicans Killed	Age/Gender Mex. Killed	# Mexicans Wounded	# Mexican Captives Taken	Age/Gender of Captives	# Mexican Animals Killed	# Indians Killed	# Indians Captured	Mexican Captives Re-taken/Esc.	Type of Encounter	Source
0304	D: Santiago Papasqiaro; R. de Flores	C		3			2	b					1	447
0305	D: Porrono del Barrial	C											1	448
0309	D: H. de Bocas area	C								4		2	3	449
0314	Tam: Reynosa	C		3			2						1	450
0400	NL: S. Francisco de Cañas	C		4	m								1	451
0428	D: H. de Torreón, H. de Canutillo	C											1	452
0428	D: Partido de Oro	C		1	m		1	b					1	453
0500	Coa: Valle de Santa Rosa	C											1	454
0505	Chi: Rosales; Cerritos Colorado/Jaco	C	10										1	455
0518	Chi: Norte; Bacilio/ Maravillas, Ojo	C	3										4	456
0520	Chi: Jiménez; Charco del Miliagro	C									1		3	457
0520	Chi: Jiménez; H. de la Ramada	C											1	458
0523	Chi: Jiménez; Cerro Blanco	C	14										3	459
0528	Chi: Jiménez; Puerto de las Liebres	C	14										3	460
0600	D	C		5		3	2						1	461
0600	D: Cuencamé	C	200	38		7	20						1	462
0600	D: Mapimí	C		29	m								3	463
0616	Chi: Hidalgo; Roncesvalles/Santa Barbara	C											4	464
0701	D: H. de la Boca de S. Julian	C		2	m	2							1	465
0704	D: H. de Sestin	C	30	2	1m, 1p					9			1	466
0717	D: La Sierra de S. Francisco	S	21	2	m		2		40	3		2	3	467
0723	Chi: Chuvíscar; H. del Fresno	C											1	468
0800	D: Oro	C		8		6	2				1	2	1	469
0800	D: Santiago Papasquiaro	C	500										4	470
0810	Chi: Hidalgo; S. Isidro/ H. de la Ramada	C	47	5	m					16			3	471
0810	D: Mapimí	C		1	w	2	2						1	472

337

Date	Place	Indian Name	# of Indians	# Mexicans Killed	Age/Gender Mex. Killed	# Mexicans Wounded	# Mexican Captives Taken	Age/Gender of Captives	# Mexican Animals Killed	# Indians Killed	# Indians Captured	Mexican Captives Re-taken/Esc.	Type of Encounter
18460826	D: Guanesevi	C	400	5		4				4			1
18460903	D: Mapimí	C	7	1	m	2							1
18460920	D: H. de la Zarca	C	100	10		9	5			2			1
18461000	Chi: Río Florido	C	800	16					##	1	1		1
18461000	D: R. de los Pinos	C		11		1	2						1
18461000	D: S. Juan del Río; Aviníto	C	400	10			5	2b, 3w					1
18461001	Chi: S. Carlos; Río del Vado/Los Chisos	C	1000										4
18461004	Z	C	500										4
18461010	Chi: Jiménez; Jiménez	C	4000	3									1
18461011	Chi: Jiménez; H. de Concepción	C	300	2	m								1
18461011	Chi: Jiménez; H. de Guadalupe	C	800+										1
18461011	Chi: Jiménez; H. de Río Florido	C	##	14									1
18461013	D: Indé; R. de Pelnados	C	400	11		3	4	1w, 3g					1
18461013	D: Indé; R. de Tres Vados	C	400	19	incl. 7c		12						1
18461016	D: H. de Madgalena	C?	500										1
18461017	D: R. de Gigantes	C		30									1
18461020	D	C	400	11		26				19			3
18461024	Chi: Hidalgo; Hidalgo	C	1							1			1
18461105	D: Mapimí	C	70										4
18461123	Chi: Hidalgo; Laguna Blanca/Allende	C	##										3
18461123	Chi: Hidalgo; Punto de Burro/Allende	C	20	3	m					4			3
18461130	D: Indé; Punto de S. Silvestre	C	##	15									1
18461201	Chi: Hidalgo; Punto de Morito	C	1							1			1
18461218	D: Indé	S	#	5		3							1
18461227	Chi: Conchos; Pilar de Conchos	C	70+	1	m		3	b					1
18470100	D: Indé	C		2	m								1
18470100	D: Indé; H. de S. Salvador	C		2	m					2			1
18470100	D: S. Juan del Río; Labor de la Trinidad	C	300										4

Place	Indian Name	# of Indians	# Mexicans Killed	Age/Gender Mex. Killed	# Mexicans Wounded	# Mexican Captives Taken	Age/Gender of Captives	# Mexican Animals Killed	# Indians Killed	# Indians Captured	Mexican Captives Re-taken/Esc.	Type of Encounter	Source
Chi: Hidalgo; Tuorachi Pueblo/Balleza	C		6									1	501
Chi: Balleza; Balleza area	C		50									1	502
Chi: Hidalgo; Hidalgo	C	##							1			3	503
Coa: S. Blas	C					1	male					1	504
D: Cerrogordo; la Estancia de Tescate	C	70				1		35				1	505
D: Santiago Papasquiaro; el Pachon Abajo	C		2	m	2							1	506
D: Camino de los Reales	C	50	2	m								1	507
D: S. Javier del Nuevo	C	50	1	m	1							1	508
D: Santiago de Papasquiaro	C		2	m								1	509
Coa:	C					18			15		18	3	510
Chi: Chihuahua; Cuevas Pueblo/Chihuahua	C	##	1	m					15			3	511
D: Tinaja	C					1	c					1	512
D: Victoria de Durango	C	400										4	513
D: Oro; H. de Sestin	C	30	1						1	#	1	1	514
D: Indé and Oro	C	700	10	2p, 4m, 2w, 2c	1							1	515
D: Indé	C		8			2						1	516
D: Indé	C	#				1					3	3	517
D: Mapimí; Aguaje del Sarnoso	C					1					1	3	518
D: Oro; Oro	C	100	2	m		5			1			1	519
D: Partido de S. Dimas	C	15	9	m								1	520
D: R. de S. Augustín	C	500	1	m		6						1	521
D: S. Lucas	C	70	1	w		3						1	522
D: Santiago Papasquiaro	C	80	4	1c, 1w, 2m	#						1	1	523
D: S. Bernardo; R. de Auga Caliente	C	100	14		#							1	524
D: Cuencamé; H. de S. Bartolo	C		2									1	525
D: Indé; H. de la Zarca	C	200+										4	526
D: Indé; el Mineral de Coneto	C		6	3m, 3p		4						1	527
D: Indé	C		5					#				1	528
D: Mapimí	C	500										4	529
D: Nazas	C				3	2						1	530

Date	Place	Indian Name	# of Indians	# Mexicans Killed	Age/Gender Mex. Killed	# Mexicans Wounded	# Mexican Captives Taken	Age/Gender of Captives	# Mexican Animals Killed	# Indians Killed	# Indians Captured	Mexican Captives Re-taken/Esc.	Type of Encounter
18471100	D: Nazas	C	10	7	m	3							3
18471100	SLP:	C	140	546		5	40						1, 3
18471100	Z: R. de Salado	C	340			#	141			42		200	3
18471102	D: Oro; H. de Sestin	C	50	3	m	9				2			1
18471214	D: Cuencamé	C								1			3
18480114	D: Cuencamé	C	30										4
18480115	Coa:	L								2			2
18480301	Coa: Guerrero	S		2	w, c								1
18480400	D: Mapimí; Aviles	A	7	1	m	1	1						1
18480410	D: H. de Ramos	A		1	m								1

NOTES

ABBREVIATIONS

AGEC	Archivo General del Estado de Coahuila, Ramos Arizpe, Coahuila
AGENL	Archivo General del Estado de Nuevo León, Monterrey, Nuevo León
AGENL-MGM	Correspondencia con la Secretaría de Guerra y Marina, AGENL
AMG	Archivo Municipal de Guerrero, AGEC
Ancla	*El Ancla, Seminario de Matamoros*
Arredondo Collection	Pablo Salce Arredondo Collection, Nettie Lee Benson Latin American Collection, University of Texas, Austin
Despatches	*Despatches from United States Consuls in Matamoros, 1826–1906* (microfilm, 12 reels, National Archives Microfilm Publications, 1964)
Diario	*Diario del Gobierno de la República Mexicana*
Diplomatic Instructions	*Diplomatic Instructions of the Department of State, 1801–1906: Special Missions*. Volume 1: *December 15, 1823–November 13, 1852* (microfilm, National Archives Record Service, M77).
FSXIX	Fondo Siglo XIX, AGEC
Globe	*The Congressional Globe*
Lafragua	Colección Lafragua, Biblioteca Nacional, Universidad Nacional Autónoma de México, Mexico City
MANM	Mexican Archives of New Mexico (microfilm)
MAP	Matamoros Archives Photostats, Center for American History, University of Texas, Austin
Mercurio	*El Mercurio de Matamoros*
Niles	*Niles National Register*
Registro	*Registro Oficial del Gobierno del Departamento de Durango*
Republicano	*El Republicano: Periodico Oficial del Gobierno de Coahuila*
Seminario	*El Seminario Político de Gobierno de Nuevo León*
SUI	Uncataloged Imprints, W. B. Stephens Collection, Nettie Lee Benson Latin American Collection, University of Texas, Austin

341

Telegraph   *Telegraph and Texas Register*
U.S. Despatches   *Despatches from United States Ministers to Mexico, 1823–1906* (microfilm,
                            179 reels, National Archives Microfilm Publications, 1955).
Voto   *El Voto de Coahuila*

INTRODUCTION: A LITTLE DOOR

1. For treaty, Richard Griswold del Castillo, *Treaty,* 183–99. For quote, see Luis de la Rosa to
John M. Clayton, Washington, March 20, 1850, in Manning, ed., *Diplomatic Correspondence: Inter-America* 9:350–52.

2. The historiography bearing on Indians and interimperial conflicts is large. Important works since
1990 include White, *Middle Ground;* Weber, *Spanish Frontier;* Richter, *Ordeal;* Usner, *Indians, Settlers, and Slaves;* Hinderaker, *Elusive Empires;* Anderson, *Indian Southwest;* Adelman and Aron, "Borderlands to Borders"; Anderson, *Crucible;* Richter, *Facing East;* Dowd, *War under Heaven;* Gallay, *Indian Slave Trade;* Calloway, *Vast Winter Count;* Anderson and Cayton, *Dominion,* 1–246; Weber, *Bárbaros;* Taylor, *Divided Ground;* Aron, *American Confluence;* DuVal, *Native Ground;* Barr, *Peace Came;* Blackhawk, *Violence over the Land.* U.S. and Canadian scholars are only now beginning to take Indians more seriously in regard to international relations after 1815. See, for example, McManus, *Line which Separates;* Anderson, *Conquest,* which discusses Indians and Texan–Mexican relations; and McCrady, *Living with Strangers.*

3. Ralph Adam Smith and Isidro Vizcaya Canales long ago tapped into northern Mexico's periodical material to give scholars on both sides of the border glimpses into the devastation suffered by parts of northern Mexico prior to the U.S. invasion. Their work, ignored by scholars of the U.S.–Mexican War, helped spark my interest in this topic. See especially Smith, "Indians in American-Mexican"; Vizcaya Canales, ed., *La invasión.* For an early but durable article on Indians in U.S.–Mexican relations after 1848, see Rippy, "Indians." For passing reference to independent Indians in the U.S. literature on the war with Mexico, see, for example, Bishop, *Our First,* 142; Smith, *War with Mexico* 1:298, 479, 521; Bernard Augustine De Voto, *Year of Decision,* 156, 249–50, 388–92, 417; Bill, *Rehearsal for Conflict,* 126, 130; Henry, *Story,* 131; Connor and Faulk, *North America Divided,* 95; Pletcher, *Diplomacy,* 76; Bauer, *Mexican War,* 19, 136–37; Weems, *To Conquer,* 315; Hietala, *Manifest Design,* 145–46; Johannsen, *To the Halls,* 33; Eisenhower, *So Far,* 220–21, 234, 249; Christensen and Christensen, *U.S.–Mexican War,* 113; Richmond, "A View," 136, 140–41; Paul Foos, *Short, Offhand, Killing Affair,* 140; Meed, *Mexican War,* 41, 89. An insightful new book on the war seeks to explain "why Mexico went to war with the United States in 1846, and why that war went so badly for Mexico" but never mentions the problems associated with Indian raiding below the river prior to 1848. See Henderson, *Glorious Defeat.* Quote is from xvii. Hall, *Social Change,* 147–203, contains keen insights both about independent Indians and the U.S.–Mexican War but does little to combine the two.

4. For recent work integrating indigenous peoples into early national Mexican history, see, for example, Mallon, *Peasant and Nation;* Guardino, *Peasants;* Eric Van Young, *Other Rebellion;* Guardino, *Time of Liberty,* 122–291. For thoughts on the place of nomads in Mexican memory, see Aboites, "Nómadas." For older Mexican literature that mentions briefly Indian raids in the context of the U.S.–Mexican War, see, for example, Bustamante, *El nuevo Bernal Díaz,* 57–58; García Cantú, *Invasiones,* 163–79; Jordán, *Crónica,* 221–30, esp. 27; Martínez Caraza, *Norte*

bárbaro, 130–31. For recent works of Mexican scholarship attentive to the effects of Indian raids upon particular states before and during the U.S.–Mexican War, see Pacheco Rojas, "Durango entre"; Almada Bay, Medina Bustos, and Córdova Rascón, "Medidas"; Navarro Gallegos, "Una 'Santa Alianza.'" I use the terms *autonomous* or *independent* to distinguish Comanches, Kiowas, Apaches, and Navajos from the large majority of indigenous peoples in North America, those in Mexico who by the nineteenth century had long since come under some kind of subordination by nonnative political authorities. Mexican officials also came into conflict with semiautonomous peoples like the Yaquis and Mayos of northwestern Mexico, but for Mexican and American observers these "rebellions" generally occupied a different conceptual space and had a different political significance than raids by los indios bárbaros. These conflicts are explored in Hu-DeHart, *Yaqui Resistance*, 18–65; Radding, *Wandering Peoples*, 288–301.

5. Weber, *Mexican Frontier*. For an important recent exception to the generalizations about the Mexican period and neglect of the state, see Reséndez, *Changing*. The border as a dividing line has been particularly obstructive for scholars of southern plains Indians. For an exciting new exception, see Rivaya Martínez, "Captivity and Adoption." Overall, scholars of Apaches have been better about transcending the divide. See, for example, Sweeney, *Mangas Coloradas*. For discussion about the border in borderlands literature, see Weber, "John Francis Bannon"; Cuello, "Beyond the Borderlands." Focused on the late nineteenth and early twentieth centuries, Truett, *Fugitive Landscapes*, is a model transnational study of the borderlands. For the argument that recent ethnohistorical literature has neglected the ideology, actions, and power of the state, see Ostler, *Plains Sioux*, 4–5. For efforts by historians of American foreign relations to interest their colleagues in borderlands, see Rosenberg, "Considering Borders;" Hogan, "Next Big Thing;" and Citino, "Global Frontier."

6. Ned Blackhawk (*Violence over the Land*, 1) observes that the narrative of American history "has failed to gauge the violence that remade much of the continent before U.S. expansion." I hope my book will contribute to the recovery of the more capacious, inclusive, and ultimately painful continental narrative Blackhawk rightly calls for.

7. For "Apache eye," see "Comunicado de José Agustín de Escudero," 1839, in Orozco, *Antología*, 263–73. For "immense deserts," see Juan N. Almonte, "Memoria del Ministro de Guerra y Marina presentada a las cámaras de Congreso General Mexicano en enero de 1841," 35–37, doc. 517, Lafragua.

8. Ruxton, *Adventures*, 117, 127.

9. Ibid., 127–29. Ruxton misspelled Jaral as "Jarral." Josiah Webb, who had met Ruxton on the road a short time before, recalled, "I thought then, and ever since, that no man of common sense who had any knowledge of Indian character, would think of taking such a trip, with such an outfit, for pleasure." Webb, *Adventures*, 239–40.

10. For two recent works that reverse the familiar pattern and stress native dominance in regions of Euro-American interest and colonization, see Duval, *Native Ground*; and Barr, *Peace Came*.

11. For "no more policy," see letter from Chihuahua signed "a contributor," in Orozco, *Antología*, 247–48. Here I abbreviate the influential definition of politics in Swartz, Turner, and Tuden, *Political Anthropology*, 7: "the study of the processes involved in determining and implementing public goals and in the differential achievement and use of power by the members of the group concerned with those goals." For more on politics, see chapter 4, below.

12. Coahuila and Texas formed a single state between 1824 and 1836. But because they became sepa-

rated after 1836 and because raiding patterns before then varied considerably between the two, I
have counted them individually in this tally.

13. For Chihuahua, see Griffen, *Utmost*. Giffen's appendix includes valuable data on Comanches
as well as Apaches. See also Orozco, *Primeras fases*; Orozco, *Antología*; Aboites, "Poder político." Sweeney, *Mangas Coloradas*, illuminates Sonora as well as Chihuahua. For Coahuila,
Rodríguez, *Historias*; Rodríguez, *La guerra*. For Nuevo León, Vizcaya Canales, ed., *La invasión*; Vizcaya Canales, *Incursiones*. For Tamaulipas, see Vigness, "Indian Raids." Ralph Smith
dedicated years to tracing out the activities of Indian raiders in Chihuahua and Durango. See
"Comanche Invasion"; "Apache Plunder"; "Indians in American-Mexican"; "Apache Ranching";
"Comanche Bridge"; and, most recently, *Borderlander*. For northeastern Mexico and Texas to
1841, see Velasco Avila, "Amenaza Comanche." Babcock, "Trans-National Trade," 81–123, discusses Comanche activities below the Rio Grande, focusing on Coahuila and Chihuahua. For
Comanche activities above the Rio Grande during the 1830s and 1840s, see especially Kavanagh,
Comanche Political History, 193–294; and the superb monograph by Brooks, *Captives*, 216–303.

14. Quote is from Daniel Dewey Barnard, in Stephanson, *Manifest Destiny*, 56–57.

PROLOGUE. EASY STORIES

1. On Burr introducing Jackson to good wine, see W. J. Rorabaugh, *Alcoholic Republic*, 102–03. For
Burr's conspiracy, see Remini, *Course of American Empire*, 144–64; Burstein, *Passions*, 62–86.
For the cellar, see Remini, *Life*, 323.

2. For Butler and Jackson, see Remini, *Course of American Empire*, 160.

3. For the Louisiana boundary, see Weber, *Spanish Frontier*, 291–301. For Adams-Onís, see Meinig,
Continental America, 72–74.

4. For Jackson's support of the treaty and for quotes, see Remini, *Course of American Empire*, 387,
353, 364. For precedents, see Cayton, "Blount Conspiracy." For reaction in Washington, see
Anderson and Cayton, *Dominion*, 238–44.

5. For Adams-Onís and for Jackson's initial approval, see Lewis, *American Union*, 126–54; quotes on
Texas are from 145–46. For "regain," see Remini, *Course of American Freedom*, 202. For Butler
on the Nueces, see Astolfi, *Foundations*, 119.

6. On security, see Lewis, *American Union*, 194–95; Remini, *Course of American Freedom*, 218–19.
Mexican political thinkers also worried about "natural" boundaries. See Reséndez, *Changing*,
18–19.

7. For the Red Stick War, see O'Brien, *In Bitterness*. On relocation prior to 1830, see La Vere, *Contrary Neighbors*, 30–61; Everett, *Texas Cherokees*, 3–48; Gregory and Strickland, *Sam Houston*,
17–18.

8. For Indian removal figuring into Jackson's desire for Texas, see Remini, *Course of American Freedom*, 219. For conflicts and for complaints by immigrant Indians, see La Vere, *Contrary Neighbors*, 30–61; Agnew, *Fort Gibson*, 7–54.

9. For colonization, see Weber, *Mexican Frontier*, 158–78. For the adaptations and shared interests
that allowed men like Austin to work well with Mexican counterparts, see Reséndez, *Changing*,
61–74. For Texas's perceived advantages, see Cayton, "Continental Politics."

10. For Jackson's note, see Remini, *Course of American Freedom*, 202. Austin's quote is from Cayton,
"Continental Politics," 307.

11. For arguments regarding sale, see Astolfi, *Foundations*, 118–23. Edwards quote comes from his letter to Jesse Thompson, Nacogdoches, Dec. 26, 1826, in Barker, ed., *Austin Papers* 2:1548–49. For Fredonia, see Reséndez, *Changing*, 40–45; Anderson, *Conquest*, 50–64; Austin's quote is on 63.

12. Remini, *Course of American Freedom*, 218–19; Astolfi, *Foundations*, 121–22.

13. Stenberg, "Jackson, Anthony Butler," 265.

14. For Clay and Comanches, see Manning, *Early Diplomatic Relations*, 288–89; Joel R. Poinsett to Martin Van Buren, Mexico City, Aug. 2, 1829, letter no. 175 in *U.S. Despatches. Tribute* is underlined in Poinsett's original. For an early American description of Comanches as scourges of northern Mexico, see Kavanagh, *Comanche Political History*, 213. Butler likewise thought Comanches useful in pressuring Mexico to sell Texas. See Astolfi, *Foundations*, 121. Quotes are from Martin Van Buren to Joel R. Poinsett, Washington, D.C., Aug. 25, 1829, in *Diplomatic Instructions*, reel 152.

15. For conflicts in the old northwest, see White, *Middle Ground*, 413–68.

16. For complaints from the old southwest, see Cayton, "Separate Interests"; quote is from 62.

17. For Jackson's moment of weakness, see Rothman, *Slave Country*, 128–39. For European events and tepid British support for Indians, see Calloway, *Crown and Calumet*, 223–39.

18. Casualty estimate includes 557 Indians dead on the field and 250–300 more drowned in the Tallapoosa River. See O'Brien, *In Bitterness*, 150. For Tecumseh's death, see Sugden, *Tecumseh*, 375–80.

19. Clark quote is in Prucha, *Great Father* 1:32.

20. For early Spanish advances to the north, see Powell, *Soldiers*; Powell, *Mexico's Miguel Caldera*. For the "colonial pact," see Radding, *Wandering Peoples*. For Indians from central Mexico, see Adams, "Embattled Borderlands"; Simmons, "Tlaxcalans." Population ratios varied across the north. Indian communities still predominated in the northwest in the late colonial era, whereas people of mixed parentage were in the majority in the northeast. See Gerhard, *North Frontier*, 23–31, 54, 65–66, 169–72, 250, 332.

21. For Spanish reactions to the plains, see Almaráz, "Uninviting Land." For Apache–New Mexican relations in the seventeenth century, see Forbes, *Apache*, 3–130. For "Apaches del Navaju," see Brooks, *Captives*, 84.

22. For anxieties about expansion, see the classic accounts in Smith, *Virgin Land*, 174–83; Slotkin, *Fatal Environment*, 199–222; and the insightful discussion in LeMenager, *Manifest and Other*, chap. 1; Pike quote is from 31. Rathbun, "Representation," explores ongoing tensions between those who feared expansion and those who embraced it.

23. Weber, *Spanish Frontier*, 147–71; quote is from 149. For a fascinating discussion of these Spanish anxieties in the eighteenth century and their interimperial consequences, see Mapp, "European Geographic Ignorance," 197–221.

24. This complicated history is discussed thoroughly in the classic by John, *Storms*, 226–531. See also Anderson, *Indian Southwest*, 105–44, 204–15; and the rich new interpretation in Barr, *Peace Came*, 109–96.

25. For Nueva Vizcaya, see Aboites, *Norte precario*, 76. See also the subtle contemporary analysis by Cortés y de Olarte, *Views from the Apache Frontier*. For New Mexico, see Frank, *Settler to Citizen*, 34–45. For Texas and for Comanche casualties, see Anderson, *Indian Southwest*, 208–11.

26. For Rubí, see Jackson and Foster, eds., *Imaginary Kingdom*. A translation of the regulations that

resulted from Rubí's tour can be found in Brinckerhoff and Faulk, eds., *Lancers*. For Spain's tenuous presence in Texas, see Barr, *Peace Came*, 2–7. Changes in the conceptualization and implementation of Spanish frontier policy are explored in Moorhead, *Apache Frontier*, and Weber, *Spanish Frontier*, 204–35. For Louisiana, see Mapp, "French Geographic."

27. Quotes are from Gálvez, *Instructions*, 36–39.

28. Translations of relevant Spanish documents for this period can be found in Thomas, ed., *Forgotten Frontiers*. For smallpox in 1780 and 1781, see Frank, *Settler to Citizen*, 71–75; Simmons, "New Mexico's Smallpox." The outbreak was part of the continental pandemic described by Fenn, *Pox Americana*. For interpretations of the peace, see John, *Storms*, 655–97; Kavanagh, *Comanche Political History*, 93–121; Brooks, *Captives*, 73–78. For war and peace in Texas during these years, see Barr, *Peace Came*, 197–286. For gifts given in New Mexico, see Frank, *Settler to Citizen*, 132–36.

29. For the emerging alliance against Apaches, see Moorhead, *Apache Frontier*, esp. chaps. 7 and 8; Reeve, "Navaho-Spanish Diplomacy." For Apaches and peace establishments, see Griffen, *Apaches*, 53–118. For a sketch of the imperfections in the peace, see Moorhead, *Apache Frontier*, chap. 11; and for efforts of Comanche leaders, see John, "Nurturing."

30. It is often assumed that its sparse population and security problems made northern New Spain a perpetual drain on imperial coffers. But by at least 1786, thanks in large part to the renewed peace, the region as a whole was producing a considerable surplus for the crown. See Tenenbaum, "Making of a Fait Accompli."

31. Weber, *Spanish Frontier*, 290–96.

32. For Wilkinson, see Kavanagh, *Comanche Political History*, 162–63; Prucha, *Great Father* 1:73.

33. For "Captain Merry," see Nasatir, *Borderland*, 137. For the thirty-three headmen, see Weber, *Bárbaros*, 259.

34. For Comanches helping royalists, see Weber, *Bárbaros*, 261. For hostilities in the 1810s, see Almonte, "Statistical Report," 181; Anderson, *Indian Southwest*, 251–55; Kavanagh, *Comanche Political History*, 157–61; Harris, *Mexican Family Empire*, 52–56. For the toll from smallpox in the 1810s, see Berlandier, *Indians*, 84 n. 87; Brooks, *Captives*, 181. For a more detailed discussion of the crisis in Comanche politics during these years, see Anderson, *Indian Southwest*, 251–65.

35. For background, see Andrews, "Bustamante," 7–13. For a nineteenth-century survey of Bustamante's career, see Cubas, *Diccionario* 1:451–60. For Iturbide's brief reign, see Anna, *Mexican Empire*.

36. For Bustamante's position, see Andrews, "Bustamante," 64. For northern Indians, see Bustamante to [Iturbide?], Nov. 21, 1821, in *Gaceta Imperial de México*, Dec. 4, 1821, reprinted in Velasco Avila, "Nuestros obstinados," 447.

37. For Lipanes, see Berlandier, *Indians*, 133. For a brief biography of Ruiz, see McLean, ed., *Papers* 4:31–35. The treaty may be found in ibid., 427–33.

38. Quotes are from ibid., 428, 431. For the press, see Velasco Avila, "Amenaza Comanche," 152–53. For Iron Button, see Kavanagh, *Comanche Political History*, 195.

39. For "barbarian nations," see Berninger, *Inmigración*, 28–29. On Texas colonization, see also Hatcher, *Opening of Texas*; Kelly and Hatcher, "Tadeo Ortiz"; Weber, *Mexican Frontier*, 158–78; Chávez, "Colonización como instrumento."

40. Stephen F. Austin to Anastacio Bustamante, Mexico City, May 10, 1822, in Barker, ed., *Austin Papers* 2:507–10. There is a large primary and secondary literature on the schemes and activities

of Anglo-Americans affecting the southern plains in the early nineteenth century. See, for example, Jackson, ed., *Journals of Pike*; Owsley and Smith, *Filibusters*; Flores, ed., *Jefferson*; Flores, ed., *Journal*. For an excellent discussion of U.S. market penetration into the region, see Isenberg, "Market Revolution."

41. For Iturbide's fall and the constitution of 1824, see Green, *Mexican Republic*, 31–51. For Bustamante in this period, see Andrews, "Bustamante," 69–109.

42. For Hoyoso, see Kavanagh, *Comanche Political History*, 198–99. For the variously hostile and friendly relations during these years, see Rodríguez, *La guerra*, 148; Griffen, *Utmost*, 139; Falcón, "Estado incapaz"; Gaspar de Ochoa to the comandante principal de Nuevo México, Durango, Jan. 29, 1825, MANM 4:658; same to same, March 8, 1825, MANM 4:665; El Baron de Bastrop, "Memorial on condition and needs of Texas," Saltillo, March 6, 1825, in Barker, ed., *Austin Papers* 2:947–52; Micasio Sánchez to alcalde de Refugio, Laredo, September 29, 1845, in MAP 14:34–37. For returning captives and blaming Kiowas, see Kenner, *Comanchero Frontier*, 71. For "a class" and for talks in San Antonio, see Velasco Avila, "Amenaza Comanche," 163–64. For the new treaties, see Kavanagh, *Comanche Political History*, 202–03. For rumors, see Stephen Austin to [José Antonio] Saucedo, San Felipe de Austin, Aug. 14, 1826, and Richard Fields to Stephen Austin, Pueblo de Charaqui, Aug. 27, 1826, both in Barker, ed., *Austin Papers* 2:1424, 1440.

43. For an excellent review of the Fredonia rebellion in Texas and its significance for the Comanche–Mexican alliance, see Velasco Avila, "Amenaza Comanche," 183–212. For "what now remains," see Anastacio Bustamante to Stephen Austin, Bahia, April 7, 1827, in Barker, ed., *Austin Papers* 2:1626–27. For defenses, see Anastacio Bustamante to the ayuntamiento de Matamoros, March 7, 1827, in MAP 7:141. For Cherokees and final quote, see Jackson, *Indian Agent*, 86, 91.

44. For the initial armistice, see Antonio Elosua, copy of the armistice celebrated with the Comanche capitans, San Antonio, Aug. 8, 1827, in MAP 8:104. The first of the three quotes above comes by way of a Mexican official in Texas, and the last two come from Berlandier, all in Kavanagh, *Comanche Political History*, 198–201. The description of the peace in San Antonio and the conferences in New Mexico, see ibid., 200–205.

45. For the commandant, see Velasco Avila, "Amenaza Comanche," 219. For primary accounts of the expedition, see Sánchez, "Trip"; Berlandier, "Cacería del oso"; Berlandier, *Indians*. For Berlandier's artifact collection see ibid., 167–89, and figs. 11 and 13, below. For more on his travels in the northeast, see also Berlandier, *Journey*.

46. For Terán and his writings, see Jackson, *Texas by Terán*.

47. For "there remain" see Green, *Mexican Republic*, 190–91. For Calderón de la Barca, see Fisher and Hall, eds., *Life in Mexico*, 107.

48. For consensus on broad postindependence goals, see Pani, *Para mexicanizar*, 359–60.

49. For demographics, see Green, *Mexican Republic*, 52–55 and n. 4, 53. For social stratification, see Di Tella, *National Popular Politics*, 15–42. For antecedents to the constitution's equality for Indians, see Weber, *Bárbaros*, 263–67. Mora's quote is from Hale, *Mexican Liberalism*, 218.

50. War dead are variously estimated at two hundred to six hundred thousand. See Anna, "Iturbide," 185. For economy, see Coatsworth, "Obstacles." The classic work on government finances is Tenenbaum, *Politics of Penury*.

51. Green, *Mexican Republic*, 31–51. For Bustamante's contingent federalism, see Andrews, "Bustamante," 71–105. For a discussion of ideology at independence, see Di Tella, *National Popular Politics*, 43–72. For an argument that ideological divides have been overdrawn in the literature

and that Mexican elites were much more concerned with protecting their own hegemony, see Fowler, "Dreams of Stability." Mexican scholars are problematizing the supposed dualities of centralist/federalist, conservative/liberal that long dominated characterizations of the period. See, for example, Palti, "Legitimacy"; Pani, *Para mexicanizar*; Palti, *La nación como problema*.

52. Green, *Mexican Republic*, 87–111, 140–49.

53. Andrews, "Bustamante," 110–20; Green, *Mexican Republic*, 154–59.

54. The Jackson cartoon, "Richard III," is by David Claypoole Johnston. See Bumgardner, "Political Portraiture," 90.

55. Green, *Mexican Republic*, 140–88; Andrews, "Bustamante," 121–32. For thoughts on how Guerrero's coup helped melt the "boundaries that distinguished legitimate and illegitimate governments," see Palti, "Legitimacy," 7–36, 60–65.

56. Green, *Mexican Republic*, 189–99.

57. For population, see Weber, *Mexican Frontier*, 166. For Terán and Alamán, see Cantrell, *Stephen F. Austin*, 219. For "lazy," "the spark," and Gross [Groce], see Sánchez, "Trip," 271, 274. For settlement patterns and "be the cause," see Manuel Mier y Terán to President Guadalupe Victoria, San Antonio, March 28, 1828, in Jackson, *Texas by Terán*, 27–39, at 32–33.

58. For Poinsett, see Pletcher, *Diplomacy*, 39–40. For Butler, see Astolfi, *Foundations*, 143–80; quote is on 144. For an insightful discussion of the period surrounding Butler's mission, see Soto, "Texas en la mira."

59. For Jefferson, see Rathbun, "Representation," 57. For Benton and the chargé d'affaires, Astolfi, *Foundations*, 62. For the Committee, see Kelly and Hatcher, "Tadeo Ortiz," 79–80. For Poinsett, Benson, "Texas as Viewed," 249.

60. For newspaper reaction, see Benson, "Texas as Viewed," 264. Manuel Mier y Terán to the Minister of War [Moctezuma], November 4, 1829, in Jackson, *Texas by Terán*, 178–79. For Mexican reluctance to sell territory, see also Suárez Arguello and Bosch García, eds., *El nombre del destino manifiesto*, 15–22.

61. Manuel Mier y Terán to the Minister of War [Moctezuma], November 4, 1829, in Jackson, *Texas by Terán*, 178–79.

62. Alamán's speech is in Bosch García, ed., *Documentos*, 172. For the law, see Cantrell, *Stephen F. Austin*, 219–21. For the political context surrounding passage of the law, see Benson, "Territorial Integrity." For Butler's quixotic efforts, see Astolfi, *Foundations*, 143–80.

CHAPTER 1. DANGER AND COMMUNITY

1. McLean, ed., *Papers* 6:66–69.

2. For conflict with Tawakonis and Wacos, see Smith, *From Dominance*, 140–43.

3. For "so energetically," see McLean, ed., *Papers* 6:67. For Guonique, see Velasco Avila, "Amenaza Comanche," 219. For Ruiz, see José Francisco Ruiz to Antonio Elosúa, Tenoxtitlan, Aug. 6, 1831, in McLean, ed., *Papers* 6:334. For a dark portrait of the cultural intermediary that resonates with Ruiz's sentiment, see Merrell, *Into the American Woods*.

4. For Chuparú, see Velasco Avila, "Amenaza Comanche," 218. For order regarding Paruakevitsi, see Manuel de Mier y Terán to Antonio Elosúa, Matamoros, Aug. 23, 1831, in McLean, ed., *Papers* 6:379–80. For returning animals, see Antonio Elosúa to Manuel de Mier y Terán, Bexar,

January 8, 1831, in McLean, ed., *Papers* 5:396. For "most celebrated," see Berlandier, "Cacería del oso," 145.

5. "Diary of the events which have occurred in the picket of civic militia and settlers who are marching voluntarily today, October 18, 1831, in the expedition against the Tahuacano Indians, under the orders of Capitan Manuel Lafuente," in McLean, ed., *Papers* 6:557–71.

6. Ibid.

7. For the assertion that Paruakevitsi had been working "to make his voice heard for peace and friendship," see Kavanagh, *Comanche Political History*, 232.

8. For Tawakonis, see Smith, *From Dominance*, 142. For Bustamante, see José Mariano Guerra to Antonio Elosúa, May 1, 1832, n.p., in McLean, ed., *Papers* 7:196.

9. For trading visit, see Ramón Músquiz to the governor of Coahuila y Texas, Bexar, Jan. 30, 1832, in McLean, ed., *Papers* 7:119. For the visit of "Isayona" [Yzazona], see Antonio Elosúa to Manuel de Mier y Terán, San Antonio, Dec. 3, 1831, in McLean, ed., *Papers* 6:589. For the son, see Kavanagh, *Comanche Political History*, 232.

10. For the peace, see Mooney, *Calendar*, 162–64. Neither Ruiz nor Berlandier say anything of significance about Kiowas. Both men had considerably more information about the "Chariticas," whom John C. Ewers identifies as Arapahos but who were more likely Kiowas. See Ruiz, *Report*, 16; Berlandier, *Indians*, 108–10; Manuel de Mier y Terán, "Noticia," 131. Mooney (164) states that the compact between Kiowas and Kiowa-Apaches and Comanches excluded the Hois. In 1844 the Hois *paraibo* Potsanaquahip told Sam Houston that his people could not stop Kiowa raiders: "They are more powerful than the Comanche [meaning the Hois] and we fear them." It is unclear whether this was earnest or simply flourish to distance his people from Kiowa raiding, but the comment does suggest an uneasy relationship. See "Minutes of the council at the falls of the Brazos," in Winfrey and Day, eds., *Texas Indian Papers* 2:103–14. Kavanagh misreads Potsanaquahip's statement that there were "nine different tribes who have not yet made peace" to mean peace with the Hois; the context makes it clear that Potsanaquahip meant the Kiowas and the eight other "tribes" had not yet made peace with Texas. Kavanagh, *Comanche Political History*, 272.

11. Scholars continue to debate Comanche population figures. José Francisco Ruiz was the most informed nonnative Comanche observer in the second quarter of the nineteenth century, and in 1828 he put the total Comanche population at ten to twelve thousand. Berlandier, *Indians*, 121. During his tour of Texas in 1834, Colonel Juan Nepomuceno Almonte likewise estimated a Comanche population of ten thousand. Almonte, "Statistical Report," 222. Charles Bent, another informed observer, suggested twelve thousand in 1846. [Charles] Bent to W. Medill, Santa Fe, Nov. 10, 1846, in Abel, ed., *Official Correspondence*, 6–9. Brown, "Comanchería Demography," argues that la comanchería could have supported enough bison to sustain between seven and eight thousand people in the early 1830s. This strikes me as low, because Comanche resource acquisition was not as geographically confined as Brown's model suggests and because they could and did consume herd animals in time of scarcity. On ethnic diversity, see Anderson, *Indian Southwest*, 220–26. For the peace and for Kiowa and Kiowa-Apache population estimates, see Mooney, *Calendar*, 53, 162–63, 236.

12. For horse breaking, see Babcock, "Trans-National Trade," 49. On Kiowa and Comanche animal wealth, see Mishkin, *Rank and Warfare*, 19; Berlandier, *Indians*, 44. See also David G. Burnet,

quoted by Ewers in Berlandier, *Indians*, 44 n. 21. For Mexico as the ultimate source for horse wealth on the plains, see Jablow, *Cheyenne in Plains*, 15–16.

13. Quote is from Tixier, *Tixier's Travels*, 268.

14. For a brief sketch of Cheyenne culture and history, see West, *Contested Plains*, 68–93.

15. For Bent's recollections, see Hyde, ed., *Life of George Bent*, 33–40. For other reports of Blackfeet, Arikaras, and Pawnees below the Arkansas, see Kavanagh, *Comanche Political History*, 235.

16. For Burnet, see Wallace, "Burnet's Letters," 134. For five hundred, see Tixier, *Tixier's Travels*, 268. For Long, see James, *Long's Expedition* 3:233–34. For complaints about arms, see Kavanagh, *Comanche Political History*, 211–12. On slain captives, see Berlandier, *Indians*, 140. See also Sánchez, "Trip," 262.

17. Mooney, *Calendar*, 257–60.

18. Berlandier, *Indians*, 122; *Texas Gazette*, June 12, 1830. For Mexican interest in Comanche–Shawnee hostilities, see Velasco Avila, "Amenaza Comanche," 227. See also Kavanagh, *Comanche Political History*, 232–33. For Comanche complaints about eastern Indian hostility, see La Vere, *Contrary Neighbors*, 53. La Vere states that Comanches and Kiowas were instigators of these conflicts (71), but the lure of the sprawling Comanche herds, the fact that the removed Indians were far better armed, and the comments of observers on the southern plains all suggest that removed Indians were more often the aggressors. In 1829, Sam Houston characterized Cherokee attacks on southern plains Indians as "unjust and impolitic" and claimed that Wichitas and Comanches had never "dared" to invade the frontiers of the United States. See Houston to Col. Matthew Arbuckle, Bayou Maynard, C.N., July 8, 1829, in Williams and Barker, eds., *Writings of Houston* 1:136–39. For the Koasati, whom Berlandier refers to as Cutchaté, see Berlandier, *Journey*, 560–61; and Ewers's identification in Berlandier, *Indians*, 124 n. 67.

19. For temperature and precipitation on the southern plains, see Leathers, "Climate." For the challenges of keeping horse herds on the plains, see James E. Sherow, "Workings of the Geodialectic," esp. 69–74; Moore, *The Cheyenne*, 49; West, *Way West*, 20–37.

20. My discussion of Comanche social and political structure in the early nineteenth century is informed by the following primary accounts of Comanche life: Ruiz, *Report*; Berlandier, *Indians*; Berlandier, "Cacería del oso"; Wallace, "Burnet's Letters"; Cameron, "Comanche Indians"; Sánchez, "Trip"; Neighbors, "The Na-Uni." Hoebel's classic ethnographies depend upon informants who were young in the 1880s and need to be used carefully, but I have benefited from them: Hoebel, *Political Organization*, 9–44; Wallace and Hoebel, *Comanches*, 209–44. For kinship, see Gladwin, "Comanche Kin." Among contemporary students of Comanches, I have particularly relied upon Kavanagh, *Comanche Political History*, 28–62; and Foster, *Being Comanche*, 31–74.

21. For the acquisition of honor, see Kavanagh, *Comanche Political History*, 28. For a comparative analysis of marriage and power in Comanche, Kiowa, and Cheyenne societies (based mainly on ethnographic sources from the early twentieth century), see Collier, *Marriage*.

22. For arguments about the significance of the Comanche division, see Thurman, "New Interpretation"; Gelo, "On a New"; Thurman, "Reply"; Kavanagh, "Comanche: Paradigmatic Anomaly"; Meadows, *Enduring Veterans*, 251–368; Davis, *Ecology*, 120–24, 62–72. Morris Foster insists that divisions were less a formal political unit than a seasonal gathering of residence bands that shared a particular territory and that their primary political function was to periodically impose restraints upon band leaders vis-à-vis other band leaders. See Foster, *Being Comanche*, 52–74.

My reading of the sources leans toward Fosters' interpretation. To maintain that the division was "the maximal level of aboriginal Comanche political organization" (Kavanagh, *Comanche Political History*, 51) or that divisions were "politically independent tribes" (Meadows, *Enduring Veterans*, 303) seems to impose too much structure on an extremely fluid social system. Given that band and division membership fluctuated regularly, that divisions came and went over the decades, that leaders at all levels were obliged to be exquisitely sensitive to popular opinion, and that there were no coercive mechanisms to restrict cooperation in hunting, raiding, or warfare at any social level, it would seem more accurate to say that the individual family was the unit of political independence. Comanches clearly identified with particular divisions, and the strength of this identification no doubt varied over time. But these units were expressions of kin relations, regional proximity, and shared cultural traits rather than firm barriers beyond which meaningful political cooperation was impossible. Moreover it does not seem that cooperation was essentially different across divisions than at any other level. That said, Kavanagh has demonstrated that divisions regularly elected principal leaders and were units of more political substance than Foster allows.

23. Historians commonly use the term *Penatekas* (Honey Eaters) to refer to the southernmost Comanche division. This is problematic for the 1820s and 1830s because it seems that the term *Penateka* does not appear in the written sources until 1843; see Report of P. M. Butler, April 29, 1843, 7, Pierce M. Butler Papers, Huntington Library. Butler himself is confusing on this point. In the document above he lists seven "bands or lodges" and identifies Hois and Penatekas as distinct groups occupying different ranges. But in a later (and presumably more informed) report, Butler enumerates only five Comanche bands/lodges, omitting Penatekas but identifying the Hois as "honeyeaters" (see Report of P. M. Butler, Fort Gibson, Jan. 31, 1844, 13, Butler Papers). Moreover Butler identifies Potsanaquahip (Buffalo Hump), whom scholars usually identify as a Penateka, as a Hois. As late as 1848, another informed Indian agent referred to the paraibo Mopechucope as the leader of the "friendly band of Penatekas or Hois"; see Robert S. Neighbors to W. Medill, Trading Post no. 2, March 2, 1848, in Senate Rep. com., no. 171, 30th Cong., 1st sess. The best evidence is therefore ambiguous about whether Hois and Penatekas were ever separate groups and, if so, for how long. If, as it seems to me, the names refer to the same division, it is unclear exactly when and for whom the later name supplanted the former. For the sake of consistency, and given that Penateka is absent from the record for the bulk of period examined in this book, I will use *Hois* throughout to refer to the southernmost Comanche division.

24. For kinship reckoning, see Gladwin, "Comanche Kin," 78.

25. For the policing functions of divisional gatherings, see Foster, *Being Comanche*, 67.

26. In Wallace and Hoebel's phrase, "The man made the office, and not the office the man." *Comanches*, 211. For Paruakevitsi, see Kavanagh, *Comanche Political History*, 5.

27. I follow Foster, *Being Comanche* and occasionally use the term Comanche *community* to refer collectively to all Comanches. *Community* is certainly preferable to *tribe*, which is freighted with stereotypes and in the strict sense is a better term for divisions than for the larger linguistic group. *Nation* is a better alternative than *tribe*, in part because Euro-Americans of the time often used the term *nation* to refer to an allied indigenous linguistic community. Nonetheless, that term too carries assumptions about political structure that are inappropriate to the Comanche case prior to the reservation era. See Kavanagh, *Comanche Political History*, 489–90.

28. On mutual use of land and resources throughout la comanchería, see, for example, Neighbors,

"The Na-Uni," 131; Wallace, "Burnet's Letters," 123. For mid-nineteenth century divisions and locations, see Kavanagh, *Comanche Political History*, 384. On death and the movement of kin, see, for example, Ruiz, "Comanches"; Berlandier, *Indians*, 96. The quote is from Burnet, "Comanches and Other Tribes," 88.

29. Mishkin, *Rank*, 24–27; Foster and McCollough, "Plains Apache."

30. For Wichita alliance and amalgamation with Comanches, see Anderson, *Indian Southwest*, 225–26; Sánchez, "Trip," 263. For Wacos campaigning in Mexico, see "Statement of Luis Sánchez as taken by Walter Winn" [May 1844], in Winfrey and Day, eds., *Texas Indian Papers* 2:64–66. For the Shoshones, see Berlandier, *Indians*, 143; Joaquín Rivaya Martínez, "Captivity and Adoption," 154–56. As late as 1844 Texan authorities were noting that hundreds of "Snakes," or Shoshones, were camping with Comanches. See "Notes, Council Ground, Tehuacana Creek," July 22, 1844, in Winfrey and Day, eds., *Texas Indian Papers* 2:80–82. Plummer describes her capture during an attack of several hundred Indians upon Parker's Fort in 1836, and most of the attackers do seem to have been Comanches. After the raid, however, the Indian family who claimed her took her north and northwest, to "the Snow Mountains, where it is perpetual snow." She describes huge mountain ranges, an "abundance" of beaver, "mountain sheep . . . who live along the brows of the mountains, and . . . feed on the brinks of the steepest precipices," and camping with her captors in a deep valley, "the mountains on either side being incredibly high." Plummer was eventually purchased by New Mexican traders somewhere, by her reckoning, five hundred miles north of Santa Fe. Considering her descriptions of animals, landscapes, and distances, along with what we know about Shoshone–Comanche kinship, it seems clear that Eastern Shoshones participated in the raid on Parker's Fort and took Plummer back to their home ranges, perhaps as far north as southwestern Wyoming. If this is indeed the case, Plummer's narrative sheds new light on the Comanche–Shoshone relationship. More important, it forces researchers to reevaluate the scope of New Mexican trading in North America and provides the earliest intimate ethnographic account of Shoshones. The first edition of the narrative is reproduced in Plummer, *Narrative*; quotes are from 9, 12–13.

31. For Comanche retaliatory raids against Cheyennes, see Hyde, ed., *Life of George Bent*, 40. For Ruiz's account of the Osage campaign of 1824, see Berlandier, *Indians*, 73. For the regularity of these "yearly wars" against the Osage, see Berlandier, *Indians*, 67. See also testimony of Dionisio Santos, Lampazos, July 11, 1873, in Velasco Avila, ed., *En manos*, 40–43.

32. Kiowa vocabulary in the following paragraphs is taken from Mooney, *Calendar*, 391–430, though I have eliminated hyphens. Mooney's informants told him that a literal translation of *t'a'ka'i* would be "prominent or flapping ears," in reference to the fact that men's short-cut hair makes their ears look more prominent. Laurel Watkins of Colorado College notes that this translation would require a very unusual loss of a vowel and finds more convincing the definition given by Harrington, *Vocabulary*, linking the word to "mule" (Mooney also noted the connection to "mule" but stressed the other translation). Where I deviate from Mooney's translation I rely on Watkins's personal communications to me on Aug. 2 and Aug. 4, 2007. I am grateful to her for kindly (and patiently) helping me to make sense of these matters—though of course any errors are my own. The best Comanche vocabulary from the nineteenth century, Manuel García Rejón, *Comanche Vocabulary*, while valuable in other regards, gives little indication of how Comanches differentiated between Mexican communities. New Mexican population estimates are taken from Colonel Antonio Narbona's census of 1827, reproduced in Carroll and Haggard,

eds., *New Mexican Chronicles*, 88. This census lumps La Cañada together with surrounding pueblos, prohibiting comparison with Santa Fe, but a document from 1824 put La Cañada's population at 5,743. See Janet Lecompte, *Rebellion in Río Arriba*, 158 n. 3. Anton Chico had been founded in 1822 but was temporarily abandoned between the late 1820s and 1834 because of Indian hostilities. See Brooks, *Captives*, 220.

33. For the El Paso population figure, see Timmons, "El Paso," 2 n. 3.

34. Berlandier, *Journey*, 262, 426–34; Alonzo, *Tejano Legacy*, 73.

35. Kiowas used the word *Tehä´no*, from the Spanish *tejano*, to refer to Anglo-Americans in Texas—whom they distinguished from Americans. It is unclear from Mooney's glossary whether they also used the word for Spanish speakers in Texas. See Mooney, *Calendar*, 425. Berlandier put the population of San Antonio and Goliad in 1828 at 2,075, though it seems he did not include any surrounding populations in the figure, and he likewise excluded presidial soldiers and their families in Goliad. Berlandier, *Journey*, 293, 374. Almonte's report from 1835 estimated that the municipalities of San Antonio, Goliad, Victoria, and San Patricio were home to 4,000. Almonte, "Statistical Report," 186. It seems that the Mexican population of Texas, like that of the communities on the lower Rio Grande, expanded somewhat during peace with the Comanches and their allies in the late 1820s and early 1830s.

36. For animals in New Mexico, see Narvona, "Report." Sugar was key to Nuevo León's economy. See J. Jesús Ávila Ávila, "Entre la jara," 206. For the importation of grains and vegetables, see Alonzo, *Tejano Legacy*, 66; Jackson, *Texas by Terán*, 159–68. For salt, see Valerio-Jiménez, "Indios Bárbaros," 57; Alonzo, *Tejano Legacy*, 68. Berlandier commented that "all the women on the banks of the Río Bravo" used cochineal to dye the woolen textiles they manufactured. Berlandier, *Journey*, 460. For dowry payments and for mules, see Graf, "Economic History," 18, 60.

37. On the limits of the ranching economy, see Harris, *Mexican Family Empire*, 28. On drought in the 1810s, see Anderson, *Indian Southwest*, 103. For the decrease in the population of Mexican Texas, see Almonte, "Statistical Report," 186. For out-migration from the lower Rio Grande in the early nineteenth century, see, for example, Velasco Avila, "Amenaza Comanche," 152, 212. For the 1.5 million figure, see Berlandier, *Journey*, 455. The estimates of animals in Texas in 1806 are from Almonte, "Statistical Report," 181. Those for 1828 are from Berlandier, *Journey*, 293, 429.

38. Berlandier met several farmers in the northeast who complained that the drought they were then suffering through had lasted for several years. See Berlandier, *Journey*, 231. On the wet cycle, see Flores, "Bison Ecology," 475. For Coahuila drought history, see Harris, *Mexican Family Empire*, 200. For the assertion of livestock recovery in Coahuila as early as 1819, see Velasco Avila, "Amenaza Comanche," 212–13.

39. On the establishments of new ranches in the late 1820s and early 1830s, see Berlandier, *Journey*, 429, 439; Alonzo, *Tejano Legacy*, 61. For three million, see ibid., 78. For testimony on growth in this period from Laredo, see Juzgado de Laredo to Secretario del Superior Gobierno del Departamento de Tamaulipas, Laredo, July 31, 1837, in Sánchez, *Frontier Odyssey*, 74–75. On landholding patterns in the lower Rio Grande, see Graf, "Economic History," 16–17; Valerio-Jiménez, "Indios Bárbaros," 52–60.

40. On the establishment and size of the Sánchez Navarro latifundio, see Harris, *Mexican Family Empire*, 166–67. On peonage, see ibid., 217–20. While studies elsewhere in Mexico have generally discredited the notion that debt peonage was common on haciendas, the sparse popula-

tion of northern states apparently led hacendados to adopt extraordinary methods in securing labor. See Katz, "Labor Conditions," 7–8. An observant traveler noted in 1846 that debt peonage existed in New Mexican haciendas as well. See Wislizenus, *Memoir*, 23. Another scholar working in Zacatecas has found that workers on one of that state's large haciendas carried little debt, were remarkably well fed, and had a near absolute right to pick up and move; so it is difficult to generalize about "the north" in this respect. See Cross, "Living Standards."

41. For the Comanche raids into Chihuahua in the 1820s, begun as raids on Apaches, see Kavanagh, *Comanche Political History*, 201; Gaspar de Ochoa to Comandante Principal de Nuevo México, Durango, March 8, 1825, MANM 4:665.

42. For Lipán ranges and population estimates, see Berlandier, *Indians*, 128 and n. 178; Sánchez, "Trip," 252; Mier y Terán, "Noticia," 129. For the Lipán–Comanche rapprochement, see Cameron, "Comanche Indians," 476; Ruiz, *Report*, 7. For Lipanes guiding Comanches, see Berlandier, *Indians*, 119–20, 132–33. For Lipán raids in Coahuila in the 1810s, see Harris, *Mexican Family Empire*, 52–56.

43. Berlandier, *Indians*, 42 n. 16, 63, 133. Berlandier cryptically states that Lipanes turned against the Comanches "because the Comanches have shown bad faith toward them, and because they have no respect for the law of hospitality, which the Lipanes observe so scrupulously." Ibid., 66.

44. For quote, see Mier y Terán, "Noticia," 129. For Comanche fear of Lipanes, see Berlandier, *Indians*, 32; Berlandier, "Cacería del oso," 150.

45. For the raid in 1799, see Babcock, "Trans-National Trade," 54. For Paruakevitsi, see José Francisco de la Garza to the Ayuntamiento of Matamoros, Laredo, Nov. 1, 1824, MAP 9:22–23. See also testimony of Dionisio Santos, Lampazos, July 11, 1873, in Velasco Avila, ed., *En manos*, 40–43. For "remain neutral," see Gaspar de Ochoa to the Comandante Principal of New Mexico, Durango, March 8, 1825, MANM 4:665. For Comanches crossing the river to get at Apaches, see Kavanagh, *Comanche Political History*, 201. Quote from Lipán mother is in Velasco Avila, "Amenaza Comanche," 299–300.

46. For political structure, see Alicia Hernández Chávez, *Tradición republicana*, 30; Weber, *Mexican Frontier*, 15–42; Martín González de la Vara, "La política." Perhaps because the constitution of 1824 gave states such latitude in organizing themselves, internal divisions and terminology varied. Terminology is all the more complicated because "states" became "departments" in the mid-1830s, as explained below. The above division of states into departments and *partidos* comes from the Tamaulipas constitution of 1825: *Constitución política del estado libre de Tamaulipas*. Zacatecas, to choose another example, divided its territory into *partidos* and each *partido* into *distritos*. Daniel Gutiérrez, personal communication, Oct. 20, 2003.

47. Population comparison is based on a Mexican population in 1830 of 7,996,000. See Aboites, *Norte precario*, 49.

48. For "communities of interest," see Brooks, "This Evil," 280. For marriages at San Miguel del Vado, see Brooks, *Captives*, 196. For San Carlos, see Vizcaya Canales, ed., *La invasión*, 57–58. For names, see Mooney, *Calendar*, 417, 429.

49. In 1846 plain buffalo hides were selling for $3.00 in Houston, while "fancy ones," that is, painted ones, could fetch as much as $10.00. See Roemer, *Texas*, 192. For trade goods, see Berlandier, *Indians*, 47, 31 n. 3. For bear grease, see Berlandier, *Indians*, 46 n. 23. In 1831 the going price in Mexico City was $1^{1}/_{4}$ to $2^{1}/_{2}$ pesos per jar. See Benson, "Texas as Viewed," 281. On the captive trade in the early 1830s, see Berlandier, *Indians*, 75.

50. For Mexican trade items, see Berlandier, *Indians*, 31, 47–48; Barreiro's observations in Carroll and Haggard, eds., *New Mexican Chronicles*, 110; and Kavanagh, *Comanche Political History*, 205–06. There are a number of references in Mexican documents to textiles taken from fallen Comanches and Kiowas. In 1841, for example, a Comanche warrior captured and later executed in Nuevo León was carrying two woven blankets and a new cotton shirt among his other possessions. He also had a leather work shirt "of Christian production." See *Seminario*, June 24, 1841. In 1840, Anglo-Texan officials reported "New Mexican blankets" among the spoils taken from a defeated Comanche party; these may have been made by Navajos or Navajo captives. See *Telegraph*, Oct. 14, 1840.

51. For eighteenth-century Comanche trading visits to New Mexico, see Foote, "Spanish-Indian Trade." For a glimpse of their range, see Kavanagh, *Comanche Political History*, 205. For the comancheros generally, see Kenner, *Comanchero Frontier*; Brooks, *Captives*, 211–22, 269–71, 265–73.

52. On the San Antonio hide exports, see Almonte, "Statistical Report," 192. For the relative significance of the hide trade in New Mexico during the eighteenth century, see Baxter, *Carneradas*, 59. Final quotes are from Barreiro, *Ojeado*, reprinted in Carroll and Haggard, eds., *New Mexican Chronicles*, 110.

53. Bazaar quote is from Berlandier, *Indians*, 48. While Comanches were at war with most of their Indian neighbors in the late 1820s and early 1830s, they still enjoyed peace and commerce with a few native communities. In the late 1820s, for example, Manuel Mier y Terán remarked on the trade that Comanches conducted through other Indians. See Mier y Terán, "Noticia," 130. He may have had in mind the Skiri Pawnees, six hundred of whom traveled to la comanchería to make peace and open trading relations with Comanches in 1822. See Berlandier, *Indians*, 103.

CHAPTER 2. BUFFALO-HIDE QUIVER

1. For requests and refusals, see Joel R. Poinsett to Henry Clay, Mexico City, July 16, 1828, letter no. 145 in *U.S. Despatches*; Kavanagh, *Comanche Political History*, 204–05. It is possible that *local* authorities provided some help. On May 28, 1834, the *Road Island Republican* published a letter from an American in San Antonio who claimed that tejano forces had helped Comanches recover horses from Shawnees.

2. For the raids in Chihuahua, see Manuel Mier y Terán to Antonio Elosúa, Matamoros, Aug. 2, 1830; Principal Commandant of Coahuila y Texas to Commandants of Rio Grande, Aguaverde, Bavia, Bahía, the Major of the Plaza de Béxar, and the Commandant at Tenoxtitlan, Sept. 4, 1830, both in McLean, ed., *Papers* 4:337, 449. For raids during the years 1831–33, see, for example, Mariano Cosío to Antonio Elosúa, Goliad, Aug. 17, 1831, in McLean, ed., *Papers* 6:356–61; José J. Calvo, circular, Chihuahua, Oct. 16, 1831, MANM 13:483; Kavanagh, *Comanche Political History*, 233; Velasco Avila, "Amenaza Comanche," 267. For a Chihuahuan declaration of war against Comanches, see José J. Calvo, circular, Chihuahua, Oct. 16, 1831, MANM 13:483. I infer the results of Ronquillo's campaign from the governor's comment in 1833 that the Comanches' "arguments could be reduced to vengeance for the deaths of five men of their nation on the Rio Pecos." See Kavanagh, *Comanche Political History*, 206–07. For the campaigns of 1833 and 1834, see also Griffen, *Utmost*, 141.

3. In 1831, New Mexico's governor refused requests to arrange the release of a Comanche pris-

oner unless the Indians stopped raiding settlements in Chihuahua and elsewhere on the frontier. See Comandante Principal to Comandante General, Santa Fe, Oct. 30, 1831 [letter book], MANM 13:521. For Bustamante, see José María Letona to Ramón Músquez, Saltillo, Oct. 20, 1831, in McLean, ed., *Papers* 6:486. See also José Isidro Madero, circular, Chihuahua, Oct. 31, 1831, in Orozco, *Antología*, 206–07. For the Tamaulipas plan, see Manuel Reducindo Barragán to Antonio Elosúa, Guerrero, Feb. 27, 1832, in McLean, ed., *Papers* 7:134. Reducindo agreed with the governor of Chihuahua that Comanches from multiple divisions were responsible for the raiding. For campaigns against Comanches in 1832 and 1833, see Smith, *From Dominance*, 143–44.

4. For the ban in Coahuila, see Babcock, "Trans-National Trade," 98. For the comanchero ban, see Kavanagh, *Comanche Political History*, 205. For penalties against unlicensed comancheros, see Brooks, *Captives*, 274–75.

5. Alejandro Ramírez to Governor of Chihuahua, El Paso, July 23, 1834, in Orozco, *Antología*, 237–39.

6. For Mexican requests that the United States stop cross-border raiding, see Joel R. Poinsett to Henry Clay, Mexico City, July 16, 1828, letter no. 145 in *U.S. Despatches*.

7. For Houston's early life and sojourn out west, see Gregory and Strickland, *Sam Houston*. For Rachael Jackson and for "would conquer," see Remini, *Course of American Freedom*, 153, 202. There is an ongoing debate about Houston's motives; an important debate, insofar as it speaks to the character of U.S. expansion into Mexican territory. For an early salvo, see Mayo, *Political Sketches*. See also Stenberg, "Jackson, Anthony Butler"; Astolfi, *Foundations*, 148; Gregory and Strickland, *Sam Houston*, 143; Agnew, *Fort Gibson*, 87; Anderson, *Conquest*, 81–82. For "the most supreme" and "if anything," see Sam Houston to Henry L. Ellsworth and Others, Natchitoches, Feb. 13, 1833, in Williams and Barker, eds., *Writings of Houston* 1:272.

8. Material about the dragoon expedition in this and the following paragraph is taken from Mooney, *Calendar*, 261–69; La Vere, *Contrary Neighbors*, 72–78; Agnew, *Fort Gibson*, 115–39; Mayhall, *Kiowas*, 63–70; Kavanagh, *Comanche Political History*, 237–40.

9. Catlin quote is in Mooney, *Calendar*, 268. For the significance of horses among the Choctaw, see Carson, "Horses," 495–513.

10. For the council quote, and for later Comanche complaints over hunting and (in early 1845) over violence, see Kavanagh, *Comanche Political History*, 242–43, 274. See also P. L. Chouteau to Gov. M. Stokes and Brig. Gen. M. Arbuckle, April 20, 1836, reprinted in *Globe* (June 13, 1836). In 1836 an Osage man killed a Comanche woman, but Osage leaders sent word that it was a mistake and offered to "cover" the dead with gifts. Comanches agreed. See Rollings, *Osage*, 271.

11. For Comanche raids in Chihuahua in 1834 and 1835, see appendix, below, and Griffen, *Utmost*, 143.

12. Ibid., 142.

13. Ibid., 143; Gregg, *Commerce*, 250. I have modified slightly Gregg's translation of Saenz's quote (Gregg provides the original Spanish in his text). Chihuahuan authorities reported that Comanches burned nine houses at Las Animas. See Orozco, *Primeras fases*, 89.

14. For a "certified list" of the tribes who had made peace with Comanches, see letter of Juan L. Velázquez de León [Saltillo?], Jan. 14, 1835, in C1, F3, E3, f2, AGEC-FSXIX. This document contains information that was originally taken from a letter written from San Antonio on Dec.

15, 1834. For the decline in trade, see Velasco Avila, "Amenaza Comanche," 259. American negotiators were not oblivious to the fact that their diplomatic mission might have implications for Mexico. In 1835 Comanches, Wichitas, Osages, and eastern Indians signed a treaty at Fort Holmes, codifying the understanding they arrived at through Dodge's good offices the year before. Article 9 of that treaty reads: "The Commanche and Witchetaw nations and their associated bands or tribes, of Indians, agree, that their entering into this treaty shall in no respect interrupt their friendly relations with the Republic of Mexico, where they all frequently hunt and the Comanche nation principally inhabit; and it is distinctly understood that the Government of the United States desire that perfect peace shall exist between the nations or tribes named in this article and the said republic." See Kappler, *Laws and Treaties*, 2:436.

15. For Almonte's observations on the Indians of Texas, see his "Statistical Report." For Mexican attempts at aligning Mexicans, Anglos, and eastern Indians against Comanches, see Jenkins, ed., *Papers* 1:44, 47, 55, 67; Velasco Avila, "Amenaza Comanche," 272–75, 280. Authorities in Chihuahua also had hopes of launching a campaign onto the southern plains. See Comandante General de Chihuahua to Comandante Principal de Nuevo México, Chihuahua, Jan. 21, 1835, MANM 19:757.

16. For Chihuahuan mules being sold in Texas, see José J. Calvo to Luis Zuloaga, Chihuahua, Sept. 10, 1835, in *Diario*, Oct. 11, 1835. For "quietude," see Kavanagh, *Comanche Political History*, 289; for treaty talks, 234.

17. Green, *Mexican Republic*, 210–20, 227–30.

18. Fisher and Hall, eds., *Life in Mexico*, 107. See also Fowler, "Repeated Rise."

19. Tenenbaum, *Politics of Penury*, 37–40; Costeloe, *Central Republic*, 31–51.

20. The following sketch of the context and events of the Texan rebellion is drawn from Weber, *Mexican Frontier*, 158–76, 242–55; Reichstein, *Rise*, 133–47; DePalo, *Mexican National Army*, 24–65; and, especially, Reséndez, *Changing*, 146–70. For the political dispute in Coahuila, see also Prieto, "Coahuila y la invasión," 162–64; López López, *La ciudad*, 274–87.

21. Austin quote is taken from Reséndez, "Caught," 105.

22. Texas historians still debate casualty figures from the Alamo. See Hardin, "Battle of the Alamo"; Anderson and Cayton, *Dominion*, 268. The claim that several men survived the Alamo siege only to be executed later is still resisted by some. For a contemporary report of the survival, see letter in *United States Telegraph*, July 13, 1836. For Goliad figures, see Davenport and Roell, "Goliad Massacre."

23. For the long-term consequences of Texan independence for Mexico–Indian relations, see the important insights in Velasco Avila, "Amenaza Comanche," 292–93. For visits to San Antonio, see Kavanagh, *Comanche Political History*, 185. Ruiz and Bean have been discussed above. For Seguín's function as an ambassador to Comanche leaders, see, for example, Jesús F. de la Teja, ed., *Revolution Remembered*, 20. For evidence of *bexareño* traders cooperating in Mexican campaigns against Indians on the lower Rio Grande, see, for example, a report from Coahuila praising "the volunteers from Bexar, for their patriotic conduct," in Rafael de la Fuente to Sr. Secretario del Superior Gobierno del Departamento, Monclova, Oct. 27, 1841, in *Voto*, Nov. 13, 1841. For tejanos acting as spies, see, for example, Santiago Rodríguez to Ministro de Guerra y Marina, Saltillo, Oct. 13, 1845, in *Republicano*, Sept. 20, 1845.

24. For consequences of raiding in Laredo, see Hinojosa, *Borderlands Town*, 50–52. For raids be-

tween the Nueces and Rio Grande, see D. W. Smith to U.S. Secretary of State, Matamoros, August 4, 1837, *Despatches* 1:700. For Kiowa participation, see Mooney, *Calendar*, 271. For details of Comanche raiding in 1836–40, see appendix, below.

25. For quote, see J. de Jesús D. y Prieto to the Secretaría de Guerra y Marina, Monterrey, April 1, 1838, C15, AGENL-MGM. Mexican officials in Saltillo seemed to have regarded the treaty with considerable skepticism but reasoned that it might reduce the number of raiders they had to face. See Gregorio Uruñuela to the Comandancia del distrito de Monclova y su frontera, Leona Vicario, May 24?, 1838, in *Gaceta del Gobierno de Coahuila*, May 26, 1838. The Comanche signatories were few and otherwise unknown; it is therefore doubtful they represented an important faction.

26. For firsthand accounts of Comanche attacks on Anglo frontier settlements during the rebellion era, see, for example, Rister, *Comanche Bondage*, 123–28; Plummer, *Narrative*, 5–7. This period is most thoroughly discussed in Anderson, *Conquest*, 153–94; for Shawnees, see 163.

27. For Lipanes in Nuevo León, see Velasco Avila, "Amenaza Comanche," 301–03. For the peace treaty with Texas, see Winfrey and Day, eds., *Texas Indian Papers* 1:30–32. Castro apparently continued to play Texans and Mexicans off of one another even after this agreement. See "Report of G. W. Bonnell, Commissioner of Indian Affairs, third Congress, first session, Houston, Nov. 3, 1838," in Senate Rep. Com., #171, 30th Cong., 1st sess., 38–50. It is possible that the "excursion" mentioned in the newspaper was a campaign into Nuevo León, one of the few raiding campaigns of that season. See Joaquín García to Ministro de Guerra y Marina, Dec. 9, 1838, C 12, E 44, AGENL-MGM; same to same, March 23, 1839, C13, E 34, AGENL-MGM. For reports of Lipán scouts encouraging and guiding Texan raiding parties, see *Telegraph*, Jan. 2, 1839; ibid., Jan. 12, 1839; ibid., Jan. 30, 1839. For the slaughter in the Comanche camp, see J. H. Moore to Albert Sidney Johnston, LaGrange, March 10, 1839, in Winfrey and Day, eds., *Texas Indian Papers* 1:57–59.

28. For retaliatory action by Potsanaquahip and others, see Schilz and Schilz, *Buffalo Hump*, 18. For initial emissaries and orders to detain later negotiators, see H. W. Karnes to A. Sidney Johnston, San Antonio, Jan. 10, 1840, Winfrey and Day, eds., *Texas Indian Papers* 1:101–02; Sidney Johnston to W. S. Fisher, Austin, Jan. 30, 1840, Winfrey and Day, eds., *Texas Indian Papers* 1:105–06.

29. *Pittsfield Sun* (April 23, 1840), *New Hampshire Patriot* (April 27, 1840), *New York Post* (April 27, 1840), *Pensacola Gazette* (April 18, 1840), *Mobile Register*, and *New Hampshire Sentinel* (April 29, 1840) were among the papers that ran the news of the "horrible massacre of the Cumanche Indians." For Maverick's description, see Fehrenbach, *Comanches*, 325. Cutting off the tip of a woman's nose was the traditional Comanche punishment (perhaps more often threatened than enforced) for adulterous wives, but, according to Maverick, Lockhart claimed it was the Comanche women who had tortured her and mutilated her face. For the critique of Maverick's claims and for the Council House Massacre generally, see Anderson, *Conquest*, 182–83, 409. Dolly Webster was held captive with Lockhart for some time and spoke often with her, yet Webster's captivity narrative says nothing about the young woman being disfigured. For the coastal raid and its interception, see *Telegraph*, Aug. 19, 1840. Some eyewitnesses believed that other Indians accompanied Comanches on the raid. See *New York Spectator*, Sept. 23, 1845 (reprinting a letter that appeared in *New Orleans Commercial Bulletin*). For the attack on the Comanche camp, see Anderson, *Conquest*, 190–91.

30. For Yellow Wolf, see Halaas and Masich, *Halfbreed,* 9–10, 27. For Bent's activities among Comanches in 1835, see Lecompte, "Bent, St. Vrain," 274.

31. Kiowa dates come from Mooney, *Calendar,* 271–74. For the casualties during the attack on the camp at Wolf River (Creek), see Moore, *The Cheyenne,* 134–35. For Lokota, see Halaas and Masich, *Halfbreed,* 31. Auguste Pierre Chouteau commented on Cheyenne/Comanche hostility for his superiors in the War Department. See Kavanagh, *Comanche Political History,* 245.

32. For Choteau, see Lecompte, "Bent, St. Vrain," 275–79. It is possible that the Panic of 1837 and the resulting depression in the United States had negative repercussions for southern plains trade. Still, the Panic of 1819 actually drove American merchants like William Becknell onto the plains and, temporarily at least, into the Indian trade. For smallpox, see Mooney, *Calendar,* 274–75. For the epidemic of 1837 on the northern plains, see Robertson, *Rotting Face.*

33. The description of the great peace of 1840 comes from Grinnell, *Fighting Cheyennes,* 63–69.

34. For a discussion of the motivations behind the great peace, see Jablow, *Cheyenne in Plains,* 72–77. Jablow concludes that Arapaho and Cheyenne warriors agreed to the peace because they could simply continue their accustomed raiding in New Mexico, but that explanation is insufficient. The New Mexican sources indicate that raids by these Indians were a very minor problem in the 1840s, except in 1841 during a disagreement between the New Mexican governor and Arapahos over captives. For the dispute, see Reeve, "Bent Papers," 29:4, pp. 311–17, and 30:2, pp. 155–59. For the bison buffer zone created by hostility between the Indians of the central and southern plains, and the significance of access to this zone for the peace, see Flores, "Bison Ecology," 476, 483; and West, *Way West,* 61–62.

35. See, for example, Flores, "Bison Ecology," 483; West, *Contested Plains,* 77; La Vere, *Contrary Neighbors,* 143. Anderson, *Conquest,* 186–87, takes this speculation to extremes, asserting without evidence that the Great Peace "came as a direct result" of the infamous Council House Massacre in San Antonio; that Comanches sought peace in order to obtain from Bent's Fort the firearms they needed to fight Texans; and that following the peace ceremonies Kiowas accompanied Comanches in attacks on the Texan settlements of Linnville and Victoria. For a similar interpretation, see Mayhall, *Kiowas,* 92. Possibly, but it is equally possible that the Great Peace occurred during or even after the attacks on Linnville and Victoria and, in any case, most if not all of the men participating in those attacks were surely Hois who lost kin in the Council House Massacre (see Report of P. M. Butler, April 29, 1843, 8, Butler Papers).

36. For details on these campaigns, see appendix, below. For an excellent edited anthology of newspaper reports on the raids in Nuevo León, see Vizcaya Canales, ed., *La invasión.* Though almost nothing is known about the consequences of the eight-hundred-man campaign into Chihuahua (and possibly from there into Durango), one small, incidental reference offers a slender but nonetheless suggestive hint. The author of a journal of a U.S. military expedition that passed by Bent's Fort in 1842 wrote that "last year" (1841), the Comanches had taken one hundred and fifty women and children captive "near Chihuahua . . . having slain the men." See Connelley, "Journal," quotation on 240.

37. For Houston's reelection and Indian policies, see Anderson, *Conquest,* 195–211. Quote is from Antonio Sánchez Muzquiz to Sr. Secretario del Despacho del Superior Gobierno de Durango, Parras, Aug. 31, 1842, in *Registro,* Sept. 8, 1842. The line of transmission (from raider—presumably in Spanish—to captive to official to official) obviously opens this quote to question. But it is

worth noting that Kiowas considered grace and good looks to be an important quality in a man, regardless of age. It was assumed that all men of highest rank should be "handsome on a horse," and in 1870 four of the twenty-five most prominent Kiowas made the list because they were hand-some. See Mishkin, *Rank and Warfare,* 36, 54–55.

38. For the "Hide-quiver war expedition winter," see Mooney, *Calendar,* 276. Comanche activities in this period resonate with the findings in Wallace and Hoebel, *Comanches,* 276, that "Comanches worked out a sort of national policy of defensive alliances" to safeguard their home territory and keep other regions "open for far-ranging aggressive action."

39. For peace among high plains tribes, see West, *Contested Plains,* 77; Brooks, *Captives,* 263–64.

CHAPTER 3. PLUNDER AND PARTNERS

1. Juan Antonio de Olaciregui to Juan N. Meléndez, Torreon, Sept. 12, 1843, *Registro,* Sept. 28, 1843.
2. For San Carlos's reputation, see Vizcaya Canales, ed., *La invasión,* 57–58.
3. Lipán Apaches used gunpowder to efface brands in order to get around laws that prohibited Mexicans from buying branded animals from them. See Berlandier, *Indians,* 132; Ruiz, *Report,* 6.
4. For horses and mules purchased by the U.S. Army, see Rives, *United States and Mexico* 2:214.
5. For Horn's observations, see Rister, *Comanche Bondage,* 134–49. For looking glasses, see Dolbeare, *Captivity and Suffering,* 8.
6. For books and shields, see Wallace and Hoebel, *Comanches,* 106. For silver coin, see testimony of Francisco Treviño, Hacienda de las Hermanas, Coahuila, Sept. 21, 1873, in Velasco Avila, ed., *En manos,* 44–49; Smith, "Comanche Bridge," 64. For Webster, see Dolbeare, *Captivity and Suffering,* 20. For plundering textiles, see, for example, El Juez Primero de paz de Agualeguas to el Prefecto del Distrito de Cadereyta Jiménez, Sept. 8, 1840, in Vizcaya Canales, ed., *La invasión,* 71–75; Roemer, *Texas,* 271.
7. For Comanches seeking ransom, see Berlandier, *Indians,* 76. For the Bents, see Hyde, ed., *Life of George Bent,* 68–69. Redemption did not necessarily mean freedom. Soon after Horn was purchased by a kindly Mexican she came under the power of an American in New Mexico who kept her in bondage and compelled her to make several linen shirts. See Rister, *Comanche Bondage,* 162–75. For Parker's search, see his *Narrative,* 33–39. For newspaper notices of Anglo and Mexican captives purchased in border settlements in the United States, see, for example, the following issues of *Telegraph:* Oct. 3, 1841; March 6, 1844; Dec. 4, 1844; July 16, 1845; Dec. 31, 1845. See also Moser, ed., *Papers of Webster,* 486, 91; Thomas H. Harvey to Commissioner for Indian Affairs, St. Louis, Sept. 10, 1845, in Senate Doc. 1, 29th Cong., 1st sess., 538.
8. Burnet added that the two hundred dollars in goods he paid for each of his four captives was "estimated at *their* market value." Of the four captives, "one of them very soon stole a horse and ran away; two were worthless idlers; and one old man rendered some remuneration by personal services." See Burnet, "Comanches and Other Tribes," 88. For Taylor, see *Pensacola Gazette,* Nov. 12, 1842. For the captive purchased in Jasper County, see *Weekly Despatch,* March 16, 1844. For Gillis Doyle, see Foreman, "Journal," n. 2. For the Mexican boy from Presidio de Rio Grande, see Roemer, *Texas,* 194–95. Kiowa informants in the early twentieth century insisted that, unlike Comanches, they never sold captives as chattels. See Mishkin, *Rank and Warfare,* 42.

9. For Horn's son, see Rister, *Comanche Bondage*, 183. For estimation of animal charges per captive herder, see Sherow, "Workings of the Geodialectic," 73. For the mule breakers, see Roemer, *Texas*, 193. For captive Mexican husbands, see Gladwin, "Comanche Kin," 84.

10. For a sampling of chores required of captive women, see Horn's recollections in Rister, *Comanche Bondage*, 156–58. For the hide market in the 1830s and 1840s, see Lecompte, *Pueblo, Hardscrabble*, 21.

11. For the Blackfeet estimate, see Jablow, *Cheyenne in Plains*, 20. Though plains communities processed buffalo in distinctive ways, a lucid description of the basic task may be found in Moore, *The Cheyenne*, 54–56, 60–65. On polygamy, see, for example, Neighbors, "The Na-Uni," 132. José Francisco Ruiz remarked that for the protection of the baby, Comanche mothers remained chaste until they weaned their children. Ruiz, "Comanches," 221. According to Berlandier, Comanche children were nursed for three or four years (though he says a few sentences later that they were nursed until the end of the fourth year). Berlandier also remarked that if a nursing mother died, her infant was buried with her, unless he or she already had teeth: "They believe that no one should be forced to shoulder the burden of so little an existence." See Berlandier, *Indians*, 33, 117.

12. For the Mexican boys, see Dolbeare, *Captivity and Suffering*, 23. For "desert life," see Berlandier, *Indians*, 35. Captives' lives and their diverse positions within southern plains communities are discussed sensitively throughout Brooks, *Captives*. See also the comprehensive new work by Rivaya Martínez, "Captivity and Adoption," esp. 150–364

13. Berlandier observed that Mexican captives rarely spoke Spanish in the settlements, though they conversed in Spanish on the plains. He suspected that they remained silent to be more effective spies. See "Cacería del oso," 148. For Comanches intercepting written material from Mexico, see, for example, Eugenio Fernández to alcalde de Guerrero, Nava, Aug. 13, 1839, C2, F10, E5, 2f, FSXIX-AGEC; and J. Andrés Marin to governor of Durango, Durango, Aug. 7, 1845, in *Registro*, Aug. 10, 1845. For captive literacy, see, for example, Berlandier, *Indians*, 83; and testimony of Sabás Rodríguez, Guerrero, June 28, 1873, in Velasco Avila, ed., *En manos*, 55–59. For typical observations that captives became the cruelest of warriors, see, for example, Ruiz, *Report*, 15; Berlandier, *Indians*, 75; Wallace, "Burnet's Letters," 130–31. "Formidable savages" quote is from Gregg, *Commerce*, 436. For Lyons, see Dolbeare, *Captivity and Suffering*, 12, 24–25; Roemer, *Texas*, 242–43. In the fall of 1847 it was reported that a captive named Warren Lyons captured by Comanches in 1837 had been returned to his widowed mother. The account claimed that upon seeing her son, the mother burst into tears: "Young Lyons sprang forward and caught her in his arms, and in a loud, shrill tone, cried, 'Oh, my mother!'" *Mississippi Free Trader and Natchez Gazette*, Aug. 17, 1847.

14. A report from Coahuila maintained that Indians had stolen 28,165 horses from that state between 1835 and March 1845. See Rodríguez, *La guerra*, 111. Losses of animals were probably even higher in Tamaulipas, Chihuahua, and Durango. For Burnet, see Wallace, "Burnet's Letters," 132. Burnet wrote at a time when Comanche raids were mostly confined to the lower Rio Grande. By the 1840s raiders were probing hundreds of miles south of the Rio Grande, and animal casualties during the long homeward rush would presumably have been even higher. Josiah Webb doubted that raiders got home with as many as half of the animals they stole. Webb, *Adventures*, 241.

15. For the predicament of young men needing horses for bride price, see Brooks, *Captives*, 175–79. See also Ruiz, *Report*, 14; Wallace and Hoebel, *Comanches*, 132–34. For horses needed on the

plains, see West, *Contested Plains*, 72. On the division of herds, see also Mishkin, *Rank and Warfare*, 20–21.

16. Mishkin, *Rank and Warfare*, 19–22, 35–41.

17. My discussion of gifts and political economy in la comanchería is informed by the classic study by Mauss, *Gift*; the later critique and elaboration by Sahlins, *Stone Age* (esp. 149–314); and by a suggestive case study from west Africa: Miller, *Way of Death*, 40–70.

18. In Sahlins' phrase, "Generosity is usefully enlisted as a starting mechanism for leadership *because it creates followership*." See Sahlins, *Stone Age*, 208. Quote on profits into people is from Miller, *Way of Death*, 46. "Gift economy" has been suggested by Mary Douglas as a better term than traditional or premarket economy. See Douglas, "Forward." End quote comes from Neighbors, "The Na-Uni," 134. On liberality, see also Wallace and Hoebel, *Comanches*, 131; Mishkin, *Rank and Warfare*, 51.

19. On the "shakedown dance," see Wallace and Hoebel, *Comanches*, 272. For gifts going to mourners, see Wallace and Hoebel, *Comanches*, 153; Neighbors, "The Na-Uni," 133; Berlandier, *Indians*, 96.

20. For war as a catalyst for changes in the social landscape of personal status, see Wallace and Hoebel, *Comanches*, 216.

21. The identification of Pia Kusa as the well-known Santa Anna comes from the testimony of a Mexican who spent years as Pia Kusa's captive. See Rivaya Martínez, "Captivity and Adoption," 180. My thanks to the author for sharing this information with me. For other memories of the captive, see "Testimony of Cornelio Sánchez, born and residing in Lampazos, forty-eight years old," June 4, 1873, in Velasco Avila, ed., *En manos*, 52–54. Kendall's letter is reprinted in *Boston Daily Atlas*, June 5, 1846. For the German, see Roemer, *Texas*, 269.

22. The captive who identified Pia Kusa as Santa Anna claimed it had been Pia Kusa's son who had captured him in 1838 (and that this son died soon after). If the captor was indeed the paraibo's biological son, then Pia Kusa must have been at least in his late thirties at the time. An observer who spent several days with him in December of 1843 estimated that Potsanaquahip was only twenty-five to thirty years old. For this and for quote on Pahayuco, see Report of P. M. Butler, Fort Gibson, Jan. 31, 1844, 4, Butler Papers. For Potsanaquahip's place of prominence, see, for example, "Talk of Pah-hah-yuco and Roasting Ear, Trading House," January 19, 1845, in Winfrey and Day, eds., *Texas Indian Papers* 2:172–75. For newspapers, see, for example, *Telegraph*, Sept. 3, 1845; *Weekly Ohio Statesman*, Oct. 22, 1845. The description is from Roemer, *Texas*, 269: I have eliminated the redundant words "countenance of" after "expression of" from the original quote. The painting is mentioned in John Mix Stanley, *Portraits*, 53.

23. For the distribution of booty following a raid, see, for example, Mishkin, *Rank and Warfare*, 32; Wallace and Hoebel, *Comanches*, 266–67; Kavanagh, *Comanche Political History*, 61. Rivaya Martínez, "Captivity and Adoption," 226–27, notes that captives belonged to their individual captors.

24. Kavanagh groups Pahayuco with the Tenewas (*Comanche Political History*, 5), but I have included him with the Hois because in negotiations with Texans he referred to Potsanaquahip (a Hois) as one of his war chiefs (see "Talk of Pah-hah-yuco and Roasting Ear, Trading House," January 19, 1845, Winfrey and Day, eds., *Texas Indian Papers* 2:172–75). Pierce Butler likewise identified Pahayuco as a Hois; see Report of P. M. Butler, Fort Gibson, Jan. 31, 1844, 4, Butler Papers. For customer competition in the gift economy, see Sahlins, *Stone Age*, 297–301. For paraibos

and trade, see Kavanagh, *Comanche Political History*, 282–83. For the custom of dealing with the resident paraibo specifically, see also Chacón, *Legacy of Honor*, 106–07; Gregg, *Commerce*, 250–51.

25. For trade connections before 1830, see Hämäläinen, "Western Comanche."

26. Smith, *Wichita Indians*, 92–154.

27. For Gregg's trading among Comanches, see Gregg, *Commerce*, 250–51. See also the experiences of Thomas James while doing business along the Santa Fe Trail, described in Kavanagh, *Comanche Political History*, 210–11. For the centrality of gifts in trade relations between Comanches and non-Indians, see La Vere, "Friendly Persuasions." For Anglo traders killed in la comanchería, see Berlandier, *Indians*, 48; Kavanagh, *Comanche Political History*, 220; and testimony of Francisco Treviño, Hacienda de las Hermanas, Coahuila, Sept. 21, 1873, in Velasco Avila, ed., *En manos*, 44–49.

28. For alarms about Coffee, see Angel Navarro to Domingo de Ugartechea, Bexar, June 1, 1835; James Bowie to Henry Rueg, Natches [Neches] Aug. 3, 1835; Peter Ellis Bean to Domingo de Ugartechea, Nacogdoches, Aug. 11, 1835, all found in McLean, ed., *Papers* 10:347, 11:250, 280. For Coffee's initial activities and his death, see Middlebrooks and Middlebrooks, "Holland Coffee"; and Britton, "Holland Coffee." Had Mexican authorities attacked Coffee's post, they might have provoked a serious quarrel with the United States. Upon hearing in May of 1835 that Mexican forces intended to evacuate Coffee's establishment, Colonel Matthew Arbuckle of Fort Gibson ordered a subordinate to protect the post, which was one of the army's most important sources of intelligence on southern plains Indians. Agnew, *Fort Gibson*, 142–44. Twice during her captivity Dolly Webster saw large parties of "American" traders come in to trade with Comanches, and she assumed they were from Coffee's establishment. See Dolbeare, *Captivity and Suffering*, 22–24. Coffee and his post still seem to have been important features of the southern plains in early 1846. See Foreman, "Journal," 69, 79.

29. For background on Chouteau and his famous family, see Arrell M. Gibson, "Chouteau, Auguste Pierre"; and Joseph Giovinco, "Chouteau Family," both in Lamar, ed., *Encyclopedia*, 211–12. For "Soto," see Mooney, *Calendar*, 422. For his activities among the Comanche and Kiowa, see Kavanagh, *Comanche Political History*, 172, 242–46.

30. For competition, see Kavanagh, *Comanche Political History*, 248. For Bent's expectations and activities, see Lecompte, "Bent, St. Vrain." The winter of 1841–42 was the best hide season the Bents ever had; they even lacked wagons enough to transport all their hides and skins back east. See Lecompte, *Pueblo, Hardscrabble*, 17–21.

31. For diplomacy leading to peace, see, for example, J. C. Eldredge to Sam Houston, Washington on the Brazos, Dec. 8, 1843, in Winfrey and Day, eds., *Texas Indian Papers* 1:251–75; Armistice signed by Comanche and J. C. Eldredge, Aug. 9, 1843, in ibid., 1:228–30; John Conner and James Shaw to Sam Houston, Council Spring Tehuacana Creek, Oct. 2, 1844, in ibid., 2:101–03; Mopechucope to Sam Houston, near the head of the Colorado, March 21, 1844, in ibid., 2:6–9; Minutes of the Council at the Falls of the Brazos, Oct. 7, 1844, in ibid., 2:103–14. For the Torreys, see Armbruster, "Torrey Trading Houses."

32. For the profits in the mule trade in 1827, see Smith, *Borderlander*, 38.

33. For complaints during the 1820s, see, for example, Joel R. Poinsett to Henry Clay, Mexico City, June 20, 1826; and same to same, July 14, 1828, letters 87 and 133 in *U.S. Despatches*. See also Manning, *Early Diplomatic Relations*, 298–99. For the Santa Anna quote, see Antonio López de

Santa Anna to José María Tornel, Guerrero, Feb. 16, 1836, in Castañeda, ed., *Mexican Side*, 64–70. For the classic articulation of the guns-for-animals thesis, see Weber, "American Westward Expansion." For the recollection of the Mexican captive, see Testimony of Dionisio Santos, Lampazos, July 11, 1873, in Velasco Avila, ed., *En manos*, 40–43. The testimony in Velasco's book was given as part of an investigation by the Mexican government relating to a dispute with the state of Texas and with the U.S. government over culpability for damages incurred from Indian raiding. The claims of former captives about the direct influence of American traders are certainly plausible but need to be viewed in light of these circumstances. For commissioner's lament, see "Report of G. W. Bonnell, Commissioner of Indian Affairs, third Congress, first session, Houston, Nov. 3, 1838," in Senate Rep. Com., #171, 30th Cong., 1st sess., 38–50. For Texan traders and Indian agents distributing ammunition, often following explicit instructions from Texan officials, see, for example, Thomas G. Western to Benjamin Sloat, Washington, May 12, 1845, and "Report of a Council with the Comanche Indians," Trading House Post No. 2, Nov. 23, 1845, both in Winfrey and Day, eds., *Texas Indian Papers* 2:238–40, 410–13. For "to carry on the war," see *Telegraph*, May 21, 1845. For the manifold ways in which American traders disrupted relations between New Mexicans and Utes, see Blackhawk, *Violence over the Land*, 121–33.

34. One of the Bents' most dedicated critics, Father Antonio José Martínez from Taos, complained in a letter to President Santa Anna in 1843 that establishments like Bent's Fort encouraged Indians to raid Mexican settlements, but the author kept his emphasis on alcohol rather than firearms. See Martínez, *Esposición*, in Weber, ed., *Northern Mexico on the Eve*, n.p. There is no evidence that alcohol was a commodity (or a social problem) of significance among the Comanches or Kiowas in the first half of the nineteenth century. Indeed, Euro-American commentators often remarked upon Comanche sobriety and disinclination to drink. See, for example, Sánchez, "Trip," 262.

35. For Warren, see Kavanagh, *Comanche Political History*, 285; and Hart, "Warren, Abel." On Gregg's trade bundle, see Gregg, *Commerce*, 250. For examples of Torrey's merchandise, see Account of Indian Bureau with Torrey and Brothers, May 17, 1844, in Winfrey and Day, eds., *Texas Indian Papers* 2:56–57. For another trade bundle, see Roemer, *Texas*, 237–38.

36. For British guns, see Berlandier, *Indians*, 119. For Mier y Terán, see his "Noticia," 130. For similar comments, see "Tribus bárbaras: Idea general," in *Calendario de Ignacio Cumplido*, 1841. In the early 1830s, Sam Houston was amazed to find that the influence of the Northwest Fur Company extended as far south as Texas, presumably via central plains Indian intermediaries. See Kavanagh, *Comanche Political History*, 235–36. For buckets, see Burns, *History of the Osage*, 216.

37. For Sioux pressure on Mandans, Hidatsas, and Arikaras, see White, "Winning of the West." For the allegation that Mexicans in Matamoros were supplying eastern Indians with guns, see D. W. Smith to U.S. Secretary of State, Matamoros, Jan. 1, 1840, in *Despatches* 2:1–2. For Texan complaints, see Barnard E. Bee to John Forsyth, Washington, Dec. 15, 1840, in William R. Manning, *Diplomatic Correspondence, Inter-America* 12:208–11. This same document mentions one of the Indians at Matamoros by the name Jim—possibly the Delaware trader Jim Shaw, mentioned below. For the Creeks, see Smith, "Traffic in Scalps," 99. For Shawnees, see Ethan Allen Hitchcock to J. C. Spencer, New Orleans, March 20, 1842, in Hitchcock, *Traveler*, 255–60; comment about Tecumseh is on 216. Shawnee arms traders ventured beyond the plains, supplying even Mescalero Apaches with guns and ammunition. See *Diario*, Aug. 9, 1838. For Omahas, see Kava-

nagh, *Comanche Political History*, 281. For captive testimony, see account of Francisco Treviño, Musquiz, Sept. 21, 1873, in Velasco Avila, ed., *En manos*, 44–49.

38. Bailey, "Osage." For horses among the Choctaw, see Carson, "Horses."

39. La Vere, *Contrary Neighbors*, 114–15.

40. For the role of Shawnees, Kickapoos, and Delawares in this trade generally, see ibid., 115–18. There are numerous references to Jim Shaw in Texan sources from the 1840s and 1850s. See, for example, Thomas G. Western to Benjamin Sloat, Washington on the Brazos, Dec. 14, 1844, in Winfrey and Day, eds., *Texas Indian Papers* 2:152–53; Roemer, *Texas*, 235–39. See also Richardson and Anderson, "Jim Shaw."

41. For the Shawnee traders, see R. A. Irion to Sam Houston, Houston, March 14, 1838, in Winfrey and Day, eds., *Texas Indian Papers* 1:43. For the captives, see Testimony of Cornelio Sánchez, Lampazos, June 4, 1873; and of Francisco Treviño, Musquiz, Sept. 21, 1873, both in Velasco Avila, ed., *En manos*, 52–54, 44–49. For the Delawares, see letter reprinted in *Daily Missouri Republican*, Oct. 15, 1841.

42. For the agent's observations, see J. C. Eldredge to Sam Houston, Washington on the Brazos, Dec. 8, 1843, in Winfrey and Day, eds., *Texas Indian Papers* 1:251–75.

43. For Cheyenne trading position, see Jablow, *Cheyenne in Plains*, 58–60; Moore, *The Cheyenne*, 70–103. For the Western Sioux and their need for horses, see White, "Winning of the West." For Cheyenne among the Hois, see J. C. Eldredge to Sam Houston, Washington on the Brazos, Dec. 8, 1843, in Winfrey and Day, eds., *Texas Indian Papers* 1:251–75. For a comparison of equestrian cultures across the plains, see Hämäläinen, "Rise and Fall."

44. The three million figure comes from Bailey, *Take My Sheep*, 112. For horses and mules, see Antonio Narvona, "Report of the Cattle and Caballada found in the territory of New Mexico," Santa Fe, April 8, 1827, in Carroll and Haggard, eds., *New Mexican Chronicles*. See also Baxter, *Carneradas*, 89–90.

45. For Durango, see Escudero, *Noticias estadísticas del estado de Durango*, 33. Before giving his estimate the author observed that "this sector of the economy is being ruined by the incursions of barbarians." For a visual of Spanish and Mexican settlement expansion in New Mexico, see Nostrand, "The Spread." See also Baxter, *Carneradas*, chap. 5.

46. For comanchero trade goods, see Kenner, *Comanchero Frontier*, 85. For firearms and ammunition, see Gregg, *Commerce*, 437.

47. For Ruiz, see Isidro Vizcaya Canales, *Tierra*, 58. For a peaceful Comanche visit to Rosas in 1838, see Velasco Avila, "Amenaza Comanche," 307; for a visit to Nava, see Rodríguez, *La guerra*, 194.

48. Hyde, ed., *Life of George Bent*, 69.

49. Horn's account provides some evidence that the Comanches were acutely aware of the contest raging at the time between Texas and Mexico and used it as an opportunity to raid the lower Rio Grande. She claims the Indians told the captured Mexican man they were friends of the Mexicans but hated the Americans. They told him they had killed Horn's male relatives but would not kill Horn and the other women in her party before they spoke with Santa Anna (presumably the president, not the Hois). They further probed the captive man for information on "all the news of the country." See Rister, *Comanche Bondage*, 140–41.

50. For decree against talking with Comanches, see Mariano Arista a sus subordinados y a los habitantes de los tres Departamentos de Oriente, circular, Dec. 19, 1840, MAP 39:151. In 1841 Mexi-

can forces defeated a party of Comanches and found among their spoils a copy of a decree in Spanish banning trade with Comanches. See Vizcaya Canales, ed., *La invasión*, 202–08. For the Indian spy, see copy of letter from Mariano Arista to Governor of Tamaulipas, Victoria, Jan. 7, 1841, MAP 39:166. For more on the Coahuiltecan speakers of the lower Rio Grande, see Campbell, "Coahuiltecan Indians." For the Durango article, see *Registro*, Aug. 17, 1845.

51. For Najar, see Vizcaya Canales, *Tierra*, 140.

52. El Juez Primero de paz de Agualeguas al Prefecto del Distrito de Cadereyta Jiménez, Sept. 8, 1840, in Vizcaya Canales, ed., *La invasión*, 71–75; for the confession, see Smith, "Comanche Bridge," 65. For the boys, see Francisco Oyarzu to Sr. Secretario del Despacho del Superior Gobierno de Durango, Mapimí, Jan. 9, 1846, in *Registro*, Jan. 25, 1846. It is possible that the Mexican "Indians" in these cases were in fact acculturated captives rather than free vecinos, though such captives who went on to raid with their captors were famous for cruelty rather than mercy.

53. For "thieves and contrabandists," see *Gaceta del Gobierno de Tamaulipas*, Oct. 26, 1844. For the attack on Bustamante, see Juez Primero de Paz to Subprefecto del Partido de Salinas Victoria, Oct. 5, 1840, in Vizcaya Canales, ed., *La invasión*, 94–98. For the subterfuge and raid at Cuatro Ciénegas, see Babcock, "Trans-National Trade," 108. For the "white flag," see *Voto*, Dec. 8, 1842.

54. For Agustín Garza, see General en gefe del ejército del norte to Vicente Filísola, Matamoros, Dec. 11, 1837, in *Diario*, Jan. 3, 1838. For Montelongo, see J. N. Armendáriz, Diario de las operaciones militares de la sección en campaña contra los comanches sobre el Bolsón de Mapimí, Cierrogordo, Aug. 21, 1842, in *Registro*, Sept. 1, 1842. For the "old thief," see José Francisco Terán to Marcellino Castañeda, Labor del Rodeo, Oct. 15, 1845, in *Registro*, Oct. 19, 1845. For more on Mexican collaborators, see Vizcaya Canales, *Tierra*, 155–59.

CHAPTER 4. THE POLITICS OF VENGEANCE

1. Rafael de la Fuente to Ignacio de Arizpe, Monclova, Dec. 30, 1840, in *Voto*, Jan. 8, 1841.

2. For the Hacienda del Salado, see Orozco, *Primeras fases*, 153. For Patos, see Harris, *Sánchez Navarros*, 8. For the initial steps taken by regional authorities to intercept the raiders, see Mariano Arista to Governor of Coahuila, Monterrey, Dec. 28, 1840, in *Voto*, Feb. 13, 1841; and Vizcaya Canales, ed., *La invasión*, 182, n. 51.

3. For "inconceivable," see editorial in *Voto*, quoted in Vizcaya Canales, ed., *La invasión*, 181. For Goribar, see article by "a bumpkin" [un patán] in *Voto*, Feb. 13, 1841.

4. "Estado que manifiesta las víctimas sacrificadas por los bárbaros," Saltillo, Feb. 6, 1841, C 86, E13, 1f, Presidencia Municipal, Archivo municipal de Saltillo, Saltillo, Coahuila. A letter from Juan Ramos Valdez (see note 11, below) indicates that while many Mexicans were wounded in the prolonged battle that finally drove the raiders away, only one was killed. Thus the great majority of the Mexican casualties were locals killed by Comanches before the final battle took place.

5. For two classic studies that pioneered economic explanations for plains Indian conflict while the scholarly mainstream was focused on other issues, see Mishkin, *Rank and Warfare*; and Jablow, *Cheyenne in Plains*. See also Ewers, *Blackfeet*, esp. 126. Mishkin argued that one must take seriously the inequalities of wealth and status within individual tribes. For a more recent and comprehensive application of this viewpoint, see Collier, *Marriage*. For discussions of the tension in plains scholarship between cultural, ecological, and economic explanations for intergroup con-

flict, see Morris W. Foster's introduction to the editions of the two works cited above, as well as Albers and James, "Historical Materialism"; and Albers, "Symbiosis." For a brief survey of existing work on Comanche politics, see McCollough, *Three Nations*, 30–35.

6. Quotes are from Brooks, *Captives*, 179. Kavanagh, *Comanche Political History*, likewise emphasizes the material motivations of raids, stressing that raiding was one of several key "resource domains" available to Comanches. While Kavanagh's pioneering study emphasizes politics and is based on a remarkable array of sources, he did not consult the copious sources produced below the Rio Grande (on 286 he includes the curious observation that "after the 1820 revolution, Mexico attempted to maintain the Spaniards' Comanche policies; unfortunately, few documentary records survive from that period"). Consequently he has little to say about Comanche activity below the river and makes misstatements like "the year 1847 also brought the start of the major horse raids south of the Rio Grande" (483), when these major raids began in the mid-1830s.

7. Anderson, *Indian Southwest*, 254, 264.

8. Rivaya Martínez, "Captivity and Adoption," is an important new exception to my observation about plains scholars. Gerald Betty notes that students of Comanches have "generally overstated" the economic function of violent rivalries and suggests that historians need to pay more attention to vengeance. But his own analysis relies too exclusively on kinship: "As far as Comanches were concerned, those persons with whom they had no relationship whatsoever did not require their benevolence. Consequently, they felt no need for self-restraint when it came to stealing livestock, abducting women and children, robbing traders, and taking the lives of anyone unrelated to them." See *Comanche Society*, 121–38; quote is from 128.

9. See table A.1 for details. This figure and casualty figures throughout the chapter are somewhat higher than those I gave in previous publications (DeLay, "Independent Indians"; DeLay, "Wider World") because I consulted additional evidence after the articles went to press. My comments below about the seasonality of raiding also reflect this expanded source base.

10. For other postcontact wars of extreme brutality, see, for example, discussions of the Iroquois' Beaver Wars in White, *Middle Ground*, 1–49, and Richter, *Ordeal*. See also Lepore, *Name of War*, 71–124; Moore, *The Cheyenne*, 112–13. My thoughts on contextualizing the violence in northern Mexico have been influenced by the work of three archaeologists: Bamforth, "Indigenous People"; Keeley, *War before Civilization*; LeBlanc, *Prehistoric Warfare*; LeBlanc, *Constant Battles*.

11. See letters from Blanco and Juan Ramos Valdez, both in Alessio Robles, *Coahuila y Texas* 2:234–36, 242 n. 9. The battle naturally became an event of great importance in regional history. In 1847 a lieutenant in the U.S. Army Corps of Engineers drafted a map of the route from Monterrey to Saltillo and included on it several key landmarks, among them the location of the "fight between Mexicans and Indians in 1841." See Saxon, "Henry Washington Benham," 146.

12. Antonio Tenorio to Mariano Arista, Venadito, Jan. 14, 1841, quoted in Arista, *Oficio y documentos*; José María Ortega to Mariano Arista, Monterrey, Jan. 18, 1841, in ibid.; Juan J. Galán to Mariano Arista, San Fernando de Rosas, Jan. 21, 1841, in *Ancla*, Jan. 24, 1841.

13. On the need to take internal politics seriously before drawing conclusions about how a community confronts outside powers, see Ortner, "Resistance."

14. Gledhill, *Power*, 8–14, discusses the problematic tendency of older writings in political anthropology to begin with western states as the normative baseline. An important component of this

bias is that it starts from a Weberian definition of politics stressing subordination and violence, when nonstate societies typically foreswore violent coercion as a tool for internal organization. My definition of politics follows Swartz, Turner, and Tuden, *Political Anthropology*, 7, but puts less emphasis on the role of leaders: leaders obviously matter, but in egalitarian societies political initiatives could come from almost anyone. For an overview of paradigms in political anthropology, see Kurtz, *Political Anthropology*. For an introduction to how scholars have written about politics in North American Indian societies, see Fowler, "Politics."

15. For Kiowa military societies, see Meadows, *Enduring Veterans*, 33–95. For lobos, see Berlandier, *Indians*, 70–72, 117. The three Indians who ran screaming through the streets of Nadadores may have been lobos. Berlandier wrote of certain lobos that "if they hold no weapon at all it means they have volunteered only to make warlike noises in the place where the fighting is hottest and most dangerous." See Berlandier, *Indians*, 72. The connection here is obviously tenuous but worth mentioning because the lobos Berlandier describes in such detail for the late 1820s are otherwise invisible in later sources. My understanding of "face" in Comanche society and, more broadly, of the necessity of putting Comanche–Comanche relationships at the center of any discussion of their history relies upon Foster, *Being Comanche*, 19–30.

16. For dances that proceeded raiding expeditions, see Roemer, *Texas*, 270; Smithwick, *Evolution*, 122; Wallace, "Burnet's Letters," 131. For "some young men," see John Conner and James Shaw to Sam Houston, Council Spring Tehuacana Creek, Oct. 2, 1844, in Winfrey and Day, eds., *Texas Indian Papers* 2:101–03. For victory dances, see Wallace and Hoebel, *Comanches*, 272.

17. Berlandier, *Indians*, 36. See also Ruiz, *Report*, 14; Wallace and Hoebel, *Comanches*, 254.

18. Rape is rarely recorded in accounts of Indian raiding from this period, and it seems to have been unusual, though the norm may simply have been that honor-conscious Mexicans did not report it or that authorities refrained from mentioning it in official letters. The relevant Spanish passage from the account cited above reads, "El 22 a las ocho de la mañana sorprendieron la Ranchería del Tanque, y en ella hicieron prisoneras tres mugeres que habian ido al agua y dos de ellas fueron forzadas por todos de cuyas," which seems to suggest that the women were raped by several raiders. Both were badly injured, and one later died of her wounds in Matamoros. See Francisco Lofero to Jorge D. de Lara, Matamoros, July 4, 1844, in MAP 50:184–89. For other instances of reported rape, see, for example, Anderson, *Indian Southwest*, 259; Wallace and Hoebel, *Comanches*, 262. In the spring of 1842 raiders killed a thirteen- or fourteen-year-old girl because, according to a state official, she refused their "iniquitous and indecent pretensions." The official considered the girl an example "for her class" because she chose death before dishonor. See *Siglo XIX*, May 1, 1842. Joaquín Rivaya Martínez has assembled a remarkable database on Comanche captivity. In a sample that includes 350 female captives from the early 1700s through 1875, he finds evidence of rape in only nine cases; but he notes that "there are suggestions that sexual abuse was at least attempted by some Comanche male in all of the available narratives of women's captivities." See "Captivity and Adoption," 207–11.

19. For the woman in the elaborate dress, see Smith, "Comanche Bridge," 65. For the "india brava capitana," see Manuel Ignacio Fierro to Sr. Secretario del Superior Gobierno del Departamento, Durango, Oct. 28, 1845, in *Registro*, Oct. 30, 1845. James Hobbs, who had been captured by Comanches and accompanied them on raids into Mexico, claimed that a young woman rode at the front of a four-hundred-man campaign into Coahuila and that the warriors all looked upon her as an "angel of good or ill luck." The herald was reported to be an expert rider, highly skilled

with a bow, and fearless enough to lead charges against the enemy. For the above and for the connection between the woman in Smith's piece and Hobbs's memoir, see Noyes, *Los Coman-ches*, 97–98. Hobbs claimed this raid reached nearly to Monclova and took place in the winter of 1835–36, but I have found no evidence of such a raid in this season. Though the mention of the female herald is intriguing, especially in light of the Durango parallels, Hobbs's account often seems implausible in light of other contemporary sources, and I have chosen not to use it as a source for direct information on Comanches.

20. For the "drafting" chanters, see Gregg, *Commerce*, 438.

21. For the matron and the scalp pole, see ibid.; Wallace and Hoebel, *Comanches*, 269. For sexual gifts following raids, see Berlandier, *Indians*, 70–71; Ruiz, *Report*, 13. For leggings and Kiowa scalp dances, see Mooney, *Calendar*, 260, 290–92; Mishkin, *Rank*, 31.

22. For the return of a failed campaign, see Wallace and Hoebel, *Comanches*, 268. There are many primary references to Comanche wailing and self-mutilation in mourning. See, for example, Horn, *Narrative*, 58–59; Neighbors, "The Na-Uni," 134; Brant, ed., *Jim Whitewolf*, 72; Dolbeare, *Captivity and Suffering*, 11, 21; and Barreiro, *Ojeado*, appendix, 9, facsimile in Carroll and Hag-gard, eds., *New Mexican Chronicles*, 263–318. For quotes on shamed lobos, see Berlandier, *Indi-ans*, 70–71.

23. Berlandier, *Indians*, 74, 68, 85. See also Ruiz, *Report*, 12.

24. My emphasis on the latent potential for cooperation in times of mutual threat or opportunity is inspired by Sahlins, "Segmentary Lineage"; and by the injunction in Swartz, Turner, and Tuden, *Political Anthropology*, 8, to "center our attention on [political] processes rather than on the groups or fields within which they occur. This means, for example, that a political study follows the development of conflicts for power (or for acquiring support for proposed goals) into what-ever groups the processes lead—rather than examining such groups as lineages, villages, or coun-tries to determine what processes they might contain."

25. For the distinction between a raid executed simply to obtain horses, captives, and plunder and a raid motivated by revenge, see Berlandier, *Indians*, 71–72. See also Hoebel, *Political Organi-zation*, 23–24; Anderson, *Indian Southwest*, 238–39; Meadows, *Enduring Veterans*, 313. Wallace and Hoebel, *Comanches*, 256, admits some ambiguity between the two categories but observes that "with the taking of a single scalp, the revenge raid accomplished its mission and was in-evitably turned back by its leader, even if bigger prospects were near at hand." The notional distinction seemed to be even sharper among Kiowas. Mishkin, *Rank and Warfare*, 28, notes that Kiowas had two variations of the word for warfare, distinguishing between horse raids and revenge expeditions. He observes that "in native thought war parties are differentiated at every point according to whether they are for horse raiding or for revenge." For similar distinctions in Blackfeet culture, see Ewers, *Blackfeet*, 124–44. As this chapter argues, the distinction lost meaning below the Rio Grande in the 1830s and 1840s; hence I use the terms *raid* and *raiding campaign* throughout this book to mean endeavors in which acquisition of animals or captives or both and intense, widespread violence often went hand in hand.

26. Quotes are from Sánchez, "Trip," 262; Berlandier, *Indians*, 67.

27. Like Comanches, Blackfeet mourners could call upon a huge network to seek aid in avenging the dead. See Ewers, *Blackfeet*, 136–37. For quotes, see Berlandier, *Indians*, 71–72; Ruiz, *Report*, 10.

28. William Bent probably witnessed a divisional gathering in early 1835, when he traded with two thousand Comanches. See Lecompte, "Bent, St. Vrain," 274. As a Comanche captive in 1838

or 1839 (the dates remain uncertain), Dolly Webster visited a camp that by her estimation contained two thousand people. See Dolbeare, *Captivity and Suffering*, 12. Rachael Plummer described a "general war council" that may have been multidivisional. It took place, by her recollection, in March of 1837 on the Arkansas River, and included "all the Indian bands, that is the Cammanchees with all the hostile tribes." The encampment was "the greatest assemblage of people [Plummer] ever saw," so large she could not see its outer edge. See Plummer, *Narrative*, 11. The Mescalero Apache chief Espejo de Enmiedo reported another in May of 1838. He told Chihuahuan authorities it was the largest group he had ever seen, representing nineteen nations and frightening away all the game in the region. See Griffen, *Utmost*, 55. He likely saw the gathering led by Tabequena and twenty-two other paraibos representing the four Comanche divisions as well as Kiowas, Kiowa Apaches, Shoshones, and Wichitas. The group went to Camp Holmes in May of 1838 to meet with Chouteau. See Kavanagh, *Comanche Political History*, 245. In December 1847 and January 1848 a Texan Indian agent reported a meeting of between five and six thousand members of "upper" Comanche divisions, Kiowas, and a few Mescalero Apaches: "The avowed intention of the present assembling is to make preparation for a descent upon the northern provinces of Mexico, Chihuahua, and others, early in the spring." See Robert S. Neighbors to W. Medill, U.S. Special Indian Agency, Dec. 13, 1847, in Senate Rep. Com., #171, 30th Cong., 1st sess; and same to same, Jan. 20, 1848, House Ex. Doc. #1, 30th Cong., 2nd sess., 573–75. Considering the coincidences by which these events were documented at all, it is likely that similar gatherings happened in other years during the 1830s and 1840s. For Sun Dances as occasions to recruit for revenge expeditions, see Mishkin, *Rank and Warfare*, 29.

29. Berlandier, *Indians*, 73–75; Meadows, *Enduring Veterans*, 269.

30. Berlandier, *Indians*, 73–75; Ruiz, *Report*, 10–11.

31. For the Osage campaign, see Berlandier, *Indians*, 73.

32. For the Comanche war trail system and quotes concerning it, see T. N. Campbell and William T. Field, "Identification." For "immense," see *Richmond Enquirer*, Nov. 3, 1837. End quote is from Alejo G. Conde to Ministro de Guerra y Marina, Durango, Feb. 14, 1845, in *Registro*, March 2, 1845.

33. For the topography and history of the Bolsón, see Rodríguez, *La guerra*, 97–99; Gerhard, *North Frontier*, 325–27. See also description in Fulton and Horgan, eds., *Diary*, 151–52. For the process whereby Comanches gained priority in the Bolsón over the Apaches, see Babcock, "Trans-National Trade," 124–25. Mescaleros continued using the Bolsón for their raids into Durango, Chihuahua, and Coahuila during the 1840s, and this sometimes led to violent clashes with Comanches. See *Diario*, Oct. 19, 1841. The Bolsón is still a mysterious place. Compass readings in the region are erratic, there are high levels of radiation and odd lights at night, and radio communication is impossible in the Bolsón because of local peculiarities in the ionosphere. See William Goetzmann's editorial note #513 in Chamberlain, *My Confession*, 369.

34. For the Mexican expedition, see J. N. Armendáriz to Comandante General de Durango, Cerrogordo, Nov. 29, 1843, in *Registro*, Dec. 14, 1843. For a very unusual instance of an extended Comanche family (consisting of twenty-two *casas*, or tents) camping below the Rio Grande but outside the Bolsón de Mapimí, see Rafael de la Fuente to Sr. Secretario del Superior Gobierno del Departamento, Monclova, Oct. 27, 1841, in *Voto*, Nov. 13, 1841. For "surrender," see José Francisco Terán to Marcelino Casteñeda, Labor del Rodeo, Oct. 15, 1845, in *Registro*, Oct. 19, 1845.

35. For animal remains, see, for example, *Registro*, May 24, 1846.

36. For mountain environments of Coahuila and Nuevo León, see Muller, "Vegetation."
37. For inactivity in winter, see, for example, Mishkin, *Rank and Warfare*, 25. Bison hunting was especially intense in the late summer and early fall, when the animals came together during rut, their coats were starting to fill out for winter, and the mosquitoes and flies were fewer than in early summer. Roe, *North American Buffalo*, 94–118. For watering holes, see Almonte, "Statistical Report," 195–96. For the observation that most water disappears from the Bolsón de Mapimí in summer, see Fulton and Horgan, eds., *Diary* 2:151–52.
38. For Kiowa deaths, see Mooney, *Calendar*, 269–71. For Webster, see Dolbeare, *Captivity and Suffering*, 24. For Hois, see Thomas G. Western to A. Coleman, Washington on the Brazos, May 11, 1845, in Winfrey and Day, eds., *Texas Indian Papers* 2:236–37; and *Telegraph*, Sept. 3, 1845. Some Mexican authorities also understood that Pia Kusa and Potsanaquahip were bent on revenge. See Santiago Rodríguez to Ministro de Relaciones Exteriores, Gobierno y Policia, Saltillo, Sept. 13, 1845, in *Republicano* Sept. 20, 1845. For another, later declaration by Potsanaquahip concerning revenge, see Robert S. Neighbors to W. Medill, Torrey's Trading House, Sept. 14, 1847, Senate Doc., #734, 30th Cong., 1st sess.
39. For intriguing instances of Comanches seeking vengeance on particular individuals, see letter from Santiago Rodríguez in *Republicano*, Sept. 20, 1845; and Betty, *Comanche Society*, 131–33.
40. See Mishkin, *Rank and Warfare*, 29. For norms concerning vengeance in other contexts, see White, *Middle Ground*, 75–82; Goldschmidt, "Inducement"; Reid, *Law of Blood*, 153–62; Reid, *Patterns*.
41. M. Paino, "Los Comanches," Mexico City, Nov. 1, 1841, in *Siglo XIX*, March 9, 1842.
42. The vast majority of Comanche casualties in Mexico were men, but occasionally women who accompanied raiding campaigns were killed as well. See, for example, Orozco, *Primeras fases*, 160–61. For figures, see appendix, below.
43. For examples of great battles for which Indian losses are unknown, see report of a clash near Marín, Nuevo León, in *Diario*, Feb. 5, 1840; and Manuel Meneses to Sr. Secretario del Superior Gobierno del Departamento de Durango, Cuencamé, Oct. 12, 1845, in *Registro*, Oct. 16, 1845.
44. Gesturing toward blood for lack of bodies was common. See, for example, Miguel Guerra to D. Francisco Casteñeda, Santa Rosa, Dec. 10, 1843, in *Voto*, Dec. 16, 1843. My estimate of Comanche deaths is drawn from data in the appendix, below, subtracting those entries that refer to raids in the Comanche theater executed by peoples identified as other than Kiowas or Comanches. For Comanches absconding with their dead, see, for example, José María de Ortega to Governor of Nuevo León, Monterrey, March 1, 1841, in *Seminario*, March 4, 1841; Sánchez, "Trip," 262. Ethnographers among Comanches in the early twentieth century reported that if a warrior's corpse was scalped he was forever barred from heaven. See Wallace and Hoebel, *Comanches*, 188. Calculation of mourning families is based on an average extended family size of twenty (Foster puts extended families at ten to thirty persons [see Foster, *Being Comanche*, 59]) and a total population of ten to twelve thousand.
45. Berlandier wrote, "When the war is a general one, with the entire people gathered in tribes to go on the warpath, public authority intervenes." On such occasions, "the most experienced captains from each tribe are put in command." He was evidently referring to the kind of campaign Ruiz observed when twenty-five hundred warriors cooperated against the Osage, and not, perhaps, to revenge campaigns involving only hundreds of men. Nonetheless, the precedent existed for established leaders to co-opt the revenge process. See Berlandier, *Indians*, 69.

46. For Kiowas, see Mooney, *Calendar*, 282; "Report of P. M. Butler," Fort Gibson, Jan. 31, 1844, 7–8, Butler Papers. The Texan source quote is *Telegraph*, February 5, 1845. The first Neighbors quote is in Foster, *Being Comanche*, 49. It was a common (and confusing) practice for Anglo-American officials to refer to Comanche divisions as bands; I have reversed this in the above quote for clarity. Burnet likewise remarked that the different Comanche divisions unite and cooperate for raids into Mexico. See Wallace, "Burnet's Letters," 133. For "proposing to," see Neighbors to William Medill, U.S. Special Indian Agency, Jan. 20, 1848, House Ex. Doc. #1, 30th Cong., 2nd sess., 573–75.

47. For "Spanish war," see "Statement of Luis Sánchez as taken by Walter Winn," Winfrey and Day, eds., *Texas Indian Papers* 2:64–66. For Pahayuco, see also Report of P. M. Butler, Fort Gibson, Jan. 31, 1844, 7, Butler Papers. For Pia Kusa, see "Report of a Council held with Comanche Indians," Trading House Post no. 2, Nov. 23, 1845, in Winfrey and Day, eds., *Texas Indian Papers* 2:410–13. For "war expedition," see Thomas G. Western to [A.] Coleman, Indian Bureau, Washington [Tex.], May 11, 1845, in ibid., 2:236–37. For "going to war," see Report of Benjamin Sloat, July 12, 1845, in ibid., 2:283–86; for "to make war," see L. H. Williams to Thomas G. Western, Trading House Post 2, August 20, 1845, in ibid., 2:326–27.

48. By most definitions (see, for instance, Centeno, *Blood and Debt*, 21), the mobilizations of Comanche and Kiowa societies and the activities of their warriors below the river in the 1830s and 1840s certainly rise to the level of "total war."

49. For 1837, see Vizcaya Canales, *Incursiones*, 11–12. For Saltillo, see "Estado que manifiesta las víctimas sacrificadas por los bárbaros," Saltillo, Feb. 6, 1841, C 86, E13, 1f, Presidencia Municipal, Archivo municipal de Saltillo, Saltillo, Coahuila. For Durango, see J. M. Iglesias de Orduña to governor of Durango, Hacienda de San Salvador de Horta, Sept. 19, 1845, in *Registro*, Sept. 28, 1845. For El Paso, see *Siglo XIX*, May 19, 1845, cited in Escobar Ohmstede and Rojas Rabiela, eds., *La presencia del indígena*, 2:100.

50. The report has five thousand fanegas of maize destroyed, and I convert one fanega into roughly two bushels. For the raid on La Pilla, see *Registro*, Oct. 19, 1845.

51. For references to Mexicans taken and later found dead, see, for example, J. N. Armendáriz, Diario de las operaciones militares de la sección en campaña contra los comanches sobre el Bolsón de Mapimí, Cierrogordo, Aug. 21, 1842, in *Registro*, Sept. 1, 1842; Francisco Lofero to Jorge D. de Lara, Matamoros, July 4, 1844, in MAP 50:184–89; and articles in *Registro* for March 12 and Sept. 20, 1846. For Comanches "immolating" prisoners, see Juan J. Galán to Mariano Arista, San Fernando de Rosas, Jan. 21, 1841, in *Ancla*, Jan. 24, 1841. *Inmolar* can mean to sacrifice as well as to burn or set on fire. Dolly Webster wrote that her Comanche captors killed a young captive, a girl, so that they could bury her alongside a chief's mother. Dolbeare, *Captivity and Suffering*, 21.

52. The estimate of three Mexicans killed for every one captured comes from data in the appendix, below, and is based on numbers of Mexicans Comanches or Kiowas captured initially, regardless of whether these people later escaped or were redeemed from their captors. For total casualties see appendix. For modern surveillance methods, see Burnham, Lafta, Doocy, and Roberts, "Mortality." The authors of that study note that "other than Bosnia, we are unable to find any major historical instances where passive surveillance methods (such as morgue and media reports) identify more than 20% of the deaths which were found through population-based survey

methods." For the Coahuila figure, see Rodríguez, *La guerra*, 111. Apaches executed raids into Coahuila as well, but my data indicate that Comanches and Kiowas were responsible for the vast majority of raiding deaths in that state during the 1830s and 1840s.

53. For "torn to pieces," see Ramón de la Bastida to ?, San Juan del Río, Oct. 19, 1845, in *Registro*, Oct. 23, 1845. For "when reproved," see Wallace, "Burnet's Letters," 134. My data suggest that Comanches and Kiowas killed more than one Mexican woman or child for every four Mexican men they killed in their raids. This calculation excludes Mexican casualties in outright battles (which were almost entirely adult males) and includes only those casualties for which I have breakdowns of gender or age or both. Were it not for imperfections with the data, the ratio of men to women and children killed would probably be tighter. See introduction to the appendix, below.

54. For the Los Moros and La Palmita raids, see *Gaceta del Gobierno de Tamaulipas*, Oct. 19 and Oct. 26, 1844; Francisco Lofero to los jueces de secciones 6, 12, 15, 16, 17, and 18–23, Matamoros, Oct. 12, 1841, MAP 51:8–9.

55. For the Kiowa version of events, see Mooney, *Calendar*, 282. The calendar includes the intriguing detail that in the building along with the doomed Mexicans there were "two Indians, who wore feathered crests upon their heads."

56. For the argument that scholars have been too focused on resistance, diluting the term and missing other aspects of peoples' histories, see Brown, "On Resisting."

CHAPTER 5. INDIANS DON'T UNMAKE PRESIDENTS

1. Berlandier, *Indians*, 120.

2. There is a growing literature on the rise of nationalism and nation-states in Latin America. See especially Centeno and López-Alves, eds., *The Other Mirror*; Centeno, *Blood and Debt*; Dunkerley, ed., *Studies*; Castro-Klarén and Chasteen, *Beyond Imagined Communities*. For a sketch of the consensus among Latin American scholars regarding the ephemeral quality of the nation, see Castro-Klarén and Chasteen, *Beyond Imagined Communities*, xviii–xxiv.

3. Quote is from Reséndez, *Changing*. Some of the most exciting recent work on the troubled emergence of nation-states in Latin American concerns native peasants and mixed-race peoples in urban areas. See Mallon, *Peasant and Nation*; Guardino, *Peasants*; Guardino, *Time of Liberty*. For a more skeptical view of peasant engagement with national politics, see Van Young, *Other Rebellion*. I take inspiration from Mallon's observation that "in any particular case, nationalism would become a series of competing discourses in constant formation and negotiation, branded by particular regional histories of power relations" and share with her the goal of "reinserting [popular political cultures] into so-called national political history." See *Peasant and Nation*, 4, xv. See also Joseph and Nugent, eds., *Everyday Forms*.

4. For rations and their reduction, see Griffen, *Apaches*, 89, 131–33. Jones, "Comparative Raiding," 104–05, calculates that the total costs of the treaty system with Apaches in Chihuahua, including rations, amounted to only 4 percent of the overall military budget for the frontier in the late Bourbon period. The budget declined after 1810, so the percentage devoted to rations likely increased. Before cutting back on rations in the 1820s, Mexican officials spent on average 180 pesos per Apache per year (see Stevens, "Apache Menace," 121). In 1848, a survey in a northern

Chihuahua town found that 85 percent of the population earned less than 240 pesos per year. See Orozco, *Tierra de libres,* 20.

5. For the initial years of the conflict, see Griffen, *Utmost,* 21–41; Sweeney, *Mangas Coloradas,* 44–67. For early raids in southern New Mexico, see, for example, Cayetano Martínez to Governor of New Mexico, March 9, 1836, MANM 21:535. For Mescaleros in Durango, see "Ofensas a la nación por bárbaros que la invaden," folder 10, SUI.

6. For sketches of social organization, see Opler, "Apachean"; id., "Mescalero"; id., "Chiricahua"; Basso, "Western Apache"; and Basso's introduction to Goodwin, *Western Apache Raiding,* 9–25. Population estimates for Apaches in the first half of the nineteenth century are educated guesses. The ten thousand figure comes from rough estimates for c. 1850 putting the Chiricahua population at three thousand, Mescalero at twenty-five hundred to three thousand, and Western Apache at forty-four hundred to forty-nine hundred: see essays above. Given the terrific warfare between these Apaches and Mexicans during the period 1831–50, it would be reasonable to assume that the total population could have been higher in 1830 than at midcentury. For a rare glimpse into Chiricahua efforts to recruit other Apache allies in the early 1830s, see monthly report of José Grijalva, Tucson, Oct. 1, 1831, in McCarty, ed., *Frontier Documentary,* 32–33.

7. For an early appeal to reinstitute the ration program, see a letter from 1831 reprinted in Escudero, *Noticias estadísticas,* 245–46. For "cruel," see Manuel Escalante y Arvizu to José Isidro Madero, Arizpe, June 27, 1832, in McCarty, ed., *Frontier Documentary,* 35–36.

8. Chihuahua has been the focus of the most creative and important work available on the dynamics and the consequences of Indian–Mexican conflicts in the nineteenth century. Víctor Orozco, especially, has demonstrated the long-term consequences of the Apache war for Chihuahua's social, economic, and political development, and for the state's central role in the Mexican Revolution. See his *Antología; Primeras fases;* and *Tierra de libres.* Other contributions to this line of interpretation include Alonso, *Thread;* Nugent, "Are We Not?"; id., "The Center"; Aboites, "Poblamiento"; id., "Poder político." The early decades of the conflict are most thoroughly explored in Griffen, *Apaches,* 119–266; id., *Utmost,* 21–126; Sweeney, *Mangas Coloradas,* 44–158.

9. Quote and instructions are from José Isidro Madero, circular, Chihuahua, June 16, 1832, in Orozco, *Antología,* 213–17. For decree on executions, see Orozco, *Primeras fases,* 82. It is doubtful that authorities ever enforced this severe measure.

10. Manuel Escalante y Arvizu, circular, Arizpe, Sept. 7, 1835, doc. 435, Pinart Prints. José Joaquín Calvo, circular, Chihuahua, Oct. 23, 1834, MANM 20:572.

11. On tax relief for the poor, see Governor José J. Calvo, circular, Chihuahua, May 18, 1835, MANM 19:469. For Coyame, see Calvo, circular, Chihuahua, May 30, 1835, in Orozco, *Antología,* 246. For abolition of duties, see Calvo, circular, Chihuahua, Aug. 19, 1835, MANM 19:482.

12. For appeals on presidios, see, for example, Zúñiga, *Rápida ojeada,* 21–26; Barreiro, *Ojeado,* 33–36; Escudero, *Noticias estadísticas,* 125, 249. For a definition of *presidio,* see Weber, *Spanish Frontier,* 438 n.30. For presidio locations, see Moorhead, *The Presidio,* 62–63. On the institution's effectiveness, see Faulk, "Fortress or Farce?" For a brief but insightful analysis of the problems facing presidios following independence, see Pedro García Conde, "Memoria del Secretario de Estado y del Despacho de Guerra y Marina Leída en la Cámara de Senadores el día 10 y en el de Diputados el día 11 de Marzo de 1845," doc. 501, Lafragua. The author insists that the presidio system had been effective because it was a *system,* with the companies working in concert and with local populations cooperating closely with troops. Political squabbling after independence

prevented the reemergence of the system, even as lack of funding undermined the effectiveness of individual presidios.

13. For the 1826 law, see Weber, *Mexican Frontier*, 108. For abuses by officers and for *pagares*, see Zúñiga, *Rápida ojeada*, 21–25. For the Chihuahua decree, see José Joaquín Calvo, circular, Chihuahua, Oct. 23, 1834, MANM 20:572. For Sánchez quote and plight of presidial soldiers, see Velasco Avila, "Amenaza Comanche," 248–53.

14. For the half-million-peso figure, see editorial from Chihuahua, Oct. 14, 1834, in "Ofensas a la nación por bárbaros que la invaden," folder 10, SUI. For Sonoran fundraising, see Manuel Escalante y Arvizu, circular, Arizpe, Oct. 11, 1833, doc. 261, Pinart Prints. For salary cuts, see José Joaquín Calvo, circular, Chihuahua, Dec. 1, 1834, MANM 20:574; and Manuel Escalante y Arvizu, circular, Arizpe, July 19, 1834, doc. 315, Pinart Prints.

15. Barreiro published his book in Puebla rather than Mexico City, though the dedication (to Bustamante) leaves little doubt about who his intended audience was. The biographical sketches are drawn from the following: Escudero: *Noticias de Sonora*, 23–27; Barreiro: Carroll and Haggard, eds., *New Mexican Chronicles*, xx–xxi; Zúñiga: Weber, ed., *Northern Mexico on the Eve*, 23. For a shorter appeal from senators and deputies from multiple states, see García, *Exposición*.

16. For quote on remote Sonora, see Zúñiga, *Rápida ojeada*, 15–16. For quotes on New Mexico, see Barreiro, *Ojeado*, 17–23, facsimile in Carroll and Haggard, eds., *New Mexican Chronicles*, 263–318. New Mexico had enjoyed its own period of rapid growth, following peace with the Comanches in the 1780s. The economic and cultural consequences of that peace are explored in detail in Frank, *Settler to Citizen*, 119–75.

17. Escudero's actual estimate of Chihuahua's annual produce and animal production is 903,019 pesos. See Escudero, *Noticias estadísticas*, 102. For Sonora, see Zúñiga, *Rápida ojeada*, 14–15, 18 n. 17.

18. Escudero, *Noticias estadísticas*, 125.

19. Zúñiga, *Rápida ojeada*, 15. For the two hundred figure, see Manuel Escalante y Arvizu, circular, Arizpe, Oct. 11, 1833, doc. 262, Pinart Prints; Escudero, *Noticias estadísticas*, 125.

20. Zúñiga, *Rápida ojeada*, 17; Barreiro, *Ojeado*, 30–31; editorial from Chihuahua, Oct. 14, 1834, in "Ofensas a la nación por bárbaros que la invaden," folder 10, SUI. Last quote is from Jan. 3, 1835, in Orozco, *Primeras fases*, 79.

21. While New Mexicans may not have contemplated secession, the governor warned national authorities as early as 1825 of the potential for "treason" if they did not provide the province with effective protection against Indians. See Weber, *Mexican Frontier*, 243.

22. Tenenbaum, *Politics of Penury*, 17–28. For an excellent overview of Mexico's early fiscal history, see also Marichal, "Una difícil."

23. Numbers are rounded averages taken from figures for individual fiscal years in table B of Tenenbaum, *Politics of Penury*, 180–81. No data are included in any category for 1821 or for 1822/23 for collection costs. War Department figures include the navy.

24. DePalo, *Mexican National Army*, 25–30; Costeloe, *Central Republic*, 5–6.

25. DePalo, *Mexican National Army*, 163; Tenenbaum, *Politics of Penury*, 36–37; Costeloe, *Central Republic*, 8.

26. For Latin American militaries and fears of social unrest, see Centeno, *Blood and Debt*. For the plight of the Mexican army, see Costeloe, *Central Republic*, 5–9; DePalo, *Mexican National Army*, 30–32. For conscription, see Serrano Ortega, *El contingente de sangre*. For the view that

regular soldiers would be ineffective against Indians, see, for example, Governor of Tamaulipas to the Ayuntamiento de Matamoros, May 12, 1837, MAP 25:146–47. For a northern appeal for regular military forces, see Barreiro, *Ojeado*, 30–31.

27. Tenenbaum, *Politics of Penury*, 24–37; Jáuregui, "Los orígenes," 79–85. For fiscal studies of particular regions in this period, see also Serrano Ortega and Jáuregui, *Hacienda y política*.

28. For Nuevo León, see J. M. Tornel to Juan N. de la Garza y Evia, Mexico, March 31, 1835, c10, e6, AGNL-MGM. For comments on New Mexico, see Tornel to Albino Pérez, Mexico City, Jan. 21, 1835, MANM 19:349–51. For New Mexican arms and for presidios, see law of Jan. 8, 1835, in Dublán and Lozano, eds., *Legislación Mexicana* 3:9–12. It is unclear whether these supplies ever reached New Mexico.

29. Dublán and Lozano, eds., *Legislación Mexicana* 3:9–12

30. For "beneficial," see Sweeney, *Mangas Coloradas*, 46; Escudero, *Noticias estadísticas*, 240–50. Escudero mistakenly attributed the landmark instructions of 1786 to José de Gálvez, longtime secretary of the Indies and Bernardo's uncle. For quote, see "Ofensas a la nación por bárbaros que la invaden," folder 10, SUI.

31. Escudero, *Noticias estadísticas*, 242.

32. For the Sonoran campaign, see McCarty, ed., *Frontier Documentary*, 43–47. For Tutije's execution, see Sweeney, *Mangas Coloradas*, 58–60.

33. Ignacio Mora to Governor of Sonora, Mazatlan, Feb. 28, 1835, doc. 373, Pinart Prints. See also Stevens, "Mexico's Forgotten Frontier," 127–28.

34. Ignacio de Bustamante to Ignacio Mora, Arizpe, March 31, 1835; Ignacio Mora to Governor of Sonora, Culiacán, April 25, 1835, both in doc. 373, Pinart Prints.

35. Ignacio de Bustamante to Ignacio Mora, Arizpe, May 13, 1835, doc. 373, Pinart Prints. Zúñiga made Bustamante's private critique of Mora public a few months later. See Zúñiga, *Rápida ojeada*, 7 n. 7.

36. J. Joaquín G. Herreros, circular, Arizpe, June 30, 1835 (copy of notice from June 2), doc. 405, Pinart Prints. For the peace negotiations, see Griffen, *Utmost*, 157–63.

37. For an excellent discussion of this point, see Orozco, *Antología*, 19–20.

38. For los indios bárbaros as Mexicans, see Weber, *Mexican Frontier*, 103. For a broader discussion of the conceptual place of Indians in postindependence Mexico, see Hale, *Mexican Liberalism*, 215–47. For an insightful discussion of how Indian identities complicated the national project in Latin America, see Héctor Díaz Polanco, *Indigenous Peoples*, 3–22, 65–82. Quotes are from Joel R. Poinsett to Henry Clay, Mexico City, April 13, 1827 [private], in *U.S. Despatches*. For the Mexican "pact," see Valerio-Jiménez, "Indios Bárbaros," 165–66.

39. For Sonoran responses to rebellions among the Yaquis, Mayos, and Opatas, see Voss, *On the Periphery*, 48–67. For Apaches as sublevados, see, for example, the treaty Chihuahua signed with Comanches and Kiowas in 1834, in Alejandro Ramírez to the Governor of Chihuahua, El Paso, July 23, 1834, in Orozco, *Antología*, 237–39; García, *Exposición*, 3; letter by Pedro Armendáris, *Siglo XIX*, April 19, 1843.

40. For the Chihuahuan query and the president's quote, see law of Jan. 8, 1835, in Dublán and Lozano, eds., *Legislación Mexicana* 3:9–12.

41. For declarations about breaking from Spanish precedent, see, for example, the comments of deputies from Zacatecas in Benson, "Texas as Viewed," 233. For Mexican opinions about Spain's Indian policies, see Weber, *Mexican Frontier*, 104.

42. For the Chihuahua plan, see Smith, *Borderlander*, 71. For income, see Orozco, *Tierra de libres*, 20.

43. For Johnson, see Strickland, "Birth and Death." For the captive's report, see *Diario*, Aug. 9, 1838. For the definitive biography of Kirker, see Smith, *Borderlander*.

44. For the cancellation of Chihuahua's scalp-hunting program, see Smith, *Borderlander*, 71.

45. For Santa Anna and the centralists, see Costeloe, *Central Republic*, 48–65. For the constitutional changes, see ibid., 100–107.

46. For the nine thousand pesos, see Rafael Revilla, circular, Chihuahua, June 26, 1833, #31, wallet 9, Pablo Salce Arredondo Collection. For the federalist tax structure, see Tenenbaum, *Politics of Penury*, 46–47. For changes under centralism, see Sánchez Rodríguez, "Política fiscal." For the contingente, see Castañeda Zavala, "Contingente Fiscal."

47. Tenenbaum, *Politics of Penury*, 39–42, 46–47.

48. For complaints about centralism depriving the frontier of resources, see, for example, Voss, *On the Periphery*, 90; *Diario*, Oct. 17, 1842, as described in Escobar Ohmstede and Rojas Rabiela, eds., *La presencia del indígena*, 215. For the British firearms, see *Diario*, Sept. 3, 1836. For Bustamante's fiscal woes, see Tenenbaum, *Politics of Penury*, 55–58; Costeloe, *Central Republic*, 127–34.

49. For rebellions, see Vázquez, "Texas Question."

50. *Diario*, Sept. 1, 1835. The rebellion in Zacatecas began when the governor of that state seized a shipment of weapons the central government had intended for Chihuahua. Though strongly profederalist, the governor of Chihuahua denounced the Zacatecas rebellion, furious that guns intended to save Chihuahua from raiders would instead be used by brothers to kill one another. See Orozco, *Primeras fases*, 85.

51. For Jackson's speech, see Senate Doc. 160, 24th Cong., 2nd sess., 1–2. For the so-called Pastry War with France, see summaries in Rives, *United States and Mexico* 1:436–50; Costeloe, *Central Republic*, 144–46, 154.

52. A systematic review of Sonoran documents and periodicals for quantifiable data on Apache–Mexican hostilities needs to be done. For the jump in Chihuahuan casualties, see Griffen, *Utmost*, 237–38.

53. Though the exchange took place in 1836, officials in Chihuahua remembered the minister's telling phrase for years. The quote was taken from a Chihuahuan newspaper article, reprinted in *Diario*, Jan. 24, 1840.

CHAPTER 6. BARBARIANS AND DEARER ENEMIES

1. Material on Zapata in this and the following paragraph comes from Salmón, "Antonio Zapata." For Péréz, see Reséndez, *Changing*, 171–73.

2. Charles Bent estimated there were seven thousand Navajos in 1846. See Charles Bent to W. Medill, Santa Fe, Nov. 10, 1846, in Abel, ed., *Official Correspondence*, 6–9. A few years later the New Mexico Indian agent James S. Calhoun thought that five thousand was a more likely number, but another local authority (Colonel John M. Washington) insisted there were between seven and ten thousand. See McNitt, *Navajo Wars*, 153. For organization, see Witherspoon, "Navajo Social Organization." For the naach'id, see Brugge, "Documentary Reference."

3. For a lucid survey of Navajo–New Mexican conflicts, see the trio of articles by Reeve: "Navajo–

Spanish Peace," "Navaho–Spanish Diplomacy," and "Navaho Foreign Affairs"; and McNitt, *Navajo Wars*. These should be supplemented with Brugge, *Navajos in the Catholic*, which relies upon a different source base and offers superb quantitative analysis of casualties over time; for baptisms, see 22–23. Brooks, *Captives*, offers a fascinating analysis of Navajo–Mexican relations. See also two books that summarize extant documents bearing on Navajo conflict with Mexicans through 1848: Jenkins and Ward, *Navajo Activities*, and Correll, *Through White Men's Eyes*. The second is the more complete.

4. Albino Chacón's recollections of the context and events of the rebellion of 1837 may be found in Chacón, *Legacy of Honor*, 23–34. New Mexicans had long cherished the notion that their activities against Indians, while naturally self-serving in many regards, were also acts of self-sacrifice to further the glory, security, and prosperity of New Spain and, later, the Mexican republic. See, for example, Pino, *Exposition*, 17–18.

5. For "annihilate," and "the ruin," see Chacón, *Legacy of Honor*, 23–34. For a revealing glimpse into how the governor viewed Navajos, see Albino Pérez to alcaldes of Taos, Ojo Caliente, Cochití, Santa Clara, Sandía, Abiquiu, Jemez, Laguna, and Socorro, Santa Fe, February 19, 1836, MANM 21:669. For discontent over Pérez's campaigns, see Reséndez, *Changing*, 181–83. For "toy" quote, see Vigil, "Maladministration," 19.

6. The context for the rebellion in this and the following paragraph is taken from Lecompte, *Rebellion in Río Arriba*; Brooks, *Captives*, 273–80; and from the excellent discussion in Reséndez, *Changing*, 171–96, to which my interpretation of the revolt is indebted. For New Mexico's precarious fiscal situation and the role of new taxes in sparking rebellion, see Martín González de la Vara, "Entre el subsidio."

7. For the rebel proclamation, see Lecompte, *Rebellion in Río Arriba*, 20.

8. For Gonzales's identity, see ibid., 36–38, and notes 54, 56; Brooks, *Captives*, 278.

9. The descriptions come from Gregg, *Commerce*, 93. Whether or not these reports were accurate, they do capture the flavor of ricos' anxiety about a potential social war.

10. For general fears about alliances between Pueblos and nomadic Indians, see Reséndez, *Changing*, 186–88. For "reestablish order," see proclamation of José Caballero, Sept. 9, 1837, quoted in Lecompte, *Rebellion in Río Arriba*, 50. For Armijo's background, see Lecompte, "Armijo's Family"; Perrigo, *Hispanos*, 36–38. Armijo's quote is from Reséndez, *Changing*, 188. For the western Pueblos, see Brugge, "Pueblo Factionalism," 196. The notion of rebel–bárbaro conspiracy would become part of Mexico City's narrative of the rebellion. The prolific Mexican writer Carlos María Bustamante, who dedicated a book to Armijo, wrote that the rebels "decided to ally themselves with the wild Indian nations surrounding them and to destroy everything, preferring to live the wandering life of the savages." See Lecompte, *Rebellion in Río Arriba*, 152.

11. Reséndez, *Changing*, 185–86.

12. For tax exemption, see Minge, "Frontier Problems," 105.

13. Zúñiga quoted in Voss, *On the Periphery*, 96.

14. For the context of the revolt, see ibid., 95–97. See also Vázquez, "Texas Question," 318. For the petition from Arizpe, see *Diario*, Nov. 19, 1837. For authorization to coordinate Indian policy, see José Urrea, circular, Arizpe, March 26, 1838, doc. 508, Pinart Prints. In October 1837 a decree was issued forbidding Sonorans from purchasing weapons from presidial soldiers. See Rafael Elías González, circular, Arizpe, Aug. 10, 1837, Pinart Prints.

15. Quote is from Zúñiga, taken from Voss, *On the Periphery*, 96. For the events of the rebellion, see

ibid., 97–101. For allied Apaches, see Quijada Hernández and Ruibal Corella, *Historia general*, 66.

16. Voss, *On the Periphery*, 97–101.

17. For *Mercurio* quote, see Vigness, "Lower Rio Grande," 74. For Bravo's comments, see Velasco Avila, "Amenaza Comanche," 297. For the federalist/centralist contest in the northeast, see also López López, *La ciudad*, 274–92.

18. For the "sufferers," see *Mercurio* [supplement], Aug. 5, 1836. For similar concerns in Monterrey, see Ridout, "Anti-National," 42–43. For presidio requests, see, for example, *Mercurio*, Sept. 15, 1837. Final quote is from *Mercurio*, Oct. 20, 1837. For more on tensions between northeasterners and the army after 1836, see Valerio-Jiménez, "Neglected Citizens," 289–95.

19. "Manifiesto de los generales y gefes del ejército del norte (March 6, 1838)" in Jiménez Codinach, Ulloa, and Hernández Santiago, *Planes* 3:151–52.

20. This summary of events is taken from Vázquez, "La supuesta"; and Nance, *After San Jacinto*, 145–60; for "wish to make," see 155. Nance's account is highly detailed but must be used with care given his uncritical use of Texan sources to access events in Mexico. For a window onto how unending raids pushed one town into supporting Urrea, see "Acta de la ciudad de Monclova" (Jan. 19, 1839), in Jiménez Codinach, Ulloa, and Hernández Santiago, *Planes* 3:173.

21. Mexicans often referred to Indian warriors as *gandules*, or layabouts. For quotes from presidial commander, see Velasco Avila, "Amenaza Comanche," 298–99. For conversation about funds see J. de Jesús D. y Prieto to the Secretaría de Guerra y Marina, Monterrey, April 1, 1838, C15, AGENL-MGM.

22. Joaquín García to the Secretaría de Guerra y Marina, Monterrey, Dec. 9, 1838, C12, E44, AGENL-MGM; José María Tornel to Joaquín García, Mexico City, Dec. 21, 1838, C12, E54, AGENL-MGM. Tornel's report from Jan. 1839 may be found in *Diario*, May 6, 1839. For the report of eighty casualties, see Velasco Avila, "Amenaza Comanche," 311.

23. For the weapons inquiry, see Pedro del Valle, circular, Monterrey, Jan. 12, 1839, #5, wallet 12, Arredondo Collection. On June 3, 1833, the central government had issued a decree empowering governors to confiscate all firearms and to fine heavily anyone who refused to hand over or who concealed their weapons. See *Gaceta del Supremo Gobierno de Durango*, Aug. 22, 1833. I have found no evidence that northern governors exercised this power in the early 1830s, but suspicion seems to have been warranted nonetheless. In June 1839 Arista would order civilians in Tamaulipas to surrender their arms to the government as a consequence of the federalist rebellion (see Ridout, "Anti-National," 42). Still, Arista understood the political and military implications of Indian raiding, and this order probably aimed above all at rattling settlements contemplating rebellion. For the "poor government" correspondence, see Joaquín García to José María Tornel, Monterrey, Feb. 11, 1839, C13, E13, AGENL-MGM; José María Tornel to Joaquín García, Mexico City, Feb. 21, 1839, C13, E18, AGENL-MGM. For María de Llano, see Roel, *Nuevo León*, 135–52.

24. For María de Llano's quote, see Mendinichaga, *Los cuatro tiempos*, 233. For Canales, see Ridout, "Anti-National," 44–45.

25. Vázquez, "La supuesta," 53–55; Nance, *After San Jacinto*, 158–70.

26. For Canales's career, see Ridout, "Anti-National." Justin Smith simply dismissed Canales as "a border ruffian and conspirator." Smith, *War with Mexico*, 158. For his efforts in late 1839, see Nance, *After San Jacinto*, 205–51.

27. For the pesos, see Joaquín García to José María Tornel, Monterrey, March 23, 1839, C13, E34, AGENL-MGM; and José María Tornel to Joaquín García, Mexico City, April 8, 1839, C13, E43, AGENL-MGM. For arms, see Juan N. Almonte to J. de Jesús Davila y Prieto, Mexico City, Nov. 25, 1839, C14, E45, AGENL-MGM; for the draft, see J. de Jesús Davila y Prieto to Juan N. Almonte, Monterrey, Feb. 12, 1840, C15, E33, AGENL-MGM; and Juan N. Almonte to J. de Jesús Davila y Prieto, Mexico City, Feb. 25, 1840, C15, E38, AGENL-MGM.

28. Minister's quote is from "Memoria del Ministro de Guerra y Marina presentada a las Cámaras de Congreso General Mexicano en enero de 1840," 45–46, doc. 517, Lafragua. For the museum, see Juan N. Almonte to J. de Jesús Davila y Prieto, Mexico City, Dec. 31, 1839, C14, E66, AGENL-MGM. For the governor's response, see J. de Jesús Davila y Prieto to Juan N. Almonte, Monterrey, Jan. 22, 1840 [draft], C14, E66, AGENL-MGM. The governor sent Almonte a Comanche lance two months later. See J. de Jesús Davila y Prieto to Juan N. Almonte, Monterrey, March 18, 1840, C15, E45, AGENL-MGM.

29. See *Diario,* Feb. 5, 1840; Velasco Avila, "La Amenaza," 313. As was so often the case, Mexican observers were unable to determine the number of Comanche dead and simply inferred great casualties because of the quantity of blood left on the ground. Webster's observation is the closest thing there is to a casualty count. Dolbeare, *Captivity and Suffering,* 19–20. The *New Orleans Commercial Bulletin* ran a translation of Arista's account of the battle, which was itself reprinted in other papers, including the *Pensacola Gazette* (Feb. 29, 1840). Interestingly, the editors of the *Bulletin* believed that the battle had been between centralists and federalists and that Arista called the federalists Comanches to insult them.

30. For Arista's quotes and his policy regarding private property and for reports of Texan looting, see Nance, *After San Jacinto,* 347, 336–37. A writer in Texas claimed Mexican hatred of Comanches accounts for "the origin of the epithet expressing odium so general in all parts of Mexico: to denote the greatest degree of degradation, they call a person a Comanche." Edward, *History of Texas,* 108–09.

31. For Berlandier's observations, see his *Journey,* 243–46, 429. See also Campbell, "Coahuiltecan Indians." For inflated figures of Indians riding with the federalists, see, for example, J. de Jesús Davila y Prieto to Juan N. Almonte, Monterrey, Nov. 6, 1839, C14, E33, AGENL-MGM.

32. Letter from Governor Mateo Quiroz in *Concordia: Semanario del gobierno departamental de Tamaulipas,* July 13, 1839. Arista quoted in Nance, *After San Jacinto,* 257; and in Ridout, "Anti-National," 90. For federalists requisitioning weapons, see for example J. de Jesús Davila y Prieto to Juan N. Almonte, Monterrey, Sept. 9, 1839, C14, E28, AGENL-MGM; and same to same, Monterrey, Nov. 13, 1839, C14, E37, AGENL-MGM. It was rumored in Nuevo León that Comanche raiders released a Mexican girl they captured near Higueras as soon as she lied to them and said she was Antonio Zapata's daughter. See Vizcaya Canales, *Tierra,* 80.

33. For Caddos, see Dolbeare, *Captivity and Suffering,* 17–18. For Zapata and Ramos, see Ridout, "Anti-National," 60–61. For Canales's proclamation about controlling Indians, delivered in February 1840, see Ridout, "Anti-National," 44. For federalist offers to protect frontier towns, see, for example, an article from *Seminario,* reprinted in *Diario,* Dec. 7, 1839. In March of 1839, Zapata led a force that seems to have turned back a five-hundred-man Comanche campaign. See Vizcaya Canales, *Tierra,* 75–76. For Zapata's delay and Canales's two squadrons, see Nance, *After San Jacinto,* 260–65. Galán was the same officer who in January 1841 would surprise and

rout the Comanche force that orchestrated the bold raid on Saltillo, as described in chapter 4, above.

34. Vázquez, "La supuesta," 73–75; Nance, *After San Jacinto*, 326–72.

35. Sonora complicates this generalization because of its on-again, off-again civil war between forces under Manuel María Gándara and José Urrea, which had less and less to do with federalism and centralism, as well as a series of Indian uprisings involving Yaquis, Papagos, and others. None of these later conflicts, however, began as protests against Mexican policy toward Indian raiding. See Voss, *On the Periphery*, 95–129; Katz, ed., *Riot*, 523–24; Hernández Silva, "Sonora y la Guerra." For the centralist habit after the Texas revolt of branding all federalist uprisings treasonous, see Reséndez, *Changing*, 186. For the Chihuahua quote, see *Diario*, Aug. 2, 1840.

36. For New Mexican–Arapaho conflict, see Reeve, "Bent Papers," 30:2, pp. 155–59.

37. For newspaper stories, see Escobar Ohmstede and Rojas Rabiela, eds., *La presencia del indígena*, cuadros 1 and 2. For quotes, see Fisher and Hall, eds., *Life in Mexico*, 509, 52. People in the capital maintained their fascination with Comanches for years. In 1846, for instance, a popular bullfighter named Tómas Rodríguez tried to thrill his crowds by dressing as a Comanche when he fought his bulls. See the *Boston Daily Atlas*, April 6, 1848.

38. Ignacio de Arizpe to Juan N. Almonte, Saltillo, Jan. 11, 1841 [draft], C1, F1, E6, 5f, FSXIX-AGEC. Editorials in *Voto*, Feb. 13 and Feb. 20, 1841.

39. For the request from San Luis Potosí, see the editorial from that department's paper, *Gaceta*, reprinted in *Diario*, Jan. 13, 1841. For the complaint from Chihuahua, see Orozco, *Primeras fases*, 160.

40. See Bustamante, *El gabinete* 2:108.

41. For the congressional debate, see the following issues of *Diario* for 1841: Jan. 31, Feb. 2, Feb. 3, Feb. 4, Feb. 12, Feb. 15, Feb. 20, and Feb. 21. For communication to northern governors, see, for example, Juan L. Velázquez de León to J. de Jesús Davila y Prieto, Mexico City, Feb. 16, 1841, C16, E4, AGENL-MGM. For the new tax (presidential decree of March 8, 1841), see *Diario*, May 18, 1841. Final quote is from Almonte, "Memoria del Ministro de Guerra y Marina presentada a las Cámaras de Congreso General Mexicano en enero de 1841," pp. 35–37, doc. 517, Lafragua.

42. Arista deserves a modern biography. For a brief sketch, see Cubas, *Diccionario* 1:246–48. For "embarrassed the revolutionaries," see Juan N. Almonte to the governor of Nuevo León, Oct. 30, 1840, C-16, AGENL-MGM.

43. For the distances Comanches could travel, see J. N. Armendáriz to Comandante General de Durango, Cerrogordo, Nov. 29, 1843, in *Registro*, Dec. 14, 1843. For Arista's appreciation of their speed and endurance, see Mariano Arista to the governors of the eastern departments, circular, Monterrey, Aug. 1, 1841, enclosed in D. W. Smith to Daniel Webster, Matamoros, Aug. 30, 1841, *Despatches* 2:127. For the important observation that the huge Comanche campaigns meant Mexicans had to be highly organized just to take the field, see Velasco Avila, "Amenaza Comanche," 310.

44. For "infested," see Juan N. Armendáriz, "Diario de las operaciones militares de la sección en campaña contra los comanches sobre el Bolsón de Mapimí," Cerrogordo, Nov. 1, 1844, in *Registro*, Nov. 10, 1844. On dead animals and captives thrown into water holes, see also Meyer, *Water*, 96–97.

45. For "pitiless campaign," see Vizcaya Canales, *Tierra*, 175. The quote on the Spanish precedent

is in *Ancla*, Feb. 8, 1841, MAP 38:64–65. For a penetrating analysis of the debates in Bourbon Spanish America about offensive or defensive war against independent Indians, see Weber, *Bárbaros*, 138–77. For Spanish campaigns, see Anderson, *Indian Southwest*, 209–12. For "defensive war," see letter of Pedro Armendáris in *Siglo XIX*, April 19, 1843. End quote is from Coahuila in 1849, taken from Rodríguez, *La guerra*, 52.

46. For González's campaign, see Simón González, circular, Chihuahua, May 18, 1838, in Orozco, *Antología*, 253–55; Orozco, *Primeras fases*, 113–23.

47. Mariano Arista to governors of the northern departments, Monterrey, Dec. 15, 1840, in Arista, *Oficio y documentos*. For provisions, see "relación del cuerpo del ejército del norte, que combatirá a las tribus salvajes," Guerrero, Dec. 15, 1840, E92, C3, AGEC-AMG.

48. For Arista's appeals to governors, see, for example, Arista to Ignacio de Arizpe, Monterrey, Jan. 17, 1841, in *Voto*, Feb. 13, 1841. Governor Ignacio de Arizpe of Coahuila caused the general enough embarrassment in the press that Arista felt compelled to have published in Mexico City a lengthy refutation of charges that he had neglected frontier defense. See Arista, *Oficio y documentos*.

49. For the "attention" quote, see Arista's letter in *Ancla*, March 15, 1841. For "having set," see Arista to the inhabitants of the eastern departments, circular, Matamoros, April 2, 1841, in *Ancla*, April 5, 1841. For the remaining quotes, see Arista to the governors of the eastern departments, circular, Monterrey, Aug. 1, 1841, enclosed in D. W. Smith to Daniel Webster, Matamoros, Aug. 30, 1841, *Despatches* 2:127. Arista was obviously not alone in looking to hated outsiders to foster national unity. For war against outsiders as an important part of the "iconographic solution" to the problem of weak nationalism in Latin America, see Centeno, *Blood and Debt*, 174–75.

50. Arista to the inhabitants of the eastern departments, circular, Matamoros, April 2, 1841, in *Ancla*, April 5, 1841.

51. Mariano Arista to the inhabitants of Coahuila, Nuevo León, and Tamaulipas, circular, Monterrey, Jan. 8, 1841, MAP 39:151.

52. For the shortfall in men, see Velasco Avila, "Amenaza Comanche," 333. For Tabasco and the quote, see Arista to the governors of the eastern departments, circular, Monterrey, Aug. 1, 1841, enclosed in D. W. Smith to Daniel Webster, Matamoros, Aug. 30, 1841, *Despatches* 2:127.

53. For the advisory panel, see *Ancla*, May 3, 1841. For "the Indians enter," see copy of Arista's letter in D. W. Smith to Secretary of State, Aug. 30, 1841, *Despatches* 2:127. For the proposal to Lamar, see *Telegraph*, July 28, 1841. As distasteful as it was for Arista to request anything of the Texan leader, he would not bring himself to address the man as "President," for that might imply some recognition of Texan independence. "Mr." Lamar consequently refused to receive Arista's communication.

54. Coahuila's governor only stepped up his public criticism in the wake of Arista's failed campaign. See Alessio Robles, *Coahuila y Texas* 2:237–43.

55. For "entirely forgetting," see "Manifiesto y Plan del General Paredes (Guadalajara, Aug. 8, 1841)," in Iglesias González, *Planes políticos*, 193. For "bloody and barbaric," see "Acta del pronunciamiento del ayuntamiento y vecindario del estado de Monterrey y de Nuevo León para secundar el Plan de Paredes (Sept. 20, 1841)," in Jiménez Codinach, Ulloa, and Hernández Santiago, *Planes* 4:84. For Santa Anna, see Fisher and Hall, eds., *Life in Mexico*, 65–66.

56. For Santa Anna's resurrection and his subsequent administration, see Costeloe, *Central Republic*, 145–253; Tenenbaum, *Politics of Penury*, 41, 45. For a later plan to wage war in la comanchería from multiple states, see letter of Pedro Armendáris in *Siglo XIX*, April 19, 1843.

57. Scholars from the United States (and, occasionally, Mexico) have long assumed that Canales and the other leaders of the northeastern rebellion sought to break the northeast away from Mexico and form a nation called the Republic of the Rio Grande. This assumption had been based on numerous Texan sources that spoke of this new republic as if it either existed already or was on the verge of coming into being. See, for example, Vigness, "Republic"; Nance, *After San Jacinto*, 252–315; Alessio Robles, *Coahuila y Texas* 2:209–28. Josefina Vázquez has convincingly argued that the Texan talk of the Republic of the Rio Grande was "wishful thinking." Though leaders of the rebellion desperate for aid might have given vague flattery to the Texan wish to see a friendly republic between Texas and Mexico, there is no evidence that these leaders ever seriously raised the possibility of secession with the people of northeastern Mexico. See Vázquez, "La supuesta." More recently an attempt has been made to again argue that the rebels intended secession, but the author does not provide evidence of such a plan in Mexican–Mexican correspondence. See Ridout, "Anti-National."

CHAPTER 7. AN EMINENTLY NATIONAL WAR?

1. My data record 414 injuries in the Comanche theater from 1831 to 1846. Mexican authorities were less likely to mention the number of their people wounded in raids or battles if the losses to death and capture were high; therefore the actual number of wounded would have been considerably higher, almost certainly surpassing numbers of killed and captured combined. When Mexican sources did mention wounds they rarely described them, so it is impossible to assess the "average" severity of Indian-inflicted injuries. For the poultice, see Harris, *Sánchez Navarros*, 79.

2. For the three Sonoran cities, see Almada Bay, Medina Bustos, and Córdova Rascón, "Medidas," 230. For the report, see Hatfield, *Chasing Shadows*, 16. For the journalist, see Kendall, *Narrative* 2:55–61. Final quote is from *Registro*, Aug. 26, 1847.

3. For the abandoned Hacienda de Nacimiento, see Miguel Guerra to Francisco Castañeda, Santa Rosa, Dec. 10, 1843, in *Voto*, Dec. 16, 1843; Harris, *Mexican Family Empire*, 194. For Lipanes, see Antonio Tijerina to governor of Coahuila, Santa Rosa, July 13, 1845, in *Republicano*, Sept. 20, 1845. For Laredo, see Hinojosa, *Borderlands Town*, 50–52. An estimate of 1827 put New Mexico's population at 43,433: see Carroll and Haggard, eds., *New Mexican Chronicles*, 88. In 1847 the Mexican government estimated from the very poor data available to them that there were 57,000 New Mexicans. For slightly higher numbers, see Weber, *Mexican Frontier*, 195 and n. 58. New Mexico enjoyed increase despite the fact that three epidemics between 1837 and 1840 together killed perhaps 10 percent of its population. For this and for population flight, see Bloom, "New Mexico Under," 2:21, 39; Minge, "Frontier Problems," 275, 284, 288. California enjoyed an even higher rate of growth during these years: 5 percent. See Weber, *Mexican Frontier*, 206.

4. The data for northern Mexico come from Aboites, *Norte precario*, 49. Aboites's calculations derive from figures for all the northern states (including Sinaloa and Baja California, which are outside the bounds of this book, but excluding New Mexico) for the years 1800, 1830, and 1857. The author attributes much of the decrease in population growth to Mexican emigration to Texas, California, and central Mexico after 1848 but reminds readers that Indian raids continued into the 1850s, in some cases becoming even more severe than before. The direct and indirect consequences of this raiding do much to explain the "push" behind the emigration. A German traveler

to northern Mexico, styling himself something of a poor man's Humboldt, described population loss in Chihuahua. According to his numbers, the state's population had increased by nearly eighteen thousand in the five years between 1827 and 1832, but that in the ten years between 1832 and 1842 it grew by less than ten thousand. See Wislizenus, *Memoir*, 59.

5. For Chihuahua, see *Siglo XIX*, March 9, 1842.

6. For disease, see José María de la Fuerte to Quirino Benavente, San Lorenzo, June 8, 1847, doc. 1635, Sánchez Navarro Collection. For "agriculture paralyzed," see *Voto*, July 9, 1842. For the traveler, see Pattie, *Personal Narrative*, 66–71. For famine, see Escudero, *Noticias estadísticas*, 125.

7. Harris, *Sánchez Navarros*, 79–80. To the long list of evils produced by Indian raiders, hacendados added the fact that murdered peons usually died in debt, leaving their creditors with no way to collect. See Vizcaya Canales, *Tierra*, 70. For the Chihuahua law and for hacendados and arms, see Orozco, *Primeras fases*, 69.

8. For Indians attacking pack trains, see, for example, J. M. Iglesias de Orduña to ?, Hacienda de San Salvador de Horta, Sept. 18, 1845, in *Registro*, Sept. 25, 1845. For complaints about Indians driving up freighters' fees, see Rafael Delgado to Jacobo Sánchez Navarro, San Luis Potosí, Aug. 25, 1851, doc. 374 in Sánchez Navarro Collection. For *productos del campo* in Tamaulipas, see Francisco V. Fernández, circular, Victoria, February 11, 1842, MAP 40:187. For raids decreasing overland trade out of Matamoros, see Valerio-Jiménez, "Neglected Citizens," 294. For the indirect effect of raiding upon tax revenues, see Prieto, "Coahuila y la invasión," 165.

9. Population estimate for northern Mexican states based on the following figures from 1830, taken from Aboites, *Norte precario*, 49: Coahuila, 77,795; Chihuahua, 138,133; Durango, 288,184; Nuevo León, 95,022; Sonora, 347,000; Tamaulipas, 80,000. A contemporary estimate from New Mexico put the population at 43,433. See Colonel Antonio Narbona's census of 1827, reproduced in Carroll and Haggard, eds., *New Mexican Chronicles*, 88. Total c. 1830 population would therefore be 1,069,567. Note that, if included, the much larger populations of San Luis Potosí and, especially, Zacatecas, departments also affected by raiding, would obviously increase the 30:1 ratio. For estimates of Comanche population, see note 11, chapter 1, above. For estimates of Mescalero, Chiricahua, and Western Apache populations, see note 6, chapter 5, above. For Navajos, see note 2, chapter 6, above.

10. For relationships between Mexicans and native peoples in California during this period, see Phillips, *Indians and Intruders*, 65–134; and the remarkable work by Hackel, *Children of Coyote*, 369–419. For Apache raids on New Mexico in the early 1830s, see, for example, Cayetano Martínez to Governor of New Mexico, March 9, 1836, MANM 21:535; Brugge, *Navajos in the Catholic*, 30–31. Many of these attacks seem not to have been directed toward New Mexicans per se but were rather occasional raids by Chiricahuas upon travelers moving south down the Jornada del Muerto and thus outside of the effective bounds of New Mexico (see Griffen, *Utmost*, 49). For New Mexican reactions, see Report of a junta re measures to be taken for defense, Santa Fe, Jan. 9, 1834, MANM 18:180–89. Apache raids in the region continued into 1836. See Pablo Salazar to Antonio Pérez, Tomé, May 3, 1836, MANM 21:576. After 1836, Apaches and southern New Mexicans were much more likely to be trading with each other than fighting. See, for example, Armijo to Justice of the Peace in Socorro, Santa Fe, March 12, 1846 [letter book], MANM 41:182. For the "unrighteous compact," see Kendall, *Narrative* 1:400–01; Webb, *Adventures*, 191–92. Armijo did

make efforts to broker peace between Apaches and Chihuahua. See Minge, "Frontier Problems," 55–57.

11. Reeve, "Bent Papers," 30:2, pp. 155–57.

12. For Armijo's refusal, see Weber, *Mexican Frontier*, 114–15. For a later elaboration on his concerns, see Manuel Armijo to the departmental assembly, June 27, 1845, MANM 38:740–45. In 1835, amid similar talk about joint campaigns against Comanches, *taoseños* openly refused to attack these neighbors who had "guarded . . . the most faithful friendship . . . and true peace in this territory." See Kavanagh, *Comanche Political History*, 280. For Armijo's seventeen hundred men, see Minge, "Frontier Problems," 123. For 1774, see Anderson, *Indian Southwest*, 211. The editorial is from *La Olivia* [Victoria, Tamaulipas], June 16, 1841, reprinted in *Diario*, July 4, 1841.

13. For animals, see Santiago Vidaurri, circular, Monterrey, Sept. 12, 1842, #127, wallet 13, Arredondo Collection. For the defensive lines, see José María Ortega to Secretaría de Guerra y Marina, Agualeguas, Oct. 12, 1842, C16, E74, AGENL-MGM; José María Ortega to Secretaría de Guerra y Marina, Lampazos, Oct. 27, 1842, C16, E78, AGENL-MGM. For the entry through neighboring departments, see José María Ortega to Secretaría de Guerra y Marina, Lampazos, Oct. 30, 1842, C16, E79, AGENL-MGM.

14. For the order to cooperate, see José María Tornel to José María Ortega, Mexico, Nov. 12, 1842, C16, E82, AGENL-MGM. For northern proposals about coordinating defense, see, for example, an editorial from Nuevo León's *Seminario* reprinted in *Diario*, Aug. 19, 1842; editorials in *Registro* from Jan. 19, 1843 and Oct. 30, 1845; and a letter from José Urrea to Governor of Durango, Ures, Feb. 3, 1845, *Registro*, March 6, 1845. For calls for funding assistance from more southerly departments, see *Diario*, Sept. 11, 1836; editorial in *Gaceta del Gobierno de Tamaulipas*, Feb. 20, 1841, MAP 39:176. For the success against Comanches, see Juan N. Armendáriz, Diario de las operaciones militares de la sección en campaña contra los comanches sobre el Bolsón de Mapimí, Cerrogordo, Nov. 1, 1844, in *Registro*, Nov. 10, 1844. For another unusual (and apparently improvised) instance of cooperation between departmental forces, see Vizcaya Canales, *Tierra*, 170.

15. For Chihuahua's forces "abandoning this department [Durango] to its fate," see Francisco Padilla to the Governor of Durango, Oct. 27, 1845, in *Registro*, Oct. 30, 1845. For the reluctance to cross borders, see also Governor of Coahuila to Secretaría de Guerra y Marina, Dec. 5, 1842 (draft), C4, F2, E12, 3f, AGEC-FSXIX; Pedro Rengel to Governor of Coahuila, Parras, April 30, 1845, in *Republicano*, May 10, 1845. For Durango's unaccepted offer of assistance, see José María Acebal to Sr. Secretario del Despacho del Superior Gobierno de Durango, Cuencamé, Dec. 2, 1842, in *Registro*, Dec. 28, 1842. For information sharing, see Governor of Nuevo León to Governor of Coahuila, Monterrey, Feb. 11, 1844, C1, F5, E11, 2f, AGEC-FSXIX; Governor of Zacatecas to Governor of Coahuila, Zacatecas, Feb. 6, 1845, C1, F5, E7, 2f, AGEC-FSXIX; Governor of San Luis Potosí to Governor of Coahuila, April 28, 1845, C2, F7, E5, 2f, AGEC-FSXIX; Governor of Zacatecas to Governor of Durango, Zacatecas, Oct. 15, 1845, in *Registro*, Oct. 30, 1845.

16. For the treaty, see *Registro*, May 12, 1842. For Durango's complaint, see editorial in *Registro*, Sept. 25, 1842. Padre Antonio José Martínez from New Mexico also criticized Chihuahua's Apache treaties. See Aboites, "Poder político," 30. For the conflict with Sonora, see McCarty, ed., *Frontier Documentary*, 101–06.

17. For "numbed the spirit," see Manuel Escalante y Arvizu, circular, Arizpe, Oct. 11, 1833, doc. 262,

Pinart Prints. For "civic virtue" and "scandalous egotism," see Santiago Vidaurri, circular, Monterrey, Aug. 15, 1842, #110, wallet 13, Arredondo Collection. For Escudero, see "Comunicado de José Agustín de Escudero, 1839," in Orozco, *Antología*, 263–73.

18. The Sonoran disputes are discussed throughout Voss, *On the Periphery*; see also Hernández Silva, "Sonora y la Guerra." For Saltillo and Monclova, see Alessio Robles, *Coahuila y Texas* 1:513–38; Prieto, "Coahuila y la invasión." For charges of negligence against Monclova, see *Voto*, Nov. 19, 1842.

19. For "repugnance," see *Registro*, Nov. 2, 1845. For the Sánchez Navarros, see Antonio Tijerina to juez de paz, Monclova, Dec. 18, 1837, doc. 696, and juez de paz to Antonio Tijerina, Dec. 19, 1837, doc. 1263, in Sánchez Navarro Collection. For Chihuahua, see Orozco, *Primeras fases*, 42–43. For New Mexican complaints, see Lecompte, *Rebellion in Río Arriba*, 11.

20. For official complaints about such behavior, see, for example, T. Juan José Champa Guerra to ayuntamiento de Camargo, Reynosa, May 10, 1842, Archivo Histórico de Camargo, AGEC. If animals had been stolen locally or within the same department, authorities often went to considerable lengths to see them returned to their owners. See, for example, "Relación de las bestias caballares y mulares que les quitó a los indios el capitán Manuel Leal comandante del escuadrón auxiliary de Bejar, el día 7 del presente mes," Rio Grande, Oct. 10, 1845, E142, C4, AGEC-AMG, which contains a careful list of brands and descriptions.

21. For false alarms, see Smith, *Borderlander*, 46. For Mexicans helping Indians, see, for example, Ruxton, *Adventures*, 168. For thieves disguised as Indians, see, for example, a letter from Nuevo León condemning the problem, reprinted in *Diario*, Feb. 17, 1843; and Jesús Cárdenas to Sr. Secretario del Superior Gobierno del Departamento de Tamaulipas, Matamoros, March 14, 1846, in *Gaceta del Gobierno de Tamaulipas*, March 22, 1846.

22. For Coahuila's donation campaign, see Francisco García Conde to José María Santos Coy, Saltillo, Aug. 18, 1838, in *Gaceta del Gobierno de Coahuila*, Aug. 24, 1838. For local donations, see, for example, Mariano de la Garza to prefecto de Monclova, Abasolo, Sept. 11, 1838, C3, F1, E5, 3f, AGEC-FSXIX; same to same, Abasolo, Sept. 19, 1838, C3, F1, E7, 3f, AGEC-FSXIX; Jesús de la Garza to prefecto de distrito, Cuatro Ciénegas, Sept. 25, 1838, C3, F1, E12, 4f, AGEC-FSXIX; Anastacio Santos to the "Junta recaudadora de suscripciones del Partido de Río Grande," Nava, Sept. 29, 1838, C3, F1, E14, 2f, AGEC-FSXIX. For list of Paula López's redeemed captives, see Francisco Padilla to Governor of Durango, Durango, Oct. 29, 1845, in *Registro*, Nov. 6, 1845. For redeemed captives, see discussion of Mexican captives retaken and escaped in introduction to the appendix, below. For casualties following the redemption, see *Republicano*, Nov. 8, 1845 (reprinting a letter from San Juan del Río that originally appeared in *Registro*); Manuel Ignacio Fierro to Sr. Secretario del Despacho del Superior Gobierno de Durango, Durango, Oct. 28, 1845, in *Registro*, Oct. 30, 1845. For Paula López's death, see Smith, "Comanche Invasion," 18.

23. For towns making security arrangements with each other, see *Diario*, June 3, 1840. For collective petitions locals made to departmental authorities concerning common defense, see, for example, the documents transcribed in Ignacio Arizpe to Ministro de Relaciones Exteriores, Gobierno y Policia, Saltillo, Jan. 27, 1842, C1, F3, E11, 14f, AGEC-FSXIX.

24. Francisco Lofero to juez de policía de Matamoros, Matamoros, June 9, 1844, MAP 46:97–98; Agapito Vela to Francisco Lofero, Estero, June 9, 1844, MAP 46:99–100; Francisco Lofero to José María Liendo, Matamoros, June 15, 1844, MAP 46:50–51; Manuel de Cela to Francisco Lofero, Matamoros, June 15, 1844, MAP 46:54–56; Francisco Lofero to Gen. D. Manuel Rodríguez

de Cela, Matamoros, June 22, 1844, MAP 46:71; Francisco Lofero to Luis Longoria, Matamoros, June 25, 1844, MAP 46:78–79; [no signature] to juzgado primero de Matamoros, Matamoros, July 4, 1844, MAP 50:71–78.

25. For the raid on San Juan del Río, see Ramón de la Bastida to Sr. Secretario del Superior Gobierno del Departamento de Durango, San Juan del Río, Oct. 19, 1845, *Registro*, Oct. 23, 1845. For San Francisco Xavier, see José de la Bárcena to Governor of Durango, Victoria de Durango, Oct. 27, 1845, in *Registro*, Oct. 30, 1845.

26. Frontier racism is a rich theme in American historiography. This sketch benefits from the subtle insights in Silver, *Savage Neighbors*, concerning the mid-Atlantic colonies in the mid- to late eighteenth century. The power of racism imported from the American south into Texas is a key argument in Anderson, *Conquest*. For early colonial gropings toward conceptions of race in British North America, see Chaplin, *Subject Matter*, 157–98; id., "Race."

27. For illuminating discussions of race in the colonial north, see, for example, Gutiérrez, *When Jesus Came*, 193–206; Frank, *Settler to Citizen*, 176–81; Cuello, "Racialized Hierarchies." The so-called Indian problem facing would-be reformers in newly independent Andean republics is a governing theme of Larson, *Trials*. See also Díaz Polanco, *Indigenous Peoples*, 3–22, 65–82. For an unusual Mexican reference to raiders killing "whites," see M. Paino, "Los Comanches," Mexico City, Nov. 1, 1841, in *Siglo XIX*, March 9, 1842.

28. For "caribe," see, for example, editorial in *Gaceta del Gobierno de Tamaulipas,* Dec. 12, 1841. For Navajo ears, see Reeve, "Navaho Foreign Affairs," n. 30. For the display of Comanche heads in Durango, see *Ancla*, Aug. 31, 1840; and Juan N. Flores to Sr. Subprefecto del Oro, Hacienda de Ramos, Feb. 22, 1845, in *Registro*, March 13, 1845. For mercenary plans, see Smith, *Borderlander*, 86. Apache scalps are mentioned throughout Smith's book; see especially 161–67.

29. For transporting bodies, see Silver, *Savage Neighbors*, 75–79. Silver notes that his subjects in the late eighteenth century mid-Atlantic rarely fretted over the implications of their own wartime barbarization, in contrast to seventeenth-century New Englanders in the midst of King Philip's War (see 315). Lepore, *Name of War*, finds New Englanders supremely anxious over their barbaric deeds. The emerging racial discourses in eighteenth-century Pennsylvania help explain the difference. In the nineteenth century Cherokees who had relocated to the Arkansas Valley employed a discourse of barbarism and savagery in an effort to forge common cause with local non-Indians against tribes on the plains and prairies. They enjoyed some success, until "whites" started migrating in large numbers and denouncing all Indians as untrustworthy racial inferiors. It quickly became clear that race talk trumped appeals based solely on barbarism and savagery. See DuVal, "Debating Identity." For "pulled some," see Rafael de la Fuente to D. Ignacio Arizpe, Monclova, Dec. 30, 1840, in *Voto*, Jan. 8, 1841.

30. For "to save," see editorial, *Registro*, Oct. 5, 1845. For "do not cover," see Antonio Sánchez Muzquiz to governor of Coahuila, Arizpe, Jan. 24, 1842, in *Voto*, Jan. 29, 1842. For "these enormous," see editorial, *Voto*, Jan. 29, 1842. "We see that" is from *La Olivia* [Victoria, Tamaulipas], reprinted in *Diario*, July 4, 1841.

31. For Escudero, see "Comunicado de José Agustín de Escudero, 1839," in Orozco, *Antología*, 269. For "slaves to some," see letter from Chihuahua signed "a contributor," in Orozco, *Antología*, 247–48. For "what is a miserable handful," see Carlos Pacheco to the permanent deputation of the congress of Chihuahua, Chihuahua, Dec. 13, 1833, in Orozco, *Antología*, 227–29.

32. The circumstances surrounding these negotiations and the treaty itself may be found in an ac-

count written by the general in chief of the northern army, Jan. 10, 1843, reprinted in *Gaceta del Gobierno de Tamaulipas*, Feb. 16, 1843. For "the bones," see Anderson, *Conquest*, 203.

33. In May of 1838, five Comanches signed a peace treaty with authorities in Monclova. Unlike Pia Kusa, none were known to Mexicans as prominent leaders, and the agreement seems not to have been taken very seriously in Coahuila. Nonetheless, it is the case that the treaty of 1838 happened at the same time that older, senior Comanche paraibos like Muguara were finalizing peace negotiations with Texas near the end of Houston's first term. See Winfrey and Day, eds., *Texas Indian Papers* 1:50–52. It is possible that the five represented a faction unhappy with the prospect of peace with Texas.

34. For Pia Kusa on the Texans, see Calixto Bravo to Adrian Wool, Laredo, April 27, 1843, in *Diario*, May 29, 1843. For "toil" and "children," see Arista's letter in *Gaceta del Gobierno de Tamaulipas*, Feb. 16, 1843. For Santa Anna's qualified approval, see Bustamante, *Apuntes*, 116. Representatives of western Comanches echoed Pia Kusa's concerns in conversation with the Mexican general Francisco Conde in Santa Fe in August 1845. They told Conde they would side with the Mexicans against the Texans because Mexicans did not aspire to take Comanche lands or destroy the buffalo, as the foreigners had already tried to do. See Francisco G. Conde to Gov. of Durango, Santa Fe, Aug. 20, 1845, in *Registro*, Sept. 25, 1845. However heartfelt these sorts of arguments were among some Comanches, they obviously failed to convince most Plains Indians to stop campaigning against Mexico.

35. For Jesuits, see *Voto*, July 22, 1843. For "this work is slow," see Interim President [Valentín Canalizo] to the commander generals of Nuevo León, New Mexico, Coahuila, Chihuahua, Durango, Sonora, and to the chief of the Army of the North, Mexico City, Nov. 25, 1844, in *Diario*, Nov. 30, 1844.

36. For colonization plan, see law of Oct. 3, 1843, in Dublán and Lozano, eds., *Legislación Mexicana* 4:620–21. For select presidial cadets, see law of May 31, 1842, in Dublán and Lozano, eds., *Legislación Mexicana* 4:216–17. For a law of March 29, 1844, concerning presidio funding, see Dublán and Lozano, eds., *Legislación Mexicana* 4:750. A law of March 20, 1826, following colonial precedents, set out strict guidelines as to how many men and horses each presidio was to have. Data from presidios is taken from the annual reports of the ministers of war for the years 1841, 1844, 1845, and 1846, available as docs. nos. 517, 494, 501, and 499, respectively, in Lafragua. There were no reports for the years 1842 and 1843, when congress was not in session.

37. For Santa Anna's downfall, see Vázquez, "Texas Question," 334–40; Costeloe, *Central Republic*, 242–60.

38. For the evaluation of Herrera's government, see Vázquez, "Texas Question," 343.

39. For connections in the 1830s, see, for example, Barreiro, *Ojeado*, appendix, p. 10; piece from *El Mosquito*, translated in part in *Texas Republican*, Oct. 31, 1835.

40. For New Mexico, see Minge, "Frontier Problems," 141–50. For the general pattern of rebellions or foreign threats generating more alarm in Mexico than Indian troubles, see also Weber, *Mexican Frontier*, 110–11. For Tamaulipas, see *Gaceta del Gobierno del Tamaulipas*, Oct. 26, 1844.

41. For Durango, see Smith, "Comanche Bridge," 69. For Tamaulipas, see *Gaceta del Gobierno de Tamaulipas*, Feb. 15, 1845. For the Nuevo León request, see Juan N. de la Garza y Evia to Ministro de Guerra y Marina, Monterrey, July 25, 1845, in C18, E4, AGENL-MGM. For the reply, see Pedro García Conde to Juan N. de la Garza y Evia, Mexico, Aug. 4, 1845, C18, E5, AGENL-MGM.

42. For Mexican complaints, see, for example, the documents in Expediente H/610 "837"/2, Legajo 16-3-31, Archivo Histórico de la Secretaría de Relaciones Exteriores, Mexico City.

43. M. Paino, "Los Comanches," Mexico City, Nov. 1, 1841, in *Siglo XIX*, March 9, 1842.

44. *Diario*, Feb. 24, 1841, as described in Escobar Ohmstede and Rojas Rabiela, eds., *La presencia del indígena*, 168. For the coat of arms, see Dublán and Lozano, eds., *Legislación Mexicana* 4:198–99. For congressional appeal, see "Contestación del presidente de la cámara de diputados," July 4, 1844, doc. 1519, Lafragua.

45. For diplomacy between Mexico and the United States in these years, see Pletcher, *Diplomacy*, 113–311. For Apaches, see Griffen, *Utmost*, 91–114. For Utes, see Minge, "Mexican Independence Day"; Ned Blackhawk, *Violence over the Land*, 121–33. Interestingly, George Bent claimed that the dispute with the Utes began when Governor Armijo commissioned a party of American mercenaries to hunt Navajos. Bent claimed these mercenaries massacred a party of Utes when they failed to find Navajos. When angry Ute leaders came into Santa Fe to demand restitution from their supposed Mexican allies, the visit degenerated into a fight and provoked a period of outright hostilities. See Bent's letter in the *New Orleans Picayune*, Nov. 9, 1844.

46. For the treaty, see "Minutes of the Council at the Falls of the Brazos," Oct. 7, 1844, in Winfrey and Day, eds., *Texas Indian Papers* 2:103–14. For passports, see, for example, Thomas G. Western to L. H. Williams, Washington, May 12, 1845, in ibid., 2:237–38.

47. For "talk," see "report of a council with the Comanche Indians," Trading House Post No. 2, Nov. 23, 1845, in Winfrey and Day, eds., *Texas Indian Papers* 2:410–13. In July of 1843, Santa Anna and his ranchería visited the town of Rio Grande, preceded by two heralds. See Manuel Menchaca to el juez de paz de Río Grande, July 8, 1843, in C2, F6, E5, AGEC-FSXIX. Martha Rodríguez notes that the "Kiowa," whom the soldiers call "Col. Santa Anna," visited Guerrero in April of 1844. This was likely the Hois Pia Kusa (known to Mexicans as Santa Anna). See Rodríguez, *La guerra*, 194. For Pia Kusa's men, see Robert S. Neighbors to Thomas G. Western, San Antonio, Jan. 14, 1845, in Winfrey and Day, eds., *Texas Indian Papers* 2:166–68. For the sixty killed, see *Telegraph*, Nov. 13, 1844. The same article falsely reported that Mexican fighters had later killed Pia Kusa; wishful thinking, perhaps, given his ongoing resistance to dialogue with Houston. Intriguingly, Pia Kusa told Texan negotiators in 1845 that "the cause of the war with Mexico was the Spaniards breaking a treaty that was made some years since." See Report of a Council with the Comanche Indians, Trading House Post No. 2, Nov. 23, 1845, in Winfrey and Day, eds., *Texas Indian Papers* 2:410–13.

48. For dietary overlap, see Isenberg, *Destruction*, 26. For the padre's observation, see Martínez, *Esposición*. For the quote, see Report of P. M. Butler, Fort Gibson, Jan. 31, 1844, 11, Butler Papers. For the suggestion that escalating Comanche raids into Mexico were driven in part by shrinking buffalo herds on the southern plains, see Flores, "Bison Ecology," 480. See Hämäläinen, "First Phase," for the suggestion that such pressures were encouraging raiding as early as the 1820s. While the spike in campaigning in 1844 may well have reflected food shortages in la comanchería, it is unlikely that declining herds had much to do with raiding before then. The timing of increasing raiding into Mexico coincided with diplomatic and political developments that were, through the early 1840s at any rate, largely independent of shifts in bison populations. Moreover, the dramatic increase in raiding in the early 1840s, for example, came at a moment when Comanche and Kiowa hunters had just obtained safe access to dense bison populations on the high plains between the Arkansas and Platte rivers. The region had been a de facto game preserve

until 1840 because of the bitter conflict between Cheyennes and Arapahos against Kiowas and Comanches. As Flores remarks, the Kiowa Calendar for 1841 includes the rare notation "many bison." See Flores, "Bison Ecology," 483. As Flores demonstrates and Hämäläinen affirms, increased hunting to supply the growing hide market, together with habitat destruction and other factors, was clearly weakening bison populations on the southern plains well before 1850. But there is little evidence that this steady, early decline translated into serious meat (as opposed to trade hide) shortages for southern plains families any earlier than 1842 or 1843, after long-distance raiding had already become an annual pattern.

49. For the events in northern Tamaulipas, see Francisco Lofero to judges of sections 6, 12, 15, 16, 17, 18–23, Matamoros, Oct. 12, 1844, in MAP 51:8–9; Jorge L. de Lara to Francisco Lofero, Matamoros, Oct. 13, 1844, MAP 51:11–13; and editorial and list of dead in *Gaceta del Gobierno de Tamaulipas*, Oct. 26, 1844.

50. For Chihuahua, see Smith, "Comanche Bridge," 67–68. For "men of reason," see José Francisco Terán to Marcelino Castañeda, Labor del Rodeo, Oct. 15, 1845, in *Registro*, Oct. 19, 1845.

51. For "more advanced objectives," see *Gaceta del Gobierno de Tamaulipas*, Oct. 26, 1844. For "the barbarians have not been so formidable," see *Registro*, Dec. 11, 1845. For the U.S.–Indian connection reported elsewhere in Mexico, see, for example, the article from *La Prudencia*, the official paper of Guanajuato, reprinted in *Registro Oficial*, Oct. 9, 1845; Bustamante, *El gabinete* 2:13–14.

52. For a magisterial overview of U.S. political history in this period, see Wilentz, *Rise*, 547–76; quote is from 568. The significance of Texas to gathering tensions in U.S. politics is the subject of Joel H. Silbey, *Storm over Texas*.

53. For Adams quote, see Stephanson, *Manifest Destiny*, 43. For Polk's early life and career, see Sellers, *Polk: Jacksonian*.

54. For a wonderful meditation on the significance of the U.S.–Mexican War, see Kornblith, "Rethinking the Coming"; Clay quote is from 83.

55. For the minister's report, see Secretaría de Guerra y Marina, "Memoria del Secretario de Estado y del Despacho de Guerra y Marina Leída en la Cámara de Senadores el día 10 y en el de Diputados el día 11 de Marzo de 1845," doc. 501, Lafragua. For García Conde's biography, see Cubas, *Diccionario* 3:130–31.

56. For Herrera, see Costeloe, *Central Republic*, 261–75. *Siglo XIX* quote is from Nov. 30, 1845, in Henderson, *Glorious Defeat*, vii. For the prominent general [Francisco García Conde], see Minge, "Frontier Problems," 294–95. For a lucid exploration of Mexican attitudes about the prospect of war in the mid-1840s, see Brack, *Mexico Views*.

57. *Tropic* quoted in *Boston Daily Atlas*, Sept. 11, 1845. *New Orleans Commercial Bulletin* quotes taken from *Registro*, Aug. 17, 1845.

58. For the *Registro*'s response, see *Registro*, Aug. 17, 1845. For last quote, see *Registro*, Sept. 25, 1845.

59. For the steps taken by the central government, see *Diario* for Oct. 26, Oct. 28, Nov. 5, and Nov. 7, 1845, as described in Escobar Ohmstede and Rojas Rabiela, eds., *La presencia del indígena*, 287–90.

60. For the formation of Herrera's council on frontier defenses, see *Registro*, Aug. 12, 1847.

61. For military reforms, see DePalo, *Mexican National Army*, 87–91. For Herrera's vulnerability

over Texas policy, see Vázquez, "Texas Question," 338. For an excellent discussion of the broader problems facing Herrera's administration, see Santoni, *Mexicans at Arms*, 9–99.

62. The material in this paragraph come from Pletcher, *Diplomacy*, 139–394; quotations are from 354. There is a large literature on the diplomacy and immediate origins of the war. Pletcher's book is still the best and most balanced treatment available. See also Vázquez, "Texas Question," 343–44.

63. For newspaper opinion, see Santoni, *Mexicans at Arms*, 40–99; Márquez, *La Guerra del 47*, 17. For quotes on newspaper reports on raiding and the political utility of such reports for Herrera's enemies, see Bustamante, *El nuevo Bernal Díaz*, 57–58.

64. For the coup, see Costeloe, *Central Republic*, 263–82. For northern complaints, see, for example, *Registro*, Jan. 1, 1846. Most northerners denounced the coup. Arista refused to support it, and Paredes consequently removed him from command of the Army of the North (Smith, *War with Mexico* 1:149). Angel Trías, governor of Chihuahua, was likewise removed from his position for refusing Paredes his support (Timmons, "El Paso," 15). For Paredes's order about presidios, see Castillo Lanzas to governor of Coahuila, Mexico City, Jan. 17, 1846, C1, F5, E2, 3f, AGEC-FSXIX.

65. For the quote from Zacatecas, see J. Llaguno to Governor of Zacatecas, Hacienda de Santa Cruz, Oct. 24, 1845, in *Registro*, Nov. 2, 1845. For Durango quote, see *Registro*, Dec. 11, 1845; quote from Coahuila taken from *Republicano*, Nov. 1, 1845.

66. Martínez, *Esposición*, n.p., reproduced in Weber, ed., *Northern Mexico on the Eve*.

CHAPTER 8. HOW TO MAKE A DESERT SMILE

1. Kearney and Knopp, *Boom and Bust*, 31–32; Graf, "Economic History," 2, 9, 435.

2. For the circulars, see Manuel Rodríguez, Aviso, Matamoros, July 4, 1844, MAP 50:190. For the consul's quote, see Richard Belt to John C. Calhoun, Matamoros, July 5, 1844, *Despatches* 2:369, no. 4.

3. For Quincy Adams and for newspapers, see Rives, *United States and Mexico* 1:362 n. 1. For the boomlet of attention in 1829, see Astolfi, *Foundations*, 125–41. As soon as word got out about the war in Texas there were public meetings in support of the rebels in New Orleans, Mobile, Montgomery, Boston, New York, and likely many other cities. The earliest debates in Congress over recognition were taken up partly in response to petitions from several different states. See Rather, "Recognition," 171, 213. For Austin's tour, see Cantrell, *Stephen F. Austin*, 332–47.

4. "Address of the Honorable S. F. Austin, Delivered at Louisville, Kentucky, March 7, 1836," in Holley and Hooker, *Texas*; quote is from 254. The address was quickly printed in New York. See Rather, "Recognition," 181. For Austin's trip, see Cantrell, *Stephen F. Austin*, 329–47.

5. Newell, *History of the Revolution*, 14–15; Pease, *Geographical*, 252–54; Wharton, *Texas*, 3. Written under the pen name Curtius, most of Wharton's Texas pamphlets were sent directly to Washington, D.C. See Lee, "Austin's Louisville Address," 430. Some also went south: Mexico's official newspaper reprinted pamphlet #5 in the midst of the Texas revolt. See *Diario*, March 7, 1836.

6. Field, *Three Years*, 6; Kennedy, *Texas*, 297, 338. For other renditions of the "herdsmen" theme, see Muir, ed., *Texas in 1837*, 110–11; Gregg, *Commerce*, 135.

7. For "more and more," see Field, *Three Years*, 6. For "had given security," see Newell, *History of the*

Revolution, 20. For "under the smiles," see Wharton, *Texas*, 5. For a later rendition of the Texas Creation Myth, complete with quotes from Austin, see Owen, *Justice*, 92–96.

8. In defining the larger story that these individual works contributed to as a Creation Myth, I have been influenced by the discussion of "mythogenesis" in Slotkin, *Regeneration*, 3–24. Following Carl Jung, James Frazier, Claude Lévi-Strauss, Joseph Campbell, and others, Slotkin defines myth making as "simultaneously a psychological and a social activity. The myth is articulated by individual artists, and has its effect on the mind of each individual participant, but its function is to reconcile and unite these individualities to a collective identity." "[A] tale that, through the course of several generations—or even several retellings within one generation—acquires this kind of evocative power has evolved into myth." "The myth–artist, priest, or fabulist uses the artifacts of myth to evoke the 'sense' of the myth and its complex of affirmations in the audience. He may use these artifacts in two ways—either deliberately, in an effort to make propaganda for his cause, or unconsciously, under the compelling association of perceived event and inherited mythology." Slotkin, *Regeneration*, 8.

9. Memucan Hunt to John Forsyth, Washington, Aug. 4, 1837, in Manning, *Diplomatic Correspondence, Inter-America* 12:129–40.

10. For envoy, see Henry M. Morfit to John Forsyth, Velasco, Aug. 22, 1836, in ibid., 11:104–05. For Austin, see Rathbun, "Representation," 197–98.

11. For "the lands of Texas," see Wharton, *Texas*, 5. For grievances and for "lost her right," see Henry M. Morfit to John Forsyth, Velasco, Aug. 22, 1836, in Manning, *Diplomatic Correspondence, Inter-America* 12:104–05.

12. Newell, *History of the Revolution*, 15.

13. Speech of Sen. Robert Walker, Dem., Mississippi, April 26, 1836, *Globe*, 24th Cong., 1st sess., 401. Speech of Rep. E. W. Ripley; Jacksonian, Louisiana, May 7, 1836, *Globe*, 24th Cong., 1st sess., appendix, 369–70.

14. Speech of Rep. Adam Huntsman, Jacksonian, Tennessee, March 2, 1837, *Globe*, 24th Cong., 2nd sess., appendix, 226–28. For the debate over annexation, see Silbey, *Storm over Texas*, 52–91.

15. John C. Calhoun to Wilson Shannon, Washington, Sept. 10, 1844, in Manning, ed., *Diplomatic Correspondence: Inter-America* 8:155–61. Speech of Rep. William Preston, Whig, South Carolina, April 24, 1838, *Globe*, 25th Cong., 2nd sess., 557.

16. On the decision to open Texas to foreign colonists, see also Hatcher, *Opening of Texas*; Kelly and Hatcher, "Tadeo Ortiz"; Weber, *Mexican Frontier*, 158–78.

17. For "to beat back," see speech of Rep. Adam Huntsman, Jacksonian, Tennessee, March 2, 1837, *Globe*, 24th Cong., 2nd sess., appendix, 226–28. For woodland settlement, see Meinig, *Imperial Texas*, 29. For Terán's quote, see Manuel Mier y Terán to Guadalupe Victoria, San Antonio, March 28, 1828, in Jackson, *Texas by Terán*, 33–34. For Indian campaigns, see Smith, *From Dominance*, 120–53. For suspicions of Anglo colonists trading with Indian raiders, see Antonio López de Santa Anna to Ministro de Guerra y Marina, Guerrero, Feb. 16, 1836, in Castañeda, ed., *Mexican Side*, 64–70. For the critique of Kennedy, see *Diario*, Feb. 29, 1840.

18. Channing, *Letter*, 69. I thank Andrea Boardman for bringing this to my attention. Speech of Archibald Linn, Whig, New York, June 4, 1842, *Globe*, 27th Cong., 2nd sess., 513–18. The indispensable text for antislavery opponents of Texan annexation was Lundy, *War in Texas*. See also id., *Origin*. For the role of slavery in arguments against annexation, see Rathbun, "Representa-

tion," 202–07, 229–34; and, more broadly, Silbey, *Storm over Texas.* For northern fears about the influence of slaveholders in national politics, see Richards, *Slave Power.* For "to reclaim," see speech of Rep. James Belser; Dem., Alabama, May 21, 1844, *Globe*, 28th Cong., 1st sess., appendix, 521.

19. Sometimes consular reports about Indian raids in Mexico were leaked to the press. See, for example, *Globe*, Aug. 17, 1836, which ran a letter from D. W. Smith in Matamoros to the Secretary of State (without attribution). For reprints of the Picayune piece, see *Greenville Mountaineer*, Nov. 22, 1844; *New York Herald*, Nov. 19, 1844; *Mississippi Free Trader and Natchez Gazette*, Nov. 20, 1844; *North American and Daily Advertiser*, Nov. 19, 1844; *Boston Daily Atlas*, Nov. 20, 1844; and *Cleveland Herald*, Nov. 23, 1844. Kennedy's work was often cited as authoritative in the U.S. Congress. See, for example, the speeches of Sen. Levi Woodbury, Dem. NH, in *Globe*, 28th Cong., 1st sess., appendix, 760–75; Rep. Robert Owen, Dem. Indiana, in ibid., 696–701.

20. Memorial of the Assembly of Missouri, Senate Doc. 225, 25th Cong., 3rd sess., 1–4. W. H. Emory wrote something similar in 1844 concerning Texas: "A silver mine has been worked near the mouth of the San Saba River, but the jealousy of the Camanches has prevented any recent attempts to carry on permanent operations." See Emory's report, Senate Doc. 341, 28th Cong., 1st sess., 59–62.

21. Connelley, "Journal," 254; Gregg, *Commerce*, 200; Emory's Report, Senate Doc. 341, 28th Cong., 1st sess., 59–62; Kennedy, *Texas*, 331. See also *Scioto Gazette*, April 24, 1845; *Niles*, May 31, 1845, 193.

22. *Boston Courier*, June 27, 1839. For Emory, see his report from April 26, 1844, in Sen. Doc. 341, 28th Cong., 1st sess., 59–62; Gregg, *Commerce*, 203; Kendall, *Narrative* 2:61–62; *Boston Daily Atlas*, June 14, 1843.

23. Kennedy, *Texas*, 330; Gregg, *Commerce*, 203; *Niles*, April 4, 1840, 66.

24. *Pennsylvania Inquirer and Daily Courier*, Feb. 25, 1841. For "unlike those," see Report of the Secretary of War, Nov. 29, 1845, in Sen. Doc. 1, 29th Cong., 1st sess., 194. For quotes on captives, in order, see Richard Belt to John C. Calhoun, Matamoros, July 5, 1844, *Despatches* 2:369, no. 4; Smith to Secretary of State, Matamoros, May 26, 1840, *Despatches* 2:166, no. 20; *Niles*, Nov. 23, 1844, 178; letter of Mirabeau Lamar reprinted in Foote, *Texas* 1:293–99.

25. For "at pleasure," see Speech of Rep. Adam Huntsman, Jacksonian, TN, March 2, 1837, in *Globe*, 24th Cong., 2nd sess., appendix, 226–28. For the commissioner, see Report of P. M. Butler, April 29, 1843, 8, Butler Papers. For the governor's daughter, see Farnham, *Travels*, 59. Gregg also recounts this story: *Commerce*, 249. For the five thousand figure, see Thompson, *Recollections*, 172.

26. For Wise's speech, see *Telegraph*, May 11, 1845. It is very difficult to determine numbers of Mexican captives among the Comanche, especially since captives taken as early as the late eighteenth century could still have been living on the southern plains in the 1830s and 1840s. Still, the data collected for this study indicate that Comanches and Kiowas captured 626 Mexicans between 1831 and 1846 and that all but 268 of these escaped or were rescued before the raiders recrossed the Rio Grande. As is the case with numbers of Comanches and Mexicans killed in this period, 268 captives is an underestimate. Still, increasing the figure by a factor of three (any more than that seems unlikely to me) puts the total captured well below Thompson's estimate. See appendix for more about counting captives. For an exception to the tendency to downplay or under-

estimate Mexican deaths, see Thomas Falconer, who, writing about Chihuahua, informed his readers that Indians there had killed upward of ten thousand Mexicans between 1832 and 1841. Falconer and Hodge, *Letters and Notes,* 100. For Roman analogy, see *Telegraph,* Jan. 27, 1841.

27. For Wilkinson, see Kavanagh, *Comanche Political History,* 163. American efforts to secure Comanche goodwill in the months before the U.S.–Mexican War are discussed in the following chapter. For the commissioner's estimates, see his reports for 1836: House Ex. Doc. 2, 24th Cong., 2nd sess., 402–03; 1838: Senate Doc. 65, 25th Cong., 2nd sess., 17–19; 1840: Senate Doc. 379, 26th Cong., 1st sess., 13; 1841: Senate Doc. 1, 27th Cong., 2nd sess., 268–69; 1842: Senate Doc. 1, 27th Cong., 3rd sess., 389–90; 1843: Senate Doc. 1, 28th Cong., 1st sess., 277–79; 1844: Senate Doc. 305, 28th Cong., 2nd sess., 321–23. The report for 1845 duplicated the population estimates from 1844. Farnham suggested there were ten thousand Comanche warriors, which would obviously put the total population at several times that number: Farnham, *Travels,* 15–16. For a forty thousand figure, see Muir, ed., *Texas in 1837,* 110. For Butler's estimate, see "Report of P. M. Butler, April 29, 1843," 7, Pierce M. Butler Papers. Butler later revised his figure down to seven thousand. See "Report of P. M. Butler, Fort Gibson, Jan. 31, 1844," Butler Papers.

28. *Barre Patriot,* Aug. 15, 1845; Farnham, *Travels,* 15–17, 59; Gilliam, *Travels,* 238, 295–305.

29. Moore, *Map and Description,* 32. Moore was the editor of the popular and durable Houston newspaper *The Telegraph and Texas Register.* Gregg, *Commerce,* 204–05; Thompson, *Recollections,* 172. On Oct. 19, 1843, the *Pittsfield Sun* reported on another lopsided victory that Shawnees supposedly enjoyed over Comanches. While the editors could not vouch for the accuracy of the story, they were "not surprised to hear that a small number of Shawnees can whip any number of Comanches. The Shawnees and the Delawares are the greatest warriors on this continent."

30. *Arkansas State Gazette,* Jan. 2, 1838; Smith, *Col. Crockett's Exploits,* 173. For similar notions about Comanches fearing Americans, see article on Texas and Mexico in *Herald* (March 10, 1836).

31. For "and sixty," see Bonnell, *Topographical Description,* 133; Field, *Matt Field,* 269; Kennedy, *Texas,* 332–33; Moore, *Map and Description,* 31–33. For "recede as fast," see Fisher, *Sketches.* Gregg, *Commerce,* 436. "Report of G. W. Bonnell, Commissioner of Indian Affairs, third Congress, first session, Houston, Nov. 3, 1838," in Senate Rep. Com. 171, 30th Cong., 1st sess., 38–50.

32. Smith to Secretary of State, Matamoros, July 1, 1836, *Despatches* 1:585–96; same to same, Nov. 11, 1837, ibid., 1:744; same to same, Matamoros, May 12, 1841, ibid., 2:90; same to same, Aug. 30, 1841, ibid., 2:127; Richard Belt to John C. Calhoun, Matamoros, July 5, 1844, ibid., 2:369. Matamoros was notoriously unhealthy. In less than two months in 1829, for instance, more than five hundred residents (of a population of sixty-seven hundred) died of "malignant and putrid fevers." See Graf, "Economic History," 32.

33. Pattie, *Personal Narrative,* 40–45; Pike, *Prose Sketches,* 137–51. David Weber suggests that Pike's informant may have been the mountain man Alexander Le Grand. See Weber, ed., *Albert Pike,* 149 n. 3.

34. For the New Mexican–Comanche relationship, see Manuel Armijo to the departmental assembly, letter book copy, Santa Fe, July 5, 1845, MANM 38:740–45. A number of scholars have worked to assemble the recorded instances of Navajo–New Mexican conflict. The most comprehensive is Correll, *Through White Men's Eyes.* See also Jenkins and Ward, *Navajo Activi-*

ties; Reeve, "Navaho Foreign Affairs"; Brugge, *Navajos in the Catholic*. None cite evidence of a Navajo raid upon Taos in the mid-1820s.

35. For Kirker's tally, see Smith, *Borderlander*, 170. For newspapers, see, for example, *Pensacola Gazette*, Feb. 22, 1844. For admirers, see Kendall, *Narrative* 2:57–58; Gregg, *Commerce*, 228; Kennedy, *Texas*, 726; Field, *Matt Field*, 190–93. See also Smith, *Borderlander*, 121–22. Benton quoted in Smith, *Borderlander*, 199. Despite his Scotch-Irish heritage, Kirker was seen as eminently American in his deeds and prowess. In 1847, for example, *St. Louis Weekly Reveille* ran a piece on Kirker: "If ever a man was un-irished, as far as appearance goes, it is Don Santiago—otherwise Master Jim!" Quoted in Smith, *Borderlander*, 193. Matt Field simply referred to "Kurker" as an American. *Matt Field*, 190.

36. *Picayune*, Nov. 17, 1844. For medals, see reprint of *Picayune* piece in the *Greenville Mountaineer*, Nov. 22, 1844. *Richmond Whig* quote was transcribed by Brian J. MacPhee for the website *The Mexican American War and the Media, 1845–1848*, http://www.history.vt.edu/MxAmWar/Newspapers/RW/RW1845aJanJune.htm, accessed December 12, 2005. For the interaction that the paper refers to, see Thomas G. Western to Benjamin Sloat, Washington [Tex.], May 12, 1845, Winfrey and Day, eds., *Texas Indian Papers* 2:238–40. Ironically, this was a rare instance when Texan authorities clearly provided ammunition to Comanches in advance of a raid into Mexico. Western ordered Sloat to "inspect your powder before you start and report its condition that part of it which may be condemned by yourself and by Williams may be distributed among the friendly tribes, but only in quantities purely for hunting purposes."

37. Falconer and Hodge, *Letters and Notes*, 100; Speech of Rep. Adam Huntsman, Jacksonian, Tennessee, March 2, 1837, *Globe*, 24th Cong., 2nd sess., appendix, 226–28; Gilliam, *Travels*, 238.

38. My thanks to Matthew Restall for helping me see this particular irony. Quotes are from Gregg, *Commerce*, 203–04; Edward, *History of Texas*, 106; Pike, *Prose Sketches*, 131.

39. The most complete exponent of the historiography on race and expansion is Horsman, *Race*; quotations are from 190 and 213. See also an early articulation of similar ideas in Merk, *Manifest Destiny*, 237–47; and Ferrand, "Cultural Dissonance," 98–138; Hietala, *Manifest Design*, 132–72; id., "Splendid Juggernaut"; Belohlavek, "Race, Progress."

40. Horsman, *Race*, 208–12; Speech of Sen. Robert Walker, Dem., Mississippi, May 9, 1836, *Globe*, 24th Cong., 1st sess., 461.

41. *Boston Daily Atlas*, June 12, 1845.

42. Thompson, *Recollections*, 172, 239.

43. James Buchanan to John Slidell, Washington, Nov. 10, 1845, Senate Doc. 52, 30th Cong., 1st sess., 71–80. Unless otherwise noted, I have based the following sketch of the coming of the war on Pletcher, *Diplomacy*, 139–394, and Sellers, *Polk: Continentalist*, 213–34, 398–444.

44. In 1837 the U.S. consul in Matamoros remarked upon the exodus of Mexicans from the region: "These hostile incursions of the Indians, repeated almost every full moon, have compelled the greater part of the frontier inhabitants to abandon their stock farms and remove on the south side of the Rio Grande." See D. W. Smith to Secretary of State, Matamoros, Aug. 4, 1837, in MAP 1:700. In 1842 the prefect of the northern district of Tamaulipas ordered all Mexicans living north of the river to cross over and congregate in the town of Reynosa because of approaching Indian raiders. See T. Juan José Champa Guerra to alcalde de Camargo, Reynosa, March 28, 1842, Archivo histórico de Camargo, AGEC. Texan newspapers often reported on the difficulty of send-

ing traders through the Nueces–Rio Grande region because of Comanche raiders. Following fights with the Indians at Corpus Christi and San Antonio, one editor had this to say: "If we intend to keep our paper claim to any portion of this delightful region, the Government certainly ought to assist its citizens in keeping possession of one or two points at least, so that we may have the color of reason to justify our claims." See *Telegraph*, July 24, 1844. For a scathing critique of the Texan claim, see speech by Thomas Hart Benton, Dem., Missouri, in *Globe*, 28th Cong., 1st sess., 475.

45. For Polk's speech, see Senate Doc. 337, 29th Cong., 1st sess., 1–6.

46. Pletcher, *Diplomacy*, 352–94; Schroeder, *Mr. Polk's War*, 3–19.

CHAPTER 9. A TROPHY OF A NEW KIND IN WAR

1. Initially there was talk of Taylor pushing south to San Luis Potosí. See, for example, W. L. Marcy to Zachary Taylor, Washington, Sept. 2, 1846, in House Ex. Doc. 60, 29th Cong., 1st sess., 339–40.

2. For Polk's prediction of a short war, see Smith, *War with Mexico* 1:347. Smith's book is a polemical defense of U.S. motives and actions in the war. Still, despite its early publication date and its biased interpretation, no book has yet surpassed *The War with Mexico* in its exhaustive use of sources, comprehensiveness, and attention to detail. It is a measure of the war's place in collective memory that the reigning masterpiece is nearly a century old. Unless otherwise noted, the following sketch of the northern campaign is drawn from the correspondence in House Ex. Doc. 60, 30th Cong., 1st sess; Smith, *War with Mexico* 1:156–400; DePalo, *Mexican National Army*, 92–116; and the lucid summary in Winders, *Crisis*, 91–118. See also Eisenhower, *So Far*, 71–250.

3. Tyler, "Gringo Views." For Bent, see Charles Bent to Manuel Álvarez, Taos, Jan. 7, 1843, in Reeve, "Bent Papers," 165. The most widely read account of the Santa Fe expedition came from the *Picayune*'s Kendall, *Narrative*. For analysis of the competing discourses surrounding the expedition, see Reséndez, *Changing*, 197–236.

4. For Armijo, see Daniel Tyler, "Armijo's Moment." For the citizens, see Moorhead, "Report." "A dwarf" comes from Rafael Chacón, cited in Tyler, "Gringo Views." Mexicans later told a U.S. officer that the Navajos had taken advantage of the fact that the men had organized in Apache Canyon to raid the northern settlements and that besides horses they had carried off fifteen or sixteen of the "prettiest women." See Calvin, ed., *Emory Reports*, 84. Another American wrote that the Navajos had captured some twenty families while New Mexico's men were occupied in the canyon. See Drumm, ed., *Down the Santa Fe*, 110. For the relief of the U.S. Army that they did not have to fight in the canyon, see, for example, Robinson, *Journal*, 25–26.

5. For Cortes, see *North American*, June 26, 1847. For Xenophon, see Eisenhower, *So Far*, 250. See also Johannsen, *To the Halls*, 132. For Kirker, see Smith, *Borderlander*, 176–78. U.S. officials represented the Mexican force at Sacramento to be 3,000–4,000, while officials in Chihuahua later put the number at only 1,565. Part of the discrepancy concerns the unknown number of rancheros who participated in the battle. For the high figure, see Smith, *War with Mexico* 1:306 and 519 n. 12. For the low figure, see "La Diputación de Chihuahua a la Nación," March 25, 1847, in Ponce de León, ed., *Reseñas*, 350–57.

6. For deserted settlements, see Balbontín, *Invasión americana*, 21–22.

7. For previous attempts, see Foreman, "Texas Comanche Treaty." For Potsanaquahip and Stanley,

see *North American and Daily Advertiser*, Feb. 6, 1844. Polk quote is in Kavanagh, *Comanche Political History*, 294.

8. For Taylor's worries, see Taylor to the Adjutant General of the Army, Corpus Christi, Nov. 19, 1845, in House Ex. Doc. 60, 30th Cong., 1st sess., 114–15. For the composition of the party and help from traders, see Foreman, "Texas Comanche Treaty," 318–19. For Coacoochee, see Foreman, ed., "Journal," 75.

9. For apprehensions surrounding the treaty, see P. M. Butler and M. G. Lewis to W. Medill, Washington, Aug. 8, 1846, in Senate Rep. Com. 171, 30th Cong., 1st sess. For "make many promises" and for treaty terms, see Kavanagh, *Comanche Political History*, 295–97.

10. For the Senate's changes, see Kavanagh, *Comanche Political History*, 300–03. For the White House meeting, see Quaife, ed., *Diary* 2:3–5; *South Carolina Temperance Advocate and Register of Agriculture and General Literature*, Aug. 13, 1846.

11. Kendall, *Dispatches*, 77–79.

12. Chamberlain was a liar and a braggart, but, paradoxically, he was also one of the most honest chroniclers of the war because he embraced its small, crude moments of meanness, brutality, and atrocity instead of ignoring or minimizing them. We cannot know whether Chamberlain actually witnessed this event or whether it happened as he claimed (his editor, William Goetzmann, was able to discount at least one element of the story, the presence of Texan ranger Bill McCulloch). There is also some controversy as to whether the Indian leader was indeed Pia Kusa/Santa Anna. Chamberlain refers to him a Comanche named "Santana," and Goetzmann interprets this to be the renowned Kiowa leader Satanta. Satanta did not come into prominence until the 1860s and would have been in his early to mid twenties in 1846, likely too young to be at the head of several hundred warriors or to be described as an "old wolfish greasy cuss." Pia Kusa seems a much more likely candidate. See Chamberlain, *My Confession*, 71, 73, and nn. 151, 152.

13. For the Mexican boy, see W. L. Marcy to Taylor, Washington, July 27, 1846, in House Ex. Doc. 60, 30th Cong., 1st sess., 395.

14. Quaife, ed., *Diary* 2:5. See also Smith, *Magnificent Missourian*, 214–15.

15. For the instructions regarding divisions, see W. L. Marcy to Taylor, Washington, June 3, 1846, in House Ex. Doc. 60, 30th Cong., 1st sess., 153–55. For fears of Mexicans depriving the U.S. Army of provisions, see Taylor to the Adjutant General of the Army, Matamoros, July 2, 1846, in House Ex. Doc. 60, 30th Cong., 1st sess., 329–32. These were realistic anxieties. In August and September 1846, for example, military authorities in Nuevo León ordered residents of Cerralvo and Marín to abandon their homes and carry their belongings with them, to hide their animals and deprive the enemy of all resources, and to attack them when possible. See González Quiroga, "Nuevo León ante," 431. For orders to encourage separatism, see W. L. Marcy to Taylor, Washington, June 9, 1846, in Senate Doc. 19, 29th Cong., 2nd sess., 9. Months before the fighting began, Taylor's informants told him that Tamaulipas, Nuevo León, and Coahuila would likely secede as soon as the war started. See Taylor to the Adjutant General of the Army, Corpus Christi, Sept. 6, 1845, in House Ex. Doc. 60, 30th Cong., 1st sess., 105–06.

16. For proclamation, see "Translation of the Spanish proclamation given to Generals Taylor and Kearny," in Senate Doc. 19, 29th Cong., 2nd sess., 17. For quote on "delicate movements" and "policy and force," see W. L. Marcy to Taylor, Washington, June 3, 1846, in House Ex. Doc. 60, 30th Cong., 1st sess., 153–55.

17. For "great fear," see Doubleday, *My Life*, 4. For Mier, see Dana, *Monterrey Is Ours*, 115. For Rey-

nosa, Smith, *War with Mexico* 1:204, 479. For Guerrero, Ridout, "Anti-National," 136. For China, Chamberlain, *My Confession*, 259; *Matamoros Reveille*, June 27, 1846.

18. Kendall's reports for the *Picayune* were reprinted in papers across the United States. The quote about Comanches is from the *Liberator*, Sept. 4, 1846. For the general's concerns, see Taylor to the Adjutant General of the Army, Matamoros, Aug. 3, 1846, in House Ex. Doc. 60, 30th Cong., 1st sess., 402. For his communication with Wool, see John E. Wool to Taylor, San Antonio, Sept. 15, 1847, in House Ex. Doc. 60, 30th Cong., 1st sess., 424–26.

19. *Niles*, Oct. 24, 1846, 119; Baylies, *Narrative*, 65.

20. For the consul, see Manuel Álvarez to James Buchanan, Santa Fe, Sept. 4, 1846, in *Despatches from U.S. Consuls at Santa Fe*. For Kearny's proclamation, see Calvin, ed., *Emory Reports*, 50.

21. Quote is from S. W. Kearny to R. Jones, Santa Fe, Sept. 16, 1846, in House Ex. Doc. 60, 30th Cong., 1st sess., 174–75. For observations of deserted homes and tales of raiding, etc., see, for example, Abert, *Report*, 49, 62, 66, 125, 135–36; Calvin, ed., *Emory Reports*, 80, 82–84, 88. Two groups of Utes visited Kearny. See Hughes, *Doniphan's Expedition*, 127, 76. Jicarilla representatives made it clear they had their own expectations of Kearny. They were unable to farm, they explained, and game had become scarce in and around the mountains where they lived: "You must, therefore, if you wish us to be peaceable, speak a good word to the Comanches, the Yutas, the Navajos, and the Arapahoes, our enemies, that they will allow us to kill buffalo on the Great Plains." See Hughes, *Doniphan's Expedition*, 128–29.

22. Hughes, *Doniphan's Expedition*, 187–90.

23. For Chihuahua, see ibid., 326.

24. For Kearny and Mangas Coloradas, see Cutts, *Conquest of California*, 184–85; Calvin, ed., *Emory Reports*, 100. For the Mormon battalion, see Smith, *Borderlander*, 170; Officer, *Hispanic Arizona*, 202. Final quote is from Bancroft, *History of Arizona*, 478.

25. After the capture of Monterrey U.S. forces seeking reliable supplies made friendly arrangements with certain hacendados in Coahuila, particularly the Sánchez Navarros, and one by-product of these arrangements was that U.S. soldiers patrolled a handful of properties to guard against Indians. See Harris, *Mexican Family Empire*, 194, 286–90. I take the details of the fight at Hacienda del Pozo from Reid's report. See John W. Reid to John E. Wool, Camp at Encantada, May 21, 1847, in House Ex. Doc. 60, 30th Cong., 1st sess., 1144–45. Some writers claimed that the Indians were Lipanes, others Comanches. Reid called them Lipanes, and Frederick Wislizenus did the same after speaking with the Mexicans at the hacienda, so apparently the Mexicans thought they were Lipanes as well. The fact that none seemed to have firearms might also argue that they were not Comanches, since Comanches were better armed by this time. But the Hois *paraibo* Potsanaquahip later complained about soldiers from Missouri attacking Comanches while they raided Mexicans near Parras, so Comanches were at least associated with the event. As we will see, Lipanes and Comanches had effected a rapprochement by the summer of 1846, so this may have been a joint operation. The circumspect Josiah Gregg saw the dead Indians himself and was unsure whether they were Comanches or Lipanes. See Wislizenus, *Memoir*, 71; Robert S. Neighbors to W. Medill, Torrey's Trading House, Sept. 14, 1847, Senate Doc. 734, 30th Cong., 1st sess; Fulton and Horgan, eds., *Diary* 2:123–25.

26. Wislizenus, *Memoir*, 71. For Morton, see Horsman, *Race*, 125–35.

27. Hughes, *Doniphan's Expedition*, 363–65. For other soldiers' accounts, see Cutts, *Conquest of California*, 87–88; Robinson, *Journal*, 85.

28. Fulton and Horgan, eds., *Diary*, 123–25.

29. For "the Mexicans on a sudden," see *North American and United States Gazette*, July 22, 1847. For "it affords," see letter in *Mississippi Free Trader and Natchez Gazette*, June 19, 1847. Other newspapers that reported on Reid's sortie include *Vermont Patriot* (July 1, 1847), *Raleigh Register and North Carolina Gazette* (July 24, 1847), and *Boston Daily Atlas* (June 22, 1847).

30. For Benton's anxiety over the war, see Smith, *Magnificent Missourian*, 210–15.

31. Benton's speech can be found in Cutts, *Conquest of California*, 89–98.

32. The Lipán–Comanche rapprochement started gradually. Some of its stages may be glimpsed in "Minutes of the Council at the Falls of the Brazos," Oct. 7, 1844, in Winfrey and Day, eds., *Texas Indian Papers* 2:103–14; L. H. Williams to Thomas G. Western, Trading House Post 2, Aug. 20, 1845, ibid., 2:326–27; "Report of a Council with the Comanche Indians, Trading House Post No. 2, Nov. 23, 1845, ibid., 2:410–13; and, for news that the Southern Lipanes had finally moved onto the Colorado, see *Telegraph*, Oct. 15, 1845. A smaller group of Southern Lipanes under Chief Flacco had moved back south of the Rio Grande a few years before, in 1842, after Flacco's son was murdered by Texans. See Smith, *From Dominance*, 188. My thanks to Todd for sharing his research on this point with me before his book's publication. The evidence on Northern Lipanes is thinner than that regarding their southern kinsmen. These Indians had lived at peace in northern Coahuila and did not come into conflict with the Mexicans of that department until 1845, apparently over a misunderstanding. See J. Antonio Tijerina to governor of Coahuila, in *Republicano*, March 15, 1845; "Expediente que contiene queja del juez de paz de Santa Rosa, relativo a la forma con que el general D. José Juan Sánchez ha reclamado la licencia concebida al Reo Diego cupian, para pasar por los indios Lipanes," May 28, 1845, C2, F9, E6, 11f, AGEC-FSXIX. For indication that the Northern Lipanes moved onto the southern plains, see Robert S. Neighbors to W. Medill, Austin, Jan. 6, 1847, House Ex. Doc. 100, 29th Cong., 2nd sess.

33. For Mescalero population figures, see note 6, chapter 5, above. In August 1846 Butler and Lewis reported that five hundred Mescaleros and thirty-five hundred "Esreequetees" (a Mescalero ethonym) had "formed an alliance and acquisition to" a Comanche division they called the "Nocoonees," referring to the Nokonis, a division that begins to appear in the documents only around this time. The authors added that the Mescaleros "have heretofore been at war with the Camanches, but recently become their allies, and are now at war with Mexico." See P. M. Butler and M. G. Lewis to W. Medill, Washington, D.C., Aug. 8, 1846, in Senate Rep. Com. 171, 30th Cong., 1st sess. For similar observations, see Robert S. Neighbors to W. Medill, Austin, Jan. 6, 1847, House Ex. Doc. 100, 29th Cong., 2nd sess. For Mescalero–Mexican cooperation against Comanches, see, for example, Mauricio Ugarte, to comandante general of Chihuahua, El Norte, May 18, 1841, in *Diario*, June 14, 1841. For Mescalero–Comanche conflict in the Bolsón, see *Diario*, Oct. 19, 1841. For Ramón Castro, see Smith, *From Dominance*, 188. For Arista's information, see Santiago Rodríguez to Ministro de Relaciones Exteriores, Gobierno y Policia, Saltillo, Sept. 13, 1845, in *Republicano*, Sept. 20, 1845.

34. For the drought and the decline in the herd, see Flores, "Bison Ecology," 482. See also Hämäläinen, "First Phase." For the loss of habitat along the Arkansas (and for the shrinking herd), see West, *Way West*, 13–83. For the consumption of horses and mules, see Robert S. Neighbors to W. Medill, Torrey's Trading House, June 22, 1847, in Senate Doc. 734, 30th Cong., 1st sess. For the antelope drive, see Mooney, *Calendar*, 287–89.

35. For the absence of Indians in Nuevo León's archives during the war, see Vizcaya Canales, *Incur-*

siones, 21. For mention of raids in the late summer of 1846, see Dana, *Monterrey Is Ours,* 103; Giddings, *Sketches,* 68; and especially Kendall, *Dispatches,* 77–79.

36. For letters, see *Registro,* June 11, 1846. For data on raiding in 1846–47, see appendix, below. For the trade fair, see La Vere, *Contrary Neighbors,* 118.

37. The records from Chihuahua are much less complete at this time, so casualty figures there are unknown. Quote is from José de la Bárcena, Durango, Oct. 17, 1846, in *Registro,* Oct. 22, 1846. For the fight on the twentieth, see editorial in ibid. For final battle, see Gamiz, *Historia,* 185.

CHAPTER 10. POLK'S BLESSING

1. Quote from Chihuahua's governor taken from *Niles,* Aug. 29, 1846, 401. For Durango quote, see *Registro,* October 22, 1846. On Nov. 11, 1847, *Registro* reported that hundreds of raiding Comanches wore uniforms similar to those of the U.S. Army.

2. For biographical information, see the introduction by Crawford Buell to Ruxton, *Adventures.*

3. Ibid., 75–87, 102. See also Webb, *Adventures,* 231–42.

4. Ruxton, *Adventures,* 110. For Armijo's sojourn in Chihuahua and visit to Mexico City, see Tyler, "Armijo's Moment," 307–16. For Armijo's service in Durango, see *Registro,* Oct. 22, 1846; *Registro, alcance,* Oct. 22, 1846; *Registro,* Oct. 29, 1846.

5. Ruxton, *Adventures,* 113–17.

6. Ibid., 117–29.

7. For the emerging peace, see Griffen, *Utmost,* 117–18. For the massacre, see Smith, *Borderlander,* 161–67. An American passing through the far north in 1846 heard that the residents of Galeana pursued a terrified pregnant Apache woman who sought refuge in the town church. The attackers reportedly tore the unborn child from her womb and gave it mock baptism. See Abert, *Report,* 121. See also the graphic secondhand description of the massacre in Ruxton, *Adventures,* 151–54.

8. The quotes are in Smith, *Borderlander,* 168. For the effect on Apache policies, see Sweeney, *Mangas Coloradas,* 135–58.

9. For Bent to Benton, see Correll, *Through White Men's Eyes,* 214, 216. Ruxton, *Adventures,* 161, 168, 185–209.

10. For continued violence, see Ruxton, *Adventures,* 214–30; McNitt, *Navajo Wars,* 122–31. For the *St. Louis Republican* letter, see reprint in *Niles,* Nov. 6, 1847, 155. For another, similar lament, see *Niles,* June 19, 1847, 252.

11. For disarmament, see Hughes, *Doniphan's Expedition,* 272; Robinson, *Journal,* 68. For New Mexico, see Hughes, *Doniphan's Expedition,* 399. For Camargo, see Ridout, "Anti-National," 147. For Pelayo, see Wislizenus, *Memoir,* 67. For Chihuahua quote, see La Diputación Permanente de la Honorable Legislatura de Chihuahua a sus comitentes, Villa de Allende, April 6, 1848, in Ponce de León, ed., *Reseñas,* 344–46. For Sonora, see Kessell, *Friars,* 305.

12. For Canales's role in fighting Texans between 1842 and 1846, see Ridout, "Anti-National," 107–16. For his service in the first two battles of the war, see Smith, *War with Mexico* 1:165–66, 171–76. For the call for guerrillas, see Antonio Canales, circular, Camargo, May 20, 1846, in *Registro,* June 21, 1846. For the arson near Camargo, see Ridout, "Anti-National," 154. For the murders in Monterrey, see Foos, *Short, Offhand, Killing Affair,* 121.

13. For "shameful atrocities," see Zachary Taylor to the Adjutant General of the Army, Matamoros, Oct. 6, 1846, in House Ex. Doc. 60, 30th Cong., 1st sess., 430. For the group executions, see Ridout, "Anti-National," 153–56. For a graphic description of the guerrilla attack on the teamsters, see Giddings, *Sketches*, 303–05. For execution of Mexican men traveling the roads, see Robinson, *Journal*, 89. For destroyed settlements in Nuevo León, see González Quiroga, "Nuevo León ante," 454. For Chamberlain's claim, see Foos, *Short, Offhand, Killing Affair*, 121. For Taylor's complaints, see Zachary Taylor to the Adjutant General of the Army, Monterrey, June 16, 1847, in House Ex. Doc. 60, 30th Cong., 1st sess., 1178. For Grant, see Anderson and Cayton, *Dominion*, 283. For "American deserters," see Baylies, *Narrative*, 57. Concluding quote is taken from Foos, *Short, Offhand, Killing Affair*, 120. One antiwar minister, A. A. Livermore, claimed American soldiers had committed such atrocities that northern Mexicans were fleeing to Comanches for protection. See Slotkin, *Fatal Environment*, 190.

14. For "Comanches of the north," see Hill, *Fighter*, 60. For "illustrious Comanches," see *Diario*, Aug. 20, 1847, as described in Escobar Ohmstede and Rojas Rabiela, eds., *La presencia del indígena*, 313. For the Mexican general's complaint, see Ignacio de Mora y Villamil to Zachary Taylor, San Luis Potosí, May 10, 1847, in House Ex. Doc. 60, 30th Cong., 1st sess., 1139–41. Much of the war literature from both sides of the border maintains that Mexican guerrillas destroyed villages just like Americans did (see, for example, González Quiroga, "Nuevo León ante," 456) but presents little hard evidence for these assertions. There is, however, good evidence of thefts and casual abuse by guerrillas in Tamaulipas. See Herrera Pérez, "Tamaulipas ante."

15. For "barbarous yankees," see Robinson, *Journal*, 76. For Cerralvo and the dozen inhabitants, see Hill, *Fighter*, 59–60. For "an over portion," see Hughes, *Doniphan's Expedition*, 362. For "from Saltillo," see Foos, *Short, Offhand, Killing Affair*, 119.

16. For Gregg's references to abandoned or depopulated ranches and villages, see Fulton and Horgan, eds., *Diary* 2:98, 99, 108, 109, 112, 119, 139, 140, 142, 143, 148, 149. See also Wislizenus, *Memoir*, 63, 66, 71, 76–78.

17. For mention of refugees being attacked by Comanches, see Hill, *Fighter*, 59. For newspaper accounts of raids, see, for example, *Boston Daily Atlas*, May 22, 1847. Quote is from letter written in Buena Vista on May 15, 1840, reprinted in the *North American*, June 11, 1847.

18. While U.S. forces focused less on protecting Mexicans from Indians in 1847 than they had in the summer of 1846, there is scattered evidence of continued intervention. Reid's fight at hacienda del Pozo is the most obvious example. Another came in November of 1847, when a detachment of soldiers was sent in pursuit of two hundred Indians raiding the properties of the powerful Sánchez Navarros, who had close ties to General Wool. See Eduardo Gonzáles to D. Jacobo Sánchez Navarro, Saltillo, Nov. 21, 1847, doc. 896, Sánchez Navarro Collection. For reports of extensive depredations in Coahuila, see José María de la Fuerte to Quirino Benavente, San Lorenzo, June 8, 1847, doc. 1635, Sánchez Navarro collection. For the corporation, see Miguel Lobo to the ayuntamiento de San Buenaventura, Monclova, Oct. 23, 1847, in C1, F9, E4, 2f, AGEC-FSXIX.

19. See petition of Luisa Huerta, Tomasa Toysoque, Magdalena Butierras, Ramona González, Antonia Siqueiros, Mariana Romero, Petra Ocoboa, María Telles, and Francisca Bayesteros, Tucson Presidio, July 6, 1848, in McCarty, ed., *Frontier Documentary*, 119–21.

20. For the draft order, see Juan N. Almonte to Juan N. de la Garza y Evia, Mexico City, August 28,

1846, C18, E10, AGENL-MGM. For failures to supply requested men, see González Quiroga, "Nuevo León ocupado," 341–42; id., "Nuevo León ante," 429. An official in Chihuahua blamed his inability to field men against U.S. soldiers on the fact that Indians had stolen all of the horses: "This land is plagued with savages." See *Registro*, Jan. 10, 1847. For the arms exemption, see José Ignacio Gutiérrez, circular, Mexico, April 9, 1847, in C18, AGENL-MGM. For Gregg, see Fulton and Horgan, eds., *Diary* 2:141. There was intense debate in Mexico about whether or not to formally support a system of guerrilla war. See Ramsey, ed., *Other Side*, 439–42, for the argument that sustained guerrilla activity would have driven the U.S. Army out of Mexico.

21. For Santa Anna's efforts at raising men, see DePalo, *Mexican National Army*, 108–09. The government's order called for 1,600 men from Zacatecas, 600 from Durango, and 560 from Chihuahua. See Calvillo Unna and Monroy Castillo, "Entre regionalismo," 423.

22. For the refusal of these states to send men, see Ramsey, ed., *Other Side*, 85–86; Smith, *War with Mexico* 1:376. For the 500 men, see Isidro Reyes to governor of Durango, San Miguel del Mesquital, Nov. 1, 1846, *Registro*, Nov. 8, 1846.

23. For minister's quote, see José María Lafragua, circular to the governors of the states, Mexico, Nov. 27, 1846, doc. 857, Pinart Prints. Durango quote is from *Registro*, April 8, 1847.

24. Bustamante, *El nuevo Bernal Díaz*, 226. For Chihuahua's response to the minister of war, see La Diputación de Chihuahua a la Nación, March 25, 1847, in Ponce de León, ed., *Reseñas*, 350–57; and Jáuregui, "Chihuahua en la tormenta," 145–47. The minister of internal and external relations was enough impressed with the defense that he ordered it reprinted across the nation. For the final quote, see La Diputación Permanente de la Honorable Legislatura de Chihuahua a sus comitentes, Villa de Allende, April 6, 1848, in Ponce de León, ed., *Reseñas*, 344–46.

25. George Wilkins Kendall thought that U.S. war planners should have taken even more notice of northern Mexico's Indian problems; that it was senseless to divert men and materials to conquering Chihuahua since "that whole section is now in the hands of the Comanches, as it were." See Kendall, *Dispatches*, 115.

26. For the decision to open up another front, see Smith, *War with Mexico* 1:347–51. After discussing the reasons for opening Scott's campaign, Smith offered a final, revealing rationale for why Polk was right not to have followed the advice of Taylor, Calhoun, and others to simply hold on to the conquered northern states and assume a defensive posture: "Simply to seize and hold, with no legal title, provinces which Mexico had not been able to protect against the Indians would have seemed to place the United States in the class of mere pilferers." See Smith, *War with Mexico* 1:348.

27. This sketch is taken from Winders, *Crisis*, 120–30.

28. For Santa Anna, see Smith, *War with Mexico* 2:181. For a discussion of the debate over continuing the war with guerrillas, see Guardino, *Peasants*, 169–71.

29. For the governor's prowar position and the final vote to negotiate, see Calvillo Unna and Monroy Castillo, "Entre regionalismo," 445–47; Smith, *War with Mexico* 2:236. For the "war to the knife" quote, see Hill, *Fighter*, 145. Details from the Comanche campaign are taken from letter from San Luis Potosí, Nov. 16, 1847, in *Monitor Republicano*, Nov. 26, 1847; José María Ortega to Governor of San Luis Potosí, Nov. 18, 1847, San Luis Potosí, in *Monitor Republicano*; Francisco Avalos to Governor of Zacatecas, San Juan del Salado, Nov. 20, 1847, in *Registro*, Nov. 28, 1847; Mariano Hermosillo to Sr. Secretario del Supremo Gobierno del Estado de San Luis Potosí,

Rancho de San Juan del Salado, Nov. 20, 1847, in *Registro*, Dec. 2, 1847. The delegates were informed of Comanche raids into Durango and Zacatecas, but it is not known whether they knew about the raids into San Luis Potosí at the time of the meeting. For an excellent description of Mexico's prospects for continuing the war, as they stood at the time of the governors' conference, see Rao Bárcena, *Recuerdos de la invasión* 3:244–58. For insurgency more broadly, see Levinson, *Wars within War.*

30. For Polk's desire for California, see Sellers, *Polk: Continentalist*, 213. On the centrality of the Pacific, see Graebner, *Empire*. For the interest of opponents of the war in acquiring San Francisco through "honorable means," see, for example, speech of Rep. George Ashmun, July 27, 1846, *Globe*, 29th Cong., 1st sess., appendix, 809–12; and Schroeder, *Mr. Polk's War*, 6–7. For Mexican willingness to part with Upper California, see Senate Doc. 52, 30th Cong., 1st sess., 342–44.

31. For the generally underappreciated effect of Anglophobia in U.S. policy during the era, see Haynes, "Anglophobia." For population figures, see Weber, *Mexican Frontier*, 195, 206. For initial Mexican refusal to part with New Mexico, see J. R. Pacheco to the Mexican treaty commissioners, Mexico, Sept. 5, 1847, in Senate Doc. 52, 30th Cong., 1st sess., 342–44. In 1844, Special Agent Duff Green reported that the Rio Grande (which with typical hyperbole he likened to the Mississippi) was navigable by steamboat up to the Rio Conchos and that from there a railroad could be constructed to move people and goods to the Gulf of California. See Duff Green to John C. Calhoun, Velasco, Sept. 27, 1844, in Manning, *Diplomatic Correspondence, Inter-America* 12:368–69. See also article 6 of the Treaty of Guadalupe Hidalgo.

32. For the treaty votes, see Schroeder, *Mr. Polk's War*, 142–59; Merk, *Manifest Destiny*, 183–91; Griswold del Castillo, *Treaty*, 43–55.

33. For Jackson's attempted purchase, see John Forsyth to Anthony Butler, Washington, Aug. 6, 1835, in Manning, ed., *Diplomatic Correspondence: Inter-America* 8:33–34. For "would justify," see Jackson's speech to Congress on Feb. 7, 1837, in Senate Doc. 160, 24th Cong., 2nd sess., 1–2.

34. Quote is from *New York Morning News*, in Slotkin, *Fatal Environment*, 183–84. For a fascinating discussion of the notion of improvement in multiple Anglo contexts, see Weaver, *Great Land Rush*, especially 81–87.

35. Speech of Rep. Timothy Pillsbury, Dem., Texas, June 16, 1846, *Globe*, 29th Cong., 1st sess., 980–82; speech of Sen. Sam Houston, Dem., Texas, Feb. 19, 1847, *Globe*, 29th Cong., 2nd sess., 456.

36. For "essential to us," see speech of Sen. Edward Hannegan, Dem., Indiana, Feb. 26, 1847, in *Globe*, 29th Cong., 2nd sess., 516. For "believe it practicable," see speech of Sen. Robert Hunter, Whig, Virginia, Feb. 7, 1848, 30th Cong., 1st sess., 310.

37. For "savages and an impassible," see Rep. Truman Smith, Whig, Connecticut, March 1, 1848, *Globe*, 30th Cong., 1st sess., 416–17. For "well-known fact," see S. W. Downs, *Speech*.

38. For the desire on the part of Polk, Secretary of the Treasury Robert J. Walker, and Secretary of State James Buchanan to make the Sierra Madre rather than the Rio Grande the new boundary, see Merk, *Manifest Destiny*, 186–87. Others championed the wildly unrealistic notion of annexing all of Mexico. For the "all Mexico" movement, see Fuller, *Movement*; Schroeder, *Mr. Polk's War*, 120–41. Quotes are from speech of John C. Calhoun, Dem., South Carolina, Feb. 9, 1847, *Globe*, 29th Cong., 2nd sess., 357; Calhoun, March 17, 1848, *Globe*, 30th Cong., 1st sess., 496–97. Calhoun's dilemma is discussed at length in Lander, *Reluctant Imperialists*.

39. For congressional opposition during the war, see Schroeder, *Mr. Polk's War*, 3–88, 160–67.

40. Speech of Sen. John C. Calhoun, Feb. 9, 1847, *Globe*, 29th Cong., 2nd sess., 357; Speech of Sen. T. J. Rusk, Dem., Texas, Feb. 17, 1848, *Globe*, 30th Cong., 1st sess., 375.

41. Polk's address is in Senate Doc. 1, 30th Cong., 1st sess. See pages 7–11 for Mexico material; quote is from 11.

42. For precedents, see article 5 of the Treaty of Friendship, Limits, and Navigation between the United States and Spain, Oct. 27, 1795, in Miller, ed., *Treaties* 2:318–45, and article 33 of the Treaty of Amity, Commerce, and Navigation between the United States and Mexico, Dec. 17, 1831, in ibid., 3:599–640. For northern insistence on article 11, see Nicholas P. Trist to James Buchanan, Mexico, Jan. 25, 1848, in Senate Doc. 52, 30th Cong., 1st sess., 280–94. Mexican negotiators thanked Trist particularly: "In his well-known love of mankind he has viewed our cause as the cause of all cultured nations, that of civilization versus barbarism." See Bernardo Couto Miguel Atristain and Luis G. Cuevas, "Exposición dirigida al supremo gobierno por los comisionados que firmaron el tratado de paz con los Estados-Unidos," Mexico, March 1, 1848, in *Registro*, May 25, and May 28, 1848. Even with the article, Coahuila and Tamaulipas declared in early May of 1848 that they would not recognize the treaty even if it were ratified—an empty threat but clearly a heartfelt complaint from two states that lost much territory through the cession. See Griswold del Castillo, *Treaty*, 52.

43. For "encumbered by," see speech of Sam Houston, Feb. 28, 1848, Senate Doc. 52, 30th Cong., 1st sess., 5. For the votes on article 11, see Senate Doc. 52, 30th Cong., 1st sess., 12–13. For the secretary's apology about firearms, see James Buchanan to the Minister of Foreign Affairs in Mexico, Washington, March 18, 1848, in Manning, ed., *Diplomatic Correspondence: Inter-America* 8:221–28.

EPILOGUE. ARTICLE 11

1. Quote is from *Correo Nacional*, in Ridout, "Anti-National," 124.

2. For the two hundred thousand pesos and their distribution among the northern states, see decree of Oct. 16, 1846, in Dublán and Lozano, eds., *Legislación Mexicana* 5:487–88. For military colonies, see decree of July 19, 1846, ibid., 5:422–26. For Seminoles, Creeks, and Kickapoos, see Buckingham Smith to Daniel Webster, Mexico City, Feb. 16, 1851; and William Rich to Daniel Webster, Mexico City, Sept. 11, 1852, both in *U.S. Despatches*; Mulroy, *Freedom*; Miller, *Coacoochee's Bones*. Representatives from these peoples began negotiating with northern Mexican authorities in 1843 if not before. See Vizcaya Canales, *Tierra*, 164–65. For an excellent review of Mexico's efforts to fortify its frontier, see Rippy, *U.S. and Mexico*, 76–80. The "Sierra Gorda rebellion" refers to a series of Indian peasant or mestizo uprisings in the Sierra Gorda Mountains of San Luis Potosí, Guanajuato, and Querétaro. See Reina, "Sierra Gorda." For bounties, see Smith, "Comanches' Foreign War."

3. For compacts between states, see, for example, Agapito García, Circular, Monterrey, April 28, 1852, #102, Wallet 16, Arredondo Collection; Israel Cavazos Garza, "Las incursiones," 353–55. Northerners also tried to organize offensive campaigns, with mixed results. See Harris, *Sánchez Navarros*, 84–86.

4. For drought, see W. H. Emory, *Report*, 85. For cholera, see Orozco, *Primeras fases*, 61–62. For cholera and food shortages in Durango, see Buckingham Smith to Daniel Webster, Mexico City,

Sept. 14, 1851, in *U.S. Despatches*. For newspaper articles, see Escobar Ohmstede and Rojas Rabiela, eds., *La presencia del indígena*, cuadro 2. For Durango casualties, see Vallebueno, "Apaches y Comanches," 681. For quotes, see Emory, *Report*, 86, 51. For a vivid account of Comanche activities below the river in the early 1850s, see Smith, "Comanche Sun." For a remarkable essay on the meanings of such borderlands violence, see Brooks, "Served Well."

5. Bushnell and Macaulay, *Emergence*, 80–81. For a sympathetic exploration of the intellectual and ideological roots of monarchism in this period, see Pani, *Para mexicanizar*.

6. For the coup against Arista, see Bushnell and Macaulay, *Emergence*, 81. For Arista's death, see Fowler, *Mexico*, 293. For the Chihuahuan charge, see Froebel, *Seven Years'*, 347.

7. Buchanan's letter is in Senate Doc. 60, 30th Cong., 1st sess., 70.

8. For this period of American political history, see Wilentz, *Rise*, 594–632.

9. Ibid., 633–42. For slavery in the New Mexican borderlands after the U.S.–Mexican War, see Brooks, *Captives*, 292–68. For the standoff over New Mexico, see Lamar, *Far Southwest*, 70–82; Texan quote is from 75.

10. Wilentz, *Rise*, 642–45.

11. For Mexican complaints, see, for example, Luis de la Rosa to Daniel Webster, Washington, Sept. 4, 1850, in Manning, ed., *Diplomatic Correspondence: Inter-America* 9:367–68; same to same, Dec. 5, 1850, in ibid., 375–76; same to same, March 17, 1851, in ibid., 387–88; same to same, Nov. 13, 1851, in ibid., 426–32; Manuel Robles to Buckingham Smith, Mexico City, July 11, 1851, in Bosch García, ed., *Documentos*, 167–69. On continued raiding below the Rio Grande after 1848, see the detailed report made by the Mexican government, based on interviews as well as archival and periodical sources from northern states, *Informe de la comisión pesquisidora de la frontera del norte al ejecutivo de la unión, en cumplimiento del artículo 3 de la ley de 30 de septiembre de 1872*, 15–108. For the U.S. Army and frontier defense generally in these years, see Bender, *March of Empire*. For the postwar problem of raiding in international perspective, see Hatfield, *Chasing Shadows*. For a discussion of U.S. failures, see Rippy, *U.S. and Mexico*, 68–84.

12. For New Mexico, see Abel, ed., *Official Correspondence*; Loyola, *American Occupation*, 74–99. For Laredo and the "melancholy disasters on the Rio Grande," see R. P. Letcher to John M. Clayton, Mexico City, April 8, 1850, in *U.S. Despatches*. On the predicament of Mexican frontier officials wishing to pursue Indians across the new border, see, for example, Juan Manuel Maldonado to Antonio María Jáuregui, Colonias de Guerrero, July 3, 1850, C7, F9, E117, 2f, Fondo Colonias Militares de Oriente, AGEC; same to same, March 28, 1851, C12, F6, E66, 3f, Colonias Militares.

13. For Letcher's first warning on lawsuits, see R. P. Letcher to John M. Clayton, Mexico City, April 8, 1850, *U.S. Despatches*. For congressmen and the secretary of war, see Loyola, *American Occupation*, 96. Enterprising Americans lawyers encouraged Mexican claims against the United States. One warned his would-be Mexican clients that the United States would seek release from article 11: "*Take my advice as you value the interests of your country never do it. It is worth more than all the gold removed of California to you.*" See Robert P. Letcher to Daniel Webster, Mexico City, Dec. 14, 1851, *U.S. Despatches*.

14. Daniel Webster to Robert P. Letcher, Washington, Aug. 19, 1851, in Manning, ed., *Diplomatic Correspondence: Inter-America* 9:89–92. For "G-d only knows," see Letcher to Webster, Mexico City, Jan. 24, 1852, in Manning, ed., *Diplomatic Correspondence: Inter-America* 9:460–62. For twelve million dollars, see Letcher to Webster, Mexico City, March 18, 1852, *U.S. Despatches*.

For "that miserable," see Letcher to Webster, Mexico City, Feb. 15, 1852, in Manning, ed., *Diplomatic Correspondence: Inter-America* 9:465–66. For twenty million dollars, see Alfred Conkling to William L. Marcy, Mexico City, June 20, 1853, in Manning, ed., *Diplomatic Correspondence: Inter-America* 9:591–93. For Letcher's hope for a dictator, see Letcher to Webster, Mexico City, March 18, 1852, in *U.S. Despatches*. The U.S.–Mexican controversy over Indian raiding following the war is explored in close detail in Rippy, "Indians"; id., *U.S. and Mexico*, 68–84, 126–47. Arguments over depredations continued into the 1870s. In 1868, the Mexican government appealed to a joint U.S.–Mexican commission, asking restitution for Indian raids totaling thirty-one million dollars. The commission allowed none of the claims, insisting that the Gadsden Treaty had released the United States from all liability. See Harris, *Sánchez Navarros*, 87–94.

15. The context of the Gadsden Purchase is described in detail in Faulk, *Too Far North*.

16. For Santa Anna's downfall, see Bazant, "From Independence."

17. The change is best reflected in data assembled by a Mexican claims commission in the 1870s. See *La comisión pesquisidora*, appendix. See also testimony of Manuel Menchaca before that commission, in Velasco Avila, ed., *En manos*, 119–24. Menchaca testified that Comanches and Lipanes alike changed their raiding patterns after 1848, crossing the river in smallish parties of fifty to seventy and subdividing into even smaller groups while raiding.

18. For the nine-hundred-man campaign and the one hundred killed, see Smith, "Comanches' Foreign War," 31, 37.

19. For the assumption that the epidemic came from forty-niners, possibly via Osages, and for Kiowa memories, see Mooney, *Calendar*, 173, 288. For the assertion that the Hois Pia Kusa brought the sickness to his own people after a raid into Mexico, see Richardson, "Santa Anna." For the epidemic in northern Mexico, see Orozco, *Antología*, 23–24. For the insight about epidemics and campaigns, see Rivaya Martínez, "Captivity and Adoption," 142, 146–47. In estimate of Comanches killed vs. Mexicans captured, I exclude captives who either escaped or were redeemed before crossing the river. See figure A.1 and appendix, below. For a similar conclusion, based on sources from a longer time period, see the excellent discussion in Rivaya Martínez, "Captivity and Adoption," 136–47.

20. For ranger attacks, see, for example, Anderson, *Conquest*, 302–17. For an enlightening comparison between the efforts of rangers and mounties on the plains to control indigenous peoples, see Graybill, *Policing the Great Plains*, 23–63. For declining bison, see Isenberg, *Destruction*, 93–122. For growing demand for cattle, see Brooks, *Captives*, 336.

21. For the 1850s on the southern plains, see Anderson, *Conquest*, 226–317.

22. The sketch in this and the following paragraph relies on Bushnell and Macaulay, *Emergence*, 193–202; Bazant, "From Independence," 31–48. For U.S. sympathy for Juárez, see Anderson and Cayton, *Dominion*, 305–06.

23. For Yaquis, see Hu-DeHart, *Yaqui Resistance*; and the new comparative work, Haake, *State, Removal*. For reinvigorated efforts against Apaches, see Alonso, *Thread*, 119–56. For the northeast, see Rodríguez, *La guerra*, 215–67. Joseph Ridout has observed that Mexico City reached accommodation with regional elites in the northeast "largely on the basis of ethnic solidarity in campaigns to exterminate the northeastern Indians." See Ridout, "Anti-National," 174. Miguel Centeno notes that Chile, Argentina, and Mexico all undertook climactic frontier wars against indigenous peoples in the 1870s–1880s, precisely at the moment when centralized authority began consolidating power: "These campaigns not only served to unite white opinion, but also

often provided new resources and territories that could be distributed so as to consolidate consensus." Centeno, *Blood and Debt*, 65.

24. For the coming of the war, see Wilentz, *Rise*, 668–788.

25. Brooks, *Captives*, 331–35.

26. For the final campaigns against raiders in northern Mexico, see Vizcaya Canales, *Tierra*, 384–401. The link in Chihuahua between frontier violence, honor, rights to land, and (eventually) the Mexican Revolution is a key theme in work by Ana Alonso and Daniel Nugent. See Alonso, *Thread*; Nugent, "Are We Not?"; id., "Center at the Periphery"; id., "Two, Three, Many Barbarisms." For a haunting transnational exploration of how Apaches frustrated the visions of Mexicans and Americans alike in the Sonora–Arizona borderlands and of the tenuous nature of development there even after Geronimo's surrender, see Truett, *Fugitive Landscapes*.

27. For the southern plains, see Brooks, *Captives*, 341–60; Kavanagh, *Comanche Political History*, 404–77; Anderson, *Conquest*, 345–61. For Potsanaquahip's later life, see Schilz and Schilz, *Buffalo Hump*, 35–47. For horses and bison, see Hämäläinen, "Rise and Fall," 843–45. For slaughters of bison, see Isenberg, *Destruction*, 130–43. For the enduring Comanche community, see Foster, *Being Comanche*.

28. For the early reservation era, see Hagan, *U.S.–Comanche Relations*, 139–65. The stories of the ill raiders appeared in *El Monitor Republicano*, as cited in Ramos et al., eds., *Indio en la prensa* 1:332, 340. To my knowledge the last notice of Comanches in the Mexican press came in August of 1881, when it was reported that a Comanche–Lipán ranchería had been attacked by Mexican troops in Coahuila (presumably inside the Bolsón de Mapimí). See Escobar Ohmstede and Rojas Rabiela, eds., *La presencia del indígena* 1:537. A few small groups of Indians maintained a fugitive existence in northern Mexico even after Geronimo and his people had been shipped to Florida in boxcars. A shadowy Indian figure called the Apache Kid executed small-scale raids in the northwest in 1894, for example, and nineteen independent Lipanes were apprehended in northeastern Chihuahua in 1903. See Chávez, "Retrato," 418 n. 1; Vizcaya Canales, *Tierra*, 399.

APPENDIX

1. Antonio Elosúa to Mariano Cosío, San Antonio, Aug. 24, 1831, in McLean, ed., *Papers* 6:356–61.

2. Mariano Cosío to Antonio Elosúa, Goliad, Aug. 17, 1831, in ibid.

3. Isidro Vizcaya Canales, *Tierra*, 37.

4. Ibid.

5. José J. Calvo, circular, Chihuahua, Oct. 16, 1831, MANM 13:483.

6. Smith, *From Dominance*, 143. These casualties were inflicted on a Comanche ranchería by a mixed force of presidial soldiers from San Antonio and allied Shawnees.

7. Ibid., 144. The attacking force consisted of Mexicans, with allied Lipán and Tonkawa auxiliaries.

8. Ibid. The attacking Comanche party killed a party of Mexicans from Goliad out gathering wood. I render this as two deaths.

9. Ibid.

10. Kavanagh, *Comanche Political History*, 233.

11. Ibid.

12. Ibid., 207.

13. Vizcaya Canales, *Tierra*, 43.

14. Ibid.

15. Griffen, *Utmost*, appendix.

16. Smith, *From Dominance*, 144. The attacking party consisted of Mexican troops and Lipanes.

17. Velasco Avila, "Amenaza Comanche," 267.

18. Kavanagh, *Comanche Political History*, 207. A later document suggests that thirteen of these Comanche captives soon escaped. See Alejandro Ramírez to Governor of Chihuahua, El Paso, July 23, 1834, in Orozco, *Antología*, 237.

19. Griffen, *Utmost*, appendix.

20. Ibid.

21. Ibid.

22. Ibid.

23. Ibid.

24. Ibid.

25. Ibid.

26. Ibid.

27. Ibid.

28. Ibid.

29. Ibid.

30. Ibid.

31. Ibid.

32. Ibid.

33. Ibid.

34. Ibid.

35. Ibid.

36. Ibid.

37. Ibid.

38. Ibid.

39. Ibid.

40. Ibid.

41. Ibid.

42. Ibid.

43. Ibid.

44. Ibid.

45. Ibid.

46. Ibid.

47. Ibid.

48. Ibid.

49. Ibid.

50. Ibid.

51. Ibid.

52. Ibid.

53. Ibid.

54. Ibid.
55. Ibid.
56. Ibid.
57. Ibid.
58. Ibid.
59. Ibid.
60. Ibid.
61. Ibid.
62. Ibid.
63. Ibid.
64. Ibid.
65. Ibid.
66. Ibid.
67. Ibid.
68. Ibid.
69. Ibid.
70. Ibid.
71. Ibid.
72. Ibid.
73. Ibid.
74. Ibid.
75. Velasco Avila, "Amenaza Comanche," 285.
76. Griffen, *Utmost*, appendix.
77. Hinojosa, *Borderlands Town*, 50–52. Number comes from a town tally for 1836, minus four deaths cited in note 79, below.
78. Griffen, *Utmost*, appendix.
79. Francisco V. Fernández in Matamoros, to Juan L. Molano in Matamoros, March 9, 1836, in MAP 26:75.
80. Griffen, *Utmost*, appendix.
81. Velasco Avila, "Amenaza Comanche," 294.
82. Juan L. Molano to Governor of Tamaulipas, Matamoros, April 21, 1836, in MAP 26:176.
83. Vizcaya Canales, *Tierra*, 53. I have added a captive taken for the one redeemed.
84. Ibid., 53–54. I have added a captive taken for the one redeemed.
85. Griffen, *Utmost*, appendix.
86. Vizcaya Canales, *Tierra*, 53.
87. Griffen, *Utmost*, appendix.
88. Ibid.
89. Ibid.
90. Ibid.
91. Ibid.
92. Ibid.
93. Vizcaya Canales, *Tierra*, 56.
94. Griffen, *Utmost*, appendix.
95. Ibid.

96. Ibid.

97. *Mercurio, alcance,* Aug. 5, 1836.

98. Griffen, *Utmost,* appendix.

99. Joaquín Velarde to Gobernador y Comandante General, Chihuahua, Aug. 7, 1836, in *Diario,* Sept. 9, 1836.

100. Griffen, *Utmost,* appendix.

101. *Diario,* Sept. 16, 1836.

102. José A. Heredia to M. de Guerra y Marina, Durango, Aug. 28, 1836, in *Diario,* Sept. 16, 1836.

103. *Mercurio,* Sept. 9, 1836.

104. Velasco Avila, "Amenaza Comanche," 294.

105. Vigness, "Indian Raids." Vizcaya Canales, *Tierra,* 59, notes that sixteen people were killed or captured in this incursion, but these casualties do not appear in my data since they are undifferentiated.

106. Isidro Vizcaya Canales, *Incursiones,* 12–13.

107. Vigness, "Indian Raids."

108. Vigness, "Lower Rio Grande," 71.

109. *Diario,* April 29, 1837.

110. *Diario,* Aug. 10, 1837; D. W. Smith to U.S. sec of state, Matamoros, Aug. 4, 1837, in *Despatches* 1:700. The dead include one Mexican officer and seven (or more) Cherokee Indian allies.

111. Velasco Avila, "Amenaza Comanche," 298.

112. Ibid.

113. General en gefe del Ejército del Norte to Vicente Filisola, Matamoros, Dec. 11, 1837, in *Diario,* Jan. 3, 1838.

114. Velasco Avila, "Amenaza Comanche," 305.

115. Rodríguez, *La guerra,* 109.

116. Velasco Avila, "Amenaza Comanche," 305.

117. Babcock, "Trans-National Trade," 108.

118. Rodríguez, *La guerra,* 110.

119. Velasco Avila, "Amenaza Comanche," 307.

120. *Diario,* July 2, 1838. I have added the figure of nine captives taken to adjust for those redeemed.

121. Vizcaya Canales, *Tierra,* 71.

122. Velasco Avila, "Amenaza Comanche," 311, recounts the governor's estimate that raiders had killed more than eighty people in the recent raids; I put the figure at fifty because of a different report of thirty deaths from the same period (see note below).

123. Joaquín García in Monterrey to M. de Guerra y Marina, Dec. 9, 1838, in C12, E44, AGENL-MGM.

124. Velasco Avila, "Amenaza Comanche," 310–11.

125. Joaquín García in Monterrey to M. de Guerra y Marina, March 27, 1839, in C13, E34, AGENL-MGM; Vizcaya Canales, *Tierra,* 76. This is a curious campaign, as it seems to have been unusually short-lived and restricted to a small corner of Nuevo León.

126. Eugenio Fernández to alcalde de Guerrero, Nava, Aug. 13, 1839, in C2, F10, E5, 2f, AGEC-FSXIX.

127. Vizcaya Canales, *Tierra,* 79. Mexican search parties located the twelve bodies throughout the countryside.

128. Ibid.

129. Ibid.

130. *Diario*, Feb. 5, 1840. Mexican forces claimed to have killed many Comanches in this engagement but provided no exact figure as the raiders absconded with their dead. Comanche dead in this entry therefore comes from Dolly Webster, who as a captive noted that in February of 1840 a war party returned to her village from Mexico. Of the forty-five who went out, only fifteen survived. See Dolbeare, *Captivity and Suffering*, 19–20.

131. Griffen, *Utmost*, appendix.

132. Ibid.

133. Smith, *Borderlander*, 106–08.

134. Griffen, *Utmost*, appendix.

135. Ibid.

136. Ibid.

137. Ibid.

138. Vizcaya Canales, *Tierra*, 88.

139. Ibid.

140. Griffen, *Utmost*, appendix.

141. Vizcaya Canales, *Tierra*, 88.

142. *Ancla*, Aug. 31, 1840.

143. Griffen, *Utmost*, appendix.

144. Vizcaya Canales, ed., *La invasión*, 67–68. The captive figure given here is probably an underestimate. The original report claimed that two "families" were taken captive and that the raiders later captured seven others. I add four to that number to account for the smallest number that might constitute those families.

145. Ibid., 66–67.

146. Ibid., 67–68.

147. Ibid., 71–75.

148. Ibid., 77–79.

149. Ibid., 82–83. The author of this document stated that the two men might be gravely wounded rather than killed.

150. Vizcaya Canales, *Tierra*, 103.

151. Ibid.

152. Ibid. In this attack raiders killed "don Juan Treviño and of all his family no one was left alive." I render this as four deaths.

153. Vizcaya Canales, ed., *La invasión*, 85–89; Vizcaya Canales, *Tierra*, 98.

154. Vizcaya Canales, ed., *La invasión*, 94–98.

155. Ibid., 89–94.

156. Ibid., 99–100.

157. Ibid., 101.

158. Ibid., 106–07.

159. Ibid., 108. In this attack, raiders took a family of five captive, of whom they later killed four, and then captured a *pastorcito*. Hence the figures of four dead and two captured.

160. Ibid., 110–12.

161. Ibid., 109–10.

162. Ibid., 114.

163. Ibid., 115.

164. Ibid., 120.

165. Ibid., 119.

166. Griffen, *Utmost*, appendix.

167. Ibid.

168. Ibid.

169. Vizcaya Canales, ed., *La invasión*, 132.

170. Ibid., 131.

171. Ibid., 133–34.

172. Ibid., 141–43.

173. Ibid., 143–47.

174. Ibid., 152–53.

175. Ibid., 181–85. This number is Victor Blanco's estimate of total destruction of the raid, excluding casualties from Nuevo León. Blanco's letter is reprinted in Alessio Robles, *Coahuila y Texas* 2:234–36. Without data from Zacatecas and San Luis Potosí this very imperfect estimate is the best number available. Numbers of Comanche dead and animals killed come from Blanco, above; from Rafael de la Fuente to Ignacio de Arizpe, Monclova, Dec. 30, 1840, in *Voto*, Jan. 8, 1841; and from "Estado que manifiesta las víctimas sacrificadas por los bárbaros." Feb. 6, 1841, C 86, E13, 1f, Presidencia Municipal, Archivo Municipal de Saltillo, Saltillo, Coahuila. These sources often mention animals being killed; the figure presented here includes only those they enumerated.

176. Vizcaya Canales, ed., *La invasión*, 161–64.

177. Ibid., 161–64.

178. Ibid., 177.

179. Ibid., 189–90.

180. Ibid., 181–85. This entry concerns only the Indian casualties at Saltillo. For Mexican casualties, see Blanco's estimate above.

181. Juan T. Galán to Mariano Arista, San Fernando de Rosas, Jan. 21, 1841, in *Ancla*, Jan. 24, 1841. Galán found five Comanche dead on the field but noted that the retreating Indians carried other dead with them; I therefore calculate seven dead, though the figure was likely higher.

182. Vizcaya Canales, *Tierra*, 121–22.

183. Vizcaya Canales, ed., *La invasión*, 192–93.

184. Juan J. Galán to Mariano Arista, San Fernando, Jan. 24, 1841, in Arista, *Oficio y documentos*.

185. Vizcaya Canales, ed., *La invasión*, 202–08.

186. *Diario*, March 2, 1841.

187. Vizcaya Canales, *Tierra*, 123.

188. Griffen, *Utmost*, appendix.

189. Vizcaya Canales, ed., *La invasión*, 213.

190. Ibid., 213.

191. Ibid., 215–16.

192. Ibid., 216.

193. Ibid., 217.

194. Ibid., 218.

195. Vizcaya Canales, *Tierra*, 123.
196. Vizcaya Canales, ed., *La invasión*, 220, 224. A servant was captured on the twenty-sixth and found dead a day later.
197. José María de Ortega to Governor of Nuevo León, Monterrey, March 1, 1841, in *Seminario*, March 4, 1841.
198. Vizcaya Canales, *Tierra*, 124.
199. Vizcaya Canales, ed., *La invasión*, 228.
200. *Seminario*, April 1, 1841.
201. Griffen, *Utmost*, appendix.
202. Ibid.
203. Vizcaya Canales, ed., *La invasión*, 242–43.
204. Ibid., 244–45.
205. Mariano Arista to M. de Guerra y Marina, Matamoros, July 15, 1841, in *Diario*, July 24, 1841.
206. José Antonio Heredia to M. de Guerra y Marina, Durango, April 19, 1841, in *Diario*, May 6, 1841.
207. *Ancla*, June 22, 1841. This party supposedly included Lipanes, Anglo-Americans, and "Tancahues" (Tonkawas).
208. Mauricio Ugarte to Comandante general de Chihuahua, El Norte, May 18, 1841, in *Diario*, June 14, 1841. In this rare instance one of the Comanche dead was a woman.
209. *Gaceta del Gobierno de Tamaulipas*, June 26, 1841.
210. *Seminario*, June 17, 1841.
211. *Gaceta del Gobierno de Tamaulipas*, June 26, 1841.
212. *Voto*, July 10, 1841.
213. *Seminario*, June 17, 1841.
214. Ibid., June 24, 1841.
215. *Gaceta del Gobierno de Tamaulipas*, June 26, 1841.
216. *Seminario*, July 1, 1841.
217. Ibid.
218. *Gaceta del Gobierno de Tamaulipas*, July 31, 1841.
219. Ibid.
220. Griffen, *Utmost*, appendix.
221. Ibid.
222. *Seminario*, Aug. 12, 1841.
223. *Gaceta del Gobierno de Tamaulipas*, Sept. 4, 1841.
224. Griffen, *Utmost*, appendix.
225. *Seminario*, Sept. 24, 1841.
226. *Siglo XIX*, Oct. 26, 1841.
227. Ibid. Drawing on newspaper accounts from Durango, the paper notes that the raiders attacked a mule train and "killed all the drivers," which I count here as two deaths. In Goma the attackers killed twelve adults and captured six children. The account goes on to say that the Indians "destroyed men, women, children, and animals" in their progress. On the twenty-seventh ten bodies were recovered from the countryside.
228. Gregorio Reyes to Governor of Coahuila, Patos, Sept. 27, 1841, C2, F5, E4, 3f, AGEC-FSXIX.
229. Griffen, *Utmost*, appendix.

230. Rafael de la Fuente to Sec. del supremo gobierno del departamento, Monclova, Oct 27, 1841, *Voto*, Nov. 13, 1841. I have added the figure of one captive taken to account for the captive redeemed. This event was an attack on a Comanche family's camp somewhere near the Rio Grande. The deaths were two men, two women. Captives included four women and a boy.

231. Griffen, *Utmost*, appendix.

232. Ibid.

233. Ibid.

234. Ibid.

235. Ibid.

236. Ibid.

237. Ibid.

238. Vizcaya Canales, *Tierra*, 133.

239. *Gaceta del Gobierno de Tamaulipas*, Dec. 16, 1841. The author noted that raiders killed "several defenseless people," which I render as three deaths.

240. Vizcaya Canales, *Tierra*, 135. The Indians seem to have been a family group: of the four dead, two were Indian women. To my knowledge, Comanches almost never sojourned below the Rio Grande in small family groups during this period—hence my identification of Apaches. Mexican forces also reported seizing four people during this encounter, though it remains unclear whether some or all of these four were Indians or Mexican captives.

241. José María Tornel to Governor of Coahuila, Mexico City, Feb. 15, 1842, C1, F5, E1, 4f, AGEC-FSXIX; Vizcaya Canales, *Tierra*, 135. Tornel's letter puts the number of Comanches at three hundred; Vizcaya Canales's sources say five hundred.

242. *Voto*, Jan. 29, 1842.

243. Pedro de Ampudia to Sr. General en Gefe, Monterrey, Feb. 19, 1842, *Registro*, March 31, 1842.

244. Ibid. The Indians were Lipanes and Tonkawas [Tancahues].

245. Vizcaya Canales, *Tierra*, 136. Mexicans estimated the number of Comanches at three to four hundred.

246. Jesus Cárdenas [to Governor?], Guerrero, Feb. 16, 1842, MAP 43:198–200. I have added the figure of one captive taken to account for the captive redeemed.

247. *El Seminal* [Victoria, Tamaulipas], March 3, 1842, cited in Martha Rodríguez, *Fuentes para la historia de la Guerra entre Mexico y los Estados Unidos*. Saltillo, 1999. [CD-ROM].

248. Jesus Cárdenas [to Governor?], Guerrero, March 23, 1842, MAP 44:60–62. I have added the figure of one captive taken to account for the captive redeemed.

249. Vizcaya Canales, *Tierra*, 140.

250. *El Seminal*, April 7, 1842, cited in Rodríguez, *Fuentes*.

251. Vizcaya Canales, *Tierra*, 141. Antonio Canales, leader in the northeastern federalist uprisings, led this attack. I have added one captive taken to account for the captive redeemed.

252. Ibid. Casualty figures here encompass two battles on the same day.

253. *Voto*, June 11, 1842.

254. *Voto*, June 9, 1842.

255. Francisco G. Conde to Comandante Gen. del Dept. de Durango, Chihuahua, Aug. 11, 1842, *Registro*, Aug. 25, 1842.

256. Vizcaya Canales, *Tierra*, 146.

257. *Registro*, Aug. 21 and Aug. 25, 1842.
258. Juan Nepomuceno Meléndez to Juan Nepomuceno Armendáriz, Campo Ponte de la Quemada, Aug. 14, 1842, *Registro*, Aug. 28, 1842.
259. J. N. Armendáriz, Diario de operaciones, Cerrogordo, Aug. 21, 1842, *Registro*, Sept. 1, 1842.
260. J. Miguel Velasco to Com. Gen. de Durango, Cerrogordo, Aug. 19, 1842, *Registro*, Aug. 25, 1842.
261. J. N. Armendáriz, Diario de operaciones, Cerrogordo, Aug. 21, 1842, *Registro*, Sept. 1, 1842; and Antonio Ponce de León to Comandante General de Chihuahua, San Carlos, Sept. 5, 1842, *Registro*, Sept. 22, 1842.
262. J. N. Armendáriz, Diario de operaciones, Cerrogordo, Aug. 21, 1842, *Registro*, Sept. 1, 1842.
263. Ibid.
264. Ibid.
265. Cayetano Justiniani to Comandante General de Chihuahua, Hidalgo, Sept. 2, 1842, *Registro*, Sept. 22, 1842.
266. Antonio Sánchez Muzquiz to Sr. Secretario del Despacho del Superior Gobierno de Durango, Parras, August 31, 1842, *Registro*, Sept. 8, 1842.
267. Ibid.
268. Ibid.
269. Vizcaya Canales, *Tierra*, 146.
270. Antonio Ponce de León to Comandante General de Chihuahua, San Carlos, Sept. 5, 1842, in *Registro*, Sept. 22, 1842. I have added six captives taken to account for the six redeemed.
271. Griffen, *Utmost*, appendix.
272. José María de Ortega to M. de Guerra y Marina, Lampazos, Oct. 30, 1842, C 16, E79, AGENL-MGM.
273. Vizcaya Canales, *Tierra*, 149.
274. Ibid., 150.
275. Ibid.
276. Ibid.
277. Ibid., 148.
278. Ibid., 149.
279. Governor of Coahuila to M. Relaciónes Exteriores y Gobierno, Oct. 31, 1842, C4, F2, E12, 3f, AGEC-FSXIX.
280. *Voto*, Nov. 19, 1842.
281. Ramón Jiménez to Sr. Secretario del Despacho del Superior Gobierno de Durango, Mapimí, Nov. 25, 1842, *Registro*, Dec. 1, 1842.
282. José María Acebal to Sr. Secretario del Despacho del Superior Gobierno de Durango, Cuencamé, Nov. 25, 1842, *Registro*, Dec. 1, 1842.
283. Juan Miguel Velasco to Comandante General de Durango, Hacienda de Torreón, Dec. 6, 1842, *Registro*, Dec. 15, 1842. I have added three captives taken to account for the three redeemed.
284. Antonio Tejada to Comandante General de Durango, Cerrogordo, Dec. 9, 1842, *Registro*, Dec. 15, 1842.
285. Vizcaya Canales, *Tierra*, 155.
286. Smith, "Comanche Bridge," 57.

287. *El Seminal*, March 4, 1843, cited in Rodríguez, *Fuentes*.

288. Juan Martínez to Juez de paz de Guerrero, Rio Grande, Feb. 16, 1843, C1, F4, E8, 2f, AGEC-FSXIX.

289. Vizcaya Canales, *Tierra*, 156.

290. Ibid.

291. Juan Miguel Velasco to Comandante General de Durango, Cerrogordo, March 14, 1843, *Registro*, March 19, 1843.

292. Juan Miguel Velasco to Comandante General de Durango, Cerrogordo, March 7, 1843, *Registro*, March 19, 1843. Raiders killed an unspecified number of people on the road: I render this as two deaths.

293. *El Seminal*, March 4, 1843, cited in Rodríguez, *Fuentes*.

294. Antonio Soto to Juan José Elguezabal, camp in the cabecera de Jacalitos, July 18, 1843, *Voto*, July 29, 1843. I have added the figure of one captive taken to account for the captive redeemed.

295. Juan José Elguezabal to Comandante Gen. y inspector de Coahuila, Monclova, July 19, 1843, *Voto*, July 29, 1843.

296. *Diario*, Sept. 9, 1843, cited in Escobar Ohmstede and Rojas Rabiela, eds., *La presencia del indígena*, 249.

297. Juan Antonio de Olaciregui to Juan N. Meléndez, Torreón, Sept. 12, 1843, *Registro*, Sept. 28, 1843.

298. Ibid.

299. Juan N. Meléndez to Sr. Secretario del Despacho del Superior Gobierno de Durango, Indé, Sept. 13, 1843, *Registro*, Sept. 28, 1843.

300. *Registro*, Sept. 28, 1843.

301. Griffen, *Utmost*, appendix.

302. Ibid.

303. *Registro*, Dec. 24, 1843; Jan. 4, 1844. One of these two accounts puts the Mexican dead at thirty-five: neither contains information about Comanche casualties.

304. Miguel Guerra to Francisco Casteñeda, Santa Rosa, Dec. 10, 1843, *Voto*, Dec. 16, 1843.

305. Smith, "Comanche Bridge," 60.

306. J. Miguel Velazco to Comandante General of Durango, Cerrogordo, Jan. 30, 1844, *Registro*, Feb. 4, 1844. I have added a captive taken for the one redeemed.

307. Governor of Nuevo León to Governor of Coahuila, Monterrey, Feb. 11, 1844, C1, F5, E11, 2f, AGEC-FSXIX.

308. *Registro*, March 24, 1844.

309. Smith, "Comanche Bridge," 61. Smith says that the raiders left "dead cowboys," which I have interpreted as two deaths.

310. Ibid. The passage refers to "dead freighters," which I interpret as two deaths.

311. Francisco Lofero to Manuel Rodríguez Cela, Matamoros, March 14, 1844, MAP 52:90.

312. Griffen, *Utmost*, appendix.

313. Smith, "Comanche Bridge," 61

314. Griffen, *Utmost*, appendix.

315. Ibid.

316. J. Miguel Velasco to Comandante General of Durango, Cerrogordo, April 2, 1844, *Registro*, April 7, 1844. The document says that in addition to two women, one soldier was killed. I count

two men killed because a second soldier was mortally wounded, and the author was certain he would not survive.

317. Griffen, *Utmost*, appendix.

318. Ibid.

319. *Diario*, May 22, 1844, cited in Escobar Ohmstede and Rojas Rabiela, eds., *La presencia del indígena*, 265. The source identifies these Indians as Caddos, though given the number of Indians it is likely either a misidentification or evidence that Caddos were working with Comanches or Kiowas or both.

320. Francisco Lofero in Matamoros to Jorge D. de Lara, Matamoros, July 4, 1844, MAP 50:184–89.

321. Manuel Rodríguez, Aviso, Matamoros, July 4, 1844, MAP 50:190.

322. Griffen, *Utmost*, appendix.

323. Smith, "Comanche Bridge," 62.

324. Manuel Menchaca to juez de paz de Rio Grande, Sept. 10, 1844, C5, F1, E7, 2f, AGEC-FSXIX.

325. *Gaceta del Gobierno de Tamaulipas*, Oct. 19, 1844.

326. Vizcaya Canales, *Tierra*, 169.

327. *Gaceta del Gobierno de Tamaulipas*, Oct. 19, 1844.

328. Smith, "Comanche Bridge," 65. Smith says here that Comanches engaged in "the routine of killing men, grabbing children." I have interpreted this in the lowest possible numbers.

329. *Gaceta del Gobierno de Tamaulipas*, Oct. 26, 1844.

330. Ibid. Francisco Lofero in Matamoros al jueces del secciones 6, 12, 15, 16, 17, 18–23, Oct. 12, 1844, MAP 51:8–9, claims that more than thirty Mexicans died in the fire at Los Moros.

331. Griffen, *Utmost*, appendix.

332. *Gaceta del Gobierno de Tamaulipas*, Oct. 19, 1844.

333. Smith, "Comanche Bridge," 63.

334. Ibid., 63–64.

335. *Gaceta del Gobierno de Tamaulipas*, Oct. 26, 1844; Vizcaya Canales, *Tierra*, 168–69. Mexican dead included ten fighters and nine captive children whom the Mexicans claimed the Comanches killed when they began their retreat. Mexican authorities believed that the raiders suffered many more casualties in this battle than the twenty-nine dead they left on the field.

336. Griffen, *Utmost*, appendix.

337. Smith, "Comanche Bridge," 64.

338. Ibid.

339. Ibid., 64–65.

340. Ibid., 65.

341. Ibid., 66.

342. Ibid., 66–67; and Juan N. Armendáriz, "Diario de las operaciones militares de la sección en campaña contra los comanches sobre el Bolsón de Mapimí," Cerrogordo, Nov. 1, 1844, *Registro*, Nov. 10, 1844.

343. Smith, "Comanche Bridge," 69. Smith says, "The raiders actually killed only a few," which I have interpreted as three dead.

344. Vizcaya Canales, *Tierra*, 170.

345. Ibid.

346. Griffen, *Utmost*, appendix.

347. Smith, "Comanche Bridge," 68.

348. Ibid.

349. Griffen, *Utmost*, appendix.

350. Ibid.

351. Ibid.

352. Ibid.

353. *Registro*, Feb. 2, 1845.

354. Ibid.

355. Ibid.

356. Juan N. Flores to subprefecto del Oro, Hacienda de Ramos, Feb. 22, 1854, *Registro*, March 13, 1845.

357. Griffen, *Utmost*, appendix.

358. Ibid.

359. Governor of Coahuila to M. Relaciones Exteriores y Gobierno, March 24, 1845, C2, F3, E9, 2f, AGEC-FSXIX.

360. Pedro Rengel to Governor of Coahuila, Parras, April 30, 1845, *Republicano*, May 10, 1845.

361. Vizcaya Canales, *Tierra*, 175.

362. Griffen, *Utmost*, appendix.

363. Smith, "Comanche Invasion."

364. Cuevas to Governor of Coahuila, Mexico City, July 10, 1845, C3, F4, E3, 2f, AGEC-FSXIX.

365. J. Antonio Tijerina to Governor of Coahuila, *Republicano*, July 26, 1845.

366. J. Andrés Marin to Governor of Durango, Durango, Aug. 7, 1845, *Registro*, Aug. 10, 1845.

367. Vizcaya Canales, *Tierra*, 175. The source says that the party of two hundred broke into smaller groups soon after entering Nuevo León.

368. Santiago Rodríguez to M. de Relaciones Exteriores, Gobierno y Policia, Saltillo, Sept. 13, 1845, *Republicano*, Sept. 13, 1845.

369. Smith, "Comanche Invasion," 9.

370. Ibid.

371. *Registro*, Sept. 25, 1845.

372. Rafael Gonzales to Governor of Coahuila, Saltillo, Sept. 12, 1845, C4, F6, E7, 13f, AGEC-FSXIX.

373. Smith, "Comanche Invasion," 9.

374. Ibid.

375. Ibid.

376. Ibid.

377. Griffen, *Utmost*, appendix.

378. Smith, "Comanche Invasion," 11.

379. Ibid., 10.

380. Ibid., 11.

381. J. M. Iglesias de Orduña to ?, Hacienda de San Salvador de Horta, Sept. 18, 1845, *Registro*, Sept. 25, 1845; and J. M. Iglesias de Orduña to governor of Durango, Hacienda de San Salvador de Horta, Sept. 19, 1845, *Registro*, Sept. 28, 1845. The figure nineteen dead includes ten killed at the hacienda, a shepherd who died soon after from severe wounds, three freighters killed soon after, and two killed on a nearby road. Escaped captives reported seeing other Mexicans killed by these

raiders, and the author names several pastors who are missing and presumed dead: I render these conservatively, as three additional deaths.

382. Smith, "Comanche Invasion," 11.

383. Hermenegildo de Villa to Sr. Secretario del Despacho del Superior Gobierno de Durango, Cinco Señores, Sept. 30, 1845, in *Registro*, Oct. 9, 1845.

384. Smith, "Comanche Invasion," 12.

385. Griffen, *Utmost*, appendix.

386. Ibid.

387. Ibid.

388. Ibid.

389. Smith, "Comanche Invasion," 13.

390. Ibid.

391. Ibid., 20.

392. Ibid., 19.

393. Ibid., 15. The death toll here was likely higher than five. The ranch administrator reported twenty-five people missing. At the time of writing he had located only five—all corpses and all men. Three children from Ochoa would be rescued soon after but this still leaves seventeen unaccounted for in these sources.

394. Ibid. Smith notes that the raiders killed shepherds in this area but gives no firm number. I count this as two deaths.

395. *Registro*, Oct. 23, 1845.

396. Smith, "Comanche Invasion," 18.

397. Ibid., 17. Six or eight soldiers were killed in this battle, but I have not included the figure here because it may have been part of the overall casualty estimate given by Manuel Gonzáles Cosío, below, n. 413.

398. Ibid., 15.

399. Ibid., 14.

400. Ibid.

401. Ibid., 12.

402. Griffen, *Utmost*, appendix.

403. Ibid.

404. José María de Jesus de Villareal to Governor of Coahuila, Monclova, Oct. 1, 1845, *Republicano*, Oct. 4, 1845.

405. Griffen, *Utmost*, appendix.

406. Smith, "Comanche Invasion," 13.

407. Ibid., 12.

408. Ibid., 13.

409. Rodríguez, *La guerra*, 117.

410. Smith, "Comanche Invasion," 14.

411. *Republicano*, Oct. 18, 1845.

412. Manuel Meneses to Sr. Secretario del Despacho del Superior Gobierno de Durango, Cuencamé, Oct. 12, 1845, in *Registro*, Oct. 16, 1845. Meneses notes that after a long gun battle the Comanches fled with their dead; hence he offers no figure on their casualties. There were just enough people captured prior to this event to account for the seventy redemptions.

413. Manuel González Cosío to Valentín Gómez Farís, Zacatecas, Oct. 17, 1845, doc. # 1288 in the Valentín Gómez Farías Collection, Benson Latin American Collection, University of Texas, Austin. My thanks to Daniel Gutiérrez for sharing this document with me. The author estimated two hundred killed when he wrote the letter. I use this haphazard estimate only because there are as yet no better data for this campaign into Zacatecas. The author noted that the six hundred Indians operated in separate parties of two hundred.

414. "unos adoloridos" to the editors, Nombre de Dios, Oct. 24, 1845, in *Registro*, Nov. 20, 1845.

415. Ibid.

416. Ibid.

417. Ibid.

418. Ibid.

419. Ibid.

420. Smith, "Comanche Invasion," 20.

421. Ibid.

422. Ibid., 21.

423. Alejo García Conde to Sr. Secretario del Despacho del Superior Gobierno de Durango, Porfias, Oct. 17, 1845, in *Registro*, Oct. 19, 1845; and Conde to editors of Registro, Durango, Oct. 21, 1845, in ibid., Oct. 30, 1845.

424. *Republicano*, Nov. 8, 1845 (reprinting a letter from San Juan del Río that originally appeared in *Registro*). This source notes that 32 villagers were killed in the initial raid; that Mexican reinforcements arrived, and ambiguously notes that in the aftermath of the battle that followed 68 Mexicans lay dead on the ground. Thus total Mexican deaths may have been 100, but I give the smaller number above. (Another account put the Mexican dead at eighty-four. See Manuel Ignacio Fierro to Sr. Secretario del Despacho del Superior Gobierno de Durango, Durango, Oct. 28, 1845, in *Registro*, Oct. 30, 1845.)

425. Smith, "Comanche Invasion," 23.

426. Ibid., 24.

427. Manuel Ignacio Fierro to Sr. Secretario del Despacho del Superior Gobierno de Durango, Durango, Oct. 28, 1845, in *Registro*, Oct. 30, 1845.

428. Smith, "Comanche Invasion," 24.

429. Ibid.

430. *Registro*, Nov. 2, 1845. Adding captives taken in this campaign and subtracting redemptions up to this point, there were at least three captures unaccounted for. Consequently, I add three here.

431. Santiago Rodríguez to Mariano Arista, Saltillo, Oct. 24, 1845, in *Republicano*, Nov. 1, 1845.

432. *Republicano*, Nov. 8, 1845.

433. Rodríguez, *La guerra*, 120.

434. *Republicano*, Dec. 13, 1845.

435. Vizcaya Canales, *Tierra*, 177.

436. José Rafael Montes to Subprefecto del Partido de Santiago, Guanaceui, Dec. 23, 1845, in *Registro*, Jan. 1, 1846.

437. Francisco Oyarzu to Sr. Secretario del Despacho del Superior Gobierno de Durango, Mapimí, Jan. 9, 1846, *Registro*, Jan. 25, 1846.

438. Griffen, *Utmost*, appendix.

439. Ibid.
440. Ibid.
441. Jesus Cárdenas to Governor of Tamaulipas, March 7, 1846, MAP 56:61–62.
442. *Registro*, March 5, 1846.
443. Ibid., March 12, 1846.
444. Ibid.
445. Ibid., March 8, 1846.
446. Ibid., March 12, 1846.
447. Ibid.
448. Ibid.
449. Ibid.
450. Jesus Cárdenas to ?, Matamoros, March 14, 1846, *Gaceta del Gobierno de Tamaulipas*, March 22, 1846.
451. Antonio Fernández to Governor of Nuevo León, Pesquería Grande, April 25, 1846, C44, Fondo Militares, AGENL.
452. José María de Arlegui to Governor of Durango, Durango, May 4, 1846, *Registro*, May 7, 1846.
453. *Registro*, May 24, 1846.
454. Governor of Coahuila to M. de Guerra y Marina, Saltillo, May 11, 1846, C2, F10, E9, 1f, AGEC-FSXIX.
455. Griffen, *Utmost*, appendix.
456. Ibid.
457. Ibid.
458. Ibid.
459. Ibid.
460. Ibid.
461. *Registro*, June 28, 1846.
462. Francisco Elorriaga to comandante general del departamento de Durango, Victoria, June 4, 1846, *Registro*, June 7, 1846; Manuel Meneses to Sr. Secretario del Despacho del Superior Gobierno de Durango, Cuencamé, June 5, 1846, *Registro*, June 11, 1846; Rafael G. y Contreras to Sr. Secretario del Despacho del Superior Gobierno de Durango, Mapimí, June 3, 1846, *Registro* June 14, 1846; and same to same, Mapimí, June 7, 1846, ibid.
463. Rafael G. y Contreras to Sr. Secretario del Despacho del Superior Gobierno de Durango, Mapimí, June 8, 1846, *Registro*, June 14, 1846; and Rafael G. y Contreras to Sr. Secretario del Despacho del Superior Gobierno de Durango, Mapimí, June 14, 1846, *Registro*, June 25, 1846.
464. Griffen, *Utmost*, appendix.
465. José María de Arlegui to governor of Durango, Durango, July 1, 1846, *Registro*, July 5, 1846.
466. *Registro*, July 19, 1846. Another man, not included in the tally here, was missing and presumed dead by the author.
467. José María de Arlegui to governor of Durango, Durango, July 20, 1846, *Registro*, July 26, 1846. The informants did not identify the Indians but did note that three of the twenty-one were *gente de razón*. I have added two captives taken for the two redeemed.
468. Griffen, *Utmost*, appendix.
469. *Registro*, Sept. 13, 1846. I have added two captives taken for the two redeemed.

470. *Diario*, Sept. 26, 1846, cited in Escobar Ohmstede and Rojas Rabiela, eds., *La presencia del indígena*, 299.

471. Griffen, *Utmost*, appendix.

472. *Registro*, Aug. 27, 1846. The editors note that another man, not included in this tally, is missing and presumed dead.

473. Victorino de la Riva to Tomas Araujo, Campo en San Javier, Aug. 28, 1846, and editorial in *Registro*, Sept. 6, 1846.

474. *Registro*, Sept. 20, 1846.

475. José María de Arlegui to governor of Durango, Durango, Sept. 22, 1846, *Registro* Sept. 27, 1846. The authors note that these Indians also stole 120 silver pesos.

476. *Registro*, Oct. 18, 1846.

477. Estevan del Campo to Sr. Secretario del Supremo Gobierno del Estado de Durango, Pinos, Oct. 28, 1846, *Registro*, Nov. 1, 1846. This raid occurred midmonth.

478. *Registro*, Nov. 5, 1846. The author notes that in addition to killing and capturing the residents of Aviníto, the raiders also robbed all the houses.

479. Griffen, *Utmost*, appendix.

480. Ruxton, *Adventures*, 86–87.

481. Griffen, *Utmost*, appendix. The four thousand number is inflated—other sources make it clear that the Indian force involved in this campaign was closer to one thousand men. Griffen notes "several" Mexican deaths: I render that as three.

482. Ibid.

483. Ibid.

484. Ibid.

485. *Registro*, Nov. 5, 1846.

486. Ibid. The editors note that the six *criaturas* (children or infants) were burned alive.

487. Griffen, *Utmost*, appendix.

488. *Registro*, Oct. 22 and Oct. 29, and *alcance*, Oct. 22, 1846.

489. Ibid. The *alcance* contains a list of the dead and the weapons that killed them. One Mexican killed in the battle died from an arrow wound, another was killed by a lance, and the rest lost their lives to gunfire.

490. Griffen, *Utmost*, appendix.

492. *Registro*, Nov. 12, 1846.

493. Griffen, *Utmost*, appendix.

494. Ibid.

494. *Registro*, Dec. 3, 1846. The report called this the start of a new invasion and said that the raiders had "destroyed almost entirely" the inhabitants of San Silvestre. I render this as fifteen deaths.

495. Griffen, *Utmost*, appendix. These Indians may have been Comanches or Apaches.

496. *Registro*, Dec. 31, 1846. These Indians may have been Lipanes.

497. Griffen, *Utmost*, appendix.

498. *Registro*, Jan. 31, 1847.

499. *Registro*, Feb. 7, 1847.

500. *Registro*, Jan. 31, 1847.

501. Griffen, *Utmost*, appendix.

502. Ibid. Total casualties amounted to fifty—no indication how many of this number were killed vs. captured.
503. Ibid.
504. Rodríguez, *La guerra*, 131.
505. *Registro*, Feb. 2, 1847. The editors mention that with this raiding party is a man whose look and dress suggest he is not an Indian.
506. *Registro*, Feb. 7, 1847.
507. *Registro*, Feb. 11, 1847.
508. Ibid.
509. Ibid.
510. John W. Reid to John E. Wool, Camp at Encantada, May 21, 1847, [U.S.] House Ex. doc. 60, 13th Cong., 1st sess., 1144–45. I have added the figure of eighteen captives taken to account for the captives redeemed. One of the accounts of the Hacienda del Pozo fight mentioned that at least some of the captives had been taken from San Luis Potosí. Robinson, *Journal*, 85.
511. Griffen, *Utmost*, appendix.
512. Ibid.
513. *Registro*, Aug. 26, 1847.
514. *Registro*, Sept. 26, 1847.
515. Ibid.
516. *Registro*, Oct. 7, 1847.
517. *Registro*, Oct. 3, 1847. I have added a captive taken to account for the three redeemed (there is evidence for two of the three being captured the day before in Indé).
518. *Registro*, Oct. 14, 1847. I have added a captive taken to account for the one redeemed.
519. *Registro*, Oct. 10, 1847.
520. *Registro*, Dec. 2, 1847.
521. *Registro*, Oct. 14, 1847.
522. Ibid.
523. *Registro*, Oct. 17, 1847.
524. *Registro*, Nov. 1, 1847. These fourteen people were killed when Comanches set their homes on fire.
525. *Registro*, Oct. 28, 1847.
526. Ibid.
527. Ibid.
528. *Registro*, Nov. 14, 1847.
529. *Registro*, Nov. 11, 1847.
530. *Registro*, Dec. 12, 1847.
531. Ibid.
532. Letter from San Luis Potosí, Nov. 16, 1847, in *Monitor Republicano*, Nov. 26, 1847. The author claims that at the time of writing the authorities knew of more than 400 Mexicans killed by these raiders throughout the state. The other 146 Mexican deaths came in two calamitous engagements between soldiers and Comanches prior to the confrontation below.
533. This battle involved forces from San Luis Potosí and Zacatecas. I have added 141 captives taken to account for the 200 redeemed, minus 19 captured in Durango during the previous weeks and

40 captured in San Luis Potosí. Comanche dead includes 1 Anglo-American and 2 Mexicans who rode with them. José María Ortega to Governor of San Luis Potosí, Nov. 18, 1847, San Luis Potosí, in *Monitor Republicano*, Nov. 26, 1847, transcribes a letter from Gen. Francisco Avalos, who claims that the Mexican force trapped 340–60 Indians at San Juan del Salado and notes that after a battle lasting several hours there were 30 to 40 Indians remaining (the 42 that *Registro* later reported killed and that I include in the data); these survivors defended themselves "barbarously" inside a building. He then notes ambiguously that "all have perished." If by "all" the general meant the three hundred plus that his forces originally encountered, it would have been by far the worst calamity Comanches ever suffered below the Rio Grande. For Comanche casualties and more on the incident, see *Registro*, Nov. 25, 1847; Francisco Avalos to Governor of Zacatecas, San Juan del Salado, Nov. 20, 1847 in *Registro*, Nov. 28, 1847; and Mariano Hermosillo to Secretario del Supremo Gobierno del Estado de San Luis Potosí, Rancho de San Juan del Salado, Nov. 20, 1847, in *Registro*, Dec. 2, 1847.

534. Victoriano Salas to gefe de partido del Oro, Hacienda de Sestín, Nov. 2, 1847, *Registro*, Nov. 14, 1847.

535. *Registro*, Dec. 23, 1847.

536. *Registro*, Jan. 23, 1848.

537. Rafael de la Fuente to the presidente municipal de San Buenaventura, Monclova, Jan. 27, 1848, C1, F1, E1, 1f, AGEC-FSXIX.

538. Francisco de la Garza to Luis Lombraña (?), Guerrero, March 1, 1848, C1, F3, E1, 2f, AGEC-FSXIX. It is unclear who these Indians were.

539. *Registro*, May 25, 1848.

540. *Registro*, April 23, 1848.

BIBLIOGRAPHY

ARCHIVAL COLLECTIONS

Archivo General del Estado de Coahuila; Ramos Arizpe, Coahuila.
  –Fondo Siglo XIX.
  –Archivo Histórico de Camargo.
  –Fondo Colonias Militares de Oriente.
  –Archivo Municipal de Guerrero.
Archivo General del Estado de Nuevo León; Monterrey, Nuevo León.
  –Correspondencia con la Secretaría de Guerra y Marina.
  –Fondo Militares.
Archivo Histórico de la Secretaría de Relaciones Exteriores; Mexico City.
Archivo Municipal de Saltillo; Saltillo, Coahuila.
Colección Lafragua, Biblioteca Nacional, Universidad Nacional Autónoma de México, Mexico City.
Despatches from United States Consuls in Matamoros, 1826–1906 (microfilm, 12 reels, National Archives Microfilm Publications).
Despatches from United States Consuls at Santa Fe, 1830–1846 (microfilm, 1 reel, National Archives Microfilm Publications), M-199.
Despatches from United States Ministers to Mexico, 1823–1906 (microfilm, 179 reels, National Archives Microfilm Publications), M97.
Hemeroteca Nacional, Mexico City.
Matamoros Archives Photostats, Center for American History, University of Texas, Austin.
Mexican Archives of New Mexico (microfilm).
Nettie Lee Benson Latin American Collection, University of Texas, Austin.
  –Pablo Salce Arredondo Collection.
  –Uncataloged imprints, W. B. Stephens collection.
  –Sánchez Navarro Collection.
Pierce M. Butler Papers, Huntington Library; San Marino, California.
Pinart Prints, Bancroft Library, University of California, Berkeley, microfilm set.

PERIODICALS

Ancla, Seminario de Matamoros
Arkansas State Gazette (Little Rock)
Barre Patriot (Barre, Mass.)
Boston Daily Atlas
Boston Courier
Calendario de Ignacio Cumplido (Mexico City)
Cleveland Herald
Concordia: Seminario del Gobierno Departamental de Tamaulipas (Victoria de Tamauli-
    pas)
Daily Missouri Republican (St. Louis)
Diario del Gobierno de la República Mexicana (Mexico City)
Gaceta del Gobierno de Coahuila (Saltillo)
Gaceta del Gobierno de Tamaulipas (Victoria de Tamaulipas)
Gaceta del Supremo Gobierno de Durango (Victoria de Durango)
Globe (Washington)
Greenville Mountaineer (Greenville, S.C.)
Matamoros Reveille
Mercurio de Matamoros
Mississippi Free Trader and Natchez Gazette (Natchez)
Mobile Register
Monitor Republicano (Mexico City)
New Hampshire Patriot (Concord)
New Hampshire Sentinel (Keene)
New Orleans Picayune
New York Herald
New York Post
New York Spectator
North American (Philadelphia)
Niles' National Register (Washington)
North American and Daily Advertiser (Philadelphia)
North American and United States Gazette (Philadelphia)
Pennsylvania Inquirer and Daily Courier (Philadelphia)
Pensacola Gazette
Pittsfield Sun
Raleigh Register and North Carolina Gazette
Registro Oficial del Gobierno del Departamento de Durango (Victoria de Durango)
Republicano: Periódico Oficial del Gobierno de Coahuila (Saltillo)
Richmond Enquirer
Road Island Republican (Newport)
Scioto Gazette (Chillicothe, Ohio)
Seminario Político de Gobierno de Nuevo León (Monterrey)
Siglo XIX (Mexico City)

South Carolina Temperance Advocate and Register of Agriculture and General Literature (Columbia)

Telegraph and Texas Register (Houston)

Texas Gazette (San Felipe de Austin)

Texas Republican (Brazoria)

United States' Telegraph (Washington)

Vermont Patriot (Montpelier)

Voto de Coahuila (Saltillo)

Weekly Despatch (Matagora, Tex.)

Weekly Ohio Statesman (Columbus)

BOOKS, ARTICLES, AND THESES

Abel, Annie Heloise, ed. *The Official Correspondence of James S. Calhoun while Indian Agent at Santa Fé and Superintendent of Indian Affairs in New Mexico.* Washington: Government Printing Office, 1915.

Abert, James William. *Abert's New Mexico Report, 1846–'47.* 1848. Reprint Albuquerque: Horn and Wallace, 1962.

Aboites, Aguilar Luis. "Poder político y 'bárbaros' en Chihuahua hacia 1845." *Secuencia* 19 (1991): 17–32.

———. "Poblamiento y estado en el norte de México, 1830–1835." In *Indio, nación y comunidad en el México del siglo XIX,* edited by Antonio Escobar Ohmstede, 304–13. Mexico: Centro de Estudios Mexicanos y Centroamericanos; Centro de Investigaciones y Estudios Superiores en Antropología Social, 1993.

———. *Norte precario: Poblamiento y colonización en México, 1760–1940.* Mexico: Colegio de México Centro de Estudios Históricos; Centro de Investigaciones y Estudios Superiores en Antropología Social, 1995.

———. "Nómadas y sedentarios en el norte de México: Elementos para una periodización." In *Nómadas y sedentarios en el norte de México: Homenaje a Beatriz Braniff,* edited by Beatriz Braniff C. and Marie-Areti Hers, 613–21. Mexico: Universidad Nacional Autónoma de México, Instituto de Investigaciones Antropológicas, 2000.

Adams, David B. "Embattled Borderlands: Northern Nuevo León and the Indios Bárbaros, 1686–1870." *Southwestern Historical Quarterly* 95 (1991): 205–20.

Adelman, Jeremy, and Stephen Aron. "From Borderlands to Borders: Empires, Nation-States, and the Peoples in between in North American History." *American Historical Review* 104 (1999): 814–41.

Agnew, Brad. *Fort Gibson: Terminal on the Trail of Tears.* Norman: University of Oklahoma Press, 1980.

Albers, Patricia C. "Symbiosis, Merger, and War: Contrasting Forms of Intertribal Relationship among Historic Plains Indians." In *The Political Economy of North American Indians,* edited by John H. Moore, 94–132. Norman: University of Oklahoma Press, 1993.

Albers, Patricia C., and William R. James. "Historical Materialism vs. Evolutionary Ecology: A Methodological Note on Horse Distribution and American Plains Indians." *Critique of Anthropology* 6 (1986): 87–100.

Alessio Robles, Vito. *Coahuila y Texas: Desde la consumación de la independencia hasta el tratado de paz de Guadalupe Hidalgo.* 2 vols. Mexico: Porrúa, 1946.

Almada Bay, Ignacio, José Marcos Medina Bustos, and José René Córdova Rascón. "Medidas de gobierno en Sonora para hacer frente a la guerra con los Estados Unidos, 1846–1849." In *XXI Simposio de historia y antropología de Sonora: Sonora y la región*, 229–63. Hermosillo: Departamento de Historia y Antropología, 1997.

Almaráz, Félix D. "An Uninviting Land: El Llano Estacado, 1534–1821." In *Spain and the Plains: Myths and Realities of Spanish Exploration and Settlement on the Great Plains*, edited by Ralph H. Vigil, Frances W. Kaye, and John R. Wunder, 70–89. Niwot: University Press of Colorado, 1994.

Almonte, Juan Nepomuceno. "Statistical Report on Texas, 1835." *Southwestern Historical Quarterly* 28 (1925): 177–222.

Alonso, Ana María. *Thread of Blood: Colonialism, Revolution, and Gender on Mexico's Northern Frontier.* Tucson: University of Arizona Press, 1995.

Alonzo, Armando C. *Tejano Legacy: Rancheros and Settlers in South Texas, 1734–1900.* Albuquerque: University of New Mexico Press, 1998.

Anderson, Fred. *Crucible of War: The Seven Years' War and the Fate of Empire in British North America, 1754–1766.* New York: Knopf, 2000.

Anderson, Fred, and Andrew Cayton. *The Dominion of War: Empire and Liberty in North America, 1500–2000.* New York: Viking, 2005.

Anderson, Gary Clayton. *The Indian Southwest, 1580–1830: Ethnogenesis and Reinvention.* Norman: University of Oklahoma Press, 1999.

———. *The Conquest of Texas: Ethnic Cleansing in the Promised Land, 1820–1875.* Norman: University of Oklahoma Press, 2005.

Anderson, H. Allen. "Jim Shaw," in *Handbook of Texas Online*, http://www.tsha.utexas.edu/handbook/online/articles/view/SS/fsh11.html, accessed Nov. 30, 2002.

Andrews, Catherine. "The Political and Military Career of General Anastasio Bustamante (1780–1853)." Ph.D. diss., University of St. Andrews, 2001.

Anna, Timothy E. "The Iturbide Interregnum." In *The Independence of Mexico and the Creation of the New Nation*, edited by Jaime E. Rodríguez O., 185–200. Los Angeles: UCLA Latin American Center Publications, 1989.

———. *The Mexican Empire of Iturbide.* Lincoln: University of Nebraska Press, 1990.

Arista, Mariano. *Oficio y documentos que el general Mariano Arista dirige al Escmo. Sr. Gobernador de Coahuila, en contestación a las especies que se vierten en la Iniciativa que dirige a las cámaras de aquella Junta Departamental, con motiva de la última incursión de los bárbaros.* Mexico: Y. Cumplico, 1841.

Armbruster, Henry C. "Torrey Trading Houses," in *Handbook of Texas Online*, http://www.tsha.utexas.edu/handbook/online/articles/TT/dft2.html, accessed Sept. 24, 2002.

Aron, Stephen. *American Confluence: The Missouri Frontier from Borderland to Border State.* Bloomington: Indiana University Press, 2006.

Astolfi, Douglas M. *Foundations of Destiny: A Foreign Policy of the Jacksonians, 1824–1837.* New York: Garland, 1989.

Ávila Ávila, J. Jesús. "Entre la jara del salvaje y el rifle del extranjero." In *La Guerra México-Estados Unidos: Su impacto en Nuevo León, 1835–1846*, edited by Leticia Martínez

Cárdenas, César Morado Macías, and J. Jesús Ávila Ávila, 201–94. Mexico: Senado de la República, 2003.

Babcock, Matthew McLaurine. "Trans-National Trade Routes and Diplomacy: Comanche Expansion, 1760–1846." M.A. thesis, University of New Mexico, 2001.

Bailey, Garrick. "Osage." In *Handbook of North American Indians*. Vol. 13, *Plains*, edited by Raymond J. DeMallie, 476–96. Washington: Smithsonian Institution Press, 2001.

Bailey, Lynn R. *If You Take My Sheep . . . : The Evolution and Conflicts of Navajo Pastoralism, 1630–1868*. Pasadena: Westernlore Publications, 1980.

Balbontín, Manuel. *La invasión americana 1846 a 1848: Apuntes del subteniente de artillería Manuel Balbontín*. Mexico: Tipografía de Gonzalo A. Esteva, 1883.

Bamforth, Douglas B. "Indigenous People, Indigenous Violence: Precontact Warfare on the North American Great Plains." *Man* 29 (1994): 95–115.

Bancroft, Hubert Howe. *History of Arizona and New Mexico, 1530–1888*. San Francisco: History Company, 1889.

Barker, Eugene C., ed. *The Austin Papers*. 2 vols. Washington, D.C.: American Historical Association, 1919–28.

Barr, Juliana. *Peace Came in the Form of a Woman: Indians and Spaniards in the Texas Borderlands*. Chapel Hill: University of North Carolina Press, 2007.

Barreiro, Antonio. *Ojeado sobre Nuevo-México*. Puebla: José María Campos, 1832.

Barrett, Elinore M. *Conquest and Catastrophe: Changing Rio Grande Pueblo Settlement Patterns in the Sixteenth and Seventeenth Centuries*. Albuquerque: University of New Mexico Press, 2002.

Basso, Keith H. "Western Apache." In *Handbook of North American Indians*. Vol. 10, *Southwest*, edited by Alfonso Ortiz, 462–88. Washington, D.C.: Smithsonian Institution Press, 1983.

Bauer, K. Jack. *The Mexican War, 1846–1848*. New York: Macmillan, 1974.

Baxter, John O. *Las Carneradas: Sheep Trade in New Mexico, 1700–1860*. Albuquerque: University of New Mexico Press, 1987.

Baylies, Francis. *A Narrative of Major General Wool's Campaign in Mexico in the Years 1846, 1847, and 1848*. Albany: Little and Company, 1851.

Bazant, Jan. "From Independence to the Liberal Republic, 1821–1857." In *Mexico Since Independence*, edited by Leslie Bethell, 1–48. Cambridge: Cambridge University Press, 1991.

Belohlavek, John M. "Race, Progress, and Destiny: Caleb Cushing and the Quest for American Empire." In *Manifest Destiny and Empire: American Antebellum Expansionism*, edited by Sam W. Haynes and Christopher Morris, 21–47. College Station: Texas A&M University Press, 1997.

Bender, Averam Burton. *The March of Empire: Frontier Defense in the Southwest, 1848–1860*. Lawrence: University of Kansas Press, 1952.

Benson, Nettie Lee. "Texas as Viewed from Mexico, 1821–1834." *Southwestern Historical Quarterly* 90 (1987): 219–91.

———. "Territorial Integrity in Mexican Politics, 1821–1833." In *The Independence of Mexico and the Creation of the New Nation*, edited by Jaime E. Rodríguez O., 275–307. Los Angeles: UCLA, 1989.

Berlandier, Jean Louis. *The Indians of Texas in 1830*. Translated by Patricia R. Leclercq. Edited by John C. Ewers. Washington, D.C.: Smithsonian Institution Press, 1969.

———. *Journey to Mexico during the Years 1826 to 1834*. Translated by Sheila M. Ohlendorf, Josette M. Bigelow, and Mary M. Standifer. Austin: University of Texas Press, 1980.

———. "Cacería del oso y del cíbolo en el no. de Tejas." In *Crónica de Tejas: Diario de viaje de la comisión de límites*, edited by Mauricio Molína, 145–70. Mexico: Instituto Nacional de Bellas Artes, 1988.

Berninger, Dieter George. *La inmigración en México*. Mexico: Secretaría de Educación Pública, 1974.

Betty, Gerald. *Comanche Society: Before the Reservation*. College Station: Texas A&M University Press, 2002.

Bill, Alfred Hoyt. *Rehearsal for Conflict: The War with Mexico, 1846–1848*. New York: Knopf, 1947.

Bishop, Farnham. *Our First War in Mexico*. New York: C. Scribner's Sons, 1916.

Blackhawk, Ned. *Violence over the Land: Indians and Empires in the Early American West*. Cambridge: Harvard University Press, 2006.

Bloom, Lansing Bartlett. "New Mexico under Mexican Administration, 1821–1846." *Old Santa Fe* 1–2 (1913–14): various.

Bonnell, George W. *Topographical Description of Texas, to Which is Added, an Account of the Indians*. Austin: Clark, Wing, and Brown, 1840.

Bosch García, Carlos, ed. *Documentos de la relación de México con los Estados Unidos*. Vol. 5, part 2, *Documentos desde la caída de la concesión de Garay hasta la entrega a la empresa privada, 1848–1853*. Mexico: Instituto de Investigaciones Históricas Universidad Nacional Autónoma de México, 1994.

Brack, Gene M. *Mexico Views Manifest Destiny, 1821–1846: An Essay on the Origins of the Mexican War*. Albuquerque: University of New Mexico Press, 1975.

Brant, Charles S., ed. *Jim Whitewolf: The Life of a Kiowa Apache Indian*. New York: Dover, 1969.

Brinckerhoff, Sidney B., and Odie B. Faulk, eds. *Lancers for the King: A Study of the Frontier Military System of Northern New Spain*. Phoenix: Arizona Historical Foundation, 1965.

Britton, Morris L. "Holland Coffee," in *The Handbook of Texas Online*, http://www.tsha.utexas.edu/handbook/online/articles/CC/fco12.html, accessed Oct. 28, 2003.

Brooks, James F. "'This Evil Extends Especially to the Feminine Sex': Captivity and Identity in New Mexico, 1700–1846." *Feminist Studies* 22 (1996): 279–309.

———. "Served Well by Plunder: La Gran Ladronería and Producers of History astride the Rio Grande." *American Quarterly* 52 (2000): 23–58.

———. *Captives and Cousins: Slavery, Kinship, and Community in the Southwest Borderlands*. Chapel Hill: University of North Carolina Press, 2002.

Brown Jr., William R. "Comanchería Demography, 1805–1830." *Panhandle-Plains Historical Review* 59 (1986): 1–17.

Brown, Michael F. "On Resisting Resistance." *American Anthropologist* 98 (1996): 729–49.

Brugge, David M. "Documentary Reference to a Navajo Naach'id in 1840." *Ethnohistory* 10 (1963): 186–88.

———. "Pueblo Factionalism and External Relations." *Ethnohistory* 16:2 (1969): 191–200.

———. *Navajos in the Catholic Church Records of New Mexico, 1694–1875.* 2d ed. Tsaile, Ariz.: Navajo Community College Press, 1985.

Bumgardner, Georgia Brady. "Political Portraiture: Two Prints of Andrew Jackson." *American Art Journal* 18 (1986): 84–95.

Burnet, David G. "The Comanches and Other Tribes of Texas; and the Policy to be Pursued Respecting Them." In *The Indian Papers of Texas and the Southwest, 1825–1916,* edited by Dorman H. Winfrey and James M. Day, 3:84–99. Austin: Texas Historical Association, 1995.

Burnham, Gilbert, Riyahd Lafta, Shannon Doocy, and Les Roberts. "Mortality after the 2003 Invasion of Iraq: A Cross-Sectional Cluster Sample Survey." *The Lancet* 368 (2006): 1421–28.

Burns, Louis F. *A History of the Osage People.* New ed. Tuscaloosa: University of Alabama Press, 2004.

Burstein, Andrew. *The Passions of Andrew Jackson.* New York: Knopf, 2003.

Bushnell, David, and Neill Macaulay. *The Emergence of Latin America in the Nineteenth Century.* 2d ed. New York: Oxford University Press, 1994.

Bustamante, Carlos María. *El gabinete mexicano durante el segundo periodo de la administración del exmo. señor presidente d. Anastasio Bustamante.* 2 vols. Mexico: J. Mariano Lara, 1842.

———. *Apuntes para la historia del gobierno del General Antonio López de Santa Anna, desde principios de octubre de 1841 hasta 6 de diciembre de 1844, en que fué depuesto de mando por uniforme voluntad de la nación.* Mexico: J. Mariano Lara, 1845.

———. *El nuevo Bernal Díaz del Castillo, o sea historia de la invasión de los anglo-americanos en México.* 1847. Reprint, Mexico: Secretaría de Educación Pública, 1949.

Calloway, Colin G. *Crown and Calumet: British–Indian Relations, 1783–1815.* Norman: University of Oklahoma Press, 1987.

———. *One Vast Winter Count: The Native American West before Lewis and Clark.* Lincoln: University of Nebraska Press, 2003.

Calvin, Ross, ed. *Lieutenant Emory Reports: A Reprint of Lieutenant W. H. Emory's Notes of a Military Reconnaissance.* 1848. Reprint, Albuquerque: University of New Mexico Press, 1951.

Cameron, John. "Comanche Indians: The Country West of the Colorado." In *The Papers of Mirabeau Buonaparte Lamar,* edited by Charles Adams Gulick, Jr., 1:475–80. Austin: Pemberton Press, 1968.

Campbell, T. N. "Coahuiltecan Indians," in *The Handbook of Texas Online,* http://www.tsha.utexas.edu/handbook/online/articles/CC/bmcah.html, accessed June 9, 2003.

Calvillo Unna, Tomás, and María Isabel Monroy Castillo. "Entre regionalismo y federalismo: San Luis Potosí, 1846–1848." In *México al tiempo de su guerra con Estados Unidos (1846–1848),* edited by Josefina Zoraida Vázquez, 417–54. Mexico: Secretaría de Relaciones Exteriores, 1997.

Campbell, T. N., and William T. Field. "Identification of Comanche Raiding Trails in Trans-Pecos Texas." *West Texas Historical Association Year Book* 44 (1968): 128–44.

Cantrell, Gregg. *Stephen F. Austin, Empresario of Texas*. New Haven: Yale University Press, 1999.

Carroll, Horace Bailey, and Juan Villasana Haggard, eds. *Three New Mexico Chronicles: The Exposición of Don Pedro Bautista Pino, 1812; The Ojeada of Lic. Antonio Barreiro, 1832; And the Additions by Don José Agustín de Escudero, 1849*. Albuquerque: Quivira Society, 1942.

Carson, James Taylor. "Horses and the Economy and Culture of the Choctaw Indians, 1690–1840." *Ethnohistory* 42 (1995): 495–513.

Castañeda, Carlos E., ed. *The Mexican Side of the Texan Revolution*. Dallas: P. L. Turner, 1928.

Castañeda Zavala, Jorge. "El contingente fiscal en la nueva nación mexicana, 1824–1861." In *De colonia a nación: Impuestos y política en México, 1750–1860*, edited by Carlos Marichal and Daniela Marino, 138–88. Mexico: Colegio de México, Centro de Estudios Históricos, 2001.

Castro-Klarén, Sara, and John Charles Chasteen. *Beyond Imagined Communities: Reading and Writing the Nation in Nineteenth-Century Latin America*. Washington, D.C.: Woodrow Wilson Center Press, 2003.

Cavazos Garza, Israel. "Las incursiones de los bárbaros en el noreste de México, durante el siglo XIX." *Humanitas* 5 (1964): 343–56.

Cayton, Andrew R. L. "'Separate Interests' and the Nation State: The Washington Administration and the Origins of Regionalism in the Trans-Appalachian West." *Journal of American History* 79 (1992): 39–67.

———. "'When Will We Cease to Have Judases?' The Blount Conspiracy and the Limits of the 'Extended Republic.'" In *Launching the "Extended Republic": The Federalist Era*, edited by Ronald Hoffman and Peter J. Albert, 156–89. Charlottesville: University Press of Virginia, 1996.

———. "Continental Politics: Liberalism, Nationalism, and the Appeal of Texas in the 1820s." In *Beyond the Founders: New Approaches to the Political History of the Early American Republic*, edited by Jeffery L. Pasley, Andrew W. Robertson, and David Waldstreicher, 303–27. Chapel Hill: University of North Carolina Press, 2004.

Centeno, Miguel Angel. *Blood and Debt: War and the Nation-State in Latin America*. University Park: Pennsylvania State University Press, 2002.

Centeno, Miguel Angel, and Fernando López-Alves, eds. *The Other Mirror: Grand Theory through the Lens of Latin America*. Princeton: Princeton University Press, 2001.

Chacón, Rafael. *Legacy of Honor: The Life of Rafael Chacón, a Nineteenth-Century New Mexican*. Edited by Jacqueline Meketa. Albuquerque: University of New Mexico Press, 1986.

Chamberlain, Samuel E. *My Confession: Recollections of a Rogue*. Edited by William H. Goetzmann. Austin: Texas State Historical Association, 1996.

Channing, William E. *A Letter to the Hon. Henry Clay, On the Annexation of Texas to the United States*. 4th ed. Boston: James Munroe, 1837.

Chaplin, Joyce E. *Subject Matter: Technology, the Body, and Science on the Anglo-American Frontier, 1500–1676.* Cambridge: Harvard University Press, 2001.

———. "Race." In *The British Atlantic World,* edited by David Armitage and Michael J. Braddick, 154–72. New York: Palgrave Macmillan, 2002.

Chávez, Jorge Chávez. "La colonización como instrumento para pacificar a los llamados indios bárbaros." In *Actas del Primer Congreso de Historia Regional Comparada,* 235–49. Ciudad Juárez: Universidad Autónoma de Ciudad Juárez, 1989.

———. "Retrato del Indio Bárbaro: Proceso de Justificación de la Barbarie de los Indios del Septentrión Mexicano y Formación de la Cultura Norteña." *New Mexico Historical Review* 73 (1998): 389–425.

Chávez, Thomas E., ed. *Conflict and Acculturation: Manuel Alvarez's 1842 Memorial.* Santa Fe: Museum of New Mexico Press, 1989.

———. *Manuel Alvarez, 1794–1856: A Southwestern Biography.* Niwot: University Press of Colorado, 1990.

Christensen, Carol, and Thomas Christensen. *The U.S.–Mexican War.* San Francisco: Bay Books, 1998.

Citino, Nathan J. "The Global Frontier: Comparative History and the Frontier-Borderlands Approach." In *Explaining the History of American Foreign Relations,* edited by Michael J. Hogan and Thomas G. Paterson, 194-211. Cambridge: Cambridge University Press, 2004.

Coatsworth, John H. "Obstacles to Economic Growth in Nineteenth-Century Mexico." *American Historical Review* 83 (1978): 80–100.

Collier, Jane Fishburne. *Marriage and Inequality in Classless Societies.* Stanford: Stanford University Press, 1988.

Connelley, William E., ed. "A Journal of the Santa Fe Trail." *Mississippi Valley Historical Review* 12 (1925): 72–98, 227–55.

Connor, Seymour V., and Odie B. Faulk. *North America Divided: The Mexican War, 1846–1848.* New York: Oxford University Press, 1971.

Constitución política del estado libre de las Tamaulipas. Ciudad Victoria: C. Contreras, 1825.

Correll, J. Lee. *Through White Men's Eyes: A Contribution to Navajo History—A Chronological Record of the Navaho People from Earliest Times to the Treaty of June 1, 1868.* Window Rock: Navajo Times, 1976.

Cortés y de Olarte, José María. *Views from the Apache Frontier: Report on the Northern Provinces of New Spain.* Translated by John Wheat. Edited by Elizabeth A. H. John. Norman: University of Oklahoma Press, 1989.

Costeloe, Michael P. *The Central Republic in Mexico, 1835–1846: Hombres de Bien in the Age of Santa Anna.* Cambridge: Cambridge University Press, 1993.

Cross, Harry E. "Living Standards in Rural Nineteenth-Century Mexico: Zacatecas, 1820–1880." *Journal of Latin American Studies* 10 (1978): 1–19.

Cubas, Antonio García. *Diccionario geográfico, histórico y biográfico de los Estados Unidos Mexicanos.* 2 vols. Mexico: Antigua Imprenta de Murguia, 1888.

Cuello, José. "Beyond the 'Borderlands' Is the North of Colonial Mexico: A Latin-Americanist Perspective to the Study of the Mexican North and the United States Southwest." *Proceedings of the Pacific Coast Council on Latin American Studies* 9 (1982): 1–24.

———. "Racialized Hierarchies of Power in Colonial Mexican Society: The *Sistema de Castas* as a Form of Social Control in Saltillo." In *Choice, Persuasion, and Coercion: Social Control on Spain's North American Frontiers*, edited by Jesús F. de la Teja and Ross Frank, 201–26. Albuquerque: University of New Mexico Press, 2005.

Cutts, James Madison. *The Conquest of California and New Mexico, by the Forces of the United States, in the Years 1846 and 1847*. 1847. Reprint, Albuquerque: Horn and Wallace, 1965.

Dana, Napoleon Jackson Tecumseh. *Monterrey Is Ours!: The Mexican War Letters of Lieutenant Dana, 1845–1847*. Edited by Robert H. Ferrell. Lexington: University Press of Kentucky, 1990.

Davenport, Harbert, and Craig H. Roell, "Goliad Massacre," in *Handbook of Texas Online*, http://www.tsha.utexas.edu/handbook/online/articles/GG/qeg2.html, accessed Jan. 20, 2006.

Davis, Michael G. *Ecology, Sociopolitical Organization, and Cultural Change on the Southern Plains: A Critical Treatise in the Sociocultural Anthropology of Native North America*. Kirksville, Mo.: Thomas Jefferson University Press, 1996.

De Voto, Bernard Augustine. *The Year of Decision, 1846*. Boston: Little Brown, 1943.

de la Teja, Jesús F., ed. *A Revolution Remembered: The Memoirs and Selected Correspondence of Juan N. Seguín*. Austin: State House Press, 1991.

DeLay, Brian. "Independent Indians and the U.S.–Mexican War." *American Historical Review* 112 (2007): 35–68.

———. "The Wider World of the Handsome Man: Southern Plains Indians Invade Mexico, 1830–1846." *Journal of the Early Republic* 27 (2007): 83–113.

DePalo, William A. *The Mexican National Army, 1822–1852*. College Station: Texas A&M University Press, 1997.

Di Tella, Torcuato S. *National Popular Politics in Early Independent Mexico, 1820–1847*. Albuquerque: University of New Mexico Press, 1996.

Díaz Polanco, Héctor. *Indigenous Peoples in Latin America: The Quest for Self-Determination*. Translated by Lucia Rayas. Boulder: Westview Press, 1997.

Dolbeare, Benjamin. *A Narrative of the Captivity and Suffering of Dolly Webster Among the Camanche Indians in Texas: With an Account of the Massacre of John Webster and his Party, as Related by Mrs. Webster*. 1843. Facsimile ed. New Haven: Yale University Library, 1986.

Doubleday, Abner. *My Life in the Old Army: The Reminiscences of Abner Doubleday: From the Collections of the New-York Historical Society*. Edited by Joseph E. Chance. Ft. Worth: Texas Christian University Press, 1998.

Douglas, Mary. "Forward: No Free Gifts." In *The Gift: The Form and Reason for Exchange in Archaic Societies*, vii–xviii. New York: W. W. Norton, 1990.

Dowd, Gregory Evans. *War under Heaven: Pontiac, the Indian Nations and the British Empire*. Baltimore: Johns Hopkins University Press, 2002.

Downs, S. W. *Speech on the Mexican War, Delivered Before the Senate on January 31, 1848*. Washington: Congressional Globe Office, 1848.

Drumm, Stella M., ed. *Down the Santa Fe Trail and into Mexico: The Diary of Susan Shelby Magoffin, 1846–1847*. Lincoln: University of Nebraska Press, 1982.

Dublán, Manuel, and José María Lozano, eds. *Legislación Mexicana; o Colección completa de las disposiciones legislativas expedidas desde la independencia de la República*. 22 vols. Mexico: Imprenta del Comercio, 1876–93.

Dunkerley, James, ed. *Studies in the Formation of the Nation-State in Latin America*. London: Institute of Latin American Studies, 2002.

DuVal, Kathleen. "Debating Identity, Sovereignty, and Civilization: The Arkansas Valley after the Louisiana Purchase." *Journal of the Early Republic* 26 (2006): 25–58.

———. *The Native Ground: Indians and Colonists in the Heart of the Continent*. Philadelphia: University of Pennsylvania Press, 2006.

Edward, David Barnett. *The History of Texas; or, the Emigrant's, Farmer's, and Politician's Guide to the Character, Climate, Soil, and Productions of that Country; Geographically Arranged and from Personal Observation and Experience*. Cincinnati: J. A. James, 1836.

Eisenhower, John S. D. *So Far from God: The U.S. War with Mexico, 1846–1848*. New York: Random House, 1989.

Emory, W. H. *Report of the United States and Mexican Boundary Survey, Made under the Direction of the Secretary of the Interior*. Washington: Government Printing Office, 1858.

Escobar Ohmstede, Antonio, and Teresa Rojas Rabiela, eds. *La presencia del indígena en la prensa capitalina del siglo XIX*. Mexico: Instituto Nacional Indigenista, 1992.

Escudero, José Agustín. *Noticias estadísticas del estado de Chihuahua*. Mexico, 1834.

———. *Noticias estadísticas de Sonora y Sinaloa*. 1849. Reprint, Hermosillo: Universidad de Sonora, 1997.

———. *Noticias estadísticas del estado de Durango reunidas, aumentadas, y presentadas a la comisión de estadística militar*. Mexico: R. Rafael, 1849.

Everett, Dianna. *The Texas Cherokees: A People between Two Fires, 1819–1840*. Norman: University of Oklahoma Press, 1990.

Ewers, John Canfield. *The Blackfeet: Raiders on the Northwestern Plains*. Norman: University of Oklahoma Press, 1958.

Falcón, Ramona. "El estado incapaz. Lucha entre naciones: Poder, territorio, 'salvajes' y jefes de departamento." In *Las formas y las políticas del dominio agrario*, edited by Ricardo Ávila Palafox, Carlos Martínez Assad, and Jean Meyer, 189-214. Guadalajara: Universidad de Guadalajara, 1992.

Falconer, Thomas, and Frederick Webb Hodge. *Letters and Notes on the Texan Santa Fe Expedition, 1841–1842*. 1842. Reprint, New York City: Dauber and Pine Bookshops, 1930.

Farnham, Thomas Jefferson. *Travels in the Great Western Prairies, the Anahuac and Rocky Mountains, and in the Oregon Territory*. Poughkeepsie: Killey and Lossing Printers, 1841.

Faulk, Odie B. *Too Far North, Too Far South*. Los Angeles: Westernlore Press, 1967.

———. "The Presidio: Fortress or Farce?" In *New Spain's Far Northern Frontier*, edited by David J. Weber, 67-78. Albuquerque: University of New Mexico Press, 1979.

Fehrenbach, T. R. *Comanches: The Destruction of a People*. New York: Knopf, 1974.

Fenn, Elizabeth A. *Pox Americana: The Great Smallpox Epidemic of 1775–82.* New York: Hill and Wang, 2001.

Ferrand, Andrew Delinton. "Cultural Dissonance in Mexican–American Relations: Ethnic, Racial and Cultural Images of the Coming of the War, 1846." Ph.D. diss., University of California, Santa Barbara, 1979.

Field, Joseph Emerson. *Three Years in Texas: Including a View of the Texan Revolution, and an Account of the Principal Battles, Together With Descriptions of the Soil, Commercial and Agricultural Advantages, &c.* Boston: Abel Tompkins, 1836.

Field, Matthew C. *Matt Field on the Santa Fe Trail.* Collected by Clyde Porter and Mae Reed Porter. Edited by John E. Sunder. Norman: University of Oklahoma Press, 1960.

Fisher, Howard T., and Marion Hall, eds. *Life in Mexico: The Letters of Fanny Calderón de la Barca.* New York: Doubleday, 1966.

Fisher, Orceneth. *Sketches of Texas in 1840; Designed to Answer, in a Brief Way, the Numerous Enquiries Respecting the New Republic, as to Situation, Extent, Climate, Soil, Productions, Water, Government, Society, Religion, etc.* Springfield: Walters and Weber, 1841.

Flores, Dan, ed. *Jefferson and Southwestern Exploration: The Freeman and Curtis Accounts of the Red River Expedition of 1806.* Norman: University of Oklahoma Press, 1984.

———. *Journal of an Indian Trader: Anthony Glass and the Texas Trading Frontier, 1790–1810.* College Station: Texas A&M University Press, 1985.

———. "Bison Ecology and Bison Diplomacy: The Southern Plains from 1800 to 1850." *Journal of American History* 78 (1991): 465–85.

Foos, Paul. *A Short, Offhand, Killing Affair: Soldiers and Social Conflict during the U.S.–Mexican War.* Chapel Hill: University of North Carolina Press, 2002.

Foote, Cheryl. "Spanish–Indian Trade along New Mexico's Frontier in the Eighteenth Century." *Journal of the West* 24 (1985): 25–30.

Foote, Henry S. *Texas and the Texans: or, Advance of the Anglo-Americans to the South-West; Including a History of Leading Events in Mexico, from the Conquest by Fernando Cortes to the Termination of the Texan Revolution.* Philadelphia: Thomas Cowperthwait, 1841.

Forbes, Jack D. *Apache, Navaho, and Spaniard.* Norman: University of Oklahoma Press, 1960.

Foreman, Grant, ed. "Journal of Elijah Hicks." *Chronicles of Oklahoma* 13 (1935): 68–99.

———. "The Texas Comanche Treaty of 1846." *Southwestern Historical Quarterly* 51 (1948): 313–32.

Foster, Morris W. *Being Comanche: A Social History of an American Indian Community.* Tucson: University of Arizona Press, 1991.

Foster, Morris W., and Martha McCollough. "Plains Apache." In *Handbook of North American Indians,* edited by Raymond J. DeMallie, 926–40. Washington: Smithsonian Institution Press, 2001.

Fowler, Loretta. "Politics." In *A Companion to the Anthropology of American Indians,* edited by Thomas Biolsi, 69–94. Malden: Blackwell, 2004.

Fowler, Will. "Dreams of Stability: An Analysis of the Beliefs of the Creole Intelligentsia (1821–1853)." *Bulletin of Latin American Research* 14 (1995): 287–312.

———. "The Repeated Rise of General Antonio López de Santa Anna in the So-Called 'Age of Chaos.'" In *Authoritarianism in Latin America since Independence*, edited by Will Fowler, 1–30. Westport: Greenwood, 1996.

———. *Mexico in the Age of Proposals, 1821–1853*. Westport, Conn.: Greenwood Press, 1998.

Frank, Ross. *From Settler to Citizen: New Mexican Economic Development and the Creation of Vecino Society, 1750–1820*. Berkeley: University of California Press, 2000.

Froebel, Julius. *Seven Years' Travel in Central America, Northern Mexico, and the Far West of the United States*. London: R. Bentley, 1859.

Fuller, John Douglas Pitts. *The Movement for the Acquisition of All Mexico, 1846–1848*. Baltimore: Johns Hopkins University Press, 1936.

Fulton, Maurice G., and Paul Horgan, eds. *Diary and Letters of Josiah Gregg*. Norman: University of Oklahoma Press, 1941.

Gallay, Alan. *The Indian Slave Trade: The Rise of the English Empire in the American South, 1670–1717*. New Haven: Yale University Press, 2002.

Gálvez, Bernardo de. *Instructions for Governing the Interior Provinces of New Spain, 1786*. Translated and edited by Donald E. Worcester. Berkeley: Quivira Society, 1951.

Gamiz, Everardo. *Historia del estado de Durango*. Mexico: n.p., 1953.

García, José Pascual. *Exposición hecha al supremo gobierno de la union por los representantes de los estados de Chihuahua, Sonora, Durango, y territorio del Nuebo-Mejico, con motivo de los desastres que sufren por la guerra de los bárbaros*. Mexico: Galvan, 1832.

García Cantú, Gastón. *Las invasiones norteamericanas en México*. Mexico: Ediciones Era, 1971.

García Rejón, Manuel, and Daniel J. Gelo. *Comanche Vocabulary*. Austin: University of Texas Press, 1995.

Gelo, Daniel J. "On a New Interpretation of Comanche Social Organization." *Current Anthropology* 28 (1987): 551–55.

Gerhard, Peter. *The North Frontier of New Spain*. Rev. ed. Norman: University of Oklahoma Press, 1993.

Giddings, Luther. *Sketches of the Campaign in Northern Mexico in Eighteen Hundred Forty-Six and Seven, by an Officer of the First Regiment of Ohio Volunteers*. New York: George P. Putnam, 1853.

Gilliam, Albert M. *Travels over the Table Lands and Cordilleras of Mexico during the Years 1843 and 44; Including a Description of California . . . and the Biographies of Iturbide and Santa Anna*. Philadelphia: J. W. Moore, 1846.

Gladwin, Thomas. "Comanche Kin Behavior." *American Anthropologist* 50 (1948): 73–94.

Gledhill, John. *Power and Its Disguises: Anthropological Perspectives on Politics*. 2d ed. London: Pluto Press, 2000.

Goldschmidt, Walter. "Inducement to Military Participation in Tribal Societies." In *The Anthropology of War and Peace: Perspectives on the Nuclear Age*, edited by Paul R. Turner and David C. Pitt, 15–31. South Hadley, Mass.: Bergin and Garvey, 1989.

González de la Vara, Martín. "La política del federalismo en Nuevo México, 1821–1836." *Historia Mexicana* 36 (1986): 81–112.

————. "Entre el subsidio y la autonomía fiscal: Las finanzas públicas de Nuevo México, 1800–1846." *New Mexico Historical Review* 79 (2004): 31–59.

González Quiroga, Miguel A. "Nuevo León ante la invasión norteamericana, 1846–1848." In *México en guerra (1846–1848)*, edited by Laura Herrera Serna, 425–72. Mexico: Consejo Nacional para la Cultura y las Artes, 1997.

————. "Nuevo León ocupado: El gobierno de Nuevo León durante la guerra entre México y los Estados Unidos." In *México al tiempo de su guerra con Estados Unidos (1846–1848)*, edited by Josefina Zoraida Vázquez, 333–59. Mexico: Secretaría de Relaciones Exteriores, 1997.

Goodwin, Grenville. *Western Apache Raiding and Warfare*. Edited by Keith H. Basso. Tucson: University of Arizona Press, 1971.

Graebner, Norman A. *Empire on the Pacific: A Study in American Continental Expansion*. New York: Ronald Press, 1955.

Graf, Leroy P. "The Economic History of the Lower Rio Grande Valley, 1820–1875." Ph.D. diss., Harvard University, 1942.

Graybill, Andrew. *Policing the Great Plains: Rangers, Mounties, and the North American Frontier, 1875–1910*. Lincoln: University of Nebraska Press, 2007.

Green, Stanley C. *The Mexican Republic: The First Decade, 1823–1832*. Pittsburgh: University of Pittsburgh Press, 1987.

Gregg, Josiah. *Commerce of the Prairies*. Edited by Max L. Moorhead. 1844. Reprint, Norman: University of Oklahoma Press, 1954.

Gregory, Jack, and Rennard Strickland. *Sam Houston with the Cherokees, 1829–1833*. Austin: University of Texas Press, 1967.

Griffen, William B. *Apaches at War and Peace: The Janos Presidio, 1750–1858*. Albuquerque: University of New Mexico Press, 1988.

————. *Utmost Good Faith: Patterns of Apache–Mexican Hostilities in Northern Chihuahua Border Warfare, 1821–1848*. Albuquerque: University of New Mexico Press, 1988.

Grinnell, George Bird. *The Fighting Cheyennes*. Norman: University of Oklahoma Press, 1958.

Griswold del Castillo, Richard. *The Treaty of Guadalupe Hidalgo: A Legacy of Conflict*. Norman: University of Oklahoma Press, 1990.

Guardino, Peter F. *Peasants, Politics, and the Formation of Mexico's National State: Guerrero, 1800–1857*. Stanford: Stanford University Press, 1996.

————. *The Time of Liberty: Popular Political Culture in Oaxaca, 1750–1850*. Durham: Duke University Press, 2005.

Gutiérrez, Ramón A. *When Jesus Came, the Corn Mothers Went Away: Marriage, Sexuality, and Power in New Mexico, 1500–1846*. Stanford: Stanford University Press, 1991.

Haake, Claudia B. *The State, Removal and Indigenous Peoples in the United States and Mexico, 1620–2000*. New York: Routledge, 2007.

Hackel, Steven W. *Children of Coyote, Missionaries of Saint Francis: Indian–Spanish Relations in Colonial California, 1769–1850*. Chapel Hill: University of North Carolina Press, 2005.

Hagan, William Thomas. *United States–Comanche Relations: The Reservation Years*. New Haven: Yale University Press, 1976.

Halaas, David Fridtjof, and Andrew Edward Masich. *Halfbreed: The Remarkable True Story of George Bent: Caught between the Worlds of the Indian and the White Man.* Cambridge, Mass.: Da Capo Press, 2004.

Hale, Charles A. *Mexican Liberalism in the Age of Mora, 1821–1853.* New Haven: Yale University Press, 1968.

Hall, Thomas D. *Social Change in the Southwest, 1350–1880.* Lawrence: University Press of Kansas, 1989.

Hämäläinen, Pekka. "The Western Comanche Trade Center: Rethinking the Plains Indian Trade System." *Western Historical Quarterly* 29 (1998): 485–513.

———. "The First Phase of Destruction: Killing the Southern Plains Buffalo, 1790–1840." *Great Plains Quarterly* 21 (2001): 101–14.

———. "The Rise and Fall of Plains Indian Horse Cultures." *Journal of American History* 90 (2003): 833–62.

Hardin, Stephen H. "The Battle of the Alamo," in *Handbook of Texas Online,* http://www .tsha.utexas.edu/handbook/online/articles/AA/qea2.html, accessed Jan. 20, 2006

Harrington, John Peabody. *Vocabulary of the Kiowa Language.* Washington: U.S. Govt. Print. Off., 1928.

Harris, Charles H. *The Sánchez Navarros: A Socioeconomic Study of a Coahuilan Latifundio, 1846–1853.* Chicago: Loyola University Press, 1964.

———. *A Mexican Family Empire: The Latifundio of the Sánchez Navarros, 1765–1867.* Austin: University of Texas Press, 1975.

Hart, Brian. "Warren, Abel," in *Handbook of Texas Online,* http://www.tsha.utexas.edu/ handbook/online/articles/WW/fwa57.html, accessed May 14, 2007.

Hatcher, Mattie Austin. *The Opening of Texas to Foreign Settlement, 1801–1821.* Austin: University of Texas, 1927.

Hatfield, Shelly Bowen. *Chasing Shadows: Indians along the United States–Mexico Border, 1876–1911.* Albuquerque: University of New Mexico Press, 1998.

Haynes, Sam W. "Anglophobia and the Annexation of Texas: The Quest for National Security." In *Manifest Destiny and Empire: American Antebellum Expansionism,* edited by Sam W. Haynes and Christopher Morris, 115–45. College Station: Texas A&M University Press, 1997.

Henderson, Timothy J. *A Glorious Defeat: Mexico and Its War with the United States* (NY: Hill and Wang, 2007).

Henry, Robert Selph. *The Story of the Mexican War.* Indianapolis: Bobbs-Merrill, 1950.

Hernández Chávez, Alicia. *La tradición republicana del buen gobierno.* Mexico: El Colegio de México; Fideicomiso Historia de las Américas; Fondo de Cultura Económica, 1993.

Hernández Silva, Héctor Cuauhtémoc. "Sonora y la guerra con Estados Unidos." In *México al tiempo de su guerra con Estados Unidos (1846–1848),* edited by Josefina Zoraida Vázquez, 481–98. Mexico: Secretaría de Relaciones Exteriores, 1997.

Herrera Pérez, Octavio. "Tamaulipas ante la guerra de invasión Norteamericana." In *México al tiempo de su guerra con Estados Unidos (1846–1848),* edited by Josefina Zoraida Vázquez, 524–58. Mexico: Secretaría de Relaciones Exteriores, 1997.

Hietala, Thomas R. *Manifest Design: Anxious Aggrandizement in Late Jacksonian America.* Ithaca: Cornell University Press, 1985.

———. "'This Splendid Juggernaut': Westward a Nation and Its People." In *Manifest Destiny and Empire: American Antebellum Expansionism,* edited by Sam W. Haynes and Christopher Morris, 48–67. College Station: Texas A&M University Press, 1997.

Hill, D. H. *A Fighter from Way Back: The Mexican War Diary of Lt. Daniel Harvey Hill, 4th Artillery, USA.* Edited by Nathaniel Cheairs Hughes, Jr., and Timothy D. Johnson. Kent: Kent State University Press, 2002.

Hinderaker, Eric. *Elusive Empires: Constructing Colonialism in the Ohio Valley, 1673–1800.* Cambridge: Cambridge University Press, 1997.

Hinojosa, Gilberto Miguel. *A Borderlands Town in Transition: Laredo, 1755–1870.* College Station: Texas A&M University Press, 1983.

Hitchcock, Ethan Allen. *A Traveler in Indian Territory: The Journal of Ethan Allen Hitchcock, Late Major-General in the United States Army.* Edited by Grant Foreman. Norman: University of Oklahoma Press, 1996.

Hoebel, E. Adamson. *The Political Organization and Law-Ways of the Comanche Indians.* Menasha, Wis.: American Anthropological Association, 1940.

Hogan, Michael J. "'The Next Big Thing': The Future of Diplomatic History in a Global Age." *Diplomatic History* 28 (2004): 1-21.

Holley, Mary Austin, and William Hooker. *Texas.* Lexington: J. Clarke, 1836.

Horn, Sarah Ann. *A Narrative of the Captivity of Mrs. Horn and her Two Children with Mrs. Harris by the Camanche Indians, after they had Murdered their Husbands and Traveling Companions, with a Brief Account of the Manners and Customs of that Nation of Savages, of Whom so Little is Generally Known.* St. Louis: C. Keemle, 1839.

Horsman, Reginald. *Race and Manifest Destiny: The Origins of American Racial Anglo-Saxonism.* Cambridge: Harvard University Press, 1981.

Hu-DeHart, Evelyn. *Yaqui Resistance and Survival: The Struggle for Land and Autonomy, 1821–1910.* Madison: University of Wisconsin Press, 1984.

Hughes, John T. *Doniphan's Expedition: Containing an Account of the Conquest of New Mexico; General Kearny's Overland Expedition to California; Doniphan's Campaign against the Navajos; His Unparalleled March upon Chihuahua and Durango; and the Operations of General Price at Santa Fe.* Cincinnati: J. A. and U.-P. James, 1848.

Hyde, George E., ed. *Life of George Bent, Written from His Letters.* Norman: University of Oklahoma Press, 1968.

Iglesias González, Román. *Planes políticos, proclamas, manifiestos y otros documentos de la independencia al México moderno, 1812–1940.* Mexico: Universidad Nacional Autónoma de México, Instituto de Investigaciones Jurídicas, 1998.

Informe de la comisión pesquisidora de la frontera del norte al ejecutivo de la union, en cumplimiento del artículo 3 de la ley de 30 de septiembre de 1872. Mexico: Díaz de Leon y White, 1874.

Isenberg, Andrew C. *The Destruction of the Bison: An Environmental History, 1750–1920.* Cambridge: Cambridge University Press, 2000.

———. "The Market Revolution in the Borderlands: George Champlin Sibley in Missouri and New Mexico, 1808–1826." *Journal of the Early Republic* 21 (2001): 445–65.

Jablow, Joseph. *The Cheyenne in Plains Indian Trade Relations, 1795–1840.* 1951. Reprint, Lincoln: University of Nebraska Press, 1994.

Jackson, Donald, ed. *The Journals of Zebulon Montgomery Pike: With Letters and Related Documents.* Norman: University of Oklahoma Press, 1966.

Jackson, Jack, ed. *Texas by Terán: The Diary Kept by General Manuel de Mier y Terán on His 1828 Inspection of Texas.* Translated by John Wheat. Austin: University of Texas Press, 2000.

———. *Indian Agent: Peter Ellis Bean in Mexican Texas.* College Station: Texas A&M University Press, 2005.

Jackson, Jack, and William C. Foster, eds. *Imaginary Kingdom: Texas as Seen by the Rivera and Rubí Military Expeditions, 1727 and 1767.* Austin: Texas State Historical Association, 1995.

James, Edwin. *James' Account of S. H. Long's Expedition, 1819–1820.* Edited by Reuben Gold Thwaites. 4 vols. Cleveland: Arthur H. Clark, 1905.

Jáuregui, Luis. "Chihuahua en la tormenta, su situación política durante la Guerra con los Estados Unidos: Septiembre de 1846–julio de 1848." In *México al tiempo de su guerra con Estados Unidos (1846–1848)*, edited by Josefina Zoraida Vázquez, 134–56. Mexico: Secretaría de Relaciones Exteriores, 1997.

———. "Los orígenes de un malestar crónico: Los ingresos y los gastos públicos de México, 1821–1855." In *Penuria sin fin: Historia de los impuestos en México, siglos XVIII–XX*, edited by Aguilar Luis Aboites and Luis Jáuregui, 79–114. Mexico: Instituto de Investigaciones Dr. José María Luis Mora, 2005.

Jenkins, John Holmes, ed. *The Papers of the Texas Revolution, 1835–1836.* 10 vols. Austin: University of Texas Press, 1973.

Jenkins, Myra Ellen, and Alan Minge Ward. *Navajo Activities Affecting the Acoma–Laguna Area, 1746–1910.* New York: Garland, 1974.

Jiménez Codinach, Estela Guadalupe, Berta Ulloa, and Joel Hernández Santiago. *Planes en la Nación Mexicana.* 11 vols. Mexico: Senado de la República, 1987.

Johannsen, Robert Walter. *To the Halls of the Montezumas: The Mexican War in the American Imagination.* New York: Oxford University Press, 1985.

John, Elizabeth A. H. "Nurturing the Peace: Spanish and Comanche Cooperation in the Early Nineteenth Century." *New Mexico Historical Review* 59 (1984): 345–69.

———. *Storms Brewed in Other Men's Worlds: The Confrontation of Indians, Spanish, and French in the Southwest, 1540–1795.* 2d ed. Norman: University of Oklahoma Press, 1996.

Jones, Kristine L. "Comparative Raiding Economies: North and South." In *Contested Ground: Comparative Frontiers on the Northern and Southern Edges of the Spanish Empire*, edited by Donna J. Guy and Thomas E. Sheridan. Tucson: University of Arizona Press, 1998.

Jordán, Fernando. *Crónica de un país bárbaro.* 5th ed. Chihuahua: Centro Librero La Prensa, 1978.

Joseph, Gilbert M., and Daniel Nugent, eds. *Everyday Forms of State Formation: Revolution and the Negotiation of Rule in Modern Mexico.* Durham: Duke University Press, 1994.

Kappler, Charles J. *Indian Affairs: Laws and Treaties*. 2 vols. Washington: Government Printing Office, 1904.

Katz, Friedrich. "Labor Conditions in Porfirian Mexico: Some Trends and Tendencies." *Hispanic American Historical Review* 54 (1974): 1–47.

———. "Peasants and the Mexican Revolution of 1910." In *Forging Nations: A Comparative View of Rural Ferment and Revolt*, edited by Joseph Spielberg and Scott Whiteford. East Lansing: Michigan State University Press, 1976.

———, ed. *Riot, Rebellion, and Revolution: Rural Social Conflict in Mexico*. Princeton: Princeton University Press, 1988.

Kavanagh, Thomas W. "The Comanche: Paradigmatic Anomaly or Ethnographic Fiction?" *Haliksa'i* 4 (1985): 109–28.

———. *Comanche Political History: An Ethnohistorical Perspective, 1706–1875*. Lincoln: University of Nebraska Press, 1996.

Kearney, Milo, and Anthony K. Knopp. *Boom and Bust: The Historical Cycles of Matamoros and Brownsville*. Austin: Eakin Press, 1991.

Keeley, Lawrence H. *War before Civilization*. Oxford: Oxford University Press, 1996.

Kelly, Edith Louise, and Mattie Austin Hatcher, trans. and eds. "Tadeo Ortiz and the Colonization of Texas, 1822–1833." *Southwestern Historical Quarterly* 32 (1929): 74–86, 152–64, 222–51, 311–43.

Kendall, George Wilkins. *Narrative of the Texan Santa Fé Expedition*. 2 vols. New York: Harper and Brothers, 1844.

———. *Dispatches from the Mexican War*. Norman: University of Oklahoma Press, 1999.

Kennedy, William. *Texas: The Rise, Progress, and Prospects of the Republic of Texas*. 1841. Reprint, Fort Worth: Molyneaux Craftsmen, 1925.

Kenner, Charles L. *The Comanchero Frontier: A History of New Mexican–Plains Indians Relations*. 1969. Reprint, Norman: University of Oklahoma Press, 1994.

Kessell, John L. *Friars, Soldiers, and Reformers: Hispanic Arizona and the Sonora Mission Frontier, 1767–1856*. Tucson: University of Arizona Press, 1976.

Kornblith, Gary J. "Rethinking the Coming of the Civil War: A Counterfactual Exercise." *Journal of American History* 90:1 (2003): 76–105.

Kurtz, Donald V. *Political Anthropology: Power and Paradigms*. Boulder: Westview Press, 2001.

La Vere, David. "Friendly Persuasions: Gifts and Reciprocity in Comanche–Euroamerican Relations." *Chronicles of Oklahoma* 71 (1993): 322–37.

———. *Contrary Neighbors: Southern Plains and Removed Indians in Indian Territory*. Norman: University of Oklahoma Press, 2000.

Lamar, Howard R. *Far Southwest 1846–1912: A Territorial History*. New Haven: Yale University Press, 1966.

———, ed. *The New Encyclopedia of the American West*. New Haven: Yale University Press, 1998.

Lander Jr., Ernest McPherson. *Reluctant Imperialists: Calhoun, the South Carolinians, and the Mexican War*. Baton Rouge: Louisiana State University Press, 1980.

Larson, Brooke. *Trials of Nation Making: Liberalism, Race, and Ethnicity in the Andes, 1810–1910*. Cambridge: Cambridge University Press, 2004.

Leathers, Daniel J. "Climate." In *Encyclopedia of the Great Plains*, edited by David J. Wishart, 624–25. Lincoln: University of Nebraska Press, 2004.

LeBlanc, Steven A. *Prehistoric Warfare in the American Southwest*. Salt Lake City: University of Utah Press, 1999.

LeBlanc, Steven A., and Katherine E. Register. *Constant Battles: The Myth of the Peaceful, Noble Savage*. New York: St. Martin's Press, 2003.

Lecompte, Janet. "Bent, St. Vrain and Company among the Comanche and Kiowa." *Colorado Magazine* 49 (1972): 273–93.

———. "Manuel Armijo's Family History." *New Mexico Historical Review* 48 (1973): 252–56.

———. *Pueblo, Hardscrabble, Greenhorn: Society on the High Plains, 1832–1856*. Norman: University of Oklahoma Press, 1978.

———. *Rebellion in Río Arriba, 1837*. Albuquerque: University of New Mexico Press, 1985.

Lee, Rebecca Smith. "The Publication of Austin's Louisville Address." *Southwestern Historical Quarterly* 70 (1967): 424–42.

LeMenager, Stephanie. *Manifest and Other Destinies: Territorial Fictions of the Nineteenth-Century United States*. Lincoln: University of Nebraska Press, 2004.

Lepore, Jill. *The Name of War: King Philip's War and the Origins of American Identity*. New York: Knopf, 1998.

Levinson, Irving W. *Wars within War: Mexican Guerrillas, Domestic Elites, and the United States of America, 1846–1848*. Fort Worth: Texas Christian University Press, 2005.

Lewis, James E. *The American Union and the Problem of Neighborhood: The United States and the Collapse of the Spanish Empire, 1783–1829*. Chapel Hill: University of North Carolina Press, 1998.

López López, Alvaro. *La ciudad y su tiempo histórico: Saltillo siglos XVIII–XIX*. Saltillo: Instituto Tecnológico de Saltillo, Instituto Estatal de Documentación, 1996.

Loyola, Sister Mary. *The American Occupation of New Mexico, 1821–1852*. Albuquerque: University of New Mexico Press, 1939.

Lundy, Benjamin. *The Origin and True Causes of the Texas Insurrection, Commenced in the Year 1835*. Philadelphia: Merrihew and Gunn, 1836.

———. *The War in Texas: A Review of Facts and Circumstances, Showing That This Contest Is the Result of a Long Premeditated Crusade Against the Government, Set on Foot by Slaveholders, Land Speculators, etc. with the View of Re-establishing, Extending, and Perpetuating the System of Slavery and the Slave Trade in the Republic of Mexico*. Philadelphia: Merrihew and Gunn, 1837.

Mallon, Florencia E. *Peasant and Nation: The Making of Postcolonial Mexico and Peru*. Berkeley: University of California Press, 1995.

Manning, William R. *Early Diplomatic Relations between the United States and Mexico*. Baltimore: Johns Hopkins University Press, 1916.

———, ed. *Diplomatic Correspondence of the United States: Inter-American Affairs, 1831–1860*. Vol. 8, *Mexico, 1831–1848 (Mid-Year)*. Washington: Carnegie Endowment for International Peace, 1937.

———, ed. *Diplomatic Correspondence of the United States: Inter-American Affairs, 1831–*

1860. Vol. 9, *Mexico, 1848 (Mid-Year)–1860*. Washington: Carnegie Endowment for International Peace, 1937.

———, ed. *Diplomatic Correspondence of the United States: Inter-American Affairs, 1831–1860.* Vol. 11, *Texas and Venezuela.* Washington: Carnegie Endowment for International Peace, 1939.

Mapp, Paul. "European Geographic Ignorance and North American Imperial Rivalry: The Role of the Uncharted American West in International Affairs, 1713–1763." Ph.D. diss., Harvard University, 2001.

———. "French Geographic Conceptions of the Unexplored American West and the Louisiana Cession of 1762." In *French Colonial Louisiana and the Atlantic World*, edited by Bradley G. Bond, 134–74. Baton Rouge: Louisiana State University Press, 2005.

Marichal, Carlos. "Una difícil transición fiscal: Del régimen colonial al México independiente, 1750–1850." In *De colonia a nación: Impuestos y política en México, 1750–1860*, edited by Carlos Marichal and Daniela Marino, 19–58. Mexico: Colegio de México, Centro de Estudios Históricos, 2001.

Márquez, Jesús Velasco. *La Guerra del '47 y la opinión pública (1845–1848)*. Mexico: Secretaría de Educación Pública, 1975.

Martínez, Antonio José. *Esposición que el presbítero Antonio José Martínez, cura de Taos de Nuevo México, dirije al Gobierno del Exmo. sor. General Antonio Lópes de Santa Anna. Proponiendo la civilisación de las naciones bárbaras que son al contorno del Departamento de Nuevo México.* Taos: n.p., 1843.

Martínez Caraza, Leopoldo. *El norte bárbaro de Mexico.* Mexico: Panorama, 1983.

Mauss, Marcel. *The Gift: The Form and Reason for Exchange in Archaic Societies.* New York: W. W. Norton, 1990. (1925, in French)

Mayhall, Mildred P. *The Kiowas.* Norman: University of Oklahoma Press, 1962.

Mayo, Robert. *Political Sketches of Eight Years in Washington: In Four Parts, with Annotations to Each; Also a General Appendix; An Alphabetical Index; and a Series of Charts, Giving a Comparative Synopsis of the Constitutions of the Several States, and the United States.* Baltimore: F. Lucas, 1839.

McCarty, Kieran. *A Frontier Documentary: Sonora and Tucson, 1821–1848.* Tucson: University of Arizona Press, 1997.

McLean, Malcolm Dallas, ed. *Papers Concerning Robertson's Colony in Texas.* 18 vols. Fort Worth: Texas Christian University Press, 1974–95.

McCollough, Martha. *Three Nations, One Place: A Comparative Ethnohistory of Social Change among the Comanches and Hasinais During Spain's Colonial Era, 1689–1821.* New York: Routledge, 2004.

McCrady, David G. *Living with Strangers: The Nineteenth-Century Sioux and the Canadian–American Borderlands.* Lincoln: University of Nebraska Press, 2006.

McManus, Sheila. *The Line Which Separates: Race, Gender, and the Making of the Alberta–Montana Borderlands.* Lincoln: University of Nebraska Press, 2005.

McNitt, Frank. *Navajo Wars: Military Campaigns, Slave Raids, and Reprisals.* Albuquerque: University of New Mexico Press, 1972.

Meadows, William C. *Kiowa, Apache, and Comanche Military Societies: Enduring Veterans, 1800 to the Present.* Austin: University of Texas Press, 1999.

Bibliography 445

Meed, Douglas V. *The Mexican War, 1846–1848.* New York: Routledge, 2003.

Meinig, D. W. *Imperial Texas: An Interpretive Essay in Cultural Geography.* Austin: University of Texas Press, 1969.

———. *The Shaping of America: A Geographical Perspective on 500 Years of History.* Vol. 2, *Continental America, 1800–1867.* New Haven: Yale University Press, 1993.

Mendinichaga, Rodrigo. *Los cuatro tiempos de un pueblo: Nuevo León en la historia.* Monterrey: Instituto Tecnológico de Monterrey, 1985.

Merk, Frederick. *Manifest Destiny and Mission in American History: A Reinterpretation.* New York: Knopf, 1963.

Merrell, James Hart. *Into the American Woods: Negotiators on the Pennsylvania Frontier.* New York: Norton, 1999.

Meyer, Michael C. *Water in the Hispanic Southwest: A Social and Legal History, 1550–1850.* Tucson: University of Arizona Press, 1984.

Middlebrooks, Audy J., and Glenna Middlebrooks. "Holland Coffee of Red River." *Southwestern Historical Quarterly* 69 (1965): 146–62.

Mier y Terán, Manuel de. "Noticia de las tribus de salvajes conocidos que habitan en el Departamento de Tejas, y del número de familias de que consta cada tribu, puntos en que habitan y terrenos en que acampan." In *Crónica de Tejas: Diario de viaje de la Comisión de Límites,* edited by Mauricio Molina, 129–39. Mexico: Instituto Nacional de Bellas Artes, 1988.

Miller, Hunter, ed. *Treaties and Other International Acts of the United States of America.* 8 vols. Washington: U.S. Government Printing Office, 1931–48.

Miller, Joseph C. *Way of Death: Merchant Capitalism and the Angolan Slave Trade, 1730–1830.* Madison: University of Wisconsin Press, 1988.

Miller, Susan A. *Coacoochee's Bones: A Seminole Saga.* Lawrence: University Press of Kansas, 2003.

Minge, Ward Alan. "Frontier Problems in New Mexico Preceding the Mexican War, 1840–1846." Ph.D. diss., University of New Mexico, 1966.

———. "Mexican Independence Day and a Ute Tragedy in Santa Fe, 1844." In *The Changing Ways of Southwestern Indians: A Historic Perspective,* edited by Albert Schroeder, 107–22. Glorieta, Tex.: Rio Grande Press, 1973.

Mishkin, Bernard. *Rank and Warfare among the Plains Indians.* 1940. Reprint, Lincoln: University of Nebraska Press, 1992.

Mooney, James. *Calendar History of the Kiowa Indians.* Washington: Government Printing Office, 1898.

Moore, Francis. *Map and Description of Texas, Containing Sketches of Its History, Geology, Geography and Statistics: With Concise Statements, Relative to the Soil, Climate, Productions, Facilities of Transportation, Population of the Country; and Some Brief Remarks upon the Character and Customs of Its Inhabitants.* Philadelphia: Tanner and Disturnell, 1840.

Moore, John H. *The Cheyenne.* Cambridge: Blackwell, 1996.

Moore, John H., Margot P. Liberty, and A. Terry Straus. "Cheyenne." In *Handbook of North American Indians.* Vol. 13, *Plains,* edited by Raymond J. DeMallie, 863–85. Washington: Smithsonian Institution Press, 2001.

Moorhead, Max L. *The Apache Frontier: Jacobo Ugarte and Spanish–Indian Relations in Northern New Spain, 1769–1791*. Norman: University of Oklahoma Press, 1968.

———. *The Presidio: Bastion of the Spanish Borderlands*. Norman: University of Oklahoma Press, 1975.

———. "Report of the Citizens of New Mexico to the President of Mexico, Santa Fe, September 26, 1846." *New Mexico Historical Review* 26 (1951): 69–75.

Moser, Harold D., ed. *The Papers of Daniel Webster: Correspondence*. Vol. 5, *1840–1843*. Hanover: University Press of New England, 1982.

Muir, Andrew Forest, ed. *Texas in 1837: An Anonymous, Contemporary Narrative*. Austin: University of Texas Press, 1958.

Muller, Cornelius H. "Vegetation and Climate of Coahuila, Mexico." *Madroño* 9 (1947): 33–57.

Mulroy, Kevin. *Freedom on the Border: The Seminole Maroons in Florida, the Indian Territory, Coahuila, and Texas*. Lubbock: Texas Tech University Press, 1993.

Nance, Joseph Milton. *After San Jacinto: The Texas–Mexican Frontier, 1836–1841*. Austin: University of Texas Press, 1963.

Narvona, Antonio. "Report of the Cattle and Caballada Found in the Territory of New Mexico." In *Three New Mexico Chronicles: The Exposición of Don Pedro Bautista Pino, 1812; The Ojeada of Lic. Antonio Barreiro, 1832; and the Additions by Don José Agustín de Escudero, 1849*, edited by Horace Bailey Carroll and Juan Villasana Haggard, 43. Albuquerque: Quivera Society, 1942.

Nasatir, Abraham Phineas. *Borderland in Retreat: From Spanish Louisiana to the Far Southwest*. Albuquerque: University of New Mexico Press, 1976.

Navarro Gallegos, César. "Una 'Santa Alianza': El gobierno duranguense y la jerarquía eclesiástica durante la intervención norteamericana." In *México en guerra (1846–1848): Perspectivas regionales*, edited by Laura Herrera Serna, 233–51. Mexico: Consejo Nacional para la Cultura y las Artes, 1997.

Neighbors, Robert S. "The Na-Uni or Comanches." In *Information Respecting the History, Conditions and Prospects of the Indian Tribes of the United States*, edited by Henry R. Schoolcraft, 125–34. Philadelphia: Lippincott, Grambo, 1852.

Newell, Chester. *History of the Revolution in Texas, particularly of the War of 1835 and '36: Together with the Latest Geographical, Topographical, and Statistical Accounts of the Country, from the Most Authentic Sources, also, An Appendix*. New York: Wiley and Putnam, 1838.

Nostrand, Richard L. "The Spread of Spanish Settlement in Greater New Mexico: An Isochronic Map, 1610–1890." *Journal of the West* 34 (1995): 82–87.

Noyes, Stanley. *Los Comanches: The Horse People, 1751–1845*. Albuquerque: University of New Mexico Press, 1993.

Nugent, Daniel. "'Are We Not [Civilized] Men?': The Formation and Devolution of Community in Northern Mexico." *Journal of Historical Sociology* 2 (1989): 206–39.

———. "The Center at the Periphery: Civilization and Barbarism on the Northern Mexican Frontier." *Identities: Global Studies in Culture and Power* 1 (1994): 151–72.

———. "Two, Three, Many Barbarisms? The Chihuahuan Frontier in Transition from Society to Politics." In *Contested Ground: Comparative Frontiers on the Northern and*

Southern Edges of the Spanish Empire, edited by Donna J. Guy and Thomas E. Sheridan, 182–200. Tucson: University of Arizona Press, 1998.

O'Brien, Sean Michael. *In Bitterness and in Tears: Andrew Jackson's Destruction of the Creeks and Seminoles*. Westport: Praeger, 2003.

Officer, James E. *Hispanic Arizona, 1536–1856*. Tucson: University of Arizona Press, 1987.

Opler, Morris Edward. "The Apachean Culture Pattern and Its Origins." In *Handbook of North American Indians*. Vol. 10, *Southwest*, edited by Alfonso Ortiz, 368–92. Washington: Smithsonian Institution Press, 1983.

———. "Chiricahua Apache." In *Handbook of North American Indians*. Vol. 10, *Southwest*, edited by Alfonso Ortiz, 401–18. Washington: Smithsonian Institution Press, 1983.

———. "Mescalero Apache." In *Handbook of North American Indians*. Vol. 10, *Southwest*, edited by Alfonso Ortiz, 419–39. Washington: Smithsonian Institution Press, 1983.

Orozco, Víctor Orozco. *Las guerras indias en la historia de Chihuahua: Primeras fases*. Mexico: Consejo Nacional para la Cultura y las Artes, 1992.

———. *Tierra de libres: Los pueblos del distrito de Guerrero en el siglo xix*. Ciudad Juárez: Universidad Autónoma de Ciudad Juárez, 1995.

———, ed. *Las guerras indias en la historia de Chihuahua: Antología*. Ciudad Juárez: Universidad Autónoma de Ciudad Juárez; Instituto Chihuahuense de la Cultura, 1992.

Ortner, Sherry B. "Resistance and the Problem of Ethnographic Refusal." *Comparative Studies in Society and History* 37 (1995): 173–93.

Ostler, Jeffery. *The Plains Sioux and U.S. Colonialism from Lewis and Clark to Wounded Knee*. Cambridge: Cambridge University Press, 2004.

Owen, Charles Hunter. *The Justice of the Mexican War*. New York: G. P. Putnam's Sons, 1908.

Owsley, Frank Lawrence, and Gene A. Smith. *Filibusters and Expansionists: Jeffersonian Manifest Destiny, 1800–1821*. Tuscaloosa: University of Alabama Press, 1997.

Pacheco Rojas, José de la Cruz. "Durango entre dos guerras, 1846–1847." In *México al tiempo de su guerra con Estados Unidos (1846–1848)*, edited by Josefina Zoraida Vázquez, 189–212. Mexico: Secretaría de Relaciones Exteriores, 1997.

Palti, Elías José. "Legitimacy and History in the Aftermath of Revolutions (Latin America, 1820–1910): A Journey through the Fringes of Liberal Thought." Ph.D. diss., University of California, Berkeley, 1997.

———. *La nación como problema: Los historiadores y la "cuestión nacional."* Buenos Aires, Argentina: Fondo de Cultura Económica, 2003.

Pani, Erika. *Para mexicanizar el Segundo Imperio: El imaginario político de los imperialistas*. Mexico: Colegio de México Centro de Estudios Históricos: Instituto de Investigaciones Dr. José María Luis Mora, 2001.

———. "Dreaming of a Mexican Empire: The Political Projects of the 'Imperialistas.'" *Hispanic American Historical Review* 82 (2002): 1–31.

Parker, James W. *Narrative of the Perilous Adventures, Miraculous Escapes and Sufferings of Rev. James W. Parker, During a Frontier Residence in Texas, of Fifteen Years . . . to Which Is Added a Narrative of the Capture, and Subsequent Sufferings of Mrs. Rachel Plummer*. Louisville: Morning Courier Office, 1844.

Bibliography

Pattie, James O. *The Personal Narrative of James O. Pattie: The 1831 Edition, Unabridged.* Lincoln: University of Nebraska Press, 1984.

Pease, L. T. *A Geographical and Historical View of Texas, With a Detailed Account of the Texian Revolution and War.* Hartford: H. Huntington, Jr., 1837.

Perrigo, Lynn Irwin. *Hispanos: Historic Leaders in New Mexico.* Santa Fe: Sunstone Press, 1985.

Phillips, George Harwood. *Indians and Intruders in Central California, 1769–1849.* Norman: University of Oklahoma Press, 1993.

Pike, Albert. *Prose Sketches and Poems, Written in the Western Country.* Boston: Light and Horton, 1834.

Pino, Pedro Baptista. *The Exposition on the Province of New Mexico.* Translated by Adrian Bustamante and Marc Simmons. Santa Fe: Rancho de las Golondrinas and University of New Mexico Press, 1995.

Pletcher, David M. *The Diplomacy of Annexation: Texas, Oregon, and the Mexican War.* Columbia: University of Missouri Press, 1973.

Plummer, Rachael. *Narrative of Twenty-One Months' Servitude as a Prisoner Among the Commanchee Indians.* Edited by William S. Reese. 1838. Reprint, Austin: Jenkins, 1977.

Ponce de León, José María, ed. *Reseñas históricas del estado de Chihuahua.* Chihuahua: Imprenta del gobierno, 1913.

Powell, Philip Wayne. *Soldiers, Indians, and Silver: The Northward Advance of New Spain, 1550–1600.* Berkeley: University of California Press, 1952.

———. *Mexico's Miguel Caldera: The Taming of America's First Frontier, 1548–1597.* Tucson: University of Arizona Press, 1977.

Prieto, Cecilia Sheridan. "Coahuila y la invasión norteamericana." In *México al tiempo de su guerra con Estados Unidos (1846–1848),* edited by Josefina Zoraida Vázquez, 157–88. Mexico: Secretaría de Relaciones Exteriores, 1997.

Prucha, Francis Paul. *The Great Father: The United States Government and the American Indians.* Lincoln: University of Nebraska Press, 1984.

Quaife, Milo Milton, ed. *The Diary of James K. Polk during His Presidency, 1845 to 1849.* 4 vols. Chicago: A. C. McClurg, 1910.

Quijada Hernández, Armando, and Juan Antonio Ruibal Corella. *Historia general de Sonora: Período del México Independiente, 1831–1883.* Hermosillo: Gobierno del Estado de Sonora, 1985.

Radding, Cynthia. *Wandering Peoples: Colonialism, Ethnic Spaces, and Ecological Frontiers in Northwestern Mexico, 1700–1850.* Durham: Duke University Press, 1997.

Rao Bárcena, José María. *Recuerdos de la invasion norteamericana (1846–1848).* Mexico: Editorial Porrúa, 1947.

Ramos, J. L., and Teresa Rojas Rabiela. *El Indio en la prensa nacional mexicana del siglo XIX: Catálogo de noticias.* Mexico: Centro de Investigaciones y Estudios Superiores en Antropología Social, 1987.

Ramsey, Albert C., ed. *The Other Side, or Notes for the History of the War between Mexico and the United States.* New York: John Wiley, 1850.

Rathbun, Lyon Oliver. "The Representation of Mexicans and the Transformation of American Political Culture, 1787–1848." Ph.D. diss., University of California, Berkeley, 1997.

Rather, Ethel Zivley. "Recognition of the Republic of Texas by the United States." *Quarterly of the Texas State Historical Association* 13 (1910): 155–256.

Reeve, Frank D. "The Navaho–Spanish Peace: 1720s–1770s." *New Mexico Historical Review* 34 (1959): 9–40.

———. "Navaho–Spanish Diplomacy, 1770–1790." *New Mexico Historical Review* 35 (1960): 200–235.

———. "Navaho Foreign Affairs, 1795–1846." *New Mexico Historical Review* 46 (1971): 101–32, 223–51.

———, ed. "The Charles Bent Papers [Letters from Charles Bent to U.S. Consul in Santa Fe Manuel Alvarez, from the Benjamin J. Read Collection, Historical Society of New Mexico, Santa Fe]." *New Mexico Historical Review* 29–31 (1954–56): various.

Reichstein, Andreas. *Rise of the Lone Star: The Making of Texas.* Translated by Jeanne R. Wilson. College Station: Texas A&M University Press, 1989.

Reid, John Phillip. *A Law of Blood: The Primitive Law of the Cherokee Nation.* New York: New York University Press, 1970.

———. *Patterns of Vengeance: Crosscultural Homicide in the North American Fur Trade.* Pasadena: Ninth Judicial Circuit Historical Society, 1999.

Reina, Leticia. "The Sierra Gorda Peasant Rebellion, 1847–1850." In *Riot, Rebellion and Revolution: Rural Social Conflict in Mexico,* edited by Friedrich Katz, 267–94. Princeton: Princeton University Press, 1988.

Remini, Robert Vincent. *Andrew Jackson and the Course of American Empire, 1767–1821.* New York: Harper and Row, 1977.

———. *Andrew Jackson and the Course of American Freedom, 1822–1832.* New York: Harper and Row, 1981.

———. *The Life of Andrew Jackson.* New York: Perennial, 2001.

Reséndez, Andrés. "Caught Between Profits and Rituals: National Contestation in Texas and New Mexico, 1821–1848." Ph.D. diss., University of Chicago, 1997.

———. *Changing National Identities at the Frontier: Texas and New Mexico, 1800–1850.* Cambridge: Cambridge University Press, 2005.

Richards, Leonard L. *The Slave Power: The Free North and Southern Domination, 1780–1860.* Baton Rouge: Louisiana State University Press, 2000.

Richardson, Rupert Norval. "Santa Anna and the Santa Anna Mountains." *West Texas Historical Association Year Book* 11 (1935): 47–55.

Richmond, Douglas W. "A View of the Periphery: Regional Factors and Collaboration during the U.S.–Mexican Conflict, 1845–1848." In *Dueling Eagles: Reinterpreting the U.S.–Mexican War, 1846–1848,* edited by Richard V. Frangaviglia and Douglas W. Richmond, 127–54. Fort Worth: Texas Christian University Press, 2000.

Richter, Daniel K. *The Ordeal of the Longhouse: The Peoples of the Iroquois League in the Era of European Colonization.* Chapel Hill: University of North Carolina Press, 1992.

———. *Facing East from Indian Country: A Native History of Early America.* Cambridge: Harvard University Press, 2001.

Ridout, Joseph B. "An Anti-National Disorder: Antonio Canales and Northeastern Mexico, 1836–1852." M.A. thesis, University of Texas, 1994.

Rippy, J. Fred. "The Indians of the Southwest in the Diplomacy of the United States and Mexico, 1848–1853." *Hispanic American Historical Review* 2 (1919): 363–96.

———. *The United States and Mexico.* New York: Knopf, 1926.

Rister, Carl Coke, ed. *Comanche Bondage: Dr. John Charles Beales's Settlement of La Villa de Dolores on Las Moras Creek in Southern Texas of the 1830s.* Glendale, Calif.: Arthur H. Clark, 1955.

Rivaya Martínez, Joaquín. "Captivity and Adoption among the Comanche Indians." Ph.D. diss., UCLA, 2006.

Rives, George Lockhart. *The United States and Mexico, 1821–1848: A History of the Relations Between the Two Countries from the Independence of Mexico to the Close of the War with the United States.* New York: Kraus Reprint, 1969.

Robertson, R. G. *Rotting Face: Smallpox and the American Indian.* Caldwell, Idaho: Caxton Press, 2001.

Robinson, Jacob S. *A Journal of the Santa Fe Expedition under Colonel Doniphan.* Edited by Carl L. Cannon. 1848. Reprint, Princeton: Princeton University Press, 1932.

Rodríguez, Martha. *Historias de resistencia y exterminio: Los indios de Coahuila durante el siglo XIX.* Mexico: Centro de Investigaciones y Estudios Superiores en Antropología Social, 1995.

———. *La guerra entre bárbaros y civilizados: El exterminio del nómada en Coahuila, 1840–1880.* Saltillo, Coahuila: Ceshac, 1998.

Roe, Frank Gilbert. *The North American Buffalo: A Critical Study of the Species in Its Wild State.* Toronto: University of Toronto Press, 1951.

Roel, Santiago. *Nuevo León, apuntes históricos.* Monterrey: Impresora Bachiller, 1955.

Roemer, Ferdinand. *Texas: With Particular Reference to German Immigration and the Physical Appearance of the Country.* Translated by Oswald Mueller. Austin: Texian Press, 1983. (1849, in German)

Rollings, Willard H. *The Osage: An Ethnohistorical Study of Hegemony on the Prairie-Plains.* Columbia: University of Missouri Press, 1992.

Rorabaugh, W. J. *The Alcoholic Republic, an American Tradition.* New York: Oxford University Press, 1979.

Rosenberg, Emily S. "Considering Borders." In *Explaining the History of American Foreign Relations,* edited by Michael J. Hogan and Thomas G. Paterson, 176-93. Cambridge: Cambridge University Press, 2004.

Rothman, Adam. *Slave Country: American Expansion and the Origins of the Deep South.* Cambridge: Harvard University Press, 2005.

Ruxton, George F. *Adventures in Mexico and the Rocky Mountains.* 1848. Reprint, Glorieta, Tex.: Rio Grande Press, 1973.

Sahlins, Marshall. "The Segmentary Lineage: An Organization of Predatory Expansion." In *Comparative Political Systems: Studies in the Politics of Pre-Industrial Societies,* edited by Ronald Cohen and John Middleton, 89–120. Austin: University of Texas Press, 1967.

———. *Stone Age Economics.* New York: Aldine, 1972.

Salmón, Roberto Mario. "Zapata, Antonio," in the *Handbook of Texas Online,* http://www.tsha.utexas.edu/handbook/online/articles/ZZ/fza3.html, accessed July 17, 2007.

Sánchez, José María. "A Trip to Texas in 1828." *Southwestern Historical Quarterly* 29 (1926): 249–88.

Sánchez Rodríguez, Martín. "Política fiscal y organización de la hacienda pública durante la república centralista en México, 1836–1844." In *De colonia a nación: Impuestos y política en México, 1750–1860*, edited by Carlos Marichal and Daniela Marino, 189–214. Mexico City: Colegio de México, Centro de Estudios Históricos, 2001.

Sánchez, Ramiro. *Frontier Odyssey: Early Life in a Texas Spanish Town*. Austin: Jenkins, 1981.

Santoni, Pedro. *Mexicans at Arms: Puro Federalists and the Politics of War, 1845–1848*. Fort Worth: Texas Christian University Press, 1996.

Saxon, Gerald D. "Henry Washington Benham: A U.S. Army Engineer's View of the U.S.–Mexican War." In *Mapping and Empire: Soldier-Engineers on the Southwestern Frontier*, edited by Dennis Reinhartz and Gerald D. Saxon, 130–55. Austin: University of Texas Press, 2005.

Schilz, Jodye Lynn Dickson, and Thomas F. Schilz. *Buffalo Hump and the Penateka Comanches*. El Paso: Texas Western Press, 1989.

Schroeder, John H. *Mr. Polk's War: American Opposition and Dissent, 1846–1848*. Madison: University of Wisconsin Press, 1973.

Sellers, Charles Grier. *James K. Polk, Jacksonian: 1795–1843*. Princeton: Princeton University Press, 1957.

———. *James K. Polk: Continentalist, 1843–1846*. Princeton: Princeton University Press, 1966.

Serrano Ortega, José Antonio. *El contingente de sangre: Los gobiernos estatales y departamentales y los métodos de reclutamiento del ejército permanente mexicano, 1824–1844*. Mexico: Instituto Nacional de Antropología e Historia, 1993.

Serrano Ortega, José Antonio, and Luis Jáuregui. *Hacienda y política: Las finanzas públicas y los grupos de poder en la primera República Federal Mexicana*. Mexico: El Colegio de Michoacán, 1998.

Sherow, James E. "Workings of the Geodialectic: High Plains Indians and Their Horses in the Region of the Arkansas River Valley, 1800–1870." *Environmental History Review* 16 (1992): 61–84.

Silbey, Joel H. *Storm over Texas: The Annexation Controversy and the Road to Civil War*. New York: Oxford University Press, 2005.

Silver, Peter. *Our Savage Neighbors: How Indian War Transformed Early America*. New York: W. W. Norton, 2007.

Simmons, Marc. "Tlaxcalans in the Spanish Borderlands." *New Mexico Historical Review* 39 (1964): 101–10.

———. "New Mexico's Smallpox Epidemic of 1780–1781." *New Mexico Historical Review* 41 (1966): 319–26.

Slotkin, Richard. *Regeneration through Violence: The Mythology of the American Frontier, 1600–1860*. Middletown, Conn.: Wesleyan University Press, 1973.

———. *The Fatal Environment: The Myth of the Frontier in the Age of Industrialization, 1800–1890*. New York: Atheneum, 1985.

Smith, Elbert W. *Magnificent Missourian: The Life of Thomas Hart Benton.* Philadelphia: J. B. Lippincott, 1958.

Smith, F. Todd. *The Wichita Indians: Traders of Texas and the Southern Plains, 1540–1845.* College Station: Texas A&M University Press, 2000.

———. *From Dominance to Disappearance: The Indians of Texas and the Near Southwest, 1786–1859.* Lincoln: University of Nebraska Press, 2005.

Smith, Henry Nash. *Virgin Land: The American West as Symbol and Myth.* New York: Vintage Books, 1950.

Smith, Justin H. *The War with Mexico.* 2 vols. New York: Macmillan, 1919.

Smith, Ralph A. "The Comanche Invasion of Mexico in the Fall of 1845." *West Texas Historical Association Year Book* 35 (1959): 3–28.

———. "Mexican and Anglo-Saxon Traffic in Scalps, Slaves, and Livestock, 1835–1841." *West Texas Historical Association Year Book* 36 (1960): 98–115.

———. "The Comanche Bridge between Oklahoma and Mexico, 1843–1844." *Chronicles of Oklahoma* 39 (1961): 54–69.

———. "Apache Plunder Trails Southward, 1831–1840." *New Mexico Historical Review* 37 (1962): 20–42.

———. "Apache 'Ranching' below the Gila, 1841–1845." *Arizoniana* 3 (1962): 1–17.

———. "Indians in American–Mexican Relations before the War of 1846." *Hispanic American Historical Review* 43 (1963): 34–64.

———. "The Comanche Sun over Mexico." *West Texas Historical Association Year Book* 46 (1970): 25–62.

———. "The Comanches' Foreign War: Fighting Headhunters in the Tropics." *Great Plains Journal* 24–25 (1985–86): 21–44.

———. *Borderlander: The Life of James Kirker, 1793–1852.* Norman: University of Oklahoma Press, 1999.

Smith, Richard Penn. *Col. Crockett's Exploits and Adventures in Texas . . . Written by Himself.* Philadelphia: T. K. and P. G. Collins, 1836.

Smithwick, Noah. *The Evolution of a State, or Recollections of Old Texas Days, Compiled by His Daughter, Nanna Smithwick Donaldson.* 1899. Reprint, Austin: W. Thomas Taylor, 1995.

Soto, Miguel. "Texas en la mira: Política y negocios al iniciarse la gestión de Anthony Butler." In *Política y negocios: Ensayos sobre la relación entre México y los Estados Unidos en el siglo XIX,* edited by Ana Rosa Suárez Argüello, Marcela Terrazas y Basante, and Miguel Soto, 19–63. Mexico: Universidad Nacional Autónoma de México, Instituto de Investigaciones Doctor José María Luis Mora, 1997.

Stanley, John Mix. *Portraits of North American Indians, with Sketches of Scenery, etc.* Washington: Smithsonian Institution, 1852.

Stenberg, Richard R. "Jackson, Anthony Butler, and Texas." *Southwestern Social Science Quarterly* 13 (1932): 264–84.

Stephanson, Anders. *Manifest Destiny: American Expansionism and the Empire of Right.* New York: New York University Press, 1995.

Stevens, Robert C. "Mexico's Forgotten Frontier: A History of Sonora, 1821–1846." Ph.D. diss., University of California, Berkeley, 1963.

———. "The Apache Menace in Sonora, 1831–1848." *Arizona and the West* 6 (1964): 220–22.

Strickland, Rex W. "The Birth and Death of the Johnson 'Massacre' of 1837." *Arizona and the West* 18 (1976): 265–86.

Suárez Arguello, Ana Rosa, and Carlos Bosch García, eds. *En el nombre del Destino manifiesto: Guía de ministros y embajadores de Estados Unidos en México, 1825–1993*. Mexico: Instituto Mora, Secretaría de Relaciones Exteriores, 1998.

Sugden, John. *Tecumseh: A Life*. New York: Henry Holt, 1998.

Swartz, Marc J., Victor Witter Turner, and Arthur Tuden. *Political Anthropology*. Chicago: Aldine, 1966.

Sweeney, Edwin R. *Mangas Coloradas: Chief of the Chiricahua Apaches*. Norman: University of Oklahoma Press, 1998.

Taylor, Alan. *The Divided Ground: Indians, Settlers and the Northern Borderland of the American Revolution*. New York: Knopf, 2006.

Tenenbaum, Barbara. *The Politics of Penury: Debts and Taxes in Mexico, 1821–1856*. Albuquerque: University of New Mexico, 1986.

———. "The Making of a Fait Accompli: Mexico and the Provincias Internas, 1776–1846." In *The Evolution of the Mexican Political System*, edited by Jaime E. Rodríguez O., 91–115. Wilmington: Scholarly Resources, 1993.

Thomas, Alfred Barnaby, ed. *Forgotten Frontiers: A Study of the Spanish Indian Policy of Don Juan Bautista de Anza, Governor of New Mexico, 1777–1787; From the Original Documents in the Archives of Spain, Mexico and New Mexico*. Norman: University of Oklahoma Press, 1932.

Thompson, Waddy. *Recollections of Mexico*. New York: Wiley and Putnam, 1846.

Thurman, Melburn D. "A New Interpretation of Comanche Social Organization." *Current Anthropology* 23 (1982): 578–79.

———. "Reply." *Current Anthropology* 28 (1987): 552–55.

Timmons, W. H. "The El Paso Area in the Mexican Period, 1821–1846." *Southwestern Historical Quarterly* 84 (1980): 1–28.

Tixier, Victor. *Tixier's Travels on the Osage Prairies*. Edited by John Francis McDermott and Albert Jacques Salvan. Norman: University of Oklahoma Press, 1940.

Truett, Samuel. *Fugitive Landscapes: The Forgotten History of the U.S.-Mexican Borderlands*. New Haven: Yale University Press, 2006.

Tyler, Daniel. "Gringo Views of Governor Manuel Armijo." *New Mexico Historical Review* 45 (1970): 23–46.

———. "Governor Armijo's Moment of Truth." *Journal of the West* 11 (1972): 307–16.

———. "Mexican Indian Policy in New Mexico." *New Mexico Historical Review* 55 (1980): 101–20.

Usner, Daniel H. *Indians, Settlers, and Slaves in a Frontier Exchange Economy: The Lower Mississippi Valley before 1783*. Chapel Hill: University of North Carolina Press, 1992.

Vallebueno, Miguel G. "Apaches y Comanches en Durango durante los siglos XVIII y XIX." In *Nómadas y sedentarios en el norte de México: Homenaje a Beatriz Braniff*, edited by Marie-Areti Hers, 669-81. Mexico: UNAM, 2000.

Valerio-Jiménez, Omar S. "Indios Bárbaros, Divorcées, and Flocks of Vampires: Identity and Nation on the Rio Grande, 1749–1894." Ph.D. diss., UCLA, 2001.

———. "Neglected Citizens and Willing Traders: The Villas del Norte (Tamaulipas) in Mexico's Northern Borderlands, 1749–1846." *Mexican Studies/Estudios Mexicanos* 18 (2002): 251–96.

Van Young, Eric. *The Other Rebellion: Popular Violence, Ideology, and the Mexican Struggle for Independence, 1810–1821*. Stanford: Stanford University Press, 2001.

Vázquez, Josefina Zoraida. "La supuesta República del Río Grande." *Historia Mexicana* 36 (1986): 49–80.

———. "The Texas Question in Mexican Politics, 1836–1845." *Southwestern Historical Quarterly* 89 (1986): 309–44.

Velasco Avila, Cuauhtémoc José. "La amenaza comanche en la frontera mexicana, 1800–1841." Ph.D. diss., Universidad Nacional Autónoma de México, 1998.

———. "'Nuestros obstinados enemigos': Ideas e imágenes de los indios nómadas en la frontera noreste mexicana, 1821–1840." In *Nómadas y sedentarios en el norte de México: Homenaje a Beatriz Braniff*, edited by Beatriz Braniff C. and Marie-Areti Hers, 441–59. Mexico: Universidad Nacional Autónoma de México, Instituto de Investigaciones Antropológicas, 2000.

———, ed. *En manos de los bárbaros*. Mexico: Breve Fondo Editorial, 1996.

Vigil, Donaciano. "On the Maladministration of New Mexico under Governors Pérez and Martínez and under Commanding General García Conde." In *Arms, Indians, and the Mismanagement of New Mexico*, edited by David J. Weber. El Paso: Texas Western Press, 1986.

Vigness, David M. "The Lower Rio Grande Valley, 1836–1846." M.A. thesis, University of Texas, 1946.

———. "The Republic of the Rio Grande: An Example of Separatism in Northern Mexico." Ph.D. diss., University of Texas, 1951.

———. "Indian Raids on the Lower Rio Grande, 1836–1837." *Southwestern Historical Quarterly* 59 (1955): 15–23.

Vizcaya Canales, Isidro. *Incursiones de indios al noreste en el México independiente (1821–1885)*. Monterrey: Archivo General del Estado de Nuevo León, 1995.

———. *Tierra de guerra viva: Incursiones de indios y otros conflictos en el noreste de México durante el siglo XIX, 1821–1885*. Monterrey: Academia de Investigaciones, 2001.

———, ed. *La invasión de los indios bárbaros al noreste de México en los años de 1840 y 1841*. Monterrey: Publicaciones del Instituto Tecnológico y de Estudios Superiores de Monterrey, 1968.

Voss, Stuart F. *On the Periphery of Nineteenth-Century Mexico: Sonora and Sinaloa, 1810–1877*. Tucson: University of Arizona Press, 1982.

Wallace, Ernest, ed. "David G. Burnet's Letters Describing the Comanche Indians." *West Texas Historical Association Year Book* 30 (1954): 115–40.

Wallace, Ernest, and E. Adamson Hoebel. *The Comanches: Lords of the South Plains*. Norman: University of Oklahoma Press, 1952.

Weaver, John C. *The Great Land Rush and the Making of the Modern World, 1650–1900*. Montreal: McGill-Queen's University Press, 2003.

Webb, James Josiah. *Adventures in the Santa Fé Trade, 1844–1847.* Edited by Ralph P. Bieber. Philadelphia: Porcupine Press, 1974.

Weber, David J. "American Westward Expansion and the Breakdown of Relations Between *Pobladores* and '*Indios Bárbaros*' on Mexico's Far Northern Frontier, 1821–1846." *New Mexico Historical Review* 56 (1981): 221–38.

———. *The Mexican Frontier, 1821–1846: The American Southwest under Mexico.* Albuquerque: University of New Mexico Press, 1982.

———. "John Francis Bannon and the Historiography of the Spanish Borderlands: Retrospect and Prospect." *Journal of the Southwest* 29 (1987): 331–63.

———. *The Spanish Frontier in North America.* New Haven: Yale University Press, 1992.

———. *Bárbaros: Spaniards and Their Savages in the Age of Enlightenment.* New Haven: Yale University Press, 2005.

———, ed. *Northern Mexico on the Eve of the United States Invasion: Rare Imprints Concerning California, Arizona, New Mexico, and Texas, 1821–1846.* New York: Arno Press, 1976.

———, ed. *Albert Pike: Prose Sketches and Poems Written in the Western Country (with Additional Stories).* Albuquerque: Calvin Horn, 1967.

Weems, John Edward. *To Conquer a Peace: The War between the United States and Mexico.* Garden City: Doubleday, 1974.

West, Elliott. *The Way West: Essays on the Central Plains.* Albuquerque: University of New Mexico Press, 1995.

———. *The Contested Plains: Indians, Goldseekers, and the Rush to Colorado.* Lawrence: University Press of Kansas, 1998.

Wharton, William H. *Texas: A Brief Account of the Origin, Progress, and Present State of the Colonial Settlements of Texas, Together With an Exposition of the Causes Which Have Induced the Existing War With Mexico.* Nashville: Printed by S. Nye, 1836.

White, Richard. "The Winning of the West: The Expansion of the Western Sioux in the Eighteenth and Nineteenth Centuries." *Journal of American History* 25 (1978): 319–43.

———. *The Middle Ground: Indians, Empires, and Republics in the Great Lakes Region, 1650–1815.* Cambridge: Cambridge University Press, 1991.

Wilentz, Sean. *The Rise of American Democracy: Jefferson to Lincoln.* New York: Norton, 2005.

Williams, Amelia W., and Eugene Campbell Barker, eds. *The Writings of Sam Houston, 1813–1863.* 8 vols. Austin: The University of Texas Press, 1938.

Winders, Richard Bruce. *Crisis in the Southwest: The United States, Mexico, and the Struggle over Texas.* Wilmington: Scholarly Resources, 2002.

Winfrey, Dorman H., and James M. Day, eds. *The Indian Papers of Texas and the Southwest, 1825–1916.* 5 vols. Austin: Pemberton Press, 1966–95.

Wislizenus, Frederick Adolph. *Memoir of a Tour to Northern Mexico.* 1848. Reprint, Fairfield, Wash.: Ye Galleon Press, 1992.

Witherspoon, Gary. "Navajo Social Organization." In *Handbook of North American Indians.* Vol. 10, *Southwest,* edited by Alfonso Ortiz, 524–35. Washington: Smithsonian Institution Press, 1983.

Zúñiga, C. Ignacio. *Rápida ojeada al estado de Sonora.* Mexico: Juan Ojeda, 1835.

ACKNOWLEDGMENTS

Over the course of this project I discovered that one of the best ways to procrastinate was to daydream about writing my acknowledgments. Now that the moment is finally here I'm realizing that these simple thanks won't live up to the prose of my daydreams, nor certainly will they do justice to the debts I've acquired over the past decade that I've been at work on this book.

Many mentors, friends, and colleagues helped me push this project out of the muck of imagination into final reality. My first debts are to my mentors at Harvard, where this book began. First and foremost my advisor Laurel Thatcher Ulrich has been a professional and personal inspiration, a demanding critic, a steady advocate, and, for every minute that I've been fortunate enough to be around her, a teacher in the very best sense of the word. Though I came to work with her on New England, she supported and encouraged me with her typical generosity and enthusiasm when my interests began to turn south and west. John Coatsworth helped me decide to make that intellectual migration in the first place. I never once left John's office without feeling smarter and an inch taller. Jack Womack contributed enormously to my thinking by spending his time with me when I needed it and by continuously opening my eyes to larger problems outside my field of vision. Two of my mentors, Bill Gienapp and Leroy Vail, passed away during the course of this project. I miss them both and wish they were here to thank in person. The shifting members of Harvard's Early American Seminar broadened my intellectual horizons and contributed to this project in many ways. The community at Cabot House sustained me for five years and deepened my life in Cambridge. I'm also grateful to various organizations for providing me with generous funding: the Charles Warren Center for American History, the David Rockefeller Center for Latin American Studies, Harvard's History Department and Graduate School of Arts and Sciences, the Department of Education, the American Philosophical Society's Philips Fund Grant for Native American Research, and the Packard Foundation.

Several librarians, archivists, and curators have generously guided me through their collections, making my work richer and my life easier. I especially want to thank the research staff at Widener Library, everyone at the late, great Hilles Library, and the kind folks at the

457

DeGolyer Library at Southern Methodist University. I had all a historian could possibly ask for at the underutilized Instituto Estatal de Documentación [el Archivo General del Estado de Coahuila] in Ramos Arizpe, Coahuila. The archive is supremely organized, and the kind and knowledgeable staff made the experience a genuine pleasure. I particularly want to thank Director Alfonso Vázquez Sotelo, Miguel Angel Muñoz Borrego, and Maria Eugenia Galindo Marines. Evan Hocker helped me a great deal at the University of Texas at Austin's Center for American History, as did Michael Hironymous and Ann Lozano at the Nettie Lee Benson Latin American Collection. I also want to thank the staff at the Hemeroteca Nacional in Mexico City, Felicia Pickering at the Smithsonian Department of Anthropology, Russ Ronspies at the Frontier Army Museum, and Penelope Smith at the Joslyn Art Museum.

For the past four years I have enjoyed the pleasure and privilege of teaching at my alma mater, the University of Colorado at Boulder, where I've received much support and friendship. In particular I'd like to thank Virginia Anderson, Francisco Barbosa, Scott Bruce, Lee Chambers, Lucy Chester, Bob Ferry, Matthew Gerber, Julie Green, Martha Hanna, Susie Jones, Padraic Kenny, Susan Kent, Anne Lester, Patty Limerick, Eric Love, Gloria Main, Ralph Mann, Marjorie McIntosh, Mark Pittenger, Mary Ann Villareal, Tim Weston, John Willis, and Marcia Yonemoto. Peter Boag has been chair during my years at Colorado and with his tremendous kindness and energy has gone out of his way to help me more times than I had any right to expect. My comrades in Hellems 363 have helped keep me sane. Susan Kent and Deans Graham Oddie and Todd Gleeson kindly made it possible for me to take advantage of a residential fellowship during my second year. One of the best things about returning to CU is that I now have an office on the same floor as my undergraduate mentor, Fred Anderson. Fred first opened my eyes to the craft of what good historians do, has been a great friend ever since, and with his characteristic generosity and insight read and critiqued the manuscript (most of it more than once) with care and good humor. I would never have started down this path were it not for Fred, and, beyond the fact that he still won't let me buy the beers, I owe him more than his modesty will permit him to acknowledge.

Much of what is good in this book I attribute to the happy year I spent at the Clements Center for Southwest Studies at Southern Methodist University in Dallas. The donors, faculty, and staff associated with the center and SMU's History Department were tremendously welcoming to me and my family and provided the support—intellectual, financial, and otherwise—that I needed to revise the manuscript. I owe special thanks to Andrea Boardman and Ruth Ann Elmore, who did so much to make my time there productive and enjoyable. I also want to thank John Chávez, Ed Countryman, Christa DeLuzio, John Mears, Dan Orlovsky, Bob Righter, and Sherry Smith. My fellow fellows Dave Adams and Eric Meeks supplied good company and even better advice and inspired me with their own work. One of the things that makes the Clements Center so special is that it convenes workshops to critique fellows' manuscripts. During my workshop I was bombarded with more insightful, sensible, and useful advice than I had the wherewithal to process. I can only hope that the participants have recognized something of their labors in the final product. In addition to Andrea, Eric, and Dave, I thank Matt Babcock, Anna Banhegyi, Gregg Cantrell, George Diaz, Sam Haynes, Ben Johnson, Todd Meyers, Eduardo Moralez, David

Rex Galindo, and F. Todd Smith. Dan Richter and Richard White traveled to Texas for the workshop and gave me penetrating critiques of the manuscript. I'm grateful for their advice and have tried to do good by it. Last, I have David Weber to thank, for my year in Dallas and for much else. With his famous generosity David encouraged me from the earliest stages of this project. Since then he has continued to amaze me with his kindness, good sense, and sharp eye. David read the manuscript at two different stages, gave me insightful feedback each time, and in many other ways has done more for me than I can possibly repay.

James Brooks, Andrés Reséndez, and Pedro Santoni all read an early version of the manuscript and challenged me to make it better. Leor Halevi and Dan Gutiérrez read later versions and helped me see problems and opportunities I'd missed. Joyce Chaplin, Jonathan Conant, Cathy Corman, Amy Greenberg, Erika Pani, Steve Hackel, Jane Mangan, and Janna Promislow read and listened to parts of the manuscript along the way and gave me helpful and insightful feedback. Material from this book has previously appeared in the *American Historical Review* and the *Journal of the Early Republic*. I thank the editors of those journals and their anonymous readers for helping me to refine my ideas. Elizabeth John and Gary Anderson both encouraged me at an early stage. Barbara Tenenbaum responded kindly to my many questions about taxes and fiscal policy in nineteenth-century Mexico. Laurel Watkins patiently answered several questions about Kiowa names. Matt Babcock helped me navigate a trip to archives in northeastern Mexico and carefully read and commented on an early version of part 1. Joaquín Rivaya Martínez read and commented on the manuscript and shared with me his fascinating dissertation about Comanche captivity. I'd also like to thank Catherine Andrews for sending me her dissertation on Anastacio Bustamante. Patrick Florance from Harvard's Map Collection guided me through mapping software and, over numerous visits, taught me how to create the maps for the project. Lara Heimert signed this book to Yale, and when she left the press Chris Rogers stepped in. Chris gave me terrific feedback on the manuscript, encouraged my progress along the way, and championed the project at the press. My remarkable editor Lawrence Kenney saved me from errors of various kinds and helped me refine my prose.

My parents, Mary and Larry DeLay, have always helped me keep things in perspective with their kindness, humor, wisdom, and love. My mom even joined me in Mexico City for a break from research. Marla, Ryan, Emma, and Colton Smith, Kim DeLay, Nikola Anguelov and Vessela Anguelova have always made me feel both needed and taken care of, and they make me laugh.

Finally I have the sweet task of thanking the three people I owe most. The best of my daydream acknowledgments have been about Diliana Angelova, my wife. She is often my most insightful critic, always my firmest advocate, and in every way my best friend. Through her own exacting work, her gentle patience, her strength, and her irrepressible joy, Diliana makes me want to be better, at everything—including fatherhood. Our beautiful children, five-year-old Noah and two-year-old Alethea, have brought more love, happiness, and wonder into my life than I could ever put into words. As they've grown up with this project I've come nearer to understanding what was at stake for so many of the people in this book. For that, and for so much else, I'm profoundly grateful.

INDEX

Italic page numbers refer to figures and tables.

Index